Mubarak Al-Sabah

Founder of Modern Kuwait
1896–1915

Also by B. J. Slot

Scheseis metaxu Ollandias kai Ellados apo ton IZ' aiona mechri ton Kapodistria
Keimena kai Meletai Neoellenikes Filologias, Athenai, 1978.

Archipelagus turbatus
Les Cyclades entre colonisation latine et occupation ottomane, c. 1500–1718
Nederlands Historisch Archaeologisch Instituut, Istanbul, 1982

Amitié et soupçons
Deux siècles de relations diplomatiques franco-néerlandaises
Ambassade de France/Museum Meermanno Westreenianum, La Haye, 1988

Nederlanders aan de kusten van Oman
Museon, Den Haag, 1992

Abel Tasman and the Discovery of New Zealand
Cramwinckel, Amsterdam, 1992

The Arabs of the Gulf, 1602–1784
An Alternative Approach to the Early History of the Arab Gulf States and Their
Relations with the European Powers, Mainly Based on Sources of the Dutch East India
Company
Leidschendam, 1995

The Origins of Kuwait
Center for Research and Studies on Kuwait, 1998

Lale ile Bashladi … It Began with the Tulip
Turkiye ve Hollanda arasindaki dört yüzyillik ilishkilerin resimli tarihçesi
(with A.H. de Groot and Z. Çelikkol), Türk Tarih Kurumu, Ankara, 2000

Kuwait: The Growth of A Historic Identity
Ed. B. J. Slot. Arabian Publishing, London, 2003

Mubarak Al-Sabah

Founder of Modern Kuwait
1896–1915

B. J. Slot

_AP_

Arabian Publishing

Mubarak Al-Sabah
Founder of Modern Kuwait, 1896–1915

© B. J. Slot, 2005

English edition first published in 2005 by Arabian Publishing Ltd
3 Devonshire Street, London W1W 5BA
Fax 020 7580 0567

Editor: William Facey

A catalogue record for this book is available from the British Library

ISBN 0 9544792 4 6

Typesetting and digital artwork by Jamie Crocker, Baldock, UK
Printed and bound in the UK by Creative Print and Design (Wales), Ebbw Vale

Contents

Illustrations

The Photographs

Between pages 142 and 143:

1. Shaikh Miz'al of Muhammara, 1880s. Jane Dieulafoy, *La Perse, la Chaldée et la Susiane: relation de voyage*, Paris 1887.

2. The Konak, the official government building of the Wali of Basra, 1890s. Max von Oppenheim, *Vom Mittelmeer zum Persischen Golf*, Berlin, 1900.

3. "Politically blind." Cartoon satirizing Salisbury, Broderick, Balfour and Lansdowne. *Punch*, London 1900.

4. Shaikh Mubarak's palace, Kuwait, 1901–2. F.L.B., "Voyage du *Catinat* dans le Golfe Persique", *Le Monde Illustré* 1902, p. 202.

5. Portrait of Shaikh Mubarak Al-Sabah, Kuwait, 1901–2. F.L.B., "Voyage du *Catinat* dans le Golfe Persique", *Le Monde Illustré* 1902, p. 202 .

6. The Imam Abdul Rahman bin Faysal Al-Saud at Kuwait, 1901–2. F.L.B., "Voyage du *Catinat* dans le Golfe Persique", *Le Monde Illustré* 1902, p. 202.

7. Kuwaitis, 1901–2. F.L.B., "Voyage du *Catinat* dans le Golfe Persique", *Le Monde Illustré* 1902, p. 202.

8. Shaikh Mubarak with officers of the *Varyag*, December 1901. The Russian State Naval Archives, St Petersburg.

9. Jabir bin Mubarak Al-Sabah on board the *Varyag*, December 1901. The Russian State Naval Archives, St Petersburg.

10. Shaikh Mubarak, Kuwait, 1901–2. Henry J. Whigham, *The Persian Problem*, London, 1903.

11. *De Koweit-zaak en Engeland* (The Kuwait Affair and England). Cartoon by Johan Braakensiek. *De Amsterdammer*, Amsterdam, 1902.

12. Shaikh Mubarak in his palace, Kuwait, December 1903. Hermann Burchardt, "Ost-Arabien von Basra bis Maskat auf Grund eigener Reisen", *Zeitschrift der Gesellschaft für Erdkunde zu Berlin*, Berlin, 1906, pp. 305–22.

13. S. G. Knox, first British political agent to Kuwait (1904–9), with his wife. British Embassy, Kuwait.

14. The bazaar in Kuwait. "Aldebaran", *Times of India, Illustrated Weekly*, 16 January 1907.

15. Shaikh Mubarak's palace, Kuwait. *Times of India, Illustrated Weekly*, 16 January 1907.

16. The British Agency in Kuwait. *Times of India, Illustrated Weekly*, 16 January 1907.

17. Shaikh Mubarak standing on the bridge joining the old and new parts of the Sif Palace, Kuwait, 1907–9. Lt-Cmdr A. N. Gouldsmith, National Maritime Museum, London.

18. Shaikh Mubarak with his friend Shaikh Khaz'al of Muhammara, 1907–9. Lt-Cmdr A. N. Gouldsmith, National Maritime Museum, London.

19. Shaikh Khaz'al of Muhammara. Arnold T. Wilson, *Loyalties, Mesopotamia 1914–1917*, Oxford/London, 1930.

20. Talib Pasha, son of the Naqib of Basra and friend of Shaikh Mubarak. Arnold T. Wilson, *Loyalties, Mesopotamia 1914–1917*, Oxford/London, 1930.

Between pages 270 and 271:

21. Shaikh Mubarak holding court in public in the open air, with Kuwaitis and British representatives, 1907–9. Lt-Cmdr A. N. Gouldsmith, National Maritime Museum, London.

22. Shaikh Mubarak in 1908. Abdul Masih Al-Antaki, *Al-Riyadh al-muzhira bayn al-Kuwayt wa 'l-Muhammara*, Cairo, 1908.

23. Mubarak's steamer *Mishrif*. Abdul Masih Al-Antaki, *Al-Riyadh al-muzhira bayn al-Kuwayt wa 'l-Muhammara*, Cairo, 1908.

24. Percy Zachariah Cox, political resident in the Persian Gulf 1905–14, in front of his office in Bushire. Private collection.

25. Mubarak Al-Sabah with Abdul Aziz Ibn Saud and members of his family, British Political Agency, Kuwait, March 1910. Capt. W. H. I. Shakespear, Royal Geographical Society, London.

26. A sample of Mubarak's private correspondence with friends. Center for Research and Studies on Kuwait.

27. The palace, Kuwait, flying the Ottoman flag, 1909–13. Capt. W. H. I. Shakespear, private collection.

28. Captain Shakespear, British political agent in Kuwait 1909–14. Arnold T. Wilson, *Loyalties, Mesopotamia 1914–1917*, Oxford/London, 1930.

29. Shaikh Mubarak, Kuwait, 1912. Barclay Raunkiaer, *Gennem Wahhabiternes Land paa Kamelryg*, Copenhagen, 1913.

30. Mubarak's palace, Kuwait: the old part. Barclay Raunkiaer, *Gennem Wahhabiternes Land paa Kamelryg*, Copenhagen, 1913.

31. Mubarak's palace, Kuwait: the new part. Barclay Raunkiaer, *Gennem Wahhabiternes Land paa Kamelryg*, Copenhagen, 1913.

32. Town plan of Kuwait in 1912. Barclay Raunkiaer, *Gennem Wahhabiternes Land paa Kamelryg*, Copenhagen, 1913.

33. A street in Kuwait, 1912. Barclay Raunkiaer, *Gennem Wahhabiternes Land paa Kamelryg*, Copenhagen, 1913.

34. The Turkish fortress at Fao on the Shatt al-'Arab. *The Times History of the World War,* Part 29, London, 1915.

35. The British Royal Marine guard of honour that accompanied Admiral Bethell on his visit to Kuwait on the occasion of the award of the K.C.I.E. to Shaikh Mubarak, Sif Palace, 16 April 1912. Maidstone Museum and Art Gallery, Maidstone, Kent, UK.

36. Portion of the British Admiralty chart of the Upper Gulf of 1862. C. G. Constable and A. N. Stiffe, *The Persian Gulf, Western Sheet.*

37. Map mentioning the "Republic of Kuwait", 1867. *Arabien zu C. Ritter's Erdkunde, bearbeitet von H. Kiepert,* Reimer Verlag, Berlin, 1867.

38. Russian map of the Kuwait region showing the planned railway to the Gulf. *Novoye Vremiye,* St Petersburg, 19/6 February 1902.

39. The borderline of Kuwait as originally proposed by the Foreign Office on the basis of Lorimer's *Gazetteer.* India Office Records, R/15/5/65.

40. The borders of Kuwait on the map accompanying the Anglo-Ottoman Convention of 1913. Auswärtiges Amt, Berlin, R 13890.

Abbreviations

AA   Auswärtiges Amt, Politisches Archiv, Berlin
AD   Archives Diplomatiques, Nantes
AE   Ministère des Affaires Étrangères, Paris
AVPR   Arkhiv Vnesknei Politikii Rossii, Moscow
BA   Bashbakanlik Arshivi, Istanbul
EI(2)   Encyclopaedia of Islam, 2nd edition, 11 vols., Leiden, 1980–2003
HHSA   Haus, Hof und Staatsarchiv, Vienna
IOLR   India Office Library and Records, British Library, London
NA   Nationaal Archief, The Hague
NAI   National Archives of India, New Delhi
PRO   Public Record Office, Kew, London (now The National Archives)
SHM   Service Historique de la Marine, Château de Vincennes, Paris

Maps

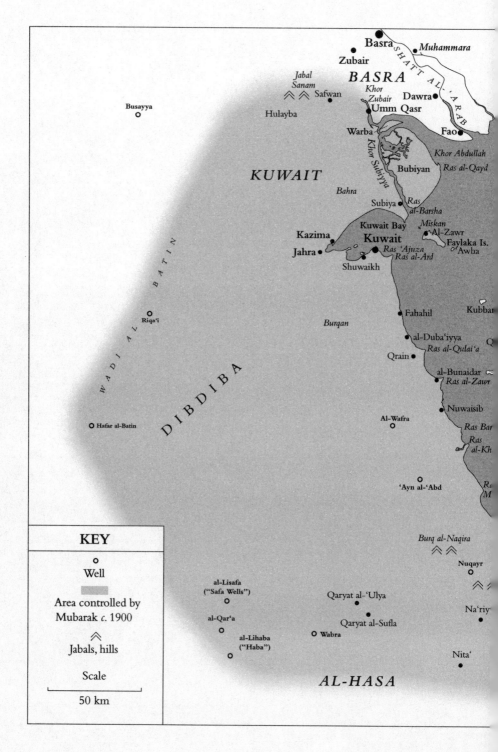

Basra
Zubair
Muhammara
SHATT AL-'ARAB

BASRA

Busayya ○

Jabal Sanam
Safwan ●
Khor Zubair
Dawra ●
Hulayba
Umm Qasr
Fao ●

Warba

Khor Subiyya
Bubiyan
Khor Abdullah
Ras al-Qayd

KUWAIT

Bahra
Subiya ●
Ras al-Barsha

Kazima ●
Kuwait Bay
Miskan
Al-Zawr ●
Faylaka Is.
Jahra ●
Kuwait
Ras 'Ajuza
○Awha
Shuwaikh
Ras al-Ard

W A D I   A L   B A T I N

Riqa'i ○

Burqan
Fahahil ●
Kubbar

al-Duba'iyya
Ras al-Qulai'a

Qrain ●

D I B D I B A

al-Bunaidar
Ras al-Zawr

Nuwaisib ●
Ras Bar
Ras al-Kh

Hafar al-Batin ○

Al-Wafra ○

'Ayn al-'Abd ○

Burq al-Naqira

Nuqayr ○

KEY

○
Well

Area controlled by
Mubarak *c.* 1900

Jabals, hills

Scale

⊢————⊣
50 km

al-Lisafa
("Safa Wells")
○

Qaryat al-'Ulya ●

Na'riy

al-Qar'a
○

Qaryat al-Sufla ●

al-Lihaba
("Haba")
○

Wabra ○

Nita' ●

AL-HASA

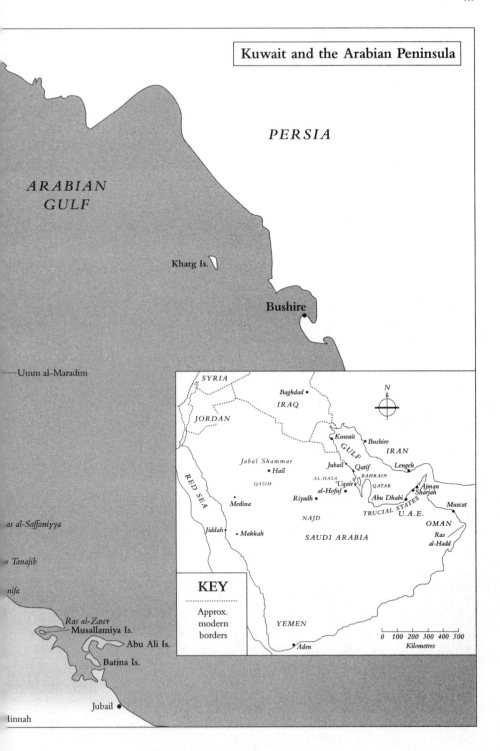

Kuwait and the Arabian Peninsula

PERSIA

ARABIAN GULF

Kharg Is.

Bushire

—Umm al-Maradim

as al-Saffaniyya

Tanajib

nifa

Ras al-Zawr
Musallamiya Is.
Abu Ali Is.
Batina Is.

Jubail

innah

SYRIA

Baghdad
IRAQ

N

JORDAN

Kuwait • Bushire
IRAN

Jabal Shammar
• Hail
Jubail • Qatif
Lengeh
QASIM
AL-HASA *BAHRAIN*
Uqair•
al-Hofuf *QATAR*
Ajman
Abu Dhabi *Sharjah*
RED SEA
Riyadh •
TRUCIAL STATES *U.A.E.*
Muscat

Medina
NAJD
OMAN
Ras al-Hadd

Jiddah • *Makkah*
SAUDI ARABIA

KEY

....
Approx.
modern
borders

YEMEN

Aden

0 100 200 300 400 500
Kilometres

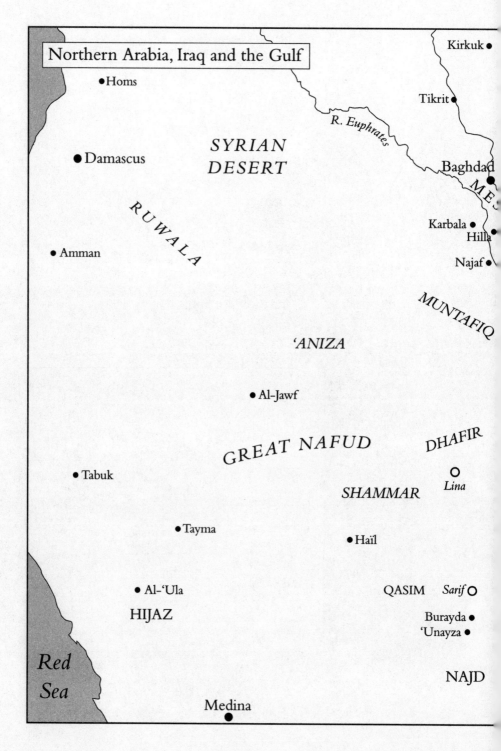

Northern Arabia, Iraq and the Gulf

Kirkuk •

• Homs

Tikrit •

R. Euphrates

SYRIAN DESERT

Baghdad

• Damascus

MES

Karbala •

Hilla

RUWALA

Najaf •

• Amman

MUNTAFIQ

'ANIZA

• Al-Jawf

GREAT NAFUD

DHAFIR

• Tabuk

○

Lina

SHAMMAR

• Tayma

• Haïl

• Al-'Ula

QASIM   *Sarif* ○

HIJAZ

Burayda •

'Unayza •

Red Sea

NAJD

Medina
●

KEY

'AJMAN
Tribe

O
Well

Scale

100 km

Teheran

Hamadan Qum

Isfahan

R. Tigris

TAMIA
Samawa
R. Euphrates
Nasiriyya
Amara
Qurna
Ahwaz
R. Karun

Basra
Zubair
Safwan
Umm Qasr
Muhammara
Fao
Bubiyan Is.

Shiraz

Jahra Kuwait
Kharg Is.
Bushire

DIBDIBA
O
Hafar
al-Batin

DAHNA SANDS

MUTAYR

'AJMAN

AL-HASA

Musallamiyya Is.

Jubail
Qatif
Dammam

Gulf

Manama

Zubara

'Uqayr
Hasa
Oasis
Hofuf

Bida (Doha)

Riyadh

Harad

Introduction

MUBARAK AL-SABAH, Ruler of Kuwait between 1896 and 1915, once described himself as "just an Arab sitting on the edge of the desert". Described by other observers as "an immensely sly fox", he often tried to deceive Europeans or Turks who had to deal with him by pretending to be less clever than he was. His self-portrayal as Arab perched on the desert edge is none the less a telling one in other respects. It is highly appropriate to regard him as an Arab sitting on the ill-defined desert edge of the decaying Ottoman Empire, as also on the edge of the just as vaguely defined British sphere of interest. It also aptly encapsulates Kuwait's situation between the desert and the sea.

In Kuwait, Mubarak is sometimes known as Mubarak I. This is incorrect, as there had been an earlier Ruler of Kuwait of the Al-Sabah family by the name of Mubarak in 1756. Hence the Mubarak of this book should properly be known as Mubarak II. His reign marked a crucial period in Kuwait's history. During it Mubarak, an autocratic ruler who in a substantial sense "was" Kuwait, operated on a complex international stage and was successful in countering the Ottoman claims which, in the 19th century, had come to pose a real threat to Kuwait's existence. The prospects of survival for small entities, such as Kuwait, caught up in areas of international tension were unpromising, but Mubarak managed to extricate Kuwait from the main snares. The game was so complicated that none of his contemporaries were able to form a clear picture of what was happening. As a result the information available to us on events, from the various powers involved in the affair, is often wildly contradictory.

Mubarak is first mentioned in a British report of 1854, which gives a short list of the ruling family of Kuwait. The ruler of the day was Jabir, then said to be 102 years of age. His son, Sabah, acted as deputy ruler. Sabah had seven sons of whom the eldest, Abdallah, was forty; the second, Muhammad, fifteen; and the fourth, our Mubarak, nine.[1] Mubarak must have been fifty or fifty-one when he became Ruler of Kuwait in 1896. By that time important changes had affected Kuwait's position. Its colossal neighbour, the Ottoman Empire, had never been able to exert much influence in the region, chiefly because of the enormous logistic problems inherent in maintaining a military presence in the remote province of Basra. However, with the growing propensity of the Ottoman Sultans to merge their status as Caliph with their position as Head of the Ottoman state, came a tendency to regard the entire Arabian Peninsula as legitimate Ottoman territory. This acquired practical meaning as, during the course of the 19th century, the establishment of telegraph and shipping lines facilitated communications between Basra and the centres of Ottoman power. That brought growing pressure to bear on Kuwait's independence, as well as competition with Britain, the other great power laying claim to control of the Persian Gulf.

It was Mubarak's crowning achievement as ruler that Kuwait's status as a sovereign state became clearly defined and established. It is not possible to arrive at a clear understanding of Mubarak's actions without a proper appreciation of Kuwait's situation, not only in its legal basis but also in actual political practice. In performing an astute balancing act aimed at maintaining as much of Kuwait's independence as possible, Mubarak exploited to the full the tensions between Ottoman ambitions and the British position, as well as the other intricate international circumstances of his time. For this he was obliged to accept a kind of British protectorate; but at that time Britain was a much safer partner than the unreliable Ottoman Empire.

Mubarak was an innovator in many fields. He was the only Arab ruler in the region capable of manipulating the international situation effectively. He was an ardent gatherer of information and a reader of forbidden newspapers. He even tried to exploit the press to manipulate public opinion outside Kuwait. He introduced the first public services into

---

[1] Report by Kemball in Hughes Thomas (ed.), *Selections from the Records of the Bombay Government*, p. 295.

his country. When it suited him, he could be a very charming and sociable companion, to Kuwaiti friends and foreigners alike. But he was also a very forceful and authoritative character who could appear wise and well-informed. One could hardly expect a man of his time and background to be a democrat. Mubarak was an autocrat; his private interests and those of Kuwait he regarded as identical.

He was also a consummate actor. Clever and lucid, knowledgeable and imposing, he impressed a German visitor as the only Gulf shaikh who could be described as a true ruler. However he was also able, when appropriate, to present himself as just a simple fellow, no more than "an Arab sitting on the edge of the desert".

Mubarak was the vital ingredient in the evolution of his desert shaikhdom into a modern state, and it is very well worth examining how this clever old manipulator managed to score an approximately eighty-per-cent success in his dealings. In trying to show the reader why and how events unfolded, this book will be primarily descriptive. If the reader wishes to make moral judgements, he is welcome to do so; but it is not necessarily the role of the historian to pass moral judgements on events in an era when a different moral outlook applied.

From the early 19th century, claims began to make themselves felt that Kuwait was in some sense part of the Ottoman Empire. Such claims were finally extinguished by Mubarak in 1914, when he received full British protection and rejected all ties with the Ottoman Empire. Before that time, the 19th-century state of affairs is usually summed up somewhat as follows: Kuwait's Ruler recognized the supremacy of the Ottoman Sultan, while the Ottomans did not interfere in Kuwait's affairs or levy any regular taxes or customs duties there.

The first two chapters of this book try to correct the existing conception of the status of Kuwait in the 19th century and of the crisis of Ottoman rule in the region at the century's end. The third chapter presents an analysis of Kuwait under Shaikh Muhammad and its takeover by Mubarak. The following chapters give a roughly chronological description of Mubarak's rule, in the context of the relationship with the British and the Ottomans as well as with other external powers. At the same time, these chapters deal with Mubarak's policy of establishing and maintaining an equilibrium of power on his desert borders – the only way in which the small city state of Kuwait could maintain a degree of autonomy.

This biography of Mubarak is based on a wide selection of sources. Naturally the British sources are of paramount importance, but sources of other origin often serve to modify or correct the image of him. He was not simply an ally of the British, but an independent operator who enjoyed great prestige and power in the region, and whose chief priorities were security and independence.

Previous authors have dealt in some detail with Mubarak's life and activities. There is one recent biography by Salwa Al-Ghanim (1998), the basic flaw of which is that it relies entirely on British sources and so presents a somewhat partial and therefore distorted picture. Another biography of Mubarak, by Bondarevsky (1994), is also based principally on British sources, but adds important Russian material. Both these works exhibit a certain bias. Bondarevsky is over-enthusiastic about Mubarak, while Salwa Al-Ghanim tends to be excessively severe in her judgements. A very detailed account of Mubarak, for the period 1896–1907, is presented in an older work by Jens Plass (1969). This relies chiefly on British sources, but presents other material too. Plass is better at placing events in their historical context. Busch's work, *Britain and the Persian Gulf* (1967), is rather more summary in its treatment, but covers a longer period, and uses printed French and German sources as well. In his recent book on the Ottomans in the Gulf, Anscombe (1997) brings the chief Ottoman archival sources into the purview of history, and so makes a most important contribution to our knowledge of Mubarak. Finally, in 2004, Al-Qasimi published a number of Ottoman documents that had escaped Anscombe. The present work is intended to complete the image by the use of sources from France, Germany, Austria and various other countries.

A historian is, to some extent, a mere messenger who relates what his sources tell him. These sources may be more or less reliable, and it is certainly the historian's task to subject them to critical appraisal. He must ask whether such-and-such a source was really in a position to know, and whether he may have been biased or even deliberately misleading. In the absence of clear evidence that the source is less than reliable, the historian is under an obligation to quote it, however contrary to accepted views or even unpalatable to some readers the story may seem. The historian has a further obligation, to explain and place his material in a wider context. He has to utilize the full panoply of documentary evidence to shed a dispassionate light on the motives of his personalities, whether friend or foe, and in doing so he must resist the temptation to act as prosecutor or to sit in judgement. In a case like Mubarak, about whose life there is an abundance of conflicting evidence, it is inevitable that a detailed historical study such as this will from time to time cast doubt on the conventional version of history and on readers' firmly held convictions and fondly held views. It is the proper role of the historian to replace, where necessary, the conclusions and full-stops of his predecessors with new issues and question-marks.

B. J. Slot
2005

1

Kuwait's Emergence in the 19th Century

1.1 The question of Kuwait's origins

There is no need in this work to go into detail on the question of Kuwait's origins and whether or not it was an Ottoman administrative district, as the earliest contemporary historical sources on Kuwait have been investigated in a previous publication.[1] For the purposes of the present work, the most important such source is an undated report addressed to Jacob Mossel, the Governor-General of the Dutch East Indies. Internal evidence points to a date for this of 1756, and to its authorship as either solely by Tiddo Frederik van Kniphausen, head of the Dutch East India Company's establishment on Kharg island, or jointly by Kniphausen and his deputy Jan van der Hulst.[2] We know from other contemporary sources that Kniphausen knew the ruler of Kuwait personally, which gives this report particular credibility.[3] Kniphausen describes Kuwait as one of the largest Arab towns in the Gulf, and notes that it was ruled at that time by several shaikhs, of whom the first in rank was Mubarak bin Sabah. Mubarak, however, was poor, and another shaikh, Muhammad bin Khalifa, who was wealthy, enjoyed almost equal influence. The report makes the important point that, already by 1756, the Al-Sabah family apparently enjoyed a prominence based on tradition, rather than on actual wealth. It

[1] Slot, *Origins of Kuwait* (1998).
[2] The part of the text relevant to Kuwait is published in Slot, *Origins*, pp. 127–31.
[3] See the texts of the travel accounts of Piggot and Ives quoted in Slot, *Origins*, pp. 135–42.

cannot be verified exactly how far back this goes, but such traditional prestige could not have been of recent origin. The Kniphausen report accords with other sources available to us on the early history of Kuwait, that there existed at that time a nominal dependency upon the Banu Khalid tribal rulers of al-Hasa.

Kuwait, as it first appears in 18th-century sources and emerges more clearly in those of the 19th century, was essentially a littoral city-state with a desert hinterland. It functioned as a market linking the Gulf with the desert routes into Arabia and to the Mediterranean. Its maritime economy derived a considerable income from pearl-diving and long-distance shipping; while land-based livelihoods were drawn from desert transport to the interior, including the escorting of pilgrims, and to the Mediterranean, especially when the Mesopotamian routes were obstructed by the frequent disorders in the Ottoman provinces. It appears that the interests of the Al-Sabah were connected more with the landward aspect, and that ruling Kuwait was a matter of compromise between the ruling family and the merchants who controlled pearling and shipping.[4]

There was limited scope for investment in the small Kuwaiti economy. The town was situated in the arid desert, and outside it the only fixed settlement was at Jahra at the western end of the Gulf of Kuwait. The town of Kuwait lacked even a sufficient water supply, and water had to be brought in from far away. Kuwaitis tended to invest surplus funds in two ways: profits from the sale of pearls in India, for example, could be invested either there (which was open to risks), or in the purchase of date groves on the Shatt al-'Arab, which were vulnerable to the chicanery of Ottoman officials.[5]

The desert is like the sea: it is difficult to delineate precise borderlines there. Nomadic peoples move amongst each other and tribal loyalties may shift from one paramount shaikh to another. The years before the First World War saw disputes over all Kuwait's borders. The northern one was relatively well-defined. To the south-west the Qasim region of central Arabia was usually disputed between the surrounding powers, and Kuwait

[4] This situation is already indicated by observations by Niebuhr (around 1766) and Kniphausen (1756), see Slot, *Origins*, pp. 131 and 152. The tension between desert and maritime interests becomes very clear in sections 9.7 and 10.3 below.

[5] For an interesting view of the economic functions of Kuwait in the region, see a report by the Austrian consul in Baghdad, Rappaport, of 24 July 1901: Vienna HHSA, PA XXXVIII K 318.

itself exercised some influence there. The southern border of Kuwait was a de facto undefined area. Here the only border was the shifting line between tribes loyal to the Al-Sabah and those loyal to whichever ruler controlled Najd, and tribal loyalties were not always stable.[6] The northern border was the subject of diplomatic dispute in Mubarak's time. There was usually a clear distinction in the north between the "regular" territory of Kuwait and the right bank of the Shatt al-'Arab, where Kuwaitis owned most of the land. Nevertheless this situation caused the most authoritative map of Arabia of the 19th century to show the Fao peninsula as part of the "Republic of Kuwait".[7] The more established view was that the border of Kuwait ran outside Bubiyan and Warba islands along the Khor Abdallah, a shallow creek south-west of the Shatt al-'Arab, up to Umm Qasr where, according to one source, the rulers of Kuwait had lived in the distant past.[8] From there the border ran along the Jabal Sanam (which already by 1600 had been considered to be the border of the Ottoman province of Basra) to the Wadi al-Batin, which formed a clear boundary to the west of Kuwait. The area of Safwan, just outside the line between Jabal Sanam and the Wadi al-Batin, was controlled before 1902 by Kuwait.

What we know about the early history of Kuwait precludes any role for the Ottoman Empire in its creation. The Banu Khalid tribe were outside the sphere of Ottoman influence and it was they who, in 1662/3, put an end to the Ottoman province of al-Hasa.[9] There are no indications of any relationship between Kuwait and the Ottomans at that time. In the 18th century the Ottomans had great difficulty in maintaining themselves in Basra, and the only firm sources we have of that period record an incident in which the Kuwaitis assisted the enemies of the Ottoman Empire.[10] A

---

[6] Tribal loyalties had been the basis of drawing (or changing) borders in the region even before the arrival of the Europeans. A typical example is the region between the Shatt al-Ama and the Shatt al-'Arab: this belonged to the Ottoman Empire, but since the Ka'b tribe recognized Persian authority the lower Shatt al-'Arab became a boundary: Slot, *The Arabs of the Gulf*, pp. 11–12.

[7] *Arabien zu C. Ritter's Erdkunde, bearbeitet von H. Kiepert,* Berlin, Reimer Verlag 1867, later reprinted.

[8] Pelly, "Remarks on the Tribes", p. 72. Mubarak wrote in 1902 that a certain Bin Raziq, a man under Kuwait's authority, had built a fortress there in the time of Mubarak's grandfather Jabir: IOLR, R/15/1/475, Mubarak 7 February 1902.

[9] *EI*(2), Vol. 4, pp. 363–4, *i.v.* Katif; *cf.* the 18th-century list of Ottoman administrative districts in Marsigli, *Stato Militare*, pp. 124–5, where al-Hasa figures no longer as a province, but as a (purely titulary) *sancak*, a subdivision of a province.

second point about the Kniphausen report is that it shows conclusively that the traditional genealogy of the Sabah family is not exactly as it was recorded by British visitors in the first half of the 19th century: the British genealogies contain no mention of the Mubarak of 1756.[11]

In this context we should turn to one interesting source on the early history of Kuwait. This is Mubarak's own version of it, a typical product of oral tradition written down a long time after the events. As a general rule, such sources can be fairly reliable in recording historical facts, but are rather weak in locating those facts in their correct historical context. This seems to apply to this case: Mubarak appears to count down to the beginning of the 17th century, but as he apparently locates Sabah I there, he conflicts with other sources as well as with the Kniphausen report. Sabah I is usually located around 1750, and this tallies with the Kniphausen report which locates a young son of Sabah I as ruler in 1756. Moreover the document mentions a relationship of Kuwait with an Arab ruler of Qatif, which also suggests a period after *ca.* 1663.[12] But whenever it may be that Mubarak's ancestors began their rule in Kuwait, no link with the Ottoman Empire is apparent.

The later Ottoman claim to Kuwait, on the grounds that it was *ab antiquo* an Ottoman administrative district, was based not on any historical documentation but rather on a feeling that the entire Arabian Peninsula properly belonged to the Ottoman Empire. This feeling arose from a mixture of the concept of the Ottoman Empire as Caliphate and universal Islamic monarchy, with shadowy memories of sporadic Ottoman military expeditions around the coasts of the Peninsula in the 16th century. Kuwait was considered Ottoman in its origins much as Oman was considered to be originally Ottoman. This claim rested on thin ice. There is a noteworthy comment by the Austrian consul in Baghdad that the Ottoman claim to the Caliphate was not readily accepted by the Arabs of the Peninsula. The consul informed his minister that, while Hanafite Islam accepted a non-Arab Caliph, such a Caliph was unacceptable to the Hanbali school of Islam prevalent in the Arabian Peninsula, whose people thus found it

[10] Slot, *Origins of Kuwait*, p. 156.
[11] Hughes Thomas (ed.), *Selections from the Records of the Bombay Government*, pp. 295–6.
[12] IOLR, R/15/1/65, fols. 102(89)–106(94), Mubarak to Cox 28 Rabi' I 1331; the same in a shorter form in a letter of Mubarak from 1899, R 15/1/471, fols. 290–291 (Arabic version), fols. 293v–294.

difficult to accept the Ottoman claim to the Caliphate.[13]

The claim to authority over the entire Arabian Peninsula was promoted by the Ottomans despite the lack of cogent arguments to support it. But it was deployed with a certain force and conviction in a debate in which the other participants had no knowledge of the history of the region, and so it came to be widely accepted.

1.2 Kuwait before 1870

Kniphausen's remark about the political and social structure of Kuwait in 1756 accords very well with the 19th century references to Kuwait as a kind of aristocratic republic.[14] Thus it appears that the state of Kuwait was originally based on a kind of compact between an aristocracy of tribal leaders in which the chief member of the Al-Sabah family, even if he was not the most wealthy or powerful person in Kuwait, was considered to be head of state. This structure is quite unique for the Gulf at that time.

Kniphausen was a typical official of the Dutch East India Company, in that he was only interested in nautical activities, which were by then little developed. Fishing and pearl diving were still the principal pursuits. His report noted that the Kuwaitis played a very prominent role in pearling, having obtained a privileged position in Bahrain in 1753. There was, however, by that time another dimension to the economy of Kuwait: it had become the point of departure for caravans between the Gulf and the Mediterranean.[15] After 1756 the maritime business of the inhabitants of

---

[13] Vienna HHSA, PA XXXVIII K 318, Rappaport 26 March 1901. See also Berlin AA, R 13840 A 11796 (3 November 1895): trouble in Arabia where they are contesting the Ottoman Sultan's claim to the Caliphate.

[14] Slot, *Origins of Kuwait*, p. 131: "Several Shaikhs rule them, all living in relative unity. The highest ranking Shaikh is Mobarak eben Saback [Mubarak bin Sabah], but because he is poor and still young, another, called Mahometh Eben Khalifa, who is rich and owns many vessels, enjoys almost equal respect among them." The reference to the "Republic of Kuwait" first appears on a German map, *Arabien zu Carl Ritter's Erdkunde Buch III West-Asien theil XII u. XIII bearbeitet von H.Kiepert, Neu nerichtigte Ausgab, die Orthographie revidiert von H. Noeldeke, mit Nachtraegen aus den neuesten Berichten von Guarmani und Palgrave.* This map was published by D. Reimer in Berlin in 1867. No mention of a "Republic of Kuwait" occurs in any of the sources quoted in the title of this map. The German orientalist Oppenheim mistakenly credits Palgrave with the invention of the term "Republic of Kuwait": Berlin AA, R 14558 A 11184, Oppenheim 17 July 1901.

Kuwait seems to have expanded rapidly. Niebuhr, who was nearby in 1765, reports on the much-increased level of seafaring activity, and by the early 1780s the Kuwaitis had become the dominant Arab naval power in the Gulf. This increase may have been connected with Basra's decline as a result of the temporary Persian occupation of that town in 1775–9.

All these activities had their ups and downs. Trade routes could be closed by wars on land or sea, and pearl diving was subject to periodic dips during years of "bad harvest". Kuwait was a desert region with virtually no natural resources.[16] It is no wonder that, probably at an early stage, the Kuwaitis began to acquire date groves in Ottoman territory on the banks of the lower Shatt al-ʿArab to provide an extra prop for their vulnerable economy. It is not clear when exactly this started. Kuwaiti tradition ascribes it to the 18th century, and there are indications in written sources that it went back at least to the first half of the 19th century.[17] The date groves were important for the Kuwaiti economy but, as they were situated in regular Ottoman territory, they could – and would – provide the Ottoman government of Basra with a handy means of bringing pressure to bear on the rulers of Kuwait.

In the 18th-century Gulf the rulers were the principal entrepreneurs. During the course of the 19th century the ruler/entrepreneur disappeared: Saʿid bin Sultan of Oman was the last example of this kind. In most places around the Gulf, Persians and Indians dominated international commerce. Kuwait stands out as rather an exception to this. It was a typically Arab town, and there seems to have been considerable

[15] The overland trade aspect is duly noted by the German traveller Carsten Niebuhr, who made a scientific expedition to the Arabian Peninsula in the service of the King of Denmark and who obtained information from the Dutch East India Company officials on nearby Kharg. See Slot, *Origins of Kuwait*, pp. 127–31 and 145–53. It had already been noted by Dutch observers in 1750, ibid. pp. 117–20. The passage on Kuwait is in Niebuhr's *Beschreibung*, pp. 341–2.

[16] It is, however, interesting that in 1758 there were plans to exploit sulphur ore for the Dutch East India Company, a plan that was shelved and forgotten (see Slot, *Origins of Kuwait*, pp. 132–4). The possibilities were reconsidered much later, in the 20th century.

[17] The possessions were there long before 1870 (see Anscombe, *Ottoman Gulf*, p. 21), and the agreement on the division of some property between different branches of the Al-Sabah in 1903 indicates that the possessions dated from the common ancestor of these branches, who was probably Jabir I (d. 1859 or earlier).

resistance to the establishment of foreign merchants there.[18] The temporary sojourn of the British East India Company in Kuwait in 1793–5 does not undermine this view, for the importance of this presence has been much exaggerated – it was not a trading post, but simply a station for the forwarding of mail overland between India and the Mediterranean. Manesty, the British representative in Basra, used Kuwait as a temporary base for his blockade of the access to Basra when, in 1793–5, he was in conflict with the Pasha of that city. This affair was politically important given the international tensions of that time, but it was of no great economic significance.[19]

1.3 Kuwait and the Ottoman Empire up to 1866

The sources we have for the 19th century differ markedly on the question of Kuwait's status. Geographical manuals of the day speak of a "Republic of Kuwait", an aristocratic republic, prosperous, well-administered and independent of the Ottoman Empire.[20] The term "republic" somehow echoes the structure as described in Kniphausen's report of 1756. On the other hand there are texts, originating from the expeditions of the British Indian Navy to chart the Gulf in the 1820s, that mention Kuwait as a de facto independent state acknowledging some sort of undefined supremacy of the Ottoman Sultan. This supremacy seems to have been entirely nominal, as there was no effective Ottoman presence in Kuwait and no Ottoman taxes or customs duties were imposed there. Some of these references also state that Kuwaiti ships flew the Ottoman flag. One further detail is relevant to the status of Kuwait. One source states that Kuwait paid a nominal tribute to the Turks, while other sources say the opposite, that the Ottomans paid a kind of protection money to the Kuwaitis to keep the Shatt al-'Arab safe.[21]

The naval texts reveal that it was the Kuwaitis themselves who informed the officers of the Indian Navy exploring the Gulf that they recognized

[18] A report of the Dutch consul-general in the Gulf, Keun van Hogerwoerd, of 15 April 1870, states that "Kuwait is the only truly Arab trading town on the Gulf": The Hague NA, Foreign Ministry, Verbaal 15 June 1870, 4469(4409).
[19] Abu Hakima, pp. 42–3; Fontanier, *Voyage dans l'Inde*, Vol. 1, pp. 222–3.
[20] E. Reclus, *Nouvelle géographie universelle*, Vol. 9, pp. 891–2; Vivien de Saint Martin, *Nouveau dictionnaire de géographie universelle*, Vol. 3, p. 215 *i.v.* Koveit.

the vague supremacy of the Ottoman Sultan. Just at the time the naval reports were written, there was a rather impressive British presence in the upper Gulf, and the British were contemplating the occupation of Kuwait or Faylaka.[22] The Kuwaitis may well have been inspired to say what they said through fear of British intervention in Kuwait's affairs; in later incidents this fear is explicitly mentioned. In the 1860s Pelly, the British political resident at Bushire, had an explanation for it: the Ottoman flag was used by Kuwaiti ships because, if they used their own flag, they would have to pay high customs duties in Bombay. Pelly opines that the ruler of Kuwait demonstrated his adherence to the Ottoman Empire because he feared that, if Kuwait were independent, the British would subjugate it.[23] Pelly's remarks cannot be dismissed as being inspired by sinister British imperialist designs on Kuwait, although the Ottomans appear to have suspected him of such ambitions. In his reports, Pelly is actually sympathetic to Ottoman desires to annex Kuwait, and shows no interest in bringing Kuwait under British influence, so he has no reason to colour his arguments. But that his intelligence about the state of affairs in Kuwait was not especially reliable is shown by his erroneous statement that the Turks had apparently established a customs office in Kuwait.[24]

One may conclude that Kuwaitis used the Ottoman flag (among other flags, as mentioned by Ottoman sources) as a kind of flag of convenience.[25] Whatever may have been written in the 19th century about some kind of allegiance to the Ottoman Sultan, there is no evidence that this ever

[21] Hughes Thomas (ed.), *Selections from the Records of the Bombay Government,* p. 576 (Kuwait pays), as opposed to pp. 110 and 296 (the Turks pay).

[22] Kelly, *Britain,* p. 338. Also letters of the French consul in Basra in Nantes AD, consul at Basra, Vol. 6, fo. 44 (7 June 1839), old p. 128 (24 December 1839) and old p. 131 (26 December 1839; here the name Faylaka is also given in Arabic script).

[23] Pelly in J. Saldanha, *Précis of Kuwait Affairs,* p. 2.

[24] IOLR, LPS/9/19, p. 299, Pelly on the advantages of opening Kuwait to international trade by Ottoman occupation: "The Turks, it seems, have established the long-dreaded customs house at Kowait, a circumstance however which, as indirectly tending to open up the port of Kowait to the enterprise of our steamers, which have hitherto been discouraged by the Arab chief of Kowait – under pretence of their presence attracting the notice of the Turks." On the other hand it seems that some circles in India expected the establishment of British authority in Kuwait, as was announced in Bombay newspapers: Paris AE, CPC Bagdad 5, fos. 306–307, report French consul 17 December 1866.

[25] Midhat Pasha: 54 Kuwaitis occasionally used Dutch and British flags, *cf.* Pelly's remark in Saldanha, *Précis of Kuwait Affairs,* p. 2.

entailed Ottoman control over Kuwait's interior or exterior policy, or over the appointment of its rulers. This all makes it very difficult to express the status of Kuwait in any modern terminology. Western observers of that time tended to resort to concepts borrowed from Western feudal law. The relationship of the Sultan to the ruler of Kuwait was described as that of a suzerain to a vassal. This description matches the state of affairs rather well, because it applies to such vague relationships as those in the 18th century between the emperor and the fully sovereign states of the German Empire; these states would even occasionally declare war against their suzerain. In short, a state's recognition of the supremacy of a suzerain is no bar to the sovereignty of that state.

The crucial point in the relationship between Kuwait and the Ottoman Empire is that the Ottoman Empire was not a normal territorial state in the modern sense of the phrase. In the 17th and 18th centuries there had been Ottoman provinces such as Algeria and Tunisia that conducted their own independent diplomacy and went as far as declaring war and concluding peace treaties in their own name with no mention of the Grand Signor in Constantinople. Of the Arabian Peninsula the Ottoman Empire seems to have nurtured a concept that had little basis in reality. The entire Arabian Peninsula was regarded as Ottoman imperial territory, even though in fact Ottoman rule in the Gulf region had only a patchy history. In the 16th century an Ottoman navy had made a few rather unsuccessful sorties into the Gulf. It had plundered Muscat and Khor Fakan and there had been some skirmishes with the Portuguese on the mainland opposite Bahrain. Al-Hasa had been an Ottoman province in the 16th century, but this was no more than a much-besieged enclave within the territory of Arab tribes hostile to Ottoman rule, and it soon became limited to the town of Qatif. The *pashaliq* of al-Hasa had ceased to exist when the Banu Khalid Arabs conquered Qatif in 1663–4. By the 18th century there remained the paper titles of Beys of al-Hasa under the Pasha of Basra, but these had no real meaning on the ground.[26] In short, the Ottoman Empire, like the German Empire before 1804 though to a lesser extent, contained states where the local potentates, not the Emperor, enjoyed full sovereign rights, while still recognizing the Emperor as their nominal overlord. Moreover, the Ottoman Sultan claimed authority over territories such as Bahrain and Oman where not even this authority had been exercised, or

[26] Marsigli, *Stato Militare*, pp. 124–5.

where these claims had no practical meaning. As a result there existed a kind of fringe where the Ottoman Empire laid claim to a vague authority, but where the practical effect of the claim varied from very little to nothing at all. The Ottoman authorities were ambiguous in their attitude to the Western notion of a sovereign state with clearly defined borders. They could argue for the existence of one when it was to their advantage to do so, but were also able to point, when it suited them, to the supranational authority of the Sultan as Caliph to lay claim to frontiers that did not in reality exist.

The question of Ottoman authority over the littoral states of the Gulf was discussed in its general context by the celebrated German geographer Ritter in Vol. 11 of his great manual on geography. Ritter stated that the Ottomans and Persians were unable to exert any real authority over the coastal Arab shaikhdoms. He observed that, while French consuls and Russian diplomats might press the Ottomans to assert their claim, the Arab rulers behaved as if they were independent, and were supported in this stance by the tendency of the British to make agreements with them as if they were fully independent.[27]

Britain's position originated at the beginning of the 19th century, when it had felt its communications through the Gulf with India to be threatened. It had intervened in regions of the Arabian Peninsula, such as the coast of the present-day United Arab Emirates or the island of Bahrain, where the Ottomans had never ruled. These interventions had been limited to obliging the local rulers to accept some degree of British arbitration in conflicts with each other or with the outside world. The British right of intervention had been vaguely codified in a series of treaties on a "Maritime Truce". Even Kuwait had been briefly a party to such a treaty. There has been some subsequent discussion about the question of the legitimacy of the British position, but the fact remains that the British had treaties on paper, were present in fact, and took decisions that were enforced. The Ottoman claim was much weaker: they could point to no actual presence apart from a few raids in the 16th century.

Ritter seems to have been influenced by continental European opinions that disapproved of British attempts to monopolize trade and navigation in

[27] Ritter, *Erdkunde*, Vol. 11/3, pp. 1059–60. Ritter's principal source for this sketch of the situation was a rather anti-British book by the French consul in Basra, Victor Fontanier's *Voyage dans l'Inde*, Vol. 1, pp. 154–5.

the Gulf, and so hoped for an Ottoman or Persian counterweight to British supremacy. The trouble with this legalistic approach is that it is divorced from the political reality. The Ottoman Empire was not a unitary sovereign state in the European sense, and since the 17th century European states (not just Britain, but virtually all of them) had concluded treaties and declared war on Ottoman provincial governments without this affecting on their relations with the Sultan. This state of affairs originated in the early 17th century when European powers in diplomatic relations with the Ottoman Empire tried to pressure the Sultan into curbing the activities of North African corsairs. The Sultan's actual power over the provinces of Tunis, Algiers and Tripoli was limited, and nothing happened. Then the Europeans entered into separate arrangements with the provincial authorities in these places, without even informing the Ottoman Government in Constantinople, and the Turks accepted this.[28] The same situation obtained in the Gulf. The Turks and the Persians had no military or administrative presence in the coastal Arab states, which went about their business as if the Sultan and the Shah scarcely existed. Hence the British, if they were to protect their interests, had no option but to deal with these states as if they were independent. As the Ottomans had never really been in these areas (with the exception of the short-lived province of al-Hasa), Ottoman claims of sovereignty were no more than empty words.

In the 19th century the Kuwaitis found themselves in a delicate position, having to maintain their independence in an extremely unstable environment. In 1808 there had been a hostile British naval intervention in the southern Gulf and others over the years that followed, many of them directed against Arabs. The interior of Arabia was by turns unstable and under the sway of successive Saudi states. Kuwaitis appear to have countered this menace by claiming a vague relationship with the Ottomans that was in essence a kind of alliance: Kuwait offered services to the Ottomans in areas where the Ottomans had little military power, and

---

[28] Fontanier is not entirely correct in accusing the British of being the only Europeans to behave in this way. He claims that the French were better behaved, for example when they informed the Turks before their war of conquest against the Ottoman province of Algiers in 1830, see Fontanier, *Voyage*, Vol. 1, p. 155. This, however, was a rather special case: France (like Holland, Sweden, Denmark, Austria and Spain) also made treaties with Ottoman provinces without informing the Porte.

in exchange were able to call upon Ottoman protection for its own interests.[29]

For most of the 19th century the relationship between Kuwait and the Ottoman Empire remained a mere formality with no practical significance. In 1841 it did not prevent the Shaikh of Kuwait from signing, with the British, the so-called convention against piracy. This was a declaration by Arab shaikhs of the Gulf by which they granted Britain what ultimately amounted to control over their maritime relations. The signing of the convention by Kuwait has received little attention, but it is no less than a discreetly formulated protectorate treaty. The undertaking of Shaikh Sabah, who acted on behalf of his old and infirm father Jabir, contained the clause:

> Should, God forbid, anyone commit an act of aggression on my subjects and dependents at sea, I will not proceed immediately to retaliate but will inform the aforesaid Resident [of Bushire], so that he may proceed to carry out the necessary punishment and retaliation after enquiring into the matter.

The promise was for the term of one year, and no renewal appears to have been implemented.[30] It was a limitation of his sovereignty for the Shaikh to undertake that, if attacked at sea, he would not retaliate but instead call on the British to decide whether to take action. As an Ottoman subject one would expect him to alert the nearest Ottoman official, but Shaikh Sabah of Kuwait knew as well as anybody that this would be a dangerous and futile step, and an expensive one too as presents would be expected. One significant point in this episode was, however, that Shaikh Sabah, when offered the treaty with the other Gulf states to add his signature, refused to do so and demanded a separate agreement for Kuwait alone, stating that he did not wish to be put on an equal footing with the rulers of the Trucial States.[31]

---

[29] Kemball stated in 1854 that Kuwait received a payment of 200 *karrah* of dates in exchange for protecting Basra against foreign aggression: Hughes Thomas (ed.), *Selections from the Records of the Bombay Government*, pp. 110, 296.

[30] The treaty was rediscovered in 1913: see IOLR, R/15/5/59, fo. 131.

[31] New Delhi NAI, Foreign Department, Secret, 12 July 1841, no. 42. The conclusion of the agreement was in fact merely intended by the British to provide a pretext for a warship to visit Kuwait in order to appraise its suitability as a naval station!

Little wonder then that the French consul in Basra could report in 1839 that the British were negotiating with Kuwait about the establishment of a British base on Faylaka without even mentioning that this might be in Ottoman territory.[32] Nor, it seems, did the British feel any legal qualms on this point; they were merely unsure of the suitability of Kuwait or Faylaka.[33] Even more significant in this light are the events of 1841–2 involving the Ka'b. There had been a struggle over the leadership of the Ka'b, on the Persian bank of the Shatt al-'Arab. Their Shaikh, Thamir, had been removed with Persian support, Thamir had fled to Kuwait, and the Persians requested the Turks to arrest him there. But events totally confounded this plan: Shaikh Sabah, son of the ruler of Kuwait, took a Kuwaiti force to the other side of the Shatt al-'Arab to re-instate Shaikh Thamir.[34]

Fontanier narrates a very telling story about Kuwait's status. Though his book is weak on chronology, the story does appear to relate to the events involving Shaikh Thamir. Fontanier remarks that the Ottomans had on that occasion also decided to attack Kuwait:

> Next he [the Pasha of Baghdad] wanted to go to the coast and force the Shaikh of Gren into submission, even ordering him to present himself before him, but the Shaikh who was old and clever, while declaring his loyalty, announced that on His Excellency's approach, he would flee with his people to an island which was his capital. The Pasha would be unable to pursue him because he had no ships and so was forced to abandon his plan. Finally the Pasha decided, as a good Turk, to resign himself to Providence and to stay where he was."[35]

For Kuwait to maintain its independence at that juncture was easy, because of the parlous position of the Ottoman authorities in Basra. They were threatened just then by the Egyptian presence in Arabia, and a serious economic crisis in Mesopotamia was imminent. Basra at that time had only 7–8000 inhabitants left, and thus must have been a much smaller

---

[32] Nantes AD, consulat Bassora, Vol. 6, fo. 44, letter of French vice-consul in Basra to French consul in Baghdad of 7 June 1839.

[33] Kelly, *Britain*, p. 347.

[34] Nantes AD, consulat Bassora, Vol. 7, letters of 31 December 1841 and 21 April 1842.

[35] Fontanier, *Voyage*, Vol. 1, pp. 377–8.

town even than Kuwait was.[36] One can agree with the conclusion in Kelly's book, by far the best work on the period:

> Kuwait's position in relation to the Ottoman Empire was obscure. At the time that Ottoman rule extended down the eastern coast of Arabia the shaikhdom as such did not exist. Kuwait town was not founded until after the disappearance of effective Ottoman rule in the region. Yet the Ottoman Sultan or at least his representative in Baghdad, persisted in claiming suzerainty over the shaikhdom. Since the Turks were incapable of enforcing their claim the attitude of the Al Sabah towards them was much like that of the Al Khalifah towards the Persians, viz. to ignore the claim on most occasions, to deny it on others, and to tolerate it when danger threatened from another quarter.[37]

1.4 The Ottoman attempt to gain control, 1866–7

It had been impossible for the Ottomans to intervene in Kuwaiti affairs during the first half of the 19th century, because of the weakness of their position in Basra. They began to show a greater interest in Gulf affairs after 1841, when Western pressure had obliged Muhammad Ali to withdraw his Egyptian forces from the Arabian provinces. However, considerable time was to pass before the Ottomans showed much interest in the difficult Basra region. Basra oscillated between being an independent province and just part of the province of Baghdad. The Basra province or district was a rather marginal region. Most of its area was controlled by Arab tribes, and the port of Basra was not thriving. Hence state income from customs and land taxes was small. Problems became apparent in 1866 during Namiq Pasha's second term as Wali of Baghdad. The thrust of Namiq's policy was to break the power of the Arab tribes in Iraq, but the province produced insufficient means to execute such a policy.[38]

Namiq Pasha was confronted by growing British activity in the region. The British position in Iraq was, strictly speaking, anomalous: under the Ottoman system the British representative in Baghdad should have been

[36] Paris AE, CPC Bagdad 4, fo. 55, consul Baghdad to Minister 15 February 1836.
[37] Kelly, *Britain*, p. 33.
[38] Longrigg, *Four Centuries*, p. 284. Paris AE, CPC Bagdad 5, fos. 240–252, Peretié to Minister 12 October 1864, mentions that Arab tribal leaders sought the support of the British against Namiq Pasha in vain.

simply a consul, but he called himself the Political Resident, and enjoyed accessories such as a large armed guard that made him more like a colonial official. In 1861, just before Namiq Pasha's arrival in Baghdad, a British shipping line began operating on the Tigris between Baghdad and Basra. During Namiq's time, furthermore, there were signs of increasing British involvement in the Gulf, and contacts between the British and various Arab tribes which, while not appearing very significant in the British sources, none the less caused the Turks some anxiety.[39] The Turks' attitude is understandable: in Iraq they were a long way from their supply bases and they constituted a minority amongst the unruly tribes.

At that juncture the Al-Sabah family became embroiled in a troublesome affair. When Shaikh Abdallah, the ruler's eldest son, arrived at the date groves in Basra province to collect the revenues, he was suddenly arrested and held prisoner in the Basra kaymakam's residence. This arose from a conflict between the Al-Sabah and the Zuhair family of Zubair over ownership of an island in the Shatt al-'Arab. The Al-Sabah claimed to have bought it legitimately from Ya'qub Al-Zuhair, while the other party claimed that the Al-Sabah had simply occupied it. The kaymakam had taken the Zuhair side, for merely political reasons according to the British consul in Basra. In the end Abdallah Al-Sabah had to go to Baghdad to defend his interests in the provincial capital, Basra at that time not being an independent province. There he won his case, but the upshot was that the attention of the Ottoman administration was now fully focused on Kuwait.[40]

Rumours of British designs on Kuwait may have inspired Ottoman measures to integrate the shaikhdom. At least the French consul in Baghdad, Pélissier, warned his government on 3 November 1866 of a risk of Ottoman intervention in Kuwait fuelled by rumours in Baghdad about British intrigues:

---

[39] See for instance the following quote from the British consul in Basra, letter of 26 June 1866: "Adverting to the peculiar position politically considered of the Sheikhs and people of Koweit [...] and to the suspicions and apprehensions which recent events in the Persian Gulf have excited in the mind of Namik Pasha, I venture to submit [...] the expediency of inviting the British Indian Steam Navigation Company, to suspend for a while its visits to that port": Saldanha, *Précis*, Vol. 5 (Kuwait Affairs), p. 5.

[40] Saldanha, *Précis*, Vol. 5 (Kuwait Affairs), pp. 4–5.

Colonel Pelly, English Resident of Bushire, who continually runs to and fro through the Gulf on a small official ship and who maintains intensive relations with the inhabitants of both shores of the Gulf has, according to the information I was able to collect, recently persuaded the Shaikh of Kuwait (who on the other hand was advised by the Imam of Muscat) to request the Queen's Government to place him under its protection. He has proposed to make the place a free port. Kuwait, situated at the far end of the Persian Gulf, has at present as its Shaikh a certain Sba Ibn Gaber who succeeded his father a few months ago. The district of this town is independent of the authority of the Porte, and the kaymakam of Basra has even paid it for a long time a kind of disguised tribute in order not to have its navigation disrupted by these valiant sailors. The non-payment of this tribute in recent times and fears that the Turks might interfere in their affairs have convinced the inhabitants of Kuwait, if I am properly informed, to accept the suggestions of Colonel Pelly. The Government of Baghdad, which pretends to have some authority over this town, has been alarmed by the British moves and has requested instructions from the Porte.[41]

Pélissier slightly modified his story six weeks later. While some people confirmed the news about British intrigues over Kuwait, others, including the British consul, completely denied it. Despite that, the French consul came across the following item in the Bombay newspapers: "The shaikhs of Kuwait in the Persian Gulf have offered their port and their town to the British Government as a present in order to make a free port of it and have consented to fly the British flag."[42] Such newspaper reports are also mentioned in a British consular report from Basra, and the news even reached *The Times* of London and French newspapers during 1866. It all appears to stem from an informal contact in 1864 between Pelly and a certain Kuwaiti named "Aboo Esaw". Pelly's very short report on this meeting had been discussed by the Government of India and printed in its secret proceedings:

When Aboo Esaw was with me a few days ago he stated, among other matters, that he was deputed as a confidential agent on behalf of the Sheikhs of Koweit to tender their township and harbour in free gift to

[41] Paris AE, CPC Bagdad 5, fos. 302–303.
[42] Paris AE, CPC Bagdad 5, fos. 306–307, Hadjoute Pélissier to Ministry 17 December 1866.

the English Government as a free port and to hoist the English flag. I replied simply that it was a question which had never before come under my consideration and one upon which I could not enter. Koweit is the best administered chieftainship of the Gulf and one of the wealthiest. It is the point of export for Arab horses and the point which our sea-going steamers may one day select as a terminus in preference to Busrah river.[43]

Kemball, the British political agent in Turkish Arabia, reported from Baghdad at the end of November 1866 that the Shaikhs of Kuwait had until then succeeded in evading compliance with Namiq Pasha's demand that an Ottoman customs office be established in Kuwait, but that the Turks were just waiting for the arrival of some of their warships in the Gulf to force the issue. In the meantime the visits of steamships of the B.I.S.N.Co. to Kuwait had been suspended.[44]

The French, who had a traditional interest in Oman, Baghdad and Basra, found the rumours of British activity in the Gulf sufficiently intriguing to warrant verification. A small warship, the *Diamant*, was sent to the Gulf. The *Diamant* visited Kuwait but Bosc, its commander, discovered the Shaikh of Kuwait to be "not enthusiastic" about the British and poured cold water on the reports in the Bombay newspapers. According to Bosc, the Arabs found the prospective advantages of relations with the British quite tempting, but feared their "encroaching tendencies".[45]

The cooling of Kuwaiti sympathy with the British as reported by Bosc may well have been due to the fact that, in the meantime, the Ottoman reaction predicted by Pélissier had taken place. On 5 January 1867 Johnston, the British agent in Basra, reported unease in Kuwait provoked by fears that the Turks intended to extend their control along the coast of

[43] New Delhi NAI, Foreign, Consultations August 1866 no. 55.
[44] New Delhi NAI, Foreign Political A, January 1867, no. 150–151.
[45] Paris AE, CPC Bagdad 6, report of the consul in Baghdad, 21 March 1867. A report of the *Diamant* on Kuwait was not found, but the archives of the French naval station Lorient contain one earlier report (Lorient, Services historiques de la Marine 4 C 5 document 6 B) stating that on his arrival at Basra the captain had found a letter from the consul in Baghdad "about rumours in newspapers that the Shaikhs and inhabitants of Kuwait had offered their town and port to the English, but up to now I heard nothing of the sort and here [in Basra] it seems that the most perfect harmony exists between the Shaikh of Kuwait and the Sultan his *suzerain*. I will visit the place after I have left here."

the Gulf, down to Muscat, as soon as the current tribal unrest in Lower Iraq had been quelled. The Governor of Basra had summoned Shaikh Abdallah to explain the newspaper reports about the offer to the British. A most extraordinary discussion then took place between Johnston, Salim Al-Badr (the Al-Sabah agent in Basra) and a certain "Abdulla ibn Esa el Ibrahim, one of the elders of Koweit" about the future of Kuwait. Three options were seriously considered. The first was to let the Turks in, but to sabotage Kuwait's economy in such a way (by allowing trade only via Basra) that the place would become valueless and the Turks would abandon it. The second was to admit the Turks, but to establish a Kuwaiti settlement on Abadan and so let "the inevitable depopulation of Koweit take its natural course". The third option was to abandon Kuwait entirely and to settle in Abadan. The Shaikh of Muhammara, who controlled that region, thought that the Persians would welcome the Kuwaitis. Open resistance to the Turks was raised as an option, but not really considered during this debate. Johnston advised the Kuwaitis to recommend a positive response to Namiq Pasha's former invitation to come to Basra to receive formal investiture as Shaikh of Kuwait.[46]

The Kuwaitis thus seem to have been sounding out the British agent, very discreetly, about British views on the future of the region. It is clear that their inclination was to bow to Ottoman pressure, but to find a way of getting rid of the Turks again as soon as possible. Evidently Johnston, for his part, preferred stability, even if this were to involve Ottoman expansion.

A more general appraisal of the Kuwait question was given by Kemball, the British resident in Baghdad, in a letter of 23 January 1867 to the Foreign Department in Calcutta. Kemball's conclusion was:

> I am of the opinion that as long as His Excellency [Namiq] confines his demands (supported by an efficient naval force) to a moderate amount of tribute, the Sheikhs of Kowait will not demur to its payment, but that the attempt, if persisted in, to introduce any form of Turkish administration on the spot will, after a certain amount of passive resistance, lead to the secession of the inhabitants of that place. Kowait, from the circumstances of its political constitution, affords peculiar attractions to a seafaring community, composed of an agglomeration of individuals from different tribes whose resources are exclusively derived from maritime relations, but its sole physical advantage consists in its harbour which is capacious

[46] New Delhi NAI, Foreign Political A March 1867, no. 30–31.

and secure. The spot is even destitute of good water and the surrounding country is barren and improductive. As the mart of Northern Arabia it enjoys no superiority over Bussorah and its prosperity as a port is dependent upon the carrying trade which provides occupation to its vessels. The material interests of the population being thus in a very slight degree bound up with the soil, it is to the restraints imposed by this condition, I believe, that must be ascribed the mild and patriarchal rule of the dominant family and their exemption from the domestic or tribal conflicts as well as abstinence from the piratical courses which have characterized the other maritime communities of the Persian Gulf. Did Koweit, therefore, cease to be a free port, and were its Government trammeled with the forms of Turkish administration (whose ascendance is everywhere based upon the feuds of its tributaries), it is probable that the inhabitants would seek asylum in more favoured localities.

No such radical denouement came to pass, because the Turks resorted, as they would so often in future over Kuwait, to half measures. On 20 January 1867, the Ottoman corvette *Izmir* left Basra for Kuwait. On arrival, it fired a 21-gun salute.[47] Kuwait replied with the same number. Its commander bore a letter, a *firman* (a document signed by the Sultan), and presents for Shaikh Abdallah.[48] After much saluting to and fro the *Izmir* left for Basra again. The only Turks who had actually disembarked were the *Izmir*'s commander and the doctor. Sayyid Muhammad Sa'id Effendi, who had brought an order to open a customs house in Kuwait from Baghdad, had excused himself from participating in the expedition at all. The following events are described by Johnston as follows:

> Namik Pasha's letter was complimentary, it conveyed to Abdulla the firman of his appointment as Sheikh of Koweit in succession to his father, deceased, and renewed the invitation to Baghdad, which Sheikh Abdulla on the plea of preoccupation with the duties of his new office, had before declined. It contained no allusion whatever to the establishment of a Customs House, or to payment of tribute of any kind. In his reply Sheikh

---

[47] Quite exuberant on the part of the Ottomans: a 21-gun salute is for heads of state.
[48] If it was intended that the Ruler of Kuwait would become a regular Ottoman official, then one would expect that Namiq would have brought a *berat* (a diploma of appointment), not a simple *firman* which is essentially a letter. The information comes from a consular report and a consul would certainly have been aware of this distinction because he frequently had to handle both types of document.

Abdulla expresses gratitude for His Excellency's notice and presents, but he studiously avoids any reference to the proposed visit to Baghdad. Ahmed Beg was not charged with any verbal message, nor did he express a desire to see any person or place, but spent most of his time in the Sheikh's divan, visited nobody, made no allusion to the Customs House or British flag affair, and the only occasion on which he left the Shaikh's house was to view a sham fight at the town gate, which, with the aid of the Arabdar (outlaying Arab communities) had been somewhat ostentatiously prepared to impress him with the military resources of the place. I am satisfied that nothing more took place than what I have related and am consequently at a loss to suggest the object of the Izmir's voyage. As a demonstration of force I am well assured that it failed its effect. The slovenly manner in which the vessel was handled and her inefficiency as a man of war were much criticized and Shaikh Abdulla appears designedly to have treated his Turkish guests with scarcely less nonchalance than was manifested by his Grandfather Sheikh Jaabir. On a similar occasion in 1860 when Mustafa Pasha deputed a commission to Koweit and Bahrain he readily accepted the flag which was tendered to him, but betrayed much reluctance to wear the koorq (dress of investiture) and though he eventually yielded to the remonstrances of those present and put it on, throwing his old ragged cloak over it, he took an early opportunity of leaving the divan to deposit the garment elsewhere. He gave Ahmed Beg some trifling presents and a cadeau of G[rand]S[ignior] P[iastre]s 15000.[49]

The Ottoman attempt had come to nothing. The conclusion was very pithily expressed by Pélissier, who remarked: "The people of Kuwait do not wish to depend upon either the Turks or the English, but would deliver themselves voluntarily to the latter if the former were to try to dominate their country."[50]

This Ottoman initiative was not followed up. Anscombe refers to Ottoman documents indicating that the Turks did not pursue the attempt to establish an Ottoman customs office in Kuwait because the Shaikh of Kuwait had warned of strong popular opposition.[51] Here we have a conclusion shared in common by the Turks, the British and the French.

[49] Johnston report to Kemball in Basra in New Delhi NAI, Foreign Political A, March 1867, no. 191, and in IOLR, LPS/3/72 (Home Correspondence 61), Johnston to Kemball 23 January 1867.
[50] Paris AE, CPC Bagdad 6, fos. 6–, Pélissier to Minister 21 March 1867.

Ottoman pressure on Kuwait seems to have derived chiefly from a desire to increase their customs revenues. There was, however, another aspect to it too: Ottoman anxiety about British expansion in an area the Ottomans regarded as their own rightful sphere of influence. This aspect was particularly dangerous because it was based on a misunderstanding of British intentions. Fear of perceived British ambitions inspired the Ottomans to plan the occupation of Kuwait; they would encounter no British opposition, because the British had no designs on the shaikhdom. Shaikh Abdallah appears to have been able to maintain his independence, but the Ottoman threat persisted.

Shaikh Abdallah had managed this crisis rather deftly. He made just sufficient concessions to the Turks to avert armed intervention.[52] The circumstances had shown that the British had lost their interest in Kuwait and wanted to avoid a conflict with the Ottoman Empire in the upper Gulf region. Kuwait had no real allies against the Ottomans and Abdallah had no choice but to maintain good relations with them. In 1868 Namiq Pasha was recalled to Constantinople, to the general relief of the people of Iraq.[53] His successor, Taki ed-Din Pasha, showed little taste for action and so there was a brief respite.

1.5 Kuwait and Midhat Pasha

The Porte recalled Taki ed-Din Pasha of Baghdad after less than a year, and appointed Midhat Pasha, highly regarded for his expertise in governing difficult provinces. Midhat Pasha had acquired a good reputation as a reformer in the Balkans. Contemporary observers are much more critical about his tenure in Baghdad, where he embarked upon an ambitious policy of administrative reforms, improvement of the infrastructure and

[51] Anscombe, *Ottoman Gulf*, p. 21, and n. 21 referring to Istanbul BA, Ayniyat 851/20 (27 May 1867) and Ayniyat 851/27 (21 October 1867).

[52] Rush, *Al-Sabah*, p. 139, has some negative words about Abdallah which appear to be based on a lack of understanding of the situation in the 1860s and 1870s. He is mistaken in his description of Abdallah's habit of sumptuous receptions: he took this from an apparently unreliable Arab translation of a travelogue by an American author he refers to as Luther (*sic*; correctly Locher). This text, however refers to Sabah II, not to Abdallah. There is nothing in it more negative than that the old Shaikh wore expensive clothes and jewelry. Locher, *Star*, pp. 55–60.

[53] Paris AE, CPC Bagdad 6, fos. 38–39, Bagdad 15 March 1868.

expansion into the Arabian Peninsula. This policy proved to be too grandiose for the limited resources of an impoverished province. Midhat left Baghdad province worse off than it had been before.

Midhat's policy in Iraq was not particularly original to him. Much of it had already formed part of Namiq Pasha's programme: exerting control over nomadic tribes, improvement of communications, countering English influence in Iraq as well as in the Arabian Peninsula, obtaining some influence over Kuwait and acquiring its revenues. Midhat was in a much stronger position than Namiq because he was not only Wali, but also commander of the Ottoman VI Army Corps, which was stationed in Baghdad. This combination of functions was most unusual.[54] Midhat was more subtle and decisive in his pursuit of these goals, but in the end his achievements remained limited.

A central theme of Midhat's policy was the transformation of the backward Baghdad province into a regular province of the Ottoman Empire. Administrative reforms of recent years had introduced a French system of regional government into the Ottoman Empire, whereby the units corresponding to *département*, *arrondissement* and *canton* had been named *wilaya*, *mütesariflik* and *kaza*. In areas with nomad populations a newly introduced registration system of landownership served to stabilize the situation. The measure was directed especially at the Muntafiq tribes. This large tribal conglomerate on the Euphrates above Basra had constituted the main threat to Ottoman control over Basra province since the 17th century, and had even been able on occasion to conquer Basra from the Ottomans. Midhat managed to settle part of the Muntafiq and to found a city for them at Nasiriyya. This operation was less successful than claimed by Midhat's admirers, because most of the Muntafiq were to remain unruly for as long as Ottoman rule over Basra province was to last. The land registration measures were a matter not just of improving public order, but also of increasing the income of the province from land taxes.[55]

There was another important aspect to the land registration. In many parts of the Ottoman Empire a declaration of Ottoman nationality had

---

[54] *EI*(2), Vol. 6, pp. 1031–5, *i.v.* Midhat Pasha, especially p. 1033.
[55] On the Muntafiq, see Chiha, *Province de Bagdad*, pp. 242, 244–5. According to Chiha, the Muntafiq (70,000 tents or 350,000 people, by far the largest tribal group in the region) were Shiite, except the ruling family which was Sunni. *EI*(2), Vol. 7, pp. 582–3, *i.v.* Muntafik.

often been required from landowners as a condition of registration. This was originally intended to undermine the protection foreign diplomatic missions were able to extend over Christian or Jewish inhabitants of the Ottoman Empire through the so-called Capitulations. These non-Muslim inhabitants were in this way coerced into resigning their foreign protection to become ordinary Ottoman subjects. In the end this goal was not achieved because most European powers insisted on exemptions from this system for their subjects. Under the administration of Midhat Pasha and his successors, the necessity of adopting Ottoman nationality as a precondition of registering landownership was occasionally proposed to the Al-Sabah for the land they owned in Basra province, but to no avail.

Midhat also tried to restore the fortunes of Basra. Terrible epidemics had reduced its population to just a few thousand. Midhat decided to move the city to a more salubrious location. There were plans for Fao, the point where the telegraph system of British India connected with the Ottoman telegraph line down from Baghdad. The project to move Basra was grossly over-ambitious given the slender financial means of Baghdad province.[56]

The element of Midhat's policy that most concerns us here is his attempt to reassert Ottoman control over affairs in the Arabian Peninsula. This was a resumption of Namiq Pasha's old policy and implied a new threat to Kuwait. There existed an almost neurotic anxiety in Ottoman circles about supposed British intrigues in the Gulf region. This was scarcely necessary, as the British were not particularly strong in the region at that time, while the opening of the Suez Canal in 1869 enabled the Ottomans to move troops and materiel with greater speed from Constantinople to Basra. Midhat was particularly concerned to improve the communications infrastructure of his province, so empowering the Wali to control events in the Basra district, something that had been almost impossible in the past. So it is little wonder that one of his first steps was the acquisition of steamboats, with which he hoped to break the monopoly of British firms over navigation in the Gulf and on the Euphrates. But the impact was not especially resounding. The French consul was rather scathing about the limited potential of the *Assur*, laden

---

[56] Paris AE, CPC Bagdad 6, fos. 107–110, 17 November 1869; see also Geary, *Through Asiatic Turkey*, Vol. 1, pp. 93–4. One wonders whether Midhat Pasha's interest in Kuwait (soon to be so conspicuous) with its land holdings in Fao had something to do with this plan.

with cargo, it was unable to reach Basra port through the shallow Shatt al-'Arab. It was useful only as a troop transport, and the cost of acquiring the ship had drained Midhat's treasury.[57]

As we have seen, the Ottomans had always fostered a vague conception of the Arabian Peninsula as part of their territory, but had been able to do little about enforcing the claim. The opening of the Suez Canal and Midhat's attempts to improve the infrastructure of Baghdad province afforded the Ottomans the means to make their presence felt, but their claims were so grandiose and sweeping as to render a collision with British interests inevitable. Midhat activated his Arabian policy immediately after Ramadan, at the start of January 1870, when he left Baghdad for Basra.[58] He appears to have been alerted by British intervention in a quarrel amongst the ruling family of Bahrain. There the Ruler, Shaikh Muhammad, had been expelled by his brother 'Ali. Muhammad had taken refuge in Kuwait and had there appealed to the Saudis for help. With Saudi assistance Muhammad had been able to overcome 'Ali and return to Bahrain, where he wantonly plundered the capital. British subjects in Bahrain (from India) suffered heavy losses. Muhammad's reign lasted only a short time. The British resident in Bushire intervened with a small naval force, claiming compensation for the aggrieved British subjects, and Muhammad was replaced by the son of 'Ali. In Baghdad it was rumoured that this would afford the British the occasion to consolidate their hold on the Gulf.[59]

Midhat Pasha seems to have nurtured plans to enforce an Ottoman claim to Bahrain. This did not come entirely out of thin air, for Muhammad had previously appealed to the Ottomans for protection.[60] In March 1870 Midhat informed Herbert, the British consul-general in Baghdad, that Bahrain and its dependencies were an integral part of the Ottoman *kaymakamlik* of Najd. Herbert was under no illusion about Midhat's ambitions and informed London the next month that the ultimate goal of Ottoman policy was "the recovery of the Arabian coast and Muscat".[61]

---

[57] Paris AE, CPC Bagdad 6, fos. 113–118, consul Bagdad 2 March 1870; ibid., fol. 116–116v.

[58] Paris AE, CPC Bagdad 6, fol. 107, 25 January 1870.

[59] Paris AE, CPC Bagdad 6, fos. 103–105, 17 November 1869; see also Kelly, *Britain*, pp. 682–3; *EI*(2), Vol. 4, p. 953, *i.v.* Al-Khalifa; Anscombe, *Ottoman Gulf*, p. 156, n. 17.

[60] Kelly, *Britain*, pp. 399–400, 502. In 1859 Muhammad had even formally approached the Wali of Baghdad, ibid. p. 515.

[61] PRO, FO 195/949, Midhat Pasha to Herbert 6 March 1870.

Nor did the French consul in Baghdad harbour any illusions about Midhat's intentions. But he considered the scheme doomed to founder among the diplomatic toils of the time. He held the view that Midhat was over-influenced by inexperienced hotheads around him, and gives an interesting sketch of the background.[62] While Ottoman control over Baghdad province was far from complete, Midhat Pasha, he says

> wants to create problems outside because he seems intent on acquiring for his government protectorate rights over all the small Muslim states near the Persian Gulf and even those of the Arabian Peninsula that are on the Gulf of Oman, and so return to the arms of Islam the prestige which they lost a long time ago.[63]

The British, who maintained only small vessels in the Gulf, were alarmed by the Ottoman designs on Bahrain. With the limited naval means at their disposal, they feared they would be unable to control the situation in the area. Meanwhile Midhat had been warning his government that the British intended to expand their power to the Arabian mainland, where al-Hasa was, according to him, in imminent danger. One must suspect either that the Turks were badly informed, or that Midhat and the zealots in his entourage were exaggerating the British menace as a pretext for their grand design to subjugate the Arabian Peninsula. Midhat expressly informed the Grand Vizier that the British, having seized al-Hasa and Qatif, would occupy Kuwait, which was so close to Basra. Thus did Midhat urge the necessity of an Ottoman intervention in Kuwait.[64] In reality such expansionist ideas formed no part of British thinking; the British were merely apprehensive about Ottoman interference in Bahrain.

Midhat's initial steps in the Arabian arena were directed at Kuwait, which Namiq Pasha had already targeted without lasting impact. His first measure was taken under the umbrella of his general policy in Baghdad province: to acquire control over the tribes by introducing the modern system of land administration instituted by recent Ottoman legislation. The matter of the land law exposed a complication in the position of Kuwait, because the Al-Sabah family and other Kuwaitis owned

---

[62] Paris AE, CPC Bagdad 6, fo. 110, Rogier 25 January 1870.
[63] Paris AE, CPC Bagdad 6, fo. 121, Rogier to Direction Politique in Paris 26 March 1870.
[64] Anscombe, *Ottoman Gulf*, p. 21, quoting Ottoman documents of February 1870.

considerable estates in Basra province. It is not clear exactly how and when these possessions originated, but they offered Midhat an easy target. He sequestrated the Al-Sabah palm groves and waited. When representatives of the Al-Sabah came to Basra to protest, Midhat put them under pressure.

By acting thus over the palm groves and by reviving the plan for a customs house in Kuwait, Midhat Pasha's policy seems to have been inspired in part by the desire to improve the financial basis of the Basra district (there was no Basra province at that time), and in part by fear that the British might bring the "independent republic" of Kuwait under their influence. He wrote an extensive report on the shaikhdom to the Grand Vizier. This misrepresented Kuwait as having been a former dependency of Basra and thus Ottoman territory; because the Ottomans had neglected it, it had become more or less independent and the Europeans had come to consider it as an independent republic, which could lead to European interference.[65]

Kuwait town was reputed at that time to be a larger place than Basra.[66] Midhat soon made good his announcements of February 1870 and took steps to establish Ottoman control over it. Unfortunately, the sources are somewhat vague about what Midhat actually did. The British sources do not really cover the events and the French were busy with other matters in 1870. Mubarak, who was present at one important stage of the negotiations, wrote an account of them, but this was written almost 30 years afterwards. We have Midhat's official reports, but one should treat this version with some suspicion as his actions were not fully supported by the Ottoman government and he may have somewhat misrepresented them to his superiors.

The same goes for the quaint account of the events as given later by Midhat's son in his biography of his father. This depicts Midhat's intervention in Kuwait in rather rosy hues, and errors in the account betray a lack of local knowledge:

> They [the Kuwaitis] had maintained their quasi-independence under
> their own chiefs, the descendants of one Sabah who had come with his

[65] Anscombe, *Ottoman Gulf*, p. 21, quoting the letter of Midhat to the Grand Vizier of 28 Kanun-i thani 1285/9 February 1870 in Istanbul BA, Usul-i Irade Dosya 77.
[66] Basra was said to have only a few thousands inhabitants at that time, while Kuwait was said to have 6000–7000 houses: figures given by the French consul in Baghdad in 1870, Paris AE, CPC Bagdad 6, fos. 107v and 114v.

tribe of Moutayer [sic!] from Nedjed five hundred years before, and had maintained ever since with practical independence a republican form of government, choosing by election their own judges (cadis) and the professors of their religious schools (medresses). Owing to the restricted extent of their territory, the inhabitants, like those of Venice, took chiefly to maritime pursuits, and upwards of two hundred small vessels of various tonnage traversed in every direction the Indian Ocean, as far as the coasts of Zanzibar, and practically monopolised the pearl fisheries of the Persian Gulf. Although they had adopted a special flag of their own, they occasionally hoisted a Dutch or English flag, to secure certain privileges accorded to these flags by the capitulations. It seemed highly desirable to Midhat Pasha to put an end to this equivocal status of the inhabitants of Koweit, and to regularise their position. He accordingly entered into negotiations with them, and offered the full enjoyment of their autonomy and privileges under the government of their own Sheik Sabah, provided they recognised themselves as forming part and parcel of the Ottoman empire, and adopted the Ottoman flag as their national ensign. These conditions were accepted by the people of Koweit, and their territory became a sandjak[67] of the vilayet of Bagdad. A formal treaty to that effect was drawn up and signed and confirmed by berats (writs of investiture) from Constantinople, and new schools and mosques arose in Koweit.[68]

Perhaps it was no mere coincidence that the story presented by Midhat's son bears some resemblance to Midhat's own report to the Ottoman Government of 9 April 1870. According to this, Midhat simply applied blackmail by blocking the important revenue from the Basra date groves. He says that then the Kuwaiti shaikhs came to petition him and asked to be put under Ottoman authority.[69] We may believe the first part of this statement but, reading between the lines, the second part looks like the result of the blackmail. The shaikhs stated that they were proud to be Ottoman subjects but that they feared Ottoman taxes and customs duties.

---

[67] This is a little strange: a *sancak*, governed by a *Mütessarif*, is a unit of higher order than a *kaza* governed by a *Kaymakam*.
[68] Ali Haydar Midhat Bey, *The Life of Midhat Pasha*, pp. 54–5.
[69] That Midhat used dubious methods to gain Kuwait appears to be confirmed by a report by the French consul in Baghdad of 2 March 1870 (Paris AE, CPC Bagdad 6, fos. 113–118: fo. 115): "By *intrigues* it is said that Midhat Pasha had pushed some inhabitants of Kuwait to ask to be placed under Ottoman authority".

Midhat stated that he did not want to impose any such things. To establish legitimate Ottoman authority, Midhat stated that he had formally appointed Abdallah as kaymakam of Kuwait and applied for Ottoman diplomas for mosques and *qadi*s in Kuwait. The so-called appointment of Abdallah raises a question: had a *berat* to that effect already been prepared (it had to be issued by the Sultan), and how did this relate to the apparently forgotten *firman* brought by the commander of the *Izmir* only three years earlier? There is no indication that the Grand Vizier responded by sending the requested documents, and it looks as if the statement in Haydar Midhat Bey's book that these documents had been issued is based on fantasy. It appears that Midhat was not entirely certain of the Kuwaitis: the Wali asked for a garrison of *zaptiye*s (gendarmes) to be sent to Kuwait.[70] It all bears the stamp of a somewhat hasty operation that remained unfinished for the time being. And one should have deep reservations about the reliability of reports written as personal propaganda by Midhat, under pressure as he was from critics in Constantinople, and of a biography by a son penned as an apologia for the policies of his father.

The Ottoman Government expressed no great jubilation at this so-called recovery of a lost territory. The garrison was never sent because the traditional government was deemed well able to keep order according to the traditional system. As there was no revenue there were also no funds to maintain the garrison.[71] Matters in Kuwait then remained much as they had been before Midhat's intervention. It is only left to us to quote a hitherto disregarded source on this: Mubarak's own view, as expressed in 1897, many years after the event. This is essentially identical to the Ottoman sources, albeit with a slightly different colouring:

> That in the year 1287 AH at the request of Medhet Pasha the then Wali
> of Baghdad, he [Sheikh Mubarek] went to meet him at Baghdad on

---

[70] Anscombe, *Ottoman Gulf*, pp. 21–2, quoting report of Midhat of 9 April 1870 in Istanbul BA, Irade Dahiliye 42435, 851/74. See also Midhat Pasha, pp. 34–5, and Istanbul BA, DUIT 69/2–1 (report of Midhat to the Grand Vizier of 8 Zilkade 1287/13 February 1870). Four days later Midhat expressed his fears about British intervention on the coasts of Oman, Najd and Kuwait: Istanbul BA, Irade Majlis Mahsusi 1667. The Grand Vizier summarized the matter in a memorandum: DUIT 69/2–1.

[71] Anscombe, *Ottoman Gulf*, p. 187, n. 24, quoting Istanbul BA, Irade Dahiliye 44930 enclosure II p. 1.

behalf of his brother, Sheikh Abdulla, who was Sheikh of Koweit at that time. Medhet Pasha explained to him the wish of the Turkish Government to include the Koweit district amongst its possessions and offered them certain advantages and protection against outsiders. He [Sheikh Mubarek] told the Wali that the Arabs would not consent to be governed by other than their hereditary sheikhs, nor would they submit to the obligations of Turkish subjects or to the establishment of customs at Koweit and would not permit Turkish soldiers garrisoning Koweit and in fact they could not entertain Turkish interference whatsoever. But with reference to flying the Turkish flag at Koweit and the Sheikh bearing the title of Kaimmakam there would be no trouble. The matter was referred to Constantinople and instructions sent to the Wali of Baghdad regarding establishing a garrison of 100 soldiers at Koweit, the grant of the title of kaimmakam to the Sheikh and flying the Turkish flag. They consented to fly the Turkish flag and took the title of kaimmakam as they had vast properties at Busreh which they would have lost if they resisted the Turkish demands altogether. But they have stoutly refused to this day the garrisoning of Koweit by Turkish soldiers and have avoided making any formal treaty with them.[72]

The British appear to have taken virtually no interest in the Ottoman action over Kuwait. No direct British reports on it have been found, the only contemporary European source being a rather vague and inaccurate report of the French consul in Baghdad. It should be noted that this report was written before it became clear that the Ottoman government would not follow up Midhat's proposal to instal a body of gendarmes in Kuwait:

A town called Kouet of which the inhabitants are governed by their Shaikhs under the approximately nominal suzerainty of the Wahabites and lived until the most recent years in a kind of republic. It is said that by some intrigues Midhat Pasha brought several of these inhabitants to ask to be placed under Ottoman nationality, and he then hurried to send them a qaimakam [...] It appears that this annexation has not for the moment stirred any objections, but it is strongly to be feared that this will cause trouble for the Ottoman Government at a later stage. The inhabitants will only remain in submission to the Porte if the latter is not

---

[72] IOLR, R/15/1/471, p. 96, report by Gaskin of meeting with Mubarak, 6 September 1897.

too demanding and does not impose too heavy charges on them, and shows itself able to defend them against the incursions of the neighbouring tribes, especially of the Wahabites who are said to have a considerable force.[73]

1.6 Fluctuating Ottoman fortunes in Arabia

Midhat's grand design was by no means fulfilled by the ambivalent integration of Kuwait. His ambition was to revive the former Ottoman province of al-Hasa, and to use it as a base from which to replace British with Ottoman control over the coasts of the Gulf. He had to hand a pretext for action: an exploratory voyage by the Ottoman steamer *Assur* had produced a report describing British interference from Bahrain on the coast of al-Hasa. This related how, in the struggle between the Saudi brothers Sa'ud and Abdallah, Sa'ud was being supported by the British. The inhabitants were alleged to be appealing for Ottoman intervention. Contacts were duly established between Midhat and Abdallah Al-Sa'ud. Midhat put forward his views to the Porte in the usual terms about the Arab desire for Ottoman rule, and dwelt much on the British threat. The Ottoman Government decided to act. By introducing administrative reforms in al-Hasa and Najd, under the authority of Abdallah Al-Sa'ud as Ottoman Governor, the region would be pacified. Once the region was under regular Ottoman administration, any further British intervention there would be contrary to international law.[74]

Midhat was dogged by ill luck. An epidemic of cholera had broken out in Iraq. To avoid it he moved his army as soon as he could to Kuwait, where lavish entertainment was laid on, but nothing of substance carried out.[75]

The British were not caught off guard by these preparations. The Khedive of Egypt had warned the British consul-general in Cairo in December 1870 that the Ottomans were planning the occupation of Central and Eastern Arabia.[76] Wild rumours circulated, and it was said in

[73] Paris AE, CPC Bagdad 6, fos. 114v–115, French consul Rogier 2 March 1870.
[74] All this is expressed in the official Ottoman idiom in a picturesque description in Anscombe, *Ottoman Gulf*, pp. 23–5.
[75] Istanbul BA, Irade Dahiliye 44003, Midhat Pasha to Serasker (Minister of War), 11 May 1287 Rumi or 23 May 1871); ibid. 44196, 12 May 1287 or 24 May 1871.
[76] Warning mentioned in Kelly, *Britain*, p. 718.

Kuwait that Kuwaiti forces would soon move to Bahrain.[77] Pelly, much alarmed, telegraphed the consul Herbert in Baghdad for information as to whether Bahrain formed part of the Ottoman design. Pelly nurtured dark but probably unfounded suspicions that the Ottomans were supported by the Russians and so kindled alarm about Russian penetration of the Gulf.[78] Midhat then calmed British fears somewhat by notifying Herbert that Ottoman ambitions did not encompass Bahrain.[79]

It would lead us too far from our main theme to discuss the events in Najd in depth. However, from a report in the British archives it appears that Abdallah Al-Sabah played a most crucial part in the "invasion" of al-Hasa. This was scarcely a military venture, simply the appearance of the *Assur* accompanied by a Kuwaiti flotilla after which negotiations followed.[80] Meanwhile Abdallah also invited the tribal leaders there to declare themselves subjects of the Sultan, and this ignited some British concern. Abdallah soon tired of the business. Already by August he had asked to be allowed to return to Kuwait and in September he left.[81]

Pelly states that the Arab tribes of the coastal area soon found reasons to regret "their subservience to the Turks". He himself actually discerned some advantages to it: the Ottomans had according to him established a customs office in Kuwait and now this port could be open also to British navigation. Pelly was mistaken. There was no Ottoman customs house in Kuwait. But one can understand Pelly's hopes: once Kuwait had been taken over by the Ottomans, European shipping would be free.[82]

---

[77] IOLR, LPS/9/18, p. 41, Edwards to Pelly 8 June 1871. In July news reached the British residency in Bushire that the *Assur* had left for Qatar, accompanied by Shaikh Abdallah in his own boat. The original plan was that Abdallah would travel on an Ottoman vessel, but it was "in need of repair" and Abdallah had to go in his own boat. See also IOLR, LPS/9/18, fo. 375, Halil bin Ahmed to Smith 6 July 1871.

[78] Kumar, *India*, p. 119. The fears about the Russians may have been caused by the logistic support given to the Turks by the Dutch consul-general in Bushire, R. C. Keun van Hogerwoerd, who was known to be close to the Russians. Pelly expressed this fear in 1871: IOLR, L PS/9/19, fo. 306.

[79] IOLR, LPS/9/18/115, telegrams exchanged between Pelly and Herbert, 5 July 1871; Kelly, *Britain*, p. 728.

[80] News gleaning from Bahrain in IOLR, LPS/9/19, fo. 88.

[81] IOLR, LPS/9/18, fo. 208, 29 September 1871; fo. 257, 18 July 1871; fos. 654 and 737, August 1871.

[82] See above, notes 23 and 24.

Anscombe is right in stating that the Ottomans were probably inspired by a distorted view of British intentions.[83] This was, however, not just a viewpoint peculiar to Midhat. Deep-seated Ottoman mistrust of British intentions went much further back, as we have already demonstrated. Anscombe's analysis of the diplomatic stand-off over the Arabian Peninsula generated by the events of 1870–2 is broadly correct, and Britain was essentially not hostile to Ottoman expansion in large parts of Arabia. We should, however be cautious in employing, as Anscombe does, terminology such as "recognizing an Ottoman claim". Such language would be perfectly acceptable by the imperial moral standards of the time, but for all that one should constantly bear in mind that Ottoman expansion in Arabia was still no more lofty an enterprise than colonization (as a German friend of the Ottomans put it in 1916).[84] The Ottomans never opened negotiations with the British to arrive at a comprehensive settlement of their respective ambitions in Arabia. In the end the matter remained largely open – which would leave Kuwait a way out of the Ottoman sphere of influence once the Kuwaitis were able to rekindle British interest in their small principality. For the time being, however, the best policy for Kuwait would be to try to evade Turkish notice altogether.

Perhaps most revealing of the Wali's vaulting ambition was an article in the official gazette of Baghdad province, the *Zawra*. This contains a whole list of the new *kaymakamlik* of Najd, in which there figures, for example, an Ottoman district of Oman with such cities as Abu Dhabi with 2000 houses, Dubai with 1000 houses, and Sharjah with 2000 houses.[85]

The usual assessment of Midhat's Kuwait venture sees it as a promising start for an Ottoman takeover of Kuwait that was never followed up, so that Kuwait soon reverted to its status preceding Namiq and Midhat's interventions. It is clear that Midhat coerced the shaikhs into emollient murmurings along the lines of "Yes, we are delighted to be Ottoman subjects (of some kind)". But there does not appear to have been any agreement in writing. Once the Ottoman army was in the vicinity the Kuwaitis had to be on their best behaviour, and they did so in a somewhat indifferent fashion. The following year (1871) produced not much more than a short-lived military alliance, honoured by a less than enthusiastic

[83] Anscombe, *Ottoman Gulf*, p. 28.
[84] Franz Stulmann, *Der Kampf um Arabien zwischen der Türkei und England*, p. 24.
[85] PRO, FO 125/949, fos. 259–265, Herbert to Government of India 7 June 1871.

participation by Kuwaiti forces in operations in al-Hasa. The Turks never established a regular administration in Kuwait, and the plan for a garrison was jettisoned from the start. The Kuwaitis dealt with the Ottoman Empire as with any large, powerful neighbour and ally. If the Ottomans had wanted something more, they should have laid claim to it.

Midhat himself confessed that whatever he had managed to obtain from the Kuwaitis was through blackmail. One can hardly reproach the Kuwaitis for acting as if Midhat's alleged incorporation of Kuwait into the Ottoman Empire had never taken place. It was never more than an empty formality. The whole affair is very aptly symbolized by Abdallah's earlier treatment of his official Ottoman costume: to throw his Kuwaiti cloak over it and discard the vestment as soon as possible.

Finally, Midhat was recalled. The verdict on his tenure in Baghdad was negative and best expressed by the French consul Rogier. Midhat's intentions might have been worthy, but inexperienced zealots in his entourage wanted to press ahead too fast with reform and expansion of the province. The costs were crippling and the province, already poor, was reduced to dire financial straits. The sole durable results were a horse-drawn tramway in Baghdad, a few badly functioning steamers, the nebulous claim to Kuwait, and a garrison in al-Hasa that was a serious drain on the budget and little more than a beleaguered and practically worthless outpost.[86]

The Ottoman government seems to have shared Rogier's negative appraisal of Midhat. The Grand Vizier, an enemy of the Pasha, told the dragoman at the British Embassy in Constantinople that Midhat had misled the Porte in representing Abdallah bin Faysal Al-Saud as an Ottoman functionary, and that his expansionist policy was merely to gratify his own personal ambitions.[87] In the light of Rogier's remarks, we might exonerate Midhat to some extent by attributing the more extreme ambitions to the diehards around him.

---

[86] Both the British and the French consuls in Baghdad state that Midhat's policy was a heavy burden on the budget of his province, see Kelly, *Britain*, p. 738; and Paris AE, CPC Bagdad 6, fos. 119–122, Rogier to Minister, 26 March 1870. Anscombe, *Ottoman Gulf*, pp. 56–7 does not believe this, apparently on the basis of official figures of the Ottoman budget, but it seems safer to believe the French consul (France was sympathetic to the Ottoman reform movement represented by Midhat), than to believe official budgets which were not always based on reality.
[87] Kelly, *Britain*, p. 723.

A contemporary description of Kuwait survives in an unexpected neutral source. In 1870 a Dutch warship, the steamer *Curaçao*, called in at Kuwait. The *Curaçao* was on a tour to parade the return of the Dutch to the Gulf after a long absence. In recent years there had been a considerable increase in Dutch trade there. Aboard the *Curaçao* was the newly appointed consul-general in Bushire, Keun van Hogerwoerd, who used the trip to acquaint himself with the economic prospects of the region. The *Curaçao* put in at Kuwait in April 1870. Muhammad, the brother of Shaikh Abdallah, came on board to greet the Dutch captain, Bowier, and was introduced to all the capabilities of a modern warship. The Dutch also visited the town, where they found that Kuwait was the only truly Arab merchant town on the Gulf, in contrast to such places as Muscat or Basra where people from India dominated trade.[88]

1.7 After Midhat Pasha

After Midhat's recall the Ottomans apparently left Kuwait alone for the time being. Shaikh Abdallah and his brother Mubarak had again averted the danger of an actual Ottoman takeover. The Turks were too busy elsewhere to embark upon initiatives in remote regions.

Shaikh Abdallah considered it prudent to keep a low profile. Kuwait lacked the military resources to challenge the Goliath of the Ottoman Empire were the latter to opt, in a crisis, for an all-out confrontation. There are no further references in the sources to Ottoman interference in Kuwait. This is understandable, as the Ottoman hold on Basra province was precarious and it was difficult enough to maintain influence in al-Hasa. Financial resources to establish regular bureaucratic control over outlying regions were lacking. In the desert region bordering Iraq, Muhammad Ibn Rashid, Amir of Haïl in Jabal Shammar, was establishing himself as a virtually independent ruler. In 1875 the district of Basra was separated once again from Baghdad province. Superficially this might look like an Ottoman attempt to extend normal provincial government to southern Iraq, but the fact that the governor of the new province was a

---

[88] The Hague, NA, Buitenlandse Zaken 1813–1870, nr. 2706: 4469 nr. 4409, report by Dutch consul; The Hague, NA, Marine Journalen 959, journal of the warship *Curaçao* 1870; Bowier, "Zending", pp. 19–20 and 92–93, article on the visit by the captain of the *Curaçao*.

local tribal leader – Shaikh Nasir of the normally unruly Muntafiq – shows how far the province was from being regularized in this way.[89]

A small but significant gesture on the part of Kuwait is recorded from that time. In 1304 AH (AD 1886–7) Kuwait produced a small coin of its own, with no Ottoman marks on it. This makes a telling legal point for, in Western as well as Islamic legal thinking, the minting of coins is one of the principal criteria of sovereignty.

One development in this period was to resurface later in legal debates about Kuwait's independence. This was the discussion in Britain about the possibility of reaching an agreement with the Turks over the demarcation line between the two empires' spheres of influence. Concern was focused on al-Hasa, where Qatar and 'Uqayr were disputed. Bushire was most anxious to settle this matter because of recurring problems around Bahrain.[90] But to reach a formal solution would be difficult in the light of the Ottoman claim to the entire Arabian Peninsula.

In the British view this matter was bound up with the question of suppressing piracy, as the Turks exercised no real control of the coastline between Fao and al-Hasa. In 1878 the Government of India hoped that the Ottoman Empire, after defeat in its war with Russia, would be willing to reach an understanding with Britain about delimiting spheres of interest. The deal envisaged was that the Turks would surrender their spurious paper claims to Bahrain and Oman, in exchange for British recognition of their claim to the region between 'Uqayr and the Shatt al-'Arab as well as Qatar; the Turks would also be prepared to leave the policing of Ottoman territorial waters in the Gulf to the British. But in London the Foreign Secretary Salisbury, who had earlier served as ambassador in Turkey, was more realistic, and did not believe that the Turks would ever accept such a deal.[91] The India Office, however, saw the Ottoman occupation of al-Hasa as the source of anarchy in the central Gulf, and insisted on British policing of the coastal waters up to the Shatt al-'Arab. A report of 1879 from the Government of India to the India Office in London drew a clear distinction between the verbal Ottoman claim to the entire coast of the Gulf down to Ras al-Hadd, and a more realistic claim where at least theoretical Ottoman authority existed between Dammam and somewhere below Kuwait.[92]

[89] Kelly, *Britain*, p. 763.   [90] Kelly, *Britain*, pp. 767–87.   [91] Kumar, *India*, p. 121.
[92] Kelly, *Britain*, pp. 797–9; the text of the report appears on pp. 842–52.

Salisbury was looking for a compromise formula, but he clearly stated to the British ambassador in Constantinople that he could not accept extravagant Ottoman claims to sovereignty in regions where no real Ottoman control existed. Then the Conservative government in London was replaced by a Liberal one. They tried to reach an agreement with the Turks, but the Porte replied that new naval units were being despatched to the Gulf and so the British demand to police its waters was unfounded.[93] As these units did nothing, the British concluded that the Ottomans were unable or unwilling to curb piracy in the region.[94] Meanwhile Ottoman relations with Britain had grown more tense as a result of the pan-Islamist policy of Sultan Abdulhamid II, whose promotion of the dominion of the Caliphate over all Muslims was seen as an unsettling force in lands such as India. In July 1881 the British notified the Turks that their warships would continue to hunt down pirates even in Ottoman waters.[95] In the end, British offers to recognize Ottoman authority on condition of effective maritime policing either by Ottoman or British ships was never accepted by the Turks. One cannot therefore really argue for British recognition of Ottoman sovereignty over the coastal zone, but merely of a negotiating position.

Nevertheless, the British persisted in the search for some kind of agreement with the Turks about a demarcation line in the Bahrain area. This became more pressing when, in 1889, rumours began to circulate about Muhammad Ibn Rashid, the Amir of Haïl, having approached the Porte with a view to an alliance for an assault on Oman. This injected urgency into the search for an agreement with the Turks. But they

[93] Kumar, *India*, p. 124.   [94] Kelly, *Britain*, p. 795.   [95] Kelly, *Britain*, pp. 829–30.
[96] Kumar, *India*, p. 128.
[97] This is found in a memorandum by Harcourt, an official of the India Office, on the Kuwait affair of 1901: "In April 1903 [*sic*; an error for 1893] Sir C. Ford [British ambassador in Constantinople] stated officially to the Turkish Minister of Foreign Affairs that Her Majesty's Government admitted Turkish sovereignty from Bussorah to El Khateef": Gooch and Temperley, *British Documents*, Part 1, Series B, Vol. 17, pp. 196–7; see also Bidwell, *Affairs of Kuwait*, 1/1, p. 31, memo of Sanderson concerning a similar vague communication of 4 July 1889.
[98] The best summary of this matter is in Plass, *England*, pp. 481–2.
[99] Salwa Al-Ghanim's judgement (*Mubarak*, p. 12) on Abdallah, that he was too enthusiastically pro-Ottoman, is not entirely justified. At that time the only way to avert the menace of the all-too-proximate Ottoman army was to present oneself as a very good ally of the Turks.

persisted with their old hypothetical claims. No useful conclusion was reached and the threat to Oman receded when the Amir became engaged elsewhere.[96]

The British none the less doggedly tried to reach an agreement. In 1893 an official of the British embassy mentioned to the Ottoman foreign minister that the British were in any case prepared to recognize Ottoman sovereignty from Basra to Qatif.[97] What was the exact wording of this – apparently oral – communication? Nothing could be found, nor did the Ottomans ever remind the British of it in later times. This is understandable, for any limitation of Ottoman authority over the Arabian Peninsula as a whole was unacceptable to Abdulhamid. So this British communication played no part in any future Anglo–Ottoman negotiations. It came up later in internal British discussions about the status of Kuwait, but for the legal minds in the India Office it was of no more than academic significance.[98]

In conclusion, the wrangling over Ottoman legal status on the Arabian coast makes it clear that there was absolutely no realistic hope that Kuwait might rely on British support, of the sort that Bahrain was able to call upon, for its independence.[99]

2

The Regional Crisis of 1890–1895

2.1 The upper Gulf and international politics in the 1890s

An important ingredient in the build-up of tension in the upper Gulf region during the 1890s was an ancient difference between the British and the Ottoman conceptions of international law. This would become ever more manifest and would leave an indelible mark on the conflict over the status of Kuwait.

We have already encountered the Ottoman Empire's pretension to authority over the entire Arabian Peninsula. This seems to have originated in the rather vague notion that, after the Ottomans' military incursions of the 16th century, all of Arabia belonged by right of conquest to them. It would be delving too deep to investigate all the related legal concepts in detail, but the basic idea is that, according to Ottoman political theory, anything conquered for Islam belonged in perpetuity to the Dar al-Islam in which the Ottoman Sultan was sovereign, and he was thereby entitled to reassert full authority in any case where local autonomy had been conceded by a previous Sultan. This was by its very nature incompatible with European international legal concepts which, based on Roman law, required actual possession for the exercise of sovereignty.

There was, however, a grey area in 19th-century thinking on imperial expansion that blurred the normal European concept somewhat. In some sense the great powers had the right to occupy as colonies or protectorates any independent territories that were not part of the "diplomatic community", at least if they were capable of doing so. It was more or less generally accepted as part of this imperialist concept that the Ottoman Empire (more or less a European great power) had the right to occupy such territories on its borders if (and this was an important condition) it was able to impose law and order there. It was on this very point that the Ottoman version of imperialism clashed with the British version. With the Trucial System (the treaties comprising the Perpetual Maritime Peace), the British had concluded agreements with territorial principalities within the zone regarded by the Ottomans as their legitimate zone of expansion. The Trucial System made Britain responsible for the maintenance of peace and order, and it was precisely on that that the British presence in the area based its legitimacy.

In this way territories in the Gulf had become in some respects British protectorates, and Britain claimed the authority to maintain the maritime peace. During the entire 19th century, the British intervened whenever the Ottoman Empire was found to be incapable of controlling petty naval banditry on the Gulf coast of Arabia, or when tribal conflicts flared up between territories over which the British claimed control. In the 1890s two cases arose that brought British intervention. The first was a matter of tribal conflict spreading between Bahrain and Qatar. The second was more complex. There was a problem of small-time piracy, partly along the coastline between Kuwait and al-Hasa, and partly in the Shatt al-'Arab. The Shatt al-'Arab nuisance was complicated by a legal disagreement: the Ottoman Empire claimed that the Shatt was part of its territorial waters, while the British held that it was international water because it formed the border between Persia and the Ottoman Empire.

There were other ingredients too contributing to tension in the Gulf. On the one hand there was a crisis within the Ottoman Empire, whose decline was becoming increasingly apparent as European powers put pressure on the "Sick Man of Europe". There was tension between France and Britain over colonial expansion, and between Russia and Britain when Russia tried to acquire a foothold or economic contacts near the Indian Ocean. This tension was perceptible in the Gulf region. Britain was also growing nervous about German economic expansion. Germany was inclined to feel sympathy for the Ottoman Empire, and hoping to foster an economic revival there that would open up Asian markets to German exports.

In the Gulf the British were also sensitive to the growing French presence, and apprehensive that the latter would offer opportunities to their Russian friends too. They were inclined to resort to rough tactics against the Ottomans, who believed they could exploit incidents in the Bahrain region to roll back British influence in Arabia. As so often happened when the Ottomans intervened in the Peninsula, such actions might ultimately rebound to their disadvantage, but they enjoyed the sympathy of France, Russia and Germany in these matters. These three powers had become hypersensitive to all that might seem to advance the interests of the British Empire.

During the 1890s the place of the Gulf in the international trade network was undergoing a change. Before 1890 Britain, or rather India, had had by far the largest share of Gulf trade. The Dutch were the only other nation of any commercial importance at the time. The firm of Hotz in Rotterdam concentrated on Persia, but was also active in Iraq and Oman. But Hotz fell into decline in the 1890s. The Dutch carried on with considerable business in Persia, but their activities in the Ottoman area of the Gulf diminished. In 1890 there was an incident when the governor of Basra ordered the Dutch flag to be removed from the vice-consulate of the Netherlands there. A fruitless naval demonstration by the warship *Atjeh* and the closure of the vice-consulate followed. A few years later the Dutch merchant Ter Meulen, who had also acted as French vice-consul in Basra, left that town for Muhammara. The Dutch remained active in Ahwaz and Muhammara, but showed no interest in the Arabian side of the Gulf.

The French had been obliged to curtail their political activity in the Gulf region in the 1860s after the Franco-German war of 1870, but they returned in the 1890s. They were on a collision course with the British in their colonial expansion. Oman had traditional trade links with French possessions in the Indian Ocean, and in 1862 France had concluded a convention with Britain ceding them equal rights in Oman. From time to time there was some French shipping in the Gulf. A French shipping line even made an attempt to open business there, but the timing was unpropitious: an epidemic was raging and the experiment was discontinued. From 1898 a French merchant, Antonin Goguyer, became active in the Gulf. After a few months his business activities, mostly in areas such as the arms trade, drew British disapproval. Goguyer, an intellectual who spoke Arabic and had even published early Arabic legal texts, was a prolific writer of articles in the French, Egyptian and Russian press. He was very anti-British and took some delight in political intrigue, supporting everything Arab, Russian or Ottoman that was directed against British interests.

The French had been active in Baghdad and Basra since the 18th century. Their chief interest there was the protection of the Carmelite monasteries and the Christian communities dependent on them. This entailed some commercial interest too, because the Christian family of Asfar in Baghdad and Basra, which was prominent in the Basra date trade and also had contacts with Kuwait, were under French protection and kept the French consul in Baghdad informed about events in Basra and the surrounding area.[1] In 1895 the French Company Messageries Maritimes made an attempt to start a shipping line to Basra. The line was not successful and the experiment was abandoned after a single attempt.[2]

The French were the main local opponents of the British in the Gulf. This state of affairs lasted until the conclusion of the Entente Cordiale with Britain in 1904, when French agents ceased obstructing the British. The French consuls in Oman opposed every British attempt to acquire more control over the government of the Sultanate, while in Baghdad the French consul showed every sympathy with the Ottomans in any conflict with the British. French consular reports from the Gulf show a considerable anti-British bias. This serves to enhance their interest for historians, because the image of the Gulf in historiography has been greatly over-influenced by the exclusive use of British sources.

French economic activity in the Gulf came in for French government support because of a general antipathy to the idea of a part of the world being monopolized by the British. For the Russians, who were acquiring an increasing interest and influence in Persia, there were even stronger reasons for opposing a British monopoly in the Gulf. The sweeping geopolitical concepts typical of the age provoked tension with the British,

---

[1] On the Asfar family, see Nantes AD, Ambassade Turquie, série D: dossier Asfar. The activities of the Asfar could be disagreeable to the British, for instance in 1900 when one of the Asfars supplied the Russian warship *Gilyak* with coal; *cf.* Rezvan, *Russian Ships*, pp. 38, 41.

[2] Paris AE, CPC Bagdad 7, fo. 523, Pognon, 6 December 1895. According to Pognon the line was opened at a bad moment because the Dutch merchant Ter Meulen, who was French consular agent in Basra, was unreliable, being already agent of a British shipping line. An epidemic of plague in Basra soon made the line unprofitable: Nantes AD, consulat Bagdad A 57, 19 October 1897, consul in Bagdad to Caillol in Marseille.

who feared that Russian influence in Persia would ultimately result in annexation of the kind that had already taken place in the Islamic states of Central Asia such as Khiva, Bukhara and Samarkand. Such an annexation would afford the Russians an outlet to the Indian Ocean uncomfortably close to India, while it might also complicate matters when the Ottoman Empire came to be dismembered. Whatever the impracticability of all this, the fact remains that in the 1890s the Russians began to exploit their contacts in the Gulf to establish an economic foothold there. The Dutch had in the past acted for the Russians there, and the Dutch consul-general in Bushire, Keun van Hogerwoerd (whose visit to Kuwait is referred to above) had also acted for Russia.[3] The Russians used French contacts too. They opened a consulate in Baghdad in 1885, and this followed the French line in its friendly contacts with the Ottomans and sympathy with Ottoman irritation at British activities in the Gulf. During the period 1898–1904, Russian activities caused the British considerable alarm, but in 1907 Russia's defeat in the Russo-Japanese War brought its competition with Britain in the Gulf to an end.

Finally the Germans too acquired interests in the region. They were opposed to a British economic monopoly of the Gulf on the grounds that it would impede the expansion of an increasingly successful German trade network. A German trading company, Wönckhaus, was established in Linga and Bahrain in the late 1890s.[4] France and Germany still both nurtured a vision that the Ottoman Empire, with some modernization, might survive, and they hoped to gain considerable strategic advantage by assisting in the development of its communications. The Germans had no interests in the Ottoman Empire involving the protection of religious communities, as the French had with the Catholics and the Russians with the Orthodox Christians. This made them less open to Ottoman suspicion and led the Sultan to place greater trust in Germany than in France or Russia. In 1894 the Germans established a vice-consulate in Baghdad, for which they employed a certain Richarz. This Richarz had already been resident in Baghdad for some time. He was a homosexual who was

[3] Jedina, *An Asiens Küsten,* p. 79: photograph of Villa Hollandabad in Bushire. The villa later became the French consular residence.
[4] Plass, *England,* pp. 395–441, gives a good summary of Wönckhaus's manifold activities in the Gulf. The Wönckhaus business archives are kept in the State Archives in Hamburg.

reputed to find life more amenable in Baghdad than in the less tolerant Europe.[5] His Baghdad contacts, like those of his French and Russian colleagues, were excellent, especially in the military. In 1899 the Germans also established a consulate in Bushire.

The Germans were an adventurous and well-educated group. Some travelled extensively throughout the Gulf, motivated apparently more by general interest and an urge to explore than by imperialist designs. The British suspected these adventurers of more sinister aims, but there is no evidence to justify such suspicions. Nevertheless the Germans established contacts that were to cause a good deal of trouble to the British in southern Persia during the First World War. The German public's interest in foreign countries created a market in the German press for information on the Gulf region. As the German press was rather aggressive in tone, articles in German newspapers could occasionally provoke diplomatic incidents.

The Austrians established a consulate in Baghdad in 1900. It is apparent from a Russian report that one of the most conspicuous foreign articles in the Kuwait bazaar was Austrian glassware.[6] The Americans too had a consulate in Baghdad, where they were represented by a Swiss merchant.[7] They played no significant part in the events of the following years. There was also a Belgian presence in the Gulf, Belgians administering the Persian customs service. The Belgians were perceived as a nuisance by the British, because they were sympathetic to the Russian interest in Persia.

In the late 19th century the Ottoman province of Basra and its dependency in al-Hasa were in serious crisis, due in part to old-fashioned problems of communication. Baghdad was one of the remotest spots in the northern hemisphere at the time. It took almost a month to reach from Constantinople, and the only rapid contact was by telegraph line. Communication in Morse code along a single wire is time-consuming and does not lend itself to a fluent interchange of information. Basra and al-Hasa were even more remote, and were closer to British bases than to centres of Ottoman power. The Ottoman VI Army Corps in Iraq was

[5] Nantes AD, Ambassade Turquie, série D, Bagdad, dossier Asfar: letter of 10 June 1906 on the "Persian" habits of Richarz.
[6] Rezvan, *Russian Ships*, p. 137.
[7] The name of the consul was Hurner. His correspondence can be found in the National Archives of the USA, Record group 59, T 509.

notorious as the worst in the Ottoman Empire, and Basra was probably the poorest province. Any control exercised by the Wali of Basra over Arab tribes such as the Muntafiq and the Banu Lam was tenuous at best, while individuals such as Muhammad Ibn Rashid, chief of Haïl, and Qasim Al-Thani in Qatar, obeyed the Ottomans only when they felt like it. In part of Basra province, the Arab shaikh controlling Muhammara (situated on the Persian side, but whose influence extended into the Ottoman Empire) did as he pleased. In the lower part of Basra province large stretches of land, as we saw in Chapter 1, belonged to the Al-Sabah of Kuwait, who were also outside the control of the Wali.

The issue that brought Kuwait most sharply into focus on the international scene during the late 19th and early 20th century was the possible installation there of the terminus of a railway between the Mediterranean and the Gulf. Kuwait was judged the prime location for this because of its deep and accessible harbour. Basra was not accessible to large vessels because of a bar in the Shatt al-'Arab. It would be costly to remove, and a rail terminus without access for large shipping would be uneconomic.

The history of schemes for a rail link between the Mediterranean and the Gulf is long and involved.[8] The original idea for such a railway, as early as 1833, was British. In the late 1850s, French plans for cutting the Suez Canal caused alarm in Britain because it would afford the French a faster route to India. A plan for a railway to Kuwait was revived in Britain, but then dropped for various reasons. Palmerston had concluded that if Britain controlled Muscat, Bahrain, Muhammara and Kuwait, the British would have enough bases in the region.[9] In 1871 Midhat Pasha, now Grand Vizier, set in hand the planning of a rail network to cover all the Asian provinces of the Ottoman Empire, including a line from Izmit to Basra. He sought advice from the Austrians Pressel and Cernik,[10] but these plans were thwarted in 1875 by the bankruptcy of the Ottoman Empire. The Ottomans then tried to acquire a rail network through co-operation with

[8] For an interesting summary, see the report of the Austrian consul in Baghdad:Vienna HHSA, PA XXXVIII K 315, Rappaport 27 August 1900.
[9] Brünner, *Bagdadspoorweg*, p. 8.
[10] Vienna HHSA, PA XXXVIII K315, Rappaport, 27 August 1900. The German consul in Baghdad claimed in 1903 that he had seen another project in the Basra Government archives: a report by Midhat Pasha of 1871 on a British plan for a line between Basra or Kuwait and Iskenderun: Berlin AA, R 13856 A 11843 (10 August 1903), Richarz 9 July 1903.

foreign companies. Abdulhamid II placed a high priority on railway construction for military reasons. He had come to the conclusion that the lack of a rail network in the Balkans was to blame for the Ottoman failure there in 1878. Later, in 1889, negotiations opened with Germany. The Ottomans had a strong and understandable strategic interest in a line running from the Bosporus, the centre of the Empire, to the Gulf through the remote province of Iraq. Baghdad was one of the most inaccessible places in the Empire, and the rigours of communication made the Mesopotamian provinces difficult to control. In 1891 the Sultan asked the Germans, who had just completed a railway from the Bosporus to Ankara, to support his initiative for an extension from Ankara to Baghdad. Germany was keen to accept, but Britain declared its opposition on the grounds that such a railway would facilitate access to India. Britain changed its attitude in exchange for German acceptance of its policy in Egypt.[11] This railway scheme was accelerated in 1897 when von Marschall, the under-secretary who had handled the issue in Berlin, became German ambassador in Constantinople.[12]

Railway plans involving Kuwait had thus been circulating for a long time, and were the reason why Ottoman attention now turned once more to the shaikhdom. As the ideal location for the rail terminus, the Ottomans renewed their interest in establishing control over it. This took place against a general background of Ottoman anxiety about regional revolts all over the Empire. Regional nationalism, which had already caused the loss of part of the Balkans, was raising its head in the Arab provinces, and the first talk of a large Arab state was being heard. In 1890 many European newspapers were banned in the Ottoman Empire. The ban penetrated even into the distant Basra province, as we know from a rather confused list of forbidden papers given by the Wali of Basra to the British consul. In the list figure such items as the Vienna "*Naval Bars*" (*Neue Presse*), the Paris "*Matten*" (*Matin*), the "*Tarbuna*" (*Tribuna*) from Rome, the *Daily News*, and various others.[13]

This instability might not have been so serious for the Ottomans had the Porte not persisted in its unrealistic ambitions to uphold its influence in the

---

[11] Lepsius, *Grosse Politik*, Vol. 14, pp. 66–7.
[12] See Erich Lindow, *Freiherr Marschall von Bieberstein als Botschafter in Konstantinopel 1897–1912*.
[13] PRO, FO 602/42, 232 (year 1890).

tribal areas of the Arabian Peninsula. It was beyond the means of Basra province alone to accomplish this objective, and so it was also pursued by the Sultan and his close associates through bribery and the exploitation of disagreements between tribal leaders. A direct link between the Sultan and Arab elements was provided by the Sultan's well-known adviser and astrologer, Abu 'l-Huda, who was reputed to be related to the Naqib of the Rifa'iyya fraternity in Basra. This Naqib was the most powerful landowner in Basra province. There was a risk inherent in this tendency of the Sultan to employ his private contact with the Naqib, as in so doing he bypassed the proper chain of command via the Minister of the Interior and the Wali of Basra; if the Naqib and the Wali did not co-operate, the whole system could easily be paralysed.[14] The Ottoman attempt to establish contact with regions such as Oman and Bahrain, and the British presence there, meant that this policy ran the risk of British intervention – a risk increased by Britain's alertness to the schemes of other European powers at the time, which was leading it to tighten its grip on Oman, the Trucial States, and the Arabian coastline in the vicinity of Bahrain.

2.2 Kuwait in the last years of Shaikh Abdallah

The 1890s were perhaps the most critical decade in Kuwait's history. Shaikh Abdallah of Kuwait had managed to fend off the Turks, but at the high tide of imperial expansion all the great powers were evincing a voracious appetite for any "vacant" territory. Kuwait fell into this category, and in the 1890s Ottoman pressure was building up again. It looks as if, at the end of his life, Shaikh Abdallah had grown more pessimistic about the feasibility of staying outside Ottoman control. Shortly before his death, he approached the British consul in Baghdad and requested permission to hoist the British flag on his house.[15] There was no chance of such permission being granted.[16]

An excellent sketch of Kuwait's ambivalent position in the early 1890s, poised between Ottoman claim and practical autonomy, is given in a manual on the social and economic geography of the Ottoman Empire in Asia by the French geographer Vital Cuinet. This demonstrates clearly the

---

[14] On the Naqib, see Anscombe, *Ottoman Gulf*, pp. 108–9, 124–6. He is frequently mentioned, usually disparagingly, in the German and French consular reports from Baghdad.

peculiarity of Kuwait's position. On the one hand it is part of the official
Ottoman structure as a *kaza* of the Basra province, while on the other
there already appears, in the general description of Basra province, the
following telling remark: "All administrative functionaries are subordinate
to the Wali or Governor-General, with the exception of the Under-
Governor of Kuwait who is in reality independent."[17] The chapter on
Kuwait in Cuinet's book elaborates that image:

> Kuwait is governed by Shaikh Abdullah bin Sabah, who has been invested
> in the regular manner by the Ottoman Government with the title of
> Qaymmakam, Under-Governor of that *kaza*. He receives for this
> function an honorarium from the Governor of Basra consisting of 150
> *kara* or 385 tons of dates per annum. In reality this Governor, whose
> investiture has been motivated by the great services he rendered to the
> Ottoman troops on the occasion of the definitive submission of the
> *sancak* of Najd by Midhat Pasha, is absolutely independent. His relations
> with the Governor-General [the Wali of Basra] are limited to obtaining
> his honorarium. All civil lawsuits and other lawsuits are dealt with by
> himself and there is no appeal against his judgements. He does not
> impose on the local population any impost or tax, but foreigners who
> import merchandise for sale in Kuwait or in the interior of the country
> have to pay a tax of a *riyal* or Maria Theresia thaler (or 4 francs 60 cents)
> per pack.[18]

That Kuwait's position was a special one can also be seen from its
complete lack, unlike all other *kaza*s, of the usual administrative
subdivisions (*nahye*) or regular Ottoman officials, and of an administrative
council, so rendering the description of Kuwait in Cuinet's book quite
different from that of other *kaza*s.

Cuinet's book presents a general picture of Kuwait in 1890. The town
had some 20,000 inhabitants, all Muslims apart from 50 Jews, while the

---

[15] PRO, FO 602/42, 7 May 1891: "Sheikh of Koweit warns that the Turks seem [...]
to annex that country. He wants to be allowed to hoist British flag if the Turks occupy
the place." This also appears in the Basra Diary in the Baghdad Residency archives in
the National Archives of India.

[16] The request received very little attention from the British. It was reported by the
consul in Baghdad to the Constantinople embassy, but I have found no response to it.
The document seems to have escaped the attention of other historians.

[17] Cuinet, *Turquie*, Vol. 3, p. 217.   [18] Cuinet, *Turquie*, Vol. 3, p. 274.

number of nomads was unknown. There were 500 shops, three khans, six coffee shops and five storehouses for corn. Most of the population lived by working in gardens outside the *kaza* of Kuwait (apparently the Basra date groves are meant here). As there was no permanent vegetation in Kuwait, the nomads ranged far outside its territory during the year. Those inhabitants who had no gardens near Fao gained their livelihood by trading imported merchandise with the tribes of the interior, or by ship-building, wood for which came from India. The poorest inhabitants worked as sailors on the *baghala*s to pay for their passage to Bahrain where they were employed as pearl divers. The nomads brought the produce of their flocks and proceeds of their raids to Kuwait. The Jews were merchants who had come from Bushire some years previously; they had a synagogue for which they had to pay the Shaikh the sum of 20 $MT annually. There were no other foreigners in the town other than a few Persians from Bushire, who were not permanent residents of Kuwait. There were three small schools where the children were taught Islam, reading and writing.[19]

Of all foreign writers Cuinet gives the most complete image of Kuwait in the 19th century. There is just one oddity in his account: the relatively little attention paid to the role of pearls in the Kuwaiti economy. In the early 20th century pearls made an important contribution, and entrepreneurs in the pearling sector played a prominent part in Kuwait. There is no way of determining whether this was misjudgement on Cuinet's part, or whether there really was a trough in pearling's importance around 1890.

2.3 The Ottomans and the regional crisis of the early 1890s

The situation as described by Cuinet may appear stable enough, but this was not the case. There was an ongoing regional dispute between Britain and the Ottomans over policing the Gulf and its coasts and over Bahrain and its dependencies. The Ottomans were bent on tightening their grip on border areas and this posed a potential danger to Kuwait. But the threat was not only external. After the death of Shaikh Abdallah on 29 May 1892, internal wrangles about how to deal with the situation surfaced inside Kuwait too.[20]

[19] Cuinet, *Turquie*, Vol. 3, pp. 273–6.

There were two episodes that seem to have engendered an atmosphere of crisis for the Ottomans on the fringe of their Empire in the Gulf region in the 1890s and, worse, afforded the British the opportunity to encroach on Ottoman territory there. The first episode took place in the lower region of Basra province, the second in Qatar and al-Hasa.

The trouble in Basra province centred on the Ottomans' virtually complete lack of authority on the lower Shatt al-'Arab. In 1886 they had set in hand the construction of a fortress at Fao, on land belonging to the Al-Sabah and adjacent to the British telegraph station.[21] The installation of this fortress served to accentuate the rivalry with the British. There is some justification for the British claim that the Ottomans were not entitled to build a fortress on the Shatt al-'Arab because the river was a frontier and therefore constituted international water. In 1890 things came to head. British warships entered the Shatt al-'Arab in a naval demonstration to prevent the Turks mounting artillery on the fortress at Fao. The French consul in Baghdad was rather cynically amused by the brouhaha over this "miserable" mud fortress, and wondered whether Britain would resort to the old gunboat tactics they had employed against the Ottomans before the Crimean War; but he did not expect any serious consequences because he felt the Ottomans would concede. The Russian consul Ponafidin, however, was most disturbed by the events, telegraphing Petersburg that he expected a bombardment and hurrying off to Basra. At that juncture a German warship, the *Kormoran,* also arrived off Fao.[22] The French consul was inspired by the incident to suggest that his government should reopen the French consulate in Muscat and that the French shipping line Messageries Maritimes should include the Gulf in its schedules.[23]

The real context of the episode was the British effort to suppress piracy against shipping from India, but the British action had little deterrent effect because, in September 1890, pirates again struck in the Shatt al-

---

[20] New Delhi NAI, Consulate Baghdad, Basra Diary, 20 May 1892. This reference clearly reflects the view of the British consulate in Basra on Kuwait's position, which apparently was entirely based on formal Ottoman information: the diary states that "the wali of Basra has appointed temporarily Abdullah Pasha's brother Muhammad Pasha to act as kaymakam of Kuwait". The contrast with the French and German descriptions of the position of Kuwait is evident here.

[21] New Delhi NAI, Baghdad Residency, Basra Diary, 17 May 1886, 1 May 1887.

[22] The *Kormoran*: New Delhi NAI, Baghdad Residency, Basra Diary, 7 August 1895.

'Arab.[24] The feeble Ottoman grip on the lower part of the river had scarcely been strengthened by the installation of the fortress at Fao. There was an overall lack of security in the province caused by armed bands, which in May 1892 even entered the city of Basra.[25] Incidents of piracy against small shipping in the Shatt al-'Arab were inevitable in such an anarchic environment. Much of this shipping came from India and was protected by the British flag, so Britain was drawn in with its claim that the Shatt al-'Arab was an international waterway where its warships could operate freely – a natural cause of alarm to the Ottomans, who felt that events in the region below Basra were slipping out of their control.

In 1893 the Ottoman fortress at Fao was still unfinished. In April of that year a new Wali of Basra, Hamdi Pasha, arrived and resumed the works. Hamdi was a naval officer and former customs chief of Constantinople. A biographical portrait of this dignitary later appeared in the British consul Wratislaw's memoirs: "An Engineer Rear-Admiral of the Turkish navy, who possessed a bushy red beard, and if put into a kilt would have made a perfect Scotsman. He was very friendly to the English."[26] Hamdi's benevolence to the English was deceptive: in reality he was extremely suspicious of English activities in the Gulf. The appointment of a naval man with customs experience to Basra was significant in the context of the rivalry between Britain and Turkey over control of the Ottoman coasts of the Gulf. Added to which, a former customs chief would look askance at the competition offered by the free port of Kuwait to Basra, where customs revenues would have to be increased to ameliorate the bleak financial situation of the province. Hamdi showed considerable energy in dealing with Arab matters. He removed Rajab, the Naqib of the Rifa'iyya brotherhood, from office as clerk of the Shari'a court. This was a risky

[23] Paris AE, CPC Bagdad 7, fos. 144–149, Pognon 27 March 1890, including a report of the French vice-consul in Basra, Gabriel Asfar, on fos. 150–151, who mentions that "the British based their claim on the Berlin treaty ... where there is no word on anything in the Gulf". It was also at that time that the incident with the Dutch consulate in Basra took place, ibid. fos. 159–160, the Dutch warship *Atjeh* arriving at Fao in June, ibid. fo. 173. New Delhi NAI, Baghdad Residency, Basra Diary, 11 February, and 11, 18 and 30 March 1890.
[24] New Delhi NAI, Baghdad Residency, Basra Diary, September–October 1890.
[25] New Delhi NAI, Baghdad Residency, Basra Diary, 20 May 1892.
[26] Wratislaw, *Consul in the East*, p. 146.

move and Hamdi's future was jeopardized by the hostility of this powerful family.[27]

Qatar and al-Hasa were the other flashpoints for the Turks in the region. There was a law and order problem there too, with marauding tribes hampering caravan traffic. When the Ottomans reinforced their military presence in al-Hasa, the most powerful man in Qatar, Shaikh Qasim Al-Thani, who had been adorned with the title of kaymakam in a semblance of bringing Qatar under Ottoman rule, felt threatened by the enlarged Ottoman military presence. He submitted his resignation as kaymakam, only to have it refused. Hamdi Pasha's predecessor as Wali of Basra, Hafiz Muhammad Pasha, took action and imprisoned brothers and sons of Shaikh Qasim.[28] He also planned a military expedition for which he requested the aid of Shaikh Abdallah of Kuwait, and in early 1893 Mubarak was sent with a few thousand warriors, accompanied also by the Naqib. While they were en route, the Wali's troops in Qatar suffered a humiliating defeat. In the midst of these proceedings Hafiz Muhammad Pasha was recalled and the Ottoman naval commander in the region, acting as Deputy Wali, opened negotiations. Shortly afterwards Wilson, the British political resident, arrived off Doha in a warship with orders to mediate. This British intervention naturally alarmed the Turks.[29] In April 1893 Hamdi Pasha was appointed Wali and at the same time the Naqib and Mubarak, who were still on their way, were ordered to turn back.[30] Later, however, Mubarak's brother Muhammad seems to have participated in mediating between Qasim Al-Thani and the Turks, because in May 1894 he arrived in Basra with some Qatari shaikhs.[31] During 1894 and 1895 the Turks were also tied down by unrest in Zubair, situated near Basra at the start of the desert route via Kuwait to al-Hasa.[32]

---

[27] New Delhi NAI, Baghdad Residency, Basra Diary, 3 August 1894. Already just one month later there were rumours in Basra that Hamdi was to be removed from office.
[28] New Delhi NAI, Baghdad Residency, Basra Diary, 7 April 1893.
[29] Anscombe, *Ottoman Gulf*, pp. 88–9.
[30] New Delhi NAI, Baghdad Residency, Basra Diary, 24 April 1893. On 19 May the Basra Diary recorded that the recall of Mubarak and the Naqib was due to the Naqib's enemies bringing their influence to bear.
[31] New Delhi NAI, Baghdad Residency, Basra Diary, 27 May 1894; Anscombe, *Ottoman Gulf*, p. 89.
[32] New Delhi NAI, Baghdad Residency, Basra Diary, 26 May, 2 June, 20 August 1894; ibid. 13 July 1895.

In this period events in Central Arabia hardly impinged upon the coastal regions of the Gulf. The hinterland of Kuwait was dominated by the formidable Amir Muhammad Ibn Rashid, to all practical purposes an independent ruler. He kept up a polite correspondence with the Sultan in Constantinople, but was far too powerful to be controlled by the Turks.[33] His only vulnerability was his dependence for supplies and weapons on markets in Iraq (controlled by the Turks), in Kuwait (controlled by the Al-Sabah), and in the more distant and limited markets of al-Hasa (also controlled by the Turks).

To most European statesmen, the Gulf was a backwater that failed to arouse much interest. This was not the case in the three imperial Ottoman centres that were directly involved with Kuwait: Basra, Baghdad and Constantinople. The provincial administration in Basra was, barring a sole telegraph wire, very remote from any communication or assistance from the Porte.[34] Links by river steamer to the nearest military post depended on a British shipping line or else were unreliable. A handful of small, decrepit armed steamboats constituted the only local military wherewithal. Just across the river Persia was in turmoil, while downstream ungovernable Arabs and the British behaved much as they pleased. Baghdad's situation was hardly superior. There was a military capability there, but it took a month to travel from Baghdad to Constantinople, along the route that was also the principal line of communication. The military authorities were only just up to the task of maintaining order along the road between Baghdad and Basra and keeping a precarious foothold in al-Hasa. Events beyond Fao could be reported only by messenger. Distorted and often exaggerated intelligence on goings-on in such a remote region could only provoke impotent fury when it reached the Baghdad command. In Constantinople, finally, at the end of the telegraph line, the Porte received reports from its officials in Baghdad and Basra that tended

[33] On Muhammad Ibn Rashid and his position, see Nolde, *Reise,* pp. 26–94, and Musil, *Northern Negd,* pp. 242–4.
[34] Readers wishing to inhale the atmosphere of an isolated official posting in a remote and rebellious area, reachable only by a fragile telegraph wire, are referred to that vintage favourite, Jules Verne's novel *Michael Strogoff.*
[35] The ships did not of course have radio by that time, but they were never far from a telegraph station, and, as they dominated the sea, could avail themselves of rapid communication between any arena of action and the nearest telegraph.
[36] Gooch and Temperley, *British Documents,* part 1, Series B, Vol. 17, pp. 123–5.

to embellish reality just to attract attention. As the Sultan watched his empire fragmenting on its margins, he was painfully aware that any response to such reports would take months to implement, and that by then the situation might have changed anyway.

One should never lose sight of the fact that, however weak the military of British India might be, once there were British troops and a warship or two in the Gulf, they were close to their local command centre at Bushire and were in a position to act anywhere on the coast.[35] This explains the apprehensions of the Turks regarding the British. And this attitude was not entirely unjustified. When a general conflict between Britain and the Ottoman Empire seemed to be looming, and the British prime minister Lord Salisbury was already toying with plans for a general carve-up of the Ottoman Empire, the British military attaché in Constantinople came up with an analysis of options for attacking the Turks. One part of the survey covered the Gulf, and stressed the weakness of the Turks in Basra province, where no regular troops were stationed.[36]

3

Change of Rule in Kuwait, 1896

3.1 Kuwait under Shaikh Muhammad, 1892–6

Shaikh Abdallah died on 29 May 1892 and was succeeded by his younger brother Muhammad.[1] It is almost impossible to establish anything with certainty about Muhammad's short reign. The sources are contradictory, and reliable contemporary documents are scarce. The truly contemporary sources on Muhammad's reign yield just four items of significance.

The first point to emerge from them is the special relationship between Kuwait and Britain, and the Ottoman reaction to it. Pognon, the French consul in Baghdad, alerted his government in 1895 to the Government of India's treatment of Muhammad as an independent sovereign ruler: it was exchanging formal protocol correspondence with him. Pognon mentioned how, two years previously, on the occasion of the death of a relative of the Shaikh of Kuwait, a British warship had arrived amid great ceremonial to deliver a formal letter of condolence to Muhammad.[2]

[1] New Delhi NAI, Baghdad Residency, Basra Diary, 29 May 1892.
[2] Paris AE, CPC Bagdad 7, fo. 496, Pognon to Minister 1 October 1895. An attempt to find confirmation of this affair in the National Archives of India met with nil result. This proves nothing decisive, because it appeared generally impossible to find any serial record of the formal protocol correspondence of the Viceroy, which, nevertheless, must have existed. Another British action that aroused suspicion was a visit by the British resident in Bushire to his colleague in Baghdad. Pognon suspected that this meeting was intended to plan a British coup in the Gulf "although they would not dare to attack Basra": Nantes AD, ambassade Constantinople D Baghdad 1890–1913, carton 13, Pognon 4 January 1896.

Pognon considered Turkey's international credibility to be weak at that moment because of the great powers' disapproval of anti-Armenian riots, but that as soon as relations improved Turkey should occupy Kuwait with a battalion of infantry. He had raised the matter with Recep Pasha, the Ottoman military commander in Iraq, but that worthy had proved most evasive. Pognon also noted the great alarm the incident had inspired in the (acting) Russian consul Mashkov, who thought it imperative that the Ottomans should take Kuwait over before the British could do so. The Russian had travelled to Basra to investigate the incident, and told Pognon that he had confronted Hamdi Pasha with the story:

> Although he [the Wali] agreed that it would be most imprudent to acquiesce in the Government of India's sending letters to a small Shaikh who in fact is no more than an Ottoman functionary and who even does not desire to be anything else, the Wali was filled with consternation to learn that the Embassy of Russia might possibly advise the Porte to occupy Kuwait.

The wry Pognon was unimpressed by Hamdi's consternation:

> Knowing as I do the incredible venality of the Turkish administration of Iraq, I can only wonder, from the information provided by my colleague, whether it is not simple bakshish paid from time to time by the Government of India to the Walis of Basra or, if by some chance these happen to be honest men themselves, to their entourage, that has until now prevented the occupation of Kuwait, and so allowed certain cartographers to preserve the "Republic of Kuwait" on their maps.[3]

The second point to note is the confirmation in contemporary sources that, under Muhammad, Kuwait still regarded itself as entirely distinct from the Ottoman Empire. When Chapuy, the owner of a French steamship, wanted to use Kuwait as a port of call he was prevented from doing so by the Kuwaitis, who were "very protective of their independence".[4]

---

[3] Nantes AD, consulat Bagdad B29, Pognon to French embassy and Ministry 14 October 1895.

[4] Nantes AD, consulat Bagdad B 29, report on Kuwait written in 1896 by Chapuy, owner of the steamer *Esther*; for this ship, see also New Delhi NAI, Baghdad Residency, Basra Diary, 11 August 1893 and 26 January 1894.

Chapuy's report, advocating the establishment of regular Ottoman authority in Kuwait so the port could be opened to international shipping, intriguingly echoes Pelly's advocacy 25 years earlier that regular Ottoman rule should be imposed.

Later sources suggest that Muhammad was pro-Ottoman while his younger brother, Mubarak, was pro-British, but there is no proof of such an assertion.[5] One should bear in mind that Shaikh Muhammad had been obliged, during the reign of Shaikh Abdallah, to conduct painful negotiations with the Turks concerning their usurpation of land at Fao for the construction of the fortress there.[6]

The clear and present danger from the Kuwaiti point of view was always that an Ottoman military intervention would stifle its independence. There was international pressure on the Ottomans to block British expansion in the Gulf by bringing Kuwait under firm control. The Ottomans were indeed alarmed about developments in the region, and Sultan Abdulhamid II continued to be sensitive to developments in the Arabian Peninsula. Sensitivities could be aggravated by relatively minor, albeit significant, matters such as the maps of Kiepert, a leading international cartographer. The Kiepert maps, first published in 1867 but from time to time reprinted, were regarded as the international standard atlas.[7] Kiepert's map of the Ottoman Empire, however, was in Turkish eyes erroneous in the matter of frontiers. Considering the map showed a "Republic of Kuwait" covering even the Fao peninsula, this reaction was not surprising. In November 1890 the Ottoman Ministry of Defence proposed a special committee to look into the whole question of Ottoman imperial borders on maps of North Africa and Arabia.[8] Nonetheless, the

---

[5] Such opinions can be found in Dickson, who only arrived in Kuwait much later (*Arab of the Desert*, pp. 266–7), and in Hewins's confused and fanciful account (*Golden Dream*, p. 129). They consider Muhammad's crony Yusuf Al-Ibrahim to have been an Ottoman agent. There is no evidence of Muhammad siding with the Turks, and a bare mention of a visit by Muhammad to Basra in 1894 cannot serve as such. The rumour circulated from the Sultan's palace in Constantinople about a conspiracy between the British and Mubarak against the loyal Muhammad was denied by the British, and there is no source to support this rumour, related in Stavrides's report published in Bidwell, *Affairs of Kuwait*, 1/1, pp. 2–3.

[6] New Delhi NAI, Baghdad Residency, Basra Diary, 27 and 29 May 1886.

[7] *Arabien zu C. Ritter's Erdkunde* bearbeitet von H. Kiepert, Berlin, Reimer Verlag 1867.

[8] Istanbul BA, Yildiz Mutanewa 46/135.

French consul Pognon could still, in 1895, record the irritation felt in military circles in Baghdad over the large Republic of Kuwait still shown on the "standard" map. He penned a long report concerning the desirability of the Ottomans occupying Kuwait to prevent British interference there.[9]

As we have seen, the British representatives in Basra tended to regard Hamdi Pasha as a friend of Britain.[10] This was probably a mistake, as Hamdi Pasha's mission was actually to diminish British influence in the Gulf and one of his first deeds in office was to resume the interrupted construction of the fortress at Fao.[11] It is thus hard to credit Pognon's suspicion that Hamdi was bribed by the British. The French consul, in his fashionable distaste for all things British, was perhaps too inclined to discern British deviousness and to underestimate British parsimony. Bribing Ottoman officials was much too costly a course for the British. One can easily imagine Hamdi Pasha being shocked by Mashkov's news about Russian pressure for the Ottoman occupation of Kuwait. Hamdi would have been against any foreign interference at all in the running of his province. It was bad enough to have the British doing it, but the involvement of yet another power would certainly lead to disagreeable consequences.[12]

An interesting new angle on the issue of the independence of the "Republic of Kuwait" was contributed by Karl Richarz, the German consul in Baghdad. He commented in an article in the *Köllnische Zeitung* on alleged British plans for a Port Said–Baghdad railway, and on activities of British agents among the Wahhabis, aimed at loosening Ottoman control along the projected route. Richarz claimed that according to his information the terminus of the railroad would be not at Basra but in "the so-called Republic of Kuwait" and he expressed his expectation that the British were planning not just to detach Kuwait from the Ottoman Empire but to annex it.[13] Richarz also remarked in December 1895 that Britain carefully protected the independence of "the so-called Republic of Kuwait" and supplied it with arms. This intelligence may be accurate, but it may just as well have been a morbid Ottoman fiction, as the news

[9] Nantes AD, consulat Bagdad, B 29, Pognon 1 October 1895.

[10] Wratislaw, *Consul*, p. 146.

[11] New Delhi NAI, Baghdad Residency, Basra Diary, July 1893. See above, section 2.3.

[12] Nantes AD, consulat Bagdad, B 29, consul Bagdad 14 October 1895.

[13] Berlin AA, R 12895 (Türkei 165 Arabien Vol. 1) A 719, Richarz 20 December 1895.

clearly emanated from Ottoman circles in Baghdad. Richarz concluded that it was essential for the freedom of access of other nations to the region that the Ottoman administration of Mesopotamia should be strengthened by international support.[14]

The third significant item to emerge from contemporary sources centres on the Ottoman record of the Kuwaiti force sent to Qatar to assist the local Ottoman administration in its conflict with Qasim Al-Thani. The force was commanded by Mubarak who, apparently as a consequence of his services in the al-Hasa expedition of 1894, had been awarded an Ottoman military rank. As seen above, the expedition was aborted, but the consequences were interesting. In Constantinople it was mooted that Mubarak should be rewarded with a brisk promotion: two steps up to the military rank of *Mirmiran* or Brigadier. This was opposed by the Wali of Basra, Hamdi Pasha, who belittled Mubarak's services and furthermore pointed out that, were Mubarak to be promoted in this way, he would outrank his brother, the Kaymakam. In the Wali's opinion neither Mubarak nor Muhammad deserved any reward at all.[15]

A family financial dispute is the fourth episode in Muhammad's reign that we can be sure about. Russian and French reports allege that Muhammad had deposited the Al-Sabah family fortune in a bank in Bombay. This caused great concern to certain other members of the family because the money had been deposited in the name of Muhammad and his sons exclusively. According to the Russian and French reports, Muhammad drew back from this course of action after strong protests, but the episode cost him dear in terms of family hostility. German consular

---

[14] Paris AE, CPC Bagdad 7, fols. 508bis–519, Pognon 30 November 1895 (especially fos. 510–511v). The informant of the newspaper was probably the renowned scholar Oppenheim, who as German consul in Cairo was well-acquainted with the situation in Kuwait because one of his contacts was in direct touch with prominent people there: Berlin AA, R 13843 A 239, Oppenheim 2 September 1897.

[15] Anscombe, *Ottoman Gulf*, p. 93 and n. 12 on p. 216, where there are (probably not entirely accurate, given the usual unreliability of Ottoman official reports) disparaging remarks about Mubarak's methods and stirring up of trouble between the tribes near al-Hasa, taken from Istanbul BA, BEO 27268. Another Ottoman document on the subject, not quoted by Anscombe, is in the Sultan's own files: Istanbul BA, Yildiz Mutanawa 78/178 of 21 Zilkade 1310/ 5 June 1893. The expedition is also mentioned in the diary of the British Agent in Basra, New Delhi NAI, Baghdad Residency, Basra Diary, 7 and 24 April 1893.

reports too mention the transfer of the money to Bombay.[16] Whatever sound sense there may be in depositing money safely abroad in troubled times, Muhammad's methods showed a remarkable lack of tact and diplomacy.

This business also features a certain Yusuf Al-Ibrahim, a Kuwaiti in possession of considerable estates on the lower Shatt al-'Arab, who belonged to a wealthy Kuwaiti banking and merchant family active in Bombay. Yusuf was related by marriage to Muhammad: both Muhammad and his brother Jarrah had married into the Al-Ibrahim family, though the relationship was somewhat distant as the wives were cousins twice removed of Yusuf. The link with Bombay business interests may, however, have fuelled Turkish suspicions about Muhammad's relations with the British.

So much for the contemporary reports. Various other opinions appear in later sources, which should all be treated with caution. They frequently present Muhammad's rule in a negative light, but our state of knowledge is insufficient for us to pass judgement on it. The British political agent in Kuwait in the 1920s and 1930s, Harold Dickson, and others convey the impression that Muhammad was incompetent and pro-Ottoman. Muhammad was doubtless an autocrat, just as Mubarak was to be, but there is no evidence of pro-Ottoman leanings.

Some sources relate that Mubarak was made responsible for the desert tribes by Muhammad, while the fourth son of Sabah, Jarrah, was in placed in charge of finances.[17] Mubarak's function was vital for Kuwait, as the vague territorial boundaries of the shaikhdom depended on the fickle loyalty of the nomadic tribes. Implementing desert policy could be costly. One important source relates how, in 1895, armed conflict broke out

---

[16] Russian report quoted in Bondarevsky, *Kuwait*, pp. 90 and 96; French report in Nantes AD, ambassade Turquie E 288, consul Bagdad 4 June 1896. A German report of 1898 contains information given by the Baghdad Mushir, Recep Pasha, that Yusuf Al-Ibrahim had deposited 2 million riyals [Maria Theresia thalers], belonging to the *ca*. 40 members of the Al-Sabah family in common, under the single name of Muhammad (Berlin AA, R 13207 A 3687, Hesse in Baghdad 3 March 1898). In a German report from Bombay it is mentioned that Muhammad's fortune of 10 million rupees was deposited with the pearl trader Shaikh 'Ali bin Muhammad Al-Ibrahim (Berlin AA R 13843 A 2075, consulate Bombay 14 January 1898).

[17] Dickson, *Arab*, pp. 266–7; Abu Hakima, *Modern History*, p. 110, based on Rushaid, *Tarikh*, Vol. 2, pp. 37–47.

between Kuwait and the powerful Muhammad Ibn Rashid of Haïl, the
Amir of Najd.[18] It is thus not inconceivable that there were serious
disputes inside Kuwait over financial priorities, with Mubarak advocating
more spending on tribal policy. We know for certain that Mubarak had
earlier, in 1871 and 1893, been employed in delicate tribal dealings, so the
story that he was responsible for tribal relations has a certain plausibility.

In early 1896 tensions manifested themselves. The Shah of Persia was
assassinated in March, and at the same time trouble flared up again in
Qatar. The British resident, having bombarded Zubara on the Qatar coast
the year before, reappeared there with a warship in order to persuade two
nearby villages to recognize British authority. Confusion over the identity
of Zubara gave rise to garbled reports in the European press that the
British had bombarded the Ottoman town of Zubair, near Basra. The affair
set alarm bells ringing in Baghdad, and somehow the news reached the
German newspapers, which duly made much of it. The French consul
even went so far as to assume that the British had been planning to bring
Qatar under their control, but that the furore in the German *Köllnische
Zeitung* had made London think twice about it.[19] The order issued by the
Ottoman authorities for the arrest of Shaikh Qasim Al-Thani contributed
further to instability in the area.[20]

Rumours such as those disseminated by Richarz, Pognon and Mashkov
about the imminence of a British takeover of Kuwait unless the Turks took
action, are a measure of the looming prospect of an Ottoman takeover of
the shaikhdom. Suggestions that Muhammad was in contact with the
British, therefore, might very well impel the Turks to intervention. At such
a time of tension anything might happen.

3.2 Mubarak's takeover, 1896

Just as the international situation in the Gulf had become perilously
unstable, internal strife erupted in Kuwait as, in May 1896, a *coup d'état*

---

[18] Musil, *Northern Negd*, p. 244.

[19] Nantes AD, consulat Bagdad B 29, Pognon 26 May 1896.

[20] New Delhi NAI, Baghdad Residency, Basra Diary, 22 April 1896: the arrest was
because Qasim had killed the Ottoman assistant-kaymakam in Qatar – a regular
Turkish official who had been attached to Qasim, who as tribal leader bore the title
of kaymakam.

took place.[21] Muhammad and his younger brother Jarrah were killed and Mubarak, Sabah's third son, took power. This rather bald statement of events is deliberate. Some publications break into thriller-like prose at this point[22] – a temptation the historian should resist at such times, when the plethora of different versions renders certainty impossible. Nor, in the absence of conclusive proof supporting any one version, should he try his hand at detective work. Most sources identify Mubarak as the man behind the killings, and several state that he did not himself fire the shots; but they vary in the motive they ascribe to him. Historians are neither policemen nor judges. Mubarak later proclaimed his innocence.[23] An Ottoman official once remarked that Mubarak probably was behind the assassinations, but that it would be impossible to prove it.[24] This observation was made in the context of Ottoman plans to take over the government of Kuwait. If the Ottomans really thought that, having occupied Kuwait, they would be unable to prove Mubarak's guilt, how should anybody else be in a position to determine the facts of what happened?

Perhaps the best approach to an understanding of the assassination, and the initial reactions to it, is to examine some of the first reports. Detailed reports were received by the Ottoman, German, French and Russian governments, but London was informed only after considerable delay. These reports are daunting in their variety, but essentially they are of three kinds, though they are occasionally interdependent. In the first place there are the reports received by the Ottoman authorities in Constantinople, either from Kuwait or from Ottoman officials in Basra. We may regard

[21] Salwa Al-Ghanim, *Mubarak*, p. 1 (quoting no sources), gives 17 May as the date, but this is contradicted by the fact that the murder is already mentioned in Ottoman reports of 28 and 29 Nishan 1312 (10 and 11 May 1896). The Turkish documents put the date at 8 May (quoted by Anscombe, *Ottoman Gulf*, p. 93 and p. 218 n. 29). The event is noted in the British Basra Diary (in New Delhi NAI, Baghdad Residency), of 14 May, without giving the exact date on which it took place. So we should conclude that Al-Ghanim is mistaken here. Al-Ghanim's date is also contradicted by Rushaid, *Tarikh*, Vol. 2, p. 45, which puts the date at "25 Dhu'l Qade 1313" which would be 7 or 8 May.

[22] Salwa Al-Ghanim, *Mubarak*, pp. 1–4, under the heading "Murder by Night"; Bondarevsky, p. 93, quotes an even more lurid account in a journalistic book that is not, however, rooted in any substantive source: Hewins, *Golden Dream*, pp. 129–30.

[23] Anscombe, *Ottoman Gulf*, p. 100, quoting Istanbul BA, Irade Dahiliye 36/5, reports of Muhsin Pasha of 8 and 12 Temmuz 1317 Rumi (21 and 25 July 1901).

[24] Anscombe, *Ottoman Gulf*, p. 98.

these as accounts by the persons most directly involved, and it is no wonder that they contradict each other. The second group comprises reports by European consular representatives, which are also full of discrepancies. In this context we should note that there was no real reporting of the events within the British colonial system. Local Kuwaiti historiography represents a third stream of information. It should, however, be noted that this material dates from the 1920s at the earliest, and so cannot be strictly regarded as contemporary.

The most direct Ottoman sources contain no information on the background and causes of the events in Kuwait. From the start the Wali of Basra, Hamdi Pasha, made it clear in his reports to Constantinople that Mubarak had killed his brothers and that direct intervention in Kuwait was necessary to avert chaos. For chaos he used a legal term, *fitna*, denoting a state of affairs an Islamic government is obliged to avoid at all cost.[25] At the same time the Porte received a series of telegrams from inhabitants of Kuwait, including Mubarak, accusing Hamdi Pasha of such poor government in Basra that the desert tribes were out of control, with the result that some bedouin had infiltrated Kuwait and killed the brothers Muhammad and Jarrah Al-Sabah.[26] No final verdict can be reached on the basis of such contradictory versions. It is noteworthy that the Kuwaitis too complained to Constantinople that Hamdi Pasha's deplorable governance had caused "*fitna*" in the region and that this had brought trade to a standstill.[27] So the Sultan was being urged by both sides to put an end to "*fitna*".

The European sources are no less discrepant. On 27 May, the British consul in Baghdad reported to his embassy in Constantinople, sending an extract from the Basra consulate diary:

> It is reported that Sheikh Mubarak Sebah of Koweit has killed his brother Muhammad Pasha Sebah and Sheikh Jerrah and two of the children of the latter. The cause of this murder is said to have been the refusal of Muhammad Pasha to advance money to his brother Mubarak.[28]

[25] Anscombe, *Ottoman Gulf*, p. 95.
[26] Al-Qasimi, *Bayan al-Kuwait*, pp. 329–38. Al-Qasimi publishes facsimiles of documents from archival series other than those used by Anscombe. On this topic the documents reproduced by him come from the series Hariciye Mütenevvi, while for the same period Anscombe used the series Bab-i Ali evrak odasi gelen-giden.
[27] Al-Qasimi, *Bayan al-Kuwait*, p. 336.
[28] PRO, FO 195/1935, Consul Baghdad to Curry, 27 May 1896.

A note on this paper states that this information had not been sent on to London, which seems distinctly odd in view of the care with which the event was reported by every other nationality in the area. Even though so sparing, the report is not totally accurate: no sons of Jarrah were killed. It is noteworthy that London remained in the dark for some weeks, and it took some time for British officialdom to work up any interest in the affair. Well before London got to know anything about it, the French government had already received the first report of 26 May from their Baghdad consulate: "Finally trouble has erupted in Kuwait where members of the family of the Shaikh kill each other. I have no precise information as yet." London was eventually enlightened on July 13th.[29]

On 4 June the French consul in Baghdad submitted a more detailed report to his embassy in Constantinople:

> A private letter to the Russian consul in Baghdad informed him of the murder of the Shaikh of Koueit Mohammed Sabah, of his brother Jessah [Jarrah] and of the son of the latter by their younger brother Mubarrek. The letter reported the arrival of two British and one Turkish ships in sight of Kuwait and reported great anxiety in Basra. Here are details of the events as confirmed by H. E. the Marshal Redjib Pasha, commander of the VI Army Corps. Some time before Shaikh Mohammed Sabah had already aroused the animosity of several of his relatives. The custom is for Koueit to be governed by the eldest of the Sabah family. Now Shaikh Mohammed, successor to Shaikh Abdullah who died three years ago, had hatched a plan to confer power exclusively on his branch of the family. With this end in view, he sent the Al-Sabah money, the revenues of the family collective, to Bombay, and had them deposited in a bank in the name of his sons. The other members of the family, urged on by Shaikh Moubarek, protested. Finally they managed to have the money deposited in the name of all of them jointly, but this affair gave rise to their hostility towards their elder brother. The situation was even more serious because Mohammed had already alienated the tribes and stood accused of making moves towards the British, which risked bringing down a British or Turkish occupation upon Koueit, both prospects equally unpalatable to the population, which enjoys a certain degree of liberty and prosperity under the present system. Exploiting this climate of opinion, Mubarrek

[29] The French information in Paris AE, NS Turquie 149, 17–20; *cf.* the first report to London, in Bidwell, *Affairs of Kuwait*, 1/1, p. 1, Herbert in Therapia (a suburb of Constantinople) 6 July 1896; this report arrived in London on 13 July.

secretly assembled the elders and tribal leaders and reminded them of Mohammed's affronts to his relatives, and pointed out the dangers to which the unstable and excitable character of the chief exposed Koueit. He concluded with the proposal to depose the Shaikh, which was unanimously accepted. A few days later Shaikh Mohammed Sabah and his brother Jessah, with the son of the latter, were killed in circumstances which remain obscure. Mubarrek proclaimed himself ruler of Kuwait. His first act was to write a letter to Marshal Redjib Pasha in which he expressed his devotion to the person of the Sultan and asked for the favour and support of the imperial administration. At the same time H.E. Redjib Pasha received a *mazbata*, adorned with the seals of the elders and notables of Kuwait, confirming that Mubarrek Sabah was not involved in the triple murder. This fact demonstrates that Shaikh Mubarrek, a man already known for his intelligence and energy, has the sympathy of the tribes and that he will be supported by them. In this situation it may be dangerous to act too hastily in Kuwait, so shortly after the death of Shaikh Mohammed. There is no doubt that the Turkish Government would be committing a serious error if it let slip this opportunity to settle the serious and always urgent matter of Koueit. After discussing the matter, H.E. Redjib Pasha and the Russian consul have arrived at the conviction that the best course of action would be for the Ottoman Government to behave as if it found Shaikh Mubarrek's innocence entirely credible, and that it was concerned only to find the real murderers of Shaikh Mohammed (the latter bore the title of kaymakam). The investigation would be launched in this manner as a smoke-screen, until the moment were judged opportune for two Turkish battalions to arrive suddenly in Kuwait, one by sea and the other by land. Then at last the vital issue of the effective occupation by the Imperial [Ottoman] Government of the *Dardanelles* of Iraq would fall definitively into the category of *faits accomplis.*[30]

The information given here by the French consul is on the whole confirmed by the report of the other party concerned, the Russian consul. Moreover later elements in the account, especially the matter of the deposit of the family fortune in Muhammad's name being the cause of the

[30] Nantes AD, ambassade Constantinople E 288, Consul Baghdad 4 June 1896.
[31] The Russian source is summarized in Bondarevsky, *Kuwait*, pp. 96–7. Recep Pasha's information to the German consul appears in Berlin AA, R 13207 A 3687 (Hesse in Baghdad, 3 March 1898).

murder, were passed on by Recep Pasha to the German consul.[31] The Russian consul also suspected the interference of British agents, although no trace of this has been found as yet in British sources. The story as related by these consuls has the edge over all other versions of the events in having some independent corroboration: Yusuf Al-Ibrahim himself stated much later that Mubarak harboured the suspicion that the family money had been put away and disappeared in the Al-Ibrahim family bank in Bombay, and something to this effect also appears in a contemporary German newspaper.[32]

The consular reports also outdo the other sources in pointing up some highly relevant aspects of the political context that have escaped earlier historians. The first is that it was clear from the start that Mubarak had full control in Kuwait. Secondly, the feeling in Baghdad that it was time to put an end to Kuwait's independence, given its pre-eminent strategic position as the "Dardanelles of Iraq", had existed for some time. The third, and for the future most important aspect is the deviousness of Recep Pasha's planned response to leave Mubarak be for a short time, be friendly to him and then suddenly to intervene with a large military force. This looks highly astute, but such complex plans tend to fail if one small detail goes wrong. It seems a grossly over-optimistic estimate of Ottoman capabilities to believe that two battalions could be despatched discreetly and in short order to Kuwait from afar, when there were no troops in Basra.

The German consul Richarz too informed his government, even taking pains to write Mubarak's name in Arabic script in his letter. An interesting feature of Richarz's account is his supposition that the Amir of Najd, Muhammad Ibn Rashid, was somehow involved. This Amir was the most powerful Arab potentate in the Peninsula, and had in recent years been actively acquiring control over all tribes of the region. In 1895 he had been at war with Kuwait.[33]

---

[32] The British consul in Basra wrote in June 1902 that an agent of Yusuf Al-Ibrahim had approached him with the story, including the statement that Mubarak found the Kuwait treasury empty: Bidwell, *Affairs of Kuwait*, 2/4, p. 95, Wratislaw 13 June 1902. The German article is in the *Köllnische Zeitung* of 3 February 1898. It was based on a letter of 31 January 1897 from the German diplomatic resident in Egypt, Max von Oppenheim, who obtained his information from a young Arab merchant from Basra who was on a visit to Egypt (Berlin AA, R 14555 A 239).

[33] Berlin AA, R 13841, Richarz 21 May. Ibn Rashid's war is mentioned in Musil, *Northern Negd*, p. 244.

Various other accounts of the events deserve our consideration. The first is that of the contemporary Kuwaiti historian Rushaid, born in 1887 and thus almost contemporary. According to him there was, at the outset, a dispute between the brothers over the share of the budget to be allocated to Mubarak's "department" of tribal affairs. This conflict was resolved through mediation by prominent Kuwaitis. Some time later Mubarak was again in need of funds; his brothers refused, but the notables of the town persuaded Muhammad to pay. But then Yusuf Al-Ibrahim intervened and stopped the payment. The notables of Kuwait tried to convince Yusuf that his intervention could cause a disastrous split in the ruling family, but Yusuf affected indifference. Mubarak then sent a deputation of notables to his brother to arrange matters. They saw Muhammad, who told them to go to Yusuf's house where he, Muhammad, would meet them. Yusuf was reluctant at first, but then agreed to a meeting, in which the delegates explained Mubarak's desire for a true and reliable account of the revenues of the date groves in Basra province, so that he could know what his legitimate share might be. An account was vouchsafed, but Mubarak was not satisfied, demanding a new account, on the reliability of which his brother would swear an oath. Muhammad, however, did not change the figures. Afterwards there was a meeting between the brothers in which Mubarak declared that he would accept the account, if only it was confirmed by Muhammad's oath. This was not forthcoming. Muhammad agreed to grant Mubarak's request only if Mubarak signed a paper unconditionally accepting whatever Muhammad offered him. During the following weeks Mubarak persisted in his efforts directly or indirectly to change Muhammad's mind. According to Rushaid, the tactless behaviour of Muhammad's younger brother, Jarrah, who was very hostile to Mubarak, brought matters to a head. Rushaid describes in picturesque detail how Jarrah publicly warned the Kuwaitis not to advance money to Mubarak because he was broke. Rushaid, typically for him, gives us details that were visible to the Kuwaiti public at the time, and should be regarded as very reliable for that part of the story.[34]

The gist of both Rushaid's and the French consul's account is that money was the crux of the dispute. This is confirmed by the British Basra Diary. Rushaid's version tallies reasonably well with the Franco-Russian

[34] Rushaid, *Tarikh*, Vol. 2, pp. 38–44.

one.[35] The crucial difference is Rushaid's imputation that Mubarak was directly involved in the murder and that he was motivated by his personal financial difficulties. Rushaid's account of his treatment by Jarrah also provides Mubarak with a credible motive, in that it would make a violent reaction understandable. Rushaid's version is interesting, but in 1896 he was still too young to be an independent observer, and we cannot know to what extent he was disinterested and neutral.

There is a tendency in the Kuwaiti sources, such as Rushaid, to elaborate on Mubarak's frustration at being relegated to the administration of tribal matters while Muhammad and Jarrah wielded the "real" power.[36] In 1910 the French consul in Muscat gave a slightly different, but more interesting version: Mubarak claimed to have "transported his brothers to the mercy of Allah [...] because they refused to help him with the customs revenue to repel the Najdis [i.e. the followers of Muhammad Ibn Rashid], and the prominent people of Kuwait forgave him [Mubarak] because of this."[37]

A very strong version of this interpretation appears in Dickson, British political agent in Kuwait from 1929 to 1935. Dickson is far from being a contemporary source, so we should not be too credulous of his rather lurid account. According to him, Mubarak was shunted off to the desert without money at the suggestion of the "deeply pro-Turkish" Yusuf Al-Ibrahim. This embodies two assumptions: a pro-British attitude on Mubarak's part in opposition to the supposedly pro-Ottoman regime of Muhammad, and a sinister conspiracy against Mubarak. There is no contemporary evidence for a pro-British stance by Mubarak as early as 1896, apart from one highly suspect British statement of 1901.[38]

[35] New Delhi NAI, Baghdad Residency, Basra Diary, 14 May 1896. A financial motive for the killings was also given in the lurid and inaccurate description by Hewins (*Golden Dream*, pp. 127–9), who even includes the probably fanciful story that Mubarak was driven into exile in Bombay.

[36] Salwa Al-Ghanim, *Mubarak*, pp. 3–4 rightly indicates that this was an honourable position fitting to Mubarak's past. There is, however, the matter that tribal policy required considerable funds, and that Mubarak was short of money and his brothers were refusing to help him. Crucial in this is the remark by the French consul in Baghdad (in the letter quoted of 4 June 1896) that Muhammad had alienated the tribes, so necessitating an expensive desert policy, and the statement by Al-Ghanim that this was insufficient reason for murder does not stand up.

[37] Paris AE, NS Mascate 14, fo. 127, annex to the Muscat report of 8 August 1910.

A slight variation on this theme presents a Mubarak, harbouring Arab nationalist sentiments, being angered by the pro-Ottoman attitude of Yusuf Al-Ibrahim which strongly influenced Muhammad's policy. While it cannot be denied that Mubarak later used to read a newspaper of that hue, and certainly contemplated pan-Arab schemes with his friend the Shaikh of Muhammara, such issues cannot be proven to have interested Mubarak before 1902, although there is no argument against it either.[39]

Still, there is no doubt that already in 1896 Mubarak was suspected by the Sultan of trying to shape Arab coalitions in the Gulf region in disregard of political borders.[40] But there is a serious flaw in the theory of an Arab nationalist motive for the murder: it does not appear that either Shaikh Muhammad or Yusuf Al-Ibrahim, whose family business was based in Bombay, were pro-Ottoman. In 1895–6, both Muhammad and Yusuf Al-Ibrahim were accused of conspiring with the British, while Mubarak was traditionally the Kuwaiti shaikh most familiar to the Ottomans; he even held a real Ottoman knighthood as titular equerry to the Sultan.[41] It should also be recalled that Muhammad had reason to dislike the Turks because of the quarrel over the Fao fortress.

[38] Dickson, *Kuwait*, pp. 266–8. Dickson employs further qualifications, like the one that Muhammad was "a lazy and spineless Ruler", but this finds no confirmation in contemporary sources. In 1901 the British resident in Baghdad informally mentioned to the German consul Richarz that Mubarak, immediately after Muhammad's murder, had told the resident in Bushire that he would accept none other than British protection, but that "a fortnight afterwards the old swine telegraphed the Sultan at Constantinople that he was his most faithful subject". The German consul was not impressed by this "boyish" statement by the resident: Berlin AA, R 13843 A 6773 (7 May 1901), Richarz in Baghdad 10 April 1901.

[39] Anscombe, *Ottoman Gulf*, p. 217 n. 16, refutes this motive in some detail. He states that it originates from Dickson (though it is not explicitly or even implicitly to be found in Dickson's book *Kuwait*, pp. 266–73) and was most strongly expressed in Husayn Khaz'al, *Tarikh*, Vol. 2, p. 13. Anscombe is wrong, however, to state that Mubarak had no Arab Nationalist sentiments at a later date.

[40] Bidwell, *Affairs of Kuwait*, 1/1, pp. 1–2: rumours in palace circles in Constantinople that Mubarak had plans for an Arab coalition covering the area claimed by the Ottomans (Kuwait, Qatar and Ibn Rashid in Najd) and semi-British Bahrain. German sources relate rumours in 1895–6 that Ibn Rashid had suspicious alliances: Berlin AA, R 12203 A 8792, Richarz in Baghdad 9 August 1895. Ibn Rashid was also alleged to be behind Muhammad's murder: Berlin AA, R 13841 A 6317, Richarz 21 May 1896.

[41] Anscombe, *Ottoman Gulf*, p. 93.

It is thus far from certain that there was an international political motive for the events of 1896. But if there was, then it might well have owed its inspiration to dangerous pro-British tendencies in Muhammad's reign. The suggestion of a link between Mubarak and Britain at that time comes from later or unreliable sources. On the contrary, Mubarak may have been aware of the alarm felt by the French, Russian and German consuls in Baghdad at the end of 1895 about the relationship between Muhammad and India, and of the pressure on the Turks to act against British intrigues in Kuwait. Mubarak may have found Muhammad's pro-British game a perilous one, or may simply have exploited it as a handy opportunity, as he was regarded as a friend by the Turks, to carry out a coup. His suspicion of a conspiracy between Muhammad and the British would have been enhanced by the involvement of Yusuf Al-Ibrahim, a Kuwaiti merchant with strong Bombay connections.[42] One may safely disregard the wild stories on offer in Ralph Hewins' rather sensational book, in which Bondarevsky tends to place some credence. According to Hewins, Mubarak was driven into exile in Bombay and many others to Basra by the incompetent Muhammad. On Mubarak's return, his brothers refused to advance him any money and he staged his coup, all this being narrated in lurid and uncorroborated detail.[43]

The view of writers such as Dickson, that Muhammad was a weak ruler whom it was necessary for Mubarak to replace, is not corroborated by contemporary sources. However, one may assume some difference of opinion over policy priorities: either to maintain a strong tribal policy (Mubarak), or to pursue prudent financial management, perhaps against the day when it might be necessary to bribe the Turks (Muhammad and Jarrah). There were sound arguments, in view of the tense situation in the region in 1895, for expatriating the money for safekeeping in India.[44] What

[42] Al-Ghanim, *Mubarak*, p. 2, criticizes Dickson for calling Yusuf an unscrupulous Iraqi, without giving an exact reference. This seems to be a misquotation: Dickson, *Kuwait*, p. 267, uses disparaging language about Yusuf (e.g. he was an "an ambitious rogue") but does not call him an Iraqi. Yusuf possessed property on the Turkish bank of the Shatt al-'Arab, as did the Al-Sabah, but this does not make a Kuwaiti an Iraqi.

[43] Bondarevsky, *Kuwait*, p. 94, quoting the dubious source Hewins, pp. 128–31. Hewins probably embellished stories told by Dickson in his old age. The only source indicating a refusal of Muhammad to participate in a pro-British conspiracy involving Mubarak is the above-mentioned highly unreliable rumour emanating from the Sultan's circle, recorded by Stavrides: Bidwell, *Affairs of Kuwait*, 1/1, pp. 1–2.

is clear is that Muhammad may have lacked tact in his dealings with the other members of his family, and that Jarrah treated Mubarak in an extremely discourteous manner.[45] There was a difference of opinion and a financial disagreement, and those may have constituted sufficient cause for a standard palace revolution.

The widely divergent stories and interpretations quoted above make it impossible to reach a firm conclusion about what happened in Kuwait in 1896. Sources contradict each other about who fired the shots and about possible motives. The historian in the end has to leave these questions open. But a noteworthy feature is the total lack of local support, in the aftermath, for those who pointed the finger of guilt at Mubarak and called for revenge on him. This certainly diminishes the plausibility of the stories directed against Mubarak.

Whatever may be the truth of the matter, Mubarak immediately gained firm control over Kuwait and was to show himself a dynamic ruler. He gained the support of the majority of his family. Finding the treasury practically empty, he concluded that Yusuf Al-Ibrahim had taken the money. He responded to this by confiscating all the property of Yusuf that he could lay his hands on. Yusuf meanwhile took refuge in his stronghold of Dawra, between Fao and Basra. The sons of Muhammad and Jarrah were eventually allowed to leave Kuwait by Mubarak. One of them, Sa'ud, arrived in Baghdad in September 1896, while the others remained in Basra. Sa'ud asked Recep Pasha to intervene in Kuwait and punish Mubarak. He also visited the German consulate in Baghdad where he encountered some sympathy, because the German consul Richarz favoured an Ottoman occupation of Kuwait to avert British or Russian interference in that "Republic", which might lead in turn to a monopoly in the Gulf by one of those powers. Curiously enough Richarz ascribes the confused situation around Kuwait to Hamdi's lack of initiative. In this he echoes the opinions of his friend Recep Pasha.[46]

[44] The matter of the money is quite complicated. It seems to be true that Mubarak found the treasury practically empty when he took over. This is even confirmed by Yusuf Al-Ibrahim, but Yusuf denied that the money had been in his hands (see Bidwell, *Affairs of Kuwait*, 2/ 4, p. 95). But then, where had the money gone?

[45] Rushaid, *Tarikh*, Vol. 2, pp. 37–47; Qina'i, *Tarikh*, pp. 25–8, where there is also mention of a mediation by Salim al-Badr (probably the Al-Sabah Basra agent) with the result that Mubarak would receive 10,000 rupees (666 pounds sterling). This agreement became void when Salim died.

3.3 Mubarak establishes himself

Hamdi Pasha, the Wali of Basra, reacted immediately to the crisis in Kuwait and reported in strong terms to the Minister of the Interior. He expressed fears that Britain would move in – not unreasonably, in the light of the warning he had been given by the Russian consul in Baghdad, Mashkov, in 1895. According to Hamdi, the people of Kuwait had had their fill of Al-Sabah tyranny, and a force of 300 men would suffice to impose Ottoman authority. Kuwait could then become a *sancak* under Basra province (thus one degree higher than its status hitherto as a nominal *kaza* in the Ottoman system).[47] The Porte was never quick to respond, and Anscombe concludes on the basis of Ottoman documents that Hamdi's reports were regarded as exaggerated in tone. Moreover Hamdi was viewed already as having somewhat bungled the Zubara affair of 1894–5. Added to which the Mushir, Recep Pasha, who favoured Mubarak, had at various times discredited Hamdi, compounding the confusion. He was spreading a rumour that Hamdi's alleged links with the British lay behind his inaction over British ties with Muhammad Al-Sabah, and behind his lack of initiative earlier in 1896 against British naval actions against Ottoman villages in Qatar, a place over which the Ottomans claimed authority. So the Porte, confronted with conflicting reports, failed to act.[48]

[46] Berlin AA, R 13841 A 10356, Richarz 10 September 1896. Interesting is the remark by Richarz that Sa'ud's move was a break with Al-Sabah family tradition: until then the Kuwaitis including the Al-Sabah had been intent on preserving Kuwait's independence. Sa'ud, however, had no success with Recep Pasha who, as can be seen from the French report quoted above (Nantes AD, Constantinople E288, consul Baghdad 4 June 1896), considered Mubarak a competent person. See also Anscombe, *Ottoman Gulf*, p. 96.

[47] Anscombe, *Ottoman Gulf*, p. 93, depicts Hamdi's reaction in strong colours, quoting his reports of 11–12 Nishan 1312 (10–11 May 1896, BA, BEO 66196), but he cannot be right in stating that these reports arrived in Istanbul as a complete surprise, given the information contained in the French report of the end of 1895. Furthermore, already in 1893 Hamdi had uttered warnings in Constantinople about the situation in Kuwait: Istanbul BA, Yildiz Mutanewa 78/178.

[48] For the accusations against Hamdi, see Berlin AA, R 13841 A 6889, Richarz in Baghdad 3 June 1896; and ibid. A 13841, Richarz 13 August 1896. These accusations are not mentioned in the otherwise accurate description of the indecisiveness of the Porte by Anscombe, *Ottoman Gulf*, p. 96.

Hence in June 1896 Mubarak seemed comparatively secure in Kuwait. The Porte seemed inclined to accept the *fait accompli*. Whether or not the French/Russian report of provisional approval by the Kuwaiti shaikhs of Mubarak's coup was accurate, it certainly seems that Mubarak encountered little internal opposition. Few had gone onto exile – only Yusuf Al-Ibrahim and the sons of Jarrah and Muhammad. These all set about petitioning Hamdi Pasha in Basra for aid. Thanks to Anscombe's research in the Ottoman archives, we know that this took place in the early summer of 1896.[49] Hamdi was described by Mubarak in his correspondence as domineering and a "listener", a man of fickle character who heeded the advice of the last person he spoke with.[50] British sources, however, tended to a more positive opinion of Hamdi, who was said to be, if not brilliant, at least not corrupt.[51] The plea for help by Yusuf Al-Ibrahim and Mubarak's nephews offered Hamdi an intriguing opportunity. He could have used it to put an end to Al-Sabah influence in Basra province, as it lay in his power to sequestrate their possessions on the banks of the Shatt al-'Arab. Whether out of fear of Mubarak's friends in the local courts of law, or simply out of the general indecisiveness of Ottoman officials, Hamdi took no such steps, merely requesting military intervention against Kuwait itself.

Ultimately the cause of Mubarak's opponents was damaged by his nephews' plea for Ottoman support. They attracted few supporters, not just because of universal sympathy for Mubarak, but also because he represented a lesser evil than direct Ottoman rule.

Top priority for the new administration in Kuwait was to avert intervention by their mighty Ottoman neighbour. According to the Hamdi view, Ottoman annexation would be the next logical step. If Kuwait were indeed a regular Ottoman district, then the whole affair would be a simple police matter: intervention by superior authority, appointment of an interim administration, a police investigation into the crime, and the initiation of legal proceedings. It is highly significant that

[49] Anscombe, *Ottoman Gulf*, p. 219, n. 37, quoting a letter of the Minister of Interior to the Grand Vizier of 25 Haziran 1317 (7 July 1896), in BA, BEO 66196.
[50] IOLR, R/15/1/471, fo. 293, Mubarak to Resident September 1899.
[51] Wratislaw, p. 146; Bidwell, *Affairs of Kuwait*, 1/2, p. 8. The British opinion seems to have been inspired by Hamdi's politeness towards British consular officials in Basra. See also Bidwell, *Affairs of Kuwait*, 1/1, pp. 4–5, Whyte, Agent in Basra, to Baghdad 2 August 1896.

nobody ever proposed this straightforward solution, doubtless simply because Kuwait was not a regular Ottoman administrative district. But the Ottomans were still faced with a stark choice, either of interventing with the added possibility of annexation, or of decorating Mubarak with robes of honour and a kaymakam's diploma, attended by the hope that he would behave himself.

The tardy Ottoman response may also have been due to Hamdi having no military means in Basra of intervening in Kuwait. His estimate of 300 men sounds wildly optimistic, considering the low quality of Ottoman troops in Mesopotamia. Furthermore, intervention would require the services of the staff of the VI Army Corps in Baghdad. But Mubarak had friends in the Baghdad military, having helped the Ottoman army three years before, and the commander-in-chief Recep Pasha considered Mubarak a fit and worthy person to rule Kuwait.[52]

The Ottoman state was highly centralized, and local officials had limited financial and military resources at their disposal. Their every step had to have central government approval, but at the centre there was near-paralysis in decision-making. Abdulhamid II's administration operated very differently from the former, traditional style of Ottoman government in which the Grand Vizier had fully delegated powers. The zealous and neurotic Sultan interfered constantly and erratically in government business. There were, however, two consistent threads in the Sultan's policy in the region: deep distrust of the British, and a deep interest in the Arabian Peninsula. One of the Sultan's chief advisers on Arabian affairs was Abu 'l-Huda, whom we have already met (see section 2.1). Abu 'l-Huda was a Baghdadi, whose father, according to the French consul, was floor sweeper of the principal mosque there. Abu 'l-Huda was the chief of the Rifa'iyya brotherhood in Basra, and a friend (or, according to Max von Oppenheim, a relative) of the Naqib of the same brotherhood, one of the largest landowners in Iraq, who in turn was in contact with Mubarak.[53] There were rumours that both Abu 'l-Huda and his competitor as the

[52] Nantes AD, ambassade Constantinople E 288, consul Bagdad 4 June 1896.
[53] On Ebulhüda, see Oppenheim, *Reise*, p. 300; also *EI*(2), Vol. 8, pp. 525–6, *i.v.* Rifa'iyya; Anscombe, *Ottoman Gulf*, p. 218, note 26. The Austrian consul in Baghdad also confirms that the Naqib acted as intermediary between the Ottoman authorities and Mubarak: Vienna HHSA, PA XXXVIII K 315, consul Rappaport 20 September 1900. The floor sweeper is mentioned by the French consul in Baghdad on 29 December 1908: Paris AE, NS Mascate 14 fo. 23v (see Chapter 10 n. 7).

Sultan's religious adviser, the Shaikh al-Islam, had accepted bribes from Mubarak, and this too may have delayed Ottoman action.[54]

The French consular report of May 1896 sheds some light on possible causes of Ottoman confusion and inertia. First, the Ottoman establishment in Baghdad was suspicious of Muhammad and felt some confidence in their old friend Mubarak. The Russian report on the financial antics of Muhammad was known to Recep Pasha, and must have confirmed the Baghdad military commander in this view. Baghdad appears to have viewed the coup as a not undesirable development, the removal of Muhammad representing a setback for the British, who had caused so much trouble in Arabia recently. Hamdi, on the other hand, had been accused by the French and Russians in Baghdad (who were close to the military establishment there) of neglecting the situation in Kuwait.[55] It is quite probable that Hamdi's overreaction was inspired in part by fear that the Porte would reproach him for indolence.

It would be understandable for the Ottoman Government to be reluctant to assign part of the ineffective and demoralized VI Army Corps to Hamdi for a hazardous desert march. What fate would await this force at the hands of the unruly desert tribes in the event of defeat? An alternative would be to embark the troops on the few warships available, but what if the British confronted them with their superior firepower? Ottoman loss of face would be the worst aspect of such outcomes, as tribal leaders might be emboldened to assert their independence. The Porte was duly hesitant, while Hamdi persisted with his requests for armed intervention. The Porte, meanwhile, was receiving reports from other sources. There had been telegrams from Kuwaitis in support of Mubarak and against Hamdi.[56] The Minister of War had received a report from Recep Pasha, the Mushir in Baghdad.[57] We also know the Mushir's opinion from the French consular report of May 1896: he saw Mubarak's takeover as a positive development. Recep's advice was to appoint

---

[54] Bidwell, *Affairs of Kuwait*, 1/1, p. 8, Whyte's memorandum of 22 March 1897.

[55] See above, this chapter, n. 2; Nantes AD, ambassade Constantinople E 288, consul Bagdad 4 June 1896.

[56] Istanbul BA, Irade Dahiliye 1314/46 (13 Haziran and 9 Temmuz 1312 Rumi or 25 June and 21 July 1896): telegrams of the Kuwaitis and comments of the Minister of the Interior, unfriendly to Hamdi.

[57] Anscombe, *Ottoman Gulf*, pp. 96–7, and nn. 34–35 on pp. 218–19.

Mubarak forthwith as Kaymakam of Kuwait. He had received a statement from Kuwait in support of Mubarak sporting a multitude of signatures.[58]

Hamdi in the meantime continued to issue dire warnings about sinister British intrigues. On the news of Muhammad's death a warship, the *Sphinx,* had been despatched to Kuwait from Bushire to investigate the situation. Hamdi duly sent the Porte news about an alleged cordial reception,[59] but his account does not tally with the British documents. Baker, the commander of the *Sphinx,* wrote:

> Kuwait is nominally an independent Arab territory, but in reality the Turks exercise great influence over it, more especially since the new Chief acceded to power, he finds it necessary to play into their hands. I paid him a visit, but he would not come off to the ship. I also noticed that he flew the Turkish flag and taxed him with it, but I could not get any satisfactory answer from him.[60]

The Ottoman Government faced a difficult choice. It could follow Hamdi's advice and send troops to Kuwait, with all the attendant risks. If Kuwait were occupied, its economic activity and its customs revenues might evaporate, the population might decamp en masse, and a garrison stationed there would become an extra burden on the already bankrupt administration. The Porte had received vague indications that the British had been involved in some way in Kuwait. If the Turks invaded and the British reacted, the mouldering Ottoman warships in Basra would not be up to confronting a British warship. Even the ageing *Lawrence* had guns that could shoot the elderly Ottoman vessels to pieces. This energetic option must have looked foolhardy to the Turks. In reality the thought of intervention had not even occurred to the British, but the Turks were not to know that. It was actually highly unlikely that the British would have dared to confront an Ottoman army if it had descended upon Kuwait. The alternative for the Porte was to follow Recep's advice and recognize Mubarak as Kaymakam, an option having great practical advantages. Perilous and costly operations would be avoided. Mubarak would be left in control of Kuwait, but that was no setback, for Mubarak was not pro-British as far as Constantinople was aware.

[58] Nantes AD, ambassade Constantinople E 288, consul Bagdad 4 June 1896.
[59] Anscombe, *Ottoman Gulf,* p. 97.
[60] Bidwell, *Affairs of Kuwait,* 1/1, p. 3.

Such conflicting reports seem to have produced a very confused picture at Yildiz Palace. It is clear that Mubarak and his friends had neutralized Hamdi's fury. The Porte, at least temporarily, accepted the status quo as early as the end of June 1896. This is evident from a sly manoeuvre by Yildiz Palace, by the Sultan's immediate circle. From there the legal councillor of the British Embassy, a certain Stavrides (a Levantine, and therefore close to the Turks), received informal notification of the Palace's alleged thinking on the Kuwait affair. Stavrides was told that there were rumours of the British residency at Bushire being involved in a conspiracy. The story was that Mubarak had held consultations with the resident, and that the reason for Muhammad's subsequent assassination had been his refusal to join a coalition with Muhammad Ibn Rashid and Qasim Al-Thani to establish an Arab confederation in which Bahrain would also be included. Paradoxically, it was also stated that the Sultan had decided to turn a blind eye to all these rumours and planned to recognize Mubarak as Kaymakam of Kuwait.[61]

One wonders whence the rumours emanated about British involvement and the planned Arab confederation. These alleged plots are not to be found in Hamdi's reports, nor do they seem to come from Baghdad. Paranoia about national movements within the Empire, coupled with disquiet about British activities in the Gulf, were the standard ingredients of the Sultan's nightmares. It looks as if he may have wished to tip the wink to the British, just in case they were planning something, that he was aware of their games in the Gulf, and that the situation in Kuwait had been restored to normal with Mubarak as regular kaymakam; there was therefore no occasion for the British to interfere. If this is the correct interpretation, then it was a very cunning move by the Sultan to warn the British off Kuwait in a covert and deniable manner.

The contacts between Yildiz and Stavrides, however, had an entirely unexpected outcome. Stavrides wrote a report of the matter and added as an explanatory preamble a short account of Kuwait as a de facto independent little state, probably taken from one of the standard geographical manuals such as Reclus and Cuinet. The report of 30 June reached the Foreign Office on 13 July, and was the first information on the Kuwait affair to reach London, so showing that communications in the

[61] Bidwell, *Affairs of Kuwait*, 1/1, pp. 1–2.

British Empire were not always superior to those in its Ottoman counterpart.

In London the Foreign Office was slightly upset, though only after considerable delay, by the Stavrides report. London asked India to investigate the matter of the Ottoman allegation that Mubarak had consulted the Bushire resident in preparation for his coup. The following timetable of events shows the snail's pace of British officialdom putting even the Ottoman bureaucracy to shame:

- 30 June: Stavrides sends memo
- 6 July: British embassy in Constantinople sends memo to Foreign Office
- 13 July: Foreign Office sends memo to India Office
- 24 July: India Office asks Government of India to find out if the report is true
- 26 August: India asks Bushire resident to investigate
- 14 September: resident asks Gaskin to investigate
- 22 September: Gaskin reports to resident
- 3 October: resident reports to Government of India that Mubarak had never met the resident and had not been in Bushire for years. And indeed no evidence of a visit by Mubarak or contacts with Bushire have been found up to now in British sources.[62]

However, it is not possible entirely to dismiss Stavrides' account of Yildiz Palace's views as a paranoid Ottoman reaction to imagined dangers, nor Dickson's story of the coup as an anti-Ottoman, pro-British move from the start. We cannot be totally sure that the British resident Wilson's denial of personal contacts between Bushire and Mubarak means that there had been no contacts at all between Mubarak and any British representative. For the correspondence between Mubarak and a British agent in Bahrain of 1897 leaves the distinct impression that these gentlemen had had earlier dealings.[63]

In the end, the Porte was disinclined to follow Hamdi's advice. In July the Ministry of the Interior began to suggest that Hamdi should be replaced and Mubarak be confirmed as kaymakam, a proposal supported

[62] IOLR, R/15/1/471, fos. 1–6 (printed numbers).
[63] IOLR, R/15/1/471, fo. 10, note from Mubarak to Muhammad Rahim Saffer of 31 January 1314 [1898].

by the Grand Vizier.[64] The cogs of the Ottoman machine revolved slowly, so that at the end of August the Minister of the Interior had to repeat his proposal, and it was not until September that action was taken.[65] Hamdi was replaced. It remained unclear, however, whether Mubarak had really been formally appointed Kaymakam of Kuwait. It had transpired that the Porte had accepted the status quo in Kuwait, but no evidence has been found as yet in the Ottoman archives that a formal appointment, with the customary robes of honour, had been issued. Some European consuls do report such an appointment, but this news may have come from Ottoman contacts seeking to spread disinformation.[66]

This Ottoman dithering granted Mubarak a breathing-space to establish himself securely, but meant that he could not be confident of Ottoman support and might start to look around discreetly for other allies. Meanwhile the Turks were not aware that their indolence in policing the Shatt al-'Arab was generating a situation that would inevitably draw the British into the region. As we saw in section 2.3 above, the British had been anxious for some time already about "piracy" in the Shatt al-'Arab. They were under the impression that this piracy, which actually amounted to little more than demanding protection money from merchant ships, was organized from Kuwait. Anything reeking of piracy was bound to stir the British up: the Trucial system, the legal basis of their presence in the Gulf, was based on its suppression. At first they had considered putting pressure on Hamdi Pasha to suppress these "pirates" acting from "Ottoman" Kuwait but, when the Turks failed to help, the British changed tack and began to wonder whether a direct approach to the Ruler of Kuwait would infringe nebulous Ottoman "sovereignty" there. A veiled question to the Porte elicited the answer that the Turks would prefer not to enter into possible entanglements with pirates from territory that they claimed, but did not control. They told the British that they saw no problem in direct British pressure on Kuwait to end piracy. This attitude was understandable

---

[64] Istanbul BA, Irade Dahiliye 46/1314, 22 Safar and 26 Safar.

[65] Istanbul BA, Irade Dahiliye 46/1314, 22 Rabi Awwal.

[66] Appointment as Kaymakam is mentioned by the British consul in Basra: Bidwell, *Affairs of Kuwait*, 1/1, p. 8. The acting German consul in Baghdad, Rosen, even has the suspect story, probably originating from Recep Pasha, that Mubarak had accepted the appointment and that a member of the Al-Sabah family had passed through Baghdad on his way to Constantinople bearing a gift to the Sultan in thanks: Berlin AA, R 13207 A 7945, Rosen 15 May 1898.

given the Turks' well-known inability to maintain order in the countryside of Basra province, but it conflicted with the Ottoman claim of sovereignty over Kuwait. Thus while the Turks were unwittingly pushing Mubarak into dealing with the British, they also almost pushed the British into dealing with Mubarak.[67]

Hamdi Pasha's successor as Wali of Basra, Arif Pasha, set about investigating the Kuwait affair immediately on his arrival, and came to the conclusion, expressed in January 1897, that Mubarak was involved in the killings, although it might be impossible to prove this.[68]

A first threat to Mubarak's independence came about through fears of the plague. In the winter of 1896–7 there was a real danger that plague might spread from India through the Gulf. For centuries already the European powers had been trying to compel the Ottoman Empire to take action over the periodic eruptions of plague that often originated in Kurdistan, where the disease was endemic. For long there had existed a *cordon sanitaire* between the Ottoman Empire and Europe. Free movement between the Ottoman lands and the outside world had been restored only after the sanitary policy of the Ottoman Empire had been placed under the supervision of an international committee established in Constantinople: another example, like the matter of state finances, of how the Ottoman Empire had been brought under international supervision. Ottoman sanitary officials in the Empire were subordinated to this committee, but they were Turks. The risk of an epidemic spreading from India through the Gulf necessitated an extension of the network of sanitary officials and quarantine stations to the Gulf region. The international committee decided to appoint several quarantine officials in the Gulf, to be established in such places as Bahrain and Kuwait, and Mubarak accepted an official in Kuwait. It was hardly surprising that this man should act as an Ottoman observer; but he was not a regular Ottoman official, and the British resident in Bushire could later state with complete justification "that the Quarantine arrangements under the Sanitary Board in Constantinople in no way imply that the Turks have any sort of jurisdiction or rights in Kuwait".[69] At the time, nevertheless, some

[67] Bidwell, *Affairs of Kuwait*, 1/1, pp. 3–7.
[68] Anscombe, *Ottoman Gulf*, p. 98.
[69] Meade on 21 June 1899, quoted in the Harcourt memorandum of 1901, in Gillard, *British Documents*, Part I, Series 2, Vol. 17, p. 200.

observers viewed the presence of the man, who arrived in February 1897, as some proof of Ottoman influence in Kuwait.[70]

During the spring of 1897, Arif Pasha began to change his mind over Kuwait. While at first agreeing with Mubarak's "friend" the Mushir Recep that it was best to leave Mubarak in his position, in March he started to advocate a radical solution: removal of Mubarak by military means. Arif argued to the Minister of the Interior that the expenses of the operation could easily be covered by the introduction of the full Ottoman system of port administration and taxation in Kuwait. The reasons given for this U-turn were somewhat idealistic: the Ottoman Empire could not allow an injustice on its territory such as had been committed in Kuwait. There may have been less lofty considerations. The tax revenue would pass through the Pasha's hands, some of it might stick to them, and a military intervention in Kuwait could generate bribes of all kinds. There was already a rumour that Arif Pasha had received a hefty bribe from Mubarak in 1896, and it is quite plausible that a higher offer from Yusuf Al-Ibrahim might have caused him to changed sides.[71]

The Minister of the Interior supported Arif's ideas. On 25 May 1897, the Council of Ministers took a decision, and on 25 July the practical details were arranged: a force of at least 1200 men with artillery was to be sent by sea, and at the same time a body of Muntafiq and other "loyal" tribesmen would confront Kuwait from the desert.[72] It is difficult to assess the realism of this plan. Were the two small warships capable of transporting 1200 men plus artillery, and was artillery really available in the region?[73] It would take some time to get such a force to Basra, and in any case a summer campaign was inadvisable. And there was no cause to count

---

[70] Anscombe, *Ottoman Gulf*, p. 100 and, much exaggerated, Salwa Al-Ghanim, *Mubarak*, pp. 36–7. The latter author appears not to appreciate that the Sanitary Board in Istanbul was an international institution.

[71] Anscombe, *Ottoman Gulf*, p. 98. For Recep's opinion that a sudden occupation of Kuwait might cause trouble because of the violent anti-Ottoman feelings of the Kuwaitis, and possible interference by foreign powers, see Berlin AA, R 13205 A 11064, Richarz 1 October 1896..

[72] Anscombe, *Ottoman Gulf*, p. 219 n. 43.

[73] A few years later the Austrian consul in Baghdad reported that the VI Army Corps had only eight pieces of (light) mountain artillery: Vienna HHSA, PA XXXVIII K 318, Consul Rappaport 13 September 1901.

[74] Anscombe, *Ottoman Gulf*, p. 100.

on the element of surprise, for Mubarak had sufficient contacts in the region to give him advance warning of any suspicious preparations.

By the beginning of 1897, Mubarak had been in control in Kuwait long enough to have secured his position there. The confusion about him prevalent in Ottoman circles had until then prevented an Ottoman strike against him. Anscombe attributes this to "an orchestrated campaign" of bribery and the spreading of disinformation by Mubarak.[74] Perhaps this is to exaggerate Mubarak's powers of manipulation. It is too simplistic to contrast Hamdi's "honest" pressure for action with the indecisiveness of his superiors in the Ottoman system. It should really be stressed that, in the eyes of many Turks, Mubarak was a reliable and competent fellow while Muhammad had been presented, rightly or wrongly, as pro-British. To intervene militarily was to take a costly risk, and one should not wonder at the Turks' hesitation. What we are left with is that, in the circumstances and thus far, Mubarak's policy had been effective, but only for the time being.

4

The British Solution
1897–1899

4.1 Mubarak courts the British

Arif Pasha's menacing change of heart was probably the reason why
Mubarak set out to seek help from the British. His good friends inside the
Ottoman system would have warned him in good time. The archives of
the British Bushire residency show that Mubarak must have decided to
approach the British as early as January 1897. In January 1897 there were
as yet no visible signs that the Turks might take action against Mubarak,
but it was just at that time that he decided to approach the British. It is
difficult to discern the immediate occasion for this step. Maybe he
distrusted Arif Pasha, or perhaps he just wanted to prepare the ground in
case he might need foreign help in future.[1] Whatever the case, on 31
January 1897 he wrote a letter to Muhammad Rahim Safar, the British
residency agent in Bahrain, requesting a meeting with the resident. The
letter, which survives only in a clumsy translation, conveys the impression
that a good friendship already existed between Mubarak and the residency
agent.[2] The notes scribbled on the back of the agent's letter to Bushire
show that various officials at the residency considered it inadvisable for

[1] Salwa Al-Ghanim, *Mubarak*, p. 36, attributes Mubarak's overture to the appearance of
the quarantine official in Kuwait, but as this was not a genuine Ottoman official it
seems more probable that it was simply distrust of Arif that was the cause. In fact
Mubarak's first move towards the British in January pre-dates the arrival of the
quarantine official in February, while relations between Arif and Mubarak had turned
sour in January: Anscombe, *Ottoman Gulf*, p. 100.

Mubarak to meet the resident, but in the end it was decided to submit the matter to the Foreign Department of the Indian Government.[3] This took time. Mubarak sent a reminder to the agent in April – a most significant juncture, because in that very month the Turks had taken the decision to intervene in Kuwait.[4] This time Mubarak received a short reply: a lesser official of the residency, Gaskin, was to make a routine trip to Muhammara, and could meet with Mubarak there. But Mubarak demurred. The suggestion of Muhammara was a little unwise, given the frequency of communication between it and Basra. A few weeks later Mubarak expressed his intentions more explicitly, writing to the Bahrain residency agent that his object was "to come to some understanding with the British Government".[5]

Bushire was unsure how to handle Mubarak's overture. The matter was complicated by Yusuf Al-Ibrahim who, on 26 April 1897, before a reply had come from India to Mubarak's reminder, also approached the British. Yusuf proposed to Gaskin, while the latter was on a visit to Basra, that the British embassy in Constantinople should recommend his interests to the Ottoman authorities. If Yusuf's party were to win the legal battle over the possession of Kuwait, they would engage themselves to the British to put an end to piracy. In the light of this news from Basra, Gaskin counselled caution over Mubarak's overture. He stated that he had been told "that Mubarak has a very limited following and the sympathy of the Arabs is with the sons of the murdered brother". Gaskin had heard that the only reason Mubarak was still ruling Kuwait was that everybody there wanted to avoid Ottoman interference. According to Gaskin, Mubarak could only

[2] IOLR, R/15/1/471, fo. 10, translation of a letter of Mubarak to Muhammad Rahim Safar, the residency agent in Bahrain, 31 January 1897. Not having used unpublished European sources, Anscombe was unable correctly to present the chronological connection between Mubarak's approach to the British and the evolution of Ottoman policy.

[3] IOLR, R/15/1/471, fo. 8v, notes, and fo. 11, telegram to Foreign Department, India, 25 February 1897. Mubarak sent a reminder in April, but still got no answer: ibid., fo. 14, the oldest original letter of Mubarak in the British archives. We may probably disregard the mention of early contacts between Mubarak and Bushire in the spring of 1896, mentioned in 1901 by the British resident in Baghdad to the German consul in 1901: Berlin AA, R 13843 A 6773, Richarz 10 April 1901.

[4] Anscombe, *Ottoman Gulf*, pp. 98 and 219 n. 42.

[5] IOLR, R/15/1/471, fo. 20 (translated on 20 May), Mubarak's discreetly unsigned note.

hold on to the Basra possessions by bribing Ottoman officials. Gaskin concluded his memo with the remark that "though Kuwait is an independent state [it] is within the Turkish sphere of influence and it is doubtful whether a meeting as proposed by Shaikh Mubarak would lead to any good end". His advice was that the commander of the *Sphinx*, next time he put into Kuwait, should obtain some more information.[6]

The reply from India came in May: the resident should try to find out from Mubarak what he wanted.[7] But the resident Wilson, who was soon to be replaced, was busy elsewhere and no action was taken. In any case, an immediate positive response to Mubarak was too much to expect. The circumstances were not favourable. Mubarak's initiative had such implications for diplomatic relations with the Ottoman Empire that it had to be submitted to the higher authorities in India and London. Elgin, the Viceroy, did not view with much favour the expansion of British commitments in the Gulf. The military resources of the Indian Government were deemed insufficient for more tasks in that region. There was nervousness too in India that a forward policy in the Gulf might cause a conflict with the Turks. Such a conflict might also inspire Turks of Caliphate leanings to meddle with the loyalty of Muslim subjects in India.

Nor was the situation in London much better. The anti-Ottoman Lord Salisbury, at that time both Prime Minister and Foreign Secretary, appeared vaguely interested in having a deal of some kind with Kuwait.[8] But this meant little, because Salisbury was often absent and the Foreign Office was coming more and more under the control of its Permanent Under-Secretary, Sir Thomas Sanderson. Sanderson's mastery of Foreign Office routine was not matched by a flair for grand strategy, and he evinced little understanding of Ottoman affairs. He enjoyed excellent relations with the India Office, where policy was at that time directed by notably cautious and formal officials. The most important of these, when it came to the question of how to respond to Mubarak, was Sir William Lee Warner,

[6] IOLR, R/15/1/471, fos. 20v –21v, Gaskin to Resident 22 May 1897.
[7] IOLR, R/15/1/471, fos. 11–11v, 9–25 May 1897.
[8] Salisbury had been promoting a plan to carve up the Ottoman Empire between the European powers in 1895: see Preller, *Salisbury und die Türkische Frage im Jahre 1895*. He had a good knowledge of Ottoman imperial affairs, having participated in the Berlin Congress of 1878.

Secretary of the Political Department at the India Office. Lee Warner was a man of great intelligence with a singular ability to formulate complex questions in a concise and cogent fashion, but his views reveal him to be insufficiently critical of the conventional exaggerations of Ottoman claims to sovereignty in fringe regions. Nor was a forward policy in the Gulf to the liking of Sir Nicholas O'Conor, the ambassador in Constantinople. O'Conor, a man of no great ability or vision, was prone to automatic disapproval of anything that might provoke the Turks in case it ruffled his agreeable existence in Constantinople's suburb of Pera (now Beyoglu). British diplomats also tended to fear that if Britain were seen to imperil the territorial integrity of the Ottoman Empire in its nominal province of Kuwait, Britain's unpopularity in Europe would be aggravated. From 1898 there would be an increase in the British embassy's influence in Gulf matters. This was because the British representative in Basra, hitherto a military officer subordinate to the Baghdad residency (and so to the Government of India), now became a regular consul recruited from the diplomatic service, and was thus more closely linked to the embassy.

At this point the India Office in London received a report from Whyte, the former British agent in Basra, who in March 1897 had visited the embassy in Constantinople on his voyage back to Britain.[9] There Whyte had seen Stavrides's memorandum and written a response, the main purpose of which was to deny the relative independence of Kuwait and the rumours of Mubarak's contacts with the British as set out by Stavrides. Whyte stated that Mubarak, in accepting his appointment as kaymakam, had precluded "the possibility of any foreign Power recognizing under the present circumstances his independence". Whyte went on to say that Mubarak had visited the Turkish *müdür* in Fao, which was not the behaviour of an independent ruler. Whyte's arguments are weak: Mubarak's appointment as kaymakam was never confirmed and it would not be odd for him, as a landowner in Fao, to visit the local governor who was his friend. Whyte's report contained some juicy gossip about

[9] Whyte was, as agent, an official of the Government of India and subordinate via the Baghdad resident to the Viceroy. In 1898 Wratislaw arrived in Basra, and his position was different: as consul he was still subordinate to the Baghdad resident, but in the latter's function as consul-general to the British embassy in Constantinople and the Foreign Office. This adjustment did not facilitate communication between India and Basra, as Basra was more closely linked with India than with Europe.

Mubarak's bribery: Hamdi is said to have refused 10,000 lira (a huge sum, almost 9000 pounds sterling); Hamdi's successor Arif had accepted 1700 lira; and the Shaikh al-Islam (the chief religious authority in the Ottoman Empire) and Abu 'l-Huda too had accepted inducements. Whyte also reported that he had heard that Mubarak was approaching the Bushire resident to obtain British protection. Whyte's negative news of Mubarak may have come from Yusuf Al-Ibrahim's Basra agent, as it is significant that he also reports the rumour that the nephews enjoyed much support in Kuwait.[10]

Whyte's report was read with interest in London. Lee Warner thought that the resident in Bushire should reject Mubarak's suggestion of a meeting.[11] Salisbury, having no respect for the Ottomans, disagreed, and there followed the customary delay by correspondence between India Office, Foreign Office and India. Finally the India Office informed the Government of India that Lord Salisbury considered that the British should not go any further than a promise to Mubarak to "respect his independence (if in fact he is independent)". This rather resembles a refusal, but there was a second clause in Salisbury's decision that is even more masterly in its ambiguity: Salisbury was ready for Britain to give Mubarak the assurance that he would be treated with friendship *"in exchange for a promise from him that he will not accept the protectorate of any other power"*.[12] This Sphinx-like pronouncement seems to be no more than a reflection of the strong British objection to any other European power establishing a position in the Gulf.

If nothing else, Salisbury's ambivalent reaction points up the special status of Kuwait. If it was a regular Ottoman province, such a warning should have been directed, not to Mubarak, but to the Ottoman Government. And if it was a regular Ottoman province, why in the first place would there be any question of Mubarak entering into relations with a foreign power?

[10] Whyte's letter in Bidwell, *Affairs of Kuwait,* 1/1, p. 8, Whyte 22 March 1898. The same remark on the lack of support for Mubarak can be found in a letter of Yusuf Al-Ibrahim, IOLR, R/15/1/471, fo. 67 (translated 9 August 1897).

[11] Salwa Al-Ghanim, *Mubarak,* p. 46; IOLR, LPS/357/1312.

[12] Bidwell, *Affairs of Kuwait,* 1/1, p. 9, India Office to Foreign Office with draft of a telegram to Government of India containing Salisbury's opinion.

4.2 The evolution of British interest

In June 1897 Wilson was succeeded in Bushire by Meade, who appears to have favoured a more proactive policy. He was immediately confronted with a crisis in the Kuwait affair. Following the decision of the Porte to intervene in Kuwait, Arif Pasha had been pressing for action against Mubarak. The Ottoman Council of Ministers arrived at the decision to take decisive action by the end of May. Arif's campaign preparations did not proceed smoothly. A warship, the *Dawasir*, and some local forces were assembled in Basra, but the Mushir Recep (Mubarak's "friend") failed to send any regular troops from Baghdad or Nasiriyya.[13] The activities of the warship gave rise to friction with the British.[14] The planned action was an exclusively Ottoman initiative and Yusuf Al-Ibrahim was unhappy with it, his chief interest being in expropriating the Al-Sabah date groves. Unilateral Ottoman military intervention in Kuwait would only cause despoliation and it was doubtful whether, and how, the nephews would be able to acquire control over Kuwait with Ottoman troops stationed there. So Yusuf decided to take the law into his own hands.

At the end of June the resident in Bushire was informed that the "Shaikh of Fao, brother of Shaikh Mubarak" (probably Hamud, who was in charge of administering the lands there) had approached the British telegraph station at Fao with some wild stories about pirates and the dangers of an attack by Yusuf Al-Ibrahim on Kuwait. A few days later more news came from Fao, this time of a planned attack by Yusuf with warriors recruited from Persian territory.[15] It is interesting that Yusuf, himself a landowner in Ottoman territory, used Persian, not Ottoman subjects; apparently he wanted to keep his plans hidden from Arif Pasha. These irregulars came from Hindian, a port in southern Persia.[16] The attack came to grief because of a stupid mistake: Yusuf's crew of cut-throats committed

---

[13] Anscombe, *Ottoman Gulf*, p. 102.

[14] Bidwell, *Affairs of Kuwait*, 1/1, p. 19, commander of the *Pigeon* in Basra 7 July 1897: the cause of the British complaints was that the Shatt al-'Arab below Muhammara was international water and that Ottoman ships were therefore not allowed to stop any ship under a foreign flag from that point on.

[15] IOLR, R/15/1/471, fos. 25 and 26, telegrams from Fao of 29 June 1897 and 5 July 1897.

[16] The place is interesting: the Khalifat tribe inhabiting Hindian is mentioned as an ally of the 'Utub as early as an Ottoman document of 1701, see Slot, *Origins*, p. 110.

a premature act of piracy in the Shatt al-'Arab. Mubarak received a timely warning as a result of this and readied Kuwait for defence. Yusuf Al-Ibrahim abandoned his plan and thought better of returning to Basra. Thus the Kuwaiti anti-Mubarak front came to grief, just as the Ottomans were putting their final decision on paper.

The Ottoman decision to invade Kuwait was issued on 25 July 1897, just after Yusuf's failed coup attempt. In any case, action had to wait until after the summer heat. Yusuf, having found it too dangerous to stay in Basra, arrived in Bahrain on 28 July. The captain of the *Sphinx* reported from there that Yusuf had been expelled from Basra by the Turks, and that he was now appealing to Qasim Al-Thani for help.[17] This could only work to Mubarak's advantage, because the Turks regarded Qasim Al-Thani as one of the least trustworthy leaders in the region. Mubarak might be confronted by two different enemy groupings, but it was to his advantage that they were now divided by their deep distrust of each other.

How confused matters had become is best depicted in a report of Rouet, the French consul in Baghdad, of 11 August. Rouet was a friend of the chief-of-staff of the Ottoman VI Army Corps, the French-speaking Muhsin Pasha, and his opinions probably reflected those of his Ottoman friend. Rouet's report contains several interesting if not entirely specific allegations. The first charge was that Yusuf Al-Ibrahim, because his power-base was in India, was representing British interests. Secondly, Yusuf had bribed Arif Pasha not to interfere in his coup. Rouet passes on several interesting facts gleaned from the Ottoman military in Baghdad, probably from his crony Muhsin Pasha. As Yusuf's forces menaced Kuwait, the British warship *Sphinx* carried out ostentatious artillery exercises in the Shatt al-'Arab, and this was probably meant more for the Ottoman warship *Dawasir* than for Yusuf. Muhsin Pasha thought (or was bribed to think) that Mubarak was pro-Ottoman. Rouet gives an interesting description of Ottoman reactions to Yusuf's coup attempt. Muhsin criticized Arif Pasha for going against Recep's peaceful solution of the Kuwait question. Recep had instructed the Ottoman warships present to attack Yusuf's irregulars, but the commanders of the warships had found reasons not to obey. When the Turks took no action against the irregulars, Mubarak had asked Arif Pasha for permission to chase Yusuf's forces away, but this too had been refused. Then Mubarak telegraphed Recep, who immediately contacted

[17] IOLR, R/15/5/471, fo. 53, Captain Baker 28 July 1897.

the Seraskerat (War Ministry) in Constantinople for instructions. Constantinople gave an evasive answer, which is attributed by Rouet to bribery by Yusuf. According to Rouet, the Baghdad authorities harboured great suspicions about Yusuf. They were at that moment investigating telegraphic instructions sent by Yusuf from Fao to his banker in Constantinople to forward 18,000 lira (*ca.* 16,000 pounds sterling) to a mysterious lawyer. Rouet's conclusion is clear:

> Shaikh Moubarek remains exposed to the incursions of enemies who are known for their sympathy to the English, thanks to the venality of the Ottoman administration. I know from a reliable source that Youssouf Ibrahim has found asylum at present on the Bahrain islands, places that are de facto if not *de jure* under English protectorate. [...] Today its interests oblige the Porte to stop disregarding whatever happens in the *kaza* of Koueït. Between Youssouf Ibrahim, who is an English vassal, and Moubarek Sabah, who asks for its [the Porte's] help, there can be no hesitation, and it is greatly to be desired that the Porte finally decides to give the "investiture"[18] to Moubarek Sabah.

The dispute as described by Rouet was only part of a blizzard of accusations flying to and fro between Mubarak, Yusuf Al-Ibrahim and various factions in the Basra government.[19]

The confusion in Constantinople suited Mubarak. Arif's plans for invading Kuwait were shelved. Yusuf was on his way to Qasim Al-Thani, but it was hardly likely that in high summer the Qatari Shaikh would move a large body of troops to Kuwait in support of Yusuf. Meanwhile Mubarak had quietly continued his attempts to forge some relationship with the British. In a written note carried by a delegate to Bahrain, Mubarak made it clear that he wanted British protection and a flag for use on Kuwaiti ships as well as his possessions in Basra province.[20] Meade was informed of this missive only after some delay due to the inertia of subordinates such as Gaskin, but the new resident immediately showed

---

[18] Interesting use of this word: the term investiture owes its origin to the feudal system, not to an administrative hierarchy.

[19] Paris AE, NS Turquie 149, ambassador in Constantinople to Minister, 11 August 1897; cf. Anscombe, *Ottoman Gulf*, pp. 104–5.

[20] IOLR, R/15/1/471, fos. 31–33v, copy of Mubarak's letter to Bahrain residency agent with translation.

interest in Mubarak's appeal.[21] He sent a telegram to India the same day
he had been informed of the presence of Mubarak's delegate in Bahrain.
In this telegram he mentioned that he had discovered his predecessor had
done nothing with his instructions to warn Mubarak about Kuwait-
sponsored piracy in the Shatt al-'Arab. Now Meade proposed to India that
the expected visit of Mubarak's delegate could be used to issue this
warning.[22] The reply came on 26 July: the Government of India agreed
with Meade's proposal. He could issue the warning to Mubarak's man if
he appeared to be a trustworthy person, and he could try to find out from
him what Mubarak's intentions were.[23] Meade immediately tried to
organize transport for the delegate on the *Sphinx,* but its captain was
difficult to reach and further delay ensued. Confusion also intensified: on
the very same day, 26 July, Meade received a telegram from India,
informing him of the receipt of information via the India Office, from the
embassy in Constantinople, about Yusuf's failed attack on Kuwait, and of
an appeal to the Porte by the people of Zubair to remove Mubarak.[24]

On 27 July, Meade sent a telegram to the summer residence of the
Government of India in Simla, stating that he understood from Mubarak's
letters to the residency agent on Bahrain that Mubarak intended to ask for
British protection.[25] Just after Meade had sent this telegram, Gaskin
dropped a report on the resident's desk. In it, Gaskin comments
interestingly on the legal position:

> Though our Government have not formally acknowledged Turkish
> jurisdiction over Koweit there is no doubt the Sheikhs of Koweit have
> acknowledged themselves to be under Turkey and fly the Turkish flag at
> Koweit on the boats belonging to the inhabitants of that port. I have
> always had an idea that the Sheikhs of Koweit have treaties with the Turks
> and so long as the Sheikhs carry out their obligations the Turks have
> promised them self-government. Any interference on the part of the

[21] IOLR, R/15/1/471, fo. 29, note by Gaskin to Meade 21 May 1897; on fo. 29v,
Meade's reply of the same date: "Come here as soon as possible and bring the delegate
with you."
[22] IOLR, R/15/1/471, fo. 34, telegram of Meade to Government of India, 21 July
1897.
[23] IOLR, R/15/1/471, fo. 39, telegram to Meade, 26 July 1897.
[24] IOLR, R/15/1/471, fos. 40–41.
[25] IOLR, R/15/5/471, fos. 42–42v, telegram from Meade to India, 27 July 1897.

British Government will open out a big question. The Turkish
Government as far as I know have in a like manner never acknowledged
our protection over Bahrein and only a few years ago have laid claims to
the island. On the other hand this might be a good opportunity to come
to an understanding with the Turks regarding our protection over
Bahrein. Our Government might get the Turks to accept our protection
over the Island if we acknowledged their influence in Koweit [...] I do
not know whether we have in our files any copies or information of any
treaties between the Sheikhs of Koweit and the Turkish Government, if
we have not, we might address the Assistant Political Agent at Busreh ...

Meade apparently found a good pretext for disregarding this
inopportune point of view in the fact that it had arrived too late and he
had already informed India of Mubarak's move.[26] But then came a new
delay. A visit to Bahrain by Yusuf Al-Ibrahim from Qatar was announced,
and Mubarak's delegate took his departure from Bahrain in something of
a hurry.[27] Meade was apparently very anxious to see Mubarak's delegate as
soon as possible, but could find no suitable way of arranging a meeting.[28]
That Meade had an agenda regarding Kuwait is clear from a confidential
message he sent to the Head of the Foreign Department in India. In
reporting the failure of his attempt to see Mubarak's delegate, he revealed
his real intentions with the words: "... it would be a great pity to allow
the Turks to extend their influence at Koweit."[29]

During August there was yet another source of delay. This time it was
Yusuf Al-Ibrahim, trying to establish contact with the British authorities.
He made a vague request for help in his dispute with Mubarak and asked
to come to Bushire. Meade applied for instructions to India, where it was
decided that Yusuf would receive no British help against Kuwait. When
this was passed on by Gaskin to Yusuf's agent, the reply was that Yusuf did
not want British help against Kuwait, but just assistance in reaching an
agreement with Mubarak over the restitution of properties. Gaskin seems

[26] IOLR, R/15/5/471, fo. 43–43v, Gaskin to Resident 27 July 1897. On the back the
remark by Meade: "This note received after dispatch of long cypher message to
Foreign [Department] Simla, 28 July."
[27] IOLR, R/15/1/471, fos. 44–45, Gaskin to Meade 29 July 1897.
[28] IOLR, R/15/1/471, fos. 55–56v.
[29] IOLR, R/15/1/471, fos. 59–60, telegram from Meade to Sir William Cuningham,
31 July 1897.

to have liked this and proposed the Shaikh of Bahrain as arbitrator. The
matter was submitted to India and permission was given to approach
Mubarak about it. Substantive action was postponed for a planned visit by
Gaskin to Kuwait, a visit that was to come shortly.[30]

Gaskin's visit to Kuwait took place during a time of developments in
Constantinople that boded ill for Mubarak, but which remained unknown
to the British. During the summer of 1897, the Turks had come to the
decision to accept Mubarak as kaymakam of Kuwait, but under
conditions. The Shaikh would become a regular paid official of state and a
judge recruited from the Basra ulema would be sent as judge to Kuwait.
Worse still, a body of *zapti* (gendarmes) would maintain order in Kuwait.
The claims of Mubarak's nephews would also be formally investigated.[31]
These ominous developments cannot have escaped the well-informed
Shaikh, and may have induced him to be particularly forthcoming towards
British visitors.

On 3 September 1897, Gaskin received instructions to go to Kuwait, on
the elderly paddle steamer *Lawrence*, to deliver the long-delayed warning
concerning allegedly Kuwait-based piracy in the Shatt al-'Arab and to
hear what Mubarak had to say. Gaskin was under strict orders not to make
any promises to him.[32] Over the following days Gaskin had several talks
with Mubarak, who displayed a responsible attitude in the piracy matter.
During a second meeting Mubarak began to complain about the corrupt
behaviour of Ottoman officials, and asserted that Khaz'al of Muhammara's
men were behind several acts of piracy. Next day there was a meeting
during which Mubarak gave his views on the dispute with his nephews.
He stated that they had lived in perfect peace and safety in Kuwait but that
Yusuf Al-Ibrahim had "poisoned their minds". He hoped for mediation by
Shaikh 'Isa of Bahrain. On a separate sheet of paper Gaskin noted down
matters of real political substance. Mubarak had vouchsafed an account of
the events of 1870 with Midhat Pasha, in order to clarify his position vis-
à-vis the Turks, a version that tallies quite well with what we know from
the Ottoman sources. Finally he expressed, on behalf of himself and his

---

[30] IOLR, R/15/1/471, fos. 67–75, letter of Yusuf and correspondence regarding this
letter.
[31] Anscombe, *Ottoman Gulf*, p. 104. Anscombe is a little confused about the precise
chronological sequence of events.
[32] IOLR, R/15/1/471, fos. 86–89, instructions to Gaskin.

subjects, "their sincere desire to put themselves under British rule under the same conditions as those enjoyed by the Shaikh of Bahrain and the Trucial chiefs".[33]

While these negotiations were under way, there were dramatic but inconclusive developments in the Ottoman system. During the course of September all sides in the conflict had been bombarding the Porte with accusations against one other, and this surfeit of indigestible information once more paralysed the Ottoman machine.[34] The Porte first tried to find a neutral party to make sense of it all, but then a new emergency presented itself: the rumour about an alliance between Yusuf Al-Ibrahim, seen by some as an English stooge because of his business relations with India, and the notoriously unreliable Qasim Al-Thani of Qatar. So delicate a matter was this that it was decided to charge a local official with the investigation. The person selected was Mubarak's friend, the Mushir Recep Pasha. Recep assigned the ticklish task to his chief-of-staff, Muhsin Pasha.

The Minister of Defence, on receiving Muhsin Pasha's report, sent a personal memorandum to the Sultan on measures to be taken to prevent an invasion of Kuwait by Qasim Al-Thani and Yusuf Al-Ibrahim. In Muhsin's view, the Porte's problems stemmed from Arif Pasha's mismanagement; Arif had been charged with reconciling Mubarak and his nephews, but he was a man who never settled a dispute without taking a bribe. Muhsin's proposed solution was simple: to appoint Muhsin himself Wali of Basra, to appoint Mubarak Kaymakam of Kuwait, and to force a settlement between him and his nephews.[35] This policy may have been inspired by some bakshish from Mubarak, but it had the merit of simplicity and was likely to avert much trouble in future. But still the Porte continued its equivocation over Mubarak. On 5 December 1897, it decided to send troops to Basra "to be kept in readiness to go to anywhere necessary".[36] This step was probably intended to discourage Qasim Al-Thani from interfering in the Kuwait affair. If by doing so it was intended to reassure Mubarak, one can also see why it might make him feel insecure.

[33] IOLR, R/15/1/471, fos. 90–97, reports by Gaskin of 5–6 September 1897.
[34] Anscombe, *Ottoman Gulf*, pp. 104–5.
[35] Istanbul BA, Yildiz Mutanawa 59/165, report of Minister of Defence, 17 Cumada II 1315 (13 November 1897); see also information passed by Recep Pasha to the German consul in Berlin AA, R 13206 A 13896, Richarz 3 November 1897.
[36] Istanbul BA, Yildiz Bab-i Asafi resmi 30/30, 10 Recep/5 December 1897.

The Turks, being great conspirators, were also great believers in conspiracy theories, and so they had the wildest notions about what was going on around Kuwait. The Mushir Recep Pasha told the German consul that the British were behind Yusuf Al-Ibrahim's intrigues: Yusuf was one of the greatest arms dealers in Arabia; if Mubarak won the struggle, then the British would recognize him as "President of the Republic of Kuwait"; but if matters went otherwise, then the British would be glad to recognize the rule of the Bombay merchant Yusuf.[37] Recep was not the only one with such far-fetched notions. The German consul in Bombay told a story about mysterious contacts between Yusuf's brother and the British resident in Baroda, Meade, who had just been appointed British resident in Bushire. The consul wrote that, after the meeting, a British warship had been sent from Bombay to attack Mubarak, but that the plan had failed because of the appearance of an Ottoman warship![38] How could anyone effectively identify an actual problem, and proceed to a realistic solution, in so dense a thicket of rumours?

4.3 The conversion of Meade and India

While the Turks wavered, the clock kept ticking. Within the British system there was gradually emerging an inclination to respond positively to Mubarak's appeal, and the first obvious convert to this policy was Meade. Gaskin's report enabled Meade to send India a strongly-worded advice to exploit the opportunity offered by Mubarak's proposal. India sent it on 21 October to the India Office in London; implicit support for Meade's view was embodied in the enquiry whether the non-intervention policy (formally stated by London only on 13 October) should not be changed. As if to persuade London of the urgency of the matter, another report was sent claiming that if intervention was desired, it should come quickly because an Ottoman-sponsored attack on Kuwait by Qasim Al-Thani was imminent. This misrepresented the true state of affairs, as the Turks had nothing to do with Qasim's alleged plan, but one cannot be sure whether it was a genuine misinterpretation by India of the pattern of events, or whether it was deliberately misrepresenting the situation to promote its own agenda for Kuwait. Whatever India's real intentions, they had little

[37] Berlin AA, R 13206 A 14169, Richarz 8 November 1897.
[38] Berlin AA, R 13843 A 2075, consul in Bombay 14 January 1898.

effect on policy in London, where Lee Warner staunchly kept the India Office on the established course of taking no action regarding Kuwait. In any case, the matter lacked urgency at that moment. When the British warship *Pigeon* visited Kuwait in November 1897, Mubarak told its commander that he had no fears of an attack by Qasim Al-Thani. Present at the meeting were several Bedouin shaikhs who supported Mubarak's opinion.[39]

The Kuwait proposal seemed to have been shelved in India as well as London. The Foreign Department in India apparently thought the matter so completely dead that, in February 1898, its chief Sir William Cuningham felt able quite openly to discuss the position of Kuwait with the German consul in Calcutta. Cuningham told the German that Britain, while viewing with disfavour an Ottoman occupation of Kuwait, could do little against it. A few days later Cuningham even told the German consul that Mubarak had approached the British for protection, but that this had been refused.[40] One cannot but wonder at the crassness of Cuningham's indiscretion, which might easily have caused Mubarak serious difficulties.

Mubarak, meanwhile, was right to take his somewhat relaxed stance. The Porte was unable to arrive at a consistent policy towards Kuwait. Recep in Baghdad, Arif in Basra, Mubarak himself, his nephews and Qasim Al-Thani were all trying to influence the Porte in different ways. From this Mubarak could conclude that there was no present danger from the Ottomans, but that a direct Ottoman attack was not out of the question at some future time. In such circumstances Mubarak followed the prudent policy of keeping the British option open.

Meanwhile Meade found support for his views on Kuwait from Loch, his colleague in Baghdad. Both agreed that it would be a good thing to obtain an agreement with Mubarak. There was no chance of such an agreement being achieved at present in the face of London's opposition, but neither gentleman bothered to hide his views. There was in fact one factor in British Gulf policy that might influence it more in the direction advocated by Meade and Loch. This was the fear of Russia gaining a foothold in the Gulf. The Russians could achieve this through their dominance in Persia, but might also be able to acquire a port on the Gulf

[39] IOLR, R/15/1/471, fos. 148–150, Mowbray to Meade 7 November 1897.
[40] Berlin AA, R13843, Calcutta 5 and 16 February 1898.

from the Turks. British fears centred on Russia gaining a port in the Gulf in much the same way as European powers had gained ports in China, that other decaying empire. In 1897 and 1898 such fears found increasingly vocal expression in the British and Indian press, and provocative articles on the matter appeared in the German and Russian press too. Already in 1892 a leading British politician, Curzon, had published an oversized tract in two volumes entitled *Persia and the Persian Question*, which focused sharply on the Russian danger in Persia.[41] As much as anything else, it was pressure from the press that elevated the fear of Russian expansion to the Gulf into a growing factor in British policy there.

Any Russian move to establish a short route between Europe and India was always sure to cause a flurry in British public opinion and policy. Then Loch dropped a pebble in the pond, the ripples from which led the British to act in a way they had not intended. On 16 November 1897, he informed Meade that he had been warned by the British embassy that the Russians were sending a heavyweight, Kruglov, to replace Mashkov as Russian consul in Baghdad, and that Kruglov's principal mission would be the acquisition of a coaling station on the Gulf.[42] Loch was exaggerating slightly; Kruglov cannot have been so important, because we know from his French colleague that he was a Raskolnik, a member of a distinctly unprestigious religious minority.[43] Loch wrote to Meade that he strongly suspected Kuwait to be the location the Russians coveted for their coaling station. In support of this, he described how, one evening shortly after the death of Muhammad, he was interviewed by a certain Aristides Jacovidi,[44] former manager of the Banque Ottomane in Baghdad, who was trying to get him to disclose what British intentions regarding Kuwait might be. Loch suspected this of being connected with Russian designs, because he

[41] Strangely enough, in his book Curzon still regarded Kuwait as part of the expansion space of the Ottoman Empire, maybe reflecting Pelly's old dream that the Ottoman Empire would help with the new railway link to the Mediterranean: *Persia and the Persian Question*, Vol. 2, p. 462.

[42] IOLR, R/15/1/471, fos. 166–169.

[43] Paris AE, NS Mascate 9, fo. 80, Baghdad 13 August 1903. This letter refers to a murder attempt by Kruglov on his chancellor (and successor) Naumphal! Kruglov is said here to be much under the bad influence of his Armenian interpreter. See also Nantes AD, consulat Bagdad A 48, Rouet 11 February 1903.

[44] Aristides Jacovidi seems to be a Greek. Loch, who apparently had an aversion to Levantines, remarked that "the name suggests intrigue".

had also received "little hints" from others warning that if England did not take Kuwait, somebody else would. Loch feared that the Turks "if squeezed by Russia would agree to its [Kuwait's] occupation by that Power [Russia] *partly because it does not belong to them* and would form such an admirable bone of contention between England and Russia and partly *pour embêter les Anglais,* a game which everyone in these parts delights in playing."

The interest of this letter lies not only in the original (but probably entirely erroneous) view it presents of Ottoman policy, but more especially in these mysterious "hints" by others. Who can these others have been? Hardly the Russians, who had their own views on the matter; and it is highly unlikely too that the French and German consuls in Baghdad, friends of the Russians, would communicate such hints. Nor is it conceivable that Ottoman officials would try to precipitate the British into action over Kuwait. The only remaining possibility is Mubarak's circle of friends. Using the Russians to provoke the British into action was one of Mubarak's favourite tactics in later years, and perhaps we are here witness to its inception. If so, it was an extremely astute move, because it really was Loch, with his hints about possible Russian designs on Kuwait, who dropped the pebble in the pond. Loch was probably correct in ascribing dreams of Kuwait to the Russians – we have already seen that the Russian consul in Baghdad had an agent there. But he was exaggerating, for there is no sign that the Russians were really in a position to take action there.

Loch then dropped his pebble in the form of a note, which was destined to convert London to the idea of intervention in Kuwait. Curzon, by that time Under-Secretary at the Foreign Office, advised Salisbury to follow up Loch's advice. The government in London, however, was still far from stirring itself over Kuwait. Sanderson placed no credence in the Russian connection, and for the time being he won the argument, his and Lee Warner's views prevailing.[45] After some discussion a formal decision issued from London:

> Her Majesty's Government are not disposed to bring Koweit under
> British protection or to interfere with the affairs of Koweit more than is

---

[45] Plass, *England,* pp. 252–3. Interesting too is a private letter of Meade to Curzon of 28 March (Bidwell, *Affairs of Kuwait,* 1/1, p. 28) in which Meade is very outspoken in his belief that Mubarak's offer should be accepted. Meade wrote that he had no proof of Loch's fears about the Russians, but that he thought them "very likely".

necessary for the maintenance of the general peace of the Persian Gulf. There is, however, nothing in the political situation of Koweit which need hamper Her Majesty's naval officers in bringing home to the Shaikh responsibility for piratical acts."[46]

While the London viewpoint had not visibly changed, beneath the surface Curzon's conversion to an interventionist policy was to be an important factor.

Meanwhile the British continued to watch the movements of Russian travellers in the Gulf with apprehension.[47] Meade really does seem to have been looking for an opportunity to obtain a foothold in Kuwait before anybody else could do so.

4.4 False alarms tilt the balance in London

The India Office policy of non-intervention in Kuwait remained valid for as long as there was no risk of Russia or Germany meddling in the Gulf. As yet Britain showed little alarm at possible Turkish interference in Kuwait, as the Turks were believed to exercise no more than a titular authority there. As long as the Turks made no serious attempt to change the status of Kuwait the question of British action there was irrelevant. The British were unaware that the Ottomans were still contemplating intervention in Kuwait, but did not yet consider the timing right.

During 1898, the Turks were to find no clear way of settling the Kuwait question. The sudden death in 1897 of Muhammad Ibn Rashid, Amir of Haïl, had had an adverse impact on stability in Arabia. He had been succeeded by a nephew, Abdul Aziz, whose impetuous character contrasted with that of his diplomatic uncle.[48] 1898 opened to rumours of an impending alliance between this "new Ibn Rashid" and Qasim Al-Thani. The Baghdad Mushir, Recep Pasha, nursed the old Ottoman unease at the threat posed by a powerful Rashidi state. He feared Britain's possible interest in acquiring influence over the Amir, in view of the alleged plans for an Egypt–Kuwait railway. Recep's expectation was that this new Qatari-Rashidi alliance would try to attack Kuwait and that then

[46] IOLR, R/15/1/471, fo. 196, Government of India to Bushire 14 December 1897.
[47] IOLR, R/15/1/471, fos. 199–203.
[48] Berlin AA, R 12843 A 869, Richarz 23 December 1897.

Mubarak, who was still seen by Recep as anti-British, would call in Ottoman help. This would enable the Ottomans to occupy Kuwait.[49] The alliance appears to have been a false alarm, but Qasim maintained his pressure on Kuwait. In April 1898 he told the Turks that he was obliged to enforce the just claims of Mubarak's nephews by attacking Kuwait. To preempt Qasim's unilateral action, the Porte decided to divert to Kuwait the expeditionary force waiting in Basra for the mission to Qatar. This force was to investigate and settle matters in Kuwait. But nothing was done: Recep Pasha needed his troops in the north and so the force was dispersed.[50]

Mubarak, it seems, was still to a certain extent trusted by the Ottoman authorities, but Ottoman ambition remained none the less a menace to Kuwait. Rumours once again circulated from Ottoman officials in Mesopotamia that Mubarak had been formally appointed Kaymakam of Kuwait, with even the acting German consul contributing the unlikely story that a member of the Al-Sabah family was travelling to Constantinople on behalf of Mubarak, to offer the Sultan a gift in exchange for the appointment.[51]

In the course of 1898 a new ingredient was added to the mix: the possible place of Kuwait in German and Russian railway projects. During May new rumours were making the rounds in Baghdad. The German plans for the Baghdad Railway were gradually taking shape, and now Recep Pasha was urging the Ottomans to take possession of Kuwait as the future terminus of the railway on the Gulf.[52] Recep Pasha was not the only one alert to such railway plans. The French ambassador in Russia warned his minister in May 1898 about an article in the Russian newspaper *Novoye Vremiye* that the Germans were planning to build a line from Anatolia to the Gulf.[53] The French were actually involved in these plans, as the Deutsche Bank had an agreement with a French financial syndicate for participation in the section between Konya and the Gulf. The Russian newspaper exhibits much alarm at the threat of German expansion towards the Gulf.

[49] Berlin AA, R 13207 A 3677, Richarz 3 March 1898.
[50] Anscombe, *Ottoman Gulf*, p. 107.
[51] Berlin AA, R 13207 A 6692 and A7945, Consulate Baghdad, 10 and 15 May 1898.
[52] Berlin AA, R 13207 A 7204 and A 7222, Rosen in Baghdad 25 May 1898.
[53] Paris AE, NS Turquie 166, fo. 74, Montebello (French envoy in Russia) 29 April 1898.

In the end it was fear of Russia, not Germany, that jolted the British enough to cause a shift in London's policy. The *Times of India* of 8 and 9 August 1898 reported on a Russian plan to construct a railway from Tripoli to the Gulf. The project had been proposed to the Sultan by a Russian, Count Kapnist, nephew of the Russian ambassador in Vienna, and the Russians were taking it for granted that the concession would be issued. The news appeared in the context of a warning by Curzon in the House of Commons that "a Foreign Power seeks to acquire a Port in the Persian Gulf". The *Times of India* was partly right, for the Sultan did grant a provisional concession. To a modern analyst the Kapnist plan looks highly speculative, and it may be that the Ottoman concession was only intended to pressure the Germans into easing up in their bargaining over the Konya–Baghdad–Gulf railway, which was of much greater strategic importance for the Ottomans. A line from Haydar Pasha (in Anatolia opposite Constantinople) to Konya already existed, and extending this to the Gulf would greatly ease the Turks' logistic problems in Mesopotamia. At that time financial disagreements had slowed the negotiations between the Ottomans and the Germans, so it is quite conceivable that the Turks granted the Russian concession merely in order to make the Germans more amenable.

In this atmosphere the anti-Russian tendency in British policy was given a boost by the appointment, in August 1898, of Curzon as Viceroy of India. Curzon had advocated a British forward policy in the Gulf, where according to his view Russia might encroach upon the vital lines of communication between Europe and India. Curzon used the gap between his appointment and his departure for India to urge London officials to respond positively to Mubarak's overture. In the end the discussion between Curzon and Lee Warner boiled down to the validity or otherwise of the Ottoman claim to sovereignty. Lee Warner reminded Curzon of the vague British recognition of Ottoman sovereignty over the coastal area between Bahrain and Basra in the 1890s (see section 1.7 above). Curzon replied that this was a weak argument simply because a claim to any particular piece of territory in the no man's land between the Ottoman possessions of Basra and al-Hasa was nonsense.[54] Plass has discussed the matter of this British recognition of Ottoman sovereignty in some detail.[55] Curzon swept Lee Warner's legal niceties brusquely aside by stressing political necessity: Russians and Germans were coming over the horizon and, were they to gain a foothold, Britain would forfeit its supremacy in the Gulf. It is of interest too that it was in this context that the German Konya–Baghdad–Gulf railway was mentioned for the first time as a major danger for the British.

The legal argument of alleged British recognition of Ottoman sovereignty over the coastline was to keep coming up on later occasions too, but its validity is dubious. The essential point is that the Ottomans had not accepted the British statement of 1893. One should also bear in mind that Kuwait was not British territory and vague assertions by British envoys in the period 1888–93 were not binding on Kuwait's ruler. If the Ottomans wanted Kuwait as a regular province, then they should simply have imposed a regular provincial administration there. The most one can say is that Britain's behaviour in going back on earlier undertakings, even if they had not been accepted as such by the Turks, was not entirely proper. The Turks on their part never explicitly quoted this British recognition as a legal basis for their claim to Kuwait, simply stressing the Berlin and Paris treaties concerning the territorial integrity of the Ottoman Empire in general, and their vague claim that it included the entire Arabian Peninsula.

In any case, tenuous legal arguments are of negligible value when vital interests are at stake. At the end of 1898, London suddenly arrived at the conclusion that in the case of Kuwait vital British interests were threatened. The press played an important part in this volte-face. During the autumn of 1898, the British press had been regurgitating the warnings first aired in the *Times of India* of August. In September, the *Times of India* gave space to a new rumour, this time of an agreement between Balfour and the Germans for the granting of a German foothold in Kuwait or Basra for a railway to the Gulf.[56] Furthermore Curzon was vehemently urging his case, and it was difficult to deny a newly appointed Viceroy a strongly expressed wish. Added to which, regional developments really did seem to lend the matter a genuine new urgency.

[54] Busch, *Britain and the Persian Gulf*, p. 106. It is noteworthy that the Foreign Secretary of the Government of India had confirmed this recognition to the German consul in Calcutta as recently as February 1898, but in August 1898 stated that the Turks had no practical authority there: Berlin AA, R 13843 A 2448 and R 13844 A 10203, Sternburg 5 February and 11 August 1898.

[55] Plass, *England*, pp. 481–2.

[56] *Times of India*, 5 September 1898.

Underlying this British change of heart, however, was a more subtle point, which was never directly expressed. Britain would certainly not favour an Ottoman military occupation of Kuwait in circumstances that might lead to Kuwait becoming strategically important to another European power. This was indeed never enunciated in writing, but the next months would demonstrate how drastically Ottoman designs on Kuwait could influence even London's decisions as to appropriate action on the principality. Vague railway rumours and the threat of Ottoman intervention had even more impact upon British policy because of a third factor, which was the singularly low quality of British diplomatic intelligence. British reports are markedly inferior in that respect to German and French ones. Extremist opinions advanced by the Indian press were partly responsible for the poor quality, but it also appears that British representatives in Constantinople and Baghdad did not have contacts within the Ottoman system to match those of the French and Germans.

In the end the reason for British intervention was an entirely spurious one that had to do with poor British intelligence on Ottoman activities. There was a kind of panic reaction to the endlessly delayed Ottoman attempts to settle the differences between Mubarak and Qasim Al-Thani in his role as supporter of Mubarak's nephews. As we saw above, in April 1898 Qasim Al-Thani had told the Turks that he was obliged to enforce the claims of Mubarak's nephews and attack Kuwait, and, to prevent Qasim acting unilaterally, the Porte decided to divert to Kuwait the expeditionary force waiting in Basra for the mission to Qatar. This force was then instead diverted to the north.[57] Next, the Porte charged the Naqib Rajab Effendi with investigating the complaints, thus placing the matter in the hands of Mubarak's friend, and by early summer the danger had blown over for the time being. For some time nothing happened. Potentially bad news for Mubarak came in the summer of 1898 when Recep Pasha was replaced as Mushir in Baghdad.[58] Then the Sultan decided to try to settle the Kuwait affair through his Arab contacts in the region. Ahmad, the brother of the Naqib, was appointed to head a private arbitration mission to Kuwait.[59] Reports of this mission and various Ottoman troop movements, by the British resident in Baghdad, inspired

[57] Anscombe, *Ottoman Gulf*, p. 107.
[58] Berlin AA, R13207 A 8104, Rosen in Baghdad 6 July 1898.
[59] Anscombe, *Ottoman Gulf*, pp. 108–9.

the India Office to inform the Foreign Office that the moment had come to act on Kuwait.[60]

On 5 December 1898, the Foreign Office issued the reluctant statement that "the question of establishing a Protectorate over Kuwait and the responsibilities which such a Protectorate would entail is a matter primarily for the Indian Government."[61] On 24 December this verdict was telegraphed to the Government of India for consultation. Then, after new reports from Baghdad and Constantinople the Foreign Office hesitated anew. O'Conor came up once again with the old story of British recognition of Ottoman sovereignty between Basra and Qatif, recalling how the Grand Vizier had been told by a British diplomat that Britain recognized Ottoman sovereignty there.[62] But the ambassador at least judged that the repression of piracy and the slave trade "would afford ground to a direct and special arrangement with the Shaikh, which need not necessarily be made public. In the course of time this arrangement might be shaped into a more effective form which would serve all practical purposes and give the Indian Government a prior lien on Koweit".[63]

The other canard that appeared to keep Kuwait at the forefront of British concerns was the story that the Sultan had granted Kapnist a concession for his Russian railway to Kuwait. The British were unaware that the wily Sultan had only given provisional approval of this chimerical plan to exert a little leverage on the Germans to speed up the Baghdad Railway project. On 4 January 1899, the Foreign Office told the India Office that, while Salisbury agreed with O'Conor that "open steps should be avoided", it was none the less "desirable to take such precautions as possible" against Kuwait falling into the wrong hands. The method

[60] Bidwell, *Affairs of Kuwait*, 1/1, p. 29, acting consul Melvill in Baghdad 6 October 1898; India Office to Foreign Office 23 November 1898.
[61] Bidwell, *Affairs of Kuwait*, 1/1, p. 30, Foreign Office to India Office 5 December 1898. The essence of this was communicated to India on 24 December: Bidwell, 1/1, p. 31.
[62] Bidwell, *Affairs of Kuwait*, 1/1, pp. 30–1, O'Conor to Salisbury 22 December 1898. This mentions the case of a communication of this kind by the dragoman (interpreter) of the British embassy, Sandison, of 1889. See also on this matter Plass, *England*, pp. 481–2. This oral communication meant little as the Turks did not accept Sandison's attempt at a compromise over the division of the Arabian coast, and so the British compromise was rejected as such.
[63] Bidwell, *Affairs of Kuwait*, 1/1, pp. 29–30, Melvill 6 October and O'Conor 22 December 1898.

proposed was to obtain a secret promise from Mubarak not to alienate any portion of his territories without previously obtaining British consent. Sanderson clarified this two weeks later with the remark that this promise should be considered separate from the question of establishing a British protectorate over Kuwait.[64] Then followed some wrangling about the exact form and about the amount of money to be offered to Mubarak for his promise, ranging from 200 pounds per annum to a lump sum of 5000 pounds or even more.

There followed a short discussion about the shape of the agreement. India proposed as a model the one binding the Trucial Shaikhs to Britain, but London decided that it should be the 1891 undertaking signed by the Sultan of Oman.[65] This document simply stated that the Sultan would not alienate any part of his dominions without British permission. Such a promise would at least keep foreign competitors out. If Mubarak could be induced to sign a similar engagement it would allow the British to stop any foreign power acquiring land in Kuwait for a railway, while entailing no firm obligations to Kuwait. The British could still behave in international diplomacy as if they were not infringing any Ottoman prerogatives in Kuwait. This was a theoretical viewpoint. The reality was different, for the British would be de facto engaging themselves to defend Mubarak against the Turks, otherwise the engagement would be futile. It is not for nothing that during its preparation in London the question was raised whether India possessed the military means to stand by the agreement.

Seen from the Ottoman perspective there seems almost an inevitability in Britain's conclusion of a deal with Mubarak in 1899: it had been prophesied already in the 1860s by the French consul in Baghdad.[66] The irony is that it was the very measures taken by the Ottomans to prevent Kuwait falling into British hands that propelled it into becoming a de facto British protectorate. Ottoman policy had been entirely counterproductive,

[64] Bidwell, *Affairs of Kuwait*, 1/1, pp. 32–3, Foreign Office to India Office, 4 and 18 January 1899.
[65] Bidwell, *Affairs of Kuwait*, 1/1, p. 35, text of "treaty" with Oman. The difference with the Trucial Shaikhs' engagements of 1892 was that the latter also promised not to admit representatives of other states into their territory without British permission. For the correspondence about selecting either the Oman version or the Trucial version, ibid. p. 34.
[66] Paris AE, CPC Bagdad 5, fos. 302–303 (1866).

and in the case of the British there is a similar irony. Britain's desire had never been to intervene in Kuwait, but in the end she had been drawn into the role of Kuwait's protecting power.

4.5 The "Agreement" of 1899

An agreement by its very nature requires two parties. It may be that the British were under the impression that they were dealing with an illiterate tribal chief. In reality they were dealing with a person who read the Arab press of the time, a press replete with sensational reporting on impenetrable political intrigues. Mubarak had also had dealings for almost forty years with high Ottoman officials, and he was a very sagacious operator. If the British wanted an agreement precluding other powers from establishing themselves in Kuwait, then they would have to pay a price. That price would be increased by the fact that the British came to their decision at a bad moment. They had panicked over Kapnist's fanciful railway plan and over an imaginary threat to Kuwait in the autumn of 1898. All this was based on unreliable or poorly interpreted diplomatic intelligence. Mubarak was in a strong position in the winter of 1898–9 and in no danger of a direct Ottoman assault, so he could afford to insist on tough conditions.

British eagerness to reach an agreement considerably weakened their negotiating position. Their negotiator Meade and his immediate boss Curzon were both strongly in favour of an engagement and were impervious to the reservations of the India Office and Foreign Office. Under such circumstances Mubarak was able to manipulate Meade. On 21 January 1899, Meade arrived in Kuwait on board the *Lawrence*, accompanied by Gaskin and by Mubarak's friend, the Bahrain residency agent Muhammad Rahim Safar.[67] It was an inauspicious moment, for just then the Ottoman gunboat *Zuhaf* was at anchor in the port of Kuwait. It was also unavoidable that movements to and from the *Lawrence* should be observed by the Kuwait agent of the International Sanitary Committee. Mubarak observed the traditional protocol by not coming on board to visit Meade, because it was not the custom of Kuwaiti rulers to visit foreign warships, even Ottoman ones. Instead, as dictated by the same

---

[67] A detailed account by Meade of his visit to Kuwait and the negotiations that took place can be found in Bidwell, *Affairs of Kuwait*, 1/1, pp. 47–50.

protocol, a prominent member of the ruler's family came on board, in this case Mubarak's brother Hamud. Meade told Hamud that he wanted to conclude an agreement with Mubarak. Hamud raised no objections in principle, but questioned the implications for the Al-Sabah lands in Basra province; if the Al-Sabah were to accept British protection, the Turks could cause problems by claiming that foreigners were not allowed to own land. When Meade was not forthcoming with a firm commitment regarding protection of the date groves, Hamud declared that he should discuss the matter with Mubarak.

At the same time Gaskin, who had been instructed to hold out a prospect of monetary reward and British support, had visited Mubarak, who appears to have opened negotiations with a typical masterly gambit. During the conversation, Mubarak casually mentioned that he had previously received and rejected a similar French proposal.[68] This was probably untrue, but it was a very cunning ploy, in the light of Meade's current difficulties with Ottavi, the anti-British French vice-consul in Muscat.[69]

Next day the *Zuhaf* left Kuwait and Mubarak felt free to invite Meade to visit him. The negotiations appear to have been most businesslike. Meade had brought with him a draft "non-alienation" undertaking to be signed by Mubarak. But the Shaikh was intent on selling such a promise for as high a price as possible. He demanded the inclusion in the written undertaking of a firm commitment of support from the British side, to be formally ratified by the Viceroy. Meade refused, stating that the proposed document was identical to that signed by other Arab chiefs. In the end Meade proposed a draft of a letter in reply to the bond, promising Mubarak, on behalf of the Government of India, its "good offices" in exchange for Mubarak's undertakings. This British promise was not inserted in the wording of Mubarak's bond itself, but the essential fact was that this formal reply converted the bond into a fundamentally different document, by making it a real bilateral agreement.

---

[68] It is highly questionable whether this was the truth. Later in the same year, 1899, there were vague talks about French protection between a French merchant on Bahrain, Antonin Goguyer, and a delegate of Abdul Rahman Al Sa'ud, the exiled Saudi pretender: Paris AE, NS Mascate 48 (dossier non rélié 1, affaire Goguyer, correspondence of 1899). There is no evidence that either Goguyer or official French representatives at Basra or Muscat had any contacts at that time with Mubarak.

[69] Busch, *Britain*, pp. 49–93, deals in detail with the Anglo-French dispute in Oman.

Something else too occurred during the meeting. Somehow the original bond was expanded to include an article excluding foreign representatives in Kuwait without previous British permission. This article formed part of the agreements with the Trucial Shaikhs, but London had not wanted it included in the Kuwait agreement. Meade is silent on how it came to be incorporated, indicating only that it had become desirable as a result of Gaskin's report of Mubarak mentioning a French overture. It may be that Mubarak himself had proposed it, or else that Meade had been spurred by the news of the French proposal to ask it of Mubarak. The point is that this article too fundamentally transformed the agreement. Unlike the mere non-alienation bond, which was a private law contract, this was a clause that had a meaning in international law. It ultimately meant that the British could expel any foreigner from Kuwait who had the permission of the Sultan to be there, and in consequence it was a denial of Ottoman sovereignty. The clause was, of course, attractive because it effectively excluded all unwanted railway initiatives, but for all but the most resolute empire-builders its implications in international law were rather daunting. This was especially the case given that this was not just a unilateral promise on Mubarak's part, but was backed by the British reply offering "good offices", entailing that Britain was committed to upholding it, even in the face of the Turks.

The next day all was finalized, and Meade and Mubarak signed. On the British side there were the signatures of Meade and two witnesses. The question then arose as to whether Kuwaiti witnesses should also sign. There followed a clever piece of theatre that appears to have been previously choreographed in the Al-Sabah family council. Mubarak's brothers Hamud and Jabir were invited to sign, but refused, unless there came a firm undertaking that British protection would also be extended to the Basra date groves. Meade felt that he could not go that far, and refused, considering that Mubarak's signature alone was sufficiently binding on Kuwait. He did, however, promise to consult London. In the meantime London had received more disturbing news about plans for railways to the Gulf, and Salisbury gave an immediate instruction that the promise should be made.[70]

---

[70] Bidwell, *Affairs of Kuwait*, 1/1, p. 41, Foreign Office to India Office 14 February 1899.

This Kuwait agreement was of a new kind for the Gulf. Existing engagements with Arab rulers in the region had been unilateral, but Mubarak had held out for a reciprocal undertaking from the British, however vague, in writing, duly signed and to be ratified by the Viceroy. "Good offices" seemed a vague and easy thing to promise but, had the British given the matter proper consideration, they would have come to a very different view. As soon as Mubarak got into trouble with the Turks, and the British offered their "good offices", the Turks would demand what right the British had to interfere and an international incident would be born. The British wished to keep the engagement secret, but it was almost impossible to shroud in secrecy something that had been expected for quite some time. Mubarak had nothing to fear from his agreement with the British leaking out. It would simply make his enemies think twice and, once seen as his protectors, the British would be unable to abandon him without terrible loss of face. In short, Mubarak had most of the advantages of the agreement, while the British were left with the problems.

Salwa Al-Ghanim gives a very critical account of Meade's incompetence in negotiating an agreement including the second clause, and condemns his failure to observing his strict instructions.[71] Meade was not a diplomat but a colonial official, and colonial officials had more room for manoeuvre than diplomats, who always have to follow instructions to the letter. Moreover, it is not clear that Meade was entirely Mubarak's victim. Mubarak's undertaking to let the British decide on any foreign presence in Kuwait answered his very real fears about French interference and Russian travellers as expressed in his correspondence with Loch. Very probably Meade had nothing against the proposal, and enjoyed the idea of forcing the sluggish pace of London officialdom.

Meade had certainly bought more from Mubarak than he had been instructed to buy. The unexpected second clause in Mubarak's engagement, when the text reached it after some delay, rattled the London bureaucracy.[72] The India Office was angry. Lee Warner was disagreeably "surprised" and Sanderson shared his feelings. Salisbury was impervious to

[71] Salwa Al-Ghanim, *Mubarak*, p. 76.
[72] Bidwell, *Affairs of Kuwait*, 1/1, p. 59, Hamilton to Government of India 30 March 1899. Meade had been instructed to make an agreement similar to the Muscat agreement, and "was not authorized to stipulate that the Shaikh should not receive Representatives from any Power". But the article was there and Hamilton decided that it would remain in force.

such niceties and saw no problem. Curzon could not officially approve of Meade's actions, but took an attitude of "no real harm having been done". India probably did not share the ruffled feelings of London officialdom; after all, it had originally proposed an engagement including the second clause.

Mubarak's engagement superficially resembled those of Bahrain and the Trucial Shaikhs, but was different in its effects because Mubarak was in a much stronger position. The secrecy desired by the British was counterproductive. If Mubarak misbehaved there was no question of the British intervening in Kuwait with a strong hand as they did in Bahrain or the Trucial States. If they were so to intervene in Kuwait, diplomatic uproar would ensue. The British could confess publicly to a certain special business relationship with Kuwait, but not to something with a status in international law like a protectorate.

4.6 An illegal agreement?

Since 1899 there has been much tangled debate about the legality of the documents exchanged between Mubarak and Meade. The formalities of the exchange were carried through. Letters were exchanged, and the Government of India formally ratified its acceptance of Mubarak's undertaking as well as its promise of "good offices". As such it was a binding document between two parties. The main discussion has focused on whether Mubarak was in a position to sign an international agreement, and whether Britain was permitted under international law to enter into such an agreement.

In its own immediate context this issue has little historical significance. The 1899 Agreement was concluded, it was implemented in practice, and even the Ottoman Empire was eventually to accept its existence. In later times, however, it was to come repeatedly under the spotlight because it formed the point of departure for the far-fetched claims to Kuwait concocted by the State of Iraq. We may disregard publications that fall into the category of political pamphlets, but two others deserve attention, with the cautionary note that they both suffer from a lack of specific knowledge about the situation of Kuwait from its origins down to 1899.

Pillai and Kumar published an article in 1962 opposing the then recently issued Iraqi claim that Kuwait was part of Iraq.[73] In this framework they also investigated the thesis that the 1899 exchange of papers was illegal and invalid. While concluding on various grounds that the agreement itself was valid, they conceded that its conclusion may have been illegal. Kuwait appeared according to them to be a vassal entity within the Ottoman Empire albeit without interference of Ottoman officials in its government. There are sufficient precedents for vassals making international agreements, so this in itself presents no problem. But, according to Pillai and Kumar, vassals do not have the right to conclude international binding agreements which are prejudicial to the rights of the suzerain. The second article of Mubarak's undertaking was deemed by Pillai and Kumar to contravene this rule, which they abstracted from Oppenheim's *International Law: A Treatise* (1953 edition, first published 1905).[74] According to them, the exchange of promises appears, however, to have acquired legitimacy in retrospect, because in 1913 the Ottoman Sultan as suzerain accepted the existence of these agreements.[75] The weak point in Pillai and Kumar's reasoning is the use of a posterior legal manual. International law in 1899 had not really solidified on this point and, until that takes place, law should be regarded as created by practice and precedent – especially in the case of the Ottoman Empire, where the government created confusion by mixing Islamic and Western legal concepts.

The German Kuhn adopts a less formalistic and more analytical approach. Kuhn investigated the Iraqi claims in more depth and established the conditions under which those claims could be valid. In this the 1899 Agreement has an important place. Kuhn takes a more dynamic view of statehood, arguing that different "vassal" entities within the Ottoman Empire acquired over the course of time an increasing degree of statehood.[76] For him the pivotal issue hinges on the precise point in this process at which a vassal entity merits description as a state.

Kuhn observed that the 1899 exchange of undertakings included the

---

[73] Pillai, R. and Kumar, M., "The Political and Legal Status of Kuwait", *The International and Comparative Law Quarterly*, 1962, pp. 108–30.

[74] Pillai and Kumar, "Political and Legal Status", pp. 118–19. These authors, however, have set out on a completely erroneous basis by supposing (p. 117) that in the past Kuwait had "regularly" paid tribute to the Ottoman Empire.

[75] Pillai and Kumar, "Political and Legal Status", pp. 120–1.

[76] Gehrke and Kuhn, *Grenze*, pp. 123–4. The part of the book concerning the legal validity of the Iraqi claim on Kuwait (pp. 119–74) is by Kuhn.

claim of elements of territorial sovereignty on the Kuwaiti side. He considers one small feature of the promise of non-alienation to be especially significant: that it included possessions in Kuwait territory of foreign nationals.[77] This implies full jurisdiction of Kuwait over foreign nationals on Kuwaiti territory, and this is a diagnostic feature of territorial sovereignty as opposed to tribal rulership. He places this with other concessions made later by Mubarak to Britain as effective deeds of government, as opposed to formal deeds of the Ottoman Sultan regarding Kuwait that were never given effect. As the only example of Ottoman interference before 1899, Kuhn mentions the quarantine official; but this is a dubious example because Kuhn is apparently unaware that this individual enjoyed a somewhat special status as an official of the International Sanitary Board, whose existence was a limitation rather than an extension of the sovereignty of the Ottoman Empire! After considering the inconsistency of the claim brought forward from the Iraqi side, Kuhn arrives at the conclusion that Mubarak had acted from his own proprietary power as Ruler of Kuwait, not as an Ottoman official, and consequently exercised territorial sovereignty. By accepting the agreement Britain recognized Mubarak's territorial sovereignty.

Next Kuhn addresses the Iraqi claim that the 1899 Agreement was void because Mubarak did not have the right to make it. Iraq described Kuwait as a "vassal", but in doing so undermines its own argument because Ottoman vassals can be states (e.g. Egypt, the Balkan states etc.). If Kuwait was not a state, it became one simply by the very conclusion of the bond of 1899. This automatic effect of the bond could only be annulled if it was not implemented (for instance through Ottoman armed intervention), but the bond did have practical implementation. Kuhn attaches no value to Iraqi arguments such as Kuwait's use of the Ottoman flag, because in other entities on the fringes of the Ottoman Empire other, much stronger ties could co-exist with local sovereignty – for example, Egyptian subjects were legally Ottoman subjects down to 1914.[78]

Kuhn has little time for Pillai and Kumar's thesis that Kuwait as a vassal state was entitled to have a valid treaty, but was not entitled to conclude it, with the result that the 1899 papers become unlawful, but not void or invalid. Kuhn doubts this on several grounds. He again puts forward the

[77] Gehrke and Kuhn, *Grenze*, p. 132.
[78] Gehrke and Kuhn, *Grenze*, p. 138.

argument that the freedom of action of Ottoman vassals is not clearly circumscribed. One might argue that a proper treaty entered into by a vassal should not infringe the suzerain's rights. In the 1899 Agreement, Mubarak promised not to admit representatives of other powers, including the Ottomans, into Kuwait. But even the refusal to admit representatives of the suzerain is not in this case regarded as legally significant, because in the 1913 Anglo-Ottoman Convention the Turks accepted the validity of the 1899 Agreement, and were then explicitly granted the right under the Convention to have a representative in Kuwait (albeit one who was not allowed to interfere in internal affairs); this amounted to an acceptance by the Ottomans that the admission of such a representative had not automatically been part of the obligation of the vassal. Kuhn moreover rightly observes that Kuwait's acceptance of a de facto foreign protectorate is not uncommon with Ottoman vassals, citing Rumania, Samos and Egypt as examples.[79]

Even quite recently the question was discussed again by Hassan Alawi in his book *Aswar al-tin*. This author tried to draw a comparison between the Anglo-Iraqi treaty of 1921 and the Kuwait Agreement of 1899. Such a comparison is unjustified because the 1899 Agreement embodied the signing away by an existing state of part of its sovereign rights, while in 1921 Britain created a new, not entirely independent state of Iraq out of territory it had conquered. Alawi seems to have missed this fundamental point. His remark that Kuwait was " neither a state nor an emirate" is, of course, irrelevant.[80] The dynamic concept of international law regarding entities on the fringe of the Ottoman Empire as proposed by Kuhn rightly states that, if a local authority is able to conclude an agreement and to execute it, then *ipso facto* the state exists.[81]

---

[79] Gehrke and Kuhn, *Grenze*, pp. 142–3.
[80] Hassan Alawi, *Aswar al-tin*, pp. 48–53.
[81] Gehrke and Kuhn, *Grenze*, p. 138: "Kuwait could have become a territorial state simply because it started to conclude treaties. As in any case of the birth of a state authority the essential question is whether these treaties were then effectively executed [...] In the case of Kuwait this cannot be denied."

5

The Secret Agreement Partially Unveiled
1899–1900

5.1 First rumours

The 1899 Agreement was intended by Salisbury to be secret, but it had not escaped outsiders that something was afoot. The Porte soon had its suspicions that something had occurred. This is no wonder. We have already seen how, in 1897 and 1898, rumours were circulating about links between Mubarak and the British. The first ones emanated from the French consulate in Muscat.[1] If Gaskin's movements of 1897 were known to Ottavi in Muscat, then they could also very well have penetrated to the Ottoman authorities too. Nor is it likely that the speculations in the *Times of India* about Mubarak's pro-British attitude would have escaped the Turks.[2] The movements of British ships in 1899 had not gone unnoticed, though the Porte received no intelligence about them from the Wali of Basra, Anis Pasha, its official closest to the scene.[3] The Wali's indolence was of no consequence, however, as others had been alerted by the British movements. When the *Lawrence* arrived at Kuwait, the Ottoman gunboat *Zuhaf* had been at anchor there. The Ottoman consul in Bushire too had

---

[1] Paris AE, NS Mascate 36, fos. 134–135, Ottavi, French vice-consul in Muscat, 23 September 1897.
[2] Paris AE, NS Mascate 36, fos. 186–190, Ottavi 20 January 1898.
[3] Report of the French consul in Baghdad, Paris AE, NS Mascate 4, fos. 55–57v, Rouet 19 April 1899. The Turkish sanitary authority in Constantinople had been informed on 5 February by the International Sanitary Board of the strange behaviour of the British warship in Kuwait: Bidwell, *Affairs of Kuwait*, 1/1, p. 56.

reported the visit. But it was unclear to the Turks exactly what had transpired.[4]

It is hardly surprising, therefore, that the Porte's suspicions about British intentions were aroused. Hamdi's fears of 1896 had finally been vindicated and he was sent back to Basra to replace the negligent Anis. The French consul in Baghdad was particularly clear about the extra Kuwaiti factor in Anis's replacement, reporting that Anis had been replaced by Hamdi Pasha, Mubarak's old enemy, who had been charged by his chief, the Minister of Marine Hassan Pasha, to establish a regular administration in Kuwait as his main task … with the prospect that Kuwait might produce a revenue of 47,000 lira.[5] The German consul, Richarz, was less well-informed. He at first reported Hamdi's arrival as a simple fact, mentioning only that the Naqib was hostile to him. Some months later, he reported that Hamdi had been charged with reforming the military in Basra province, but was still apparently unaware of any connection with Kuwait.[6]

It is noteworthy how badly informed the British seem to have been about the Ottoman state of mind. There is no hint in British sources of any alarm over Hamdi Pasha's appointment or what the Ottomans intended by it. French reports clearly state that it was common knowledge that Hamdi had been appointed because of rumours about the British and Kuwait.[7] Wratislaw, the British consul in Basra, regarded Hamdi as a friend. While he did murmur vaguely about the potentially negative consequences of Hamdi's appointment for Mubarak's Basra possessions, he failed to spot the direct causal connection between that appointment and Meade's movements.[8] The diplomat Wratislaw did not grasp that his friendly social contact with Hamdi (whose duplicity is mentioned by

[4] Bidwell, *Affairs of Kuwait*, 1/1, pp. 48, 53. See also ibid. pp. 43 and 66–8: Constantinople may also have received the news of the mysterious actions of the British warship with Meade on board in Kuwait from the sanitary authorities in Basra (the agent of the Sanitary Board in Kuwait had informed Dr. Stiépovich, his boss in Basra, and Stiépovich telegraphed the Board in Constantinople, where O'Conor was informed by Dr Dickson, the British member of the Board. It is inconceivable that other members of the International Board would not have informed Ottoman friends.

[5] Paris AE, NS Mascate 4, fos. 55–57v, Rouet 19 April 1899.

[6] Berlin AA, R 13846 A 5651, Richarz 12 May; and R 13847 A 11077, Richarz 17 August 1899.

[7] Paris AE, NS Mascate 4, fos. 55–56, Rouet 19 April 1899. The French Foreign Minister asked the French ambassador Cambon in London to verify, ibid. fo. 95, 8 June 1899.

Mubarak) counted for little in the context of Hamdi's real mission – to counteract British influence.

There is little basis for the rumours casting suspicion on Mubarak himself for leaking news of the Agreement to the Turks as a provocation, or from primitive pride. This accusation emanated from O'Conor, who was seldom especially well-informed.[9] In theory it would be in Mubarak's interest for the Turks to know that he had strong protection, but the rather conspicuous movements of British warships would be enough to inform the Porte. There is however a strong indication that there was a leak on the British side, in Bushire. The French envoy in Teheran heard from Bushire that a protectorate agreement had been signed between the British and Kuwait.[10] Another possibility is that the leak came from Loch, the British resident in Baghdad, whose rumours of the Port Said–Kuwait railway's imminence were causing some nervousness.[11]

The press had also paid considerable attention to Kuwaiti affairs during 1898. Some of these newspaper reports had been unfounded rumours, for example that the Germans were interested in acquiring Kuwait. This story was first printed in a Russian newspaper, but in February 1899 it also appeared in the German newspaper *Börsezeitung*.[12] The first explicit press mention of an agreement between the British and Mubarak first appeared in June 1899 in the French newspaper *Liberté*, followed by the London *Morning Post*.[13]

In the meantime there occurred a small diversion. Two Russians were travelling in the Gulf, their interest apparently centred on Kuwait. They

---

[8] Bidwell, *Affairs of Kuwait*, 1/1, p. 61: the vague formula that Hamdi's appointment "may have some effect on the position of Mubarak" because of Hamdi's attitude towards Mubarak's nephews.

[9] Salwa Al-Ghanim, *Mubarak*, p. 81, based on a mere assumption by the British ambassador in Constantinople: Bidwell, *Affairs of Kuwait*, 1/1, pp. 63–4.

[10] Paris AE, NS Mascate 4, fos. 139– 139v, French envoy in Teheran 12 October 1899.

[11] Paris AE, NS Mascate 4, fos. 79–81v, Rouet 2 May 1899.

[12] Paris AE, NS Mascate 4, fos. 10–11, report of the French ambassador in Berlin, 13 February 1899.

[13] *Morning Post* of 5 June 1899: "The *Liberté* states that Coloneal Meade, British Resident at Bushire and Admiral Douglas have made an agreement with Sheik Mubarek of Koweit which causes anxiety to the Porte. Kowait is the key to the Euphrates. The Porte would like to establish its authority there, but it now fears to intervene directly and is consequently instigating the natives of Montefik to attack Sheik Mubarek and replace him by another ruler [...]".

were far from grandees: one was a Baghdad Armenian merchant, Ovanessian, who had acquired Russian nationality and since dubbed himself Ovanessov, and the other was a Russian Muslim named Abbas Aliyev. The German consul in Baghdad was told that Kuwait was the main focus of their interest. The British understood that their travels were related to Russian railway plans. Their official story was that they had come to buy sheepskins – not such a far-fetched cover, as Kuwait was the point from which sheepskins from central Arabia were exported to large industrial centres. Such news could only serve to strengthen the British decision to hold on to Kuwait.[14]

1899 brought a general certainty on one point at least: that Mubarak had made a deal of some kind with the British involving protectorate status or a British foothold in Kuwait. But there was no clue at all to the actual content of the Agreement. That was to remain a well-kept secret for many years.

5.2 First consequences of the 1899 Agreement

The 1899 Agreement with Britain afforded Mubarak some security, but did not solve all his old problems. It also created some new dangers. An important existing problem was the old quarrel between the Al-Sabah and the Rashidi Amir of Najd. For years there had been friction while the Shammar Amir, Muhammad Ibn Rashid, was establishing himself as the leading Arab potentate in the Peninsula. In the summer of 1897, Muhammad Ibn Rashid was succeeded by his nephew Abdul Aziz, a young man only thirty years old, who was less diplomatic and more hotheaded than his predecessor.[15] One longstanding quarrel between Kuwait and the Rashidis had arisen because Kuwait forbade the export of arms into the Amir's territory. In the light of reports that Mubarak's troops were well-armed with the rifles that stayed there, this arms blockade seems to have suited Kuwait. The tension between Mubarak and the Amir arose also from the presence of exiles on both sides. Since 1894, Abdul Rahman bin Faysal Al-Saud, who had been expelled from Najd by Muhammad Ibn

---

[14] Bidwell, *Affairs of Kuwait*, 1/1, pp. 56–7; Rezvan, *Russian Ships*, pp. 7–8; Berlin AA, R 13846 A 4922, Richarz in Baghdad 25 March 1899.

[15] Musil, *Northern Negd*, pp. 244–5; Berlin AA, R 14555 A 238, Oppenheim, German consul in Cairo, 29 September 1897.

Rashid, had been living in Kuwait on a pension of 230 Turkish pounds (*ca.* 250 pounds sterling, a not inconsiderable sum in the Ottoman system) from Sultan Abdulhamid II.[16] Later, tribal leaders from Qasim, notably Burayda, who were hostile to the Amir came to live in Kuwait. On the other side it seems that the Amir had received several of Mubarak's nephews.[17] At the beginning of 1899 the conflict appears to have been exacerbated. In March the Amir moved his troops to the Euphrates, reputedly to take part in an impending Ottoman attack on Kuwait. The Ottoman authorities in Mesopotamia had no reason to view this concentration of unruly elements with favour, and paid the Amir to return to his country.[18]

New problems were caused by the indiscreet way in which the British had acted at the beginning of 1899. The Ottoman response had been the appointment of Hamdi Pasha. The British were unaware that Hamdi was anti-British, but they knew from the past that he had promoted the cause of Mubarak's nephews in the dispute over the date groves. Then came the news that Mubarak's nephews, who had been living under the Amir's protection in Zubair, had gone to Hamdi immediately on his arrival in Basra. This set off alarm bells at the highest level in Britain as early as April–May 1899.[19]

Problems over the date groves would jeopardize the income Mubarak needed for the running of Kuwait. He decided that a counter-measure on the same level was called for. He came up with a scheme to generate new income that undermined his popularity with the merchant class in Kuwait, but contained a clear warning if not a provocation to Hamdi as well. He had already mentioned in vague terms to the British his plan to open his own customs office in Kuwait, but now he began to levy regular customs duties not just on merchandise entering Kuwait from the sea, but

[16] Musil, *Northern Negd*, p. 245. The Ottoman financing of the residence of an enemy so close to the Rashidi borders was probably intended to make that dangerous and virtually independent vassal of the Sultan think twice before causing trouble to his suzerain.

[17] Anscombe, *Ottoman Gulf*, p. 117.

[18] Paris AE, NS Mascate 4, fos. 55–57v, Rouet 19 April 1899. The German consul also reported the military moves of Ibn Rashid, but mentions no connection with Kuwait: Berlin AA, R 13846 A 3680, telegram from German embassy in Constantinople 29 March 1899; ibid., R 13846 A 7208, Richarz 18 May 1899.

[19] Bidwell, *Affairs of Kuwait*, 1/1, pp. 60–3.

also on merchandise coming from Basra, which had already paid customs to the Sultan's *gümrük* office. The duties were 5 per cent, the normal amount levied in the Ottoman Empire.[20] The British hardly reacted, but Hamdi must have been more alarmed: not only did Mubarak's move threaten the Basra customs revenue, because goods destined for Kuwait would in future no longer go through Basra, but at the same time it emphasized Kuwait's independence from the Ottoman Empire. In the past the Ottomans had never received any customs duties from the port of Kuwait, any minor duties levied there going directly into the Al-Sabah treasury. Duties at Kuwait, however, had always been small, and the Ottomans had been able to console themselves with the thought that Kuwait was a kind of free port on Ottoman territory. Now Kuwait had started to act as a fully independent state.

At the end of April 1899, rather belatedly, the British began to give some thought to how they should handle the Turks when Britain's good offices might be summoned to protect Mubarak or his interests. Meade was the first to propose clearly that the Turks should be formally warned.[21] O'Conor considered that if a threat appeared it might be "desirable to warn the Turkish Government that owing to the importance of British interests in the Persian Gulf, Her Majesty's Government would view with displeasure any expedition against Mubarak."[22] This was all too diplomatic and discreet, and ignored the fact that several Ottoman officials suspected that a real agreement existed. The India Office preferred the clearer approach suggested by Meade.[23] By that time a new factor had entered the equation: Hamdi had approached the British consul Wratislaw in Basra with some vague talk about Kuwait. He told Wratislaw that the Sultan would understand the British viewpoint if the British would only explain it to the Turks. This move looked far from sincere considering Hamdi's attitude in the past. The British suspected that Hamdi had permission from the highest level for his initiative.[24]

Hamdi meanwhile continued to support Mubarak's nephews in their endeavours to promote their claim to the date groves.[25] In July 1899,

[20] Bidwell, *Affairs of Kuwait*, 1/1, p. 64, Wratislaw 3 May 1899.
[21] Bidwell, *Affairs of Kuwait*, 1/1, p. 63, Meade 30 April 1899.
[22] Bidwell, *Affairs of Kuwait*, 1/1, pp. 60–1, O'Conor to Salisbury 24 May 1899.
[23] Bidwell, *Affairs of Kuwait*, 1/1, p. 61, India Office to Foreign Office 7 June 1899.
[24] Bidwell, *Affairs of Kuwait*, 1/1, pp. 64, 74–5.

Mubarak's brother Hamud arrived in Basra to keep an eye on Mubarak's interests, and called in the help of the British consul. According to instructions, Wratislaw notified Hamdi of the British interest in this dispute, but did so rather weakly and hesitantly. Hamdi maintained his cordial façade to Wratislaw, but protested to Mubarak in a letter combining fatherly reproach with covert threat. Hamdi's main objection was Hamud's "improper" involvement of the British consul.[26] This Ottoman protest had no firm basis. It had been customary for many years for European diplomatic and consular representatives to "help" friendly Ottoman subjects in courts of law and elsewhere. This was grudgingly accepted by the Ottomans. It is significant that Hamdi protested to Mubarak, not to the British consul.

August 1899 brought a new incident. A probably false report from Qatar, and thus possibly from friends of Mubarak's nephews, that Mubarak was intending to sell land in the strategic location of Fao, caused the Turks to contemplate a renewed démarche on Kuwait. Hamdi's patron, the Minister of Marine Hassan Pasha, decided to make Kuwait a regular Ottoman port and instal a regular Ottoman harbour-master there.[27] This was a risky step, as to appoint a harbour-master would constitute a profound change in the status of Kuwait. It might have been conceived as a provocation, to test whether Mubarak and the British were ready to confront the Turks openly, but the big question remained what the Turks should do if such a confrontation occurred. On 4 September, the Basra harbour-master left for Kuwait and the director of Baghdad customs was

[25] Hamdi's actions here may have been more than simple blackmail. It may be that the Turks were fearing British interference also in Fao: immediately after the first news of co-operation between Mubarak and the British had reached Basra, the Turks had sent a mission to Fao to prevent the local authorities conspiring with the British: Berlin AA, R 13207 A 4660, Richarz in Baghdad 23 March 1899.

[26] IOLR, R/15/1/471, fo. 229, Hamdi to Mubarak, 11[?] July 1899. Interesting is the view of a prominent Kuwaiti expressed to the French consul in Muscat, that Mubarak provoked the fury of the Ottomans by sending his secretary to Wratislaw over the date groves matter: Paris AE, NS Mascate 4, fo. 131, Ottavi 23 September 1899.

[27] Anscombe, *Ottoman Gulf*, p. 115. The British sources give a slightly different account of the matter, stating that Hamdi Pasha was instructed by the Porte to appoint a harbour-master: IOLR, R/15/1/471, fos. 239–240, Wratislaw to O'Conor 25 August 1899; *cf.* Bidwell, *Affairs of Kuwait*, 1/1, pp. 82–4. Mubarak's words in IOLR, R/15/1/471, fo. 266, are in strange contrast to the comforts Mubarak's European guests sometimes treated to in his palace: see Burchardt, "Ost-Arabien", p. 306.

in Basra reportedly to open a customs office in Kuwait. Mubarak was ready and immediately sent the Ottoman official back, under the graphic pretext that "he was just an Arab sitting on the edge of the desert and was unable to provide accommodation". Wratislaw took the matter up with the Basra Wali, Hamdi Pasha, and issued a vague warning about the "grave dissatisfaction" of the British Government. The Wali said that the measure was taken without consulting him, that in the past he had urged the occupation of Kuwait, that he thought that an Ottoman occupation of Kuwait would be in Britain's interest, and finally that he thought that Turkey and Britain could reach a satisfactory resolution of the matter.[28] The Minister of Marine then suggested that, after consulting Mubarak, a native Kuwaiti should be appointed. Hamdi rejected this suggestion, not without good reason, and the matter was allowed to lapse.[29] The incident had served only to alarm the British.

British anxiety was further aggravated by rumours of impending Ottoman military intervention in Kuwait, a step that had already been secretly suggested in August by Hamdi.[30] Hamdi had said that Mubarak was a stupid man – *gayet cahil*[31]– who was in danger of succumbing to British pressure, and so a military move on Kuwait would be a good pre-emptive strike.[32] Nothing much was done, but rumours of an Ottoman military strike started to go the rounds. As usual nothing came of it. For his proposed surprise attack on a September morning, Hamdi would need the co-operation of the military, and the regional commander Muhsin Pasha was strongly opposed to the scheme. According to some sources, Muhsin owed his attitude to having been bribed by his friend Mubarak. This suspicion was probably groundless, Muhsin rather belonging to the school of Ottoman officials that held that it was precisely Ottoman pressure that was driving the harmless, autonomous Kuwait into Britain's arms.

It seems that Mubarak was not wholly content to rely on the support afforded him by the British, for he had in the meantime been trying to

---

[28] IOLR, R/15/1/471, fos. 255–258, telegrams from Wratislaw to O'Conor 25 August – 8 September 1899.

[29] Anscombe, *Ottoman Gulf*, p. 115.

[30] Anscombe, *Ottoman Gulf*, pp. 115 and 225 n. 10.

[31] See Chapter 6 n. 21.

[32] Anscombe, *Ottoman Gulf*, p. 115, and p. 225 n. 14, quoting Istanbul BA, Yildiz/Bab-i Asafi Resmi 104/30.

line up more guarantees for his freedom. The Ottoman consul in Bushire notified Hamdi Pasha, probably in September, that Mubarak had appealed for Persian protection, through his friend Shaikh Khaz'al of Muhammara as intermediary. This is one of the first clear references to co-operation between Khaz'al and Mubarak, who would soon become close friends.[33]

Khaz'al and Mubarak shared a somewhat similar predicament. Both had assumed the rule as a consequence of violent events. Both had a delicate relationship with a great Islamic power. Mubarak had problems in maintaining his independence *vis-à-vis* the Ottoman Empire, while Khaz'al was in much the same relation to Persia, and also exploited British support to sustain his autonomy. Both were anxious about technological developments that might endanger their positions, Mubarak facing the Ottoman-German railway plans, and Khaz'al the Dutch-Persian plans to canalize the Karun river and the irrigation of the surrounding lands.[34] Both were sociable gentlemen who enjoyed life, and they became intimate friends. There were also differences. Khaz'al was much richer than Mubarak, and he was in the enviable position of owning land on both the Persian and the Ottoman side, and so in case of trouble he could always take refuge on the other side. But appearances can deceive. Mubarak had to fend off the Ottomans, a declining power whose claims were nebulous, whereas Khaz'al actually held the position of a Persian official. Mubarak's Kuwait was more of a unity than the tribal conglomerate controlled by Khaz'al. Khaz'al was forced to deal on occasion with tiresome tribal rebellions.

The report that Mubarak was not satisfied with Britain's protection and had been approaching the Persians was confirmed from Bahrain.[35] One cannot exclude the possibility that these rumours were spread by Mubarak himself to exert a little pressure on the British. This was hardly necessary. The British suddenly overreacted to the Turkish threats to Mubarak's independence. Following the news about the harbour-master and in view

---

[33] The first mention of close contacts between Mubarak and Khaz'al was by Meade on 14 May 1899: Bidwell, *Affairs of Kuwait*, 1/1, p. 71. There is a summary biography of Khaz'al in *EI*. See also Graves, *Cox*, pp. 113–15; and a description of Khaz'al's position in the early 20th century in Plass, *England*, pp. 486–8.

[34] Graves, *Cox*, p. 225; W. Floor, "Le Karūn et l'irrigation de la plaine d'Ahwaz", *Studia Iranica*, 28/1, pp. 95–122.

[35] Bidwell, *Affairs of Kuwait*, 1/1, pp. 90–1.

of the rumours of impending Ottoman military intervention, Bushire sent a warship to Kuwait. On 8 September Salisbury, never very patient with the Ottomans, brusquely ordered O'Conor to warn them that the British Government had no designs on Kuwait, but had friendly relations with the Shaikh, and that "a very inconvenient and disagreeable question would be raised if an attempt were made to establish Turkish authority or customs control at Kuwait".[36] So now O'Conor had to be open with the Ottoman Foreign Minister Tawfiq Pasha about the British interest. The Ottoman Minister responded in an understanding manner, but this was a charade. He also informed the Sultan. Abdulhamid sent Kostaki Anthopoulos Pasha to have informal talks with O'Conor. Anthopoulos, a glib Greek gentleman, was Ottoman ambassador in London and just at that time on leave in Constantinople. Anthopoulos told O'Conor that the Sultan was most disturbed about O'Conor's notification to Tawfiq, and enquired whether there might be some misunderstanding. O'Conor was most evasive about the position of Kuwait. He told Anthopoulos that Britain had no aggressive intentions. There were special ties with the Shaikh of Kuwait, and Britain had strong objections to the sending of a harbour-master. By way of compensation, O'Conor told Anthopoulos that Britain had no problems with the position of Mubarak as kaymakam.[37] Thus O'Conor was trying to convey the message that there was no British opposition to a purely formal Ottoman authority, but that the Turks should not put pressure on Mubarak. In a subsequent talk with Tawfiq, O'Conor hit on a cunning way to rattle the Turks a little. He warned the Ottoman minister that it was risky to embark on discussions over Kuwait, because Britain had never recognized Ottoman rule over Qatar. As British warships had several times attacked territory claimed by the Turks there, this was a thinly veiled threat.[38]

The Ottomans were not prepared for a real confrontation. They had already told O'Conor that rumours of an Ottoman military move against

[36] Bidwell, *Affairs of Kuwait*, 1/1, pp. 81–2.
[37] Bidwell, *Affairs of Kuwait*, 1/1, pp. 86–7. The question remains whether the formal appointment of Mubarak had really been issued by the Porte, but this point was not discussed. The British idea that Mubarak had a formal appointment goes back to Muhsin telling Wratislaw that he had received a telegram that an irade to that effect had been issued, but there is no indication that a formal appointment was issued to Mubarak; *cf.* Bidwell, *Affairs of Kuwait*, 1/1, p. 76.
[38] Bidwell, *Affairs of Kuwait*, 1/1, p. 88, O'Conor 15 September 1897.

Kuwait were false, and claimed that the harbour-master had been sent to Kuwait by over-zealous officials acting without instructions.[39] It looks as if the Ottomans had still not grasped the full extent of the damage done to their position, and persisted in the belief that Mubarak had not entered a formal agreement with Britain. It was only Hamdi who kept reiterating that Mubarak did have a formal agreement, and putting it about that he had sought British protection after having been refused Persian protection.[40] The Ottoman government put its faith in Muhsin's thesis that Mubarak would be loyal if only he were left alone. It was decided to send the Naqib, Hamdi's arch-enemy in Basra, to Mubarak to ask him to make his submission to the Sultan in writing. Mubarak would then be rewarded with money and presents. This decision was taken by the Ottoman council of ministers in December 1899.[41] By that time it had become urgent for the Turks to settle the Kuwait problem somehow, because plans for a railway to the Gulf were advancing.

5.3 Differing views on the 1899 Agreement

Things had not gone entirely according to British expectations. They had hoped for the Agreement to remain secret, so that the "good offices" would not be required by Mubarak. O'Conor had proposed discretion, but the conspicuous movements of warships and officials in the Gulf had been far from discreet. They provoked Ottoman measures against Mubarak and so would force the British to come forward with something stronger than mere good offices. There is no proof, but it is not unreasonable to suspect that Meade had abandoned discretion on purpose to force the issue. A visible move would commit the British openly, and make it impossible for them to entertain a loss of face.

The form of the Kuwait Agreement was a compromise between leaving Kuwait to the Turks on the one hand and establishing a formal protectorate on the other. A frequent disadvantage of a compromise between two incompatible policies is that it results in the negative

---

[39] Bidwell, *Affairs of Kuwait*, 1/1, p. 84. It is interesting that Tawfiq claimed that the harbour-master had been sent by the Ministry of Marine, Hamdi's chief contact in Constantinople.

[40] Anscombe, *Ottoman Gulf*, p. 115.

[41] Anscombe, *Ottoman Gulf*, pp. 116 and 225 n. 16.

consequences of both alternatives, while precluding the advantages of either. This is particularly true of the compromise between London and India over the shape of the Kuwait Agreement. This was a secret agreement which in form did not amount to a protectorate; however, neglecting to protect Mubarak would lead to British loss of face. The compromise solution reached by O'Conor and Salisbury was as flawed as the Ottoman policy of leaving Mubarak be without letting him feel secure as ruler of Kuwait. British protection of Mubarak would inevitably stir up Ottoman suspicions as well as the international brouhaha which secrecy had been intended to avoid, while Mubarak could do much as he liked as long as no formal protectorate existed, because the British could not openly act against him if he misbehaved.

British handling of the matter was hampered by the frequent absences of the Foreign Secretary, Salisbury. Salisbury basically agreed with Curzon, but in his absence matters were left to Sanderson and Lee Warner, formalistic people with little vision. They liked the secrecy and informality of the Agreement, because thus it offered the least risk of Ottoman protests and the complications arising from them. What these mandarins seem not to have grasped was that Mubarak would quickly understand that the Agreement had value only when the British had been forced to commit themselves, so that they could not turn back. It was in Mubarak's best interests to provoke British protective action. The British had no way of controlling Mubarak at that stage because there existed no formal protectorate, and so there could be no British agent in Kuwait to keep him from acting against British policy. The residency agent in Bahrain appointed a Muslim merchant in Kuwait as "news agent", but this gentleman was no more than a news-gatherer whose views on matters in hand were tinged by his distinct lack of understanding of the international politics. This worthy was certainly in no position to control Mubarak.[42]

The position and policy of the British consul in Basra were a source of confusion. He was closest to Kuwait and could directly observe Ottoman activity in the region. Hence, though Kuwait was a responsibility of the Persian Gulf residency at Bushire, any problem there would land first on the plate of the diplomatic network in the Ottoman Empire. If the Ottomans decided to make trouble, O'Conor and his consuls in Baghdad

[42] IOLR, R/15/1/471, fos. 299, 300, 306, 305, reports of the secret "news agent" Haji Ali bin Ghulam Ridha, summer 1899.

and Basra would be the first to feel it. Wratislaw was one of the weaker elements in the British system. His published memoirs contain only a minimal account of his role in the Kuwait question.[43] Wratislaw saw Kuwait as a rather unimportant tribal territory in the process of being regularized by incorporation into some great power's territories, and he feared that British efforts to acquire control over it would cause problems with the Ottomans in general and bring unpleasantness for him in his remote posting. He felt he had a good relationship with Hamdi Pasha, despite the latter in fact using Wratislaw to drop disinformation about Ottoman policy into the British system. In consequence, Wratislaw's information was often inaccurate, and his aversion to decisive action, shared by his chief O'Conor, was not beneficial for the relationship between Mubarak and Britain.

Seen from Mubarak's side, the situation was that the British had given him a vague commitment for good offices, mainly in case he ran into trouble with the Turks. He was, however, threatened by other local powers, such as Abdul Aziz Ibn Rashid, Yusuf Al-Ibrahim and Qasim Al-Thani, all of whom could be brought into play in an undercover way by the Turks. It was very unclear how far the British would go to protect him against such Arab enemies. With the virtue of hindsight, and knowing all the circumstances as we do now, it looks as if Mubarak's best course would be to contrive to make the Kuwait Agreement appear important to British interests, and then to force a crisis obliging them to act according to their promise – a *casus foederis*. And this is exactly what he did. It remains to be seen whether Mubarak's actions were based on cool analysis, or whether he was a naturally talented operator who attained his objectives by instinct. Some observers seemed inclined to view him as just a rather stupid tribal chief with a lucky streak, but in fact there is no reason to underestimate the subtle political nous of tribal chiefs having to chart their course through the complexities of Arabian affairs. Mubarak had seen more of the world than any other member of the Gulf ruling families. We shall see that he later distinguished himself as practically the only subscriber in the region to nationalist newspapers, and a German visitor described him as the only real leader he had met in the Gulf.[44] Mubarak himself might like to present himself as a "simple Arab sitting on the edge of the desert", but we may safely assume that these words were meant as a smokescreen.[45]

---

[43] Wratislaw, *Consul*, pp. 166–8.

It was clear almost from the start that the two parties to the Agreement of 1899 had different views about it. The British side was hoping that the treaty would never be invoked. Britain was unpopular among the other European powers and it would be damaging for it to be seen as too keenly anticipating the dismemberment of the Ottoman Empire. Most European powers agreed that at some time it might be necessary to carve up the Ottoman Empire, but that this should be arranged in an orderly manner. For the time being, the territorial integrity of the Ottoman Empire was covered by international treaties. If the British were to intervene in favour of Mubarak, in the face of loud Turkish claims that Kuwait was part of the Ottoman Empire, they would be seen to be helping themselves to a slice of the cake before it was baked. The British were aware of this sentiment, and this was the reason for the careful formulation of the 1899 Agreement. British policy-making had become muddied by the disparate priorities prevailing in different parts of the British system: Curzon's fear of Russia; Salisbury's antipathy to the Ottomans; the delicate relationship with the Germans and the Russians and the fear that the Turks might award control over Kuwait to either of them; and, perhaps in the background, a vague apprehension that a conflict with the Ottomans might cause upheaval among Muslims in the British colonies.

Mubarak on the other hand had only to consult his own interests. He had a minimal commitment from the British, no more than a promise of "good offices", and he seems to have grasped that, to make such an agreement work in his interest, he needed to make it a visible reality, not just a piece of paper languishing in an obscure file. First and foremost his concern was to ward off Ottoman attempts at annexation. Next he still had to keep his nephews and their allies off his back, and if possible to retain the possessions in Basra province that were essential for his finances. The methods available to him were of two kinds. In order to fan British concern for the protection of Kuwait, he could brandish the threat of other European powers becoming involved there. As for his Arab neighbours, he could aim to maintain a kind of equilibrium between them. To achieve the first aim, Mubarak could exploit the desire of the

[44] Burchardt, "Ost-Arabien", p. 306, where Mubarak is described as well-informed on world affairs, and the only one of the Shaikhs Burchardt met during his travels who resembled a real ruler.
[45] IOLR, R/15/1/471, fo. 266.

Russians to acquire a coaling station and the German or Russian interest in railway schemes. For the latter purpose we find him supporting the Saudi exiles against the Rashidis, who had been so ready to attack him as soon as an Ottoman attack seemed to be imminent in the spring of 1899. Understandably, Mubarak would feel more secure if the predominance of the Rashidis were to be counterbalanced by a stronger Saudi neighbour.

Various historians, such as Busch, Plass and Ravindar Kumar, have a smile for Mubarak's ingenious methods of achieving his ends. This opinion is not shared by Salwa Al-Ghanim, who squarely states Mubarak's 1899 policy as follows: "Shaikh Mubarak was using his new relationship with Britain within months of the ratification of the agreement, as a foundation for a new policy of resistance to the Ottoman authorities, and expansion of Kuwait's influence among the desert tribes of Arabia."[46] This is a slightly distorted version of the reality. As regards the first part of Salwa Al-Ghanim's statement, there was not really a new policy of resistance, as Mubarak had always opposed Turkish attempts at annexation. One might say that on this occasion Mubarak used his British alliance to force the Turks to back off from the first serious attempt to establish Ottoman authority in Kuwait, which had in any case been chiefly provoked by British indiscretions. In the second part of the statement, Salwa Al-Ghanim is too much influenced by the obvious irritation about Mubarak in her British sources. Aside from a few grumbling remarks by the British, there is no solid evidence that Mubarak had large ambitions for a tribal empire in Arabia. Mubarak was, however, confronted with a state of affairs where the "borders" of Kuwait were determined by whether or not a certain tribe was under his control, and he could hardly sit back in the extremely fluid situation pertaining in 1899. As ruler of the city-state of Kuwait his position was clear, but on the desert side there was a fringe of tribes acknowledging the authority of the Shaikh of Kuwait. They would continue to do so for as long as he was perceived by them to be strong. The British had no wish to become embroiled in a desert war and loudly let it be known, but Kuwait had an ill-defined desert border and Mubarak had no option but to uphold his influence in Kuwait's hinterland.

[46] Salwa Al-Ghanim, *Mubarak*, p. 81.

5.4 Baghdad Railway plans take shape

The British had tumbled into the 1899 Agreement with Mubarak in part because of their perception of a threat from a decidedly fanciful railway scheme. Almost instantly there appeared another plan that looked distinctly more realistic. Any railway plan in the region would pose a menace to Kuwait, both because it would make its strategic position more conspicuous and because it would afford the Ottomans more military mobility. Britain was predisposed to view any railway plan with suspicion that involved foreign control over a route to India. This suspicion could be exploited by Mubarak to enhance Kuwait's value in British eyes. As would be seen in years to come, whenever some power was to try to acquire influence over Kuwait, the British would hasten to Mubarak's aid, and the more he appeared susceptible to seduction by other offers, the faster they would rally round him. Mubarak was not above discreetly revealing that he received alluring offers from other parties, and giving the British the impression that he could be swayed. This attitude kept the British on their toes and eager to help him if need be.

For several decades already there had been sporadic railway plans involving Kuwait. These had never got beyond the proposal stage, but at the end of 1899 it looked as if a Turco–German plan might be feasible. This was the project for a line from Haydar Pasha via Baghdad to the Gulf. It would create a direct connection between the centre of Ottoman power and the Mesopotamian provinces of Mosul, Baghdad and Basra. Maybe the economic importance of this transport link between the Indian Ocean and the Mediterranean was exaggerated at the time, but its strategic significance was enormous. The Ottomans would have much easier access to Baghdad and Basra. They would be able to transport troops and equipment to the unruly Mesopotamian provinces, and that might enable them to force the Arab tribes into submission. In earlier schemes for a railway through the Arabian desert from Syria or Egypt, Kuwait had often figured as the natural and logical Gulf terminus. For a railway along the Euphrates a line to Kuwait looked a less logical extension, but it was a candidate once again because a bar in the Shatt al-'Arab rendered Basra port inaccessible to large ships unless it was removed by continuous and costly dredging. So Kuwait was still in the picture, and to its ruler this was not an attractive prospect because a railway would enable the Ottoman authorities to bring their influence to bear on it.

In 1891 the Sultan had asked Wilhelm II for his support for an extension to Baghdad of the German-sponsored Anatolian Railway. Plans did not prosper at first due to British and Russian opposition.[47] In May 1898 there were consultations about extending the projected line to the Gulf.[48] Already on 15 April 1899 the *Times of India* had identified Kuwait as the probable Gulf terminus for the Baghdad Railway.[49] In November 1899, the Deutsche Bank and the Ottoman Government reached an agreement, and an *irade* of the Sultan, granting a provisional concession, was issued on 23 December 1899.

In November 1899 the Germans got to work. A technical mission was set up to visit Baghdad, consisting of the German consul-general in Constantinople, Stemrich, and an Alsatian engineer, Kapp, who represented the French financial interest in the project (the Baghdad Railway is generally seen as a German project, but in the early stage there was a considerable involvement by French investors). The Ottomans apparently thought that this Mission offered a good opportunity to clarify Kuwait's status in the wake of O'Conor's warnings of September, and Tawfiq Pasha suggested to the German ambassador that Kuwait should be considered as terminus for the railway. This was a sly move that might – and would – cause trouble between the British and the Germans, but the Ottomans appear not to have considered the long-term consequence that the more railway plans mentioned it as terminus, the greater became Kuwait's importance for Britain.[50]

The journey of the German Mission to Kuwait did much to enhance Kuwait's status in international opinion as first choice for a railway terminus. It is not, however, easy to establish the exact course of events, because the sources are profoundly contradictory. Even before the arrival

---

[47] Lepsius, *Grosse Politik*, Vol. 3, pp. 66–8.

[48] Paris AE, NS Turquie 166, fos. 77 and 97, French embassy in Constantinople to Foreign Ministry in Paris, 10 and 15 May 1898.

[49] Berlin AA, R 13846 A 6741, Richarz 11 May 1899.

[50] Lepsius, *Grosse Politik*, Vol. 17, p. 465, Marschall, German ambassador in Constantinople, 23 December 1899. Probably, however, the mission had already conceived the plan to visit Kuwait earlier: Rouet reported on 3 January 1900 that "some weeks ago" Kapp had decided to go to Kuwait after having heard of Rouet's observations made on a visit to the region: Nantes AD, consulat Bagdad A 47, Rouet to embassy 3 January 1900. Kapp's intention to look at Kuwait is confirmed by a telegram in Berlin AA, R 13747 A 14761 (15 December 1899), Marschall 15 December 1899.

of the Mission, Richarz, the somewhat excitable German consul in Baghdad, went so far as to suggest that he should negotiate the lease of a piece of land from Mubarak. The German embassy consulted the Mission, which judged that German acquisition of land would be unwise as it would kindle Ottoman mistrust. At that juncture the Mission was already alert to possible problems arising from the ties between Britain and Kuwait, and wanted to proceed very cautiously. The German chancellor, however, was astonished that, given the unsuitability of Basra, the mission did not push more strongly for a terminus in Kuwait.[51]

In 1899, various wild suggestions of a possible German acquisition of Kuwait had appeared in the German press.[52] The German Government, however, had been very discreet and loyal to their Ottoman friends and had taken no such initiatives; the newspaper articles were mere speculation. A German warship, the *Arcona*, which visited the Gulf in 1899, did so with utmost discretion and did not call in at Kuwait.

While apprehension at German intentions spread in British circles, the Germans kept cool heads. The difference was that the British were caught up in the web of a secret and rather inconsistent policy, while the Germans had a single aim, to make the railway a reality. The Germans were perfectly aware that there was something between the British and Mubarak, and had sized up the situation from their point of view. They saw the Turks were somewhat unreliable business partners, with no navy in the Gulf capable of confronting the British, while British capital would probably be needed to realize the railway. In that context the Mission sensibly limited its activities to simply exploring the terrain between Basra and Kuwait and establishing friendly relations with Mubarak. They would leave the matter of acquiring land to a much later date when the plans were ready to be implemented. This still left the Germans some scope for a little English-baiting, for instance when Stemrich said to the British consul in Basra that he saw no reason why the Turks should not intervene in their territory of Kuwait to establish a site for the terminus.[53]

In Baghdad, the Mission discussed plans for its Gulf excursion with the

---

[51] Berlin AA, R 13847 165/8, A 14760–14761 (15 December 1899), Marschall and reply by Bülow.
[52] Paris AE, NS Mascate 4, fos. 10–11, embassy Berlin 13 February 1900.
[53] See for instance the letter of Wratislaw to O'Conor of 13 January 1900, in Bidwell, *Affairs of Kuwait*, 1/2, p. 10.

German and French consuls. The discussion was reported by Rouet to his direct superior, the ambassador in Constantinople, but not to his ministry. Richarz reported nothing. The Mission felt it vital to take a look Kuwait, but worried that its prospects might be harmed if Mubarak refused it entry into Kuwait. Neither Richarz nor Rouet considered the support of Ottoman officials to be of any value. Instead Richarz recommended using his friend the Naqib Al-Ashraf, a friend of Mubarak too. Rouet put forward some unnamed weighty religious authority in Baghdad who had helped French archaeologists, but Richarz won and a letter of introduction to the Naqib was written. The Mission also had a letter of introduction to Mubarak written by the Mushir of Baghdad, a logical step in the light of the Ottoman military's conviction of the railway's strategic importance. Rouet gave the Mission recommendations to Shaikh Sa'dun of the Muntafiq, through whose territory the Mission would pass, and to a local Christian, Gabriel Asfar, an important date exporter who acted unofficially as his agent and who was procurator of the Carmelite monastery in Basra. The Mission was to stay in Basra with Asfar, who also had business dealings with Mubarak.

Once the Mission was in Basra they found Hamdi unwilling to help, on the grounds that he had no direct instructions from the Porte to do so. The Mission then decided not to approach the Naqib in order not to irritate Hamdi, the Naqib's declared enemy. Hamdi warned the Mission that going to Kuwait was risky. One wonders why he was so obstructive. It can hardly have been from a desire to be nice to the British, as Rouet suspected, for in that case one would expect a proud report from Wratislaw trumpeting his achievement. It seems to have been nothing more sinister than bureaucratic boneheadedness, and it would cost him his job. A few days after the Mission left Basra for Kuwait Hamdi received a telegram ordering him to await instructions in Beirut. Rouet thought Hamdi had been removed as a result of German complaints, but there is no real evidence for that, though the Germans were quite content with it. Nor do British sources contain anything to suggest suspicious collusion between the British and Hamdi. Stemrich stated in his report on his visit to Kuwait that he did not credit such suspicions, instead ascribing Hamdi's refusal to furnish the Mission with a military escort to his fear that Mubarak might refuse the Ottoman military access to Kuwait territory, and so cause him considerable loss of face. The upshot was that Stemrich and Kapp finally made their way to Kuwait with a guide from Zubair provided by Asfar.[54]

Whether or not Mubarak was aware of these machinations, he exploited the Mission to best effect. He received it most cordially, giving Stemrich and Kapp the impression that they could reach a deal with him regardless of any obstruction by Ottoman bureaucracy in Iraq. According to Kapp's story, as summarized by Rouet, they formed the opinion of Mubarak as "essentially a friend of his own independence who feared British as much as Ottoman domination", and Stemrich's report too depicts his stance similarly. Mubarak was friendly, and at the same time discreetly advertised his British affiliation by letting the Mission see an abundance of British objects in his reception room. The Mission did not want to enter into premature negotiations with him before matters could be arranged on the Ottoman side, so Mubarak did not need to refuse any direct request, and could limit himself to bland assurances of good will. Better still, the Mission saw no reason to visit Basra on their return journey from Kuwait, but went from Zubair direct to Baghdad.[55] It is not clear whether this was at Mubarak's suggestion, but the desert journey would doubtless have met with his approval and support. An interesting side effect was that information about the Mission's visit reached Wratislaw only after much delay; he even thought at first that it had not visited Kuwait at all.[56]

The British were naturally nervous about the Mission, fearing that Mubarak was about to bow to Ottoman pressure. So they sent a warship to warn him. In London they were considering the option of discreetly informing Germany about their relations with Kuwait.[57] The officials in Bushire took more positive action, sending the *Melpomene* to Kuwait with Gaskin on board to talk with Mubarak. Mubarak divulged that he had

[54] French documents: Nantes AD, consulat Bagdad A 47, Rouet to embassy 3 January 1900 and 23 January 1900; *cf.* about Asfar, A 48, Rouet to embassy 21 September 1903; *cf.* Stemrich report in Berlin AA, R 13848 AA 6864, Stemrich 25 May 1900. Richarz reported Hamdi's removal on 23 January because of pressure brought on the Sultan by the Naqib through Ebülhuda (Abu 'l-Huda): Berlin AA, R 13849 A 2668 (1 March 1900), Richarz 23 January. For Wratislaw's view, see Bidwell, *Affairs of Kuwait*, 1/2, pp. 17–18.

[55] Nantes AD, consulat Bagdad A 47, Rouet to Embassy, 7 February 1900 (the quotation is from here; Rouet was informed by Kapp); *cf.* Stemrich's report, Berlin AA, R 13848 A 6864, 25 May 1900.

[56] Bidwell, *Affairs of Kuwait*, 1/2, p. 5, O'Conor to Salisbury 24 January.

[57] Bidwell, *Affairs of Kuwait*, 1/2, p. 4, Salisbury to O'Conor 19 January 1900.

received a letter from the Mushir of Baghdad advising him to be friendly to the Mission, and that he had already been informed through private channels of the German plans. He then promised not to agree to anything without consulting Meade.[58] The commander of the *Melpomene*, however, was unsure of Mubarak's attitude and fearful that "the Shaikh of Kuwait would throw us over at any moment".[59] Gaskin was sent to Kuwait again, this time on the *Lawrence*, arriving on 28 January after the Germans had left, to find out what had happened.[60] Gaskin tried to collect information from various parties. He first quizzed Mubarak's secretary, Abdallah bin Attaj, but this gentleman kept his counsel. He then discreetly asked the residency's "secret news agent" in Kuwait, Haji 'Ali bin Ghulam Ridha, but this worthy was able to vouchsafe nothing except that no agreement had been reached between the Shaikh and the Germans. Mubarak himself was the most forthcoming with information, and this was written down by Gaskin in great detail. There are some discrepancies between Mubarak's account to Gaskin and the reports emanating from the Mission. The essential elements in Gaskin's version are that Mubarak had told the Germans that he recognized the Sultan only as head of the Islamic world, but that Turkey had no authority over Kuwaiti territory; and that the Germans had asked him to use his influence over the tribes to protect the railway, and to sell them the land for it, but that he had politely refused all that, as Arabs do not sell the pastureland of their tribes. This all was appropriately phrased for British consumption. Gaskin also learned that, on their way from Basra to Kuwait, the Germans had taken a good look at the terrain and had decided that Kazima Point, inside the Gulf of Kuwait, would be the best site for the terminus.

Mubarak gave accounts of the Mission in later years too. He told several visitors, such as the French naval commander Kiésel in 1902 and Lord Curzon in 1903, and when negotiating a lease of land to the British in 1906, that Stemrich had put pressure on him to sell land, but that he had staunchly refused. No doubt Mubarak spread this myth in order to

---

[58] Bidwell, *Affairs of Kuwait*, 1/2, p. 12, Denison to Meade 15 January 1900, translation of the letter of the Mushir on p. 13.

[59] Bidwell, *Affairs of Kuwait*, 1/2, p. 14, Denison to Rear-Admiral Bosanquet 27 January 1900.

[60] Bidwell, *Affairs of Kuwait*, 1/2, pp. 19–21, report signed by Meade, but prepared by Gaskin.

demonstrate his close ties to the British and the value of Kuwait, something that for various reasons it suited him to parade in front of these visitors.

There is no sign in the information given by Rouet and Stemrich that there had been any direct reference to the acquisition of land by the railway company; on the contrary, such an overture was regarded as undesirable. Hence on this essential point the reports of the Mission and the accounts given by Mubarak to the British contradict each other. Perhaps the most plausible is that of Stemrich, as he had no reason to colour his account. Like a good solid German, Stemrich opens his report by quoting Carl Ritter's geographical manual *Erdkunde* (published in 1844) on the way in which the rulers of the small Gulf states achieved independence. Stemrich, it seems, was quite impressed by Kuwait, dwelling on the cleanliness of the town and the plentiful ships in the harbour. He nursed no illusions about the extent of Ottoman authority in places such as Kuwait: "In order to maintain their suzerainty they must apply a loose rein and negotiate (*das System von laxieren und pactieren*). This would not matter if it were not for the British exploiting the situation, and if Kuwait was not destined to be the terminus of the Baghdad railway." Stemrich depicts Mubarak as

> a man in his fifties, tall, of proud carriage and intelligent mien. The orderliness of Kuwait shows that Mubarak knows how to rule and he is widely feared by the surrounding Arabs, while he is much respected by the notables who assemble in the evening for sessions in his konak [palace]. He is wealthy, and treats almost all the land around the bay as his private property.

In his palace Mubarak showed off the many gifts he had received from the British, but after his visit there Stemrich placed no credence in the stories circulating in Basra and Baghdad that Mubarak had concluded a treaty with them. He was of the opinion that Mubarak was not in a position to conclude a treaty with a Christian power, because of the strong local opposition it would meet. Stemrich believed Mubarak to be in favour of the railway project. According to him Mubarak was virtually independent ("in practice there is no [Ottoman] Government authority in this district"), but on the other hand he had no doubt that Kuwait formed part of Ottoman territory. During the German visit Mubarak displayed considerable irritation with the Pashas of Basra, but was very loyal to the Sultan in his discourse.[61] It is not hard to see why Mubarak should tease the British by inventing the German request for a concession of land: it would boost British enthusiasm for their relationship with Kuwait.

After this episode the railway plan made little progress, because the not unimportant matter of finance remained unresolved. For Mubarak the affair had been a triumph. To the Ottomans and Germans, his positive attitude stood in stark contrast to Hamdi's obstruction. The Porte had unwittingly done Mubarak a favour by removing Hamdi. And Mubarak had grasped the golden opportunity to show the British that they needed to cultivate their relationship with him if they wanted either to exclude foreign powers, or to control the Kuwait terminus.

5.5 British revelations to the Germans

Mubarak's prospects looked bright, but in the background the ineptitude of British officialdom was sowing the seeds of future crises. On 7 January 1900, the Government of India had suggested to the India Office that, in view of the imminent visit of Stemrich and Kapp, it might be wise to warn the Germans about the British position in Kuwait.[62] This was perhaps not unconnected with some articles on Kuwait in the *Times of India* of 4 and 6 January, it being quite customary for Curzon to use the press to bring pressure to bear on London.[63] Salisbury was strongly against warning the Germans, and no official notification was made. The reason for this was that British foreign policy was under fire from the continental states over the Boer War in South Africa. O'Conor concurred but suggested that Siemens, director of the Deutsche Bank, should be privately informed in vague terms. This appears to have been done.[64] But the India Secretary Hamilton especially continued to feel uneasy, because of his view that the

[61] Stemrich report in Berlin AA, R 13848 A 6864 (part of it is also in the final report about the railway sent by O'Conor to London, see Bidwell, *Affairs of Kuwait*, 1/2, p. 33); Lepsius, *Grosse Politik*, Vol. 17, p. 469, Marschall 1 February 1900: "the project of renting land has *not* been talked about"; the word "not" is underlined in the original report. Rouet's report of 3 January 1900 in Nantes AD, consulat Bagdad, A 47.
[62] Bidwell, *Affairs of Kuwait*, 1/2, p. 2.
[63] Cuttings from *Times of India* sent by German consulate Bushire, in Berlin AA, R 13848 A 34, Bushire 24 January 1900.
[64] Bidwell, *Affairs of Kuwait*, 1/2, p. 4; Plass, *England*, p. 269.

legal basis of the British position in Kuwait was very weak. He was pressing for an official notification of the British position to the Germans and the Turks, but Salisbury opposed this. By the end of March the worst crisis in South Africa had passed, and on 9 April O'Conor approached the Ottoman foreign minister, Tawfiq, with the suitably vague statement that the British Government "did not want to interfere with the Sultan's authority in those parts", but that considering the extent of British interests in the Gulf it would be unacceptable for another power to acquire a foothold in Kuwait, where Britain had "certain agreements" with the Shaikh. According to O'Conor – we shall see below that there exists another version of this encounter – Tawfiq did not react to these vague words and O'Conor did not clarify them. Marschall, the German ambassador in Constantinople, was told informally by O'Conor that, "while Britain did not desire to interfere with the status quo or with the Sultan's authority in these parts", Mubarak might not be free to make any concession without approval of the British Government. The German reacted with polite surprise: how could an Ottoman kaymakam be tied in that way to a foreign power? O'Conor then aggravated the ambiguity of the matter by insisting that the "arrangements" did not change anything in the legal position of Kuwait.[65]

The Germans were guilty of naïveté. They presumed that, since O'Conor had confirmed the status quo and the Sultan's authority, the "arrangements" between Mubarak and the British must be a private matter without consequences for the status of Kuwait in international law. Berlin ordered Marschall not to press O'Conor any further on the subject.

The Turks had their own interpretation of O'Conor's démarche. On the 12th, one day after Marschall had been ordered to let the Kuwait matter rest, Tawfiq gave Marschall an account of his meeting with O'Conor of 9 April. Maybe O'Conor had been untruthful in his report to Salisbury of their meeting, but it is more likely that Tawfiq was embellishing it from his own point of view. According to Tawfiq, O'Conor had asked him to postpone the concession for the last section of the railway to the Gulf, on the grounds that it might lead to local trouble or foreign interference. According to his own account, Tawfiq then declared

---

[65] Bidwell, *Affairs of Kuwait*, 1/2, pp. 22–4, O'Conor 10 April 1900; *cf.* Lepsius, *Grosse Politik*, Vol. 17, p. 470, Marschall 9 April 1900. It is interesting to note that Marschall was prompter in reporting than his British colleague.

1. Shaikh Miz'al, ruler of Muhammara, 1880s. The shaikhs of Muhammara and Kuwait were old friends, and Miz'al had tried in 1895–6 to mediate in the conflict between Mubarak and his brothers.

2. The Konak, the official government building of the Wali of Basra, in the 1890s. This photograph appeared in Max von Oppenheim's *Vom Mittelmeer zum Persischen Golf* (Berlin 1899–1900).

POLITICALLY BLIND OR (UN)INTELLIGENT (NON)ANTICIPATORS.

(As seen by Mr. J-hn M-rl-y, and, possibly, by others.)

CH-MB-RL-N.   S-L-SB-RY.   BR-DR-CK.   B-LF-R.   L-NSD-WNE.

"They drifted along to the edge of the black unfathomable abyss in ignorance of where it was they were drifting to. . . . . It is true, the Government say, that whenever our foresight and our knowledge could be tested we have shown blindness, short-sightedness at all events, and ignorance. It follows from this that, whenever we cannot be tested in the future, you are bound to treat us implicitly and without asking questions."—Mr. J. Morley at Arbroath.

3. "Politically blind." Cartoon in *Punch* in 1900 satirizing several of the London politicians acting in the Mubarak comedy: Salisbury, Broderick, Balfour and Lansdowne. The cartoon itself is not connected with the Kuwait affair.

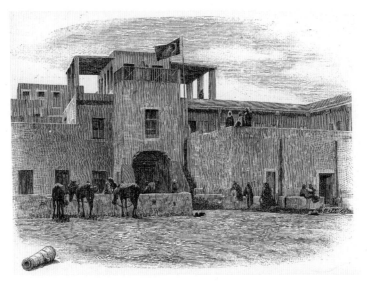

4. Shaikh Mubarak's palace, Kuwait, 1901–2. The officer of the *Catinat* took various pictures in Kuwait. This one of Mubarak's palace was not very distinct, so for publication in the magazine a wood engraving was used.

5. Shaikh Mubarak Al-Sabah, Kuwait, 1901–2. The earliest clear portraits of Mubarak date from the winter of 1901–2. This photograph was taken by an officer of the visiting French warship *Catinat*.

6. The Imam Abdul Rahman bin Faysal Al-Saud at Kuwait, winter 1901–2, by the officer of the *Catinat*.

7. Kuwaitis, winter 1901–2, by the officer of the *Catinat*.

8. Shaikh Mubarak with officers of the Russian warship *Varyag*, December 1901, taken by a Russian naval officer.

9. *Above:* Jabir bin Mubarak Al-Sabah on board the *Varyag*, December 1901, taken by a Russian naval officer.

10. *Left:* The British journalist Henry Whigham visited Kuwait at about the same time as the French ship *Catinat*, in the winter of 1901–2. In his book, *The Persian Problem*, he included this picture of "Mubarak, Sheikh of Kuweit", though the dubious likeness to other portraits of Mubarak, with the exception of the *Catinat* portrait of 1901–2, has caused some to doubt the identification.

BIJVOEGSEL van de Amsterdammer, Weekblad voor Nederland van 12 Januari 1902.

DE SULTAN: Wel thuis John! — Je hebt de vlag moeten strijken, dat doet mij en mijn vriendjes dáár oprecht genoegen!

11. De Koweit-zaak en Engeland ("The Kuwait Affair and England"). By Johan Braakensiek, this appears to be the earliest political cartoon ever made relating to Kuwait. It appeared in the Dutch newspaper *De Amsterdammer* in 1902. Braakensiek however misunderstood the Kuwait situation of the time. Like most continental European observers, he was under the impression that the international brouhaha following the flag incident of December 1901 had resulted in Britain being obliged to relinquish its intention (as manifested by the supposed hoisting of the British flag on Mubarak's palace) to establish a formal protectorate over Kuwait. In reality the British had forced the Turks to retire. The cartoon shows Sultan Abdulhamid and a servant bowing a despondent John Bull out of a Turkish coffee-house, where the German Emperor and the Russian Czar enjoy a smoke and a cup of coffee. The legend to the cartoon represents the Sultan as saying: "Have a nice trip home, John. You had to lower your flag and this will afford genuine pleasure to my friends over there."

12. The German traveller Hermann Burchardt took this portrait of Shaikh Mubarak in his palace during his visit to Kuwait in December 1903. Mubarak's ornate costume shows how much Kuwaiti fashion has changed between then and now.

13. S. G. Knox, first British political agent to Kuwait (1904–9), with his wife.

14. The bazaar in Kuwait. An illustrated article on Kuwait in the *Times of India*'s *Illustrated Weekly* of 16 January 1907 features several photographs by a certain "Aldebaran", as well as this drawing of the Kuwait bazaar by Cecil Burns after one of Aldebaran's images. The right-hand gallery was the coffee-house frequented by Kuwaitis during the afternoon.

15. Shaikh Mubarak's palace, Kuwait. The same article in the *Times of India*'s *Illustrated Weekly* also contains this picture of Mubarak's palace. The caption mentions that the first-floor room with the gallery was the one in which Mubarak gave his official receptions.

16. The British Agency in Kuwait, in the *Times of India's Illustrated Weekly* of 16 January 1907.

17. Shaikh Mubarak standing on the bridge joining the old and new parts of the Sif Palace, Kuwait, photographed by the British naval officer Lt-Cmdr A. N. Gouldsmith, 1907–9.

18. Shaikh Mubarak with his friend Shaikh Khaz'al of Muhammara, photographed by the British naval officer Lt–Cmdr A. N. Gouldsmith, 1907–9.

19. Mubarak's close friend Shaikh Khaz'al of Muhammara. This photograph, of uncertain date, but perhaps *ca.* 1920, appeared in Arnold T. Wilson's *Loyalties, Mesopotamia 1914–1917* (Oxford/London, 1930).

20. Talib Pasha, the mercurial son of the Naqib of Basra and friend of Shaikh Mubarak, was at one time Ottoman governor of al-Hasa and later member of the Ottoman parliament for Basra. This photograph, of uncertain date, but perhaps *ca.* 1920, appeared in Arnold T. Wilson's *Loyalties, Mesopotamia 1914–1917* (Oxford/London, 1930).

that he saw no danger; the Ottomans had a regular kaymakam in Kuwait and foreign interference would be a violation of Ottoman sovereignty; the Sultan could issue orders in Kuwait just as he could in Mosul. O'Conor agreed with this, according to Tawfiq, but said that Britain could not comply with the Turks granting concessions to subjects of third powers in regions where British interests were involved. Tawfiq refused to discuss this because that would be a violation of the sovereign rights of the Sultan. After this – probably heavily falsified – account of his meeting with O'Conor, Tawfiq asserted that he had agreed with the Grand Vizier that they should not inform the Sultan of it, because they considered it a British attempt to fish in murky waters or to obtain some special deal. Marschall observed that O'Conor's attitude was ambivalent: he was offering the Germans an agreement on the railway, but threatening the Turks with legal problems. He passed it off as the British seeking some interesting concession in the region and did no more about it.[66]

The Germans had been too trusting of British "honesty". O'Conor's veiled warning to the Germans and Turks had been more than a little underhand. It might have had embarrassing consequences if the true position of Kuwait had come into the open, but for a year nothing serious happened. At the end of April 1900, it looked for a moment as if the railway affair might gather momentum, when rumours spread from Bahrain that the railway company was preparing to build a pier in Kuwait. Bahraini rumours were often groundless, and this one went the rounds in British circles for a month or two without being confirmed or denied. The worst consequence of this canard was that the British ambassador in Berlin, Sir Frank Lascelles, took it upon himself to intervene in the Kuwait affair. He approached the German chancellor, Bülow, seeking confirmation of the rumour, remarking that the Shaikh of Kuwait "though technically a subject of the Sultan enjoyed a large measure of

[66] Lepsius, *Grosse Politik*, Vol. 17, pp. 470–2, correspondence between Marschall and the German Foreign Ministry 9–12 April 1900.

[67] The German attitude towards the British presence in the Gulf was still often quite relaxed. Metternich, German chargé d'affaires in London, found that Britain had an effective presence in the Gulf while the Turks had a formal claim. He advised negotiations with Britain over the position of Kuwait: Lepsius, *Grosse Politik*, Vol. 17, p. 477 (note).

[68] Bidwell, *Affairs of Kuwait*, 1/2, pp. 31–32. The words used by Lascelles were approved by Salisbury.

independence and had, as Your Lordship [Salisbury] had informed Count Hatzfeldt [the German ambassador in London] entered into special arrangements with His Majesty's Government". Bülow, who had a better memory than Lascelles, corrected the British diplomat by pointing out that the information had been given by O'Conor to Marschall and not by Salisbury to Hatzfeldt, but otherwise denied the rumour.

Much of the problem sprang from British vagueness and carelessness in their terminology, allowing the Germans to labour under a mistaken idea of the British view of the position of Kuwait. This would aggravate the crisis that would come the next year.[67] The rest of the problem stemmed from British unwillingness to be open about their relations with Kuwait. They wanted their agreement with Shaikh Mubarak to be both secret and effective all at once.[68] It could not achieve both aims, and the tension between the two was bound to burst into the open sooner or later.

In the end Mubarak was the only party to profit from this episode. The threat from the Ottomans had receded for the time being, and he had mended his relationship with them. As for the British, by means of a small deceit he had caused them to place greater value on their tie with Kuwait.

6

The Hinterland and Sarif
1900–1901

6.1 The Russian game

Mubarak's goals were simple: independence and prosperity, preferably in some relationship with the Caliph – Mubarak being a good Muslim – or, failing that, with the help of whoever might be to hand. The Ottoman Empire and the European powers had more complex and conflicting goals in their Gulf policy, and each was entangling itself in a web of its own making. This was especially the case with the Turks and the British. We have observed the Ottomans dithering between two courses, either to let Mubarak be or to occupy Kuwait. The first was the cheaper option, but did nothing to quell the decades-old fear that Mubarak might sell himself to the British. The second would add to the burdens of bankrupt Ottoman Iraq and could end in a disastrous conflict if the British turned out to be ready to resort to force. The British were hardly better off. They feared the international opprobrium that would result from such a breach of the Berlin Treaty of 1878, and their overriding reason for entering into direct relations with Kuwait was fear that, unless they did so, a rival European power might establish itself there with the Turks' blessing. So they too wavered, between respect for the territorial integrity of the Ottoman Empire and the establishment of a full protectorate over Kuwait. The outcome was an almost unworkable compromise.

This was a period when most European powers were indulging in grand geopolitical visions. Domination of vast landmasses through railway communications, control of globe-girdling sea routes, all this was the stuff of eager debate, usually conducted over a map notable chiefly for its imprecision and with little knowledge of local circumstances. The British felt entire regions, such as the Gulf and its coasts, to be "areas of particular interest to Britain" from which other Powers should be excluded, but there were no legitimate means of enforcing or maintaining a British monopoly. Other European powers held that the seas were free and that they should make some show of presence in the Gulf to prevent it becoming a de facto British lake. They had some justification for this, as non-British trade interests in the Gulf had grown to considerable importance by the beginning of the 20th century.

The previous chapter recounted the German entry onto the Gulf stage. This had sent a frisson of alarm through the British in India, but the Germans had behaved with the utmost tact. They were focused on economic matters and tended to take the view that provocation of the British was not in their commercial interests. Alarm bells rang none the less in the press, mainly in the *Times of India* – the usual mouthpiece of Curzon's friends and those like them who most feared foreign competition in Asia.[1] French activities too sometimes stirred British anxiety, but these were limited chiefly to Oman, although the French had maintained from of old a minor presence in Iraq. Relations between France and Britain were currently strained, and any French move was watched with distrust in London, provoked by fear that the French might help the Russians acquire a foothold. For decades already Russia had been viewed by the British as the real menace to their position in Asia. It was theoretically possible that the Russians, who were already entrenched in Persia, would be able to establish overland railway links to the Indian Ocean that would be much faster than British communications by sea. Such trepidation was rife in India, especially in Curzon's circle. Meanwhile the Russians were casting around for a coaling station somewhere on the Indian Ocean littoral. The Russian press had been speculating on the possibility of leasing or buying a harbour in the Gulf from the Turks, and Kuwait had been mentioned in this connection. And Russian merchants had been busily buying sheepskins in Kuwait, though this had attracted little public attention.[2]

[1] *Times of India*, 4 and 5 January 1900.
[2] Rezvan, *Russian Ships*, pp. 7–8, indicates that the visit of the two merchants, an Armenian, Ovanessian, and a Russian Muslim, Aliyev, also had a political purpose. See also Berlin AA, R 13846 A 4922 (26 April 1899), Richarz 25 March 1899.

British sources tend to present an oversimplified view of Russian motives. The reality was more complex. There can be no doubt about the general Russian desire to acquire access to the open sea and for southward expansion to the Indian Ocean, but in the Kuwait affair there were other factors too at play. A vital one was the Russian fear of British and German collusion in a joint monopoly of the Gulf: Germany through the Baghdad Railway and Britain through its India connection. The Russians believed the basic thrust of British and German policy to be to block Russian expansion through Persia to the sea, just as the British had earlier blocked Russia's advance through Afghanistan. It is small wonder, then, that the Russians showed an interest in Kuwait. The ambiguous status of that little principality could still be exploited to act as a brake on the railway plans.

Russian views on Kuwait lacked consistency. In 1895–6, fearing a British intervention there, they had urged the Turks to occupy the place. In 1899 their fear was rather that the Germans might settle there with Ottoman blessing, and they now had to act with more subtlety. The policy of the Russian representatives in Bushire and Baghdad appears to have been to acknowledge Mubarak's independence to a certain extent and to encourage him to resist any German advances[3] – a policy completely at odds with the Russian pressure on the Porte to occupy Kuwait militarily. There is no sign that the Russians were aware that their support for the Ottoman occupation of Kuwait might be at all incompatible with their opposition to the Baghdad Railway.[4]

In 1899 the Russians decided to send a warship to the Gulf. A principal purpose of this mission was to show the flag and demonstrate that the Gulf was freely accessible to ships of all nations;[5] otherwise the naval demonstration was to be discreet. This move none the less perturbed the British. The ship assigned to the mission, the gunboat *Gilyak*, was a more modern and imposing vessel than the small British gunboats named after birds such as the *Pigeon,* the *Redbreast* and the *Lapwing,* or the elderly

---

[3] Lepsius, *Grosse Politik,* Vol. 17, pp. 473–4, Richarz 19 April 1900.

[4] For the Russian pressure for the occupation of Kuwait, see Nantes AD, consulat Bagdad B29, Pognon 14 October 1895; and Lepsius, *Grosse Politik,* Vol. 17, pp. 507–9, Marschall in Constantinople 15 and 31 December 1901. Bondarevsky, *Kuwait,* pp. 219 n. 19 and 303 n. 31, refers to parts of the document published in Lepsius, *Grosse Politik,* Vol. 17, pp. 508–9, but does not mention the Russian desire for an Ottoman occupation of Kuwait and thus seems unaware of the inconsistency of the Russian policy.

[5] Rezvan, *Russian Ships,* p. 5.

paddle steamers *Lawrence* and *Sphinx*.[6] The appearance of this warship would show the people of the Gulf that Britain was not the only naval power. The Russian consul-general in Baghdad, Kruglov, was to accompany the *Gilyak* on its Gulf tour.

The *Gilyak* was to call in at Kuwait. For this the Russians, to distinguish themselves from the British, had requested the Porte's permission. This caused a diplomatic hitch because the Sultan, who distrusted Russia, was slow to grant it. It is nowhere explicitly stated what specific purpose was to be served by a Russian visit to Kuwait, but several can be suggested. The first was probably that the Russians felt it desirable to show interest in Kuwait because of the contacts already established through their trade in sheepskins. Perhaps there were vague thoughts too of acquiring Kuwait from the Turks as a coaling station. But the report of the consul Kruglov shows that the Russians wanted more precise intelligence on two matters: the British position in Kuwait, and the German railway plans. British contact with Kuwait had been observed by the Russians from afar, and had been reported in the Russian press.[7] Ironically, they had been unaware that these British moves had been provoked in part by fears of Russian expansion.[8] The French consul, Rouet, plainly stated that the Russian initiative was directed against the Germans.[9] He regarded Kruglov as intending above all to thwart the Baghdad railway scheme because the Russian was afraid of Germany establishing itself in Mesopotamia.[10] As

[6] See Wratislaw, *Consul*, p. 163: "little gunboats of the *Bird* class". The *Sphinx* was "an elderly wooden paddle-ship designed more to afford roomy and airy quarters to officers and crew in the torrid Persian Gulf where she passed her existence than for purposes of offence".

[7] Rezvan, *Russian Ships*, pp. 7–8; Bondarevsky, "Mubarak's Kuwait", pp. 49–50; Berlin AA, R 13847 A14102 (1 December 1899), German ambassador in St. Petersburg 30 November 1899.

[8] The Russians believed the British and the Germans to be conspiring against them: Berlin AA, R 13848 A 3555 (22 March 1900), German embassy in Russia 19 March 1900: the Russian newspaper *Novoye Vremiye* puts forward the view that Britain supported Germany in the Baghdad railway scheme with the intention of causing problems for Russia!

[9] Paris AE, NS Mascate 5, fos. 63–64, Rouet to Ministry 25 March 1900.

[10] It is interesting that the German consul Richarz supposed the Russian mission to be chiefly intended to counteract British plans for a railway from Egypt to the Gulf, which had been intended to frustrate Russian plans for a railway to the Gulf: see Berlin AA, R 13209 A 3587 (22 March 1900), Richarz 20 February 1900.

Rouet was telling Kruglov of the friendly welcome accorded by Mubarak to Stemrich's mission, Kruglov made a telling interruption. As Rouet began a sentence describing how Mubarak had declared himself to be "the loyal subject of ...", Kruglov interjected: "of the German Emperor." One can only speculate whether Kruglov was serious or merely intending to mislead Rouet, but Kruglov's strong dislike of Rouet's support for the railway plans is all too clear. Rouet also gained the impression that Kruglov feared Kuwait becoming a German naval station and coal depot.

Kruglov wrote a detailed report on his Kuwait visit. Having arrived there from Basra on board the *Gilyak*, he stayed on for some time after its departure as Mubarak's guest. Mubarak gave the Russians an unusually splendid and cordial reception. He then grumbled about the British, and denied having any compact with them! This was in direct contradiction of information the Russians had received from Shaikh Khaz'al in Muhammara, that there existed some kind of "conditional agreement" enabling Mubarak to call on British help in emergencies. The Russians had heard similar things in Basra, but in Kuwait Mubarak's associates denied such stories. Kruglov was not convinced. He suspected Mubarak of deceiving him about his past relations with the British in order to improve his relations with the Turks after the appointment of the friendly Muhsin Pasha. Muhsin Pasha had waxed most eloquent to Kruglov in praise of Mubarak. It appears that Muhsin and the Naqib, no doubt with Abu 'l-Huda in the background, had great plans for the Kuwaiti ruler. Kruglov's report mentions sweeping plans to establish Ottoman control over Muscat, Bahrain, Qatar and the Trucial Coast in co-operation with Mubarak. The Turks may have hoped that such dreams might cause Mubarak to forget Kuwait.[11] Such speculations recall Midhat Pasha's wilder ideas and must have been close to Abdulhamid's heart. They were not as extravagant as at first sight they might appear, for Mubarak had assisted the Turks in establishing themselves in Arabia in the past, as he would later in circumstances where the Turks posed no threat to his independence. It may very well be that the Porte's reluctance to deal decisively with Mubarak was inspired in part by the idea that he could be useful, as indeed he was to be in the desert negotiations of 1904.

Mubarak expatiated at length to Kruglov on the services he had rendered the Ottoman Government. He duly abstained from letting the

[11] Moscow AVPR, Section Constantinople Embassy 1264, fos. 74–86.

Russians know of his ties with Britain, but, in the vaguest terms, suggested that he might be willing to accept Russian protection if offered.[12] This ploy should not be taken too seriously. The idea of foreign protection was openly bandied about. During his lifetime Mubarak had toyed with the idea of British, Russian, French and Persian protection. By talking in this way to Kruglov, his main aim must have been to deceive those Ottoman officials who still believed him to be in treaty relations with the British, and at the same time to show the British that, if they failed in their commitment to him, he always had their rivals to fall back upon. That was why, with British officials, he drew a tantalizing veil of mystery over his Russian dealings. Nor from the Russian side was this a very serious proposition. The Russians were unable to give substance to a direct relationship with Kuwait without treading on Ottoman toes. And to do so would sit very oddly with the Russian ambassador's advice to the Turks, the previous year, to mount a military occupation of Kuwait.

In his report Kruglov also recorded the deep disfavour with which Mubarak viewed the German railway plan. This was confirmed to him by Mubarak's secretary, Sayyid Mahmud. Given the situation, of the Porte's support for the railway scheme, Kruglov could be expected to be happy at the measure of independence shown by Kuwait. He remarked that Ottoman authority was manifest only in the form of an Ottoman flag and the presence of an officer of the Sanitary Board. Kruglov was clearly unaware of the somewhat special international status of the quarantine officials.[13]

The visit of Kruglov and the *Gilyak* should be assessed in the framework of the vague fears that Russia might establish a presence of some sort in Kuwait with the blessing of both Mubarak and the Turks, and also in the context of nebulous Russian railway plans. There was little reality or consistency in Russian policy. At the local level it created an anomalous situation, whereby Russian designs on Kuwait were vaguely aired, just when the Russian embassy in Constantinople had been urging a military occupation of Kuwait on the Turks. The truth was that the Russians never had the slightest intention of entering the Gulf arena except in friendly

[12] According to Bondarevsky, "Russian and German Policy", p. 50, Mubarak told Kruglov: "I want you to know that if I sell out to anyone, I would sooner sell to mighty Russia than to Britain; I don't trust Britain."
[13] Moscow AVPR, Section Constantinople Embassy 1264, fos. 74–86.

co-operation with the Ottomans. This policy was not formulated in a spirit of hostility towards Mubarak, for the Russians (like other continental Europeans) were coming round to the view that he was a kind of autonomous chief of part of the Ottoman Empire, and had been forced only by misguided Ottoman officials and British pressure into relations with the latter. This was, in turn, a view that went unchallenged by Mubarak, who in this way contrived to keep all his options open.

Kruglov was tight-lipped about his meeting with Mubarak. This provoked distrust among the British, and the French consul in Baghdad too complained of his Russian ally's taciturnity on the subject. When pressed by Rouet, Kruglov opined that Mubarak was a "mediocre" man, but Rouet did not believe him. The German mission had told a quite different story and Rouet suspected that Kruglov was disappointed because this "kinglet" (the French word used was *roitelet*) was not as hostile to the German railway plans as Kruglov had hoped.[14] In this Rouet was probably mistaken. Mubarak certainly had no reason to favour the railway, while Kruglov, who also opposed it, had good reasons to withhold Mubarak's view from Rouet who was much too intimate with the German planners. Disbelief of his Russian colleague aroused Rouet's curiosity about the true Mubarak. A few months later, when a French warship called in at Kuwait, Rouet wanted to go there too "to study this interesting personality and to establish his opinion of the future railway".[15]

Rouet was not the only official to inform his foreign ministry in Paris about Kuwait and the Russian initiatives there. Reports came from the French consulate in Muscat too. Here the French consul had had a meeting with one Syromiatnikov, a Russian sent to the Gulf in the summer of 1900 by the Russian minister Witte to explore commercial possibilities. This Russian was more forthcoming to the French about his impression of Mubarak. Syromiatnikov was "quite satisfied with his dealings with the Shaikh of Kuwait and the Shaikh of Muhammara who, with good reason, he considers to be very important personalities, and to whom he has given rich presents."[16]

[14] Paris AE, NS Mascate 5, fo. 71, Rouet 12 April 1900.
[15] Nantes AD, ambassade Constantinople E 288, Rouet 7 June 1900; and Nantes AD, consulat Bagdad B 29, Rouet 12 April 1900.
[16] Paris AE, NS Mascate 5, fos. 105–106, Ottavi 29 September 1900.

Some interesting additional light on the Russian mission to Kuwait and its aims was shed by the German consul, Richarz. Richarz was convinced that the mission was "not intended to stimulate Mubarak in his submission to the Ottoman Empire" and, furthermore, was intended to harm the Baghdad Railway project. According to Richarz, who obtained his information from Ottoman officials in Baghdad, Mubarak was very discreet in his dealings with the Russians and kept his distance from them. This latter remark may be wishful thinking, but there is some truth in it too, for Kruglov's report proves that Mubarak was less than sincere to him in describing his relations with the British.

6.2 Relations with the Ottomans

Meanwhile the Ottomans were trying, amidst this web of international intrigue, to regain some measure of control over Kuwait. The replacement of Hamdi Pasha as Wali of Basra by the less aggressive Muhsin Pasha was not done in a spirit of friendship to Mubarak, for whom it was only partial compensation for the earlier loss of Recep Pasha, who himself had previously been replaced as Mushir of Baghdad by a person hostile to the Kuwaiti ruler.[17] At the end of April 1900, the German ambassador in Constantinople rightly pointed out that Muhsin's chief task was to bring Mubarak back into the Ottoman fold, and recorded the Porte's impatience with his lack of progress.[18] Muhsin was a cultivated and sociable character, but not one given to the use of force. He spoke French well and was on good terms with most of the foreign consuls in Baghdad, two of whom went to the trouble of obtaining French and Russian decorations for him.[19] Foreign observers tended to approve of him. Even Wratislaw seems to have liked him, writing warmly in his memoirs: "He was quite a superior man, well educated and a good soldier. We were always on cordial

[17] Paris AE, NS Mascate 4, fos. 55–56v, Rouet 19 April 1899. Recep had been notified of his replacement in July 1898, but he was still there at the time of the Stemrich mission: Berlin AA, R 13207 A 8904 (31 July 1898), Consulate Baghdad to Berlin 6 July 1898.
[18] Berlin AA, R 13848 A 5070 (23 April 1900), Ambassador Marschall in Pera 20 April 1900.
[19] Berlin AA, R 13848 A 12513 (7 September 1900), Richarz in Baghdad 9 August 1900. French decoration: Nantes AD, consulat Bagdad A 48, Rouet 1 December 1900.

terms and the Pasha was not averse to mixing to some extent in the social life of the British."[20] None of this, however, served to resolve the Porte's problems in Basra province.

Muhsin Pasha seems to have been caught up in a game that was rather too complex for him. On one side there was the Naqib, and behind the Naqib there was Abdulhamid's adviser Abu 'l-Huda, both of them pressing for Mubarak to be a loyal Ottoman dignitary; while on the other was Mubarak with his artful manoeuvrings in the desert and with foreign powers. The Shaikh kept Muhsin supplied with sweeteners and was always ready to pander to him with fulsome declarations of friendship for the Sultan, all the while attending to his own agenda. Those Turks who deemed themselves smarter than Mubarak simply failed to grasp how consummate a politician he was. In the upper echelons of Ottoman government there existed the mistaken view (instilled by Hamdi Pasha) that Mubarak was an ignorant boor and thus vulnerable to cunning foreign intrigues.[21] The Porte lived in hopes that if it treated him nicely Mubarak would be loyal.

Almost instantly on Muhsin's appointment in January 1900, the Naqib went to Kuwait to implement a previous decision by the Ottoman Government, of 17 April 1899, to bring Mubarak to heel by demanding his submission in writing against the promise of favours and presents.[22] The Naqib was also to warn Mubarak against foreigners. Mubarak immediately gave the desired statement of loyalty and requested the resumption of an old stipend received by his brother Muhammad. The Porte was duly duped. Mubarak was promoted to the rank of Mirmiran (a civil rank equivalent to the military one of brigadier), awarded the Mecidiye order

[20] Wratislaw, *Consul*, p. 146.
[21] Hamdi quoted by Anscombe, *Ottoman Gulf*, p. 115: Istanbul BA, Y–A Resmi 104/3. The Turkish term used was *gayet cahil*; *cahil* in Ottoman Turkish means inexperienced, as well as dumb, illiterate, ignorant. One leaves it to the reader to select a meaning or a combination of meanings. Kruglov too told Rouet that Mubarak was "a mediocre man", but that may have been an attempt to deceive his French colleague (who, however, was not deceived, recalling the words of Stemrich and von Kapp after their visit to Kuwait: Nantes AD, consulat Bagdad B 29, Rouet 12 April 1900).
[22] On the removal of Hamdi in January 1900: Berlin AA, R 13848 A2668 (1 March 1900), Richarz 23 January 1900. The sending of the Naqib by Muhsin is mentioned in a letter of the French consul in Muscat: Paris AE, NS Mascate 5, fo. 22, Ottavi 24 February 1900.

and promised a stipend of 108 tons of dates per annum.[23] He had now mended his fences with the Turks and under these circumstances it is no wonder that he wanted to keep the British a little more at arm's length. So the Shaikh cancelled his earlier permission for a British shipping line to include Kuwait in its schedule.[24] The British were not really angry: they thought life would be easier for them were Mubarak to enjoy better relations with the Turks.

6.3 Impending conflict in the desert

Mubarak had the promise of British protection at his back and, next door, a friendly Ottoman wali, so he was now in a position to seek a solution to another pressing problem. This was the hostility on the desert side from the Al-Rashid rulers of Haïl in Jabal Shammar. The chief of the Al-Rashid dynasty, usually referred to as "Bin Rashid" or "the Amir" in contemporary sources, claimed supremacy of a sort over all the Arabs within a sphere of influence that had been expanding for decades. His position in relation to the Ottoman Empire was ambiguous, as described with tolerable accuracy by the Austrian consul in Baghdad: "Neither the Ottoman Government nor the Amir find it convenient to ask the delicate question whether the latter is a vassal of the Sultan or an independent ruler." The only hint was that the Turks did not use the term Amir, but simply the general title of Shaikh.[25]

Kuwait's desert border was its most vulnerable side. Traditionally it was protected by a screen of allied nomadic tribes, who were now coming under pressure from the expansionist policies of the Amir. It is often stated that the conflict between Kuwait and the Al-Rashid was provoked by Mubarak, but one reference indicates an earlier one between the Amir and Kuwait in 1895, and thus during the rule of Mubarak's predecessor, Muhammad.[26] The contemporary German scholar and diplomat Max von Oppenheim also stated, in more general terms, that the Al-Sabah grew

[23] Anscombe, *Ottoman Gulf*, p. 116. In order to improve the atmosphere, Mubarak had built a mosque devoted to the Sultan – a nice gesture which did not imply any real or formal subordination: Istanbul BA, DUIT 69, 3–5, in the same file as the documents on Mubarak's reward.

[24] Bidwell, *Affairs of Kuwait*, 1/2, pp. 44–5, Shipley in Basra 18 August 1900; Plass, *England*, p. 273.

[25] Vienna HHSA, PA XXXVII K 318 (Bagdad 1901), Rappaport 26 March 1901.

envious of the Amir Muhammad Ibn Rashid when the latter began to extend his influence all over Arabia.[26] Anscombe states that, after Mubarak's accession, Muhammad Ibn Rashid granted sanctuary to his nephews, a decidedly unfriendly gesture, but he cites no source for this assertion, and other sources place the arrival of Mubarak's nephews in Hail at a much later date. It appears in any event that there were no new hostilities of any kind before Muhammad Ibn Rashid's sudden death in 1897.[28] His successor, Abdul Aziz, was regarded at the time as an impetuous if not foolhardy military adventurer, unlike his more politically astute uncle. And indeed his chief characteristic was his ambition to maintain and aggrandize his position as Amir by military means. This made him more of a menace, not only to Mubarak, but also to the stability of the largely nominal Ottoman authority in the region.[29] Plass ascribes two further causes to the conflict: a partly political one – as long as Mubarak was in control in Kuwait, the Amir would not have a source of supply of arms outside Ottoman control; and a partly territorial one – a dispute over the Hafar wells, claimed by Kuwait but close

[26] Plass, *England*, p. 272; Gehrke p. 252, quoting Musil, *Northern Negd*, p. 244.

[27] The German Orientalist Max von Oppenheim (who had observed events from Cairo) wrote, in the summer of 1901, a detailed historical account of the conflict between the Amir, the Saudis and Mubarak in a series of letters to the German foreign ministry, which together constitute an unpublished book. Much of the information in the letters came from a member of an Arab merchant family, Muhammad Bassam, in Damascus. The Al-Bassam were established in several places in the Middle East as well as in Bombay. They were of the party of the Amir. These letters are kept in Berlin AA, R 14558. For the remark about the Al-Sabah attitude towards the expansion of Muhammad Ibn Rashid's power "during the last decades", see letter A11184 (31 July 1901), written in Paris, 17 July 1901.

[28] That Muhammad Ibn Rashid received Mubarak's nephews is stated by Anscombe, *Ottoman Gulf*, p. 117. Plass, *England*, p. 271, states, quoting Dickson (allegedly *Kuwait and Her Neighbours*, p. 136), that the nephews came to the Amir with Yusuf Al-Ibrahim after the failed attack on Kuwait of 1897, which might also be just before Muhammad Ibn Rashid's death in 1897. This reference, however, cannot be found in that place in Dickson. From British sources it appears that Yusuf Al-Ibrahim and the nephews appeared in Hail in about May 1900: IOLR, R/15/1/473 86(124), Report from news agent 17 August 1900, that on 5 June the news reached Kuwait that the nephews and Yusuf had come to Ibn Rashid.

[29] Musil, *Northern Negd*, p. 244; Berlin AA, R 14556 A 12909 (28 September 1899), Oppenheim in Damascus 28 September 1899; and ibid., R 14558 A 11183 (31 July 1901), Oppenheim in Paris 17 July 1901, referring to the contrast in style with Muhammad and conflicts with tribes.

to the summer pastures of the Shammar.[30]

In her biography of Mubarak, Salwa Al-Ghanim puts forward the view that the conflict between him and the Shammar ruler was caused by Mubarak's megalomaniac desire to supplant the Al-Rashid as supreme leader of the Arabs. It cannot be denied that Mubarak was opposed to the Amir's position as chief regional power, but he had sound reasons for such antagonism and he was certainly not the only one to hold such a view. The maximal view of Mubarak's ambitions is given by Wratislaw, who at most asserts Mubarak's desire to challenge the Amir's supremacy among the tribes – a comment Wratislaw made only at a very late stage in the conflict.[31] Nor was Mubarak's challenge a solo venture, as it took place in co-operation with other prominent tribal leaders in the region, all of them with serious reasons to oppose the Amir.

The British woke up to the conflict rather belatedly, but non-British sources mention skirmishes between the Amir and Mubarak having taken place as early as 1898. An article in the leading German newspaper, *Köllnische Zeitung*, of 20 January 1900, sheds interesting light on the desert situation at that time, for which British sources are still extremely scanty. The article, from a correspondent in Bahrain, describes the parlous predicament of Abdul Aziz Ibn Rashid. His uncle, the Amir Muhammad, had subdued many tribes, but now the Mutayr and Qahtan had loosened their ties while the 'Utayba and 'Ajman had come out openly against Rashidi rule. The Ottoman Sultan was apprehensive about Rashidi political ambitions, seeing a potential Arab nation-state as a threat to the Caliphate, because most Arabs were sympathetic to the view that only an Arab should be Caliph. According to the *Köllnische Zeitung*, the Sultan came up with a devious means of containing the Amir: Abdul Rahman bin Faysal Al-Saud, chief of the ruling dynasty of Najd which had been ousted from Riyadh by the Al-Rashid, was living as an exile in Constantinople, and was now sent with a suspiciously fat pension to live nearer to his homeland, in Kuwait. It is not easy to verify the latter statement because the sources contradict each other over the size of the pension.[32] The paper goes on to remark that Kuwait had become the focus of all those working for the downfall of the Amir of Haïl, and that already in the summer of 1898 the Mutayr and Dhafir tribes, together with Kuwaiti forces and Saudi exiles, had attacked Shammar forces

[30] Plass, *England*, p. 272.
[31] Bidwell, *Affairs of Kuwait*, 1/2, pp. 66–8, Wratislaw 22 November 1900.

near the Lina wells and seized much plunder. The Amir had reacted by sending an envoy to the Sultan, paying over a large sum of money and promising obedience to him. According to the article, the Sultan now ordered Abdul Rahman to lie low or forfeit his pension, and by way of a threat reminded Mubarak that his fratricide had not been forgotten. These measures were effective and peace was restored for a while.[33]

The British were not entirely ignorant of the hostilities between Mubarak and the Amir. As early as April 1899, Wratislaw had listed Mubarak's principal adversaries as Qasim Al-Thani and Yusuf Al-Ibrahim, as well as Abdul Aziz Ibn Rashid. The resident, Meade, forwarded this letter to India with the remark that the three enemies might have been spurred on by the Turks, who had adopted a more aggressive stance since Hamdi's re-appointment as Basra Wali, to attack Mubarak. A few days later there was a rumour that the Turks were urging the Amir to attack Mubarak in order to contrive an occasion for intervention.[34] The French, however, offered a completely different perspective on the situation. According to Rouet, the Turks were not free to attack Kuwait, their hands being full with a conflict with the Amir, who was in Samawa claiming a huge sum of money.[35] Samawa is close to Muntafiq territory, and this move by the Amir may have pushed Sa'dun, leader of the Muntafiq, into seeking an alliance with the Amir's other enemies.[36]

[32] 90 Ottoman Lira (Turkish pounds) per month according to Plass, *England*, p. 271 n. 5. This amounts to *ca.* 80 pounds sterling, which in the Ottoman Empire was a very large subsidy. However, the news agent of the British in Kuwait puts the amount at 40 Turkish pounds (36 pounds sterling), with a small additional subsidy by Mubarak: IOLR, R/15/1/473, 119(62), news agent in Kuwait, 17 August 1900.

[33] *Köllnische Zeitung* 20 January 1900, cutting in Berlin AA, R 13847 A 238 (20 January 1900).

[34] Bidwell, *Affairs of Kuwait*, 1/1, p. 61, Wratislaw 22 April 1899; ibid. p. 69, Meade 7 May 1899; Plass, *England*, p. 271.

[35] Paris AE, NS Mascate 4, fo. 56, Rouet 19 April 1899.

[36] Berlin AA, Türkei 13846 A 3680 (29 March 1899), telegram Embassy Pera 29 March 1899. The Muntafiq had played a prominent part in the history of Ottoman Iraq since the 17th century, conquering Basra several times. Midhat Pasha had tried to defuse the threat by settling part of this nomadic tribal federation. From then on, there existed an Ottoman-controlled settled part concentrated around Nasiriyya, and a nomadic part that remained troublesome to the Ottomans. Sa'dun was the chief of this nomadic part. On Sa'dun, see also Berlin AA, R 13883 A325 (6 January 1901), Richarz in Baghdad 1 December 1900; and Vienna HHSA, PA XXXVII K 318 (Bagdad 1901), Rappaport 26 March 1901.

Rouet was right in supposing the Turks to be evenly balanced between Mubarak and the Amir. They did not trust either ruler, and so the most attractive policy option for the weak Ottoman authority in the region was to foster conflict between them. If the Amir were to triumph completely over his enemies he would become too powerful to control. However, it would also be deleterious to Ottoman control of Iraq for a great conflict to flare up between tribal leaders who were officially seen as Ottoman subjects. So the Turks were in favour of a limited, low-level conflict, with no clear victor. They were aware of the risk factor in such tribal rivalries – possible intervention by foreign powers. They had a real fear of the British in this respect, but probably knew nothing of the more outlandish attempts by tribal leaders to acquire foreign protection of their interests. As we have seen, Mubarak had created a Russian option, while Abdul Rahman Al-Saud had recently sought French protection through a French merchant in Bahrain.[37]

Mubarak was reluctant to involve the British in his desert policy, and the British did not examine the Shaikh's activities too closely. Reports came from the local merchant who acted as British "news agent" in Kuwait, but there is no sign of any reaction from the new resident, Kemball, who appears to have been a less energetic character than his more proactive predecessor, Meade. Mubarak's reception, in April 1900, of members of the former ruling family of Burayda in Qasim, who had escaped from Ibn Rashid's prison, should have triggered some alarm in Bushire.[38] Now not only were there the Saudis in Kuwait, but even more implacable enemies of the Amir too. On the other side, the Amir posed a threat to Mubarak by his support for Yusuf Al-Ibrahim and Mubarak's nephews. As we saw above (note 27), it is unclear exactly when the nephews had taken refuge with Ibn Rashid.[39] The first really firm evidence of a direct Rashidi/Al-Ibrahim coalition as a threat to Mubarak is in

[37] Paris AE, NS Mascate 5, fo. 48, Goguyer in Bahrain to consul Ottavi in Muscat 10 October 1899.

[38] IOLR, R/15/1/473, 4(6), report from news agent in Kuwait, 11 April 1900, translated on 1 May 1900.

[39] German sources seem to confirm that contacts may have taken place in the Autumn of 1897, thus just after Muhammad Ibn Rashid's death, for at the beginning of November it is mentioned that Yusuf was in Bahrain: Berlin AA, R 13206 A 14169 (4 December 1897), Richarz in Baghdad 8 November 1897. In Bahrain contacts with Ibn Rashid's agents would be easy.

Stemrich's report on his visit to Kuwait of January 1900.[40] This is confirmed by an Ottoman document of September 1900, describing the Amir's pressure on the Ottoman authorities to support the claims of Yusuf Al-Ibrahim and the nephews against Mubarak.[41]

It is also remarkable that the British took virtually no action against the rapidly escalating arms trade in Kuwait, despite the ink of Mubarak's promise to put a stop to it, of 24 May 1900, being barely dry.[42] In June or July of 1900 Mubarak penned some critical words about the Amir's character and policy to the resident in Bushire, but there was still no hint in his letters of preparations for a conflict.[43] The British wanted Mubarak to "be quiet and keep out of trouble", but Mubarak was unable to remain inactive while the Amir, in his role as protector of Yusuf Al-Ibrahim and the nephews, was becoming a direct menace to Kuwait's stability.

By the late summer of 1900, both sides were preparing for war.[44] Historiography based on British sources tends to present the Mubarak/Ibn Rashid conflict of 1900–1 too much as an isolated incident. In reality it formed part of the general process of disintegration of the Shammar Amirate under the rule of Abdul Aziz Ibn Rashid. The latter's haughtiness in his dealings with tribal leaders, to whom he displayed a conspicuous lack of generosity, was bound to offend bedouin chiefs. He appears also to have laid heavy financial burdens on subordinate tribes. All this may have kindled an opposition movement within the Al-Rashid confederation. In

---

[40] "Ibrahim Jussuf is a friend of Bin Rashid. From Bombay he has communicated with the powerful Shaikh of Najd to incite him to move against the Shaikh of Kuwait. It is said that Bin Rashid has attacked and plundered people of Mubarak last year and has killed several of them. Mubarak was unable to take revenge and looks to be intent on not getting in touch with Bin Rashid." Berlin AA, Türkei 13846 A6864 (2 June 1900), report by Stemrich 25 May 1900.

[41] Anscombe, *Ottoman Gulf*, pp. 117 and 226 n. 27, quoting a letter of the Grand Vizier of 27 September 1900.

[42] Copy of Mubarak's promise to suppress arms trade: IOLR, R/15/5/59, fo. 103.

[43] IOLR, R/15/1/473, fo. 50(70). On a small piece of paper enclosed in an undated letter translated on 20 July 1900, Mubarak describes Abdul Aziz Ibn Rashid as young, impetuous and imprudent, just as the German sources of the time did. It is doubtful whether Salwa Al-Ghanim is justified in seeing these critical words of Mubarak as heralding the great conflict to come (Al-Ghanim, *Mubarak*, pp. 84–5), if one considers them in the light of the newspaper article quoted above, Musil *Northern Negd*, pp. 244–5, and Anscombe, *Ottoman Gulf*, p. 117.

[44] Anscombe, *Ottoman Gulf*, p. 118.

areas conquered relatively recently by the Amir Muhammad, such as Qasim, considerable unrest broke the surface. Such disturbances may have given opponents like Mubarak, the Saudis and Sa'dun the idea that the time was ripe to ensure that they would not fall victim to the expansion of Shammar power. Among the Amir's adversaries Mubarak wielded the most prestige: the Saudis were exiles, and Sa'dun's reputation rather low.

Muhsin Pasha was averse to a regional conflict that would only undermine his mission to bring Mubarak back into the Ottoman fold. Mubarak indulged Muhsin with a not entirely convincing show of allegiance.[45] Nor did the British look with favour on a war involving Kuwait, though it took some time for the full implications of the rising desert tension to really register in Bushire. British concern over trouble brewing in the desert got off to a rather feeble start in July with warnings, from the consulate in Basra to O'Conor in Constantinople, that Mubarak was amassing arms. Then the news agent in Kuwait reported that the Amir was urging the Ottoman Government to support the cause of Mubarak's nephews and Yusuf Al-Ibrahim. This report was dated 17 August 1900, and on 3 September Kemball asked the British consulate in Basra to verify the news. The acting consul Shipley replied on the 12th that there had indeed been pressure on the Porte on the part of the Amir. In September 1900, Gaskin reported a rumour from Bahrain that Abdul Rahman Al-Saud had initiated operations against the Amir and had written to Mubarak appealing for help.[46] At the beginning of October both the Kuwait news agent and Shipley in Basra informed Kemball that the Amir was in hot pursuit of Saudi adherents who were retiring on Kuwait after a successful raid against the Amir's subjects. Shipley also passed on the news that the Porte had appointed a special committee to settle the dispute between

[45] Al-Qasimi, *Bayan al-Kuwayt*, p. 378, reproduces in facsimile a letter from Mubarak to Muhsin about his building of a mosque dedicated to the Caliph (omitting Sultan Abdulhamid's other more substantial titles) and by way of concession to Ottoman sensibilities signing it as Kaymakam of Kuwait, but with the more equivocal heading Kaymakam of Kuwait and Chief of its Tribes. This may appear something of a concession in comparison with Mubarak's customary way of styling himself: Hakim [Ruler] of Kuwait and Chief of its Tribes. However, to limit the Ottoman Sultan to "Caliph" and adapt his own extended title was not an entirely effective way of allaying Ottoman suspicions.

[46] IOLR, R/15/1/473, fo. 130(90), Gaskin to Bushire 9 September 1900; and ibid. fo. 133(92), news agent in Kuwait to Gaskin 4 September 1900.

Mubarak and the Amir. This news was sufficiently alarming for Kemball to send a telegram to India.[47] Curzon reacted quite strongly, proposing in a telegram to London that Kemball should be sent to Kuwait to appraise the situation on the ground and to warn Mubarak "to avoid giving the Turks an excuse for interference".[48] At the same time, the Foreign Office in London had been warned by the embassy in Constantinople about the Saudi operations, news that reached Salisbury on 3 October 1900.[49] The matter still seemed to lack urgency, but on the 14th the India Office approved Kemball's mission to Kuwait.[50] By that time clear alarm signals had sounded: Gaskin had reported on 12 October that an alliance had been concluded between the Saudis, the Muntafiq and Mubarak, and that Mubarak had issued the call-to-arms to his men.[51] In the midst of this confusion Muhsin Pasha was still trying to play things down, informing Shipley that Mubarak had shown "much prudence" and that the Amir was returning home.[52]

Clearly the British authorities had still to grasp the true scale and significance of these developments. They felt greater concern about a somewhat curious naval visit by the French warship *Drôme* to Kuwait. The *Drôme* was an elderly wooden supply ship, but its commander was a person of considerable prominence, diplomatic knowledge and ability. There was little in the event to engender British consternation. Mubarak did not meet the French commander, excusing himself by saying that he was in the desert preparing for war "because he was threatened by an attack of Abdul Aziz Ibn Rashid". If the British had been aware of this excuse they would have been less delighted by the French failure to meet Mubarak. Instead the French were cordially received by Jabir, Mubarak's eldest son.

---

[47] IOLR, R/15/1/473, fos. 156–159(107–109), news agent 2 October 1900; Shipley 5 October 1900; and Kemball 5 October 1900.

[48] Bidwell, *Affairs of Kuwait*, 1/2, p. 46, Government of India to India Secretary Hamilton, 8 October 1900.

[49] Bidwell, *Affairs of Kuwait*, 1/2, p. 45: it is about a raid of "Faysal" (*cf.* ibid. p. 47*: Abdul Rahman bin Faysal) in territory of the Amir.

[50] Bidwell, *Affairs of Kuwait*, 1/2, p. 47. The order reached Kemball on 16 October: 175/176(120).

[51] IOLR, R/15/1/473, fo. 171(117), Gaskin to Bushire 7 October 1900 (news from Kuwait of 2 October).

[52] Bidwell, *Affairs of Kuwait*, 1/2, p. 47, telegram of Bunsen in Constantinople to Salisbury 17 October 1900.

The visitors were charmed by Kuwait's neatness, order and prosperity, and by the respect shown by the inhabitants to the ruling family, but they also observed how they were deliberately kept from contact with the local population. Rouet, the French consul, who had travelled down from Baghdad to meet the *Drôme*, opined that the people of Kuwait feared contact with Europeans and "see in their isolation the best protection of their independence". He had planned to sound Mubarak out about his views on the Baghdad Railway, but thought it unwise to press Jabir for his views on it.[53]

It was only once the *Drôme* had departed on 16 October that the British became really alarmed. The Amir's activities gave good reason for this. Having pursued the Saudi raiders to Kuwait, the Amir marched with a considerable force into the Muntafiq lands on the Euphrates and demanded that Muhsin Pasha should expel Sa'dun from Ottoman territory. Sa'dun had participated in the recent Saudi raids, so there was just cause for the demand and Muhsin sent troops against him. The Muntafiq leader took refuge in flight.[54] The Amir was not satisfied, and also reiterated claims for justice on behalf of Mubarak's nephews. Wratislaw reported on 13 November that "a disturbance of the peace is considered possible". Less restrained was a report of the commander of the British gunboat *Redbreast*, on station in Basra, that the Amir claimed full satisfaction for the nephews from the Ottoman Government, without which he would mount an assault on Kuwait. In these circumstances the India Office saw reason to warn the Foreign Office that "in the event of the Amir of Najd threatening Kuwait Her Majesty's Government are bound [...] to extend their good offices to the Sheikh".[55] This admonition could not have come at a worse moment. Salisbury had just been replaced as Foreign Secretary by Lansdowne, who did not share Salisbury's sublime insouciance for what others might think of British imperial policy.

---

[53] French report in Nantes AD, ambassade Constantinople E 288, Rouet 8 November 1900; see British report Bidwell, *Affairs of Kuwait*, 1/2, p. 59. The reception by Jabir had been quite friendly, and Jabir had offered Rouet Mubarak's private yacht for the voyage back to Basra: Paris AE, NS Mascate 8, fo. 85.

[54] Bidwell, *Affairs of Kuwait*, 1/2, p. 60, Shipley to embassy in Constantinople 31 October 1900.

[55] Bidwell, *Affairs of Kuwait*, 1/2, pp. 54–5, Wratislaw 13 November 1900; ibid. p. 49, Commander-in-Chief East Indies to Admiralty 10 November; and India Office to Foreign Office 24 November 1900.

Lansdowne was profoundly unhappy when he perceived the mire into which British policy had slipped over Kuwait, and his reaction to the problem was entirely uncreative. He grumbled and protested his inability to do anything but stumble on along the treacherous path down which events, injudicious British officials and, not least, Mubarak, had led him.

London's instinct was to adopt a low-key approach, by increasing the naval presence in the Gulf and issuing discreet warnings to the Amir. But policy was overtaken by events. On 19 November 1900, Lansdowne was informed by the embassy in Constantinople of news from the Basra consulate, to the effect that the Amir was pursuing Mubarak's ally Sa'dun, who had conducted a raid on Najd, and that the Amir would desist from attacking Kuwait only if justice were done to Mubarak's nephews, and if the Amir were recognized as having authority over Kuwait.[56] Then suddenly the tension seemed to die down. The British consul in Basra reported that large Ottoman troop reinforcements had reached the region, under orders to intervene between the two adversaries. Muhsin Pasha claimed to Wratislaw that the Amir had promised to retire and that he, Muhsin, intended to force Mubarak to retire too.[57] It was a rather belated Kemball who then finally made his planned visit to Kuwait. He was unable to obtain a clear picture of the situation because Mubarak was still in the desert, but it soon transpired that the crisis was over and both parties were returning home.

Mubarak returned from the desert to Kuwait via Zubair, where he met Muhsin Pasha.[58] He accompanied the Wali to Basra and from there sent a message of loyalty to the Sultan, probably to please Muhsin whose credit at the Porte varied in proportion to his success in prevailing upon Mubarak to behave. Consul Wratislaw in Basra considered Mubarak to have been "primarily answerable" for the recent troubles by allowing the Saudis to attack the Amir from his territory. His view was that, from a

[56] Bidwell, *Affairs of Kuwait*, 1/2, p. 54, letter of Wratislaw of 15 November, received on the 19th; the text mentions the word "suzerain", which can hardly have been an accurate rendering of the Amir's wish.

[57] Anscombe, *Ottoman Gulf*, p. 118; IOLR, R/15/1/473, fo. 223(152), telegram Wratislaw to Bushire 14 November 1900; Bidwell, *Affairs of Kuwait*, 1/2, p. 56, Government of India to India Office 19 November 1900.

[58] Anscombe, *Ottoman Gulf*, p. 118; Bidwell, *Affairs of Kuwait*, 1/2, pp. 66–8, Wratislaw 22 November 1900; Nantes AD, consulat Bagdad B29, Rouet 1 December 1900; Berlin AA, R 13883 A 325 (6 January 1901), Richarz 1 December 1900.

position of strength based on the arms trade, his friendship with Muhsin
and the British guarantee in case things went awry, Mubarak had disputed
the hitherto unchallenged supremacy of the Amir over the shaikhs of
Arabia. The Amir had responded impetuously, but Mubarak was, according
to Wratislaw, the main culprit. He had been aided by the Muntafiq Shaikh
Sa'dun, according to Wratislaw a "confirmed rogue" whose livelihood was
brigandage. Wratislaw, who apparently placed too much trust in the views
expressed to him by the affable Muhsin Pasha, had a somewhat confused
idea of the outcome of the affair. He thought that Muhsin had gained
prestige by forcing the parties to disengage and accept the Sultan's
supremacy, and that the Amir had lost prestige by agreeing to retire first;
and that Mubarak had expended a lot of money for nothing in the affair
and had ended up by submitting to the Sultan. He feared, however, that
the Amir would in the end not accept his "defeat" and resume hostilities.
Kemball in Bushire had a slightly more moderate view of Mubarak's guilt,
but he agreed with Wratislaw that the conflict had effectively ended,
disregarding reports from the Kuwait news agent that Mubarak was not
intending to submit and was still deploying considerable forces in the
desert.[59]

In the event, the British representatives in Basra and Bushire had been
too complacent in their apparent disregard of dangerous developments. A
change of policy in the Ottoman administration may have been the prime
cause of the speedy resumption of hostilities. Muhsin's kid-gloved
handling had achieved a cosmetic repair of Ottoman territorial claims to
Arabia, but now intervention seemed to the Turks to be the most attractive
alternative once again. The Sultan himself, as well as the Mushir Ahmad
Fayzi Pasha, a favourite of the Sultan who called him "my lion", seems to
have been responsible for this change of policy.[60] The Mushir informed the
German consul in Baghdad, Richarz, that after talks Mubarak and the
Amir had both agreed to have their warriors transformed into
"Hamidiye" regiments, i.e. semi-regular troops retaining their tribal
structure. Richarz wrote on 29 March 1901 that the Sultan, who regarded
the strife between two of his principal "officials" in the region, Mubarak

---

[59] Bidwell, *Affairs of Kuwait*, 1/2, pp. 66–7, Wratislaw to embassy in Constantinople 22
November 1900.
[60] The words "my lion" in Nantes AD, consulat Bagdad A 48, fo. 169. Rouet, 19 August
1903, describes the Mushir as a not very competent "slit-eyed Tatar".

and the Amir, as particularly harmful, had ordered his brother-in-law Kazim Pasha to detach Yusuf Al-Ibrahim from the Amir. According to Richarz, Kazim made peace and brought Yusuf Al-Ibrahim as his "guest" with him to Baghdad.[61] This, however, did nothing to allay Mubarak's fears. That he had good reason is revealed by Rouet's report that the Amir had assigned Yusuf to Kazim Pasha on condition that Kazim would satisfy the demands of Mubarak's nephews.[62] Ottoman policy had thus shifted: Mubarak had hitherto been protected by the commander of the Ottoman VI Army Corps, but on Recep Pasha's departure the attitude of the Baghdad military establishment had changed. Kazim Pasha and the Mushir were more inclined to side with the Amir.

The Turks' policy now appears to have been to make peace between Mubarak and the Amir so as to isolate and resolve the problem of Sa'dun's faction of the Muntafiq. Muhammad Pasha Daghestanli, a rather dim and uncouth soldier none the less trusted by the Sultan, was despatched to bring Sa'dun to heel.[63] Sa'dun's hold on the Muntafiq had always been a little precarious, and he surrendered to the Ottoman army. For a moment things looked promising for the Turks, but then Sa'dun, suspecting the Ottoman commander of planning to hand him over to his mortal enemy the Amir, escaped from his keepers and took refuge with Mubarak.[64] These events of November–December 1900 can only be seen as a terrible Ottoman blunder: the Sultan's trusted officers had aroused the suspicion of both Mubarak and Sa'dun that the Turks had taken the Amir's side. All Muhsin's careful work had been undone.[65]

Mubarak now had no reason to stay his hand. Wratislaw had already supposed, not unreasonably, that Mubarak's stance sprang from his

[61] Berlin AA, R 13843 A 6678 (5 May 1901), Richarz in Baghdad 27 March 1901.
[62] Paris AE, NS Mascate 6, fos. 90–93 (fo. 91), Rouet 24 June 1901. Anscombe's view of Kazim's mission is too naïve in stating, on the basis of British documents, that Kazim was sent to make peace and that the Amir had accepted, but went to war again when Mubarak attacked. Anscombe, *Ottoman Gulf*, pp. 119 and 227 n. 39.
[63] Portrait of Muhammad Pasha Daghestanli in Oppenheim, *Vom Mittelmeer zum Persischen Golf*, p. 265.
[64] For Wratislaw's reports to the embassy of 28 November and 14 December 1900, see Bidwell, *Affairs of Kuwait*, 1/2, p. 68, and 1/3, p. 4. In the first report it is also stated that, during his visit to Basra, Mubarak had promised to sever his links with Sa'dun.
[65] Muhsin rightly saw the operation against Sa'dun as not especially intelligent: Bidwell, *Affairs of Kuwait*, 1/3, p. 4, Wratislaw 14 December 1900.

certitude that he could count on British support in the event of defeat.[66] But Wratislaw (or the British in general) do not seem to have grasped the full implications of the affair. Mubarak had his piece of paper of 1899, but he needed to test the extent to which he could call upon it. The Amir was a dangerous neighbour, and Mubarak had ill-defined borders in the desert zone. There were two ways in which Mubarak could improve this situation. He could either defeat the Amir and so rearrange the tribal hierarchy in his favour, or be defeated himself and so oblige the British to protect him from the desert side too. The situation in 1900 was such as to encourage Mubarak to force the issue without delay. The British were uncomfortably aware of the growth of international interest in Kuwait, and so their concern and willingness to pay were at their peak. At the same time Mubarak was in a strong position locally. He had a friendly Wali of Basra, and for the time being Sa'dun was his ally, though that mercurial individual could never be relied on for long. And Mubarak's hand was further strengthened when it emerged that his old enemy, Qasim Al-Thani, might be joining him and the Saudis in a general alliance of tribes of the coastal region against the Amir.[67]

Meanwhile British anxiety about what Mubarak might do was intensifying. O'Conor in particular was unhappy. He saw that if Mubarak met with defeat, Britain might be faced with three disagreeable options: either to "raise an unpleasant question with the Turks", which would imply that Britain claimed protection over Mubarak; or "to assert effective control over Kuwait", which would cause a major international row; or to tear up the 1899 Agreement.[68] O'Conor had a distorted view of the actual state of affairs. The British tended to suspect the Germans of encouraging the Turks to urge the Amir on, but there is no evidence for such collusion between the Turks and the Germans. Also it is far from certain that the Turks really controlled the Amir. The British were blind to the internal dispute within the Ottoman establishment, in which some wanted to apply the stick, while Muhsin and his friends favoured dangling the carrot. For the time being Muhsin controlled the Basra government, while the military command took the tougher line.

[66] Bidwell, *Affairs of Kuwait*, 1/2, p. 66–8, Wratislaw 22 November 1900.
[67] Berlin AA, R 13849 A 18054 (14 December 1900), Richarz in Baghdad 6 November 1900.
[68] Plass, *England*, p. 276.

After some debate in London it was decided to order India to send Kemball to Mubarak once again to warn him in the strongest terms.[69] It would be a somewhat empty gesture, as London could not really hope to control Mubarak while there was no real protectorate. The reality was even worse: Kemball had already sent Mubarak one clear warning in writing, but Mubarak had chosen not to heed it.[70] Mubarak did not want peace with the Amir as long as he was giving sanctuary to Yusuf Al-Ibrahim. Once Mubarak had already blatantly flouted Kemball's first warning, Curzon clearly risked a serious loss of face if he sent Kemball on a new mission, and so things were left to run their course.[71]

Mubarak continued with his preparations for war. He marched with a considerable army into the vague border zone to the west, where he was joined by Sa'dun and tribesmen from eastern Arabia. In this way he was able to cover the Saudis who were trying to detach the people of Najd from the Amir. Mubarak's army was very large, but it was a patchwork of disparate elements. The Amir's forces were much more homogeneous but, as seen above, the situation was such that even a defeat would have its advantages for Mubarak.

The residency in Bushire and the British consulate in Basra could do nothing but await the outcome. The same went for Muhsin Pasha, whose plans for a peaceful resolution were being shattered before his impotent gaze. The unfolding drama gave rise to a plethora of wildly contradictory reports that made their way to Kuwait and Bahrain, and later to Basra too. In short, having penetrated deep into the Amir's territory, Mubarak suffered a crushing defeat near Sarif.[72] Muhsin Pasha acted as if nothing

---

[69] Bidwell, *Affairs of Kuwait*, 1/3, p. 21, Hamilton to Government of India 26 February 1901.

[70] Bidwell, *Affairs of Kuwait*, 1/3, p. 10, Kemball to Mubarak 10 December 1900: "It seems to me that you are pursuing a dangerous policy by continuing to provoke the Amir of Nejd, and I again counsel you to keep quiet". This was in answer to a letter from Mubarak of 25 November, which contained a simple account by him of the state of affairs, ibid. p. 7. Ibid. p. 13, for the oral reply given by Mubarak to the news agent: he is unable to keep quiet while Yusuf Al-Ibrahim is staying with the Amir.

[71] Plass, *England*, p. 276; Bidwell, *Affairs of Kuwait*, 1/3, p. 11, Government of India to Hamilton 28 January 1901: Kemball's visit seeming to have no result, a second failure might be embarrassing.

[72] IOLR, R/15/1/473, fos. 402–453: a series of newsletters and other correspondence on the battle.

had happened. He told everyone that Mubarak was just inspecting his herds in the desert and would soon return. Muhsin's behaviour struck Wratislaw as an attempt to safeguard his own position: after all, his *raison d'être* as Wali of Basra was his reputed ability to control Mubarak.[73] But Wratislaw himself had no solid news either, only wild rumours.

6.4 The Battle of Sarif and its consequences

At first it looked as if all had gone well for Mubarak. Rumours circulated that he had appointed Abdul Rahman Al-Saud as governor of Riyadh.[74] At the end of March 1901, news seeped through to Bushire that Mubarak was deep inland, while Ibn Rashid was lurking close to Kuwait. Then suddenly, weeks after the events, news began to trickle in of a defeat for Mubarak between Haïl and Burayda. First came a telegram from Basra of 29 March that the Wali had received news of a defeat of Mubarak.[75] The first more detailed accounts of the battle are in letters from Gaskin, the political assistant in Bahrain, to the Bushire residency. Gaskin wrote, on 1 April 1901, that on 27 March a runner had arrived from Najd with the following news:

> A hard battle was fought between Sheikh Mubarek and Bin Rashid at a place between Buraida and Hayil and Shaikh Mubarek was routed by Bin Rashid owing to the Braih and Gahtan tribes and some of the Nejd tribes deserting Sheikh Mubarek at the last moment on the approach of Bin Rashid; Sheikh Mubarek is said to have escaped and is in full flight for Koweit.[76]

Next day Gaskin wrote another letter setting out the results of closer

---

[73] Bidwell, *Affairs of Kuwait*, 1/3, pp. 50–1, Wratislaw 22 March 1901.

[74] IOLR, R/15/1/473, fos. 378–380, news agent in Kuwait 27 February 1901. This was first confirmed, but later it was found out that only the "village of Araz" (possibly Harad, due east of al-Kharj and south of Hasa Oasis) had been conquered, see ibid. fos. 397–398.

[75] IOLR, R/15/1/473, fo. 402, telegram from Basra 29 March 1901.

[76] IOLR, R/15/1/473, fos. 419–424, Gaskin 1 April 1900. The letter contains other news that seems to confirm Mubarak's defeat: the Al-Murrah tribe was attacking the 'Ajman, something they would not have dared to do if Mubarak had had the upper hand.

investigation into the reports of the battle, having now himself spoken with the man who had brought the news from Kuwait:

> It appears that Ben Rashid had made secret arrangements with the Braih and Harb tribes to desert Sheikh Mubarek and attack him in the rear when his (B.R.) forces get within striking distance. Bin Rashid to get close to Sheikh Mubarek's army and at the same time to shield his Arabs from long range fire had herds of camels driven in front of his host and when they got within striking distance they passed through the camels and attacked Sheikh Mubarak's force at close quarters. At the same time the two tribes mentioned above attacked the Kuweit people's camp in the rear and created a great confusion. It is believed that the slaughter on Sheikh Mubarek's side was very great owing to the majority of the Koweit people being on foot and unable to escape ...[77]

On 6 April Gaskin reported on a meeting with an Arab warrior claiming to have been present at the battle:

> ... that it took place the 17th March and lasted all day. That the Ajman tribe seeing that the day was going against them bodily removed Mubarek from the field so as to prevent him from falling a victim. That Hamood the brother of Mubarek fell in the fight and that after withdrawing from the fight Mubarek was informed that Bin Rashid and two of the latter's cousins the sons of Hamud-al-Rashid had also been killed. He also states Mubarek will not return to Koweit, but intends to further press Bin Rashid. The Thafir tribe of Muntafiq failed to join Mubarek and it is stated that this tribe have been bought out by the Turks, but Saadoon with about 50 followers were with Mubarek and fought on his side to fulfil their agreement with him.[78]

A somewhat later but interesting account of events immediately following the Battle of Sarif was given in February 1903 to the captain of the Russian warship *Boyarin* during its visit to Kuwait. According to this, after Sarif the Amir had come so close to Kuwait that he could have looted Mubarak's house. Mubarak had retired from the scene of battle and entered the town dressed as a beggar, fearing his subjects' anger over the

[77] IOLR, R/15/1/473, fo. 425, Gaskin, 2 April 1900.
[78] IOLR, R/15/1/473, fos. 429–432, Gaskin 6 April 1900. The file 473 contains several Arab reports on the battle with translation into English.

defeat and being abandoned by them. This fear was unfounded, as Mubarak was sufficiently popular for a deputation of notables to appeal to him to stay on and continue the war at all costs.[79] One wonders how the Russians came by this story, and it is not impossible that it was embroidered and dropped intentionally by an agent of Mubarak. Mubarak personally gave an account of the battle to Kemball during the latter's visit to Kuwait on 14 April 1901.[80]

Anscombe claims that the Battle of Sarif extinguished Mubarak's ambition to become the foremost Arab leader in the Arabian Peninsula.[81] Maybe he did harbour such dreams, but the plain facts do not sustain much more than that he had tried to exploit the conjunction of a broad alliance with the Basra Wali's neutrality, to ward off the dangerous alliance of the Amir, Yusuf Al-Ibrahim and the Baghdad military command. In the long term the only solution was to contain the power of the Amir by reinstating Abdul Rahman Al-Saud in Najd and helping to maintain the independent power of the Muntafiq that was also endangered by Ibn Rashid. This would render Kuwait more secure by producing a balance of power in the region.

The defeat must have been a terrible personal blow to Mubarak. Some of his closest associates as well as his own brother had been killed in the battle. At the same time it appears that he rapidly recovered his poise. His first step was to assure the officer sent by Muhsin to Kuwait of his allegiance to the Sultan. Mubarak declared to the Turk that he had received the order to desist from hostilities from the Sultan just after the defeat and had hurried back to Kuwait in obedience. Wratislaw, normally far from being one of Mubarak's admirers, this time was unstinting in his praise: "It is difficult not to admire the Shaikh's self-possession."[82]

Mubarak had certainly taken a great risk in coming to blows with the Amir, by far the most powerful Arab leader in the Peninsula, but it was not an absurd risk. In the event of defeat he could count on British support. Indeed, one may speculate whether the advantages of defeat might have entered into his calculations beforehand, for they were considerable. By

[79] Rezvan, *Russian Ships*, p. 139.
[80] Bidwell, *Affairs of Kuwait*, 1/3, pp. 44–6, Kemball's account of his visit to Mubarak 20 April 1901.
[81] Anscombe, *Ottoman Gulf*, p. 118.
[82] Bidwell, *Affairs of Kuwait*, 1/3, p. 41, Wratislaw 10 April 1901.

forcing the British to protect him in an international context in which their Kuwait Agreement would figure prominently, Mubarak's claims according to the treaty would be "effectuated" in the strongest possible way. Moreover, the scope of the treaty would be incontestably extended to the desert border zone. Against this it cannot be denied that Mubarak's normally cool and calculating spirit had deserted him in the heat of battle. The sources indicate that he personally had fought his hardest in the heat of battle and sustained a wound. One wonders if it was to Sarif that he owed the scar of a sword-cut noted on his face by a later visitor.[83] One cannot but admire his courage, but his death would have been a disaster for Kuwait's independence. The first reports of the battle speak of huge losses on Mubarak's side, as well as heavy losses on the part of the Amir. In the end, however, it was reported that Kuwaiti losses were not so serious. The truth of such events can of course never be known, but one has to take into account the fact that after a chaotic desert encounter it would take some time for all the dispersed warriors to return home.[84]

The first consequence of Mubarak's defeat was that Muhsin Pasha was discredited. This was a pity for the Kuwaiti Shaikh but, if the sources are accurate, we need shed no tears for Muhsin, who is said to have gained considerable pecuniary benefit from his alliance with the Naqib and Mubarak. A weightier question is whether Sarif enabled Abdul Aziz Ibn Rashid to move more menacingly on Kuwait. In fact the Amir too had suffered heavy losses and he was in no position to exploit his victory to the full. The present danger to Kuwait would be from the Turks, and this would have to be counteracted by British support. But accurate intelligence was needed before decisions could be formulated, and accurate intelligence came slowly. The Porte heard nothing for some time, probably because Muhsin Pasha, as a good Ottoman official, wanted to be certain of his facts before informing his bosses. Ottoman officials, like others, tended to report rumours only if they tallied with their overall strategy.

The Ottoman response to Mubarak's defeat was confused. Muhsin received the first reports of the battle through Abdul Aziz Ibn Rashid's

---

[83] Antaki, *Al-Riyad*, p. 198, sees the proudly borne scar as a sign of great personal courage.

[84] Berlin AA, R 13850 A 8948 (15 June 1901), Sternburg in Simla 29 May 1901, quoting an article in the *Pioneer* newspaper that Simais, the Belgian inspector-general of the Persian customs, had stated that losses on the Kuwaiti side had been limited to 50 dead and 200 wounded.

Basra agent, who was spreading the tale that Mubarak had been killed.[85] A contradiction followed two days later, and on 31 March Muhsin Pasha sent a telegram to the interior ministry with the details: Mubarak defeated, but he and Sa'dun alive; the battle had taken place at two weeks' travel from Basra, so he had received the news rather late. Muhsin advised his minister to react prudently in order not to provoke Mubarak.[86] Thus the Turks were deflected from a rapid response.

The British response too was confused. Mubarak was the lynch-pin of their position in the upper Gulf and his death would infinitely complicate their policy. British communications were likewise slow. Wratislaw, consul in Basra, like Muhsin Pasha had first heard the news from Ibn Rashid's agent, and he passed it on, albeit with strong reservations. This time British officialdom reacted by proposing direct action. Now the 1899 bond had suddenly acquired a tremendous value! While Mubarak's fate still hung in the balance, the British were considering support for his son Jabir's succession against a possible Turkish-sponsored attempt by one of the nephews to take control, precisely because it was feared that, unlike Jabir, a Turkish-sponsored candidate would not adhere to the 1899 Agreement.[87] A warship was to be sent forthwith, to be followed soon after by another, while a third was being kept in readiness. The first ship, the *Sphinx*, sent a report that relaxed the tension a little: the Shaikh was well and there was no fear of an immediate attack on Kuwait.[88] The British reaction had been jumpy, but the reality was that such a show of force was certain to deter the hesitant Sultan from strong action. It is vital to understand too that the Turks were still uncertain about the precise nature of Mubarak's relations with the British. They had reasons to think that Mubarak had not yet obtained a formal agreement, but feared he would sign one the moment they tried to intervene.[89]

The Turks thus adopted a posture of ostensible neutrality between Mubarak and the Amir. When the Amir declared to the Sultan that "the

[85] Bidwell, *Affairs of Kuwait*, 1/3, p. 17, O'Conor to Lansdowne 29 March 1901.
[86] Istanbul BA, Y.A. Hüs 414/45, telegram of Muhsin Pasha to Minister of Interior 18 Mart 1317 = 31 March 1901. Anscombe seems to be mistaken in the sequence of the penetration of the story of Mubarak's defeat to the Ottoman Government, when he states (*Ottoman Gulf*, pp. 119 and 227–8 n. 40) that the first news reached Constantinople from a tax inspector on 3 April.
[87] Bidwell, *Affairs of Kuwait*, 1/3, p. 18, O'Conor to Lansdowne 31 March 1901; ibid. p. 19, Admiralty to Foreign Office 30 March 1901.
[88] Bidwell, *Affairs of Kuwait*, 1/3, p. 23, Capt. Phillips of *Sphinx* 10 April 1901.

punishment of God has been visited upon Mubarak because he has not obeyed the orders of the Caliph", the Sultan sent a large body of troops into the region to prevent more inter-Arab conflict. The German ambassador in Constantinople supposed that the troops would occupy Kuwait, because the Sultan sympathized with the Amir.[90] At first the situation appeared to threaten Mubarak. Units of the VI Army Corps were deployed from Baghdad to Basra, and its commander, Ahmad Fayzi Pasha, left Baghdad to meet the Amir. Wratislaw reported that the Porte had sent a strongly worded instruction to Mubarak summoning him to Basra to explain his actions.[91] Mubarak certainly had no intention of obeying such orders. This all boded ill, especially for the British, who feared that they were heading for a direct confrontation if the Turks moved against him. The realities of the situation were better appreciated by a well-informed Arab outsider, Shaikh Khaz'al of Muhammara, who told the French consul in Muscat that Mubarak's defeat had not really changed the international situation; Mubarak could safely continue to play the Turks off against the British, as the former had no navy and the latter no army; and Mubarak was safe from the Amir, because neither the Turks nor the British could permit the Amir to conquer Kuwait. Khaz'al's detached and sceptical view was to be vindicated by events.[92]

The Ottoman deployment went forth at a snail's pace and the Ottoman troops halted long before reaching Basra. The French consul in Baghdad recorded the rumour that when the Ottoman troops under the command of Muhammad Pasha Daghestanli started to arrive in Basra, they were ordered back to Amara because Mubarak had paid 7000 Turkish pounds to Muhammad Pasha and 5000 to Muhsin Pasha. The *Times of India* attributed the Ottoman retreat to the presence of the British warships *Marathon* and *Lawrence* near Kuwait.[93] There was perhaps a better explanation for the Turkish retreat. A new ally had come to Mubarak's aid:

[89] Berlin AA, R 13843 A 6773 (7 May 1901), Richarz in Baghdad 10 April 1901: Richarz quizzed the British consul in Baghdad, who denied that an agreement existed between Mubarak and Britain. Even Kazim Pasha told Richarz that no agreement existed between the British and Mubarak.

[90] Berlin AA, R 13883 A 5405 (11 April 1901), telegram Marschall in Constantinople to Berlin 10 April 1901.

[91] Bidwell, *Affairs of Kuwait*, 1/3, p. 29, O'Conor 25 April 1901; ibid., pp. 30–1, Wratislaw 27 April 1901.

[92] Paris AE, NS Mascate 6, fos. 61–66 (64v), Ottavi 10 May 1901.

Yersinia pestis, the microbe causing bubonic plague. This terrible disease suddenly broke out in Basra, forcing the Turks to halt troop movements thither, while the troops already arrived had to be put under quarantine.[94] This would postpone decisive action for months, as quarantine would keep the troops immobile until June, by which time it would be too hot to do very much.

True to form, however, Mubarak did not put all his eggs in one basket. Another potentially useful opportunity had suddenly presented itself. The European consuls in Baghdad had received vague reports about the events in the desert. They had reacted in disparate ways: the French were unconcerned as their interests were not involved; the British consul had been instructed that these were matters chiefly for Bushire; and the German consul reported, but kept a low profile. The Russian consul, by contrast, appeared not to have put the vague earlier Russian projects involving Kuwait entirely out of his mind, and sent his usual intermediary, Abbas Aliyev, to Kuwait to see what Mubarak had to say. According to Aliyev, Mubarak complained about Kazim Pasha conspiring with the Amir against him, and also repeated the old story of British ties with Yusuf Al-Ibrahim. This was a stale and largely inaccurate tale, but it was one that had been circulating earlier in Baghdad and was known to the Russians, so it could be exploited again to pull some wool over Russian eyes. Mubarak told Aliyev that, if necessary, he was ready to hoist the Russian flag.[95]

It is not too difficult to understand Mubarak's motives for what, on the surface, seems an extraordinary move. His vague suggestion that he was ready to accept some kind of Russian protection was meant, as in 1899, as a way of keeping his options open. Mubarak cannot have been so naïve as to hope that the upper echelons of the Russian diplomatic service – which was committed to preserving Ottoman territorial integrity – could be won over to so rash a venture as proclaiming a Russian protectorate over Kuwait, even in a context of Anglo-Russian rivalry. Mubarak was simply intent on manipulating his old friend, the Russian consul in Baghdad, into spreading rumours that the Amir could not be trusted because of his

[93] Paris AE, NS Mascate 6, fos. 90–93, Rouet 24 June 1901, which also quotes the *Times of India*.

[94] Anscombe, *Ottoman Gulf*, p. 119.

[95] Moscow AVPR, Section Embassy Constantinople, file 1295, fos. 194–200, report by Ovseyenko, Russian consul in Basra, 20 April 1901; Bondarevsky, *Kuwait*, p. 220.

relations with the British stooge Yusuf Al-Ibrahim, and that he, Mubarak, was still keeping his distance from the British, even though some Ottoman officials had been conspiring with the disloyal Amir. In short, it was a cunning ploy to spread disinformation among the Turks in Baghdad. If a whiff of his dealings with the Russians were to reach the British, this would be no bad thing, as the Russian approach could only elevate Kuwait's standing in British eyes. Something did indeed seep through to Wratislaw in Basra, no less than a copy of an extremely vague letter by Mubarak himself, but it caused no particular alarm, probably because British power was on the spot and ready for action, while the Russians had nothing to hand.[96]

The Russian intermezzo was interesting, but had no further consequences. The Turks hesitated, but went on with their preparations to intervene. There were no leaks to the British, and in any case leaks would have made no difference because the British had already decided to protect Mubarak, even by force, albeit with much grumbling on the part of the Foreign Office. The Russians would never have gone to such lengths, and in any case there was disharmony among those on the ground. Aliyev may have sympathized with Mubarak, but the Russian consul in Basra had a less positive view.[97]

Meanwhile the British were still fearful of Kuwait being overrun by either the Ottomans or the Rashidis, and that Mubarak might try to save his skin by rejoining the Ottoman camp. Of course the Foreign Office was most unhappy about the whole Kuwait business, but by this time their diplomatic *amour propre* had suffered such a battering over it that the significance of the tiny principality had swollen out of all proportion. In addition the British suddenly felt freer to use robust tactics with the Turks. Anglo-German negotiations over an alliance had failed in March, and so there was no more reason to spare German sensibilities. The sole problem was that, just at that juncture, British naval forces were not close enough to confront an Ottoman adventure with sufficient strength.

Lansdowne had reason to be nervous that all the pains taken over Kuwait would go for nothing were Mubarak to be expelled, and he

[96] Bidwell, *Affairs of Kuwait*, 1/3, p. 54, intercepted letter of Aliyev of early May 1901.
[97] This can be seen from the consul's report of 3 November 1901 in Moscow AVPR, Section Embassy Constantinople, file 1245, in which he arrived at the judgement that Kuwait was a British protectorate and that soon it would be "completely enslaved".

suddenly rushed into action. O'Conor was instructed to issue a warning to the Turks the moment they made a move on Kuwait.[98] So Mubarak had won his point. The British would, in case of need, reveal their tie with Kuwait. There was every sign that British warships would prevent an Ottoman occupation of Kuwait, and in the event of Turkish aggression the British would also resort to open diplomacy. As described above, the Ottoman troop movement ground to a halt, and in the end there was no need for O'Conor's warning.

Muhsin, the Wali of Basra, thought this an opportune moment to earn some credit in Constantinople by bringing Kuwait back into the Ottoman fold without recourse to the costly war machine. He came overland with a small body of troops to Kuwait, but they were not permitted to enter.[99] Muhsin proposed that Mubarak should accept a small Ottoman garrison for his protection. An Ottoman garrison was certainly not what Mubarak desired, and he turned it down, declaring that he had already acquired the protection of a foreign power. Mubarak may also have judged an Ottoman garrison to be of little practical use, as no Arab chief in the region was deterred by them. Muhsin, however, was able to persuade the Shaikh to accompany him by boat (Mubarak's) to Fao, where they sent a joint declaration of loyalty to the Sultan.[100]

Wratislaw was right not to be particularly alarmed by this step, writing of the "protestations of loyalty and devotion to the Sultan of which he [Mubarak] is habitually lavish".[101] Now, however, it was O'Conor's turn to flutter into a panic over the possibility that Mubarak might betray the British. His urgent telegram to London arrived on a Sunday afternoon (27 May), a most inconvenient time for the Foreign Office.[102] Even the

---

[98] Bidwell, *Affairs of Kuwait*, 1/3, p. 30, O'Conor 27 April 1901; ibid. p. 32, Foreign Office to O'Conor 29 April 1901.

[99] Moscow AVPR, Section Embassy Constantinople, file 1245, report of Russian consul in Basra 3 November 1901.

[100] Bidwell, *Affairs of Kuwait*, 1/3, p. 60, telegram Wratislaw 1 June 1901. The Russian Basra report of 3 November 1901, in Moscow AVPR, Section Embassy Constantinople, file 1245, expressly states that the loyalty was declared to Abdulhamid as Caliph. At that time the distinction between loyalty to the Caliph as spiritual leader and loyalty to the Ottoman administration was sufficiently clear to everybody concerned. The Ottomans desired loyalty to the administration, but Mubarak offered loyalty only to the spiritual head.

[101] Bidwell, *Affairs of Kuwait*, 1/3, p. 60, Wratislaw to Embassy 1 June 1901.

[102] Plass, *England*, p. 279, is the first to point out the comic aspect of this situation.

punctilious Sanderson was driven to contemplate actions more appropriate to a rogue state, such as the kidnapping of Mubarak and Muhsin by the *Cossack*, the British warship at station in the Shatt al-'Arab, under the pretext that Muhsin needed to have all his back-teeth drawn by a dentist in Bombay.[103] Historians with a sense of humour will be disappointed to learn that, a few days later, O'Conor sent a telegram with the news that Mubarak had returned to Kuwait, so defusing the situation.[104] Naturally the whole comedy did nothing for the Navy's conception of the competence of British diplomacy.[105] Meanwhile Mubarak was realist enough to understand that his telegram of loyalty could only temporarily delay Ottoman plans to establish a garrison in Kuwait.[106] On 28 May 1901 he asked Capt. Phillips, of the British warship *Sphinx*, for a formal protectorate of Britain over Kuwait.[107]

The Amir gave an extra stir to the pot. The punishment of defectors in Qasim had kept him busy for some time, and his proximity to Kuwait heightened the local tension. In May he approached Wratislaw through his Basra agent (one of the members of the important Bassam merchant family), with the tale that he was disgusted at the duplicity of the Turks and wanted British protection. The Amir had a splendid offer: he would leave control over Kuwait to the British and would guarantee the safety of a British railway from Egypt to the Gulf. In exchange, he wanted Mubarak expelled from Kuwait and replaced by his nephew Sabah.[108] The matter was submitted to the Foreign Office, where it met with a cool reception, but it was decided first to ask Curzon for his opinion. Curzon, never one to forget that his good advice had been rejected in the past, reminded the India Office that the present mess was a consequence of the decision of 1898 to declare a full protectorate having been withdrawn. He assumed

[103] Plass, *England*, p. 279.

[104] Bidwell, *Affairs of Kuwait*, 1/3, pp. 47–8, O'Conor 29 May 1901.

[105] Plass, *England*, p. 280.

[106] According to Richarz, the establishment of an Ottoman military administration had been Muhsin's real mission in visiting Kuwait: Berlin AA, R 13883 A 7702 (24 May 1901), telegram from Marschall in Constantinople 23 May 1901. Also, the Turks said that they were sending more warships to the Gulf. All this may have been exaggeration by the Ottoman officers in Baghdad who wanted to present the Turkish administration as more energetic than it actually was.

[107] Bidwell, *Affairs of Kuwait*, 1/3, p. 66, Capt. Phillips on the *Sphinx* 29 May 1901.

[108] Plass, *England*, p. 280; Bidwell, *Affairs of Kuwait*, 1/3, p. 61, Wratislaw 3 June 1901.

that London wanted to maintain the existing "patch-work status quo", and stated that in that case Mubarak should be urged to settle the dispute with his nephews. Curzon expected Mubarak to look to Britain to pay for this settlement (which, in the end, it would do!). His advice was not to alienate the Amir's new sympathy, but to send a discreet mission to him.[109] A discreet mission did not accord with London's idea of proper standards of diplomacy. Hamilton did not at all share Curzon's vision of the January 1899 Agreement, rather feeling that his hand had been forced by Curzon, and politely torpedoed his ideas, weakly proposing some British attempt to mediate between the Amir and Mubarak. This plan, in turn, was torpedoed by Lansdowne who – rightly – felt that the British officials lacked the necessary local knowledge to mediate.[110] Curzon, not without justification, sensed that British Cabinet policy was inspired by reluctance to offend the Germans, and indulged in some wild prophecies about a German acquisition of Kuwait.[111]

By that time the situation in the desert was also shifting. Just before Sarif, it had become clear that the Amir's grip on his own domain was slipping.[112] In the summer of 1901, both Sa'dun and the Saudis were active again on the Amir's borders. The alliance of Mubarak with Sa'dun and the Saudis appears to have enabled an effective blockade, harming Hail's trade with Basra as well as with the Amir's allies in Zubair. The Amir now had to face three fronts, which intensified his difficulties.[113]

Mubarak's request of 28 May 1901 for a formal British protectorate stood no chance of acceptance, but it had in the meantime somehow been made public and was reported in *The Times* of 19 June 1901.[114] The news in the press had diplomatic consequences. On 24 June, Berlin received from the German consulate in Simla a cutting from the semi-official Indian newspaper *Pioneer*, mentioning that a formal request by Mubarak for a protectorate had been forwarded by the Government of India to

[109] Bidwell *Affairs of Kuwait*, 1/3, pp. 47–8 and 54, O'Conor to Lansdowne 29 May 1901; Sanderson to India Office 30 May 1901; and Government of India to India Office 8 June 1901.

[110] Plass, *England*, p. 283.

[111] Plass, *England*, p. 283.

[112] Bidwell, *Affairs of Kuwait*, 1/3, p. 41, Wratislaw 10 April 1901.

[113] IOLR, R/15/1/474, fos. 93–95 (131–135), 100–101 (141–142), 112–113 (160–161), reports from British news agent in Kuwait, 13, 16 and 29 July 1901.

[114] Plass, *England*, p. 285.

London. Berlin reacted by asking Richarz in Baghdad whether the Turks had already occupied Kuwait. Richarz asked Kazim Pasha and received a negative answer. Then confirmation of Mubarak's request came from the German consulate in Simla too.[115] Until then Germany had handled the affair in a very low-key manner, but in the summer of 1901 negotiations between Germany and Britain over an alliance and about the financing of the Baghdad Railway stalled, and the Germans felt free to act more openly. So the Kuwait affair was now becoming internationalized.

Dr Rosen, chief of the Oriental Department at the German foreign ministry and a considerable authority on Middle Eastern affairs (he had even visited the Gulf), tried privately to obtain information from the British ambassador in Berlin, Sir Frank Lascelles, about the affair. Rosen reminded him of O'Conor's notification to Marschall, of 19 April 1900, that there existed some kind of agreement between Mubarak and Britain that might have some impact on the Baghdad Railway plans. He tried in a subtle way to extract from Lascelles what the status of the agreement was and whether Britain was planning to establish a protectorate over Kuwait. Lascelles denied the protectorate plan and, in order to prove his point, quoted from the very secret letter of the Foreign Office to the India Office of 15 July 1901, in which it was stated that the British Government could not follow the wish of the Indian Government for a protectorate because this would have international consequences.[116]

Interestingly, this fact is missing from Lascelles's report of the meeting.[117] And Rosen's report makes it clear that Lascelles had disclosed to him much else that he had not told London, enough to let him understand the British relationship with Kuwait to be a matter not of private but of international law. Until then the Germans had ascribed little importance to the affair because their foreign ministry had been under the mistaken impression that the British link with Kuwait was a matter merely of private law. Lascelles, not known for his perspicacity, had now revealed to

[115] Berlin AA, R 13884 A 10347 (24 July 1901), Sternburg in Simla 14 July; A 10504 (18 July 1901), telegram to Richarz in Baghdad 18 July 1901; A 10617, telegram in reply from Richarz; A 10980 (28 July), letter from Sternburg in Simla, 10 July 1901.
[116] Lepsius, *Grosse Politik*, Vol. 17, pp. 480–1, Rosen 30 July 1901. See also Berlin AA, R 13884 A 10950 (30 July 1901): the literal text (translated into German) of the clause in the Foreign Office's letter to the India Office regarding the protectorate request is included!

the Germans that Britain had an agreement under international law with somebody the Germans considered to be "merely an Ottoman kaymakam". This was a breach of the territorial integrity of the Ottoman Empire and an excellent stick with which to discomfit British diplomats. Lansdowne was certainly unhappy with Lascelles' handling of Rosen. Lascelles had reported having advised Rosen that "the Shaikh of Kuwait, although technically a subject of the Sultan, enjoyed a considerable amount of independence". Lansdowne disapproved of this formulation. Rosen reported that Lascelles had told him literally that Mubarak was "a semi-independent chief", which looks even worse from the British standpoint. Lansdowne warned Lascelles that, after a warning of 8 August by Wratislaw about Ottoman troop movements, he had confirmed to O'Conor in Constantinople that Britain would oppose an Ottoman descent on Kuwait by force.[118]

This affair, though trivial, vividly illustrates the British inability to maintain a consistent policy over Kuwait. The Turks, however, were even more inconsistent, poised as they were between two alternatives: either to follow the hard line and try to occupy Kuwait (with the risk of British intervention), or to follow Muhsin's line and try by emollient means to detach Mubarak from the British. Muhsin was most eloquent in advocating his policy. It was, he argued, the imprudent actions of the Mushir, Fayzi Pasha, that had driven Mubarak into the arms of the British, and that had led to British warships ostentatiously visiting Kuwait. The Porte in the end disagreed with Muhsin, maintaining that his lenient policy had caused the desert war.[119]

6.5 The Ottomans decide to act

Under the circumstances it is no wonder that the Turks had come to the conclusion that a softly-softly approach only compounded an already complex affair. At the end of July 1901, Muhsin was replaced by Mustafa Nuri Pasha as Wali of Basra. At the same time orders were issued for the Ottoman troops, who had been immobilized by the epidemic, to march south – distinctly odd in view of the summer heat, which made a desert

---

[117] Bidwell, *Affairs of Kuwait*, 1/3, pp. 70–1, Lascelles 30 July 1901.
[118] Bidwell, *Affairs of Kuwait*, 1/3, p. 72, Lansdowne to Lascelles 10 August 1901.
[119] Anscombe, *Ottoman Gulf*, p. 120.

march so inadvisable. The British feared a Turkish attempt to ferry troops to Kuwait on warships.[120] By the end of June it had still appeared to the British as if there was no great Turkish danger, and they had used the apparent lull to try to persuade Mubarak to agree to the British India Steam Navigation Company including Kuwait in its schedule.[121] Mubarak was certainly aware of the Ottoman threat by that time, but he had probably given up making peace with the Turks and calculated that the closer his ties with the British, the more certain he could be of their protection.

The inclusion of Kuwait in a British shipping schedule was telegraphed by Rouet in Baghdad to the French embassy in Constantinople, with the warning that it would seriously damage the Basra customs revenues, and consequently the ability of the Turks to pay their debts or finance a railway. Rouet had also alerted Constans, the French ambassador in Constantinople, to the presence of British warships in Kuwait and the hoisting of the British flag there. Constans reacted by sending his dragoman to the Ottoman Foreign Minister to raise the alarm there. The dragoman strongly advised the Turks to assert categorically their sovereignty over Kuwait. The Russian ambassador appears to have made a similar move.[122] On 31 July 1901, unequivocal orders were issued to the Wali: Mubarak was to come to Basra, and a customs office and garrison was to be established in Kuwait. A tough message was also sent by the Sultan to Mubarak.[123] Meanwhile Ottoman troop concentrations continued, but because of the summer heat this achieved no more than to give advance warning to Mubarak and his friends. Kemball visited Mubarak at the beginning of August. In his report he expressed his concern that the Turks might try to ferry troops to Kuwait by warship, and warned that the British hold on Kuwait could be maintained only if

---

[120] Bidwell, *Affairs of Kuwait*, 1/3, p. 70, Government of India 10 August 1901.

[121] PRO, FO 602/16, fo. 256, Wratislaw 6 July 1901.

[122] Paris AE, NS Mascate 6, fo. 115, Constans to Rouet 2 and 3 July 1901; fo. 117, Constans to Foreign Minister in Paris 5 July 1901; fo. 118, Rouet to Constans 3 July 1901; fo. 125, Constans to Foreign Minister 16 July 1901; Anscombe, *Ottoman Gulf*, p. 121, mistakenly writes that the démarche was made by the ambassador Constans in person, see Istanbul BA, DUIT 69/2–8.

[123] Anscombe, *Ottoman Gulf*, pp. 121 and 228 n. 51. The text of the order sent from the Porte to the Wali of Basra appears to have fallen into the hands of Mubarak, who sent it to Bushire: IOLR, R/15/1/474, fo. 147.

Mubarak could be assured of British support. The only effective measure would be a combination of plain speaking from O'Conor and naval demonstrations in the Gulf.[124]

Constans, by no means the sharpest of diplomats, may never have realized that his ill-timed intervention benefited nobody but Mubarak. O'Conor advised against an over-ostentatious naval demonstration, but at the same time promised to warn off the Ottoman foreign minister, Tawfiq, at the first possible opportunity. He did so on 20 August, but as usual Tawfiq denied all knowledge of "any intention to molest or interfere with Mubarak", and at the same time insisted that Kuwait was an integral part of the Ottoman Empire. Tawfiq pointed to how Mubarak had only just recently confirmed his loyalty to the Sultan by telegram. O'Conor nevertheless came away with the impression that the Porte would instruct the Wali of Basra not to proceed hastily.[125] Lascelles in Berlin also received clear instructions in order to avoid future misunderstandings. Remarkably it was only to his friend Lascelles that Lansdowne had explicitly announced, in August 1901, that an Ottoman attempt to occupy Kuwait would be countered by force. Such a clear statement appears not to have been issued to O'Conor, the party most directly involved. O'Conor apparently believed that, if the worst came to the worst, the British would restrict themselves to a naval demonstration.[126]

Then British diplomacy blundered again. King Edward VII had to travel to Homburg in Germany in connection with the death of his eldest sister, the mother of the German Emperor. Lansdowne foresaw that Wilhelm II would choose his moment to initiate a discussion of matters outstanding between Britain and Germany. So he composed a rather hurried *tour d'horizon* of how things stood between the two countries. This paper was intended as a confidential briefing for the King on the British position. King Edward, however, misunderstood the character of the memo and just

---

[124] Bidwell, *Affairs of Kuwait*, 1/3, p. 73, Government of India to India Office 10 August 1901.
[125] Bidwell, *Affairs of Kuwait*, 1/3, pp. 74–5 and 77, telegrams of O'Conor to Lansdowne 16 and 20 August 1901. Mubarak, of course, had kept all options open by stressing his loyalty to the Sultan for as long as the British had not given him a firm undertaking. The meeting between Tawfiq and Lansdowne was described in more detail in a letter of 20 August: ibid. pp. 85–7.
[126] Bidwell, *Affairs of Kuwait*, 1/3, p. 72, Lansdowne to Lascelles 10 August 1901; *cf.* ibid. pp. 74–5, O'Conor to Lansdowne 16 August 1901

handed it to the Emperor Wilhelm. Having thus got into the wrong hands, the paper was then revealed to have been rather carelessly composed. As regards the Kuwait affair it followed the standard Foreign Office formula that "Her Majesty's Government did not desire to interfere with the status quo or with the Sultan's authority in these parts", but the essential limiting clause, "insofar as it really exists", had been omitted.[127]

The Germans genuinely believed the document to represent the whole truth of the British position, and presumed therefore that the British accepted the Sultan's full authority over Kuwait, which would include the right of the Turks to send troops there to settle matters, and would also entitle the Germans to reach a deal with Mubarak. Holstein, the most influential German official, composed a note which was handed to Lansdowne by Metternich, the German chargé d'affaires in London. In this he reiterated that Germany had no direct interests in Kuwait, but that the port was important for the railway. He stated that the Germans did not know precisely what the arrangements between Britain and Mubarak might be. Dr von Siemens, the managing director of the railway, would be asked to conclude an agreement over the sale of land by the Shaikh. If he were unable to achieve this, then Germany would ask Britain to give her "full cognizance of the arrangements entered into between the British Government and the Shaikh of Kuwait". This somewhat menacing message only reached Lansdowne on 3 September 1901. And by then the Turks had already embarked on their first moves on Kuwait with the arrival there, on 25 August, of the warship *Zuhaf*.[128]

By the summer of 1901, Mubarak's position had clarified. His defeat at Sarif had set in train a series of events obliging the British to convert their undertakings to him into reality. By their repeated blunders the Turks and the British had tied themselves in diplomatic knots, storing up problems for the future, but Mubarak was secure. Total defeat had been transmuted into partial victory.

---

[127] Bidwell, *Affairs of Kuwait*, 1/3, p. 97, extract from memorandum "on questions which may be mentioned by the German ambassador to the King"; *cf.* Berlin AA, R 13884 A 11734 (12 August 1901).

[128] Berlin AA, R 13884 A 11734, notice on the King's memo by the chancellor Bülow, 13 August 1901, and draft of the German memorandum by Holstein of 20 August 1901; Bidwell, *Affairs of Kuwait*, 1/3, pp. 97–8, the memorandum handed to Lansdowne by Metternich.

7

The "Kuwait Crisis" and the Status Quo Understanding, 1901–1902

7.1 The *Perseus* and *Zuhaf* incident

During the course of August 1901, the Turks tried to turn the screw on Mubarak. The Wali of Basra asked Mubarak's agent whether Mubarak would oppose the occupation of Kuwait by Turkish troops. The agent gave a diplomatic answer: Mubarak would not fight against Muslim troops, but he would accept British protection. The Wali countered by warning that the British were not in a position to oppose the Ottoman army on land and that the Amir was assisting the Sultan. But the agent politely made it clear that Mubarak was adamant. In the meantime the menacing troop concentrations in Nasiriyya and Samawa continued to loom in the background.[1] And vague attempts to reconcile Mubarak and the Amir of Haïl, by Shaikh Khaz'al of Muhammara and the British consul in Basra, were of no avail.[2]

On 25 August, the elderly Ottoman warship *Zuhaf* entered the port of Kuwait. According to Anscombe, this took place as part of a routine mission from Basra to Qatar.[3] In itself the sending of an Ottoman warship to Qatar was not unexpected, for an Ottoman army unit had suffered

---

[1] IOLR, R/15/1/474, fos. 151–157, letter of Mubarak reporting on talks between the Wali and the agent, 3 August 1901; and letters received by Mubarak from Basra and Baghdad, 15 and 25 August 1901.

[2] IOLR, R/15/1/474, fos. 170–171, Wratislaw 22 August 1901; and Bidwell, *Affairs of Kuwait*, 1/3, p. 77 (Government of India to Kemball 25 July 1901) and p. 78 (O'Conor 22 August 1901).

terrible losses in al-Hasa in an attack by Arabs. This does not, however, explain why the commander of the *Zuhaf* took it upon himself to visit Kuwait, and the innocent explanation found by Anscombe in the Ottoman archives becomes less credible in the light of the German consul in Baghdad having been informed by his sources that an Ottoman warship had been sent specifically to Kuwait.[4] The German report implies that the Ottoman command in Baghdad knew very well that a warship had been sent there, and it is inconceivable, in a structure like the Ottoman state, for such orders not to have emanated from the Sultan himself.

If the *Zuhaf*'s mission was intended as the long-delayed Ottoman descent on Kuwait, then the moment was ill-chosen, as it came just a few weeks after Kemball had warned his superiors that the Turks might try to land troops from warships. As a result, the British had decided that any Ottoman attempt to land troops in Kuwait should be opposed by force.[5] Mubarak had forewarned the British that he would be unable to oppose a Turkish military intervention, and so it fell to Kemball to formulate the orders to the British naval units in the Gulf as to precisely what action to take in the event of an Ottoman warship appearing off Kuwait. Having consulted the Senior Naval Officer in the Gulf, Kemball decided that the only safe course was to warn the commander of the *Zuhaf*, the moment he appeared off Kuwait, that Britain would oppose by force any attempt to land troops.[6] Such a step would minimize the military implications.

Pears, commander of the British warship *Perseus*, which was already in the port of Kuwait, held a rather injudicious exchange with the captain of the *Zuhaf*. As no first-hand Ottoman account is yet available, we have to rely on Pears' version alone.[7] Seeing the upper deck of the *Zuhaf* loaded with stores, Pears asked its captain whether he was contemplating a long

[3] Anscombe, *Ottoman Gulf*, p. 121, where no Ottoman source for this assertion is quoted. His data probably came from a memorandum passed to the Ottoman council of ministers: Istanbul BA, Usul-i Irade, Dosya 77, of 13 and 17 Agostos 1317 Rumi (26 and 30 August 1901).

[4] Berlin AA, R 13384 A 12272 (25 August 1901), telegram from Wangenheim, German chargé d'affaires in Therapia near Constantinople, 25 August 1901 (the ambassador Marschall was on leave).

[5] Bidwell, *Affairs of Kuwait*, 1/3, p. 73, Government of India to India Office, 10 August 1901.

[6] PRO, FO 602/16, Kemball to Wratislaw 1 September 1901.

[7] IOLR, R/15/1/474, fols. 146–148, Pears 25 August 1901.

stay in Kuwait and whether the *Zuhaf*'s mission was to Kuwait only, or also to other ports. The captain replied that he had business with the Shaikh, that he did not know how long he would stay, and that his mission was to Kuwait only. The last part of this reply clearly contradicts Anscombe's source that the *Zuhaf* was destined for Qatar. In accordance with his instructions, Pears then advised the Ottoman officer that "the British Government had decided to protect Sheikh Moubarak, that the landing of Turkish troops would not be permitted and that any attempt to do so would be prevented by force if necessary". He also issued the blunt warning that, should an attempt be made to land armed forces, the *Perseus* would open fire on them. An exchange of official perspectives then calmed the meeting down. The *Zuhaf*'s commander claimed that all the coastline down to Qatar belonged to the Turks, Pears asserted Mubarak's independence, and the Turk stated that he had come not to land troops, but only to hold talks with Mubarak.

Next day the commander of the *Zuhaf* did indeed visit Mubarak. Mubarak gave Pears an account of the interview: the Ottoman commander had first tried to "cajole" him, but he, Mubarak, had made it clear that he would have nothing to do with the Turks, but was under British protection; the Turk then issued strong warnings and told Mubarak that he would not proceed with his mission to Qatar, but would immediately return to Fao to report to Constantinople. Pears pointed out in his report that this threat was at variance with the Ottoman commander's earlier statement that his mission was to Kuwait only. The commander of the *Zuhaf* had clearly been less than candid when he said that his main mission was to Kuwait, when the Ottoman Government had overtly sent him only to Qatar. It appears that he had taken it upon himself to make a special mission to Kuwait, possibly in concert with a clique of Ottoman officials or even with the connivance of the Sultan's palace, either to gain credit by acquiring a new declaration of loyalty from Mubarak, or to stir up a bit of trouble on behalf of parties with interests in the railway.[8]

[8] A slightly different account of the visit of the *Zuhaf* to Kuwait is given by Rouet, who had it from a Muslim correspondent in Basra. This version states that when the *Zuhaf* arrived in Kuwait, the commander of the *Perseus* immediately ordered it to leave. After talks between the commanders, Pears allowed the Turk four hours to visit Mubarak. When the commander of the *Zuhaf* protested to Mubarak, the Shaikh replied that the Turks' military moves had obliged him to request British protection: Nantes AD, Bagdad B 29, Rouet 25 September 1901.

A point to note in Pears' report is his assertion of Mubarak's explicit denial of all ties with Turkey and his claim to be under British protection. This is not really consistent with Mubarak's normal posture, to use Wratislaw's graphic phrase, of "lavishness with protestations of loyalty to the Sultan". Mubarak's custom was to issue profuse and ornately worded assurances of loyalty, which however fell just shy of the full acceptance of Ottoman authority so much desired by the Sultan. Ottoman documents make no mention of outrageous pronouncements such as Pears reported Mubarak to have made. It is possible that Mubarak, accurately gauging Pears' upright and rather unsubtle character, gave him a slightly inaccurate story to provoke him into taking a tough line towards the Turk, and the British into crossing the Rubicon with their informal protectorate over Kuwait. For Mubarak to increase his insurance cover in this way would be entirely typical of him.

The *Perseus–Zuhaf* encounter was no minor international incident. As the commander of the *Sphinx*, Phillips, rightly remarked to Wratislaw: "Now the fat is in the fire."[9] Kemball wearily supposed that the blame would be laid at his door, because he had interpreted "opposing the landing" to include the issuing of an advance warning.[10] The British had issued threats to use force against a warship of another power in a port claimed by that power to be under its sovereignty. They appreciated the serious repercussions that the affair might have, and set in hand a study of options for the defence of Kuwait against an Ottoman attack. Somewhat paradoxically, the Amir's recent menacing attitude worked to Britain's advantage, as it afforded a pretext to fortify Kuwait with trench work and artillery.[11] Now Kuwait was prepared not only for a landing of Ottoman troops, but also for an attack from landward.

The Porte had been informed of the *Zuhaf–Perseus* incident through various channels. There had been telegrams from the *Zuhaf* at Fao and from Muhsin, who was still in Basra.[12] As usual, Muhsin pushed his line

---

[9] PRO, FO 602/16, fos. 226–226A, Phillips to Wratislaw, dated "Monday" (the document is badly positioned in the file).

[10] PRO, FO 602/16, fos. 277–278, Kemball to Wratislaw 1 September 1901.

[11] Bidwell, *Affairs of Kuwait*, 1/3, pp. 144 8, Capt. Field of the *Marathon* 28 September 1901.

[12] Istanbul BA, Irade Dahiliye 19 Cumada Ahira 1319/50. Muhsin's report in Istanbul BA, DUIT 69/2–19, 13 August 1317/26 August 1901.

about the risk of intervention in Kuwait driving Mubarak into the arms of the British. His report downplayed the incident, and the Porte based its diplomatic response on the stronger wording of the *Zuhaf* commander's telegram. For the British simply to have warned the Turks that landing troops in Kuwait would be opposed by force was sufficient in itself to create a diplomatic incident, but the Ottoman version of events went far beyond this. Anscombe supposes that "the Ottoman captain misunderstood the warning, probably as a result of a terse meeting with Mubarak".[13] This is unlikely. In dealings involving both Ottoman and British representatives, Mubarak tended to leave the strong words to the British. It is more plausible to suppose that the Ottoman naval commander tried to cover his somewhat shamefaced retreat by exaggerating the dangers he faced.

The Ottoman diplomatic offensive opened with the Government instructing its foreign minister, Tawfiq Pasha, to protest to O'Conor. Tawfiq was to state unequivocally that Kuwait was Ottoman territory, and that if Mubarak acquired British protection this could be only as an individual (as was fairly commonplace under the Capitulations system).[14] Tawfiq met with O'Conor on 29 August and complained that the captain of the *Perseus* "had warned the Captain of the *Zuhaf* to clear out of Koweit". O'Conor countered that the affair had been misrepresented and that all the British captain had done was to issue a friendly warning not to land troops.[15] O'Conor was wrong to believe that Tawfiq had more or less accepted this explanation. On 6 September, Tawfiq told O'Conor that the Sultan now wanted to know "the terms and nature" of Britain's "arrangement" with Mubarak, but added soothingly that the Sultan knew that it was "a cardinal principle of His Majesty's Government not to do anything prejudicial to the interests and integrity of the Ottoman Empire." O'Conor issued the usual British statement about the great British interest in Kuwait and Mubarak accepting the Caliph's authority, but he reported to Lansdowne that he did not expect the Sultan to be

---

[13] Anscombe, *Ottoman Gulf*, p. 121 (without direct reference to sources).

[14] Istanbul BA, DUIT 69/2–11, Rays al Kitab 21 Jumada Awal 1319/28 August 1901. Under the Capitulations (the old Ottoman system of treaties), foreign powers could place Ottoman subjects under their protection, granting them certain exemptions from Ottoman jurisdiction and taxation.

[15] Bidwell, *Affairs of Kuwait*, 1/3, pp. 82–3, O'Conor 29 August 1901.

satisfied with the British assurances.[16]

At the same time Tawfiq also began to spread the exaggerated version of the incident, which he conveyed by telegram to the Turkish ambassador in London, Kostaki Anthopoulos Pasha, showing it to other ambassadors in Constantinople too.[17] The most controversial passage read: "The Wali of Basra telegraphs that at the arrival of the Imperial Navy's corvette *Zuhaf* in Kuwait, the commander of the British ship at anchor in the port informed him that he would declare that port to be under British protection."[18] Other versions too were communicated by the Sultan and his secretary, Tahsin Bey, to the German chargé d'affaires in Constantinople.[19]

The Germans now came to the view that the British had been deceiving them all along, but that the slow reactions of the Turks had also been to blame. Wangenheim, the chargé d'affaires standing in for Marschall in Constantinople during the summer holiday, was instructed to reproach the Ottomans for having, months previously, neglected to follow the sound German advice to occupy Kuwait immediately.[20] While grumbling about Turkish inertia, the Germans were themselves very quick with a decisive response. On 29 August, the very day of Tawfiq's protest to O'Conor, Bülow, the German chancellor, ordered Eckardstein, his chargé d'affaires in London, to ask Lansdowne whether it was true that Britain intended to declare Kuwait a British protectorate and, if so, to advise him that this would be a breach of the Treaty of Berlin and hence, given German interest in Kuwait as terminus of the Baghdad Railway, should be considered "an unfriendly act towards Germany". Eckardstein was also to

---

[16] See Bidwell, *Affairs of Kuwait*, 1/3, p 93–44, O'Conor to Lansdowne 6 September 1901. See also p. 93, Lansdowne to O'Conor 4 September 1901, about a meeting with Anthopoulos, who protested about the form of words used by O'Conor to Tawfiq. Anthopoulos stated that O'Conor had notified Tawfiq about a "convention" with Mubarak, but that the Turkish position was that Mubarak was an Ottoman official and that "the convention to which you [O'Conor] had alluded was without validity".

[17] Bidwell, *Affairs of Kuwait*, 1/3, p. 93, Lansdowne to O'Conor, 4 September 1901.

[18] A copy of Tawfiq's telegram can be found in a letter from the French embassy in Constantinople, Paris AE, NS Mascate 6, fos. 149–150.

[19] Berlin AA, R 13884 A 12428 (29 August 1901), telegram from Wangenheim 28 August 1901 (Tahsin's version of events); R 13884 A 12551 (31 August 1901), telegram from Wangenheim 30 August 1901 (the Sultan's own version of events).

[20] Berlin AA, R 13884 A 12427/II (29 August 1901), draft of a telegram to Wangenheim in Constantinople, 29 August 1901.

remind Lansdowne of the British memorandum given by the King to Wilhelm II in Homburg, in which the "Sultan's authority in those parts" was expressly confirmed. Eckardstein was absent, and Count Hatzfeldt executed the instruction, reporting on his visit to the Foreign Office the very next day.[21]

The Ottoman protest in London, by contrast, was muted. Anthopoulos, who knew how unreliable Ottoman bureaucratic reports could be, had no desire for diplomatic shenanigans in the summer season. He lodged his protest on 4 September with Sanderson at the Foreign Office (Lansdowne was absent) and then disappeared into the English countryside.[22] There was an almost spectacular discrepancy between Anthopoulos' low-key action and his instructions from Tawfiq, but it is quite possible that the former was aware of a lack of clarity in Constantinople and that the Ottoman reports may have been exaggerated. On 5 September Tawfiq ordered Anthopoulos to tell the British that making agreements with Mubarak was illegal and that, if the British wanted to protect their interests in Kuwait, they should deal with the Porte.[23]

While the Turks acted incoherently, the Germans had already set in motion a canny cat-and-mouse game with the British on behalf of their Ottoman friends. Lansdowne had wisely taken leave of absence on summer holiday, so it fell to poor Sanderson to face the German chargé d'affaires, Hatzfeldt, over a matter in which British diplomats had already thoroughly undermined their own position during previous months. Sanderson cunningly tried playing for time. In part he denied that the British had any intention of establishing a formal protectorate over Kuwait (as was the truth), and in part cast doubt on the accuracy of the report of the *Zuhaf*'s captain. He admitted that the landing of Ottoman troops had been forbidden by Pears, but he claimed that this matter was already being dealt with in friendly discussions between the Ottoman authorities and

[21] Lepsius, *Grosse Politik*, Vol. 17, p. 482, Berlin AA, R 13884 A 12428/I (29 August), draft of a telegram to Eckardstein in London, 29 August 1901; R 13884 A 12495 (30 August 1901), telegram to the embassy in London, 30 August 1901. For the British version see Bidwell, *Affairs of Kuwait*, 1/3, p. 90, Lansdowne to Lascelles 3 September 1901.

[22] Istanbul BA, Y.A. Hüs 419/81, report of Anthopoulos of 4 September; *cf.* Plass, *England*, p. 295 and Bidwell, *Affairs of Kuwait*, 1/3, p. 93, Lansdowne to O'Conor 4 September 1901.

[23] Istanbul BA, Y.A. Hüs 429/82, telegram Tawfiq to Anthopoulos 5 September 1901.

the British ambassador in Constantinople, so that he, Sanderson, could not discuss it with a third party. As usual with this kind of exchange, Sanderson later regretted that he had not been firmer, writing to Lansdowne that he should perhaps have told the German that the Turks were to blame for the incident by disturbing the status quo in Kuwait. In a later letter to Lansdowne, Sanderson proposed a typically British fudge to resolve the dispute: there should be no Ottoman garrison, harbour master or customs in Kuwait, but Britain did not desire to enter into a discussion whether Kuwait was part of the Ottoman Empire or not.[24]

7.2 The Status Quo Understanding takes shape

Plass gives a lucid summary of the views prevalent among British diplomats. O'Conor, no doubt from his closer familiarity with the Ottoman situation, wanted to avoid a term like sovereignty, which in the Ottoman and German view had an absolute meaning, and use only the vaguest phrase such as purely nominal authority; while Sanderson and Lansdowne, who cared little about words, just wanted to be sure that the Turks would have no practical power over Kuwait. For Sanderson and Lansdowne a kind of status quo was acceptable.[25] The disadvantages of this seem not to have been considered. A "status quo" would in fact mean that Britain's dealings with Mubarak would continue to be of dubious validity, and that supposed Ottoman rights were in abeyance, not denied. Maintaining a status quo might also be jeopardized by officials on the spot being unhappy with it and so trying to undermine it – which, indeed, was what would happen. For the time being, however, the diplomatic uproar over the *Perseus* incident rumbled on.

The German chancellor Bülow informed the acting ambassador in London, Count Metternich, that he was not satisfied: preventing Ottoman troops from landing in Ottoman territory was a denial of the Sultan's authority in his own lands, and was contrary to the assurances given by the King to the Emperor in Homburg. The remainder of Bülow's telegram was less forthright, containing no clear instructions and only vague threats against Britain.[26] But this hardly mattered, for Metternich was a very able

[24] Plass, *England*, p. 292.
[25] Plass, *England*, pp. 292–3.
[26] Berlin AA, R 13884 A 12495/II (30 August 1901), telegram from Bülow to Metternich.

diplomat. He was a stiff old man who spoke very, very slowly, and could repeat himself endlessly to make his point, and so was able to make himself a thorough nuisance to the Foreign Office.

Lansdowne was still absent, so Sanderson had to bear the brunt of Metternich's visit on 3 September. Sanderson deployed the precise standard formula, that Britain recognized the authority of the Sultan in Kuwait only insofar it really existed. Mubarak was "semi-independent" and had never accepted the sovereignty of the Sultan. At that point the discussion took a critical turn. Metternich, who was steeped in world affairs, retorted that in the Ottoman territory, "be it in Yemen, in large parts of Anatolia and especially in Arabia, the authority of the Sultan was not always exercised, but that nevertheless his 'Hoheitsrechte' (his rights as supreme authority) were recognized". Metternich's argument was of course of dubious validity and in fact undermined his own position, inviting as it did a critical survey of the true character of the Ottoman Empire's often imaginary authority on its fringes. When Metternich persisted in his demand for a clear British statement, Sanderson told him that only Lansdowne, on his return, could give a formal answer. But Sanderson also repeated Salisbury's old assurance that Britain would not cause problems over the Baghdad Railway.[27] On 5 September Metternich again saw Sanderson, who was most emphatic in his assurances that Britain and Germany shared the same interests in Kuwait, and that as far as the railway was concerned it was important for Kuwait not to be affected by the unhealthy trade climate prevailing in Turkey.[28]

In Berlin the affair fell into the hands of more radical spirits. The hawkish under-secretary Richthofen placed the matter before the combustible Emperor Wilhelm II. He stressed the danger that the British example might give other powers too the idea that Ottoman territorial integrity could be impugned. Another danger envisaged by Richthofen was that the loss of Kuwait would cut the Turks off from their possessions in al-Hasa and Qatar. Wilhelm II was given to scribbling ejaculations on official papers, and next to this paragraph he jotted "This is their intention!". Richthofen ended his memorandum with an expression of his regret that, just at that juncture, the Turks were mired in two conflicts – one with France over economic matters (there were strong French naval

---

[27] Lepsius, *Grosse Politik*, Vol. 17, pp. 484–6, Metternich 4 September 1901.
[28] Lepsius, *Grosse Politik*, Vol. 17, p. 487, Metternich 5 September 1901.

demonstrations in the Aegean Sea), and one with Britain over Kuwait. According to Richthofen, the Turks would be wise to settle one of the two and submit the other to the International Court in The Hague. On this the Emperor scribbled: "Bravo, this should be Kuwait, because then Russia must clarify its position concerning the Persian Gulf and make a choice between us and Britain."[29]

Richthofen's suggestion of the International Court placed the affair in an interesting new light. The British had never paid any attention to the legal implications of their Gulf activities, and hence they might sail into troubled waters at The Hague. The Turks, however, failed to follow up this sagacious proposal. Plass is of the opinion that the International Court should have been proposed much earlier in the affair, and that it was now too late for it.[30] It is true that the matter had proceeded rather too far for a quick settlement in the tranquil surroundings of The Hague, but it would still perhaps have been possible to exert considerable pressure on Britain by going down that route. Rosen, the regional expert in Berlin, concurred that the Turks should settle either of the two conflicts that beset them, so that they had their hands free for the other.[31]

The German and Ottoman protests to Britain were in striking contrast, but the Germans were not setting out to provoke a quarrel just for the sake of it. Metternich and the German under-secretary, Holstein, viewed the incident as a handy opportunity to press the British into concessions over the railway, and saw the question of Ottoman sovereignty over Kuwait as secondary.[32] But Richthofen, ever the hawk, notified Metternich on 6 September that he had found a discrepancy between Sanderson's statement that Tawfiq and O'Conor were dealing in a friendly fashion with the *Zuhaf* affair, and the communications the German foreign ministry had received from Constantinople. Richthofen nurtured an over-optimistic view of Ottoman resolve. On the same day, 6 September, a telegram from the German embassy in Constantinople announced to Berlin that the Turks had assured O'Conor that the Ottoman Government

---

[29] Lepsius, *Grosse Politik*, Vol. 17, pp. 488–9, Richthofen 6 September 1901. The description of these events in Sitki, *Bagdadbahnproblem*, p. 103, is somewhat exaggerated.

[30] Plass, *England*, p. 296.

[31] Lepsius, *Grosse Politik*, Vol. 17, p. 489, Rosen 4 September 1901.

[32] Berlin AA, R 13884 A 1314 (4 September 1901), telegram of Metternich to Baron Holstein at the Foreign Ministry, private, 4 September 1901.

no longer planned to send troops to Kuwait.[33] The news of Ottoman pusillanimity was confirmed by a report from Metternich in London that the Ottoman ambassador there, the Sultan's confidant Kostaki Anthopoulos Pasha, took a rather languid view of the whole affair and, not wishing to get involved, had pointedly retired to the countryside.[34] At that moment Holstein, the *éminence grise* of German diplomacy, decided that the German game of embarrassing the British had been fun, but that it was now time to move on to wiser courses. He sent a one-sentence telegram to Metternich: "For us the main thing is that the Sultan should reach some kind of agreement with the English."[35]

And this indeed was what was about to happen. Tawfiq Pasha was trying to tie the British down with an agreement that would salvage as much as possible of the Ottoman position. This was essentially a policy of the Ottoman ministers, the Sultan himself being inclined to wait and see.[36] The British were ready to exchange a promise not to change the status of Kuwait for an Ottoman one not to interfere militarily. Lansdowne, who took little interest in Kuwait, would be happy to dispose of the affair without losing face or provoking a tiresome quarrel with the eloquent Curzon. He made his views clear in a letter to the British ambassador Lascelles in Berlin: "Personally I have always disliked the Koweit business, and if it were not that we were somewhat committed to the Sheikh – and also on the future of the Porte –, I should have thought we had much better let the Turks have him and thank God ourselves that we were rid of a knave. But I am afraid it would give Curzon a fit to hear that anybody said so."[37] Apparently the noble Lord Lansdowne thought that Lascelles, whose blundering in giving Rosen an ambiguous formula for the British view on the Ottoman position in Kuwait had seriously weakened the British position, would be more sympathetic to his viewpoint than Curzon, who wanted a full British protectorate!

[33] Lepsius, *Grosse Politik*, Vol. 17, pp. 490–1, telegram from Wangenheim 6 September 1901.

[34] Lepsius, *Grosse Politik*, Vol. 17, pp. 491–2, private telegram from Metternich to Holstein 7 September 1901.

[35] Lepsius, *Grosse Politik*, Vol. 17, p. 492, private telegram from Holstein to Metternich 7 September 1901.

[36] Lepsius, *Grosse Politik*, Vol. 17, pp. 499–500, Marschall 2 October 1901.

[37] Busch, *Britain and the Persian Gulf*, p. 208.

By then it was as clear as day that the Turks would not dare to stand up to the British and would seek some compromise. Others were unhappy at this Ottoman attitude. The Russians grumbled that the Turks should have taken their advice of early 1900 and occupied Kuwait then.[38] Richthofen was still trying to persuade the Turks to have recourse to The Hague, but the Sultan feared that this might inspire Bulgaria to bring its Macedonia dispute with Turkey to The Hague, and so cause complications.[39] Chancellor Bülow agreed with Holstein that it was not worth risking an Anglo-German conflict over the matter. He warned the German foreign ministry that Germany had no territorial ambitions in Kuwait, and that the Baghdad Railway Company was an international business enterprise, not a German political venture.[40]

The view from Constantinople was that the crisis had passed. Marschall considered, by 2 October 1901, that matters would soon be settled unless Mubarak and the Amir started a new war, in which case the English might find a pretext to intervene. Marschall's fear was justified, as the Ottomans had few means of restraining these excitable Arab potentates.[41] Meanwhile the British "promise" not to change the status of Kuwait had been formulated. Bülow felt that, in negotiating with O'Conor without liaising with the Germans, the Turks had been insufficiently collaborative. He ordered Marschall to desist from pressing the Turks to submit the case to the International Court at The Hague. A commendably clear-sighted politician, he once again formulated Germany's political goals in the Kuwait affair in order of priority: first, the maintenance of German prestige; second, the general territorial integrity of the Ottoman Empire; and, a mere third, the uncertain future of the railway.[42]

Meanwhile the British and the Turks had agreed on the formulation of the notes to be exchanged to bring a formal end to the dispute. Tawfiq correctly gave copies of the drafts to the German ambassador Marschall on 5 October. The British press was still trumpeting that Germany had been

---

[38] Lepsius, *Grosse Politik,* Vol. 17, p. 494, telegram from Richthofen to Bülow 12 September 1901.

[39] Lepsius, *Grosse Politik*, Vol. 17, pp. 496–7, private telegram from Metternich to Holstein 7 September 1901.

[40] Lepsius, *Grosse Politik,*Vol. 17, p. 498, Bülow to Foreign Ministry 1 October 1901.

[41] Lepsius, *Grosse Politik,*Vol. 17, p. 499, Marschall 2 October 1901.

[42] Lepsius, *Grosse Politik,*Vol. 17, pp. 500–1, Bülow to Marschall 4 October 1901.

behind the dispute, so Bülow wished Metternich to inform Lansdowne unequivocally that Germany had no interests in Kuwait.[43]

The Germans tried to cover their retreat with some fancy footwork. To season his meeting with Lansdowne a little, Metternich was to draw the Foreign Secretary's attention to *Persia and the Persian Question*, Curzon's famous book in which the great man himself, in mentioning that Britain accepted Ottoman authority over the region between Basra and al-Hasa, had implied that Britain recognized Ottoman authority over Kuwait! Rosen, an avid reader, had come across this little gem. This neat diplomatic thrust was foiled by a slightly ludicrous series of events, which illustrates the workings of diplomatic bureaucracies. Lansdowne showed polite interest in the quote and asked Metternich to be shown the passage. Metternich did not have it to hand and tried to obtain a copy of the book, but it was out of print. An antiquarian bookseller offered it for ten pounds, and Metternich asked Berlin's permission to spend that sum. Berlin refused, advising Metternich to borrow the book from the Berlin foreign ministry's library. The library refused, on the grounds that the book could not be sent outside the country ... by which stage the provocative little barb had quite lost its sting.[44]

A final hitch arose from a discreet Ottoman attempt to deceive the British. Tawfiq added three words to the Ottoman promise not to intervene militarily in exchange for the British promise not to declare Kuwait a British protectorate. These words were *"en ce moment"*, "for the time being". Lansdowne was not so stupid as to fall for this ruse, which would render the entire promise worthless.[45] The necessary formal steps were now taken. Kostaki Anthopoulos conveyed Tawfiq's statement to Lansdowne, and Lansdowne replied to Tawfiq through a note by O'Conor

---

[43] Lepsius, *Grosse Politik*, Vol. 17, p. 498, Bülow to German Foreign Ministry 1 October 1901. The tone of the British press can be seen from *The Times* of 12 September 1901 in which, in an article entitled "Great Britain and Turkey", it is stated: "Any hesitation to uphold the status quo in the Persian Gulf, even should it turn out in this case that the action of the Porte was prompted or supported by a great continental Power would be viewed in India with the utmost concern."

[44] Curzon, *Persia and the Persian Question*, Vol. 2, p. 462. Berlin AA, R 13885 A 14343, note by Rosen 9 October 1901, and instruction to Metternich 10 October 1901; R 13844 A 14652, Metternich 17 October 1901; R 13885 A 15620, Metternich 2 November, and Foreign Ministry to Metternich 12 November 1911.

[45] Plass, *England*, p. 296.

which repeated Tawfiq's text without the inclusion of the words *en ce moment*, and ended with Britain's promise in exchange, that it would not occupy Kuwait nor establish a protectorate there, provided the Turks did not send troops and respected the status quo there.[46] The Turks did not quibble with this British response, and so the matter was settled in October 1901 by a formal exchange of notes in good diplomatic form. In this exchange of notes, the British form of words was now the determining one – the ultimate text to which the Ottomans had raised no objection.

Our conclusion must be that the *Zuhaf* affair throughout exemplified the Turks' bad management, which was cleverly exploited by Mubarak. A verbal flare-up between Pears and the captain of the *Zuhaf*, and the subsequent tough British line at least partly fuelled by Mubarak feeding Pears with disinformation, could only drag the British into an open defence of Mubarak from the Turks – just the thing Mubarak needed at that moment. The diplomatic exchanges that followed displayed neither British nor Ottoman diplomacy to best advantage.

The incident and the ensuing Status Quo Understanding reverberated through the world's press in wildly divergent guises. The visit of the *Zuhaf* had naturally provoked uproar in the Indian newspapers, but some European papers too voiced criticism of the Ottoman attempt to gain a foothold in Kuwait. The *Times of India* could quote with relish the Austrian *Neue Wiener Tagblatt*'s opinion that the Turkish move was calculated to disturb the peace.[47] Diplomatic secrecy was only partly maintained. The *Daily Telegraph* declared that in the final agreement Great Britain had informed the Porte that she had no intention of occupying Kuwait or interfering with the Sultan's suzerainty, but would not allow its cession to any other power.[48] This was a rather woolly and inaccurate rendering of the exchange of notes. The *Times of India* fulminated about the British recognition of Ottoman suzerainty, "an act in defiance of the interests of India that calls for the severest condemnation". Such a reproach

[46] The British note concludes verbatim: "pourvu que le Gouvernement Turc s'abstienne d'envoyer des troupes à Koweit et y respecte le statu quo le Gouvernement de Sa Majesté (le roi) n'occupera pas cette place ni y établira un protectorat brittannique."

[47] *Times of India*, 26 September 1901. The Austrian paper's stance may have been inspired by the pro-British sympathies of the Austrian consul in Baghdad.

[48] *Daily Telegraph*, 14 October 1901; a similar piece also in *The Times* of the same date.

was unjustified, for the exchange of notes made no mention of suzerainty, but only of the status quo.[49] German and French newspapers ebulliently saw the outcome of the affair as a British retreat. The *Frankfurter Zeitung* even rejoiced in a supposed British recognition of the full sovereignty of the Sultan over Kuwait and of the Ottoman right to a railway line to Kuwait, on condition that the Turks permanently gave up the right to interfere militarily in Kuwait "where they had never had a garrison".[50] The Russian press seems to have come to the precise opposite understanding of the gist of the agreement, decrying the metamorphosis of Kuwait into a British port.[51] The Egyptian Arab press too indulged in vehement denunciations. The *Liwa* of 24 September was particularly badly informed, printing false reports that the Amir had entered Kuwait city and had showed mercy to Mubarak's allies. The Amir was said to have established his administration in Jahra! The *Mu'ayyad* warned that after their action in Kuwait the British would occupy Najd, and declared hysterically that Mubarak had killed his brother and attacked the Amir with the ultimate intention of conquering Iraq![52]

7.3 The Ottomans test the status quo

The exchange of notes of October 1901 can be regarded as a de facto recognition of Kuwait's autonomy by the Porte. But the Turks appear to have regarded it as no more than a temporary undertaking to leave the Kuwait affair pending. Almost at once they seemed surreptitiously to be trying to stretch the status quo in Kuwait as far as possible to their advantage. This could be done in various ways. The general lack of cohesion within the imperial administration gave local officials scope to experiment with their own initiatives. Then there were Arab leaders regarded as more or less under Ottoman authority, who could instigate their own operations, perhaps goaded on by elements within the Ottoman

---

[49] *Times of India*, 16 October 1901. The *Times of India* took this as an opportunity to insert a long account of the history of the Kuwait affair.

[50] *Frankfurter Zeitung*, 7 October 1901; cf. *Figaro*, 8 October.

[51] *St Petersburger Herald*, 12 December 1901.

[52] Egyptian newspapers: *Liwa*, 24 September 1901, article "La révolution en Arabie et la trahison du Cheyk de Koweyt" translated in Paris AE, NS Mascate 6, fo. 187. The *Mu'ayyad* of 18 September 1901, ibid., fos. 170–171.

system. Sultan Abdulhamid seems to have thought the latter a safe and deniable method, but that was a misjudgement, because initiatives by local officials or tribal leaders could backfire by showing him to be not in control and unable to honour his agreements. The *Perseus* incident had already demonstrated how the initiative of a military officer, combined with skilful manipulation on Mubarak's part, could unexpectedly damage the Ottoman case and lead to Kuwait's status being clarified in Mubarak's favour. In the months that followed, the same combination of ill-managed Ottoman initiatives and discreet provocation by Mubarak continued to produce similar results.

As early as October 1901, it was already evident that the Turks were up to something. The long-delayed departure of Muhsin from Basra finally took place and his successor Mustafa Nuri Pasha was on his way.[53] The Turks denied any link between this and the Kuwait affair, but it was generally thought to be directly connected, as the replacement was rumoured to have been caused by the military commander Ahmad Fayzi Pasha's complaints about Muhsin's relations with Mubarak.[54] Another issue was the Ottoman force that had originally been destined for Kuwait, but that had now been marooned in Samawa for half a year. Its presence was a running source of tension. As early as 12 September the Viceroy Lord Curzon had reported to London on renewed troop concentrations in Basra. These may have been no more than manoeuvres connected with the *Zuhaf* incident, but a *Times* article, by a Turkish exile in London, about Ottoman troop deployments in the region and stormy exchanges between Mubarak and Ahmad Fayzi Pasha, conveys the impression that there was trouble brewing.[55] The British duly prepared a plan for the defence of Kuwait.[56]

In Baghdad rumours persisted that the Turks were preparing to intervene in Kuwait, and even that Ottoman troops were approaching it.[57]

[53] Paris AE, NS Mascate 7, fos. 44–45, Rouet 25 October 1901.

[54] *Neue Politische Correspondenz* of 16 October 1901, where it is also said that the Turks considered the Kuwait affair to be over.

[55] *The Times* of 2 October 1901, article entitled "The troubles at Koweyt" (not to be confused with another more general article on the situation in Kuwait in the same edition). The article gives a peculiar and somewhat primitive summary of the history of Kuwait. Of particular interest is the remark that Mubarak's last war against the Amir occurred because the Sultan "had urged the Amir to attack him".

[56] Bidwell, *Affairs of Kuwait*, 1/3, pp. 114–48, defence plan by Capt. Field of the *Marathon* in Kuwait, 28 September 1901.

Such rumours may just have been a local Ottoman attempt to keep up the pressure on Mubarak. Nonetheless the Russian ambassador in Constantinople received orders to warn the Turks to abide by the Status Quo Understanding.[58] This warning was due not to Russian sympathy with Mubarak, but to Russian fears that the Ottomans, by breaking the agreement, might hand the British a pretext for occupying Kuwait. Marschall, the German ambassador in Constantinople, correctly identified the discontent and gossip among the Ottoman military in Baghdad as the source of Russian fears. Like the Russians he was trying to defuse such tension. The Germans were not happy with Richarz's frequent intercourse with the Baghdad military, whose wild opinions he kept passing on to his superiors. In the end the ministry in Berlin ordered Marschall to suggest Richarz limit his contacts with local officers.[59] But the Germans themselves were also indulging in wild conspiracy theories. They suspected the Russians of having incited the Turks to reopen the Kuwait affair in order to foment trouble between Britain and Germany.[60] In reality it remains debatable whether the Ottoman military seriously contemplated a real confrontation over Kuwait. The only firepower available to them at Samawa was some light mountain artillery, which stood no chance against the heavy guns of the British ships.[61]

There remained another source of instability: the continuing presence of the Rashidi Amir in the region. The Government of India feared that the Amir, possibly inspired by Ottoman diehards, would make a new attempt on Kuwait. In fact Mubarak's tribal position was improving. The reconciliation between Mubarak and Qasim Al-Thani, which had taken place at the time of Sarif, had increased the vulnerability of the southern flank of the Amir's territory, where the Mutayr and 'Ajman too were

[57] Berlin AA, R 13885 A 16186, telegram from Marschall 16 November 1901.
[58] Berlin AA, R 13885 A 16602, telegram from Marschall 23 November 1901. According to Bondarevsky, Kuwait, pp. 225–6, Zinoviev did indeed at that time have a talk with Tawfiq in which both agreed that Kuwait should not be attacked.
[59] Berlin AA, R 13885 A 16186, telegram from Marschall 16 November 1901, and telegram from Berlin to Marschall 22 November 1901.
[60] Lepsius, Grosse Politik, pp. 504–6, Mühlberg to German ambassador Marschall in Constantinople, 15 November 1901; Berlin AA, R 13853 A 16408, telegram Marschall to Richarz 22 November 1901.
[61] Vienna HHSA, PA XXXVIII 318, B 1901, Rappaport in Baghdad 13 September 1901.

troublesome.[62] But from time to time there were auguries of impending hostilities between Mubarak and the Amir.[63] There is no strong evidence that the Turks were behind Rashidi hostility towards Mubarak, as the Amir seems to have concluded that an Ottoman alliance could confer no advantage. Indeed he had already approached the British when it looked as if the Turks would withhold their assistance.[64] The British Government had grasped how limited Ottoman control was over Ibn Rashid, and that it might therefore be wise to warn him off Kuwait directly. Wratislaw was instructed to do so, and wrote a letter to the Amir. He received a haughty answer, but was also told informally by an intermediary that the Amir would like contact with Britain.[65] But this time it seems to have been no more than a ruse, because the Amir sent copies of his correspondence with Wratislaw to the Porte as proof of his deep loyalty to the Sultan. The Sultan showed the correspondence to the German ambassador Marschall, and they both interpreted it as a rejection by the Amir of a British approach for an alliance with the Amir.[66] Constantinople was a hotbed of diplomatic intrigue, and the purport of the correspondence between the Sultan and the Amir about the exchange between the latter and Wratislaw was also leaked by "a reliable source" to O'Conor, but the British ambassador was not impressed.[67]

Ottoman policy towards Mubarak remained opaque. The Ottoman force of 5–6000 men, still stationed near Samawa, could not go on living

[62] There is an interesting but not always accurate description in an article in the Egyptian newpaper *Al-Mu'ayyad* of 29 September 1901, containing information given by a young Egyptian traveller, "Bayoumi Ibrahim Effendi". It shows the state of public opinion in the Arab world. The Egyptian met Mubarak, who was very explicit in his desire for revenge on the Amir because of the death of his brother Hamud. Noteworthy is the reference to Qasim Al-Thani, who had now become an ally of Mubarak and had attacked Ottoman troops.

[63] Berlin AA, R 13885 A 16438 (21 November 1901), Richarz 17 October 1901; A 16465 (21 November 1901), telegram Marschall 21 November 1901; Nantes AD, consulat Bagdad B 29, Rouet 25 October and 6 November 1901.

[64] Bidwell, *Affairs of Kuwait*, 1/3, p. 61, Wratislaw, 3 June 1901: the Amir sent a message to Wratislaw that he wanted to be taken under British protection, provided Mubarak was replaced in Kuwait by his nephew Sabah.

[65] Bidwell, *Affairs of Kuwait*, 1/3, p. 106, Wratislaw 22 August; p. 128, Wratislaw 25 September; pp. 135–6, Wratislaw 1 October; and p. 137, O'Conor 4 November 1901.

[66] Berlin AA, R 13885 A 14616 (16 October 1901), telegram from Marschall 15 October 1901; and A 14813 (20 October 1901), Marschall 17 October 1901.

off such a poor district indefinitely. The purpose of this force was ostensibly to maintain the pressure on Mubarak, but it is also possible that it was there to discourage Ibn Rashid from attacking Kuwait, as that would provoke British intervention. It was probably the proximity of this army that induced Sa'dun of the Muntafiq to give himself up to the Turks. The Ottoman military in Iraq kept pressing for an occupation of Kuwait and, now that the danger on their flank from Sa'dun had been removed, the screw could be tightened.[68] Ottoman officials told the French consul in Baghdad that they were trying to keep the Amir away from Kuwait, but on the other hand Muhammad Pasha, the commander in Samawa, had been intriguing against Mubarak. This Pasha had been advising the 'Aniza, allies of Mubarak who often feature as an important factor in the unrest of the time, to remain neutral in the conflict between Mubarak and the Amir. Part of the 'Aniza had at first sided with the Amir, but had then gone over to his opponents.[69] During September 1901, one of their shaikhs, a certain Salih bin Hasan Al-Muhanna Aba 'l-Khayl of Burayda, had been recruiting warriors among the Arabian nomads who flocked to Egypt during that season.[70] In October the 'Aniza were defeated by Kazim Pasha.[71] One catches a glimpse of the wider Ottoman strategy from a telegram from the French consul in Baghdad of 7 November, which mentions Muhammad Pasha's report of his failure to turn the Muntafiq

---

[67] Berlin AA, R 13885 A 14813 (20 October 1901), Marschall 17 October 1901; cf. Bidwell, *Affairs of Kuwait*, 1/3, p. 139, O'Conor 8 November 1901. The French consul in Baghdad was also informed by the Turks. According to Rouet's source, the Amir had assured the Sultan that he as well as Mubarak were his devoted servants, and would be so in all circumstances. The last words were seen by Rouet as a poisonous barb directed at Mubarak: Paris AE, NS Mascate 7, fos. 52–53, Rouet 14 November 1901.
[68] Berlin AA, R 13885 A 16130 (15 November 1901), Richarz 16 October 1901.
[69] Berlin AA, R 13850 A 13288, telegram of the Ministry in Berlin to Richarz in Baghdad, 17 September 1901.
[70] Paris AE, NS Mascate 7, fos. 41–42, French consulate in Cairo, 23 October 1901. Shaikh Salih was one of the Burayda shaikhs who in 1900 had escaped from the Amir's prison to Kuwait. An Ottoman document of October warning about the journey of one of Mubarak's men from Egypt to Syria may also be connected with this activity: Istanbul BA, DUIT 69/2–13, memorandum of Rays ul-Kitab, 18 Rajab 1319/31 October 1901. See also Berlin AA, R 13885 A 16560 (23 November 1901), consul Moritz in Cairo 23 November 1901, where there is mention of an article in the Egyptian newspaper *Liwa* of 24 September 1901 reporting that the Porte had ordered the arrest of Shaikh Salih, who was accused of being a British agent.

and 'Aniza against Mubarak, and states that an operation against these powerful tribes would be risky and incur more losses and expense than a direct operation against Kuwait. This seems firm evidence that, at a high level, the Ottomans were still contemplating military action against the shaikhdom.[72]

In November 1901, the Sultan devised new methods of regaining control over Kuwait without directly confronting the British. It seems that he was now trying to exploit the hostility between Russia and Britain to obtain some Russian leverage for asserting his claim to Kuwait. The Russians took up the sport of baiting the British in the Gulf with some enthusiasm, and went to some lengths to do so, suppressing even their old fears about the Baghdad Railway to sound out the Germans about a common policy. The Germans made it clear that they had once advised the Turks to submit the dispute to the court in The Hague, anticipating that the mere presentation of the case before the court would deter the British. The advice had been repeated in vain. Because of this the Germans felt they "were no longer able to advise the Porte".[73]

7.4 The *Pomone* flag incident

After his failure to obtain a satisfactory diplomatic solution of the Kuwait affair in September–October 1901, the Sultan reverted to his old ploy of trying to put pressure on Mubarak through his private network. In early November 1901, the Naqib of the Rifa'iyya brotherhood in Basra was sent on a visit to Mubarak to exhort him to return to the Ottoman fold. Mubarak was warned that Britain was powerless to protect him from the might of the Ottoman Empire. The mission fell on deaf ears.[74] Then the

---

[71] Berlin AA, R 13885 A 15017 (25 October 1901), telegram from Marschall 24 October 1901.

[72] Paris AE, NS Mascate 7, fo. 49, telegram from Rouet 7 November 1901; Berlin AA, R 13885 A 15927 (11 November 1901), Marschall 9 November 1901: high Ottoman military in Baghdad fear that the Muntafiq and the 'Aniza will become independent if the Turks do not occupy Kuwait. Meanwhile Kazim Pasha was spreading rumours in Baghdad that an attack on Kuwait by the army in Samawa was soon to be expected: Berlin AA, R 13885 A 16186, telegram from Marschall 16 November 1901.

[73] Lepsius, *Grosse Politik*, Vol. 17, pp. 504–5, Foreign Ministry to Marschall 15 November 1901.

[74] Correspondence about this mission is in IOLR, R/15/1/474, fos. 290–305.

Naqib came again to Kuwait on 28 November, together with the brother of Mustafa Nuri Pasha in the *Zuhaf*, with the demand that Mubarak should either behave as other shaikhs (apparently implying that he should accept an Ottoman garrison) or leave Kuwait, to reside either in Constantinople with the rank of state councillor, or elsewhere outside the region.[75] It is not entirely clear on whose authority such a mission was sent to Kuwait. Jabir vouchsafed, on behalf of his father, that Mubarak's agent in Basra had been informed that the Wali had received a telegram from the Sultan. But the Ottoman Government later denied having sent the mission. This may be true, as up to now no formal order has come to light in the Ottoman archives, and it was not unusual for the Sultan to bypass his own government. This new approach represented a significant development. The Sultan now dealt with Mubarak not through the imperial administration, but through the Islamic channel. This could, of course, be seen as a vindication of Mubarak's view of the Sultan as his religious and not his administrative superior.

The British were first informed of the Naqib's mission by Mubarak, who claimed to have received the text of a telegram from Constantinople, accompanied by a telegram to the Wali of Basra from the Sultan's private secretary.[76] Later the Ottomans claimed that the Naqib had come on a private visit, but this is hardly compatible with the facts: the Naqib arrived in Kuwait on the warship *Zuhaf* accompanied by the Wali's brother.[77] The French consul in Baghdad, Rouet, had no doubt about the character of the mission, reporting as early as 26 November that the Naqib had been sent by the Sultan to Mubarak on the *Zuhaf*. He also reported the rumour that

[75] IOLR, R/15/1/474, fo. 359, telegram from chief private secretary of the Sultan to the Wali of Basra, 23 November 1901; *cf.* Nantes AD, consulat Bagdad B 29, Rouet 5 December 1901.

[76] IOLR, R/15/1/474, fos. 329–331, commander *Redbreast*, Mubarak to Bushire, 29 November 1901.

[77] Bidwell, *Affairs of Kuwait*, 1/3, pp. 154–5, Lansdowne to O'Conor on a talk with the Ottoman ambassador.

[78] Paris AE, NS Mascate 7, fos. 61–62, Rouet 26 November 1901. Rouet sardonically described the *Zuhaf* as "*de triste mémoire*" ("of sad memory", referring to its failed mission in August). In a letter of 5 December, Rouet wrote that the mission of the *Zuhaf* and the proposal for a gendarmerie were "platonic satisfactions for the Turks which merely confirmed the inability of the Porte to impose its authority over Kuwait": Nantes AD, consulat Bagdad A 32, pp. 267–8.

the Naqib was under instructions to suggest that Mubarak organize a Kuwaiti Arab regiment of gendarmerie, in the uniform of Ottoman zaptis. Rouet considered this to be just another face-saving device by the Sultan – to leave Mubarak be, but to give him an Ottoman coloration.[78] Whatever the precise purport of the proposals, they could with justification be regarded as an attempt to alter the status quo. While no actual invasion might be planned, Kuwait still felt the pressure of a military intervention, either by the Ottomans directly or indirectly through the Amir.

The double threat from the Turks and the Amir gave Mubarak an opportunity to enhance Britain's commitment to Kuwait's security. He acted scared, making it clear to the British naval officers present that he needed their help. Kemball in Bushire was convinced of the need to protect him. Already before the *Zuhaf*'s first mission he had visited Kuwait to tell Mubarak that Britain intended to protect him if he kept to his promises.[79] On 30 November Mubarak wrote to Kemball that the Naqib had left Basra for Kuwait. He warned the resident that "if I see that you do not check and prevent my enemies [...] I will not be able to go against the Turkish Government and the only alternative for me will be to join them." Kemball asked Simons, the commander of the cruiser *Pomone* and Senior Naval Officer in the Gulf, to remind Mubarak of his earlier promise, and at the same time advised Mubarak to prevaricate with the Naqib.

Kemball was expecting a crisis, and ordered the British ships to oppose any attempt to infringe the status quo. When the Naqib arrived with his message, Mubarak thought it prudent to play for time and requested a few days to think about his reply. In reality this was meant to give the gunboat *Redbreast* time to warn Bushire.[80] At first the Turks acquiesced, but then they changed their mind and demanded an immediate reply. Mubarak chose this moment to act as if he was in great peril. He blankly refused to parley with the Ottoman officials unless British naval officers were present, and he appears to have impressed on the British how nervous he was about the Ottoman threat. Mubarak shrank from a direct confrontation with the Turks and the Naqib, preferring the British to bear the brunt of the encounter. The idea was to get the British to commit themselves unambiguously to the protection of Kuwait in front of Ottoman witnesses – a ploy that had already worked very well with the *Perseus* in August.

[79] PRO, FO 602/16, fos. 334–335, Kemball 23 August 1901.
[80] IOLR, R/15/1/474, fo. 345, Simons 3 September 1901.

Mubarak naturally had little use for the Ottoman offer of a comfortable sinecure as member of the Council of State. The French consul in Baghdad related how the Kuwaiti Shaikh demonstrated the risibility of the Sultan's offer. Mubarak claimed that he had over the past five years paid the sum of no less than 38,000 Turkish pounds in bribes to Ottoman officials, and now the Sultan was offering him an annual salary of 100 Turkish pounds (90 pounds sterling). Until what age, Mubarak asked, would he have to live on such a pension before he recouped the sums he had handed out![81]

The Shaikh prepared an excellent scenario. He first asked Simons for a written promise of protection and, on that being refused, agreed with Simons that the latter would warn him, in the presence of the Turks, that the *Pomone* would open fire on Kuwait if he accepted the Ottoman demands. In this way Mubarak contrived to maintain his innocence in the eyes of the Turks, while at the same time commit the British to an action that practically amounted to a protectorate. To the expostulations of the Naqib and the Wali's brother, Simons bluntly retorted that they had twice broken the status quo agreement by issuing threats to Mubarak. Simons declared that he was now entitled to order the Shaikh not to respond to their propositions.[82] The *Zuhaf* and its passengers left for Basra on 5 December. Kemball, in a letter to Wratislaw, commented: "It has been a narrow shave; if Mubarak had not received the support of the Senior Naval Officer he would, I believe, have gone over to the Turks, as he clearly was very frightened; he was determined to get something out of us."[83] Kemball was obviously preparing his defence in case of being accused by London of having acted too vigorously!

The Ottoman documents make it plain that the whole incident took the Porte by surprise. Apparently Ottoman ministers had known neither about the Naqib's mission nor that the Sultan and his Yildiz Palace clique were behind it.[84] The Grand Vizier began by ordering the Basra Wali to hold his peace.[85] The minister of foreign affairs, Tawfiq, told Anthopoulos, ambassador in London, that the Turks intended to maintain the status quo, that the Naqib had intended no mischief towards Mubarak, and that he

[81] Nantes AD, ambassade Constantinople, E 288, Rouet 13 January 1902.
[82] IOLR, R/15/1/474, fos. 348–349, a hastily pencilled report from Simons in Kuwait to Kemball, 4 December 1901.
[83] PRO, FO 602/16, fos. 345–346, Kemball to Wratislaw 8 December 1901.

had boarded the *Zuhaf* merely because it was available. But Tawfiq then went on to formulate the Turkish position in a way that would certainly be unacceptable to Britain. British opposition to the presence of an Ottoman official in Kuwait, he said, would be in breach of the Status Quo Understanding, in which case the Turks would submit the matter to arbitration (apparently by the International Court in The Hague).[86] The Turks had little diplomatic support for this, as the Russian and German embassies were just then advising the Porte to try an emollient approach to Mubarak to prevent him siding with the British.[87]

Lansdowne protested about the incident to Anthopoulos, who replied that the British "were needlessly disturbed" because the Naqib had only been on a private visit. He had not been to Kuwait on an official mission, but only as a spiritual leader (a "kind of bishop" was the term used!) and the Porte had had nothing to do with it. This was a feeble excuse. As we have seen, the Naqib had been accompanied by a brother of the Wali of Basra, which lent the group some official weight, and they had come on board the warship *Zuhaf*, hardly a way for private visitors to travel. Anthopoulos also discreetly let drop the story of another incident during the visit. According to him, the *Pomone*'s commander had hauled down the Ottoman flag from Mubarak's palace (where it had flown for "300 [!] years") and replaced it with a black-and-white striped one, proclaiming it to be the new flag of Kuwait. Anthopoulos alleged that the commander had declared Kuwait to be an independent state and that the Turks had no business there. Lansdowne was incredulous. The British archives give no indication that Anthopoulos followed his instructions to the full in threatening that the matter might be submitted to the International Court.[88]

---

[84] Berlin AA, R 13886 A 18093 (21 December 1901), telegram from Marschall 21 December 1901: Tawfiq told the German ambassador "that he had told the Sultan that if he had been informed earlier about the mission of the Naqib he would have advised against it". Anscombe, *Ottoman Gulf*, pp. 126–7, tries to explain the difference of opinion within the Ottoman system.

[85] Istanbul BA, Y.A. Hüs 422/68, 28 Saban 1319/10 December 1901.

[86] Istanbul BA, Y.A. Hüs 423/8, Tawfiq to Anthopoulos, 1 Ramadan 1319/11 December 1901.

[87] Istanbul BA, Y.A. Hüs 423/8, memorandum by Tawfiq to Grand Vizier, 4 Ramadan 1319/15 December 1901.

[88] Bidwell, *Affairs of Kuwait*, 1/3, pp. 155–6, Lansdowne to Bunsen (chargé d'affaires in Constantinople while O'Conor was on leave) 17 December 1901.

The truth about the flag incident was this. The commander of the *Pomone*, wanting to keep in communication with his ship while in Mubarak's palace, was using the palace flagpole for signalling – the black and white flag was a signal flag.[89] The Turks, however, circulated a much-embroidered version of the story among their friends. The commander of the gunboat *Zuhaf* related how he had brought the Naqib and the Wali's brother to Kuwait. On these gentlemen presenting themselves to Mubarak in the palace, a British officer and some sailors suddenly materialized, and roughly enquired of the Naqib what his business was. Then the British officer, pointing at the Ottoman flag on the palace, declared that it should not be there, ordering it to be lowered and replaced with a black-and-white striped one, which he said was the flag of Kuwait. The officer tore the Ottoman flag to shreds with his own hands.

The matter was reported by the Turks to the German ambassador Marschall who, as he had been instructed, wisely declined to comment on this lurid tale.[90] Maximov, dragoman to the Russian embassy, was also informed, but this worthy played a duplicitous role. Maximov told the German embassy that he had advised the Porte to send two or three warships to Kuwait and expel the British.[91] According to the Ottoman records, however, it appears rather that the Russian dragoman had, just like his German colleague, advised the Turks to move cautiously.[92] A few days later the Sultan's secretary Izzet Bey approached Marschall for advice as to how to respond to British misdeeds. The German ambassador, sick and tired of Ottoman chicanery, gave the barbed answer: "In the past we have given advice on the Kuwait affair. His Majesty the Sultan has, I do not doubt on weighty grounds, adopted other courses. Because of this, I am now unable to offer further advice."[93]

---

[89] Bidwell, *Affairs of Kuwait*, 1/3, p. 160, commander of *Pomone* 20 December 1901.

[90] Berlin AA, R 13886 A 17821 (16 December 1901), telegram from Marschall in Pera 15 December 1901.

[91] Lepsius, *Grosse Politik*, Vol. 17, p. 507, Marschall 15 December 1901: Mr Maximov (the dragoman of the Russian embassy) had said that the Porte should send two to three warships to Kuwait: "It is enough to open the gunports and to say to the British 'shoot first'." That would, according to Maximov, make them leave instantly, as the Russians had experienced several times [with the British] in China.

[92] Istanbul BA, Y.A. Hüs. 423/8, memorandum by Tawfiq, 4 Ramadan 1319/15 December 1901.

[93] Lepsius, *Grosse Politik*, Vol. 17, p. 508, Marschall 18 December 1901.

The "flag crisis" appears to have made most impression on the Russians.[94] It was probably coincidence that it happened just while a large Russian warship, the *Varyag*, was on a Gulf cruise. The *Varyag*, a first-class armoured deck cruiser, was the largest warship yet seen in the Gulf.[95] She arrived in Kuwait on 8 December, just three days after the *Zuhaf* had left. Mubarak trod warily in the diplomatic minefield of the time, and declined to visit the *Varyag* as he had with the *Gilyak* the previous year.[96] The officers of the *Varyag* and the Bushire consul-general, Ovseyenko, visited his son Shaikh Jabir, who was acting as deputy ruler. The Russians walked about a bit and saw Mubarak's army, which they judged a motley crew of minimal military value. They also saw trenches around Kuwait in the European manner, which must have been the British defence works of the previous summer, but few other signs of British presence, except that the *Pomone* was off the coast. They then went to Jahra to see Mubarak, who received them very cordially, telling them that he would like Russian ships to visit Kuwait more often and "that he would prefer to turn to the Russians for help than to any other nation if Kuwait got into trouble." He then reiterated his opposition to the railway.[97] According to the version given by Ovseyenko to his French colleague in Bushire, Mubarak had told the Russians that his sole desire was to remain independent.[98] The fact is that it all these warm words to the Russians were very vague and non-committal. To the British Mubarak drew a veil of mystery over the visit – predictably – with the intention of rattling them a bit.[99]

The flag affair received wide coverage in the press, which was now fully alert to the "Koweit crisis".[100] The delay of several weeks in reporting the

[94] Berlin AA, R 13886 A 17999 (19 December 1901), telegram from Marschall in Pera 19 December 1901.
[95] Vienna HHSA, PA XXXVIII K 318 (1901), Rappaport 28 December 1901.
[96] According to the French consul in Bushire, Mubarak had gone away on a hunting trip on the advice of the captain of the *Pomone*: Paris AE, NS Mascate 17, fos. 9–12, consul Bushire 21 February 1902.
[97] Rezvan, *Russian Ships*, pp. 73–6, report of the captain of the *Varyag*.
[98] Paris AE, NS Mascate 17, fos. 9–12, consul Bushire 21 February 1902.
[99] Bidwell, *Affairs of Kuwait*, 2/4, pp. 3–4.
[100] *St Petersburger Herald* 12 December; *Frankfurter Zeitung* 20 December; *The Times* 21 December. It should be noted that the Germans played a rather nasty trick on the British by hinting to the Turks that it would be wise to leak Lansdowne's "unsatisfactory" (*unbefriedigend*) explanation of the incident to a German journalist: Berlin AA, R 13886 A 18093, telegram Berlin to Marschall 22 December 1901.

Perseus incident was not repeated. The Russian press was especially excited.[101] A Dutch magazine even circulated a full-size poster with a cartoon of the "Koweit affair".[102] But the diplomatic crisis would not last long, because no European power was certain enough of the facts to intervene in favour of the Turks. Moreover the Status Quo Understanding was a bilateral matter between the Ottoman Empire and Britain, and hence other governments were not entitled to intervene.

The Turks then tried to squeeze Mubarak another way. Mustafa Nuri Pasha forbade the exportation of food from Basra province to Kuwait. O'Conor protested so vehemently this time that Tawfiq hastened to ascribe the measure to local initiative taken without consulting the Porte. By now this kind of excuse had been used so often that nobody believed it any more – although this time it may have been true.[103]

Turkish attempts to pressurize Mubarak were not the only Kuwaiti problems to preoccupy the British.[104] The end of December 1901 saw new reports of an impending assault by the Amir of Haïl. Even the German ambassador warned the Turks of the consequences of the Amir's actions.[105] His troops had approached Kuwait and camped at Safwan, prompting the

[101] Berlin AA, R 13886 A 18280 (25 December 1901), Marschall 23 December 1901. One ranting article in the *Novoye Vremiye* so caught the eye of the British Foreign Office that a translation was circulated in its confidential print (published in Bidwell, *Affairs of Kuwait*, 1/3, p. 164).

[102] Cartoon by Johan Braakensiek in the Dutch magazine *De Amsterdammer*, 12 January 1902. This was probably the only periodical to devote a cartoon to the Kuwait conflict. As was commonplace in the Continental media, the affair was also misunderstood by the *Amsterdammer* as a victory for the Turks over the British, who were thought to have been obliged to give up their plan for a protectorate. The cartoon shows John Bull (Britain) politely being bowed out of Kuwait by the Sultan, under the approving gaze of the Emperor Wilhelm II and Czar Nicholas II.

[103] Bidwell, *Affairs of Kuwait*, 1/3, p. 159, Lansdowne to Bunsen 23 December 1901; and ibid., p. 161, O'Conor 27 December 1901. An Ottoman document appears to indicate that Mustafa Nuri Pasha had ordered the blockade as a punishment measure for the incident with the Naqib: Istanbul BA,Y.A. Hüs 423/29, 11 December 1317/23 December 1901. On the other hand the British consul in Basra wrote that the blockade was ordered by an irade (an order of the Sultan): Bidwell, *Affairs of Kuwait*, 1/3, p. 166, Government of India to India Office 22 December 1901.

[104] Bidwell, *Affairs of Kuwait*, 1/3, p. 151: instructions from Lansdowne to Bunsen in Constantinople to protest about the concentration of Ottoman troops reported by Simons; ibid., p. 154, reply by Bunsen: news given by Simons is not true.

[105] Istanbul BA,Y.A. Hüs 423/29, Grand Vizier 18 Ramadan 1319/25 December 1901.

commander of the *Pomone* to station heavy artillery at Jahra to protect
Kuwait's water supply.[106] On hearing of this the Sultan was furious,
proposing that his Government should threaten force against the guns and
institute proceedings in The Hague.[107] This was preposterous, for the
Ottomans had no power to confront the British and it was now too late
for The Hague. The British withdrew the artillery as soon as the Amir
retired. The Ottoman Government finally judged the Amir's menacing
manoeuvres to be contrary to the imperial interest. Troops were deployed
to occupy positions between the Amir and Kuwait, as described below in
section 7.6.[108]

Mubarak had succeeded in sucking Britain into full military protection
of his autonomy. This was much more than envisaged by the vague
promise of "good offices" in the 1899 Agreement. Now the only
outstanding grey area was the exact extent of Mubarak's territory to be
protected against Ottoman or Rashidi incursion.

7.5 International opinion in early 1902

During the second half of 1901, the Ottomans had made inconclusive
moves towards a military resolution of the Kuwait affair, yet it was the
reverberations of the relatively trivial flag incident that continued to stir
international diplomacy and the press. There had never been much
sympathy in Europe for the regime of Abdulhamid II and Britain too was
unpopular. It is no wonder that speculation was rife about alternative
solutions to the Kuwait problem. However serious the flag incident might
appear, the Germans were reluctant to take sides in an Ottoman–British
conflict. Russia and France first wished to establish the facts and appraise

[106] Bidwell, *Affairs of Kuwait*, 1/3, p. 161, Commander-in-Chief Indian Navy, 25
December 1901; ibid., pp. 167–8, Simons 31 December 1901. As might be expected,
O'Conor grumbled about the risks of landing artillery for relations with the Turks:
ibid., p. 161, O'Conor 27 December 1901. For the Ottoman side, see Istanbul BA,
DUIT 69/2–17, 2 Shawal 1319/22 January 1901; DUIT 2/19, 8 Shawal 1319/28
January 1901; Y.A. Hüs 423/60, 21 Ramadan 1319/31 December 1901; and
Anscombe, *Ottoman Gulf*, pp. 127–8.
[107] Anscombe, *Ottoman Gulf*, pp. 127 and 230 n. 86.
[108] Istanbul BA, Y.A. Hüs, 424/25, Memorandum of the Grand Vizier, 9 Shawal
1319/19 January 1902: a defeat of Mubarak at the hands of Abdul Aziz Ibn Rashid is
not in the interest of the Ottoman Empire. Anscombe, *Ottoman Gulf*, pp. 127–8.

the local situation before they were ready to commit any support to the Turks. They both sent warships once more to gather intelligence.

The press aired much fascinating debate about Kuwait and its relation to the Ottoman Empire. The *Times of India*, subsidized by the Indian Government, had always championed the view that Britain should jump to its duty in the Gulf and declare Kuwait a protectorate.[109] German, Russian, French and Egyptian newspapers customarily supported the Ottoman viewpoint.[110] An entirely original perspective in the Egyptian newspaper *Pyramides* attracted widespread comment. It was written by Antonin Goguyer, a fanatically anglophobic French scholar and arms merchant in Muscat, who had some contact with Abdul Rahman Al-Saud.[111] Goguyer had perhaps already established contact with Mubarak too; he certainly did later, but we shall come to that in the next chapter. Goguyer analysed the entire Kuwait affair in a novel way. He identified two causal factors behind the crisis: the desire of the Turks to get their hands on the terminus of the Baghdad Railway, and the desire of the British to monopolize trade and shipping in the Gulf. His solution was simple: "The civilized states of continental Europe, Turkey included, must take the small state of Kuwait under their protection, confirming its independence, just as has been done for the Kingdom of Belgium, the Principality of Monaco, and so many other small republics of Europe or Central America." According to Goguyer this status could also be conferred upon the other small independent states of the Arabian Peninsula. The consequence of this idea would for Kuwait to acquire a status analogous to Belgium as a sovereign state, but with the obligation of neutrality and pacifism that Belgium had received under the 1839 Treaty of London. Goguyer made a second arresting point, that settlement of Arab affairs should be not only between the Arab states, but also within them. He explained that the authority of the shaikhs, in its original state, had been counterbalanced by the power of the tribal chiefs, but that British intervention had upset that balance by making the shaikhs more autocratic. Goguyer thirdly observed that British influence had also created immigration by wealthier people from India to the Gulf, who enriched themselves as bankers and merchants at the expense of the "noble race of Arabs", who were reduced to the status of serfs. This is used to good effect

[109] *Times of India*, 3 October 1901 and 2 January 1902; see the comment of the French consul Vossiou in Bombay of 23 October 1901 in Paris AE, NS Mascate 7, fo. 38.

as a stick to beat the British with: "It is clear that Europe – England excepted – has no interest in seeing the noble race of Arabs enslaved by the Hindus and hence by the masters of the Hindus." Goguyer's last two theses seem to be based on the situation pertaining in Bahrain, the Trucial States and Oman, as Kuwait had always been closed to Indian merchants. Goguyer had no standing at all in international diplomacy, and his article was no more than amateur speculation, but its proposal of a general "Arab" solution is interesting in view of his contacts.[112]

Meanwhile the French cruiser *Catinat*, which had been despatched to investigate the state of affairs in the aftermath of the flag incident, reached Kuwait on 20 February 1902. This visit was viewed with some satisfaction by the Ottoman military in Baghdad. Their hope was that visits by foreign warships such as the *Catinat* and, most recently, the *Varyag* might deter British intervention.[113] It was an idle hope. The warships had merely come to observe the situation and the British remained undeterred.

The commander of the *Catinat*, Kiésel, held talks with Mubarak, who this time did not avoid the French. Kiésel's report of the visit sheds telling light on what Mubarak judged appropriate for the French to know.[114] He even allowed a photograph to be taken during the long session, the first to be published. He gave an interesting resumé of his encounter with Stemrich and von Kapp, his quarrel with the Amir, the decline of Ottoman

---

[110] Berlin AA, R 13888 A 2871 (21 February 1902), quoting the Egyptian *Mu'ayyad*: "The influence of Al-Sabah extends among all the Arab tribes and, when we say the influence of Al-Sabah, we may as well say British influence: the Bedouins have confidence in Britain only. Now if Kuwait can be considered as lost, it can be expected that Iraq and the Hijaz will share the same fate. If Al-Sabah is punished as he deserves, Turkey can keep Britain in an attitude of respect."

[111] Goguyer's biography can be reconstructed from his personal file: Paris AE, NS Mascate 48. He also sometimes used the first name Antoine.

[112] Letter from Muscat of 15 January 1902 in *Pyramides* of 29 January 1902, cutting in Paris AE, NS Mascate 7, fos. 105–106.

[113] Nantes AD, consulat Bagdad B 29, Rouet to minister and ambassador 23 January 1902.

[114] Report of the *Catinat* in Paris AE, NS Mascate 17, fos. 24–29. The same volume contains other reports too on the visit. The same reports, with some other related papers, are in Vincennes SHM, BB4, 1857, where reside the best versions of the photographs taken by the mission. The visit of the *Catinat* to Kuwait was also reported in an article in a French magazine: F.L.B., "Voyage du 'Catinat' dans le Golfe Persique", *Le Monde Illustré* 1902, p. 202 (with photographs).

power in the Gulf. On relations with the Turks, he asserted that he had nothing to do with them. Mubarak concluded the meeting with the polite remark that he was delighted to see the French flag at Kuwait, and to have been able to explain his position to the representative of a nation with a universal reputation for justice. The French commander thought better of raising the subject of relations with Britain. He sensed the British presence everywhere, and the British commander Pelham entered as Kiésel took his leave, but Kiésel was unable to discover the precise nature of Anglo–Kuwaiti relations. His proposal to discharge a 21-gun salute (the customary number for a sovereign head of state) met Mubarak's rejoinder that he was grateful, but was unable to reciprocate this polite gesture because he had no artillery. Mubarak showed Kiésel the only flag on the palace: the Ottoman one. Kiésel regarded Mubarak as simply wishing to avoid all possible trouble.

Kiésel put his time in Kuwait to good use, sending people into the town to collect information. He also had a meeting with Abdul Rahman Al-Saud, the reason being that the latter had been in contact, through his Bahrain agent Muhammad Abdul Wahhab, with the French arms dealer Goguyer to request French protection. The anglophobe Goguyer would stop at nothing to obstruct what he regarded as perfidious British plans in Arabia, but Kiésel knew that he was in no position to instigate intrigues and admonished Abdul Rahman that Goguyer, even though he had friends among French politicians, lacked official standing as a representative of France.

Kiésel collected valuable information about the state of affairs in Kuwait. He reports that the Basra government had sent 65,000 bricks to Bubiyan to construct a building 15 metres long, and that 300 Ottoman soldiers were at Umm Qasr for the purpose of erecting a fortress there. It appeared to the French that Mubarak's approach to the British was hesitant and caused chiefly by fear of the Turks. The French caught wind of preparations by the Amir for a new assault on Kuwait. Kiésel gained the impression that Kuwaitis generally resented the British tie, but remained silent out of fear of Mubarak. But they approved of the presence of the French flag, a sentiment shared by their ruler. There was an English commercial agent in Kuwait, a certain Hajji 'Ali. Appointed by the resident in Bushire, he was a merchant who also carried on business on his own account. Since the early summer of 1901 the English had had an interpreter in Kuwait, a certain "Hajji Abdallah Kafer", who resided in Mubarak's palace.[115] According to Kiésel, Mubarak had recently proclaimed his full independence, having first recognized "the authority of the Sultan in Constantinople". Mubarak stated that he hoisted the Ottoman flag "as a simple mark of honour to the religious head he recognizes", and had never hoisted the British flag in Kuwait – a clear denial of the flag incident. Kiésel's conclusions were that Mubarak was not aware of the benefits to be reaped from the railway, that he had been intimidated by the Government of India, which tried to "shield him from all information that might enlighten him", and that the Turks had been too aggressive towards him. Ultimately, Kiésel thought, there would be only three alternatives for the future of Kuwait: conquest by the Amir, submission to the Sultan, or the acceptance of a British protectorate. Kiésel was "convinced of the sincere desire of Mubarak to remain independent", but did not think him in a position to resist the proposals of the most persuasive power. Kiésel's report boils down to the old French view that Mubarak was not a friend of the English *per se*, his actions being determined by his desire as far as possible to maintain his autonomy.[116]

France and Russia were not the only powers to pay close attention to Kuwaiti affairs. Every European power represented in Constantinople was now following them. Typical were the Netherlands, a power whose interest normally focused chiefly on the Balkans, Anatolia and, because of the Dutch East Indies, the territory with the largest Muslim population in the world, on Islamic movements. The Kuwait affair caught the eye of Baron Weckherlin, the Netherlands envoy, in January 1902. The Baghdad Railway concession had just been granted, prompting Weckherlin to ask the German ambassador Marschall whether Kuwait was to be the terminus.[117] Marschall replied that this point was left open in the concession, observing that when "people in the region see the line gradually approaching, they will squabble over whose land the track should cross, as happened in our country too". Weckherlin considered this

---

[115] Hajji 'Ali Ghulam had been, since 1899, the "secret" British news agent whose activities had become public knowledge in 1901. The other was probably a simple interpreter to serve the British warships.

[116] Kiésel's report of 24 February 1902 (the version in Paris AE, NS Mascate 17), fos. 26–28.

[117] Lepsius, *Grosse Politik,* Vol. 17, pp. 418–28, Marschall 2 February 1902.

assumption to be the reason why the Germans had not intervened in the dispute between the Ottomans and the British over the status of the Shaikh of Kuwait. What then follows in Weckherlin's report is a mixture of sound understanding and bad prophecy so typical of contemporary comment, worth quoting here *in extenso* as an example:

> I personally feel that Moubarek (that is the name of the Shaikh) feels no particular sympathy for either of the two powers [Britain and Turkey], but is only trying to play one off against the other to stay as independent of each as possible. As regards the railway, one might probably assume that, if this town [Kuwait] is really found to be the most appropriate for that purpose, Britain has little prospect of gaining exclusive control over it. In any event there is the question whether Russian ambitions in the direction of the Persian Gulf, and the actions it has already taken, do not show British dominance of those waters to be already in decline.[118]

Weckherlin's comment was not the most profound analysis of the international confusion surrounding the Kuwait affair. The real question was whether the status quo would be maintained. Pallavicini, the Austrian ambassador in Constantinople, was the most lucid in his appraisal. According to him, Britain and Turkey agreed that the "sovereignty of the Sultan" was to be upheld, but they had different interpretations of what sovereignty meant in the context of Kuwait. The Turks saw Kuwait as a normal district of Basra province, while the British regarded sovereignty there to be more of the symbolic sort they also recognized for the Sultan in Cyprus or Crete, which at that time meant merely nominal, not substantive. That type of sovereignty certainly excluded the right to send troops. Pallavicini predicted that the Turks would refrain from sending troops for the time being. But he was mistaken ...[119]

7.6 The Ottomans occupy Kuwaiti territory

There was a feeling in the outside world that in the flag incident Britain had been forced to retreat under international pressure.[120] This

---

[118] The Hague NA, Buitenlandse Zaken Kabinet, Rapporten van Hoofden van Zendingen, box 49, Weckherlin 22 January 1902, nr. 37/17.

[119] Vienna HHSA, PA XII K, 178 Bericht 4 A, Pallavicini 15 January 1902.

[120] See for instance the cartoon in the *Amsterdammer*, n. 102 above.

interpretation was misguided, but in continental European and Egyptian newspapers sympathy for the Sultan persisted. Abdulhamid felt encouraged to continue his policy of applying pressure on Kuwait. A large Ottoman force remained encamped around Samawa. It is never wise to move troops from their base and then leave them to spend the summer heat in the middle of nowhere in the vague expectation of operations at some unspecified time. For a while there had been warnings of low morale and large-scale desertion.[121] Some action ought to be taken now, while the winter season of 1901–2 lasted.

In Ottoman military circles in Mesopotamia there were continuing calls for an occupation of Kuwait, while rumours circulated that the Sultan's brother-in-law, Kazim Pasha, would be appointed commander of the troops in Samawa. On 26 November 1901, Richarz had reported that the army there had been put on alert, and at the beginning of December troops had been moved to Nasiriyya closer to Kuwait.[122] This may have been just a manoeuvre to reinforce the mission of the Naqib, who was just then preparing to leave for Kuwait, but by the beginning of 1902 there was a definite expectation that the Ottoman troops would move against the shaikhdom.[123]

Ottoman operations began with troops entering the desert city of Zubair. Ordinarily Zubair was the scene of a power struggle between two factions, for and against the Rashidi Amir. From there a small body of troops advanced to Safwan, which was regarded as part of Mubarak's territory. O'Conor reported this to Lansdowne on 3 January.[124] The same day Tawfiq announced to Marschall the remarkable, but erroneous, news that an Ottoman kaymakam had been appointed in Kazima and that a small Turkish garrison had been established in that place.[125] Two weeks later

---

[121] Paris AE, NS Mascate 6, pp. 172–3, Rouet 19 September 1901; Nantes AD, consulat Bagdad B 29, Rouet 26 February 1902.

[122] Berlin AA, R 13887 A 469 (10 January 1902), Marschall in Pera 7 January 1902.

[123] Berlin AA, R 13887 A 93 (3 January 1902), Marschall 31 December 1901: the military are angry that no action has been taken against Mubarak as yet; ibid., A 780 (16 January 1902), Marschall 13 January 1902: Ottoman occupation of Kuwait is expected within a few days.

[124] Bidwell, *Affairs of Kuwait*, 2/4, p. 5, O'Conor 3 January 1902.

[125] Berlin AA, R 13887 A 92 (3 January 1902), telegram from Marschall in Pera 3 January 1902; ibid., R 13887 A 411 (9 January 1902), telegram from Marschall in Pera 9 January 1902: there is no mention of a kaymakamlik in the official yearbook of Basra province.

the Turks occupied Umm Qasr, a deserted fortress described in a British source as the place of residence of the Al-Sabah before they came to Kuwait, at the point where the Khor Zubair joins the Khor Abdallah. Several weeks later Ottoman soldiers landed on Bubiyan near the entrance of the Khor Abdallah.[126] There seems to have been no question that the places occupied belonged to Kuwait. The pro-Ottoman Rouet expressed it like this: "the Ottoman forces ... intend now to take effective possession – if not of Kuwait – at least of all other points constituting the kaza of that name."[127]

The British sources present these actions as originating from the Sultan and not from the Ottoman Government. When the British protested, Tawfiq behaved as if he knew nothing.[128] This was, however, pure deception. The Porte had decided on a military advance to the Khor Zubair on 23 December 1902.[129] A German source makes it clear that Tawfiq knew of the Ottoman operation well in advance of the British protest.[130] The Ottoman military in Baghdad had hoped that the deployment would be a prelude to the occupation of Kuwait, but the troops halted on occupying Safwan, Umm Qasr and a point on Bubiyan, probably because the Porte had grown nervous of a British reaction.[131] This aroused considerable discontent in Baghdad.[132]

It may be that the Ottoman descent on Kuwaiti territory formed part of a larger plan. One year later the Russian newspaper *Novoye Vremiye* sparked uproar in Russia and Germany by publishing an article with a map of the region showing the railway terminus at Kazima.[133] The map also shows planned Ottoman fortresses all around Kuwait town. At first this

---

[126] Bidwell, *Affairs of Kuwait*, 2/4, p. 16, O'Conor 20 January 1901 (he has been informed by the Austrian Ambassador, Pallavicini). Pelly, "Remarks", p. 72. The text of Pelly is quoted in Whigham, *Persia*, pp. 94–6.

[127] Paris AE, NS Mascate 8, fos. 23–24, Rouet 21 April 1902.

[128] Bidwell, *Affairs of Kuwait*, 2/4, p. 25, O'Conor 27 January 1902.

[129] Anscombe, *Ottoman Gulf*, pp. 129 and 231 n. 93; Istanbul BA, Usul-i Irade Dosiye 77, Bashkatib to Grand Vizier, 12 Ramadam 1319 (22 December 1901).

[130] Tawfiq played the innocent to O'Conor on 27 January, but already on 3 January he had proudly announced the Ottoman conquests to the German ambassador: Berlin AA, R 13887 A 92 (3 January 1902), telegram from Marschall in Pera 3 January 1902.

[131] Berlin AA, R 13887 A 1072 (24 January 1902), Marschall 21 January 1902.

[132] Nantes AD, consulat Bagdad B29, Rouet to minister and ambassador 26 February 1902.

item seemed a chimera, for when challenged to name its sources the Russian newspaper came up with nothing of substance.[134] From the deeper recesses of officialdom, however, something more tangible did pop up. The German military attaché in Constantinople informed the German Government that he had indeed advised the Ottomans on plans for a modern heavy artillery battery, with earthworks, to replace the old-fashioned masonry fortress with light artillery at Fao, and for the construction of a similar installation on Bubiyan.[135] This was advice from a German military officer on his own initiative, with no support from German officials. Too much significance should not be attached to such plans, as they would meet with overwhelming British opposition. Given relations between Russian representatives and the Ottoman military in Baghdad – the previous Russian consul there, Mashkov, wrote for the *Novoye Vremiye* – the profusion of small fortifications on Kuwait territory as shown on the Russian newspaper's map may very well have emanated from Ottoman sources.[136]

Those planning the Ottoman deployment had probably been consulting a rather sketchy map. They seem to have been trying to identify an alternative route for the railway with a terminus on the Khor Abdallah, and so outside British control. An Ottoman occupation of Bubiyan might also give the Ottomans direct access to the Gulf of Kuwait. On a map the Ottoman move looks inspired. Kuwait was useless to the Turks because the Shaikh might summon British help, while the Shatt al-'Arab was an unattractive location for a terminus. The lower Shatt was an international waterway (forming the border with Persia), enabling the British to move warships there at will, and to oppose the construction of Ottoman fortresses on its bank. The strategic possibilities of the Khor Abdallah had

---

[133] Berlin AA, R13855 A2553 (21 February 1903), letter of the German ambassador in Russia including cutting of map and translation of article from *Novoye Vremiye* of 19/6 February.

[134] Berlin AA, R 13855 A 3878 (18 March 1903), newspaper article *Süddeutsche Reichskorrespondenz,* 18 March 1903, investigating the sources of the *Novoye Vremiye.*

[135] Berlin AA, R13855, A 3543 (13 May 1903), Russia 11 March 1903; ibid., A 3878 (18 March 1903), cutting from *Süddeutsche Reichskorrespondenz* of 18 March 1903 about the sources; A 5524 (18 April 1903), letter of the German Embassy in Constantinople 15 April 1903, on the report of the military attaché.

[136] Berlin AA, R 13856 A 11165 (25 July 1903), telegram of the ambassador in Constantinople 25 July 1903.

already been remarked upon by a French naval officer in the 1780s.[137]

The link between the troop deployment and the railway project was grasped as early as February 1902 by the French consul Rouet in Baghdad. He did not believe it a coincidence when the deployment was followed almost at once by Abdulhamid's decree of 21 January 1902 granting the concession for the Konya–Baghdad railway to the Deutsche Bank.[138] This was clearly intended to push matters along, but it could little more than a gesture. The final agreement for the line from Konya to the Gulf would be signed only after much intricate international wrangling in March 1903.[139]

The Ottoman invasion was something of a gamble. There were no adequate nautical charts of the area and so there was no way to be sure whether Umm Qasr had easy access to the open sea.[140] Umm Qasr would later be exposed as unsatisfactory for a terminus by the shallows in the access channel through the Khor Abdallah. But for the time being the Turks busied themselves constructing a small fortress there. This created some confusion in European consular reports, where Umm Qasr was confused with Kazima, so creating the illusion in Paris and Berlin that the site originally planned for the railway terminus was now in Turkish hands.[141] It was several months before this confusion was cleared up.

The Ottoman deployment came at a difficult moment for Mubarak. He was with some troops in the desert when the move on Safwan took place, but he wisely took no action. To confront Ottoman troops would amount to an open declaration of rebellion and would render him forever reliant on British support. It was in any case a particularly unpropitious moment for Mubarak to confront the Turks. In January 1902 he was summoned to appear before the Basra Civil Court, to be heard in the dispute with his nephews over the Basra properties. Loss of the income from the Basra

---

[137] Mention of the Khor Abdallah in Rosilly's report, in Decaen papers, municipal library of Caen, France, MS no. 92, fo. 22.

[138] Nantes AD, consulat Bagdad B 29, Rouet 26 February 1902. On the concession see Lepsius, *Grosse Politik*, Vol. 17, p. 418, Marschall 2 February 1902.

[139] These negotiations are described in Brünner, *Bagdadspoorweg*, pp. 113–20.

[140] There was at the time nothing better than the nautical chart by Stiffe and Constable of 1860, see Slot, *Origins of Kuwait*, p. 179. As early as 1786 the French captain Rosilly had already remarked that the Khor Abdallah was very shallow: see above n. 137.

[141] Nantes AD, consulat Bagdad B 29, Rouet to ambassador and minister 26 March 1902; the same error is made by Richarz, in Berlin AA, R 13888 A 3910 (10 March 1902), Marschall 7 March 1902.

estates would be a crippling blow to Kuwait's finances. One may wonder whether this sudden summons by the Civil Court was part of the routine progress of the case, or whether the Sultan had impelled the Court to act just at that moment. Mubarak's unwillingness to confront the Turks directly was prudent, as the Basra possessions would be in deep jeopardy were he to be declared a rebel. There was some difference of opinion between Mubarak and the British over how best to resolve the matter of the date groves. Mubarak was in favour of British officials applying diplomatic pressure to halt the legal machine. The British objected to such open confrontation as it would expose their own ambiguous legal standing in Kuwaiti affairs. They preferred to fight this battle in the courts of law.[142] This was a sound approach, as the wheels of Ottoman justice ground exceedingly slowly, enabling time to be gained. Furthermore it would be quite acceptable for the British to be present in the legal process as protectors of Mubarak personally: protection of litigants, even if they were Ottoman subjects, by foreign consular services was quite normal in the Ottoman legal system, and the Turks had never opposed British protection for Mubarak's person.[143]

Under these circumstances, Mubarak had to count on the British also to halt the Ottoman encroachment in the region of the Khor Abdallah. If the British could be prevailed upon to force the Turks to retire, this would have the advantage that his borders would be firmly defined as part of the status quo. Even if the Turks did not retire, but were just told by the British to halt their advance, Mubarak would have the bonus of a guaranteed minimal borderline with the Turks. The British were not really in a position to refuse Mubarak some help in this matter, either by diplomatic means or by a show of naval force. The only setback for Mubarak was that British officialdom was not ready for action just at that juncture. He had no other options open. True, he had contacts with Russians in the region, but the Russian ambassador's attitude towards Kuwait was ambivalent.[144] Mubarak could expect nothing from the Germans or the French. The only course open to him was to avoid a rupture with the Turks while crossing his fingers that the British would protect his borders.

---

[142] Bidwell, *Affairs of Kuwait*, 2/4, p. 18, O'Conor 26 January 1902.
[143] The legal status of a person, even an Ottoman subject, under foreign diplomatic protection was a common feature in many guises in the practice of law in the Ottoman Empire.

7.7 Halting the Ottoman encroachment

The British reaction to the Ottoman military move was tardy and inconsistent. There were some grounds for their attention being distracted at that moment, because they were still uncertain whether the Rashidi Amir was really retiring, and the Ottomans were protesting about British breaches of the status quo such as the erecting of a second flagstaff in Kuwait (for signalling to ships), and the landing of artillery there. Consequently it was some time before the Ottoman troop movements rang any alarm bells. For a proper understanding of the British response, we need to track the flow of information reaching the British authorities. The first warning of an imminent move by the Ottoman army by Bunsen, the number two at the British embassy in Constantinople, on 15 December 1901, elicited no reaction.[145] When the next warning came, Ottoman troops were already inside Kuwaiti territory.

On 2 January 1902, Wratislaw reported to O'Conor that Ottoman troops had moved from Zubair to Safwan, which the Amir had just vacated, and the next day the Government of India warned the India Office in London that Ottoman troops had moved into an area claimed by Mubarak as his territory.[146] On the 17th, Wratislaw notified Kemball that a battalion had moved from Safwan to "Umr inlet", but next day he complained that he had no adequate map and that it looked as if the Turks were "hemming in Kuwait".[147] No British action followed, but neither was Mubarak quick to invoke the "good offices" he had been entitled to claim since 1899, waiting until 22 January to write to the Bushire resident to

[144] Lepsius, *Grosse Politik*, Vol. 17, pp. 508–9, Marschall 31 December 1901. According to the Germans, Zinoviev, the Russian ambassador in Constantinople, was at that time still vexed that the Turks had not followed his advice to occupy Kuwait militarily in 1899. On the other hand Bondarevsky, *Kuwait*, pp. 225–6, mentions Russian documents in which Zinoviev reported that he had successfully urged Tawfiq not to attack Kuwait.

[145] Plass, *England*, p. 305.

[146] Bidwell, *Affairs of Kuwait*, 2/4, p. 5, O'Conor 3 January 1902. O'Conor did not understand that at that moment the Turks were moving into Kuwaiti territory. This is in contrast to ibid. pp. 5–6 (telegram Government of India to India Office 3 January 1902), where it is clear that the Government of India had a better understanding of the meaning of a report by O'Conor's subordinate Wratislaw.

[147] IOLR, R/15/1/475, fos. 20 and 21, Wratislaw to Kemball 17 and 18 January 1902. Wratislaw was no geographer, and by "Umr inlet" he probably meant Umm Qasr.

protest at the Ottoman incursions into his territory.[148] At the same time Kemball received alarming tidings from Muhammara of a conspiracy in Kuwait sponsored by Yusuf Al-Ibrahim to murder Mubarak.[149] Mubarak's reaction was slow, even allowing for various delaying factors such as his absence from Kuwait at the time of the first Ottoman movement, and problems of finding a ship to sail to Bushire with the message. It may be that he was governed by caution in view of the delicately poised lawsuit over his Basra properties, and first wanted to establish, through his network in Iraq, what Ottoman intentions really might be, or to procure a troop withdrawal through bribes.

Only from 25 January was there any sign that the British intended to oppose the Ottoman encroachment. On that day the Foreign Office issued a vaguely worded protest to Anthopoulos to the effect that "Ottoman regular troops in the vicinity of Kuwait continue to cause anxiety".[150] Two days later O'Conor met with the Ottoman foreign minister and "referred to news" that Ottoman troops had occupied Safwan and Umm Qasr, places he believed to be claimed by Mubarak. Tawfiq denied all knowledge of these places (he could not find them on any map) or of Ottoman troop movements there.[151] Tawfiq was deceiving O'Conor – not difficult, in view of O'Conor's scanty knowledge of the region. On the 25th, Tawfiq had informed the German ambassador Marschall that the Turks were placing garrisons in places on Ottoman territory to the south of Fao that would

---

[148] IOLR, R/15/1/475, fos. 40–43, Mubarak to Kemball 22 January 1902.

[149] IOLR, R/15/1/475, fos. 32–34, MacDouall 18 January 1902. It seems that the British journalist Whigham too refers to these rumours when he states that there was "a growing feeling against Mubarak" in Kuwait in 1902: Whigham, *Persia*, p. 104. It should be noted that Whigham was the only visitor to Kuwait to evince a low opinion of Mubarak's intelligence and knowledge: ibid., pp. 104–6, which stands in stark contrast to other eye-witness accounts.

[150] Bidwell *Affairs of Kuwait*, 2/4, p. 18*, Sanderson to Anthopoulos 25 January 1902.

[151] O'Conor's report in Bidwell, *Affairs of Kuwait*, 2/4, p. 58; Tawfiq's report of 30 Shawal 1319 in Istanbul BA, Y.A. Hüs 425/7. Tawfiq had a point. The Turks had no reliable maps of their own and depended on European products. Umm Qasr appeared on maps only after the place had become known through the events of 1902. Some older maps have Safwan, such as the Berghaus map *Reduzirte Karte vom Persischen Gulf* of 1832, and James Wyld's *Map of the Countries between England and India* of 1842 (both with the spelling Zofan). But the maps of Andree, Perthes and Kiepert, which were generally accepted as standard in 1902, did not include it.

be suitable as termini for the railway.[152] O'Conor's warning to the Turks was very feebly formulated and British resolve was not strengthened by information coming from Basra. On 30 January, O'Conor reported that Wratislaw had cast serious doubt on the validity of the borders claimed by Mubarak. According to him, Mubarak's real territory was a small strip around Kuwait town and everything else depended on the fickle loyalties of nomadic tribes.[153] That might well be the case, but the loyalty of nomadic tribes was the only way to determine territories at that time, and had served in the past to delineate the borderline between Persia and the Ottoman Empire.

The Government of India now entered the debate, forwarding to the India Office a report by Kemball of 4 February. In it Kemball was still trying to formulate proof of Mubarak's ownership of the occupied places. He also wanted to send a gunboat to check any further Turkish advance.[154] Lansdowne invited O'Conor's opinion. O'Conor as usual advised against a confrontation with the Turks, but thought that he could warn them against a breach of the status quo and that a gunboat might be sent to demonstrate British resolve. Lansdowne followed O'Conor's advice and permitted Curzon to send a warship, but only " to observe and report".[155]

The British case was somewhat nebulous. Not only was there no clear information on the frontiers of Kuwait, but British officials were in no position to demand from the Turks what precisely they meant by claiming that their troops were inside "Ottoman territory". Did the Turks mean Ottoman territory in the sense that they claimed Kuwait to be Ottoman; or did they mean "real" Ottoman territory? Whatever the case, the British diplomatic response was very sluggish. By contrast, commanders of British armed forces directly involved, in this case the Indian Navy, were keen to have a clear declaration by the British side of Kuwait's borders, because if

[152] Berlin AA, R 13887 A 1319 (25 January 1902), Marschall in Pera 25 January 1902. Marschall had already reported to Berlin on 23 January, on the basis of a report from Richarz, that the military in Mesopotamia had received orders from Constantinople to establish a garrison in "Kasr": R 13887 A 1410 (27 January 1902), Marschall in Pera 23 January 1902.

[153] Bidwell, *Affairs of Kuwait*, 2/4, p. 24, O'Conor 30 January 1902.

[154] Bidwell, *Affairs of Kuwait*, 2/4, p. 27, Government of India to India Office 7 February 1902.

[155] Bidwell, *Affairs of Kuwait*, 2/4, pp. 27–8, O'Conor to Lansdowne and Foreign Office to India Office, 8 February 1900.

Ottoman troops came too close to him, Mubarak might be expected to switch loyalties.[156]

Meanwhile the Turks advanced. On 17 February 1902, the British news agent in Kuwait reported that an Ottoman envoy was on his way to Mubarak and that the Turks had moved a small number of soldiers to Bubiyan.[157] But by then the British machine had ground slowly into action. Their wary intervention was prompted in part by fears that Mubarak might eventually turn to the Turks unless Britain demonstrated its power to protect him. According to the Commander of the Indian Navy, Mubarak was complaining to naval officers that the British "do much more for Bahrain".[158] His dissatisfaction was not entirely unjustified. Blunders and inconsistencies in British policy were to blame for many of Mubarak's problems. It is more than likely too that Mubarak paraded an exaggerated vulnerability – it was, after all, his standard ploy to show the British that his loyalty had a price. The *Sphinx* steamed up the Khor Abdallah to see what was going on. Its commander Kemp found that forty Turks had erected tents behind a decayed mud wall at Umm Qasr inlet. Kemp went up to them and then witnessed a curious incident: a number of Arabs, apparently subjects of Mubarak, assembled as if they were going to attack the Turks. The Turks were very nervous, but Kemp was able to persuade the Arabs to withdraw. The Ottoman commander was highly suspicious of the British visit and also seems to have believed that Kemp had put the Arabs up to the attack to discompose him. The worrying news for the British authorities was Kemp's opinion that, if the Khor Abdallah were to be dredged, Umm Qasr could make a good terminus for the railway.[159] Capt. Pelham of the cruiser *Fox* reported Mubarak's assertion that the Arabs were Muntafiq, not Kuwaitis, and that the Turks now seriously suspected Mubarak of having organized the Saudi capture of Riyadh in January 1902 – a not implausible suspicion.[160]

Before the end of January the British had begun searching around to discover the borders of Mubarak's territory. Until then they had been in the dark about the precise extent of what they had committed themselves

[156] Plass, *England*, pp. 306–7.
[157] IOLR, R/15/1/475, pp. 91–2, news agent 17 February 1902.
[158] Bidwell, *Affairs of Kuwait*, 2/4, p. 4, Bosanquet to Admiralty 20 February 1902.
[159] IOLR, R/15/1/475, p. 103, map by Kemp on p. 114.
[160] IOLR, R/15/1/475, pp. 95–100, Pelham 21 February 1902.

somehow to protect. They first sought Ottoman information in Basra about the boundary of the Kuwait administrative district, but nothing was to be found.[161] Here they were thwarted by the simple truth that Kuwait was not an Ottoman administrative district in any real sense. This British uncertainty is in telling contrast to the assurance with which Rouet, who was pro-Ottoman, airily described the positions occupied by the Turks as belonging to Kuwait.[162] On 17 February, Mubarak wrote to the resident setting out some proof of his claims. He stated that the uninhabited site of Umm Qasr had in the 19th century been temporarily settled by Kuwaitis (Bin Raziq), and that taxes on the harvests at Safwan had been paid to him. Such proofs were vague, but at no time did the Turks offer anything better. On 25 February, Mubarak added in a new letter that his family had always owned Bubiyan just as they owned Faylaka.[163] Kemball tried to set Kuwait's claims down on paper in proper form. From the start he had found the claim to Safwan dubious, but supported Mubarak's claim to Umm Qasr. He added Pelly's old observation about Umm Qasr being the seat of the 'Utub tribe before they made the move to Kuwait, to Mubarak's statement about the Kuwaiti settlement there in the time of Jabir I.[164] Such arguments did not cut much ice with officials, although Kemball did make the very pertinent remark in his report that "the Turkish claim does not appear much stronger".

It was obvious to the British that their position in Kuwait had suffered a setback, but they had no idea how serious it was as their local knowledge was so deficient. The first priority was to prevent further damage. Mubarak was no doubt better acquainted with the local topography, but he had his own good reasons for avoiding confrontation with the Turks. It would be to his advantage if the British, not he, put a stop to further Ottoman troop movements, and a British check to the Ottoman advance would automatically mean a firm delimitation of his border with the Turks. There was no doubt that the Ottomans had infringed the status quo, but the British could do little about this particular breach. There it ended for the

---

[161] Bidwell, *Affairs of Kuwait*, 2/4, p. 24, O'Conor 30 January 1902.
[162] Paris AE, NS Mascate 8, fos. 28–29, Rouet 21 April 1902.
[163] IOLR, R/15/1/475, pp. 85–6, Mubarak 25 February 1902.
[164] IOLR, R/15/1/475, pp. 115–18, Kemball 26 February 1902. For notes and correspondence on the borders of Kuwait of that time, see IOLR, R/15/1/475, pp. 51–9.

time being. To recapture the positions by force would mean a direct attack on the Ottoman army, and this would cause international uproar. Nor was a protest any use, as the Ottomans would simply reply that the sites they had occupied were part of their territory.

The British had been caught unawares by the Ottoman incursion, but they could move troops and equipment much faster than the Turks, and soon they had sufficient forces in the area to deter them. The Turks had no more than limited approval of their initiative from their German friends, whose advice was that it was fine to occupy points along the Gulf coast so long as they did not provoke a conflict with Britain.[165]

By that time the news had reached the press, which showed a good grasp of the affair. In the *Morning Post* of 10 February, Whigham had already commented that the Germans wanted to occupy the Khor Abdallah. On the 25th, the *Morning Post* had news from Bushire that Ottoman troops had occupied Safwan and Umm Qasr, and remarked that both places were claimed by Mubarak and that Umm Qasr was the home of his tribe.[166] In the pro-Curzon press, such as *The Times*, there was growing pressure on the government to take a firm stand against the Turks.

Now came rumours that the Turks also wanted to occupy points closer to Kuwait, on the Khor Subiya.[167] Later they acted as if they were in possession of Subiya, but this was a completely false claim serving only to sow confusion.[168] In reality the Ottoman advance had ground to a halt. It may have been that the Turks dared go no farther after the incident with the tribesmen in Umm Qasr and the appearance of the *Fox*, a big second-class cruiser.[169] On 20 February, the German ambassador in Constantinople

---

[165] Berlin AA, R 13888 A 2844, telegram from Berlin to Marschall 23 February 1902.

[166] Berlin AA, R 13888 A 2705 (18 February 1902), comments by Rosen on the *Morning Post* article of 10 February; A 3370 (28 February), cutting from the *Morning Post* 27 February 1902.

[167] Bidwell, *Affairs of Kuwait*, 2/4, pp. 45–6, Captain Pelham of the *Fox* 31 January 1902, relating rumours from Basra.

[168] As late as May 1902 Marschall was still reporting news originating from Abdulhamid's brother-in-law, Kazim Pasha, that the construction of an Ottoman fortress at Subiya had been completed! See Berlin AA, R 13888 A 7549 (15 May 1902), Marschall in Therapia 12 May 1902. At the beginning of March there were rumours of Ottoman plans to occupy "Hajeje"[Hajija] and Mubarak sent troops there, but nothing happened: see Bidwell, *Affairs of Kuwait*, 2/4, pp. 47–8, Douglas to Admiralty 14 March 1902; Foreign Office to India Office 15 March 1902.

was already reporting Turkish complaints that their troops were being "stalked" by British officers, who shadowed them under all kinds of pretexts such as tourist excursions and hunting trips.[170] In any event, the Turks dared not venture closer to Kuwait, and by the end of February the troop concentrations in Samawa were being dispersed. The Turkish public came to the forlorn conclusion that the Kuwait dispute had been lost.[171] The French consul in Baghdad considered the Ottoman encroachment a fiasco. It would solve no Ottoman problems and only burdened the bankrupt provincial administration with the extra costs of garrisoning the newly occupied sites.[172] News of the British military steps to deter a Turkish advance aroused some excitement in Russia. The newspaper *St. Petersburgskiya Wyedomosti* reported that the British were putting Kuwait on a defence footing – an item apparently derived from the report of the *Varyag* that there were European-style trenches around Kuwait. The article concluded with the words: "El Mubarek has sold his people to the British in a scandalous fashion and all Arabia is against him".[173]

For the British there remained the question of how far it might be feasible to induce the Turks to withdraw from the positions they had occupied. O'Conor had already advised Lansdowne that nothing could be done, on the basis of scanty information from Wratislaw.[174] Kemball was unhappy, feeling that the territorial losses were harming Mubarak's popularity among Kuwaitis.[175] But Kemball was a realist, settling to the view that Britain should maintain a formal claim on Umm Qasr, while the Turks "should be told to leave" Bubiyan which was effectively and clearly Kuwaiti territory. This viewpoint was forwarded to London by the Government of India. O'Conor could not be expected to be in favour of such blunt language. He stated that there was no point in risking a conflict over Bubiyan, and resurrected the old fears of Russia by warning that the use of force against the Turks might inspire the Russians to seize a port on

---

[169] Kazim Pasha had been spreading greatly exaggerated stories about the Umm Qasr incident: Berlin AA, R 13888 A 3910 (10 March 1902), Marschall 7 March 1902.

[170] Berlin AA, R 13888 A 2453, telegram Pera 20 February 1902.

[171] Berlin AA, R 13888 A 3552 (2 March 1902), Marschall 27 February 1902.

[172] Nantes AD, consulat Bagdad B29, Rouet to minister and ambassador 26 February 1902.

[173] Berlin AA, R 13888 A 4858 (27 March 1902), St Petersburg 24 March 1902.

[174] Bidwell, *Affairs of Kuwait*, 2/4, pp. 37–8, O'Conor 6 March 1902.

[175] IOLR, R/15/1/475, pp. 145–9, Kemball 16 March 1902.

the Gulf.[176] O'Conor then received a telegram from Wratislaw in which that worthy stated that Umm Qasr would make a better terminus for the railway than Kuwait, but that Mubarak's rights there were undefined. O'Conor reacted to this with masterly inertia.[177]

Other British officials in Constantinople were hardly more engaged. The Dutch envoy reported the British embassy as being so unconcerned about the Bubiyan issue that they were unofficially putting it about that Bubiyan did not belong to the Shaikh of Kuwait anyway. A British "expert" had even told the Dutch envoy that Bubiyan could make a good rail terminus because the island was so near the mainland that it could be connected by a simple dam. The Germans were also confident. The Dutch envoy reported an over-optimistic Marschall telling him that the line would find a terminus on the Gulf by some means or other, and that the English might very well have to surrender the Persian Gulf.[178]

O'Conor's lack of dynamism was less reasonable than it might seem. The Turks were not so sure of themselves, as was shown by the hesitant progress of their advance. There was scope for the British to apply a little pressure, and this had always worked in the past. The simple reality seems to be that the British officials craved a quiet life.

7.8 Britain redefines its Kuwait policy

The Ottoman encroachment of early 1902 had created an entirely new situation as well as new misunderstandings. Some European observers, for example Rouet, seem to have been correct in supposing the Turks to have relinquished Kuwait itself and thus in ascribing little significance to the military advance. The British, however, appear to have over-estimated the resolve and military might of the Turks, especially considering that, just two years later, the VI Army Corps was to prove completely incapable of dealing with tribal warriors in the desert. The essential new points in British calculations were the realization that they had no clear idea of the extent of the Kuwait they had to protect, and that Kuwait's value had

---

[176] Bidwell, *Affairs of Kuwait*, 2/4, pp. 42–3, Government of India to India Office 7 March 1902; O'Conor to Lansdowne 11 March 1902.

[177] Bidwell, *Affairs of Kuwait*, 2/4, p. 49, O'Conor 16 March 1902.

[178] The Hague, NA, Buitenlandse Zaken Kabinet, Rapporten van Hoofden van Zendingen, box 49, Weckherlin 15 March 1902, no. 145/54.

diminished with the emergence of an alternative route to the Gulf for the Baghdad Railway. And now tentative negotiations between British and German financial groups over an international consortium for the railway merely added to the complexity.[179]

In these circumstances one can hardly commend Lansdowne's actions. The navy reported the threat of new Ottoman troop movements while Lansdowne was subject to pressure from India. Curzon wanted Britain to uphold the Kuwaiti claim to Umm Qasr, and to demand a Turkish withdrawal from Bubiyan.[180] This would mean conceding the fragility of Mubarak's claim to Umm Qasr, without yielding on Bubiyan itself. O'Conor persisted in his opinion that none of Mubarak's claims could be substantiated. Lansdowne settled for a weak compromise between India and O'Conor. On 15 March, O'Conor received instructions from the Foreign Office to warn against the new Ottoman troop movements. The instructions were that he had to issue his warning "on the ground that they tend to keep the country in a state of constant disturbance and alarm and that they are an impediment to our efforts to keep the Sheikh quiet, in accordance with the agreement made between His Majesty's Government and the Government of Turkey."[181] This was done, despite O'Conor's receipt on the 16th of a delayed message from Wratislaw in Basra to the effect that Mubarak's claims on Bubiyan were quite reasonable. The same day Curzon addressed O'Conor directly, urging the ambassador to act according to the undertakings given to Mubarak in 1899.[182]

O'Conor's protest was received on 16 March by the glib Tawfiq, who feigned ignorance of an occupation of Bubiyan and even of the existence of that island. While one might concede as genuine Tawfiq's disclaimer a few weeks earlier of any knowledge of Safwan and Umm Qasr because they were not on any map, Bubiyan was shown in virtually every atlas then in use. Tawfiq duly promised to investigate the matter, but told O'Conor that the military movements might be to do with the establishment of a

---

[179] Plass, *England*, p. 310; Bidwell, *Affairs of Kuwait*, 2/4, pp. 50*, 55 and 61, Lansdowne to Monson 19 March 1902; to O'Conor 24 March 1902; and O'Conor to Lansdowne 25 March 1902.

[180] Bidwell, *Affairs of Kuwait*, 2/4, p. 47, Government of India 7 March 1902.

[181] Bidwell, *Affairs of Kuwait*, 2/4, p. 48, Lansdowne to O'Conor 15 March 1902.

[182] Plass, *England*, p. 313.

terminus for the Baghdad Railway under full Ottoman control. That is the British version of the meeting.[183] Tawfiq gave a quite different account of the very same meeting to the German ambassador. O'Conor, he said, had declared that Britain would make no complaint about the occupation of Bubiyan and various other places because they were inside Ottoman territory, but would oppose an Ottoman occupation of Kazima. It is an open question whether it was Tawfiq or O'Conor who was lying.[184] Tawfiq's version as given to the Germans looks the more unreliable, as a possible motive for it might be that he was trying to deflect German attention from Kazima. By claiming that Britain had no objection to the alternative Ottoman outlets to the Gulf, Tawfiq was promoting the Khor Abdallah option to the Germans. If this was Tawfiq's intention, it would support the view of Rouet and others that the Turks had de facto abandoned their claim to Kuwait itself.

Meanwhile the British Government was coming under growing pressure from parliament and the press.[185] Under these circumstances a meeting took place on 20 March, between the heads of the Admiralty, the India Office and the Foreign Office, to discuss a memorandum by Lansdowne. In this, overall British Gulf policy was formulated in limited and negative terms, in essence to oppose the establishment by any other European power of a military presence in the Gulf. In Kuwait's case the problem was that the Agreement of 1899 had been intended to obtain control over the only possible terminus of the Baghdad Railway, and this now appeared to have been based on a misconception, as a consequence of which Britain was continually being drawn into in disputes over Kuwait's status and undefined borders to no political advantage. Lansdowne expressed his feelings most vividly:

> The situation is becoming more and more embarrassing, and the time has come for looking it in the face. We have saddled ourselves with an impossible client in the person of the Sheikh. He is apparently an untrustworthy savage, no one knows where his possessions begin and

---

[183] Bidwell, *Affairs of Kuwait*, 2/4, p. 49, O'Conor 16 March 1902.

[184] O'Conor's report in Bidwell, *Affairs of Kuwait*, 2/4, p. 49; report of the Grand Vizier to the Sultan of 2 Zilkade 1319 in Istanbul BA, Y.A. Hüs 435/7; the German report in Berlin AA, R 13852 A 4963 (29 March 1902), telegram from Marchall 28 March 1902.

[185] Plass, *England*, p. 311.

end, and our obligations towards him are as ill-defined as the boundaries of his Principality.[186]

The final remark is an obvious dig at Lansdowne's predecessor Salisbury, while the rest of the passage displays a remarkable blindness to the fact that much of the trouble had been caused by British blunders. The meeting decided that the protection of Mubarak would be limited to the Gulf of Kuwait and its immediate surroundings. The exact extent of Kuwaiti territory would be determined in talks with Mubarak and the Porte. The meeting also decided that Britain was not interested in participating in the choice of terminus for the Baghdad Railway. The offer of participation had been made by Tawfiq in his meeting with O'Conor.[187]

The result was a new set of instructions from Lansdowne to O'Conor. In these the decision on Kuwait's borders of the 20 March meeting is not mentioned.[188] O'Conor was instructed to make it clear that Britain had "no wish to encourage the Sheikh to break away from his relations of allegiance to the Sultan". The terminology here is very precise and proper, "allegiance" being the vague acknowledgement of the suzerain in a feudal context. Britain was bound to afford Mubarak support "against attacks or attempts to encroach on his territories or diminish his privileges". Britain was not willing to be drawn into a series of tiresome disputes about Ottoman troop deployments to places to which Mubarak's claims were vague. Lansdowne reminded O'Conor that Britain had no objection to a terminus of the Baghdad Railway in Kuwait or elsewhere, provided an appropriate British share in it was assured; if not, then Britain would use its power to block the financing of the railway (under powers deriving from the control by European powers of Ottoman finances).[189] One policy shift emerges clearly: the Foreign Office view that the chief British protection against undesirable railway developments was not so much control of Kuwait, as the power to impose a financial embargo on the necessary loans. This shift diminished the importance of Kuwait to Britain. This judgement was destined later to be proved unsound.

[186] Bidwell, *Affairs of Kuwait*, 2/4, p. 54, memorandum by Lansdowne 21 March 1902; *cf.* Busch *Britain and the Persian Gulf*, p. 217; Plass, *England*, pp. 310–11.
[187] Plass, *England*, p. 312.
[188] Plass, *England*, p. 312, supposes that this point was considered not opportune because of the existing tensions with the Turks over the delimitation of Aden territory.
[189] Bidwell, *Affairs of Kuwait*, 2/4, p. 55, Lansdowne to O'Conor 24 March 1902.

This time it was O'Conor who took a more hawkish line. He had probably grasped that, if Britain allowed the Turks to employ what in the 1960s would have been called "salami tactics", he would be drawn into a series of protests to the Ottoman foreign minister that could drag on for years. On 25 March, he firmly warned Tawfiq against further encroachments that would stoke continuing unrest in the region; if on the other hand the Ottomans maintained the status quo, Britain might adopt a positive attitude to Ottoman railway plans. During the meeting, O'Conor carefully avoided letting Tawfiq know about secret contacts between Germany and Britain about the possibility of making the railway an international venture.[190] The very same day, 25 March, Wratislaw warned that the Turks planned to occupy Subiya regardless of its occupation by Mubarak's men. O'Conor, more or less on his own initiative, went to Tawfiq on the 27th to issue a stern admonition, to be told by Tawfiq that the Sultan had not given a reply to O'Conor's warnings of the 25th that would satisfy the British. O'Conor robustly told Lansdowne: "I do not think any further encroachment can be allowed without encouraging the Turks to proceed to still greater length and without losing control over the Sheikh. The presence of a gunboat in the region will hardly fail of its effect." Ironically, on the same day the Ottoman ambassador in London protested to Lansdowne about British warship movements in Ottoman waters.[191]

The 20 March meeting in London had not escaped Curzon, who had been sent a copy of Lansdowne's note about the "savage". A badly, if not stupidly, worded telegram from the India Office Secretary to the Government of India reporting a conciliatory note on the Kuwait affair to be delivered by the British ambassador to the Porte only fuelled Curzon's vexation. This telegram, of 26 March, was meant as a paraphrase of Lansdowne's instructions to O'Conor of 24 March about "allegiance", but it now opened with the ominous sentence: "Kuwait having been acknowledged as part of the Ottoman dominions, His Majesty's Government do not wish to encourage Shaikh to throw off allegiance to Sultan; they do not wish to enter into irritating discussions about movements of Turkish troops to places claimed by the Sheikh, but of which the title is difficult to prove; they must however, protect him from

[190] Bidwell, *Affairs of Kuwait*, 2/4, p. 61, O'Conor 25 March 1902.
[191] Bidwell, *Affairs of Kuwait*, 2/4, p. 58, Anthopoulos 27 March 1902.

encroachments." It was to be expected that Curzon would protest vehemently at such a capitulation: "We do not understand the policy of His Majesty's Government regarding Koweit." The Viceroy enquired, in righteous indignation, whether the line of action defined on 12 September 1901 was no longer valid, and expressed the fear that the status quo was "whittled out of existence".[192] Finally, he demanded how serious an "encroachment" needed to be, to call forth British action.[193]

It was clear that much of this uproar had been ignited by the clumsy wording of the India Office telegram of 26 March, and Bertie, under-secretary at the Foreign Office, tried to calm the irate Viceroy by explaining that the basis of the policy was the more carefully formulated telegram to O'Conor of 24 March, which did not include the offending words "part of the Ottoman dominions". Bertie stated that no new policy was intended. In fact O'Conor had stopped short of acknowledging Kuwait to be in any way part of the Ottoman Empire. Bertie tried to convince Curzon that Britain had no desire to see the status quo whittled away, and that it wished "to preserve for the Shaikh both his privileges and his territory, but that these, particularly the latter, are unfortunately not sufficiently defined".[194] Privately, Lansdowne told Curzon that it was in the British interest for the legal position of Kuwait to remain ambiguous, and that the British position "should not depend upon the extent of our hold on this barbarous personage [Mubarak]".[195] The noble Lord was mistaken: in the years that followed, the British would be repeatedly made aware that their position was based fundamentally on the personal will of Mubarak and, as we shall see, in 1906 they would even sign an agreement confirming just that.

---

[192] The Viceroy refers here to the definition of Kuwait's position used in British contacts with Berlin and Constantinople: see Salisbury's addition to Lansdowne's instructions to Lascelles of 12 September 1901: "The Shaikh belongs to a class of native chiefs in those regions who enjoy a large measure of practical independence and with whom H.M. Government have found it necessary to have direct relations for the sake of the maintenance of tranquillity and the protection of British trade." PRO, FO 78/5174.

[193] Bidwell, *Affairs of Kuwait*, 2/4, p. 65, telegrams between Hamilton and Government of India, 26 and 29 March 1902; Plass, *England*, p. 314.

[194] Bidwell, *Affairs of Kuwait*, 2/4, p. 66, Bertie to India Office 3 April 1902.

[195] Busch, *Britain and the Persian Gulf*, p. 218, quoting Lansdowne to Curzon 10 April 1902.

This confusing intermezzo illustrates all too clearly the inability of the British to make clear choices. International relations made them afraid to protect Mubarak, while regional Asian policy did not allow them to drop him, and in the meantime they still lacked any real means of controlling his actions. They still had, nonetheless, a strong geopolitical motive for wanting leverage over Kuwait: the need, albeit largely imaginary, to block other powers from gaining a foothold on the Gulf. It is little wonder that, at the beginning of 1902, the idea of having an official of the Indian Government in Kuwait to report on Mubarak's doings was already being aired. An extremely low profile would be vital, to prevent an avalanche of international protest. Various options were considered, but no solution reached.[196]

Meanwhile the Turks had quietly finished work on the new military outposts. The German consul in Baghdad reported that they had even been solemnly inaugurated. He lists the posts as Safwan, Umm Qasr, one on Bubiyan and one at Subiya, not far from Kazima, opposite the south-western point of Bubiyan. Richarz probably obtained his information from over-optimistic Ottoman officers in Baghdad, for the Turks had not occupied Subiya and the outposts were insignificant from a military point of view. Richarz quizzed Kazim Pasha about the exact location of the post on Bubiyan, but received no clear answer.[197] The Ottomans seem to have been playing their usual game with the Germans, always exaggerating their power in the region and pretending that possible routes for the railway were under their control. But by that time the Germans had lost much of their appetite for protecting the unreliable Turks.

The intricacies of all this international diplomacy must have escaped Mubarak. Its outcome was not entirely to his advantage but, ultimately, Curzon and his officials, and even to a lesser extent the British representatives in Constantinople and Basra too, were ready to protect him at vital moments. His situation would become more delicate were the railway to the Gulf actually to be built, and even more parlous if London decided its interests lay in participating in it. And so it was to Mubarak's

---

[196] For the correspondence on this subject see Bidwell, *Affairs of Kuwait*, 2/4, pp. 85–7. The official should not be too high-ranking, to avoid him being too conspicuous. The most suitable idea was for a native military man to be appointed. The idea of a native agent was in discussion from January 1902, but was dropped the following April.

[197] Berlin AA, R 13888 A 9226 (14 June 1902), Richarz 15 May 1902.

advantage that Curzon himself was opposed to the railway, seeing it as a vehicle for a possible German threat to Anglo-Indian interests.[198]

For Kuwait there were more pressing matters to hand than inchoate railway plans. In the short run the hostility of the adjacent Ottoman authorities, or Ibn Rashid's expansionism, could inflict much more immediate damage than remote railway schemes. Mubarak had his own methods of dealing with such matters. Judiciously targeted bribes might stifle Ottoman threats, and tribal alliances might hamper Ibn Rashid. There were occasional skirmishes with the latter, but he was less of a menace now that he faced a second front against the Saudis in Riyadh. The Saudis' position in southern Najd was already so strong that Abdul Rahman bin Faysal had left Kuwait to join his son, the Amir (and future King) Abdul Aziz in Riyadh.[199] One noteworthy development took place when, after raids by Ibn Rashid's allies in Zubair on Kuwaiti herdsmen near Safwan, Lansdowne decided that Mubarak should be notified that it was impossible for Britain to protect him from raids in the region of Safwan. This declaration of British non-intervention should Mubarak be attacked from the desert, certainly did not help to justify Britain's demand that if he wanted protection he had to keep out of desert politics, for he would still have to fend for himself in that area![200]

The Turks posed a greater danger, and Mubarak tried to mend his fences with them. He had some reason to be impatient with Britain's failure to help him in the border dispute and he turned to other methods. After some delay the British consul in Basra was informed that, in February 1902, Mubarak had been dangling a considerable inducement before the Wali, Mustafa Nuri Pasha, to halt further Ottoman advances and to take up his case at the Porte. On the same day that O'Conor was able to send this news on to London, he also sent a message that Tawfiq had promised him that Ottoman troops would not move to Subiya.[201] Mustafa had refused the bribe and proposed that Mubarak should instead pay the sum into the ailing provincial treasury. This had not been done, but the offer had been followed by a rather affable correspondence. It can hardly be

[198] Busch, *Britain and the Persian Gulf*, p. 218.
[199] Mubarak notified Kemball of this departure on 14 June 1902: IOLR, R/15/1/475, p. 238.
[200] Bidwell, *Affairs of Kuwait*, 2/4, p. 98, Foreign Office to India Office, 28 July 1902.
[201] Bidwell, *Affairs of Kuwait*, 2/4, p. 63, two telegrams from O'Conor, 1 April 1902.

doubted that Mubarak was the source of a rumour spread by the Turks in June 1902, that he had refused the British permission to open a coal depot in Kuwait on the grounds that the land there belonged to the Sultan.[202] The rumour was evidently false, but it is none the less symptomatic of a slow healing in Mubarak's relations with the Turks.

7.9 The affair of Mubarak's Basra agent

By March 1902, direct confrontation with Mubarak as ruler of Kuwait had become too risky a venture for the Ottomans. Now that the vendetta between Ibn Rashid and the Saudis had taken a new turn, the situation on the border of Iraq had become unstable. Legal proceedings over the date groves crept on slowly because Mubarak's friends and agents were able to exploit every legal technicality, and any flaw in the procedure was certain to provoke British protests. Mubarak's attitude towards the Turks had thus grown somewhat tougher. There was an incident when Turkish troops attempted to land on the small island of "Amayer" (Musallamiya island in the bay of the same name, off the Hasa coast), but were repelled by its inhabitants who claimed to be subjects of Mubarak.[203] However, the Turks then came up with a new wheeze to put Mubarak under pressure. On 28 May 1902, Abdul Aziz Salim Al-Badr, Mubarak's agent in Basra, was arrested because he had taken delivery by mail of some Arab newspapers that were banned in the Ottoman Empire. There was no doubt that the prominent reader these papers were destined for was Mubarak.[204]

There are two aspects to this affair: the question of Mubarak's relations with early Arab nationalist movements, and the timing and background of the arrest. Anything that could affect the Ottoman Government's grip on its Arab provinces was of vital interest to Mubarak, so banned Arab newspapers were essential reading for him. Abdulhamid II's regime exploited the concept of the Ottoman Sultan as Caliph as a device for

[202] Berlin AA, R 13888 A 9686 (22 June 1902), Therapia 18 June 1902.
[203] Bidwell, *Affairs of Kuwait*, 2/4, pp. 99–100, Kemball 26 April 1902, with a letter of Mubarak of 19 April.
[204] Bidwell, *Affairs of Kuwait*, 2/4, pp. 87, 91–3, O'Conor 30 May; Government of India to India Office, 16 June; and Wratislaw 29 May and 2 June 1902. From the correspondence it is clear that the British regarded the accusation as somewhat far-fetched.

applying pressure on Western imperial powers with Muslim subjects, and also for legitimizing Ottoman rule over the Arabs. Its effectiveness in the latter context was undermined by the lack of universal Islamic recognition of the Ottoman Caliphate claim, and the Porte tried forcibly to suppress debate on the topic as well as on the general legitimacy of its rule over Arabs. Outside the Ottoman Empire, however, newspapers and pamphlets attacked the Ottoman stance as well as the personality of the Sultan. The most incriminating item in the banned material collected for Mubarak was the *Khilafat* newspaper printed in London. Unlike later papers going by that title, this was an Arabic-language paper produced by Ottoman exiles opposed to Abdulhamid, and was linked to the Young Turk movement.[205]

The Ottoman Government was not especially renowned for its lenient treatment of dissidents, but this arrest came out of the blue and appears somewhat heavy-handed. A report in Turkish of the interrogation of Mubarak's agent by the Ottoman authorities, in the papers of the British Bushire residency, contains nothing that could be considered greatly incriminating.[206] There must have been more to the affair than met the eye. Richarz, the German consul in Baghdad, shed a more revealing light on the arrest than was available to British officials. According to Richarz's sources (usually the Baghdad military), Mubarak's agent had already aroused Ottoman suspicions in the past by acting as intermediary between Mubarak and Muhsin Pasha, and indeed had been the man who had bribed Muhsin to act against the interests of the Ottoman Empire. Mustafa Nuri Pasha had now taken the step of searching the agent's papers, and a highly incriminating correspondence had come to light containing proof of Mubarak's bribery of Muhsin. Richarz moreover reveals that Mubarak had approached the Sultan directly in order to obtain the release of his agent. According to Richarz, this was the first time since the *Zuhaf* affair that the Shaikh had directly contacted the Sultan. This unusual step shows how far Mubarak would go for the sake of his friends.[207]

[205] The *Khilafat* newspaper was published by the Pan-Islamic Society in London. According to the survey of the international Islamic press by Oppenheim (report of 30 November 1908, p. 11 in Berlin AA, R 14566) it was aimed at various kinds of Muslims in Britain.
[206] IOLR, R/15/1/475, pp. 221–3, report on interrogation, with translation.
[207] Berlin AA, R 13888 A 10580 (9 July 1902), Richarz 12 June 1902.

The arrest undoubtedly came at a delicate moment. The legal proceedings between Mubarak and his nephews over the Kutuzain estate in Basra province were gathering momentum, and the agent had Mubarak's legal papers relating to these possessions in his hands. In view of this it is highly possible that Yusuf Al-Ibrahim or the nephews were somehow implicated. The papers were briefly confiscated, but released after British protests.[208] The measures taken against his agent, especially the very harsh treatment meted out to him, seem clearly to have been aimed at putting Mubarak under indirect pressure. This interpretation is supported by the fact that the agent was freed much later, once Mubarak had demonstrated his favourable intentions towards the Turks.

It would be unfair to accuse Mubarak of recklessness in ordering dangerous literature. In his position it was wise to be well-informed, and in 1902 there was hardly any way of obtaining such material other than via Basra. It would certainly have been imprudent to obtain it through Bushire and so reveal his Arab connections to the British, even were the British to allow the transit of such material.

In the end the matter amounted to no more than a minor incident. Mubarak persisted in his efforts to obtain his agent's release. Diplomats like O'Conor and Wratislaw were reluctant to intervene in such matters. The lawsuit concerning the date groves dragged on as sluggishly as might be expected. Mubarak held the possessions and his men could only be evicted by force, and force could be resorted to only once Mubarak had lost his final appeal. Lawsuits in Ottoman Basra proceeded at a snail's pace. One problem for Mubarak was that he had never officially entered his possessions at the Ottoman land registry. The reason for this omission was obvious: as we have seen, Mubarak was unwilling to do so because registration was routinely implemented only for Ottoman subjects, and Mubarak was far from wanting to be registered among their number. In truth the legislation was full of loopholes, and foreign subjects were entitled to own land in the Ottoman Empire under certain conditions. Taken as a whole, the outlook for Mubarak was not inauspicious. Time was working in his favour, for Ibn Rashid's decline would inevitably weaken the position of his nephews and Yusuf Al-Ibrahim.

---

[208] Bidwell, *Affairs of Kuwait*, 2/4, pp. 93 and 97, India Office to Government of India 1 July 1902; and Bunsen to Lansdowne 22 July 1902.

8

Mubarak's Position Improves
1902–1904

8.1 The *Lapwing* incident, 1902

By the summer of 1902, the situation around Kuwait had stabilized considerably. Mubarak was still preoccupied by his agent's detention and the unresolved lawsuit, but on the whole he was out of danger. The Ottomans' loss of international diplomatic support rendered them unable to resume their advance into Kuwaiti territory without risking a direct confrontation with Britain, and the British were continuing to support Mubarak's legal right to Bubiyan. So Mubarak had reached something almost amounting to a defined borderline with the Ottoman Empire. Despite having been jeopardized by British errors, his legal position had remained unchanged.

At this juncture his enemies suddenly made a fatal mistake, improving his position still further, and helping to bring about a situation in which his most serious problems could be solved and his relations with the Ottomans restored from a position of strength.

Behind the scenes Yusuf Al-Ibrahim was continuing to scheme against Mubarak, but things were not going well for the Shaikh of Dawra. The faltering progress of the lawsuit over the Basra date groves led him to propose a compromise with the Kuwaiti ruler. His offer was to end the dispute in exchange for financial compensation. It was made through the Wali of Basra, who in June 1902 approached Wratislaw through his dragoman, with an interesting story: Yusuf Al-Ibrahim felt no personal hostility to Mubarak and he "really did not mind about the murder of the

Sheikh [Muhammad]" because Muhammad's wife was not his sister, but only his cousin! Yusuf averred that the conflict boiled down to an issue of money: on his assumption of power in Kuwait, Mubarak had found the treasury empty bar a mere 19,000 rupees and, jumping to the conclusion that Yusuf had appropriated the rest, had confiscated all Yusuf's property in Kuwait.

Yusuf's conciliatory approach was no doubt prompted by other factors, notably the fading power of his ally the Amir Abdul Aziz Ibn Rashid, and the friendship developing between Mubarak and Khaz'al which augured difficulties for him in the Dawra area. However, Yusuf's claims for compensation were so colossal that it is not entirely clear how serious his proposal was. Perhaps he merely wanted to present himself as the reasonable party in the conflict. In any case, Mubarak rejected the offer. Even Wratislaw, whose sympathies did not normally lie with the Kuwaiti ruler, approved of this, opining that Yusuf's claims for compensation in Kuwait were far beyond the means of Mubarak, who had huge expenses in Kuwait – most of them probably to fight Ibn Rashid and to bribe the Turks.[1]

The rebuff appears to have goaded Yusuf Al-Ibrahim to conclude that the only way of obtaining the money he claimed (or of recovering his expenses in bribing Turks and financing Ibn Rashid) would be by forcing Mubarak out of Kuwait by means of a coup d'état supported by irregulars brought in from outside – just the kind of operation he had tried some years previously with such disastrous results. The operation would have to be clandestine, otherwise the British would seize the opportunity to prevail on the Turks to oppose the plan in order to "maintain the status quo".

The Amir too played a sporadic part in the action. At the end of August 1902, rumours were rife that subjects of Mubarak had been raided by bands from Zubair under the direction of Ibn Rashid or Khalid Al-'Aun.[2] Zubair had for some time past been racked by a power struggle between two factions, one pro-Rashidi, the other favouring Mubarak, but for years now the Amir's faction had had the upper hand and Khalid Al-'Aun was in control of the place. From time to time European observers had

---

[1] Bidwell, *Affairs of Kuwait*, 2/4, p. 95, Wratislaw 13 June 1902.
[2] Bidwell, *Affairs of Kuwait*, 2/4, pp. 28–9, Wratislaw 10 January 1902, mentioning Khalid Al-'Aun as the chief supporter of the Amir in Zubair.

242   *Mubarak's Position Improves, 1902–1904*

reported efforts by Mubarak, whose mother was from Zubair, to support his adherents there. The Wali of Basra was slightly alarmed and took precautionary measures.[3]

It thus appears that there was a concerted plan by Yusuf Al-Ibrahim and the Amir for a two-pronged attack on Kuwait. But the plan did not prosper. The Turks, probably fearing British reactions, refused the Amir's requests for help against Mubarak.[4] On the Amir's other front, the Saudis were trying to emulate Mubarak by seeking British support, no doubt in expectation of repeated attempts by the Amir to expel them from Riyadh. They contacted the British with the story that the Russians, on the occasion of the *Varyag*'s visit to Kuwait, had offered Abdul Rahman Al-Saud an alliance. Rumours of Russian intrigues had occasionally inspired British panic in the past, but Kemball was unimpressed by this story, and there really was no chance of the British Government wanting to extend its involvement into central Arabia. British support was even less likely at that moment, in the light of persistent rumours of an imminent Saudi defeat at the hands of the Amir.[5] Meanwhile Mubarak was busily supporting the Saudi side with arms, while limiting himself to a purely defensive stance against the Amir's encroachments on Kuwaiti territory.[6] The Germans suspected the gun-running from Kuwait to the Saudis of being a British ploy to undermine Ottoman influence in central Arabia, but there is no firm evidence for this idea in the British sources. At the very least it was in Mubarak's interest to allow the Saudis to import arms – maybe even partly paid for with Kuwaiti subsidies – to fight the Amir.[7]

In al-Hasa the Turks had run into serious problems. In the growing insecurity of the southern borderlands a caravan had been attacked by tribesmen. This time the caravan's Turkish military escort had been wiped out, dealing a damaging blow to Ottoman prestige. The Turks were unable just then to transport sufficient reinforcements to al-Hasa and were reduced to "forgiving" the attackers. Rumours abounded of Mubarak's

[3] Bidwell, *Affairs of Kuwait*, 2/4, p. 121, Wratislaw 6 September 1902.
[4] Plass, *England*, p. 320: the Amir received only decorations; Bidwell, *Affairs of Kuwait*, 2/4, p. 107: extract from the Constantinople newspaper *Levant Herald* of 25 August 1902.
[5] Paris AE, NS Mascate 8, fos. 68–69, Rouet 31 July 1902.
[6] Bidwell, *Affairs of Kuwait*, 2/4, pp. 101–2, Kemball 23 May 1902, forwarding a letter of Abdul Rahman b. Faysal Al-Saud.
[7] Berlin AA, R 13889 A 15538 (24 October 1902), Richarz 25 September 1902.

involvement in this attack too.[8] The Porte then tried another tack. To maintain its governance of the isolated *mütesarrifliq* of Najd (the Ottoman term for al-Hasa), Talib, son of the Rifa'iyya Naqib of Basra, was appointed *mütesarrif* – a mere half-year or so after this same Talib had been summoned to Constantinople in disgrace. His appointment was ascribed to the Sultan's Rifa'iyya adviser Abu 'l-Huda's influence. It met with considerable criticism in Baghdad, where Talib had a bad reputation as corrupt and a stooge of the British.[9]

The lack of both Ottoman and Rashidi support for significant operations against Kuwait may have been one of the reasons deciding Yusuf Al-Ibrahim to go to war on his own. He had secretly prepared a force of irregulars, and at the beginning of September 1902 he once again attempted a coup. This one did not come unannounced. On 3 September, Mubarak sent a message through his brother "Sabba" to the British India telegraph office in Fao, warning that Yusuf and two sons of Muhammad were intending to attack Kuwait the next day with 200 men. The clerk of the telegraph office forwarded the message to Bushire.[10] That same day the commander of the British gunboat *Lapwing* received notification that two dhows belonging to Yusuf Al-Ibrahim "had left to attack Koweit in conjunction with a shore force".[11] The *Lapwing* steamed off in search and found two suspect dhows that had sailed from Yusuf's stronghold of Dawra, on the Ottoman side of the Shatt al-'Arab. The dhows fled to the Persian shore where a skirmish ensued. The dhows were captured and six crewmen killed, the rest of the crew of about 150 men escaping. One British sailor was killed, a matter the British authorities could not pass over lightly.[12] The *Lapwing* sailed to Basra and the British prepared a strongly-worded protest. Mubarak sent a telegram to Constantinople, which was shown by the Baghdad authorities to the German consul, Richarz. According to Richarz, Mubarak's telegram blamed the incident on Yusuf

[8] Paris AE, NS Mascate 8, fos. 44–45 and 58–60, Rouet 4 June and 15 July 1902; Berlin AA, R 13888 A 10142 (9 July 1902), Richarz 5 June 1902.

[9] Bidwell, *Affairs of Kuwait*, 2/4, p. 105, Wratislaw 3 July 1902; Paris AE, NS Mascate 8, fos. 68–69, Rouet 31 July 1902.

[10] IOLR, R/15/1/475, p. 267, 3 September 1902.

[11] Bidwell, *Affairs of Kuwait*, 2/4, pp. 107–9, Commander-in-Chief of the East India station 6 September 1902, and Wratislaw 8 September 1902.

[12] Bidwell, *Affairs of Kuwait*, 2/4, pp. 124–5, report of the commander of the *Lapwing* of 7 September.

and Ibn Rashid, and painted the Ottoman officials bribed by him in favourable colours (it is not clear who these officials were). Richarz's correspondence of this time revels in the wildest conspiracy theories current amongst the Ottoman military in Baghdad, one officer holding the rather interesting view that the British exaggerated the incident to keep their own weapons trafficking via Kuwait secret.[13] The French consul in Basra shared the opinion of his German colleague that the whole incident was trumped up by the British.[14]

For Yusuf as much as for the Ottomans this fiasco was pure disaster. It enabled the British to claim that there had been an attempt to upset the status quo by force from Ottoman territory, and Bushire intended to make the most of it. The British warship *Cossack* was sent to investigate, its commander reporting that it was clear that "the attacking party were raised and dispatched from Ottoman territory". There were no clear proofs of real Ottoman involvement, but the British considered the Ottoman authorities responsible, and as the attack had been launched from Ottoman territory they had a strong prima facie case. Wratislaw protested to the Wali and reported to O'Conor that the Wali's reply had not been satisfactory. According to Wratislaw the Wali was determined "to prevent guilt being brought home to Yusuf-ben-Ibrahim or any one for whom the Turkish Government is responsible". The consul had then confronted him with witness statements, removing virtually all doubt about the involvement of Yusuf Al-Ibrahim and some of Mubarak's nephews. The Wali then evinced a somewhat improved grasp of the gravity of the matter, but still rather hypocritically professed puzzlement to Wratislaw as to why Mubarak had not come to the Ottoman authorities with his complaints. Later, on 30 September, the Wali claimed to have received orders from Constantinople to deal with the matter in a judicial enquiry – a new attempt to delay matters.[15]

[13] Berlin AA, R 13889 A 15537 (24 October 1902), Richarz in Baghdad 19 September 1902; A 15538 (24 October 1902), Richarz in Baghdad 25 September 1902. See also the opinion of the German consul in Damascus, who thought the affair had been engineered by Mubarak: R 13889 A 18259 (19 December 1902), German consul in Damascus 4 December 1902.
[14] Paris AE, NS Mascate 8, fos. 105–106 and 116–117, Rouet 22 October and 12 November 1902.
[15] Bidwell, *Affairs of Kuwait*, 2/4, p. 110, Wratislaw 9 September 1902; ibid., pp. 130–4, Wratislaw's outline of the whole affair, with witness statements, 30 September 1902.

Mubarak wisely stood aloof from the debate between the Turks and the British. He had already garnered his profit from the affair, in the form of proof that an attack on Kuwait would be countered by the British, and of the disgrace of his enemies in Basra. He could afford to sit back and enjoy the prospect of the English getting tough with the Turks.

Bushire and the Government of India did indeed want to exploit the affair to the full, but they were thwarted. Diplomatic circles in Constantinople were unimpressed by the *Lapwing* incident, the prevailing view being that the British were exaggerating the affair. Curzon may have pressed for strong action, but O'Conor, true to form, was reluctant to put the Turks under serious pressure without incontrovertible proof of Turkish guilt. That Curzon's case was strong is undeniable: a British sailor had died and there were indications of Ottoman involvement. The British naval authorities too desired tough action in the light of the sailor's death. Curzon fulminated within the walls of his palace that the minimum appropriate response would be a bombardment, and the Foreign Secretary of India even contemplated the occupation of Fao and the proclamation of a protectorate over Kuwait. Curzon rejected the Secretary's suggestions, but with some regret, accompanied by aspersions on the pusillanimity of the Foreign Office in London.[16]

On 8 October Curzon's ideas reached London in very diluted form, all that remained being his demand for a strong protest to be lodged with the Turks.[17] Curzon had taken pains to couch this protest in cunning terms: the Turks had been warned by O'Conor on 25 March about encroachments, but the *Lapwing* incident proved that this warning had been ignored. The India Office, which apparently shared the view prevalent in the Ottoman bureaucracy that disagreeable papers lose their venom if allowed to rest for some time, spent more than a week considering what to do before passing the matter on to the Foreign Office on 17 October. Lansdowne finally instructed O'Conor to issue the protest in the form suggested by Curzon. The formulation of Lansdowne's instruction to the ambassador makes it clear that he had lost patience: "as [...] the situation does not appear to have improved, you should now make the further remonstrance made by the Viceroy."[18] But O'Conor was really

---

[16] Busch, *Britain and the Persian Gulf*, p. 220.
[17] Bidwell, *Affairs of Kuwait*, 2/4, p. 126, Government of India to India Office 8 October 1902.

resistant to taking a firm line with the Sultan and his ministers, as that would disturb the even tenor of his diplomatic routine. His predecessor, Currie, had been made of tougher stuff, the Sultan once saying of him: "So inflamed were my Ottoman sensibilities that I was barely able to control myself; my eyes welled with tears, and on the Ambassador taking his leave I burst into sobs." The Sultan had taken his revenge by making life as uncomfortable as possible for Currie.[19] So O'Conor advised Lansdowne to postpone the protest until the official Ottoman enquiries had delivered a verdict.

In the meantime discussions had taken place between Mustafa Nuri Pasha and Wratislaw about what form these enquiries should take. The Turks wanted to deal with the Kuwaiti witnesses in an Ottoman court. This was rejected by the British, who foresaw pressure on the witnesses by the Ottoman authorities or agents of Yusuf. Wratislaw came up with a compromise: to have the witnesses interrogated on board a British ship. Lansdowne would have preferred the witnesses to be heard in an Ottoman court under British safe-conduct, but reluctantly gave his permission on condition that it should be made clear that permission would be given to Ottoman officials to carry out their duties on British warships only as an act of courtesy and favour on the part of the British. But this compromise too was rejected by Mustafa Nuri Pasha. In the end, Wratislaw himself took the testimonies.[20]

Sworn statements of witnesses in Kuwait too were taken by the commander of the British warship *Cossack*. Some of these testified that Yusuf Al-Ibrahim and some of Mubarak's nephews had been present in Dawra when armed men were being embarked on the dhows. Moreover the signet ring of one of Yusuf Al-Ibrahim's closest associates had been found in one of these boats.[21] A process of Ottoman legal chicanery then ensued. Wratislaw was considerably exasperated and strongly advocated

[18] The correspondence is printed in Bidwell, *Affairs of Kuwait*, 2/4, pp. 126–7.

[19] A. E. Deniz, "The Problem of External Pressures, Power Struggles and Budgetary Deficits in Ottoman Politics under Abdulhamid II", unpublished thesis, Princeton, 1976, pp. 52–3.

[20] Bidwell, *Affairs of Kuwait*, 2/4, pp. 127, 135–6 and 152–7: Lansdowne to O'Conor 24 October 1902; O'Conor to Lansdowne 3 and 8 November 1902; and Wratislaw to O'Conor 7 November 1902.

[21] Bidwell, *Affairs of Kuwait*, 2/4, pp. 136–7, report of the commander of the *Cossack* 16 September 1902.

using the incident to get Yusuf, whom he considered a very dangerous man, and the nephews expelled from Basra.[22] The Wali's continued obstructiveness convinced Wratislaw of the futility of pursuing anything through an Ottoman court, and he advised O'Conor to use diplomatic pressure in Constantinople to have Yusuf and the nephews expelled.[23] It was only on 20 November that O'Conor sent one of his staff to Tawfiq Pasha to issue a stiff warning about Ottoman delaying tactics, and also to complain about new raids by the Amir against Kuwaiti tribes in the region of Safwan. Tawfiq promised to bring the matter to the attention of the Grand Vizier. Eventually, on 1 December, O'Conor found an occasion for a serious word with Tawfiq Pasha on the matter. He did this in his usual lofty and detached manner, alluding vaguely to a lot of reports from Basra all of which he had not yet been able to read, but which clearly demonstrated the complicity of Yusuf and the nephews in the *Lapwing* incident. He requested that they be expelled from Basra. Tawfiq was as usual very understanding, and promised to submit the matter to the Grand Vizier.[24]

Curzon fumed that he found it inconceivable that Britain should drop a case in which a British sailor had lost his life. Lansdowne, at first disinclined to take a tough line, agreed the necessity for stronger action having received a report from Wratislaw. This had originally been addressed to O'Conor, but a copy had reached London via India before the Constantinople embassy had decided to send it on to the Foreign Office. In it, Wratislaw related how a handsome bribe from Yusuf had induced the Wali to pull his punches. This incensed Lansdowne, who judged that Britain was now entitled to demand Mustafa Nuri's replacement, something that Curzon had long been urging.[25] O'Conor was again dilatory in following this through, and was forestalled by the Turks. On 29 December 1902, he was informed by Tawfiq that Yusuf and Mubarak's two nephews involved in the *Lapwing* affair – Khalid bin Muhammad and Hamud bin Jarrah – were to be expelled from Basra. The tardy O'Conor then took the liberty of suggesting to Lansdowne that it

[22] Bidwell, *Affairs of Kuwait*, 2/4, pp. 130–1, Wratislaw to O'Conor 30 September 1902.
[23] Bidwell, *Affairs of Kuwait*, 2/4, pp. 152–3, Wratislaw 7 November 1902.
[24] Bidwell, *Affairs of Kuwait*, 2/4, pp. 150–1 and 157, O'Conor 20 November and 2 December 1902.
[25] Bidwell, *Affairs of Kuwait*, 2/4, p. 162, Lansdowne to O'Conor 17 December 1902; Government of India to Hamilton 13 December 1902.

would be wise to delay the demand for Mustafa Nuri's replacement, because the Turks were showing their good intentions by halting the Amir's advance.[26] But the Turks kept dragging their heels. Yusuf had indeed left Basra, but no formal order of banishment had been issued, while the Turks suggested that the nephews should be confined to their estate in "Ghurdilan", just opposite Basra.[27] Lansdowne now lost patience, replying that Britain would demand the removal of the Wali unless adequate punishment were meted out to the guilty parties.[28]

The affair then took yet another turn. Already in early January 1903 Mustafa Nuri Pasha, fearful of being held to account for the trouble, had approached Wratislaw with the proposal that Yusuf Al-Ibrahim should be banished, but that the dispute between Mubarak and all his nephews should be ended once and for all by arbitration. In the new circumstances the nephews should now be more amenable to reason. After some time the British came round to the idea. They laid down various conditions, the chief one being that the arbitration should take place under British supervision. Mubarak too showed willing.[29] Negotiations were set in train that would last for a long time.

The *Lapwing* affair had improved Mubarak's position substantially in relation to Yusuf Al-Ibrahim and the Turks, and the British had been able to claim that the Turks had been in violation of the status quo agreement. There were still considerable dangers, however, on the desert front. While the Amir's position had deteriorated, he was far from defeated. His planning, however, seems to have left much to be desired. After his failure to recover Riyadh, a flurry of raids broke out in the region of Safwan between his and Mubarak's tribesmen. As usual the British were strongly

[26] Bidwell, *Affairs of Kuwait*, 2/5, pp. 4–6, O'Conor 29 December 1902 and 6 January 1903.
[27] "Ghurdilan" is probably the same as the place depicted on a Dutch manuscript town plan of Basra of 1672, when there was a ruined palace of the rulers of Basra of the Afrasyab family in that place: The Hague NA, 4.VEL 865.
[28] Bidwell, *Affairs of Kuwait*, 2/5, pp. 7–9, Whitehead (chargé d'affaires in Constantinople) to Lansdowne 16 January 1903; and Lansdowne to Whitehead 20 January 1903.
[29] Plass, *England*, p. 319; Bidwell, *Affairs of Kuwait*, 2/5, p. 16, Wratislaw to O'Conor 8 January 1903.
[30] Bidwell, *Affairs of Kuwait*, 2/5, pp. 14–15, Kemball to Government of India 22 December 1902.

opposed to military action by Mubarak. London once again wanted to warn him, but Kemball, while obeying orders, pointed out that as neither the Turks nor the British intended to protect Mubarak's tribes such warnings were unreasonable.[30] The Porte too was worried about the desert situation.[31] As usual one of the Porte's chief problems was the unreliability of its intelligence network. This was most obviously revealed in November 1902, when the Turks were under the illusion that the Amir had won decisive victories in battle. They prematurely rushed to announce the establishment of three new administrative districts on the coast of the Gulf between Kuwait and Qatif.[32] In reality the situation remained little changed, except that the Amir's failure to recover Riyadh had landed him in the difficulty of having to conduct a war on two fronts.

So time passed, punctuated by mutual recriminations between the British and the Turks over Mubarak's or the Amir's manoeuvrings, but with no substantive change to the situation. Meanwhile Mubarak was somehow able to convince the Ottomans of his innocence. Richarz reports that the Mushir Fayzi Pasha paid him a visit to discuss the Kuwait affair. Fayzi complained that Britain's Kuwait policy brought all Eastern Arabia into turmoil while they forbade Mubarak, under threat of bombardment, to submit to the Sultan, which he was – according to Fayzi – willing to do![33] Thus Mubarak had apparently mended his fences rather effectively on the Ottoman side, even with old adversaries like the Mushir.

8.2 After *Lapwing*: the Baghdad Railway

British efforts to obtain compensation or satisfaction for the *Lapwing* incident dragged on, only to be thwarted by Turkish delaying tactics.[34] For the British there now remained two principal matters outstanding: to arrange a settlement between Mubarak and his nephews either in or out of court, and to acquire a satisfactory degree of influence over the railway to the Gulf.

---

[31] Istanbul BA, DUIT 69/2–25, Reis ul-Kitab to Grand Vizir 2 Shawal 1320/2 January 1903: Ibn Rashid wants to move his headquarters to Safwan, but that will cause trouble with Britain because it is considered a threat to the safety of Kuwait.

[32] Berlin AA, R 13889 A 18580 (25 December 1902), Richarz 27 November 1902.

[33] Berlin AA, R 13889 A 1746 (5 February 1903), Richarz 6 January 1903; the essence of the report was forwarded by Marschall to Berlin by telegram 9 January 1903.

[34] Bidwell, *Affairs of Kuwait*, 2/5, pp. 16–18, Wratislaw to O'Conor 8 January 1903, with enclosed correspondence with Mustafa Nuri Pasha.

The first item would take time, but looked feasible. Over the railway project, however, confusion reigned. India was opposed to the whole thing anyhow (and the First World War would later vindicate India's view). But the Foreign Office feared that the railway would be built in the end and, that being the case, wanted some influence over it. Foreign Office apprehension was not entirely justified at that point. Though the German entrepreneurs were optimistic, and one of the leading personalities in the project, the President of the Deutsche Bank Dr Gwinner, intended to travel to London to arrange its financing, the realistic outlook was less auspicious. Wangenheim, the German chargé d'affaires in Constantinople, had a clear view of the differences of opinion between Britain and Turkey and how for the time being they could prevent progress. On the one hand the British would refuse to participate unless they acquired influence over the management of the railway. The Sultan, on the other hand, would not countenance any British influence, and was also insisting on Ottoman officials and police being stationed at the terminus on the Gulf. Wangenheim supposed that the British would certainly reject such an Ottoman presence in Kuwait and would, furthermore, consider any terminus on the Gulf outside Kuwait with an Ottoman presence to be a threat to the security of Kuwait and contrary to the status quo agreement. The Germans were perfectly reasonable about this and were even willing to pressure the Sultan into accepting British participation.[35]

In February 1903, a French and a Russian cruiser, the *Infernet* and the *Boyarin*, carried out a joint cruise in the Gulf. This demonstration of Franco-Russian amity may have looked impressive at first sight, but it would make no substantial impact on the Kuwait affair. The two ships arrived in Kuwait on 20 February, and next day Mubarak received the Russian and French officers in a splendid new reception room, ostentatiously adorned with portraits of the British royal family.[36] This time British protection was all too conspicuous and there was no more talk about Russian protection for Mubarak. The visitors raised the matter of the old British plan for a railway between Egypt and Kuwait, a scheme that popped up from time to time as an alternative to the Baghdad Railway.

[35] Berlin AA, R 13888 A 13360 (14 September 1902), Wangenheim 11 September 1902.
[36] Russian report in Rezvan, *Russian Ships*, pp. 136–7. The French reports can be found in the archives of the French navy in Vincennes SHM, series BB4, file 1669.

The Shaikh stated his opposition to the Baghdad Railway, but not to this alternative if it could be a collaborative venture between Russia, France and Britain.[37] Mubarak conducted himself with great aplomb – with good reason, as most of his problems were being gradually solved. The French and Russians made an intelligence-gathering tour of the town. The Russians had an economic interest in the export of sheepskins from Kuwait, and noted the sole foreign imported product as glassware from Austria (i.e. from the Czech provinces of the Austrian Empire). According to Russian observations, Kuwait town's defences had been improved, a fact that escaped the French, who remarked that it was completely unfortified.

The mirage of Russian protection for Mubarak had now definitely been dispersed by his discreet show of relations with Britain. The Russians had nothing to offer him, but it would have been against his nature for Mubarak not to try to manipulate events a little in his favour. He had in fact been inimpeachably loyal to his British friends during these latest dealings with the Russians and French, but in his talks with British officials afterwards he none the less veiled them in an aura of mystery. One never knew when relations with other powers might come in handy to keep the British guessing. It was a safety device for Kuwait which would not in the end be needed, but Mubarak always tended to err on the side of caution.[38]

During their visit the Russians and the French also tried to collect information about the situation in the interior. There had been dealings in the past between the Saudis and Goguyer, who had contacts in both France and Russia.[39] The captains paid a visit to Abdul Aziz Al-Saud, who was in Kuwait just then, but there is no sign of any serious political discussion, and the encounter seems to have been no more than an exchange of information. The French had dealt with political matters during the previous visit of the *Catinat*, when Kiésel had told Abdul Rahman Al-Saud that Goguyer had no official standing to negotiate on behalf of France.[40]

[37] Rezvan, *Russian Ships*, p. 137.

[38] Rezvan, *Russian Ships*, pp. 136–7; Bidwell, *Affairs of Kuwait*, 2/5, pp. 27–28, Commander Kemp of the *Sphinx* 14 March 1903.

[39] Vincennes SHM, BB4, file 1669, Goguyer to the commander of the *Infernet* 31 October 1902.

[40] Plass, *England*, p. 324; Rezvan, *Russian Ships*, p. 138. For the contacts of Abdul Rahman Al-Saud with the commander of the *Catinat*, see Paris AE, NS Mascate 17, fos. 28–28v.

Visits by warships coming on the heels of the *Lapwing* incident did nothing to calm the British press. At the start of 1903, a vehement debate had erupted there about the Russian position in Persia and the dangers this posed for Britain in the Gulf. Two British journalists, Chirol and Whigham, had visited the region, and both of them had subsequently bundled their articles in book form. Both advocated a decisive policy.[41] A. T. Mahan, an American naval officer and prominent publicist on matters of naval strategy, had also joined the discussion.[42] In essence the thesis of these observers was that Britain could not allow a foreign power to acquire a naval base on the Gulf. Hamilton, by contrast, who had always been the most accommodating of the British ministers, held to his view that Russia could not in the end be denied a foothold on the Gulf.

Meanwhile the Deutsche Bank proceeded with the railway preparations and, on 5 March 1903, the Sultan signed the convention on the construction of the Baghdad Railway.[43] Lansdowne now began to change his attitude. During a meeting with Gwinner in January 1903 he had stated that he would not oppose the railway. In the light of the progress made in early 1903 by the Germans he came to the conclusion that they would build the railway anyhow, and at a meeting with British bankers in February he announced that he could accept a British role in the project on condition that it was opened up to international participation. This was formally confirmed in a letter to Baring Brothers, who were leading the British financial consortium interested in joining the venture.[44] Gwinner, at the instigation of Rosen of the German foreign ministry, had notified the British bankers of a number of German wishes: permission for the Turks to increase customs duties, a substantial proportion of the mails to India to be forwarded via the railway, and finally the establishment of

[41] Berlin AA, R 13889 A 1369 (29 January 1903), Richarz in Baghdad 27 December 1902; Chirol, *The Middle Eastern Question*, pp. 241–3; Whigham, *Persia*, pp. 167–71.
[42] A. T. Mahan, "The Persian Gulf and International Relations", pp. 27–45. See also Berlin AA, R 13853 A 13250 (5 September 1902), Metternich in London, with a bundle of press comments on Mahan's article, 2 September 1902; and Paris AE, NS Mascate 8, fos. 87–91, French ambassador Cambon in London 10 September 1902, including comments by *The Times*.
[43] Gillard, *British Documents on Foreign Affairs,* Vol. I/B/17, pp. 329–48, has the text of the contract.
[44] Brünner, *Bagdadspoorweg*, pp. 147, 151; Gooch and Temperley, *British Documents*, II, no. 208, p. 181, Sanderson to Baring Brothers 24 February 1903.

railway installations and an Ottoman customs office in Kuwait.[45]

Delicate negotiations between Lord Revelstoke of Baring Brothers, Gwinner and the French participants were going on in Paris when all of a sudden, at the end of March, the British newspapers began an offensive against British participation in the plans. Among those behind the offensive was the British family of Lynch, which had a large stake in the Euphrates and Tigris Steam Navigation Company, and so risked losses were a railway to be opened. Under these circumstances Lansdowne began to reconsider his support for the railway project.[46]

On 7 April came questions in the House of Commons. The Baghdad Railway issue was raised by an MP, Bowles, who mentioned in passing that Kuwait had been brought under British influence precisely to stop the railway being constructed there. In the course of the debate, Balfour declared that it was desirable for the terminus of the railway to be within the territory of a Shaikh who was under British protection and had treaties with the British. Curzon could scarcely conceal his delight at this unexpected utterance.[47] The *Times of India* "welcomed this disclosure, which constitutes a more definite revelation of British influence in Kuwait than any previously made."[48] In Baghdad the Ottoman military too had access to the *Times of India* (possibly through the French or German consuls) and Turkish consternation was great.[49] Curzon welcomed Balfour's words as a final public declaration of the protectorate over Kuwait, which however it was not, as no protectorate had been formally declared.[50]

Finally, on 21 April, Revelstoke reported on the progress of the bankers' negotiations. Lansdowne now understood that the plan was to divide the shares equally between Britain, France, Germany and the Anatolian

[45] Brünner, *Bagdadspoorweg*, pp. 156–7; Berlin AA, R 13889 A 3742 (16 March 1903), note by Rosen 16 March 1903; and A 4523 (31 March 1903), note by Rosen 31 March 1903.

[46] Brünner, *Bagdadspoorweg*, p. 157.

[47] *Hansard* 4th Series, 120, column 1358 ff.; Plass, *England*, pp. 102–3.

[48] *Times of India*, 15 April 1903.

[49] Berlin AA, R 13889 A 7885 (1 June 1903), Richarz in Baghdad 4 May 1903, reporting that the Ottoman authorities in Baghdad were highly upset by Balfour's formal and public declaration in the House of Commons that special treaties existed with Mubarak.

[50] Plass, *England*, p. 103.

Railroad Company S.F.O.A. (which was in reality under German control). This meant in practice that the railway would be under German domination. Lansdowne finally decided to end his co-operation.[51]

On 5 May 1903, Lansdowne made an unequivocal statement in the House of Lords that he considered "the establishment of a naval base or of a fortified port in the Persian Gulf by any other Power as a very grave menace to British interests". The reaction of Russia and Germany to this statement was unexpectedly mild. Perhaps their governments even welcomed such a declaration if it helped to dampen the wild expansionist speculations doing the rounds in their countries. Hamilton, however, was unhappy with the Foreign Secretary's hawkish attitude, and still hoped for a compromise with Russia over the Gulf.[52]

8.3 After *Lapwing*: the nephews and the hinterland

By now Anglo-Russian rivalry, as far as Mubarak was concerned, had receded into the background. Visits by warships were no more than colourful interludes. The formal declaration of special ties with Britain was of far greater significance. More important still, however, was the course of the dispute with his nephews over the date groves in Basra province. Mubarak's nephews grasped how considerably their position had weakened after the *Lapwing* affair and the disappearance of Yusuf Al-Ibrahim from the scene. Negotiations between the parties about a compromise now became serious.[53] Mubarak was unhappy with the first compromise offered by the nephews and revisited an old judgement of the Sultan that the matter should be settled by arbitration.[54] This was a not unreasonable idea, as arbitration would admit British influence in the settlement of the affair to a considerably greater degree than would a case in a regular court of justice. It would also minimize any possible chicanery

[51] Brünner, *Bagdadspoorweg*, pp. 162–3.
[52] Plass, *England*, pp. 155–6; Busch, *Britain and the Persian Gulf*, pp. 256–7; see also the comment in *The Times* of 11 May 1903.
[53] Bidwell, *Affairs of Kuwait*, 2/5, pp. 21 and 24★, Whitehead 12 February 1903; India Office to Foreign Office 12 March; and Government of India to India Office, 5 and 11 March 1903.
[54] Bidwell, *Affairs of Kuwait*, 2/5, p. 24★, Government of India 5 March 1903: the Sultan's decision dated from the time of Muhammad Anis Pasha (1898–9); and ibid., p. 34, Mubarak 4 May 1903.

by Ottoman officials. Then came the crucial question of the composition of the panel of arbitrators. Mubarak created difficulties over this and also demanded that his Basra agent should be released first.[55]

July 1903 saw some progress. A new compromise was offered. After some negotiation Mubarak replied with a counter-proposal. Finally on 6 September a compromise was reached through arbitration.[56] A relatively small portion of the possessions in Basra province and a sum of money were given to the nephews. Mubarak borrowed part of the money from the Government of India.[57] So Mubarak had come out of the imbroglio with his nephews comparatively unscathed. The entire matter, barring the longstanding differences with Yusuf Al-Ibrahim, had been settled. Mubarak could now well afford to act as if Yusuf Al-Ibrahim's claims no longer existed. The final arrangements for the transfer of property and the payment by Mubarak took a few months more.

Settling with his nephews freed Mubarak to pay more attention to desert conflicts, where matters had turned out badly for the Turks and the Amir. Riyadh and southern Najd were now firmly in Saudi hands after the failure of Abdul Aziz Ibn Rashid's counterattacks. During the winter of 1902–3, the British had received frequent warnings of raids and impending attacks either by the Amir on Mubarak or by Mubarak on the Amir. Diplomatic pressure on the Porte to restrain the Amir had been reasonably effective, but it was felt that Mubarak did too much as he liked. Moreover information reaching Bushire from Kuwait about the development of the conflict looked unreliable and contradictory. O'Conor especially suffered the disadvantages of the situation, fielding Ottoman complaints about Mubarak and having to issue warnings to the Turks when the Amir moved.

Mubarak was active during the early summer of 1903 strengthening the buffer zone between himself and the Amir. He tried to reinstate the exiled shaikhs of 'Unayza in Qasim, who had come as exiles to Kuwait.[58] In

[55] The relevant correspondence can be found in Bidwell, *Affairs of Kuwait*, 2/5, pp. 33–6, 39–43, 47.

[56] The relevant correspondence can be found in Bidwell, *Affairs of Kuwait*, 2/5, pp. 51–2, 61–2, 66–7, including the text of the agreement. See also the papers in IOLR, R/15/1/483.

[57] Plass, *England*, pp. 319–20. See also PRO, FO 602/16, fo. 366, Mubarak to Resident 28 February 1904; and fo. 367, calculation by Crow (Wratislaw's successor as consul in Basra) of the sums needed by Mubarak, 7 March 1904.

August 1903 he also attacked hostile tribes south of Zubair.[59] Mubarak had some cause to feel insecure. Rumours were going around that Yusuf Al-Ibrahim was either coming to Dawra or building a fortress in Burayda in Qasim, in the Amir's territory, near 'Unayza.[60] O'Conor feared that Mubarak would renew hostilities with the Amir and, rather casually, suggested in a telegram that "the expediency of controlling his [Mubarak's] action by appointing a Resident at Kuwait" should be considered.[61] This was quite a volte-face: the ambassador had always argued that the British profile in Kuwait should be as low as possible and had vetoed the appointment of a British representative in Kuwait. The indolent ambassador, it seems, had finally understood that an unsupervised Mubarak was a cause of more trouble than Tawfiq's protests about British infringements of Ottoman sovereignty.

The Government of India consulted Bushire on O'Conor's proposal. In the past Meade would have jumped at this chance, but his successor Kemball was not keen. Kemball had repeatedly warned that it was neither reasonable nor possible to restrict Mubarak's desert activities as long as Britain was not willing to guarantee Kuwait's desert border. Were Britain to appoint a local agent to restrain Mubarak, it would entail that Britain's "undertaking to keep the Sheikh in order must involve our responsibility for affording him redress in case of internal raids". In short, Kemball was of the opinion that the establishment of an agency would mean Britain giving Mubarak a territorial guarantee. Arguably Kemball had come to understand Mubarak better than most of his contemporaries did. To involve Britain in his security was precisely the reason why Mubarak had in the past occasionally suggested the expediency of a permanent British representative in Kuwait. If Britain wanted an agent merely to stay Mubarak's hand in the desert, then Mubarak would lose interest in having an agent. The ambassador had a different perspective on the issue. He remarked that Britain could not protect Mubarak to the seaward (against

[58] Bidwell, *Affairs of Kuwait*, 2/5, pp. 43 and 54, O'Conor 18 July 1903 and Crow 20 July 1903. Crow remarked that the Amir's forces had been considerably weakened because some tribes were becoming restless.

[59] Bidwell, *Affairs of Kuwait*, 2/5, p. 69, Kemball 3 September 1903.

[60] Bidwell, *Affairs of Kuwait*, 2/5, pp. 39–40 and 44–45, Crow 8 July and 30 June 1903.

[61] Bidwell, *Affairs of Kuwait*, 2/5, pp. 43 and 54, O'Conor 18 July 1903; Plass, *England*, p. 325.

the Turks), if to the landward he kept attacking the Sultan's "vassals". This once again reveals O'Conor's overriding priority, to maintain friendly relations with the Turks.

Kemball combined his rejection of O'Conor's proposal with an alternative: to charge the British consul in Muhammara with keeping an eye on Kuwait and to assist trade there. This was an astute ploy, almost Byzantine in its subtlety. It would place Kuwait more directly under his own control as Bushire resident, the direct superior of the Muhammara consul, and thus avoid interference by British representatives in Turkey. Placing Kuwait in a *Persian* consular district would also be an obvious denial of Ottoman claims of sovereignty. Curzon was not opposed to this solution, but he also recognized the advantages of a British officer in Kuwait itself because it would clarify the British position there and improve the quality of intelligence on the Arabian Peninsula. It is obvious that the reports of the existing "news agent" in Kuwait in the Bushire archives were occasionally sensationalized, often inaccurate and possibly manipulated by Mubarak, so there was an advantage in having local reports from a reliable European. Curzon liked the idea of placing Muhammara and Kuwait under a single British official, but said that he could live with an agent in Kuwait, provided that "the connection between Koweit and Bussorah is in no way strengthened or recognized".[62] This last remark was meant as protection not only for Kuwait's independence, but also for the Government of India's freedom of action, by excluding British consular officials in Turkey and through them the Foreign Office from meddling too much in Kuwait matters.

The Foreign Office strongly opposed this plan to diminish its influence in the Kuwait affair. Sanderson notified the India Office that the Muhammara consul had other things to do and that he did not see why frequent communication with the Basra consulate might make it look as if Kuwait depended on Basra. The installation of an agent in Kuwait would constitute an unacceptable breach of the status quo.[63]

In the meantime another matter alarmed the British. Mubarak wanted to go to Fao in summer to inspect his date groves. O'Conor was unhappy

[62] Bidwell, *Affairs of Kuwait*, 2/5, p. 46, Government of India to India Office 31 July 1903.
[63] Bidwell, *Affairs of Kuwait*, 2/5, pp. 49–50, Foreign Office to India Office and India Office to Foreign Office, 13 August 1903.

with the idea, but felt that if the English opposed it they would be held responsible by Mubarak if the revenue fell short due to some kind of fraud. The consul in Basra was consulted, but this worthy reported that Mubarak's relations with the Wali of Basra were excellent and that there was no longer any danger in a visit to Basra province.[64]

8.4   Curzon's visit, 1903

Lansdowne's statement of 5 May 1903 in the House of Lords, about Britain's resolve to prevent any foreign penetration of the Gulf, created a climate conducive to a more open handling of British involvement there, and afforded Curzon the opportunity to revive the old idea of a viceregal tour of the Gulf. Such a tour would provide timely corroboration of Lansdowne's declaration.[65] Lansdowne did not oppose the general idea, though he prudently warned that it should not be an occasion for the expansion of British commitments. He also feared that the Viceroy's trip might upset the delicate balance between British and Russian influence in Persia.[66] Meanwhile Lord George Hamilton was totally unable to discern any advantage at all in such a tour.[67]

While preparations for Curzon's tour were under way, instability persisted in the wider Arabian border zone around Kuwait. Basra province too was coming under considerable pressure from the growing unruliness of the Muntafiq during the second half of 1903, and the conflict between the Turks and Sa'dun had resumed in the autumn of that year.[68] After inflicting a resounding defeat on Sa'dun, the Turks warned Mubarak not to give shelter to Muntafiq fugitives. The reports about Mubarak's involvement in the affair were just rumours, but O'Conor took the opportunity to warn the Foreign Office once again about Mubarak's

[64] Bidwell, *Affairs of Kuwait*, 2/5, pp. 59–60, India Office to Foreign Office 21 August, and Lansdowne to O'Conor 29 August 1903.
[65] Curzon had first made such a proposal in 1901, see Plass, *England*, p. 157. Salisbury had rejected the plan on the grounds that it would be seen as provocative at the time of the South African crisis.
[66] Plass, *England*, p. 158, where Lansdowne's jibe about "George Curzon's prancings in the Persian puddle" is quoted.
[67] Plass, *England*, p. 157.
[68] Nantes AD, consulat Bagdad, B 29, Rouet 18 November 1903: a good summary of the historical background concerning Sa'dun.

adventures.[69] The Foreign Office had grown used to such warnings and Sanderson limited his response to a recommendation to the India Office to make use of Curzon's planned trip to the Gulf to issue a new warning to the Shaikh.[70] O'Conor, however, continued to predict trouble despite the flimsiness of his evidence for Mubarak's involvement in the trouble between the Turks and the Muntafiq. There were indeed rumours that members of Sa'dun's family had taken refuge in Kuwait, but it was also known that relations between Mubarak and Sa'dun had cooled by that time. O'Conor, however, held to his own interpretation of events and still "feared that the Sheikh has been abetting the military adventures of Sa'dun".[71] In truth there was no indication of Mubarak's involvement, and his relations with Sa'dun were indeed strained at the time.

Sa'dun continued to be a thorn in the flesh for the Turks. The Ottoman military commander Muhammad Pasha apparently considered his three regiments inadequate to deal with the Muntafiq and requested reinforcements from the commander-in-chief.[72] But the Mushir in Baghdad was reluctant to call up reserves without the express permission of the Porte, being afraid that such an unpopular measure would fuel local discontent. In the end Muhammad Pasha resigned. British sources ascribe his hesitancy to his alleged kinship with Sa'dun's wife. By contrast Ottoman circles in Baghdad went so far as to blame Sa'dun's rebellion on British intrigues.[73] The truth cannot now be established, but the latter interpretation was perhaps just another wild Ottoman conspiracy theory of the kind that prevented the Turks from formulating an adequate and appropriate response.

The governments of the great powers may not have intended the matter of Kuwait's status to climb up the international agenda, but various

---

[69] Bidwell, *Affairs of Kuwait*, 2/5, pp. 70–1, O'Conor to Lansdowne 18 November and 15 December 1903, and Crow to O'Conor 16 November 1903; Bidwell, *Affairs of Kuwait*, 2/5, p. 71, and 2/6, pp.1–2, Crow to O'Conor 21 November 1903.

[70] Bidwell, *Affairs of Kuwait*, 2/5, p. 70, Foreign Office to India Office 25 November 1903.

[71] Bidwell, *Affairs of Kuwait*, 2/6, p. 2, O'Conor 11 January 1904.

[72] Paris AE, NS Mascate 10, fos. 78–79, Rouet 3 December 1903; *cf.* Berlin AA, R 13889 A 18239 (8 December 1903), Richarz 9 November 1903.

[73] Reported by Rouet 3 December 1903, NS Mascate 10, fo. 78, where he even mentions that Sa'dun was said to have sent messengers to Curzon. For the mention of Sa'dun's kinship with Muhammad Pasha's wife, see Bidwell, *Affairs of Kuwait*, 2/6, p. 4, Crow 28 December 1903.

hotheads had other ideas. True, Kuwait hardly figured in the press debate on the scope of Britain's domination of the Gulf in which Mahan, the American strategic theorist and naval officer, was playing a vocal part. But the press in India was arraying Curzon's projected Gulf tour in the most exotic colours. Lansdowne may have intended it to be a low-key affair, but if so he had reckoned without the Indian press – which was probably not uninfluenced by the Viceroy, as it was heavily subsidized by the Indian Government. The most extravagant rumours went the rounds and were duly denied. Perhaps the most far-fetched, in the *Pioneer*, was that Curzon would go right up to Baghdad, there to stage a grand durbar. The French consul in Baghdad wearily remarked that there would be no durbar in Baghdad, nor a visit to the Basra province, not so much because Curzon was afraid of the Ottoman reaction, but because he wanted to spare Russian feelings.[74] The *Pioneer* saw Curzon's tour as an opportunity to expand the "Trucial Zone" to the entire coast between Kuwait and Oman.[75] This was all nonsense, but it traced its origin to the Calcutta rumour-mill.

The most delicate segments of Curzon's tour would be the visits to Bushire and Kuwait. Bushire may have been the British headquarters in the Gulf, but it was Persian territory, and the Persian authorities chose to ignore the Viceroy, which made his visit there fall rather flat. This was a personal setback for Curzon, who had always placed such emphasis on the importance of Persia for India. Already before the start of Curzon's trip the visit to Kuwait had been trumpeted by the Indian press as a momentous event. Echoes of English jingoism even reverberated in the reports of the French consul-general in Calcutta.[76]

The German and French consuls in India could only report what they heard from the Indian Government and press. The French consul judged that Curzon's manifestation was intended to convert Kuwait, where the Shaikh wanted only "to keep his independence from the Turks as well as from the English", into a straightforward protectorate. He includes a

[74] *Pioneer*, quoted by Rouet Baghdad 18 Nov 1903: Paris AE, NS Mascate 10, fo. 15. It must have been the first time that Curzon showed any sensitivity to Russian feelings.

[75] *Pioneer*, report from Allahabad of 5 October, quoted in Nantes AD, consulat Bagdad B29, Rouet to embassy 15 December 1903.

[76] Paris AE, NS Mascate 10, fos. 84–93, French consul in Calcutta 5 December 1903.

cutting from an Indian newspaper which gives a vivid description of Curzon's visit to Kuwait, saying of Mubarak that "his knowledge of current affairs and the condition of his territory is great and his intelligence is striking". However there was no information available to outsiders about what Curzon had actually discussed with Mubarak.[77] Mutius, the German consul-general in Calcutta, reported from Simla his belief that Curzon's trip was intended to be no more than a show of power and splendour. He did not believe that treaties would be concluded in Kuwait or Muscat, but only that a little pressure would be applied.[78] Rouet, the French consul in Baghdad, gave his minister "all the news circulating in Baghdad, true as well as dubious, because it shows the state of public opinion at a time when the Indian Government stages a political demonstration that provokes the wildest flights of fancy". As one example, he quotes a report in the *Pioneer* that Mubarak had given a port to the north-east of Kuwait to the British. Rouet gives his own imagination full rein in supposing that this port might be in Mubarak's part of Fao![79] His German colleague Richarz in Baghdad was able to report what he heard from his Ottoman acquaintances. The Turks pretended to him that Curzon had not disembarked at Kuwait, although Richarz knew very well from the Indian newspapers that he had visited the town. Richarz attributed this discrepancy either to the indifference of the incompetent Mushir, Fayzi Pasha, who embargoed all information, or to Ottoman fear of losing face because they considered Curzon's visit a shameful affront. It was said in Baghdad that the Wali of Basra had orders to persuade Mubarak to keep his reception of Curzon as low-key as possible. Richarz did not believe that Mubarak would pay any attention to the Turks because, according to him, this Wali had never managed to prevail upon Mubarak by either friendly or forcible means. He reports that, according to the *Times of India*, Mubarak had allowed the establishment of a British post office in Kuwait. Even more painful to the Turks was a rumour which, according to Richarz, was being spread by the British consulate in Baghdad, that the Viceroy had been in Kuwait to ascertain its borders.[80] The German envoy

[77] See again Paris AE, NS Mascate 10, fos. 84–93, French consul in Calcutta 5 December 1903.

[78] Berlin AA, R 13889 A 15395 (18 October 1903), consul Mutius in Simla 23 September 1903.

[79] Paris AE, NS Mascate 10, fos. 78–79, Rouet 3 December 1903.

in Teheran had an even more spectacular tale: it was being said there that Curzon had concluded a treaty with Mubarak.[81]

Curzon's tour had also provoked unease in other European chanceries. The Austrians sent their chargé d'affaires in London to the Foreign Office to make enquiries. The under-secretary, Hardinge, told the Austrian that Kuwait's bond of dependence upon Turkey was gradually loosening, a development that could hardly be other than agreeable to the British.[82]

All these conflicting reports demand an investigation of the facts of Curzon's visit to Kuwait in November 1903. Actually very little occurred. The Viceroy arrived with great pomp and circumstance, and Mubarak, always wary of being outshone, responded in kind. Richarz recorded a telling detail to show how Mubarak's asserted his neutrality: even during the viceregal visit, he continued to fly the Ottoman flag in Kuwait. The Ottoman flag is mentioned in Curzon's report, but somewhat in passing. The anti-British French arms trader Goguyer gives a more picturesque account. Mubarak himself had told Goguyer, during the latter's stay in his palace, how on Curzon's arrival he had planted a huge Ottoman flag behind the welcoming crowd on the beach. He described the Viceroy's reaction in nice Kuwaiti dialect: "*Hua istanis fi ez-zahir, lakin ma istanis fi el-batin*" – equivalent to the Dutch expression "He was grinning like a peasant with toothache".[83]

The official British report of the private interview on board the *Hardinge* between Mubarak and the Viceroy, attended also by Kemball and the secretary of the Indian Foreign Department, Dane, commands interest as the only systematic account extant of a meeting between Mubarak and

[80] Berlin AA, R 13889 A 1322 (26 January 1903), Richarz 28 December 1903; see also news about excitement in Ottoman circles in Lepsius, *Grosse Politik*, Vol. 17, p. 515, telegram of Marschall of 2 January 1904.

[81] Berlin AA, R 13889 A 3570 (29 February 1904), German envoy Rex in Teheran 7 February 1902.

[82] Berlin AA, R 13889 A 17657 (28 November 1903), German embassy in Russia 26 November 1903.

[83] Mubarak's words are given in Latin script in a letter from Richarz to Bülow of 21 July 1904 (in Berlin AA, R 13889 A 13158 of 14 August 1904). The text in Arabic script is in Rouet's rendering of Goguyer's experiences, in Paris AE, NS Mascate 11, fos. 35–39, Rouet 28 July 1904, fo. 37v. The official British report of Curzon's visit (IOLR, R/15/1/476 fo. 183) reads: "The flag flying over his house the previous day was a red flag with the star and crescent, but this did not appear to have been hoisted on the occasion of the Viceroy's visit."

a group of Europeans.[84] The Viceroy opened by asking Mubarak if he had any observations to make. Mubarak stated that he had cut his ties with the Ottomans and had repelled Russian and French advances, so he felt justified in asking for some compensation for the Ottoman title and allowance he had relinquished, especially in view of his great expenses. Curzon then asked Mubarak to give details of his income. Mubarak replied that the bulk of it came from the date groves, but that now he had given up part of these to his nephews. The income from Kuwait (customs and a "poll tax" on tribesmen) was only 60,000 rupees, less than a quarter of his present share of the revenue of the date groves. Then Mubarak requested that Umm Qasr should be liberated from the Turks.[85] Curzon asked why Mubarak had not kept garrisons at those places – a quite unrealistic question, to which Mubarak retorted that the places were just pasture grounds used by nomads. Curzon promised to consider Mubarak's requests, but said that he was unable to commit himself to anything. There was also some discussion about the fate of Mubarak's Basra agent, and Curzon promised to do his best through diplomatic channels. Once again Curzon warned against meddling in Arabian affairs, and Mubarak as usual freely promised to do his best. After this conversation the Shaikh accompanied Dane on a visit to the *Hyacinth*, the British flagship. Mubarak showed himself much impressed and declared that he had never been on a warship before.[86]

The Viceroy offered Mubarak a sword. Apparently Mubarak, not without some justification, felt that a rather cheap gilded sword fell somewhat short of the normal standard of gifts expected from guests in

[84] The official report is in IOLR, R/15/1/476, fos. 181–183. A more informal description of Curzon's visit to Kuwait with two photographs appears in his own book, *Tales of Travel*, pp. 247–50, where it figures under the heading "Humours of Travel". The text was later republished with four photographs in P. King (ed.), *Travels with a Superior Person*, pp. 31–4. See also the articles on the visit to Kuwait in the *Times of India* of 9 and 12 January 1904. The latter article describes Mubarak's reception room with the portraits of members of the British royal family. This inspired Richarz to remark that he had heard that Mubarak had a second reception room, specially for Ottoman visitors, with the portraits of the Sultans: Berlin AA, R 13889 A 4873 (21 March 1904), Richarz 18 February 1904.

[85] A handwritten remark in the margin also mentions "some other place"; probably Bubiyan was meant, and this is confirmed by a handwritten note at the end of the report.

[86] Official report in IOLR, R/15/1/476, fo. 182.

the region, and politely asked for the *"rutbe"* to accompany it, together with a fitting allowance. Later there was some discussion among the British about the precise meaning of *rutbe*, it being understood at first that Mubarak desired some decoration. When during a later visit Kemball asked Mubarak for clarification, it was translated as "function" or "rank", perhaps something like a knighthood. Mubarak explained that the rank of *mirmiran* had been conferred upon him by the Ottoman Sultan, but that he did not use this and that he would like, as a client of the British, to have a British *rutbe* to use instead. It seems that Kemball, no expert in Ottoman rank and protocol, failed fully to grasp the implications. In the Ottoman system *mirmiran* had indeed originally denoted an administrative rank, and in the old days a very elevated one: in the 17th century it had been used for the wali of a full province. Later it was reduced to a rank in the civil service equivalent to that of lieutenant-general in the army.[87] After some further discussion the matter sank from view. It was not until April 1912 that Mubarak was at last dubbed Sir Mubarak, the British having been goaded into action by the Turks' award of a new decoration to the Shaikh. The matter of the annual allowance was agreed after some negotiation at 15,000 rupees or 1000 pounds sterling, but the British were unable to finalize a decision and the matter lapsed until further discussions in 1907.

On a later occasion Curzon claimed that during his visit Mubarak had also repeated his request for a British India post office in Kuwait. Curiously, there is no mention of this in the report of the Viceroy's visit to Kuwait.[88] A post office would be of some advantage to the British, enabling them to keep an eye on the Kuwaiti ruler. French and German Baghdad reports too claimed that Mubarak had been put under pressure by the British to allow a post office. It is impossible to establish the truth of the matter. Had Mubarak been feeding disinformation to Turkish officials in Baghdad about his opposition to a post office? Or was he genuinely opposed to the idea, and had the India officials invented, or perhaps heavily solicited, Mubarak's request in order to render the British official in Kuwait they so much desired more palatable to the resistant authorities in London? Curzon proposed a kind of discreet double function: an Indian post agent with medical training, who could combine

[87] *EI*(2), Vol. 6, pp. 95–6, *i.v.* mir i-miran.
[88] Bidwell, *Affairs of Kuwait*, 2/6, p. 5, Government of India to India Office 16 January 1904.

his mail duties with useful work in health care in Kuwait. It was thought that this was because he feared that Mubarak would otherwise deal with the American Dutch Reformed Church missionaries over establishing a medical service in Kuwait. A probably apocryphal version of Curzon's demands was given by Rouet, who reported that the Viceroy had wanted Mubarak to accept a British consul or agent; Mubarak, whose attitude to Curzon, according to Rouet, was "not that of a vassal", had refused, and had only allowed a post office.[89]

Even O'Conor saw no problem with a post office. The Porte might point to a breach of the status quo, but foreign post offices existed elsewhere on Ottoman territory.[90] In the end, however, it was not implemented, because the British did not want to irritate the Turks while they were trying to persuade them to evacuate Bubiyan.[91] The press, furthermore, had got wind of the plan and other European powers were already grumbling about it.[92]

During Curzon's visit a detailed survey was made of the feasibility of a railway terminus at Umm Qasr.[93] This was important because in 1902 O'Conor, unencumbered by any local knowledge and simply on the basis of a crude map, had claimed that it made no strategic sense to get into a dispute with the Turks over their position on Bubiyan while Umm Qasr was under their occupation. But it was now concluded that it was vital for the access to Umm Qasr not to be controlled on both shores by a foreign power. As a consequence it would be to Britain's advantage if Mubarak could be persuaded to plant a post on the northern end of Bubiyan. This would overlook and control the anchorage of Umm Qasr and shipping in the Khor Abdallah. The Government of India proposed either that the

[89] Paris AE, NS Mascate 10, fos. 150–151, Rouet 2 February 1904.
[90] Bidwell, *Affairs of Kuwait*, 2/6, p. 6, O'Conor 5 February 1904.
[91] Bidwell, *Affairs of Kuwait*, 2/6, pp. 50–2, O'Conor 13 June 1904.
[92] For German reactions, even before the matter was submitted by Curzon to London: Berlin AA, R 13889 A 221 (5 January 1904), Embassy in Constantinople 2 January 1904; and A 1322 (26 January 1904), Richarz 28 December 1903.
[93] A British officer, Smythe, had explored the route and the possibilities of Umm Qasr, thus causing the Turks some alarm. They even feared a British attack because there were only 20 Ottoman soldiers there: Berlin AA, R 13857 A 720 (14 January 1904), Richarz 10 December 1903; and R 13889 A 4873 (21 March 1904), Richarz 18 February 1904. See also Istanbul BA, Y.A. Hüs 462/94, telegram from Basra to Porte 13 November 1319 Rumi/26 November 1903.

Porte should be pressed to recognize Mubarak's claim to Bubiyan and withdraw the Turkish garrison, or that Mubarak should place a garrison of his own there.[94] The next chapter will show that nothing came of these suggestions.

On the whole Curzon's visit to Kuwait achieved little for British interests. It had been an extremely expensive way of conveying the umpteenth warning to Mubarak to stay out of trouble in the desert. Mubarak had more reason to be satisfied. He had dropped some of his demands, and others were to be granted in the future. He had also magnified his prestige locally by receiving a splendid guest with due pomp and ceremony. Next he did his best to mollify hurt Ottoman feelings. He resorted to his old expedient of playing dumb, informing the Porte that "a high British India official" had been on a pleasure trip around the Gulf and that he had given him a fitting reception. This was indeed not so far from the truth, as nothing of real substance had taken place.[95]

It is noteworthy how adverse and undesirable from the British point of view was the coverage of Curzon's visit in the Muslim press. The German consul in Egypt, reporting on an article in the pan-Islamist Egyptian newspaper *Al-Mu'ayyad*, commented: "From the reports it can be concluded that Shaikh Mubarak Al-Sabah has staged festivities in honour of Lord Curzon on much too elaborate a scale, as can also be seen in the Indian press. The Indian newspaper *Mohammedan* gives various details ... This was a political demonstration by England in the territories of the Orient. If the Ottomans had protested against such meddling in their affairs at the right moment, it would not have gone so far."[96] The British press, on the other hand, naturally presented the visit in most positive and triumphalist tones.

Just a few days after Curzon had left, the German "tourist" Hermann Burchardt visited Kuwait in December 1903. He was accommodated in Mubarak's palace and, while his observations are not political, they present

[94] Plass, *England*, p. 329; Bidwell, *Affairs of Kuwait*, 2/6, pp. 13–15 and 21, Government of India 4 February 1904, and O'Conor 5 April 1904.

[95] O'Conor reported that an informant had told him that Mubarak's report had been received at the Porte with some scepticism, but it rather looks as if it provided just the kind of face-saving some Ottoman officials needed: Bidwell, *Affairs of Kuwait*, 2/6, pp. 3–4, 20 January 1904.

[96] Berlin AA, R 13889 A 19417 (31 December 1903), Consul Janisch in Cairo 23 December 1903.

an interesting informal view of Kuwait. He described approvingly the quality of the soap and towels in the palace and the cleanliness of the town. The foreign visitor was treated with great tolerance. Though it was Ramadan, Burchardt was offered meals during daylight hours. He was much impressed by Mubarak, whom he described as "exceptionally well-informed for an Oriental", and "the only one of the Shaikhs I encountered during my journey who had the air of a monarch."[97]

8.5 The British agency in Kuwait

Mubarak's activities on his desert border, and especially his conflict with Ibn Rashid, remained the chief source of anxiety for the British. The information they received through their "news agent" in Kuwait was often sensationalized, and possibly partly fed by Mubarak himself for his own obscure reasons. Gossip circulating in the Bushire bazaar and in Basra, or emanating from the not especially reliable agent Gaskin in Bahrain, provided an inadequate basis for policy-making. Meanwhile a gradual weakening of both the Ottoman and the Rashidi position in the Arabian border area was setting in between 1902 and 1904. Ibn Rashid had been unable to recover Riyadh, and by the end of 1902 the Saudis were penetrating the region of Qasim in northern Najd, which the Rashidis had conquered in the 1890s.

Elsewhere in the vicinity, the ever-unruly Muntafiq were in open revolt against the Turks. There were rumours in Baghdad that they were being egged on by Talib Pasha, the son of the Naqib of the Rifa'iyya, who was reputed to be in contact with Mubarak and the British. During the winter of 1903–4, the Ottomans proved unable to contain Sa'dun of the Muntafiq, and to make matters worse they also suffered a resounding defeat against the Saudis when trying to support Ibn Rashid.

The British observed these developments, but their hands were tied. The most expansionist officials in British India might dream of an alliance

---

[97] Burchardt, "Ost-Arabien", pp. 306–7, with photographs of Mubarak and of the vegetable market in Kuwait. Original photographs can be found in an album in the University of Leiden originating from Rudolph Saïd Ruete (Oriental Manuscript Department, collection of the Oosters Instituut) and in the Ethnographic Museum in Berlin. Burchardt also reported on his journey in a letter to Richarz, where he says of Mubarak that "he stands far above the level of the other Shaikhs I had the occasion to visit": Berlin AA, R 13858 A 8530 (20 May 1904), Richarz 12 April 1904.

with the Saudis, but London wanted at all cost to avoid conflict with the Turks. The Turks meanwhile were receiving the most alarming intelligence on affairs in Arabia. They believed in 1904 that Ibn Saud had sent a certain Ibrahim to Bahrain to borrow money there, and that this Ibrahim had come back with the fanciful tale that, after the Ottoman defeat in Qasim, Mubarak had occupied the entire coast of Arabia between Kuwait and Qatif.[98]

Important as it might be for the British to restrain Mubarak from actively intervening in the situation, it was difficult to descry from Bushire what he was really up to. The British debate about ways of controlling him had continued during the whole of 1903. As we saw above, two options explored were the control of Kuwait by the Muhammara consul and the stationing of a British agent at Kuwait, but both had been rejected. The first was an unacceptable change in the consular hierarchy, and the second would be a breach of the status quo. In August 1903, Hamilton came up with a compromise solution that met with Lansdowne's reluctant approval. He proposed the appointment of an official who was to pay regular visits to Kuwait. O'Conor did not believe that Mubarak could be controlled in this way, but London had come to a decision.[99]

After his tour of the Gulf, Curzon followed up the conclusions he had reached regarding the alternative route of the railway: to give up Umm Qasr but to try to recover Bubiyan.[100] He met with little success. On 3 March 1904, the India Office sent his letter to Lansdowne. Lansdowne took his time, and on the 22nd asked O'Conor for his opinion of Curzon's letter. O'Conor poured cold water on Curzon's ideas. He claimed that Mubarak's claim to Bubiyan could not be separated from that to Umm Qasr, and that the Turks would in any case consider any establishment on Bubiyan to be in breach of the status quo. He did not, however, exclude the possibility of continuing from time to time to press the Turks to withdraw, and suggested finding out whether the Ottoman troops had not already retired. In that case the British could oppose their return.[101]

[98] Paris AE, NS Mascate 11, fos. 81–82, Rouet 21 October 1904; the French consul did not believe this story.
[99] Plass, *England*, p. 326; Bidwell, *Affairs of Kuwait*, 2/5, pp. 49–50, 68, India Office to Foreign Office and Foreign Office to India Office 13 August 1903, and O'Conor 16 October 1903.
[100] Bidwell, *Affairs of Kuwait*, 2/6, pp. 13–15, Government of India 4 February 1904.
[101] Bidwell, *Affairs of Kuwait*, 2/6, p. 21, O'Conor 5 April 1904.

O'Conor for once followed up his promises, and in May he did indeed bring pressure to bear on Tawfiq over the Bubiyan garrison.[102]

In the end Hamilton's proposal for an official to make regular visits to Kuwait was slightly modified. It was now decided to appoint a political agent, but one who should not be in permanent residence so as not to arouse the suspicion that a protectorate had been established. Thus O'Conor's proposal of July 1903, to send a "resident" to Kuwait to control Mubarak, became reality in the summer of 1904. By that time, preparations had been completed for the despatch of a political agent and a post official to Kuwait. O'Conor requested that the postman's despatch should be postponed to avoid irritating the Turks while Tawfiq's reply on the Bubiyan garrison issue was awaited. Then there was some misunderstanding, and the despatch of an agent too was postponed. In August 1904, however, the agent, S. G. Knox, arrived in Kuwait. He was immediately served by Mubarak with a request for Britain to obtain the release of his Basra agent from prison.[103]

Mubarak was probably unaware that the reason for the appointment of a political agent was not so much to facilitate contact between himself and the British, so that he could more easily communicate his wishes, but rather to curtail his independence of action in the desert. This did not prevent him from rising to the situation. Knox was a colonial official and expected to be able to sit with Mubarak and give him policy advice like an older and wiser brother. His nose was put somewhat out of joint when he saw that this did not conform to Mubarak's idea of his function. Mubarak followed his own policy and chose not to discuss matters with Knox, although he was friendly enough and not disobliging when Knox came to him with the clearly expressed wishes of his superiors. But for the normal running of Kuwait Mubarak kept his own counsel, going every day to his "office" and only rarely conferring with Knox. Knox spent much time sitting about in coffee houses trying to collect information and making occasional trips into the desert.

Part of the problem in their relationship lay in Britain's employment of military officers from the colonial administration as representatives in the Gulf. The proper function of these representatives was essentially a

---

[102] Bidwell, *Affairs of Kuwait*, 2/6, p. 23, O'Conor 16 May 1904.
[103] Bidwell, *Affairs of Kuwait*, 2/6, p. 68, Knox 7 August 1904; it had some effect, see p. 76, Townley to Lansdowne 15 October 1904.

diplomatic or consular one. The experience of men of military background, who had been "controllers" of native rulers in India, was inappropriate for consuls in the Ottoman Empire and management advisers to rulers who enjoyed de facto independence. The independent attitude of individuals such as Mubarak or Khaz'al of Muhammara could be somewhat offensive to them. As a result, Knox often felt humiliated by Mubarak.

The Ottoman response to this British breach of the status quo was mixed and ineffective. The Porte's first action on becoming aware of Knox's appearance was to dismiss the Wali of Basra, Mustafa Nuri Pasha. If the reports of the German and French consuls in Baghdad depict Ottoman feelings correctly, the Turks were chiefly alarmed because they thought that Knox had been sent to co-ordinate help to the Saudis through Kuwait. This nicely illustrates the Turks' misunderstanding of British intentions: while they laboured under the misapprehension that the British were behind Mubarak's support for the Saudis, the reality was that Knox had been sent to *restrain* Mubarak from supporting the Saudis! Mustafa Nuri Pasha was temporarily replaced by Fakhri Pasha, who was at first dismissed by Rouet as a salon soldier but who showed some energy in governing Basra. He clapped some robbers of the Naqib's circle into jail, an action that could be considered not so much a public order measure as a warning, because the Naqib, with his ties to Mubarak, was regarded as the leading pro-British personality in Basra.[104]

The Ottoman foreign minister sought solace with the German ambassador Marschall. As so often, Tawfiq came with an exaggerated complaint, this time that the resident agent had gone to live in Mubarak's house on which the British flag had been hoisted. This again raises the question whether Tawfiq was deliberately misleading the German or was himself poorly informed by his officials.[105] This persistent Turkish habit of exaggerating events in Kuwait, as they had done previously in the warship incidents, was a prime cause of international tension, but it was gradually becoming ineffective. The German reaction was cool. Tawfiq told Marschall during the same meeting that the Porte planned to propose international arbitration on the Kuwait affair. When Marschall reported

[104] Paris AE, NS Mascate 11, fos. 63–64v and 70–72v, Rouet 14 September and 6 October 1904.
[105] Berlin AA, R 13890 A 17809 (12 November 1904), Marschall 9 November 1904.

21. Shaikh Mubarak (seated in corner, farthest from camera) holding court in public in the open air, with Kuwaitis and British representatives, photographed by the British naval officer Lt-Cmdr A. N. Gouldsmith, 1907–9.

22. Shaikh Mubarak in
1908. This portrait
appeared in the Egyptian
Christian journalist Abdul
Masih al-Antaki's poorly
printed book on Kuwait,
Muhammara and Riyadh,
entitled *Al-Riyadh al-
muzhira bayn al- Kuwayt
wa-'l-Muhammara* (Cairo,
1908).

23. Al-Antaki's book
also contains this very
indistinct picture of
Mubarak's steam yacht,
Mishrif. This vessel
played an important
part in Mubarak's life,
affording him freedom
of movement, especially
to Muhammara, where
among other things he
was able to send
and receive telegrams
without British or
Turkish knowledge. The
Mishrif appears to have
been a surprisingly
large vessel.

24. Percy Zachariah Cox, British Political Resident in the Persian Gulf 1905–14, in front of his office in Bushire.

25. Capt. W. H. I. Shakespear took this photograph of Shaikh Mubarak with Abdul Aziz Ibn Saud and members of his family, on the veranda of the British political agency, Kuwait, in March 1910.

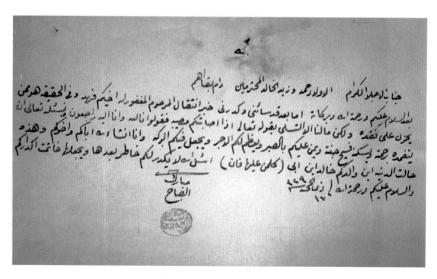

26. A sample of Mubarak's private correspondence with his friends.

27. *Above*: The palace, Kuwait, flying the Ottoman flag, photographed in the years 1909–13 by the political agent Capt. W. H. I. Shakespear.

28. *Right*: Captain W. H. I. Shakespear, British political agent in Kuwait 1909–14, who was killed at the Battle of Jarrab in Qasim in 1915. This photograph, of uncertain date, appeared in Arnold T. Wilson's *Loyalties, Mesopotamia 1914–1917* (Oxford/London, 1930).

29. Shaikh Mubarak, Kuwait, 1912, by the Danish traveller Barclay Raunkiaer. Raunkiaer visited Kuwait in 1912 under some suspicion that he was a German agent. The original Danish edition of his book, *Gennem Wahhabiternes Land paa Kamelryg* (Copenhagen, 1913), contains a number of his interesting photographs, including this portrait of Mubarak in somewhat exuberant dress.

30. The old section of Mubarak's palace, Kuwait, by Barclay Raunkiaer. In *Gennem Wahhabiternes Land paa Kamelryg*, Raunkiaer gives an interesting description of Mubarak's palace and daily routine, including two pictures of the palace. This image gives a closer view of the older part of the palace, which can also be seen in the French picture of 1902 (no. 5, above), and in the *Times of India* picture of 1907 (no. 15).

31. The new section of Mubarak's palace, Kuwait, by Barclay Raunkiaer. This, Raunkiaer's second picture, shows the new part of Mubarak's palace, the architecture of which is still visible on the outside of the Sif Palace even today.

32. Town plan of Kuwait in 1912. To Barclay Raunkiaer's *Gennem Wahhabiternes Land paa Kamelryg* we also owe the earliest town plan of Kuwait. Roman figures (not very clearly visible) refer to the legend. I (in negative in a black complex of buildings in the middle of the seafront) is Mubarak's palace. II (on the seafront halfway between the palace and the north-east end of the city) is the British political agency. At the south entrance of the city, V appears twice and VI once: VI is a coffee-house and V is the audience building of the Shaikh in the bazaar. IV (at the right-hand top of the capital W of the name "KUWEIT") is the great mosque. III (on the seafront directly to the left the palace) is the Shaikh's customs office. VII (to the right of the palace) is the American mission.

33. A street in Kuwait, 1912, photographed by Barclay Raunkiaer in 1912.

34. The Turkish fortress at Fao. This fortress at the entrance of the Shatt al-'Arab was built on Al-Sabah land in 1890, and was twice the cause of conflict between the Al-Sabah and the Basra government. The picture appeared in *The Times History of the World War*, Part 29. London, 1915.

35. The British Royal Marine guard of honour that accompanied Admiral Bethell on his visit to Kuwait, on the occasion of the award of the K.C.I.E. to Shaikh Mubarak, Sif Palace, 16 April 1912.

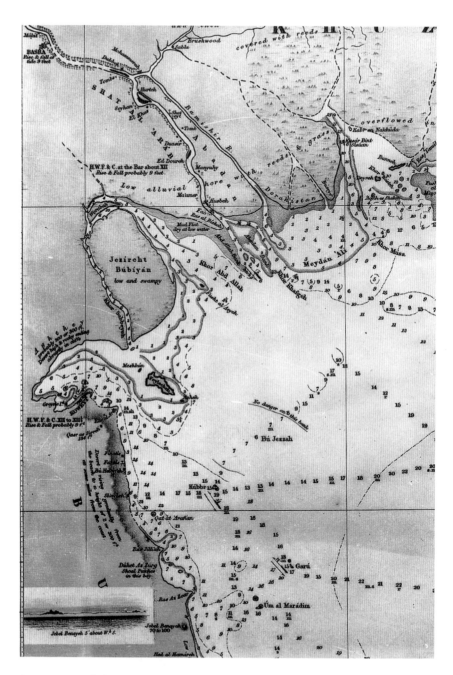

36. Portion of the British Admiralty chart of the Upper Gulf of 1862 (C. G. Constable and A. N. Stiffe, *The Persian Gulf, Western Sheet*). This chart shows few details, but clearly indicates the strategic value of Warba.

37. Map mentioning the "Republic of Kuwait", 1867. This is the original version of the German map of 1867 that mentions the Republic of Kuwait. This map (*Arabien zu C. Ritter's Erdkunde, bearbeitet von H. Kiepert*, Reimer Verlag, Berlin, 1867) and its later editions caused diplomatic trouble. Interesting too is the mention of Segwan (Safwan), a place of which Tawfiq Pasha claimed total ignorance in 1902 even as Ottoman troops were occupying it.

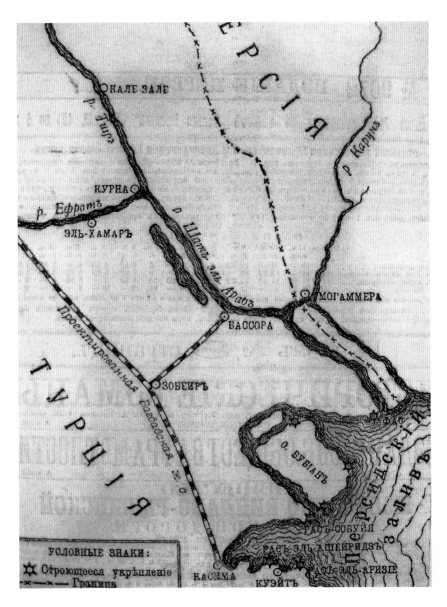

38. Russian map of the Kuwait region showing the planned railway to the Gulf. This map, which appeared in the St Petersburg newspaper *Novoye Vremiye* of 19/6 February 1902, shows two branches of the line from Zubair, one to Basra and one to Kazima. The map is based on exaggerated intelligence, and shows all possible routes of access by sea to a railway terminus on the Gulf of Kuwait or on the Khor Abdallah to be commanded by seven Ottoman fortresses (indicated by the starred dots), supposedly to be built with German help.

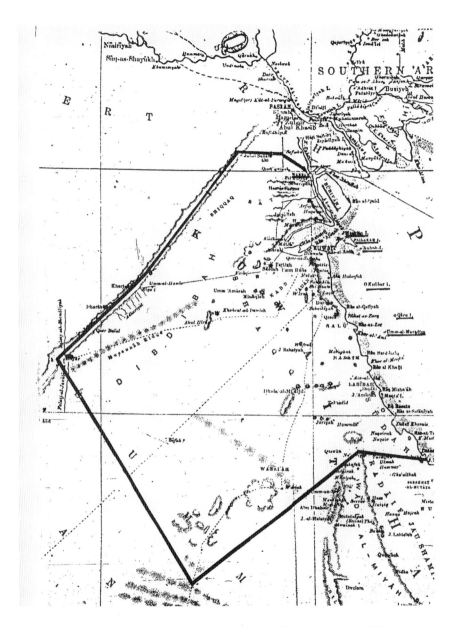

39. The borderline of Kuwait as originally proposed by the Foreign Office on the basis of Lorimer's *Gazetteer*, which was itself based on Knox's travels (IOLR, R/15/5/65). The main point of contention in the southern border area was the village of Anta'a (Nta' on the map, Antā'a in the list of names in IOLR, R/15/1/478), just south of the point where the southern borderline turns from a north-easterly to an eastward line.

40. The borders of Kuwait on the map accompanying the Anglo-Ottoman Convention of 1913. The map shows the two perimeters of the compromise: a red inner circle and a green outer arc. The main difference from the original British proposal is that Anta'a/Nta' is now included within Kuwait territory (it is shown in the small circle on the most southerly part of the outer perimeter), while some of the desert area in the south-west now falls within Ottoman territory. This product of diplomatic compromise completely lacks practical value, there being really no way with the means of the time to trace large circular perimeters on the ground with any degree of accuracy. (Map in Berlin AA, R 13890).

this to Berlin, the weary response was that Germany had already suggested that to the Turks three years before.[106]

The Turks also tried to lodge a complaint with the British as soon as they heard of Knox's posting to Kuwait. As usual this first took the form of a rather informal request for information by the Ottoman ambassador in London, which included a warning that establishing a British consul would constitute a breach of the status quo.[107] The British had foreseen this and had a reply ready: Knox's presence was temporary and was not an appointment of a permanent official. At the end of October 1904 the acting Wali of Basra complained to the Porte about Knox, who was going into coffee shops in Kuwait and mixing with people there and interfering in the government of the place.[108] In November, the Grand Vizier complained to O'Conor about Knox's presence, but the British ambassador was easily able to counter this. Knox's presence was temporary, he said, and in any case why had the Turks not yet made good their breach of the status quo on Bubiyan?[109] But the Turks reiterated their protests.[110]

In September 1904, the *Sphinx* conducted a more detailed survey of the Khor Abdallah. This brought forth the usual Ottoman protests, but also a new insistence by the Indian Government on progress with Turkish withdrawal from Bubiyan. Commander Kemp of the *Sphinx* confirmed the importance of upholding the claim to Bubiyan.[111]

By the end of 1904 Mubarak's situation had eased. The Rashidi Amir's star was on the wane. He was safe from Ottoman attacks, and no more Ottoman infringements of his boundaries were to be expected. The Ottomans might in future even be compelled to withdraw from one or more positions they had occupied in January 1903. The only fly in the ointment might be efforts by the new British agent to control him. But, as Rouet pointed out, Mubarak was no vassal and did not behave like one, and the agent would run into difficulties should he try to "guide" the Shaikh with too heavy a hand.

[106] Berlin AA, R 13890 A 17809 (23 November 1904), Berlin to Marschall.
[107] Bidwell, *Affairs of Kuwait*, 2/6, pp. 71–2, Lansdowne to Townley (chargé d'affaires in Constantinople) 20 October 1904.
[108] Istanbul BA, Y.A. Hüs 480/113, Fakhri, acting Wali of Basra, 17 October 1320 Rumi/30 October 1904.
[109] Bidwell, *Affairs of Kuwait*, 2/6, pp. 80–1, Townley to Lansdowne 3 November 1904.
[110] Bidwell, *Affairs of Kuwait*, 2/6, pp. 81–2; cf. various Ottoman documents in Istanbul BA, Y.A. Hüs 480/113.
[111] Bidwell, *Affairs of Kuwait*, 2/6, p. 77, Lansdowne to Townley 3 November 1904.

9

Mubarak's Attempts at Independence 1904–1907

9.1 The shifting international scene

The period 1904–7 saw the position of Kuwait considerably affected by fundamental changes in relations between the great powers. In 1904, France and Britain concluded an agreement on their colonial activities as part of the Entente Cordiale. In 1904–5, Russia suffered a decisive defeat by Japan and had exhausted its naval resources. And in 1907 Russia and Britain too reached a settlement of their Asian interests.[1] The consequence of this was that Britain now had a freer hand in dealing with the Turks in the Gulf. Only the Germans maintained their sympathy with the Sultan, but even they had grown weary of Ottoman unreliability and had no serious intention of making problems for Britain. The British remained none the less uneasy about German railway plans and the growth of German trade in the region.

For Mubarak the cooling of international rivalries meant fewer openings for international diplomacy. Now that the Russians were out of the game, he was restricted to his balancing act between the Turks and the British. This was now made easier for him by the serious problems the Ottomans were facing in the region. Basra province was in a state of anarchy, to the extent that the French consul in Baghdad regarded it as ripe

---

[1] It should, however, be noted that the Baghdad Railway project was a matter between Britain, Germany and the Ottoman Empire that remained outside these agreements with Russia and France.

for foreign occupation.[2] Affairs in the desert had also shifted substantially in Mubarak's favour. First there were reports that 'Unayza had been occupied by his allies Aba 'l-Khayl and Siyala, who had formerly been living in exile in Kuwait.[3] Next came the news that Burayda had fallen into the hands of the Saudis, which meant that Abdul Aziz Ibn Rashid had lost the important region of Qasim to them.[4] The Amir withdrew to the Euphrates to request Ottoman assistance, and the Porte ordered the VI Army Corps to step in as necessary. The Baghdad army command sent four battalions of infantry, mountain artillery, ammunition and arms. This force was not believed in Baghdad to be intended for real fighting, but merely to exploit the opportunity offered of demonstrating Ottoman sovereignty, which had never been effectively exercised in that region.[5] The Amir would not have greatly appreciated that idea, but at that moment he hardly had a choice. Up until now the Turks had regarded Abdul Aziz Ibn Rashid as a dangerous ally who was not to be allowed to grow over-mighty. But now there was a risk of this ally collapsing, leaving the field to the Saudis who appeared less favourably inclined to the Sultan's policy. The Turks believed the Saudi advance to be supported by the British, and to be yet another example of British expansionism in the region. The Ottoman command in Baghdad received a letter from Abdul Aziz Al-Saud in which the former exile styled himself Amir of Arabia and claimed the title "Amir al-Barr", Lord of the Desert. True, in this letter the new Amir offered his loyalty to the Sultan, but such declarations were in the same coin as those so profusely issued by Mubarak. Some Ottoman officers were already entertaining the thought that it might be wise for the Ottoman authorities to change sides and ally themselves with the Saudis.[6] With his Ottoman auxiliaries Abdul Aziz Ibn Rashid tried to regain the lost territory, only to suffer a humiliating defeat in July 1904.[7]

In this battle of "Qseibe" (Qasr Ibn 'Uqayl) the Ottoman unit of 1200 men was numerically not especially significant. The Rashidis had some 7000 men and the Saudis 20,000. The important aspect of the affair was,

[2] Paris AE, NS Mascate 11, fos. 26–27, Rouet 15 June 1904.
[3] Berlin AA, R 13858 A 8015 (11 May 1904), Richarz 12 April 1904.
[4] Paris AE, NS Mascate 10, fos. 194–195, Rouet 25 April 1904; Bidwell, *Affairs of Kuwait*, 2/6, p. 31, Abdul Aziz Al-Saud to Mubarak 10 Muharram 1322.
[5] Paris AE, NS Mascate 10, fos. 194–195, Rouet 25 April 1904.
[6] Berlin AA, R 13858 A 8277 (16 May 1904), Richarz in Baghdad 20 April 1904.

however, that a regular Ottoman army unit had been annihilated in a regular battle, only prisoners and deserters surviving. In view of this, earlier British fears of confronting smaller Ottoman units near Kuwait appear to have been groundless, for it was obvious that the Ottoman army in Iraq was of little military value. It was only just able to maintain Ottoman authority in Iraq, while interventions in Central Arabia invariably ended in disaster. The British, however, were ill-informed about such matters, which also helps to explain their reluctance to have anything to do with the Saudis.

The one avenue left to the Turks was to strengthen their hold on Iraq. Mustafa Nuri Pasha was removed from office. The main reason given for this was that he had been unable to prevent Mubarak admitting a British agent. Mustafa Nuri's successor, Fakhri, resorted to another means of countering the growth of British power in the region, by assailing the position of Talib Pasha, son of the reputedly pro-British Naqib, in Basra province. Fakhri stood little chance of success, and after a few weeks he was replaced by Mukhlis Pasha.[8]

In the autumn of 1904, meanwhile, Abdul Aziz Ibn Rashid suffered a second defeat at the hands of the Saudis.[9] By the end of the year the Turks appear to have reached the conclusion that Mubarak personally represented no great danger to them and was not helping the British to expand their influence. According to reports circulating in Baghdad, Mubarak had refused the British permission to hoist their flag on the agent's residence, and had also made it clear that he would not accept Gaskin as successor to Knox.[10] These rumours may very well have been planted by Mubarak himself in order to restore good relations with the

[7] There were first rumours that the battle had ended in a victory for the Turks: Berlin AA, R 13858 A 8822; see also Paris AE, NS Mascate 11, fo. 43, Rouet 4 August 1904. Rouet was rather sceptical about the news. The Ottoman War Minister too claimed victory: Bidwell, *Affairs of Kuwait*, 2/6, pp. 59–60, military attaché Maunsell in Constantinople 9 August 1904. The French consul reported the real result of the battle on 8 and 21 August: Paris AE, NS Mascate 11, fos. 46 and 53–54.

[8] Paris AE, NS Mascate 11, fos. 63–64 and 70–71, Rouet 14 September and 6 October 1904; Berlin AA, R 13858 A 16494 (18 October 1904), Richarz 25 September 1904.

[9] Bidwell, *Affairs of Kuwait*, 2/7, p. 2, Knox 17 October 1904; Berlin AA, R 13859 A 19492 (12 December 1904), Richarz 17 November 1904.

[10] Paris AE, NS Mascate 11, fo. 90, Rouet 22 November 1904; Berlin AA, R 13890 A 392 (18 January 1905), Richarz 1 December 1904.

Ottomans. Already in September the Turks were trying to befriend Mubarak in order to establish contacts with the Saudis through Kuwaiti mediation.[11]

The British response was somewhat indecisive. Ottoman opposition to Knox's presence in Kuwait was too vocal for the Foreign Office's liking, and it brought pressure to bear on the Indian Government to withdraw him in conformity with the agreement that the agent's posting would be temporary.[12] India dragged its heels, proposing that the Turks should be offered Knox's withdrawal in exchange for the evacuation of Ottoman forces from Bubiyan. O'Conor disapproved of this linkage, as it would concede an Ottoman say in the placement of British officials; his preference was for the British to withdraw the agent unilaterally.[13] Meanwhile the agent was experiencing difficulties as Mubarak made it clear that he expected him to work hard in promoting his interests over Bubiyan, in disputes with the Ottoman authorities in Basra and, above all, in obtaining the release of his Basra agent.[14] Eventually it was decided that Knox should leave when the summer heat set in. For health reasons, however, he left Kuwait in May 1905.[15]

9.2 The arms trade and Goguyer

A key factor in military developments in Arabia was Kuwait's importance as a centre of the arms trade. The Turks, French and Russians all supposed that the supply of arms to the Saudis via Kuwait was a sinister ploy by the British to expand their influence in the Gulf at the expense of Turkey's ally Ibn Rashid. This was a conspiracy theory too far, for in fact it was Mubarak, in his efforts to counter his enemy by helping the Saudis with arms, who was chiefly responsible for it.

[11] Bidwell, *Affairs of Kuwait*, 2/6, pp. 90–1, Knox 3 September 1904.
[12] There is a remarkable (but perhaps not entirely true) report that Mubarak himself had complained to the Wali of Basra about Knox, who behaved "like a consul" and threatened to close shops in Kuwait unless he was allowed to open a post office: PRO, FO 78/5385, fos. 385–388, Townley 14 December 1904.
[13] Bidwell, *Affairs of Kuwait*, 2/6, p. 108, Foreign Office to India Office 16 December 1904.
[14] Bidwell, *Affairs of Kuwait*, 2/6, pp. 82–3, correspondence between Mubarak and Cox 7–16 August 1904.
[15] Plass, *England*, pp. 345–6.

It is true that, since they had concluded their agreement with Mubarak in 1899, the British had turned a blind eye to the considerable firearms traffic through Kuwait, which formed an important source of the Shaikh's revenues. In May 1900 Mubarak had signed, under British pressure, an undertaking to ban the import and export of arms, but he had done little to implement it, and the British had not pressed him to do so during the difficulties of 1901–2.[16] Mubarak levied a special tax on rifles imported into Kuwait, and the arms trade contributed substantially to Kuwait's prosperity. It had been carried on there from before Mubarak's rule.[17] The British were not so much exercised about the Kuwait arms trade in itself, as about the fact that most arms arrived there via Muscat. The Kuwaiti traffic was an offshoot of the Muscat arms trade, and they did have sound reasons to disapprove of the latter.

Muscat was the hub through which arms from Europe penetrated the region. There the rifles were sold to local merchants, who either smuggled them to the Makran coast, whence they passed to the Afghan border region, or carried them to the upper Gulf where Kuwait, situated as it was outside the reach of both Ottoman and Persian customs officials, was an excellent place to disembark them. But after Knox's arrival and the decline of the Rashidis, the British wanted to disentangle Mubarak from as many political complications as possible. From the moment it became clear that arms produced in Britain were infiltrating the Afghan border to be used against the Indian army, there was pressure from India to put an end to the trade, at least in its most dangerous channel from Muscat to the opposite coast of the Gulf of Oman. The trafficking of arms through Kuwait was thus a mere part of a larger network that the British aimed to suppress. The arms business conferred on Mubarak a degree of independence from the British, and enabled him to manipulate tribal conflicts in the desert. The Government of India, while growing gradually more active in suppressing the arms trade, was hampered by the fact that French firms were prominent importers of arms from Britain into Muscat. France had a legal foothold in Oman, and the freedom of the Government of India and its

[16] For a copy of the promise of 24 May 1900, see IOLR, R/15/5/59, 103.
[17] Musil, *Northern Negd*, p. 244, about Kuwait as the place where Muhammad Ibn Rashid obtained his arms, which was ended by the war between Muhammad Al-Sabah and Muhammad Ibn Rashid. On the other hand Knox wrote in 1905 that the arms trade in Kuwait had started with Mubarak: Plass, *England*, p. 483.

Gulf representatives to act against the French was circumscribed by larger Foreign Office concerns to maintain good relations with France.[18]

The main entrepreneur in the arms trade was the French merchant Antonin Goguyer who, as we have seen in Chapter 7, also used his contacts to play a part in international intrigues. Goguyer's arms business was extensive, and he was well-connected in French political circles.[19] He was a colourful figure in other ways too. He spoke fluent Arabic, was a scholar who had published classical Arabic legal texts, and had also written anti-British articles on Gulf affairs in the press. Goguyer's opinions were typically French of the old-fashioned kind, and he was vehemently hostile to what he regarded as Britain's tendency to exclude other nations from world trade. He thus harboured some sympathy for Russian attempts to counteract Britain's monopoly in the region. His contacts were wide-ranging in France, in Russia and among Arabs of all kinds. As early as 1899 he had offered four million rupees for the lease of the customs revenue of Bahrain, and had established contact with the agent of Abdul Rahman Al-Saud there. He had had even proposed to this agent that he should seek French protection for his master.[20]

Goguyer's earlier life reads like a novel. He was born in the French village of Dun-le-Palestel in 1846 and must have learnt Arabic somewhere at an early date, because he began his career as an interpreter in the Tunisian law courts and published a number of serious scholarly studies on classical Arabic texts.[21] In Tunis he also wrote articles in a local Arab newspaper that were so disagreeable to the French authorities that they banned it. He then published similar articles in a French newspaper in Tunis, until the French authorities there decided to expel him. Next he turned to gun-running in Somalia and Ethiopia, supplying Britain's

[18] Graves, *Cox*, pp. 59–62 and 70–6; Busch, *Britain and the Persian Gulf*, pp. 154–86.

[19] Plass, *England*, p. 393; Paris AE, NS Mascate 48, a large file entitled "Affaire Goguyer".

[20] Busch, *Britain and the Persian Gulf*, p. 140; see also Plass, *England*, p. 393, and Paris AE, NS Mascate 48, Goguyer 31 July 1899.

[21] Goguyer is mentioned in the big bio-bibliographical index of scholars, *Index Bio-Bibliographicus Notorum Hominum*, Vol. 89 (Osnabrück 1998), p. 89. His scholarly works were: *Choix splendide de préceptes cueillis dans la loi [par Ahmad ibn al Khoga]: petit manuel de droit immobilier suivant les deux rites musulmans orthodoxes de la régence de Tunis*, traduit sur la première éd. du texte arabe et annoté par A. Goguyer, Paris, 1885; and a translation of Ibn Hijam, *La pluie de rosée: étanchement de la soif = Qatr al-nada wa-bal al-sada*, Leiden, 1887.

Muslim opponents. At one point he was arrested in Ethiopia and spent some time in prison. On his release he went to Bahrain as agent of Ettinghausen, a firm of Paris jewellers who had a virtual monopoly in the trade of pearls between Bahrain and Europe. There he made his first contacts with Saudi agents, with whom he discussed the possibilities of the Saudis acquiring French protection. A year later he set himself up in Muscat as an arms dealer.[22]

In 1904 he suddenly popped up in Kuwait, disguised as an Arab. This may have been connected with a disagreement with Cox, at that time British agent in Muscat. Goguyer spent three months as a guest in Mubarak's palace under the name of "Abdallah Al-Mughebi", his plan being to open a branch office in Kuwait.[23] Then he left again for Muscat. He claimed that he had received permission from Mubarak to open a business in Kuwait, and after a time his nephew Elbaz arrived there as prospective manager of it, but was asked to leave after a few weeks. The business was then left in charge of a Muslim merchant. Later Elbaz revisited Kuwait but failed to obtain permission to open a business, and left again for Muscat.[24] The precise reason for his departure is unclear, but it may have owed something to British pressure on Mubarak, or to discontent among the Kuwaitis, who were averse to the establishment of foreign competition.[25] Mubarak was unable really to allow foreign merchants into Kuwait, as that might kindle unrest among his people. At

[22] It is not entirely clear why his writings were so objectionable, but remarks by the French ambassador in London, Paul Cambon, who was French resident in Tunis during Goguyer's sojourn there, and Goguyer's later tendency to promote Arab independence from the Turks, fuel the suspicion that he may have been opposed to the existing structure of a French protectorate for Ottoman rulers over an Arab population, promoting instead direct French rule over the Arabs. See Paris AE, NS Mascate 48, especially Cambon's letter of 10 December 1906, and an internal memorandum of the Ministry concerning a Muscat telegram of 30 June 1902, no. 6, which give more details on Goguyer's career.
[23] Paris AE, NS Mascate 48, letters of Laronce, French consul in Muscat, 2 and 17 February 1904.
[24] Elbaz was a nephew of Goguyer's wife Yasmina Elbaz, a Jewish lady from North Africa. Goguyer himself was not a Jew.
[25] Paris AE, NS Mascate 48, Rouet, 25 October 1904, and Goguyer 15 October 1904; see also PRO, FO 602/16, fo. 395, Consul Crow in Basra 11 May 1905, stating that Mubarak had allowed Goguyer to open a shop in Kuwait. On 2 February Crow had described Goguyer as a Russian spy (ibid., fo. 359).

about the same time Kuwait was visited by two American missionaries. One, Miss Miller, preached in the *suq* and was soon asked to leave. The other, Samuel Zwemer, wrote a letter to Gaskin, British agent in Bahrain, complaining about the growth of anti-European sentiment, intolerance, and the strength of the Wahhabi community in Kuwait. Zwemer's picture does not tally either with Goguyer, who observed that the Wahhabi presence in Kuwait was insignificant, or with Burchardt, who found Kuwait a tolerant place.[26] Anglo-French relations may have been improving rapidly in the direction of the alliance that was to be concluded in 1907, but in the Gulf there was direct friction between the French and English over interests in Oman. Gaskin, the British assistant political agent in Bahrain, was probably the most vehemently Francophobe official in his fears of Goguyer, his sentiments being warmly reciprocated by the French consul in Muscat. If there is any truth in assertions in French sources that Mubarak had rejected Gaskin as British representative in Kuwait, then Gaskin was unpopular with the Shaikh too.[27] According to Gaskin, Mubarak and Goguyer had secretly agreed to organize the shipping of arms to Kuwait by native ships.[28] The British were unable legitimately to oppose this, as Goguyer was not a "representative of a Foreign Power", but just a private merchant.

Goguyer's arms trafficking at this time seems to have made a substantial contribution to Mubarak's income as well as to the Saudi victories over Ibn Rashid. Other sources, however, shed even more interesting light on his relations with Mubarak. The French consul in Baghdad mentions that, after the Ottoman defeats by the Saudis, Goguyer was trying to reconcile Mubarak with the Turks. At first this came up against Mubarak's deep scepticism about the reliability of Ottoman officials. A few months later, however, he showed more interest. A number of articles by Goguyer in various newspapers, as well as his correspondence, show that he and Mubarak had deep discussions about the future of the Arabs in the region, and about how to avert Ottoman and British interference in Kuwait.[29]

[26] IOLR, R/15/1/477, fo. 69, Gaskin 12 March 1904 (about Zwemer); and PRO, FO 602/16, fo. 359, Consul Crow in Basra 2 February 1904.

[27] For rumours that Mubarak had refused to accept Gaskin as agent, see Paris AE, NS Mascate 11, fo. 90, Rouet 22 November 1904.

[28] IOLR, R/15/5/476, fos. 53–54, Gaskin to Kemball 7 February 1904.

[29] Nantes AD, ambassade Constantinople E 288, Goguyer 12 April 1905.

The British tried to stir up trouble between Mubarak and Goguyer by accusing the latter of being the author of a rather wounding newspaper article in *Al-Ahram*. This started from the premise of full Ottoman sovereignty over Kuwait. It spoke of Mubarak having first accepted British protection and then having reverted to the Turks, and finally having come full circle at the time of Curzon and become a protégé of the British once more.[30] However, it differs completely in style and purport from press pieces known to be by Goguyer.[31] Knox thought that by showing the article to Mubarak he could put an end to the relationship between him and the Frenchman. He did not succeed, and the arms trade with Goguyer's firm continued.[32] When Knox later protested about the scale of Goguyer's arms exports to Kuwait, Mubarak piously denied all knowledge. He must have found it amusing to hoist Knox with his own petard when he claimed that he had expelled Goguyer from Kuwait because of the Frenchman's scurrilous articles about him in the newspapers.[33]

A significant feature of Goguyer's relationship with the Kuwaiti ruler is that it offers a different view of Mubarak. In Goguyer's account Mubarak is not the devoted friend of Britain but a politician who tried to balance the British with the Ottomans. There are predictable similarities and divergences in Curzon's and Goguyer's descriptions of Mubarak. Curzon, in his report of their meeting in Kuwait, noted how impressive a character Mubarak was. Goguyer used almost exactly the same words, but with a

[30] The article in *Al-Ahram* of 16 September 1904, by a correspondent in Muscat, was attributed by Grey, British agent in Muscat, to Goguyer. This was mainly because it was anti-British like Goguyer, and because the article revealed a certain knowledge of Kuwait affairs (and, according to Grey, Goguyer was the only person in Muscat to know Kuwait well): Bidwell, *Affairs of Arabia*, 1/2, pp. 1–4 (translation of the article and correspondence about it). The same correspondent was probably responsible for an article of 3 January 1905 which is actually contrary to Goguyer's ideas, see below n. 44.

[31] Article by Goguyer in *Pyramides* of 29 January 1902, in Paris AE, NS Mascate 7, fos. 105–106; and in the Russian *Journal de St.-Petersbourg* of 18 November/1 December 1905, in Paris AE, NS Mascate 48.

[32] See also Plass, *England*, p. 393: in 1907 the British gave Mubarak some pieces of artillery as a present because they feared that otherwise he would buy them from Goguyer.

[33] IOLR, R/15/1/477, fo. 49 (53), report by Knox on a conversation with Mubarak on 28 February 1905.

different import, in writing about Mubarak to his friend Rouet, the French consul in Baghdad. Goguyer's account of the Kuwaiti ruler's opinions is quite different from the picture given by Curzon. This is no wonder, as Mubarak could be more open and relaxed in his dealings with an adventurer who spoke his language fluently and with whom he shared business interests. Given Goguyer's high-level contacts and his abilities as a writer, Mubarak could even use the Frenchman to propagate his own opinions.

Goguyer own words about Mubarak are remarkably neutral considering the Frenchman's Anglophobia. Interesting too is his use of the terms Prince and Principality for Mubarak and Kuwait, whose status one never sees referred to in these terms in English sources:

> It is undeniable that English influence is very strong in Kuwait. English protection has saved the Principality from the loss of its autonomy, which would have been a bitter blow in that it would have entailed subjection to an Ottoman administration which I persistently heard decried in the Shaikh's entourage. The Prince of Kuwait is grateful, but he is also too well-informed to pay [to the British] more than is necessary for services rendered. Furthermore his intention to maintain [his autonomy] was already sufficient to put him on his guard against insidious demands. Naturally I did not deflect him from this stance. He flew the Ottoman flag (which is distinguished from the [regular] Ottoman flag by a white band along the mast side) and only replaced it with the British flag when a small Turkish detachment threatened to occupy the town in 1901.[34] He flies the British flag when a steamship (whether merchant vessel or warship) arrives [...]

> In actual fact Shaikh Mubarak, who lacks none of the essential qualities of a statesman, not least the dignity, has clearly refused to accept a British consul. A horseman who escorted me on my excursions showed me of his own accord (unless he did it by order of his master) the sites that the English had requested for the construction of their consulate.

[34] This reference to the subtle flying of a flag slightly different from the regular Ottoman one appears nowhere in British sources, but later another foreign observer remarked on Mubarak's use of a flag that differed slightly from the standard Ottoman one: Berlin AA, R 13891 A 34 (7 January 1910), German consul Wassmuss in Bushire, who had seen a modified Ottoman flag on Mubarak's palace from a ship in Kuwait harbour, 18 December 1909.

He also refused the English a privileged status. None but subjects of the Shaikh live in Kuwait. A third refusal has even been more painful to the Anglo-Indian Government. The latter have long since had two pretexts for meddling in the affairs of its small neighbours to the north-west of India: piracy and the slave trade. These two scourges have ceased to exist except in the Indian press ... A new pretext had to be found to place the Arab straw huts regularly under the threat of British artillery, and this pretext is the arms trade. Lord Curzon, during his visit to Muscat, had intervened in vain with the Sultan of Oman to obtain the interdiction, and the question was also raised without success in Kuwait with Mubarak [...]

Another symptom: three Turkish officers passed through Kuwait last March on their way from al-Hasa to Basra in order to avoid quarantine. I was present at their reception by the Shaikh, who received them in a perfectly correct manner. As usual he asserted his loyalty to the Ottoman state, not in explicit terms, but implicitly in phrases such as "We have our common flag". And then I heard him describe the visit of Lord Curzon in an interesting way, saying almost literally: "When the Viceroy came I gave him a quite different reception from the jubilant demonstrations with which he had been received in Muscat and Bahrain. I stationed 3000 horsemen armed with Martini rifles on the beach behind the Ottoman standard, which was surmounted by a big golden orb. He showed satisfaction, but inside he was not satisfied." [Here Goguyer gives Mubarak's words in Arabic script].

However fearsome a man he may be, he is quite capable of being agreeable. During our second meeting he told me the story of a French officer who came to Kuwait about forty years ago to buy horses, which were sold to him against a simple paper trusting in his decency as a Frenchman.[35] Next he discussed the friendly opinion the Arabs have of our nation, doing so with such eloquence that I was moved by it. Moubarek El Sabah is getting old – he is more than seventy – and his eldest son Djaber, the heir presumptive, lacks his qualities.[36]

[35] Mubarak's chronology was not entirely accurate: he must have meant the visit of the French military officer Pétiniaud to Kuwait in 1853, thus 50, not 40, years before: see Nantes AD, consulat Bagdad B 29, French consul in Baghdad 31 August 1853. Pétiniaud bought horses from a certain Bin Badr, who is described as one of the most important merchants in Kuwait at that time. "Bin Badr" was the well-known horse-dealer Yusuf Al-Badir, whom Pelly met in Kuwait.

[36] Paris AE, NS Mascate 11, fos. 35–39, Rouet 28 July 1904.

This text is quoted at length because it depicts Mubarak in more detail than any other of the time. Goguyer was a curious phenomenon, combining as he did Anglophobia with a keen interest in Arab nationalism. In 1905 he admonished Rouet that he should not view Arab nationalism through British eyes as the French were wont to do. Goguyer complained to Rouet that he was accepted in France as an expert in classical Arabic language and law, but that his advice on the policy France should adopt in contemporary Gulf affairs was ignored. This maverick's views are none the less interesting because he was the only European to study the emerging Arab nationalist movement from the viewpoint of the Gulf. He gives a list of Arab leaders in the Peninsula who stood with a sword in one hand and a declaration of loyalty to the Caliph in the other:

> In the last five years the Arab movement has grown more intense. This can come as no surprise to those who see, everywhere in the world, the secondary nationalities [meaning nationalities under foreign rule] take advantage of the spreading of democratic ideas and the resulting social evolution to free themselves from the unified states imposed in the past by the avarice of monarchies.[37]

Goguyer's view of Mubarak's relationship with the Ottomans may have derived from his earlier experiences in Tunisia. Tunisia had officially been part of the Ottoman Empire, but it was ruled by a hereditary Bey and conducted its own foreign policy and diplomacy. Ottoman administrative reforms of the 19th century had not been applied in Tunis, and the revenues of the "province" went not to the Sultan but to the Bey, who minted his own coinage. The Bey regularly assured the Sultan that he was a most loyal subject and sent presents to Constantinople, but that was more or less the extent of "Ottoman dominion" in Tunisia. The cases of Kuwait and Tunis were thus analogous. This explains why Goguyer was able to take a positive view of Mubarak's attitude towards the Turks. Goguyer did not see the Ottoman Empire as a state in the modern sense, and he did not share Richarz's opinion that Mubarak was a rebel who did not act according to his "feudal" obligations.

Most British observers tended at heart to agree with Richarz. Imperial interest led them to support Mubarak, but it gave them an uneasy

[37] Nantes AD, ambassade Constantinople E 288, Goguyer 12 April 1905.

conscience. The English seem never to have grasped the true meaning of Mubarak's declarations of loyalty to the Sultan. They saw them essentially as a symptom of his duplicitous cunning. Richarz was too naive to appreciate the subtlety of Goguyer's and Mubarak's stance. When Rouet showed Richarz some letters from Goguyer about Kuwait, Richarz reported back to Berlin that his French colleague and Goguyer had fallen for British propaganda![38] Such an accusation was very wide of the mark, as Goguyer's view of Mubarak had nothing to do with the British one.

There had been a flurry of mixed messages after 1899 about Mubarak's attitude and opinions. He had signed an undertaking to the British, but he had also intimated to the Russians that he was ready to do a deal with them. He had also from time to time issued declarations of some vague kind of loyalty to Sultan Abdulhamid II. To the various parties with which he had dealings Mubarak presented a different image of himself. To the British he denied any real subordination to the Ottomans other than a vague loyalty to the Caliph. To the Russians he claimed some kind of independence without specifying his relationship with the Ottomans; given the official Russian policy of support of the Ottoman claim to full sovereignty over Kuwait, he was unable to deny the Ottomans outright. To the French and Germans he claimed to be a loyal, but completely autonomous, vassal of the Sultan. To the Sultan, finally, he stressed his complete loyalty, while resisting any direct or indirect interference of the Ottoman administration in Kuwait and staunchly refusing to be considered part of the normal Ottoman administrative structure. To the Ottoman Empire he was an ally, even a respectful vassal, but as vassal he claimed something that in Western feudal terms would be called allodium: a kernel of sovereignty in his own right.

In the autumn of 1904, Goguyer wrote to Mubarak with the suggestion that France and Russia should be allowed to mediate between him and the Sultan. The Shaikh sent the following reply which reveals his true feelings about the Turks:

> You inform me that the Sultan is in a conciliatory mood and wishes me

[38] Berlin AA, R 13889 A 13158 (14 August 1904), Richarz 21 April 1904. Richarz was especially angry about a passage in which Goguyer wrote that British protection of Kuwait was preferable to Ottoman protection because Ottoman protection would result in a German protectorate.

to be with him in the same way as I was in the past. Be aware, my friend, that with my person and with my fortune I have done great service to the Sultan and that I have behaved towards him with sincere friendship and loyalty regarding all his interests in this region. It was I who was the cause of their conquest of Qatif and al-Hasa. Any time there was trouble, I went there with my troops at my own expense. When I was in charge of that territory it was quiet and secure and the military force there consisted of just a single battalion, whereas now there are six, which have to be maintained at great cost. Soldiers are killed there all the time and the affairs of the Sultan are in disarray. Sa'dun and suchlike people did not dare lift up their head during the times when I was co-operating with the Turks. How many times did I go to the sancak of the Muntafiq when there was trouble there? From Samawa to al-Hasa all the country was safe and quiet. But after I had placed my person and my fortune at their disposal they approached and favoured my enemies who are unruly people. They listened to their slander and they repelled me unjustly. I have certificates attesting my behaviour from the civil and military authorities, who all lavished praise upon me. Concerning the two powerful states of which you speak to me, I am their friend and there is no doubt that the agents of those powers who came here appreciated the reception I gave them. I hope that it will please God to reward me for it."[39]

Given the anti-Russian and anti-French feeling in India, Mubarak was prudent enough to keep his dealings with the Russians and Goguyer secret from the British. The true nature of his relations with the British were a well-kept secret from all the other parties, and he liked to spread uncertainty about his relations with the Turks. His goal was to have a merely nominal relationship with the Turks with complete autonomy for Kuwait. In 1870 the Ottomans had made a largely botched attempt to impose their authority on Kuwait by blackmail. It is no wonder that the Shaikh of Kuwait tried to negate the effects of 1870 whenever he had the chance, but this had to be done with care. The Ottomans were – with limitations – the pre-eminent power in the region, and much of the Al-Sabah revenues came not from Kuwait, but from land in Ottoman territory. Goguyer's view was that Mubarak, as an Arab leader of his time,

[39] Inserted in Nantes AD, consulat Bagdad A 33, fos. 272–273, Rouet 22 November 1904.

was loyal to the idea of a universal orthodox Muslim leadership, but objected to servants of the Caliph, in his other capacity as Ottoman Sultan, infringing upon the rights of the Ruler of Kuwait. As soon as the Islamic world was threatened, Mubarak was among the first to close ranks and to offer support. The Ottoman Empire's establishment, however, routinely misused the Caliph's standing by deliberately confusing Pan-Islamism with Pan-Ottomanism. Goguyer's analysis has much merit in offering an explanation of Mubarak's behaviour that fits his actions better than the British view of him, as an erratic ally who was always demanding too much in return for his co-operation.

9.3 Safwan 1905: Goguyer and desert reconciliation

At the end of 1904 the Turks were making preparations for a military expedition into Qasim, either to restore the Rashidi position or to take control for themselves. Large troop concentrations were mustered near Baghdad, but the French consul had no high opinion of the motley Ottoman force and predicted disaster were the Ottomans to proceed with their plans.[40] The defeat of the Ottoman corps from Iraq at Qasr Ibn 'Uqayl had been followed in October by another defeat by the Saudis of Ottoman troops sent from Medina.[41] A third defeat of their regular forces by Arab tribesmen would incur serious Ottoman loss of face.

According to Richarz and Anscombe, it was fear of this new force that moved the Saudis to seek a compromise with the Ottomans.[42] This interpretation does not seem entirely plausible when one considers the French reports of the sorry state of Ottoman military preparations, and the ease with which Ibn Rashid's Ottoman auxiliaries had been defeated in 1904. But the fact is that there was a rapprochement between the Saudis and the Porte. Goguyer later claimed that it was he who had suggested to both the Saudis and Mubarak that they should approach the Turks.[43] This

---

[40] Paris AE, NS Mascate 11, fos. 100–102, 28 December; see also Plass, *England*, p. 347.
[41] Bidwell, *Affairs of Arabia*, 1/1, p. 9; Paris AE, NS Mascate 11, fos. 90–92, 22 November 1904.
[42] Berlin AA, R 13890 A 1832 (2 February 1905), Richarz, 2 January 1905; Anscombe, *Ottoman Gulf*, p. 156: Anscombe tends sometimes to overestimate Ottoman power in the region.
[43] Paris AE, NS Mascate 11, fos. 100–102, Rouet 28 December 1904; Nantes AD, consulat Bagdad B 29, Goguyer 5 December 1908.

is not impossible, given Goguyer's contacts with both of them. On the other hand it was claimed by the Egyptian newspaper *Al-Ahram* that the plan emanated from Qasim Al-Thani of Qatar. This has a less probable air, but it is not impossible in view of that Shaikh's mercurial character.[44] A completely different version is given in the Saudi chronicle recorded by Musil: there the Turks are bribed by the Saudis after the latter had levied a considerable tax on all their tents to pay off the Turkish commander, so breaking the Ottoman-Rashidi alliance.[45]

The French consul in Baghdad heard a completely different story from the Ottoman military that is certainly untrue, but nevertheless sheds interesting light on the scale of Turkish paranoia. According to this version, Mubarak was angry with the British for attempting, on the occasion of Curzon's visit, to forge a confederation between Kuwait, the Saudis and the Rashidis, because he feared that this would strengthen Britain's hand too much.[46] There is no gainsaying that in such a confederation Mubarak would not only be the weakest partner, but that he would also be vulnerable to strong British pressure. According to the French consul this had moved Mubarak to make overtures for an alliance involving the Turks. Knox had already reported that the Wali of Basra had already tried to enlist Mubarak in a peaceful solution to the conflict between himself, the Saudis and Abdul Aziz Ibn Rashid.[47]

In the past the Saudis had entertained thoughts of a British alliance enabling them to expand in the direction of al-Hasa, the territory they had lost to Midhat Pasha in 1871, and so rendering the vicinity of the British in Bahrain useful to them.[48] The Ottomans had certainly provoked them by forbidding trade between al-Hasa and Najd in 1904.[49] The proposal for a British protectorate had fallen on deaf ears in 1902, and in 1904 the British were trying to choke off the supply of arms from Kuwait, so it was time for a change in Saudi policy. Abdul Aziz Al-Saud sent a messenger to Constantinople at the end of 1904 bearing messages of loyalty.[50] Anscombe

[44] *Al-Ahram* of 3 January 1905, quoted in Berlin AA, R 13890 A 3545 (2 March 1905), Consul Schröder in Beirut 17 February 1905.
[45] Musil, *Northern Negd*, p. 281.
[46] Paris AE, NS Mascate 11, fos. 120–121, Rouet 12 March 1905.
[47] Bidwell, *Affairs of Kuwait*, 2/6, pp. 90–1, Knox 3 September 1904.
[48] Bidwell, *Affairs of Kuwait*, 2/4, p. 102, Abdul Rahman Al-Saud to Kemball 5 Safar 1320/ 14 May 1902.
[49] Anscombe, *Ottoman Gulf*, p. 152.

remarks that Ibn Saud had learnt, by observing Mubarak, that "the Ottomans, although powerful, could be managed by the maintenance of an outwardly friendly attitude".[51] In this way a new Saudi-Kuwaiti-Ottoman alliance began to take shape. The British were not involved this time, and felt some unease about it.[52]

Conditions favoured such a new configuration. The Turks appear to have been open to a compromise after their defeats, and Ahmad Fayzi Pasha showed great reluctance to march with his motley force into Arabia.[53] It seems that most of the practical preparation for the deal was made by Mubarak. A meeting between the Wali of Basra, Abdul Rahman Al-Saud and Mubarak took place in Safwan on the border of Kuwait. An agreement was rapidly reached which was mainly a face-saving device for the Turks: the Ottomans would be allowed to keep a small garrison in the two main cities, 'Unayza and Burayda, of the disputed region of Qasim, as well as an army encamped in the desert, the idea being that this area would act as a kind of buffer between the Saudis and the Rashidis. The appearance so created of Ottoman control of Arabia was a mirage, given the weakness of the Ottoman garrisons.[54] French reports state that the Saudis also claimed a foothold in al-Hasa from the Turks, but that they failed to obtain this. However, in exchange for a token allegiance given by the Saudis to the Ottomans and acceptance of a token Ottoman force of occupation in Qasim, there was no mention of any Ottoman claim on the Riyadh district, where Saudi rule was implicitly recognized as

[50] Anscombe, *Ottoman Gulf*, pp. 154 and 239 n. 56, referring to the text of the message in the Istanbul archives.

[51] Anscombe, *Ottoman Gulf*, p. 155.

[52] IOLR, R/15/1/477, fo. 44 (48), acting consul Monahan in Basra 18 February 1905.

[53] Paris AE, NS Mascate 11, fos. 144–145, Rouet 10 May 1905.

[54] Bidwell, *Affairs of Kuwait*, 2/7, p. 4, Government of India to India Office 23 January 1905; Bidwell, *Affairs of Arabia*, 1/1, p. 75, Townley (British chargé d'affaires in Constantinople) 24 January 1905; and ibid. 1/2, pp. 30–2, Monahan in Basra to Townley 24 February 1905, with the remark that Mubarak's Basra agent was now being better treated in prison. See also Berlin AA, R 13859 A 1414 (26 January 1905), Richarz 17 December 1902. See also the interesting but biased comment on the impending meeting in the Egyptian newspaper *Al-Ahram* of 3 January 1905, translated in a letter of the German consul in Beirut: Berlin AA, R 13890 A 3545 (2 March 1905), Schröder 17 February 1905. The news about the conference was leaked in Basra by Mubarak's former secretary Hamid Effendi: Berlin AA, R 13859 A 5344 (30 March 1905), Puttmann, acting German consul in Baghdad, 22 February 1905.

independent.[55] The loser was Ibn Rashid, while Mubarak was now a respected arbiter in regional matters. He had been able to resist without difficulty Ottoman pressure at Safwan to submit to the Sultan.[56]

The Safwan conference is often described in rather vague terms by historians of the region. A key element in the success of the negotiations was that Mubarak was able to gull the Ottomans into believing that they should reach an agreement now, before the British began to fortify the Kuwait area.[57] Mubarak was one of the few people who knew that in reality the British in the Gulf were not allowed by London to broaden their commitments in the region, so he was deliberately playing on the persistent Ottoman fear of British expansion. Mubarak's deceit brought him great advantages. He received the credit for something that was little more than an Ottoman face-saving operation in Arabia; but, for the Sultan, face-saving was of vital importance. In the years that followed, Mubarak was able to capitalize on his improved relations with the Ottomans. The essence of the agreement was that the Turks accepted the Saudi conquest of Najd, relinquishing any formal Ottoman authority over that region, in exchange for Abdul Rahman Al-Saud's merely nominal promise of loyalty to the Sultan and the stationing of a small body of Ottoman troops to garrison the cities of Burayda and 'Unayza. The presence of troops would be merely symbolic, as the units were too small for real combat and the future would show that the Turks were unable to supply them. Within a year most of the force had melted away.[58]

The formal Ottoman authority as established at Safwan went unchallenged, and the Sultan's contentment was increased by the idea that the ideology of the Saudis forbade them entering into contracts with Christians such as the British. This assumption was over-optimistic, for his main protection in this respect was not the Saudi concept of law, but Britain's unwillingness to be seen working at the disintegration of the Ottoman Empire in Arabia. Goguyer's vague talk of a future Arab

[55] Paris AE, NS Mascate 11, fos. 120–121, Rouet 12 March 1905; Berlin AA, R 13859 A 6344 (14 April 1905), Richarz 13 March 1905.
[56] Bidwell, *Affairs of Arabia*, 1/2, pp. 28–9, O'Conor 13 March 1905.
[57] Anscombe, *Ottoman Gulf*, pp. 138 and 234 n. 122; Bidwell, *Affairs of Arabia*, 1/3, pp. 47–9, report by Knox on what Mubarak told him about the Safwan meeting.
[58] Paris AE, NS Mascate 12, fo. 100, Rouet 3 May 1906. Musil, *Zeitgeschichte*, pp. 70–1, mentions that Ibn Rashid was very hostile to the Ottoman occupation of Burayda and 'Unayza and treated the Ottoman garrisons as enemies.

confederation with only a weak nominal acknowledgement of the Ottoman Caliph and independent of the British, but perhaps sponsored by the French and the Russians, found partial expression in the Safwan agreement, but that agreement was built on sand while the balance of power among the Arabs kept shifting. Goguyer was little more than an intriguer with a bee in his bonnet. It was almost impossible to maintain unity among the Arab rulers, and external developments were moving in favour of growing British supremacy. Ottoman policy was too inconsistent, while France and Russia were moving ever closer to Britain in their European interests and thus becoming reluctant to oppose Britain in the Gulf. What remains of interest is Goguyer's revelation of another Mubarak, happy to discuss Arab national aspirations with a European over coffee – an ideology which inspired stronger feelings in many Arab Gulf leaders than the reports of British observers would lead us to believe. Finally Mubarak had, to a certain extent, restored Ottoman faith in him.

9.4 New railway alarms

The Baghdad Railway project continued to be a destabilizing factor in the background of Kuwait's historical evolution. The plan had a considerable impact on British and Ottoman policy towards Kuwait. This is not the place to repeat other works that deal with the intricate international negotiations over the project, but a summary survey of progress and delays thus far is called for at this point, because the Ottoman insistence on control of the terminus on the Gulf continued to pose a real threat to Kuwait's independence.

The Turks felt an urgent strategic need to establish a fast transport link with their Mesopotamian provinces. So vital to them was this connection that they felt unable to concede any British control of the Mesopotamian section down to the Gulf, as they lived in fear of a British plot to take over Lower Mesopotamia. Such suspicions were exaggerated: as we have seen, the British never intended to take on too many responsibilities in the Gulf. The problem was that their actions could occasionally be interpreted by the Ottomans as proof of expansionist aims.[59] The Germans viewed the railway project essentially as a purely economic venture that would strengthen their commercial position within the Ottoman Empire. But collaboration between the Germans and Turks was uneasy, chiefly because of tortuous Ottoman procedures, the parlous state of Ottoman finances, obstructive officials and corruption. The Germans were not averse to co-operating with the British, but at the same time they had to deal with the Turks, whose aim was to use the railway project to assert their claim to Kuwait.[60] In the light of the Turkish fear that British participation in the railway would reinforce British interference in Iraq, German attempts to reach an understanding with the British were doomed to fail.[61]

From the start the railway project had attracted considerable interest from French investors, but distrust of the Germans engendered a lack of enthusiasm at French government level. In some French circles the hope was that the project would open up the Gulf and so terminate Britain's economic monopoly there. There were also dreams of connecting the railways being constructed by the French in Anatolia and Syria with the German-Ottoman railway. Russia was strongly opposed to the railway, chiefly from fear of increasing German influence in the region. The British had mixed feelings. Financiers found the project promising and were interested in participating, but set against this were political misgivings, especially in the Government of India, that the railway would create a link from the Mediterranean to the Gulf that would be under Turco-German control. The British had hoped that control of Kuwait would afford an effective impediment to all undesirable developments, as Kuwait was for some time considered to be the only terminus with full access to deep-water port facilities. Then, in 1902, it had looked as if the Turks had found an alternative to Kuwait in the Khor Abdallah, so undermining Britain's one vital means of controlling the railway project.[62] In 1903 the British were already beginning to think that this alternative location might not be

---

[59] The most common causes of Ottoman distrust were: the British claim that the Shatt al-'Arab was an international waterway; British relations with Muhammara; British support for a British shipping company on the rivers of Iraq; and the special position claimed by the British consul-general in Baghdad as "political resident" (a semi-colonial title) of Turkish Arabia with a large sepoy bodyguard.

[60] Lepsius, *Grosse Politik*, Vol. 17, pp. 418–28, Marschall 2 February 1902; ibid. p. 498, Bülow to Foreign Ministry 1 October 1901; and Berlin AA, R 13885 A 14325, Foreign Ministry to Marschall 4 October 1901.

[61] Ottoman fear of British control over a railway to the Gulf had a long lineage. Richarz saw, in the archives of Baghdad province, a memorandum by Midhat Pasha of 1871 on the importance of a railway to Baghdad, but that British influence in it should be avoided: Berlin AA, R 13856 A 11843 (10 Augustus 1903), Richarz 9 July 1903.

of any great use, but not everyone agreed.[63] So there were still fears that the Turks and Germans might construct a railway to an alternative terminus. In 1904 the British resumed pressure on the Turks to evacuate their minuscule garrison from Bubiyan. This action was initiated by Curzon as a result of his trip to Kuwait, and O'Conor raised the matter again with Tawfiq, but no conclusion was reached.[64] The British believed they had yet another potential means of blocking the plan: the Ottoman Empire was technically bankrupt and was unable to finance its share in the railway, unless permission was granted by the European powers to increase customs duties. It was also thought in London that the Germans would need to float loans on the London market to finance their share.

The uproar in the press at the beginning of 1903 had forced Lansdowne to make his statement in the House of Lords that the Baghdad railway plan would be acceptable to London only if British supremacy in the Gulf were safeguarded. The first solution Lansdowne came up with was that the section of the railway between Baghdad and the Gulf could have international status, provided that the Turco-German alliance was denied a controlling interest in it. The possibility thus opened up of a new route to India outside British control provoked a storm in the British press, especially when it emerged that it would be difficult to preclude a controlling Turco-German interest.[65] In the end the British government decided that British banks should not participate in the railway. That made the financing of the railway difficult, and British hostility to a cherished German plan inflicted serious damage on Anglo-German relations.[66]

The Germans, however, managed to raise the finance in their own country to begin construction of the railway in Anatolia. The question of

---

[62] Kemp's report of 20 February 1902, in Bidwell, *Affairs of Kuwait*, 2/4, pp. 67–9, states that Umm Qasr would be a good terminus for the railway, and that the long inland shipping channel of the Khor Abdallah would protect it against an attack from the sea.
[63] Consul Crow made a trip from Basra to Umm Qasr in1903. He was of the opinion that, because of continuous silting, dredging the Khor Abdallah would require an "enormous and continuous expense": Bidwell, *Affairs of Kuwait*, 2/6, pp. 31–33, Crow 4 May 1903. On the other hand Smythe, at the time of Curzon's visit, found Umm Qasr to be a better location for the terminus than Kuwait or Kazima: ibid., pp. 50–1, O'Conor 13 June 1904.
[64] Bidwell, *Affairs of Kuwait*, 2/6, pp. 13–15 and 33–4, Government of India to India Office 4 February 1904, and O'Conor 16 May 1904.
[65] Kumar, *India*, pp. 170–3; see also *The Times* of 9 April 1903.
[66] Brünner, *Bagdadspoorweg*, pp. 151–65.

internationalizing the last stretch was left pending. The British, feeling that they had lost the first battle, now started to mend their fences, and in 1904 concluded an agreement with the French to terminate all colonial disputes. In the years that followed, complex negotiations went ahead with the Germans and the Turks on the financial question and the size of the share the British might take in the last section. The British Foreign Office, where Lansdowne was replaced by Grey after the 1906 elections, was still unable to settle on a consistent line. Grey, who felt that the railway was inevitable, had two alternatives before him. The first was to bring the entire railway under an international company involving equal shares for Britain, Germany, France and Russia. This would hardly be acceptable to the Turks. The other option was for Britain to control the final section to the Gulf.[67] This too was impracticable, because the Porte demanded effective Ottoman control over the terminus in Kuwait. In the end the British avoided a decision and set out to delay matters.

Grey's negotiations over the plan for an international company to run the Baghdad Railway soon ran into difficulties. By disclosing to the Russians and the French that whatever happened Britain would claim control over the final section, Grey angered the Russians, who rejected the plan. The French government too was unhappy, and French financiers decided to continue with the Germans on the old footing. Another problem for the British was that France and Russia had little interest in exerting pressure on the Turks by vetoing an increase in Ottoman customs duties, so the British were isolated on this issue. Worse still, international political considerations involving British interests in other parts of the Ottoman Empire made it difficult for them to maintain indefinitely their veto on raising Ottoman customs duties.[68]

However, British anxiety that the Germans and Turks would soon be able to construct the Baghdad Railway was not entirely justified. They were unaware of German and Turkish divisions and uncertainty over the Gulf terminus of the railway. There was little accurate intelligence in either Berlin or Constantinople about the alternatives to Kuwait. If the Germans and the Turks had examined the Khor Abdallah alternatives more closely, they too would have concluded that shipping movement to a terminus at

[67] Busch, *Britain and the Persian Gulf,* p. 307; Butterfield, *Diplomacy,* pp, 55–8; Brünner, *Bagdadspoorweg,* p. 267.
[68] Brünner, *Bagdadspoorweg,* pp. 347–52.

Umm Qasr could be threatened from a position on Warba Island. The Ottoman hold on the Khor Abdallah could not be secured unless new points were occupied, and it was clear that the British would not allow that. A terminus at Basra was also a possibility if funds could be found to dredge a channel through the bar in the Shatt al-'Arab. But this option was rejected. The Deutsche Bank was interested in acquiring a concession to dredge the access route to Basra, but German officials in Constantinople believed that the Turks would not allow it, for fear it might inspire the British to occupy Basra.[69]

The British never appreciated the complexities of the relationship between the Germans and the Turks, and tended to overestimate German willingness to help them. So British hypersensitivity to sudden alarms over the railway and the Kuwait situation persisted. In reality the Germans had mixed feelings about financing large projects in Turkey and experienced difficulties in reaching agreements with the Porte.

Kuwait's importance to the British was once again apparent. British handling of Mubarak, however, lacked finesse. Relations between Mubarak and the Turks had improved as a consequence of the Safwan conference in early 1905. In September 1904, Knox had told Mubarak that Britain regarded the affairs of central Arabia as of secondary importance unless they directly impinged on the security of Kuwait.[70] India was alarmed that Knox might in this way have given Mubarak the green light for engaging in desert politics.[71] In January 1905 Knox had tried to make amends, but under difficult circumstances. Mubarak opened the discussion by complaining to the agent about the arrest of some of his business associates in Basra. The arrests may have had to do with Ottoman measures against the Naqib's friends, but Mubarak presented them as proof of the feebleness of British protection. Mubarak gave Knox to understand that it was British passivity in relations with the Saudis that had led to Ottoman troops

---

[69] Berlin AA, R 13865 A 13570 (21 August 1906), Listemann, German consul in Bushire, 12 July 1906, and Tschirschky in Berlin to Marschall, 21 August 1906; ibid. A 20847, Marschall to Berlin 12 December 1906.

[70] Bidwell, *Affairs of Kuwait*, 2/6, pp. 90–1, Knox 3 September 1904. Mubarak, of course, was not happy with this viewpoint because he feared that the British lack of action would ultimately bring about a Saudi-Ottoman alliance that would be a danger to Kuwait.

[71] Bidwell, *Affairs of Kuwait*, 2/6, p. 93, Cox to Knox 8 October 1904; Plass, *England*, p. 348.

occupying Qasim. Knox made excuses for British standoffishness, telling Mubarak that Curzon had for long been proposing contact with the Saudis, but that London had forbidden it. Mubarak replied with the not wholly unjustified remark that if Curzon's hands were so tied he should resign. Curzon took all this so seriously that he despatched the elderly paddle steamer *Sphinx* to Kuwait as a demonstration of British power.[72] The discussions between Mubarak and Knox show how Mubarak made full use of an opportunity to point out to his British friends that they were failing to live up to their promises, thus putting himself in a position of strength over new British demands.

Mubarak was able to deal so confidently with the British because his relations with the Turks were gradually improving. His Basra agent received better treatment in jail and was released at the end of 1905.[73] This new warmth caused the British some disquiet. In January 1906 the British consul in Basra reported that Mubarak and Mukhlis Pasha, the Wali of Basra, were being suspiciously friendly with each other: the Wali had been allowing Mubarak to build embankments on his Fao property.[74] Mubarak made various friendly overtures to the Turks, allowing the mail for al-Hasa to pass through Kuwait and sending Ottoman deserters from the desert back to Basra. The consul reported that Mubarak signed his letters to the Wali "Your friend" and "Kaymakam of Kuwait". It is not certain that the consul was right to attach importance to this style of signature, Mubarak being rather indiscriminate in this respect. In any case, the only surviving letter from Mubarak to the Ottoman authorities of January 1906 is signed "Ruler of Kuwait and Chief of its Tribes".[75] Rumours put about by Ottoman officials were often unreliable and intended to manipulate, as is very clear from the disinformation they constantly fed to the German consul Richarz. By the end of 1905, the British were becoming

---

[72] IOLR, R/15/1/477, fos. 5–7 (5–7), Knox 23 January 1905; Bidwell, *Affairs of Kuwait*, 2/6, p. 69, Government of India to India Office, same date; Plass, *England*, pp. 348–9.

[73] Plass, *England*, p. 350.

[74] Bidwell, *Affairs of Arabia*, 1/1, p. 134, Monahan 28 January 1905.

[75] IOLR, R/15/1/478, Crow to O'Conor 4 January 1906; Plass, *England*, p. 349, quoting FO 371/146 no. 4263, O'Conor to Grey 30 January 1906. For Mubarak's letter to the Chief of Staff of the Ottoman army in Basra of 6 January 1905, which he signs in the customary way as Ruler of Kuwait and Chief of its Tribes, see facsimile in Al-Qasimi, *Bayan al-Kuwayt*, p. 363.

apprehensive about Mubarak's cordiality with the Turks, and this was to be a theme of the following years.

British disquiet was fuelled by two alarming rumours reported by O'Conor to the Foreign Office. The first was a report from Basra that Mubarak's relations with the Turks had grown so close that he might be contemplating dropping his British connection. The other was that German engineers had been spotted in the vicinity of Kuwait.[76] According to Plass, the second rumour was certainly untrue, while the first was unsupported by any serious evidence.[77] O'Conor produced various arguments to show Mubarak's newly hostile attitude to the British – enough to induce him to perform another U-turn, in suggesting that it was time to have Knox return from his leave.[78] O'Conor's perception of Mubarak's rapprochement with the Ottomans was not as misplaced as Plass would have it, for Anscombe describes various documents indicating that both the Wali of Basra and the Porte believed deals could be done with Mubarak.[79] Anscombe cites a further possible reason for Mubarak turning against the British: indignation over their interference in the affairs of the Bahrain ruling family in March 1905. This is mere supposition unsubstantiated by any documentary source, but it has a certain plausibility because the Bahrain case lost the British their reputation for honest dealing with local rulers. Overall, Mubarak seems to have been carrying out a little adjustment to his usual balancing act. Increased British pressure was inclining him a little towards the Turks, without making a decisive break.

9.5 Knox's return and change in the desert

The decision to let Knox return was taken. London, however, wanted to settle one outstanding issue once and for all before provoking the Turks by

---

[76] Report from Basra in Bidwell, *Affairs of Arabia*, 2/5, p. 10, India Office to Government of India 3 October 1905; Busch, *Britain and the Persian Gulf*, p. 305.
[77] Plass, *England*, p. 350.
[78] Bidwell, *Affairs of Arabia*, 2/5, pp. 40–1, O'Conor 31 October 1905, with a report enclosed by Crow in Basra of rumours from Kuwait concerning Mubarak's unfriendly attitude. See also ibid. p. 39, Cox to Government of India 5 October 1905, in which Cox denies the most important rumours.
[79] Anscombe, *Ottoman Gulf*, p. 138.
[80] Bidwell, *Affairs of Arabia*, 1/2, pp. 112–13, O'Conor 17 April 1905.

returning the agent to Kuwait. Lansdowne suggested it would be wise for Mubarak to assert a more decisive claim to Bubiyan by stationing a garrison there. Cox, who had succeeded Kemball as resident in Bushire in May 1904, was sent to find out what Mubarak might think about such a proposal.[80]

According to Cox, Mubarak had no military worries about the Ottoman troops who had occupied Kuwaiti territory in 1902, because they were isolated and relied on the goodwill of the Arabs to receive any supplies at all. The Shaikh formulated conditions for his participation in the scheme. According to Cox these were: first, a British guarantee that they would support his claim to Bubiyan with the Ottoman authorities at every administrative level; second, the permanent establishment of a political agent; and, third, the institution of regular visits by British warships to Kuwait and the Khor Abdallah. The whole thing, Cox maintained, was conceived by Mubarak as insurance in the event of the Ottomans making trouble over his Basra possessions as they had done in 1904. Mubarak's final condition was the not unexpected demand that the British should pay all expenses.[81] Plass cynically supposes that only this last condition came from Mubarak, and that the other three were invented by Cox because they fitted in with his schemes all too well. Plass found some support for this view in a note by Sanderson.[82] This is couched in vague terms and might be no more than an expression of an ageing official's general distaste for youthful enthusiasts in outposts, but there is another reason to concur with Plass: the first three conditions match Cox's priorities better than they do Mubarak's. Mubarak might have given the first guarantee a much wider scope, while it is hard to see how the second or third were really in his interest.[83] One might, for example, doubt whether it was really to his benefit to have a permanent agent in Kuwait. The future would show that in fact it came with considerable disadvantages.

Soon the plan to do something about Bubiyan was dropped once again because O'Conor could make no progress with the Turks.[84] Knox, however, returned to Kuwait on 25 October 1906 and resumed his

[81] IOLR, R/15/1/477, fos. 119–122 (122–125), Cox 11 June 1905.
[82] Plass, *England*, p. 352, quoting a note by Sanderson on a letter of the India Office to the Foreign Office of 3 August 1905, in PRO, FO 78/5469.
[83] Plass, *England*, p. 352.
[84] Bidwell, *Affairs of Arabia*, 2/4, pp. 73–4, O'Conor 18 September 1905.

"informal" activities. It is an open question whether he was really at all welcome in Kuwait. Mubarak had not missed him during his absence, for he had dealt reasonably well with Cox. Unfriendly comments made by Mubarak about the English to an Ottoman deserter contain the observation that he, Mubarak, kept the English agent as isolated as possible.[85]

Two matters claimed the agent's immediate attention. One was the old problem of arms trafficking. The British felt increasingly uneasy about allowing it to continue in Kuwait while suppressing it elsewhere. The other was the situation in the desert. Intervention in either of these areas was not conducive to improving Knox's relations with Mubarak. Knox insisted on Mubarak clamping down on the arms trade. Mubarak was not in a position to refuse outright, so he clamped down on it. He thus forfeited considerable income, though for quite some time he compensated for his loss by secretly allowing the smuggling of arms in return for a substantial payment. It was unavoidable in so small a place as Kuwait that Knox would get to hear of it, however hard Mubarak might try to keep him in the dark. All this militated against easy and open relations between the two men.[86]

Desert policy was the other main cause of friction between Mubarak and Knox. Knox was powerless to do anything but remonstrate when the Shaikh indulged in desert power play. Like many British officials in the Gulf, Knox felt somewhat frustrated. London forbade all British intervention in hinterland affairs, while he as well as the Indian Government felt it necessary for Britain to bring its weight to bear occasionally on local rulers. The Indian Government could see advantages in an alliance with the Saudis, and was nervous that constant rejection of his advances would in the end turn Ibn Saud against Britain. London, strongly influenced by O'Conor and fearing complications with the

---

[85] Hüsni, *Necd*, pp. 226–7; Anscombe, *Ottoman Gulf*, p. 234, n. 123; Hüsni, the deserter in question, also quoted Mubarak as saying that he refused to allow the British to execute works in Kuwait because Kuwait was Ottoman territory. British protection extended only to him as an individual and to his rights. If Mubarak really said this, he must have been deceiving the poor Turk. For Hüsni, see also IOLR, R/15/1/478, fo. 4 (5), Crow 18 November 1905.

[86] *Political Diaries*, Vol. 1, p. 202 (Kuwait, October 1905); ibid. Vol. 2, pp. 73 and 112 (February and March 1907); and IOLR, R/15/1/478, fo. 80C (105), note by Knox, undated [June/July 1906].

Ottoman Government, wanted to keep well away. It must have been most irritating for poor Knox that Mubarak gave not a fig for oft-repeated British warnings and continued to strut his prominent part upon the desert stage. But Knox, noting with admiration that he could travel safely inland as "guest" of Mubarak for more than 150 miles through wild country, would discover that Mubarak's desert policy could bring some incidental satisfactions.[87]

Desert events can be discerned at two levels. There was the minor raiding and skirmishing on the margins of bedouin grazing grounds and migration routes, and there was the great desert game being played out by the Saudi, Shammar and Muntafiq leaders. Events of the first kind were often recorded by Knox in his diary, which is replete with raids for and against Mubarak. But the second kind was of greater import. At the beginning of 1906, the seriously weakened Shammar Amir Abdul Aziz Ibn Rashid was seeking reconciliation with Mubarak. The path to easier relations between them was smoothed by the death of Mubarak's old foe Yusuf Al-Ibrahim at Haïl early that year.[88] Yusuf's brother and heir took a broadly friendly attitude to Mubarak. The Kuwaiti ruler took the opportunity to discuss the changing situation in Central Arabia with Cox on the latter's visit to Kuwait in March 1906. Cox was a personality with whom Mubarak always had much easier relations than with Knox, and Cox saw little reason to share the fears of the consul in Basra concerning Britain's relations with the Shaikh.[89] Mubarak told Cox quite openly that he favoured a double reconciliation, between himself and the Amir and between the Amir and the Saudis. An agreement should be based on the following territorial demarcation: Shammar to the Rashidis; Najd and Wadi al-Dawasir to the Saudis; and Kuwait, 'Unayza and Burayda to Kuwait. Such speculation was admirable in its opportunism, for 'Unayza and Burayda were part of the neutral zone originally conquered by the Saudis and now occupied by the Ottomans in accordance with the 1905 Safwan agreement. Mubarak calculated that such a compromise was

[87] IOLR, R/15/1/478, fos. 21–22 (25–27), Knox 7 February 1906.
[88] IOLR, R/15/1/478, fos. 61–62 (77–79): Consul Muhammara to Residency Bushire 15 March 1906.
[89] IOLR, R/15/1/478, report of Cox to Foreign Department of the Government of India, 18 March 1906. The report presents quite a positive image of relations between Knox and Mubarak, which is not entirely borne out by Knox's reports. For Basra fears, ibid., fos. 50–52 (55–57), Crow 4 January 1906.

within reach and expected only the Turks to oppose the deal. They would certainly do so because an Arab entente would spell the end of their policy of divide and rule.

By that time some new arrangement in the disputed zone of Qasim was certainly becoming necessary. The Ottoman "army of occupation" stationed there according to the Safwan agreement had evaporated. Deserters melted away in all directions, while other units started to operate more or less independently on their own behalf. This lawless situation soon claimed an illustrious victim. In April 1906, Abdul Aziz Ibn Rashid was killed. The sources closest to the event give varying accounts, the most probable being a version circulating in the Euphrates valley, related by Rouet, that his death had been at the hands of Ottoman soldiers in revenge for having been abandoned in the desert. The Turks in Baghdad obtained their first news from Mubarak and later confirmation from elsewhere. The Turkish opinion, as stated in German consular reports, was that Ibn Rashid had been "murdered". These sources moreover relate that his body, contrary to Arab custom, had been mutilated and his head exhibited around Qasim impaled on a long Bedouin spear. By contrast the diary of the British agent in Kuwait, Knox, states that Ibn Rashid was killed in battle with Ibn Saud. The Turks were shocked by this sudden event. Abdul Aziz was succeeded by his brother Mit'ab.[90] This seemed a positive development, as the Ottomans accepted the succession and Mubarak too appears to have been favourably disposed towards Mit'ab. The latter sent the powerful Shaikh Khalid Al-'Aun, who had many possessions in Zubair and Basra province, as emissary to Mubarak to draw a line under the old conflicts. But the whole situation failed to find favour with Knox, who at the time was unhappy about his relations with

[90] Paris AE, NS Mascate 12, fo. 100 (Rouet 3 May 1906); Berlin AA, R 13864 A 7656 (25 April 1906), Bodman in Constantinople forwarding telegram of Richarz that the Wali of Basra had been notified by Mubarak that Ibn Rashid had been assassinated on 19 April; A 10844 (19 June 1906), Richarz in Baghdad 25 April 1906; and A 11267 (26 June 1906), Richarz 29 May 1906. There is a less accurate version (mentioning also the death of Mit'ab) in *Political Diaries*, Vol. 1, p. 346 (April 1906), where it is stated that Abdul Aziz's signet ring was sent to Mubarak. The inaccuracy was corrected on p. 352. These contemporary sources are all more or less at variance with the standard "Saudi version", that Ibn Rashid was killed in a nocturnal skirmish with Saudi forces at Rawdat Muhanna in Qasim, to be found e.g. in Rihani, *Ibn Sa'oud of Arabia*, pp. 165–6; Philby, *Arabia*, pp. 190–1; and Philby, *Sau'di Arabia*, p. 250.

Mubarak, who seldom returned his visits, and who had kept him in the dark about the visit of Mit'ab's emissary. During Mubarak's absences, his son Jabir also ignored Knox. Little wonder that he felt deeply frustrated and suspected the Shaikh of dark intrigues.

Knox wrote that people in Kuwait were gossiping about Mubarak leaning more towards the Turks. The Kuwaiti merchants, however, were being nice to the agent, and Knox gathered from local rumour that Khalid Al-'Aun had come to discuss not only reconciling Mit'ab with Mubarak and the Saudis, but also resuming the arms traffic with the Rashidi domain. Knox complained that Mubarak had made a secret deal with the Rashidi emissary over the covert purchase of arms, which was to be hidden from the agent. This was reason enough for Knox to remonstrate once again about the arms trade. Mubarak took no pains to hide his indifference to the agent's feelings. Knox heard that Mubarak had told Kuwaiti merchants that, unlike the ruler of Bahrain, he had an undertaking from the British that they would not interfere in the running of Kuwait. Mubarak had said furthermore that if the British broke this promise he would turn against them. Cox reacted to Knox's complaints by sending a friendly letter to Mubarak exhorting the Shaikh to be pleasant to the agent, but making no mention of the arms trade or of relations with the Rashidis.[91] Mubarak was able to carry on with his policy, but he sent a friendly reply to Cox explaining that Khalid Al-'Aun had come in connection with Mit'ab's wish for peace with the Saudis; there was, however, no word about arms trafficking.[92] The Shaikh did not refrain from irritating Knox, and continued to mediate between the new Rashidi leader and the Saudis, apparently with some success because a truce was agreed.[93] It was in Mubarak's interest for Mit'ab to not entirely vanish from the scene, because then Kuwait would have an over-mighty neighbour in the Saudis. Saudi power was still in the ascendant. In November 1906 they agreed with the Turks that the Ottoman army in Qasim, inasmuch as it had not quite totally evaporated, would be

[91] IOLR, R/15/1/478, fos. 76–79, Knox to Cox (confidential) 12 June 1906, with on fos. 80–81 a report annexed on Al-'Aun's visit; ibid., Cox to Mubarak 30 July 1906.
[92] IOLR, R/15/1/478, fos. 110–114, Mubarak to Cox 3 August 1906.
[93] IOLR, R/15/1/478, fos. 197–199 (231–233), Knox to Cox 13 October 1906. Knox did not believe in the reconciliation and considered it a "hollow truce". The reconciliation had the support of Shaikh Khaz'al of Muhammara, ibid. fo. 209 (241), MacDouall to Cox 17 October 1906.

withdrawn with the exception of 40 men in the cities of Burayda and 'Unayza.[94]

The delicate equilibrium Mubarak had tried to establish was soon upset again. On 29 December 1906, Mit'ab was killed during a hunting trip by his cousin Sultan. Sultan did not last long either and was replaced by an uncle, Hamud. This upset Mubarak's careful plans for a regional balance of power. At first the Saudis went to war to avenge Mit'ab's death. Worse still, relations between the Saudis and the Turks were improving while Rashidi power was on the wane. The Saudis had by now given up all hope of some kind of agreement with the British and had established good formal relations with the Turks. The Sultan was content to let the Saudis be, as long as he was shown sufficient outward respect for Ottoman prestige to be maintained.

One of the advantages of the Safwan agreement for Mubarak had been that the token occupation by the Ottomans of Qasim, just beyond the hinterland of Kuwait, had turned it into a kind of neutral zone. Mubarak had cause to object when the Saudis, after the Ottoman garrison of Qasim had melted away, meted out rough treatment to some local 'Unayza shaikhs who were old friends and allies of his.[95] It looked as if the Amir might now simply be replaced by the Saudis in the role of dangerously strong neighbour of Kuwait. Relations between Mubarak and the Saudis became tense for a while, but improved when Saudi attention turned to problems elsewhere.[96] Mubarak headed a small merchant state that depended for its safety on a regional equilibrium. It was not in Kuwait's interest to be bordered on two sides by the Saudis alone, unbalanced by the Al-Rashid. With the decline of the Rashidis, the Saudis had become too powerful as neighbours, especially in view of their good relations with the Turks. Moreover much of the old vague and disputed borderline

---

[94] IOLR, R/15/1/478, fos. 238–239, Knox to Cox 20 November 1906.

[95] Report by the German consul in Baghdad about a letter written by Mubarak to his Baghdad agent, Mansur bin Sulayman Al-Salih: Berlin AA, R 13867 A 12894 (18 August 1906), Richarz 25 July 1906; this was the main cause of the deterioration in relations between Mubarak and the Saudis. Another incident is recorded in *Political Diaries*, Vol. 1, p. 358 (May 1906). There were also rumours that the Saudis were thinking of reviving very old imperial claims, such as the payment of *zakat* by Oman: ibid., p. 353, April–May 1906.

[96] The *froideur* between Mubarak and the Saudis is also mentioned by Knox: R/15/1/478, fos. 197–199, Knox to Cox 13 October 1906.

between Kuwait and the Amir had now become a frontier zone between Mubarak and the Saudis. Disputes between them arose over the ill-defined borders of tribal loyalty, and once again the maintenance of the network of tribal allegiances in the hinterland became vital for Kuwait's security.

In this existing pattern of alliances Mubarak could not afford to come into conflict with the Turks while the Turks were friends with the Saudis. Mubarak was sensible enough to behave in the most cordial manner towards the Ottoman authorities. In May 1907 Pertew Pasha, the German-trained Chief of Staff of the Ottoman VI Army Corps, had an "accidental" meeting with Mubarak at Fao. Mubarak seems to have communicated his views to the Pasha with some success. Pertew, a supporter of reform movements in the Ottoman Empire, foresaw no problem with Mubarak if only the Turks would treat him decently. Mubarak had complained bitterly to him about repeated British meddling in his affairs.[97]

The Ottoman Empire was in decline, but not yet dead and buried. German officers were training the Ottoman army, and little by little it was growing in effectiveness. During the First World War the British experience at Gallipoli and other places would reveal the Ottoman army as a force to be reckoned with. Pertew Pasha, a capable pupil of the German von der Goltz Pasha, was in the long term a potential threat to the more or less independent Arab rulers. In years past, corrupt incompetents had let control over Iraq slip away, but the new commander might be able to reform the Army Corps and regain control over the Iraqi Arab tribes, after which he would have his hands free for adventures in the desert. The Turks were gradually achieving an at least formal reconciliation with the obstreperous tribal rulers on the margins of Iraq. They had reached a modus vivendi of sorts with the Saudis and Mubarak, and they were now intent on acquiring Sa'dun of the Muntafiq as a new ally. Control over the Muntafiq had for centuries been a traditional priority of the Ottomans in Iraq. Midhat had partly achieved it, but the Ottomans had not managed to gain effective control over Sa'dun's group within the Muntafiq. Pacification of the entire Muntafiq confederation would considerably strengthen the Ottoman hold on Iraq, but this was certainly not in Mubarak's best interests.

[97] Berlin AA, R 13890 A 10671 (8 July 1907), Richarz 13 June 1907. Richarz heard some confidential news from Pertew himself, though the British were in the dark: *Political Diaries*, Vol. 2, p. 193 (May 1907).

The Ottomans achieved a reconciliation with Sa'dun thanks to the Naqib, and next set out to conclude a more formal tie with Mubarak. This they did at first with the help of Shaikh Khaz'al of Muhammara, who as a nominal Persian subject was a neutral go-between, and next directly through the Wali of Basra. The intention was to detach Mubarak from the British and restore him to the Ottoman fold in however vague a manner. Reconciliation with Mubarak, however, was doomed to fail because the Ottomans were not ready to pay the price for it. They were ready to accept Mubarak's position in Kuwait and even to allow him some possessions in Basra province, but they could not allow an unlimited expansion of them. Mubarak had been negotiating to buy land from Sa'dun in Basra province, and the Ottomans thus faced the prospect of Mubarak's domain continually expanding there. It was perfectly reasonable for them to fear that at any moment the British might claim some kind of authority over it. They stopped the deal.[98] Mubarak was as furious with the Ottomans as he was with Sa'dun, who refused to return his deposit, causing a rapid deterioration in their relations. This posed a further danger to Mubarak because Sa'dun always had the ability to raise a huge, albeit undisciplined, army from his tribal resources.

The British agent was only able to play a limited part in such games, and his hands were completely tied by his superiors when it came to Saudi matters. After the death of Abdul Aziz Ibn Rashid, Cox had given serious consideration to Mubarak's recommendation of an informal British protectorate for Abdul Aziz Al-Saud or, as he formulated it, "an extension of the status quo" to Najd, and Knox too had stated that the Saudis would like British protection.[99] There was no chance of such plans finding acceptance at higher level, and Mubarak left Knox little scope for action in Kuwait. So the agent spent his time trying to collect information about inner Arabia, and travelled around the countryside trying to figure out where the territory of tribes obedient to Mubarak began and ended. Relations with Mubarak remained strained. Knox maintained his equanimity in public, giving vent to his vexation in angry little remarks in his diaries and letters. Friction between the agent and the Shaikh was unavoidable. Britain had often tried to restrict Mubarak's dealings with his

[98] Anscombe, *Ottoman Gulf*, p. 139; Plass, *England*, p. 380.
[99] IOLR, R/15/1/478, fos. 168 (203) and 174–175 (208–209), Cox to Government of India 16 September 1906, and Knox to Cox 18 September 1906.

neighbours, but Mubarak needed to act despite Britain's adherence to its policy of non-intervention in Arabian affairs. In practice the British were unable to stick to this policy at all times, and were ready to jettison the principle of non-involvement when direct British interests were involved. This had occurred in August 1905, when the Saudis intervened in a quarrel in Qatar between Qasim Al-Thani and his brother Ahmad. Abdul Aziz Al-Saud had then announced that he would visit Oman and the Trucial Shaikhdoms. This served to rekindle old fears, going back to the 1870s, of Saudi intervention in an area over which the British claimed control. Cox was nervous and received instructions from India to obtain more information from Kuwait. O'Conor did not trust Mubarak as intermediary and preferred a direct warning from Cox to the Saudis. This looked too complicated and Mubarak was asked for information about Saudi intentions. The Shaikh replied that the Saudis were too weak to interfere in Oman, and wanted only to blackmail the Shaikhs of the Trucial Coast for money. He promised to write to Abdul Aziz Al-Saud. The Saudis soon made it clear that they would do nothing adverse.[100] After this incident matters reverted to normal, with sporadic attempts by Mubarak at mediation between the Saudis and Rashidis, probably because he wanted to avert Ottoman intervention in the region, and so he had to put up with occasional warnings from Knox against interference.[101]

A revealing description of the relations between Mubarak and Knox was written somewhat later, in 1908, by the French naval captain Banal on the occasion of his visit to Kuwait on the warship *Surprise*. Banal quotes one of Knox's remarks that epitomizes his somewhat arrogant attitude towards the local people: "The Bedouin are children, but sometimes they can be nice children." Knox described Mubarak to Banal in glowing terms, but ended with the rather dispirited coda: "He does not need me at all."[102] That was precisely the point. Banal was impressed by Mubarak, noting that "the Shaikh's demeanour exudes intelligence and energy". The

---

[100] Plass, *England*, pp. 353–4.

[101] See for example in 1907, IOLR, R/15/1/479, fol, 115 (143), Cox to Government of India 17 September 1907.

[102] Paris AE, NS Mascate 38, fos. 58–59, Banal 20 April 1908. The full quotation of Knox's statement to Banal is: "The Shaikh is a man who is remarkable for his intelligence, activity and authority. He is a great Arab figure. He governs his country in an admirable manner and *he does not need me at all.*"

insincerity of Mubarak's show of affection for Knox was obvious to the Frenchman, and the uneasiness of the agent's relationship with him was plain to see.

Mubarak's dissatisfaction with the British was a crucial factor in the situation. He had probably expected greater benefits from the 1899 Agreement, while he resented British attempts to control him and force him into measures that might turn out to his disadvantage. He became less willing to make concessions, and the rumours that he was trying to detach himself from the British and seeking reconciliation with the Sultan continued to circulate. Naturally it is quite possible that Mubarak himself was the source of such rumours, because they were a useful means of putting pressure on the resident in Bushire.

The uneasy relationship between Mubarak and the British was clearly demonstrated in the curious affair of Kuwait's use of flags. Mubarak, like most Kuwaitis in the past, had been completely relaxed about the Ottoman flag and whether to fly it or not. It appears, however, that at some point he had quietly modified the flag on his palace to distinguish it very slightly from the regular Ottoman one – as we saw above, in 1904 Goguyer had remarked that the flag flown in Kuwait had a white band along the mast side.[103] Somehow this modification seems never to have registered with the British. In 1904 there was trouble over the legal position of Kuwaiti vessels at Bushire. Bushire was a Persian port, while for the British it was also their headquarters in the Gulf, although they had no formal authority there. Persian officials chose to treat the Kuwaiti dhows as Ottoman vessels, and this was, of course, a provocation to the British resident. So an old plan was resurrected that Mubarak should stop flying the Ottoman flag and instead use a distinctive Kuwaiti one. The idea quickly got bogged down in differences of opinion within the British administration. Sanderson was against it, but O'Conor and the India Office viewed it with favour. In February 1905 Lansdowne gave his blessing to a compromise: a new flag could be used on boats, but the Ottoman flag should remain on Mubarak's palace.[104] Then the British spent a year discussing the design of the new flag. Finally the choice fell on an Ottoman flag with the addition of the name Kuwait in Arabic and

[103] Goguyer's remark is quoted by Rouet in Paris AE, NS Mascate 11, fos. 35–39, 28 July 1904.
[104] Plass, *England*, pp. 372–3.

Latin script. Much time and expense was spent on the plans, colour samples even being printed of ship's papers showing the new flag.[105] Then came the moment to submit the designs to Mubarak. Cox visited Kuwait in March 1906 and showed them to him, but the moment was ill-chosen. Mubarak was of the opinion that his interests were not being adequately protected by Britain, nor had there been any response to the financial matters he had discussed with Curzon in 1903. Under these circumstances the Shaikh had no reason to be particularly co-operative. He complained bitterly to Cox about trouble he was having with the Turks – problems in Fao and the offensive behaviour of the British consul in Basra to a servant of Mubarak there – which he attributed to his relationship with Britain. It would be safe to change the flag, he said, only if he could count on genuine British protection from the consequences of such an act. Cox's impression was that Mubarak's hesitancy was inspired by little more than an aversion to the Latin script, and so he proposed a modified design using Arabic script only. He believed this to be more to Mubarak's taste. But now London's approval had to be sought once more.[106]

This time it was O'Conor who appears best to have appreciated Mubarak's position. He agreed that if Mubarak were to change his flag at Britain's suggestion, Britain should be ready to protect him from the consequences.[107] And this was the issue on which the matter ground to a halt. The consultations had delayed things for almost half a year, during which time the Kuwaiti ruler had been given no reason to foster more positive feelings about the reliability of his British allies. Mubarak desired guarantees that his interests would not suffer from the change, and Knox was unable to provide them.

The British apparently took some offence at what they for their part regarded as Mubarak's unreliability.[108] True, he may twice have conditionally accepted the idea of a different flag, but this did not justify British reproaches or pressure. Cox could point the finger with some justice at the reluctance of British diplomats in the Ottoman Empire to

[105] IOLR, R/15/5/61.
[106] IOLR, R/15/1/478, Knox 8 March 1906; also in Rush, *Records of Kuwait*, Vol. 1, pp. 526–9.
[107] Rush, *Records of Kuwait*, Vol. 1, p. 531, O'Conor 23 May 1906.
[108] Rush, *Records of Kuwait*, Vol. 1, p. 532, Knox 30 September; and ibid., pp. 533–4, Cox 14 October 1906.

protect Mubarak's interests.[109] However, the chief reason why India and the Bushire residency avoided quarrelling with Mubarak just at that moment, was that Bushire needed Mubarak's goodwill in the acquisition of land in Kuwait to secure British control of plans for the terminus of the Baghdad Railway, a matter which will be amply described in the following pages. Only O'Conor still advocated the use of a special flag for Kuwait, but this time not on ships, but on the Shaikh's palace. The reasoning was that if trouble with the Turks were to flare up, it would be not in some port, but under controlled conditions on Kuwait territory. This was a policy too far and the idea was buried for the time being.[110] By 1908, entirely on his own initiative, Mubarak was using yet another flag, again resembling the Ottoman one but with three stars in a line along the mast side.[111] The whole farcical flag episode places British inconsistency in handling Kuwait affairs in no better a light than the incompetence of the Ottomans at the time. Endless delays and an inability to formulate a clear policy were common to both Britain and Turkey.

1906 brought signs of growing co-operation between Mubarak and Shaikh Khaz'al of Muhammara.[112] There had been links between Muhammara and Kuwait for some time. As early as the 1840s Shaikh Sabah had sent military assistance there.[113] There were similarities between Khaz'al and Mubarak: both had come to rule in violent circumstances, both faced a nominal overlord who wanted to extend his authority, and both counted on a degree of British protection against this overlord. The only difference was that Mubarak in the course of time had managed to commit the British to a certain guarantee on paper and to exclude Ottoman officials from Kuwait. Khaz'al, otherwise much richer and more powerful, was never able to achieve this.[114] Ultimately this would mean

---

[109] On the matter of Basra merchandise, see Plass, *England*, p. 374.

[110] Plass, *England*, p. 375; PRO, FO 371/243, no. 6373, O'Conor 18 February 1907.

[111] Berlin AA, R 13891 A 34 (7 January 1910), German consul Wassmuss in Bushire, 18 December 1909.

[112] Plass, *England*, pp. 362–3.

[113] Fontanier, *Voyage*, pp. 347–8.

[114] It seems that Khaz'al shared Mubarak's distrust of the British. The Dutch newspaper *Telegraaf* wrote in 1905 that Khaz'al "is very much afraid of British predominance" and for that reason favoured an independent means of communicating with the outside world, and a consulate-general of a small neutral power such as the Netherlands: cutting from the *Telegraaf* enclosed in a letter of the Dutch merchant Ter Meulen of 1909, The Hague NA, Ministry of Foreign Affairs, B-dossiers file 1380, letter with cutting received 28 October 1909.

that Kuwait would be able to maintain its autonomy, while Muhammara would become just a Persian provincial capital. Khaz'al's capital, as formally Persian territory, was completely beyond the reach of Ottoman power. Arab friends of Khaz'al could make use of Muhammara as a base of operations without the Turks' knowledge. Mubarak appears to have used the British vice-consul in Muhammara, MacDouall, to forward information to Bushire. In this way he was able at first to counteract the not always benign influence of the Basra consulate's reports, and later still he was able to send letters without Knox's knowledge.

Khaz'al was a large landowner in Basra province, where his status was similar to Mubarak's, but he was somewhat better placed, being able to send ruffians to enforce his rights on Ottoman territory from his safe refuge in Persia. It is little wonder the two shaikhs became cronies. Mubarak was at a disadvantage in being the less well-off of the two, but it was important to his dignity and prestige to appear equal. This involved expenses, which were sometimes difficult to cover from income that had been hit by restrictions on the arms trade. From 1906 on Mubarak developed the habit of making frequent visits to Khaz'al. To reduce the risk of delays due to bad weather, he acquired a steam yacht for speed of movement (the rulers of Muhammara had owned one as early as the 1860s).[115]

The Government of India was disquieted by the frequent contacts between Khaz'al and Mubarak, fearing that both rulers might be working towards an Arab alliance against the Sultan and the Shah. Cox did not share these fears, nor did the Muhammara consul MacDouall. Arab shaikhs made frequent visits to Muhammara because they were able to send telegrams from there without interference by the Ottoman authorities. Khaz'al, according to the consul, allowed this in order to make friends with neighbouring Ottoman Arabs and so acquire allies in case of conflict with the Shah. Even O'Conor saw nothing amiss.[116]

But the Indian Government would have been right to worry about Mubarak's policy slipping out of British control. He was playing for equilibrium in the region and, with the rising power of the Saudis, he was cultivating the Ottomans and Rashidis. It was Goguyer's scenario that at

---

[115] For a picture of Mubarak's yacht, see Illustration no. 23 (from Antaki, *Al-Riyad*, p. 144).
[116] Plass, *England*, pp. 362–3; IOLR, R/15/1/478, fo. 182 (216), Government of India to Cox with reply 8 October; and fos. 197–199 (231–233), Knox 13 October 1906.

this time most appealed to him: an agreement between Najd, Shammar and the Turks on the basis of a status quo, whereby the Turks would not interfere in Arab affairs in exchange for verbal assurances of Arab loyalty.

9.6 Negotiations over Bandar Shuwaikh

Three synchronous factors mark the history of Kuwait in the years 1904–6. In the foreground there was the relatively minor evolution in Mubarak's relations with Ottoman officials. Also to the fore were the politics of the desert, where Mubarak tried to maintain as favourable as possible a position for Kuwait in the ever-shifting pattern of relations between Najd, Shammar and the Turks. The third element, the intermittent attempts by the Germans and Turks to get the planned railway from Haydar Pasha via Baghdad to the Gulf moving again, rumbled on in the background.

The Baghdad Railway project is a recurring feature of Kuwait's history during Mubarak's career. Britain had long been confident that it could block any undesirable development in the railway scheme by its control of the Kuwait end, and through difficulties in financing the project without the participation of the City of London. Furthermore, nobody would risk constructing the line without a financial guarantee from the Ottoman Government. The Ottoman Government was in no position to give such a guarantee without raising customs duties, and the British held the power of veto over such measures. As we have seen, however, the British were aware that their financial impediments could not be maintained indefinitely, and that the Turks might be able to juggle their finances on behalf of the railway. Worse, the British also feared that Germany might be able to finance the railway to the Gulf without recourse to the City of London.[117] Such British fears were somewhat exaggerated. The Baghdad Railway might be a hobby-horse of the German Emperor, but German officialdom was wary of the Ottomans and had no illusions about the corrupt Ottoman bureaucracy. The Germans were still willing to help the Turks, but only with reservations.

British views fluctuated on the suitability of their position in Kuwait as a means of blocking undesirable railway developments. As shown above in section 9.4, the area surrounding the Gulf of Kuwait had seemed no longer

[117] Plass, *England*, pp. 378–81.

to be uniquely suitable when the Ottoman occupation of Kuwaiti territory in 1902 had opened up the possibility of a terminus on the Khor Abdallah, outside the area of British control. But by the end of 1904 the value of Kuwait to the British had returned as new and better survey data became available. The British now knew that any terminus of the railway on the Khor Abdallah, for example at Umm Qasr, would entail the same or more costly dredging work as a terminus at Basra.[118] So the vicinity of Kuwait town once again became best candidate for the terminus, the only point at issue being whether Kazima or Shuwaikh was most suitable. By the end of 1905, India had become convinced that Shuwaikh was best, but debate continued in London.[119]

Happily for Britain, Knox and Cox had already been weighing up the acquisition, by lease or sale, of a piece of coastline that had been earmarked when, after much delay, a survey of the relevant coastlines had been carried out in 1904–5. Knox had proposed in November 1905 the purchase of a site at Shuwaikh to create a coal shed for the steam launch he wanted for the agency and for British merchant ships.[120] No final decision had been made, but Grey's attempt to internationalize the railway had run into trouble with France and Russia in the early summer of 1906.[121] Now Britain's only option was to assert its hold on the location for the terminus. So the Foreign Office asked the India Office, in June 1906, to acquire the site in Kuwait where the railway terminus could be constructed.[122]

It was a rather unpropitious moment for the British to enter into negotiations with Mubarak. During the summer of 1906 formal visits between the palace and the agency had been suspended.[123] Then, in

[118] Bidwell, *Affairs of Kuwait*, 2/6, pp. 31–3, Crow 4 May 1903. This was the first indication that the Khor Abdallah had great disadvantages.

[119] Plass, *England*, pp. 375–6.

[120] Plass, *England*, pp. 376–7.

[121] Plass, *England*, pp. 382–3.

[122] The Foreign Office in London asked the India Office to initiate the matter on 12 June 1906, and in September the India Office notified the Indian Government: Plass, *England*, p. 380. Plass has by far the best and most detailed account on the events that followed. Salwa Al-Ghanim, *Mubarak*, pp. 156–61, gives another long account, but this omits some essential points and is over-judgemental about British officials exceeding their instructions.

[123] *Political Diaries*, Vol. 1, pp. 428–9 (July–August 1906). See also correspondence exchanged between Mubarak and Cox in IOLR, R/15/1/478, fos. 36–98 (123–125) and fos. 110–111 (138–141), 30 July and 3 August 1906.

August, Knox had to keep a low profile while an Ottoman army commander, returning discomfited from the garrison in Qasim, unexpectedly came to stay in Mubarak's palace.[124] In September Mubarak irritated the British on a specifically railway matter by contributing 500 liras, instead of the 200 liras requested, to the Hijaz Railway Fund and the Mecca water supply, projects dear to Abdulhamid II – a generous donation duly reported in the *Basra Gazette*.[125] Mubarak's ire was further stoked when the British consul in Basra refused, with O'Conor's acquiescence, to intervene in problems at customs over packages destined for him.[126] It was just at that juncture that Knox received orders to make his first approach to Mubarak about the possibility of Britain leasing or buying a stretch of coastline on the Gulf of Kuwait.[127] Mubarak at that point had little reason to be generous to Knox and behaved like a spider in his web. While promising to be forthcoming, he refused to name a price, and prepared the ground for a high bid by giving a newly adorned, but quite untruthful, account of an alleged offer by the Stemrich/von Kapp mission of 1900 to buy land for the railway in Kuwait.[128] In the meantime he sought the advice of Kuwaiti merchants about how best to deal with Knox.[129]

Mubarak seems to have been thoroughly aware of the British predicament and was in no hurry to advance the negotiations. He gave a further turn to the screw by discreetly revealing that he knew very well

---

[124] *Political Diaries*, Vol. 1, p. 449; and IOLR, R/15/1/478, Cox 14 October 1906.

[125] IOLR, R/15/1/478, Cox to Government of India 4 September 1906.

[126] IOLR, R/15/1/478, fos. 211–212 (243–244), Cox to Government of India 21 October 1906. Cox, while noting ironically that he did not "question the wisdom" of O'Conor's decisions, warned the Government of India that this was "just one of those incidents which Sheikh Mubarek most resents and which inevitably impress him with the timidity of our support", and that because of that one could not expect Mubarak to be "whole-hearted or single-minded" in his relations with Knox.

[127] Plass, *England*, p. 383. Salwa Al-Ghanim, *Mubarak*, p. 158, mentions two meetings between Mubarak and Knox in September and October, but this could not be verified because in the regrettably careless printing of this book the notes of an entire chapter are missing.

[128] Plass, *England*, p. 383. On this occasion Mubarak added the embellishment that Stemrich and Kapp had offered him a substantial price, and that when he turned it down the Germans had told him that the Sultan had given them the land and that they would take it.

[129] Plass, *England*, p. 383, quoting Knox to Cox 28 October 1907, in PRO, FO 406/33, p. 8f, no. 1627.

that Britain's desire to acquire just that stretch of coast was connected with the railway scheme. Knox's original idea had been a combined budget to acquire a site at Shuwaikh measuring 600 by 100 yards plus a steam launch for the agency for the total sum of 10,000 rupees (or 667 pounds sterling), of which half was to be for Mubarak. Plass remarks most aptly that since the British desire to acquire the land was a political matter, Mubarak by the same token could ask a political price. By then Knox was proposing a somewhat larger site of 1200 by 200 yards, at a lease of 320 pounds per annum, or a sale price of 3200 pounds.[130]

Mubarak's relations with Knox remained bad, as reflected in the highly critical way Knox described Mubarak's financial policy in his diary.[131] Mubarak was in no hurry, trusting in external pressures to bring the British round. He reminded Knox about his request for an annual subsidy on the occasion of Curzon's visit, claiming that he was a much poorer man than other Gulf rulers under British protection. Mubarak's income from the Kuwait customs covered only half his expenses – he apparently regarded his other income, such as that from his date groves and real estate, as private.[132] Though he did not say so, he implied that his customs revenue had been hit by the British-sponsored measures against the arms trade. Knox was given to understand that the sum he had in his mind would not cover the purchase of the land. His solution was to suggest the acquisition of a much larger stretch of land for the price desired by Mubarak. Cox was not unwilling to accommodate this, observing that a subsidy of the size apparently desired by Mubarak had already been previously considered. He was spurred to make faster progress by rumours that the powerful German shipping line Hapag might include Kuwait in its schedules, a development that would further complicate relations with the Ottoman Empire.[133]

In the meantime the India Office was dreaming of buying an even larger piece of land, thus forgetting the most elementary tactics of business negotiation. It proposed to the Foreign Office a site measuring 1800 by more than 200 yards for an annual lease of 1000 pounds. The Foreign Office agreed, but preferred to buy the land rather than to lease it.[134] Mubarak exploited the slow progress of negotiations – by now it was June

[130] Plass, *England*, pp. 384–5.   [131] *Political Diaries*, Vol. 2, *passim*.
[132] Plass, *England*, p. 384.   [133] Plass, *England*, p. 385.
[134] Plass, *England*, p. 386.

1907 – to his own advantage. He quickly built a coal storage facility for his steam boat in the exact centre of the area desired by Knox, while the British indulged in lengthy discussions among themselves about the price to be paid and how it should be divided between Britain and India. Knox was understandably vexed by Mubarak's ploy, but the Shaikh remained unmoved by the agent who was obviously an errand boy he could manipulate.[135] Meanwhile new rumours circulated about quarrels between Mubarak and Knox. It was said in Muhammara that Mubarak or Jabir had ordered the British agent to take down the British flag that had been hoisted on a mast standing on the ground. In essence this was a matter of protocol: a flag on a building meant that the building belonged to a foreign state, while a flag-pole on the ground meant that the land too belonged to the foreign state and so this was often not countenanced. The British consul in Muhammara, MacDouall, did not believe this news, but reported that during a recent visit to Muhammara Mubarak had appeared very angry with the British.[136] Knox once again registered bitter complaints about Mubarak playing tricks on him.[137]

With all this friction there was little or no progress in the negotiations over the lease of the Bandar Shuwaikh site. A crisis in relations between Shaikh and agent occurred when, once again without notifying Knox, Mubarak left with an armed force for Muhammara to help Khaz'al in a quarrel with the Banu Turuf, an Arab tribe on Persian territory opposite Amara. Knox was furious and demanded in Bushire that Mubarak should be clearly admonished that this was against the rules. He even offered his resignation. But in these delicate circumstances Cox refused to back his agent. Mubarak received no British protest and his operations in Khaz'al's territory prospered.[138] He had cause for satisfaction, as he had made it clear that the Shaikh, not the British, ruled Kuwait. Poor Knox had to make *bonne mine à mauvais jeu*, relations were restored on Mubarak's terms, and Knox still had to try to reach an agreement on the acquisition of land. This afforded Mubarak the opportunity to revive his former demands. He was in any case in need of cash, having just concluded the agreement with

[135] Plass, *England*, pp. 386–7.
[136] IOLR, R/15/1/479, fos. 59–60, Consul in Muhammara 18 May 1907.
[137] IOLR, R/15/1/479, fos. 63–68, Knox to Cox 12 June 1907 (so confidential that Knox wrote that he kept no copy in the Kuwait Agency archives).
[138] Plass, *England*, pp. 368–9.

Sa'dun described above to purchase date groves.[139]

Knox's feelings were of no account. Bushire wanted a deal and Mubarak wanted as high a price as possible. In August 1907 a basic agreement was reached for the lease of a plot measuring 3750 by 300 yards around the enclave of Mubarak's private wharf, for the price of 4000 pounds per annum, many times the sum originally contemplated by London. The Viceroy now wanted to bring the matter to a swift conclusion. The British believed Mubarak might be readier to clinch the deal in view of his renewed annoyance with the Ottoman authorities in Basra, who had refused to register his purchase of land in Basra province from Sa'dun. This was a vain hope. Just when the agreement was to be finalized, Mubarak suddenly came up with some new conditions, much to the dismay of poor Knox.

Mubarak grasped that he could increase his demands while the British were so keen to obtain the lease on the Bandar Shuwaikh site. This time he was interested not in money but in political concessions. The British had recently demonstrated what little regard they had for the rights of Arab rulers under their protection, and Mubarak wanted some safeguards for his independence from Britain. In 1905 there had been the incident on Bahrain referred to above that had damaged Britain's reputation for fair treatment of local rulers. It had involved the representative of the German firm of Wönckhaus, and Britain had felt it necessary to intervene with a heavy hand to avoid a conflict with the German Government. Plass is probably right in ascribing Mubarak's sudden demand of political guarantees from the British to his mistrust of British intentions as a result of that Bahrain incident. The new conditions imposed by Mubarak were a demand for a British guarantee for his independence in Kuwait, and a clause that the Shuwaikh lease would become void should there be a substantial change in Kuwait's relationship with Britain.[140]

After much talk the "agreement" took shape in a remarkable document. It was not a convention signed by both parties, nor even an exchange of written promises like the 1899 bond, but a unilateral letter

---

[139] Anscombe, *Ottoman Gulf*, p. 139, puts a different complexion on the affair. According to him it was Britain's cunning use of Mubarak's sudden irritation with the Ottomans over the failure of the sale of Sa'dun's land that enabled them to get Mubarak to sign the Bandar Shuwaikh deal.

[140] Plass, *England*, p. 387.

written by Mubarak in which he granted the lease and the options against the agreed sum. Included in it was a repetition of the non-alienation bond of 1899 and the confirmation by Mubarak that the British had given him extensive guarantees concerning the protection of his own and his heirs' position in Kuwait. His treatment of the guarantees was forceful: British failure to keep their promises would render Mubarak free to terminate the lease. The repetition by Mubarak of his non-alienation promise of 1899 is especially interesting, in confirming that it also extended to Mubarak's possessions outside Kuwait. In 1899 the dangerous implications of this passage had caused considerable alarm in London, but in 1906 the British were happy with its inclusion, possibly because they thought it might come in useful for Britain to have some hold on the strategic lands at Fao.[141] A further point in the final agreement covered the sharing of customs revenues from the future railway terminus between Mubarak and the British. This prognostication had interesting legal implications. It implied an extra British recognition of Mubarak's local sovereignty that could have drastic consequences in the light of German and Turkish insistence on full Ottoman control over the customs at any future terminus. If negotiations about the railway really did materialize, the British would face a problem when forced to admit that they were not free to negotiate the customs revenues without Mubarak's approval!

There was one more remarkable feature of the final agreement. This was that the British option to acquire extra land around Shuwaikh was extended to Warba and Bubiyan too. The inspiration for this inclusion had come from the Viceroy in August 1907. Cox had demurred, fearing further delay, but the India Office submitted the matter for consultation with the Foreign Office. The Foreign Office ordered O'Conor to lay the preliminary legal basis for the British option by reasserting Mubarak's claim to Bubiyan and Warba in his talks with the Turks. O'Conor refused and the consultations in London ended with the conclusion that Warba and Bubiyan were unimportant. London thus decided to drop the Bubiyan/Warba clause, but events had overtaken the policy-makers. Knox reported that he had overlooked the part of his instructions telling him not to request an option on Warba and Bubiyan, and had already asked for it. Knox felt that he could not draw back without risking Mubarak's suspicion, and had gone ahead and concluded the agreement. London

[141] Plass, *England*, pp. 387–8.

accepted.[142] In this way Mubarak unexpectedly received what was tantamount to formal British recognition of his rights to Bubiyan and Warba.[143]

Mubarak ended with a little sting in the tail. Long before, he had asked for two artillery pieces – for saluting purposes, so he claimed, despite the curious inclusion of real ammunition. He discreetly indicated that, should the British refuse, he would buy the guns from Goguyer. London agreed to supply them.[144]

9.7 Financing Mubarak's desert policy

A recurring theme in Knox's diaries for the years 1907–8 is the increasing financial burden imposed on Kuwait's inhabitants by Mubarak. It appears that taxation was considerably increased in this period. It is not easy to reconstruct the true state of affairs on the basis of Knox's version, because his frequent quarrels with Mubarak place a question mark over his neutrality as an observer. Hence it is necessary to examine the situation in more detail.

It was the custom in states such as Kuwait, and even until quite recently in other Gulf states, for no sharp distinction to be drawn between state revenues and the ruler's private purse. It does not, however, follow that there was not a vague feeling that there was some distinction between purely family capital and the state's revenues and expenditures. One should also recognize that this lack of distinction works both ways. State revenues might be applied to the ruler's private expenses (it is usually difficult to judge exactly what is private in such circumstances), but private income might also be used for the running of the state. Mubarak appears from time to time to have dipped quite deeply into his family capital, or into income from the family date groves in Basra province, to keep Kuwait running. He not infrequently pointed this out, and it was never challenged by any observer, however critical they might be about his methods of generating income. Desert diplomacy was an expensive business, Ottomans had to be

---

[142] Plass, *England*, pp. 388–92.

[143] Text of the agreement first published in Gehrke, *Grenze*, Vol. 2, pp. 15–21. See for the different stages of the contract IOLR, R/15/5/92.

[144] Plass, *England*, p. 393, indicates that the permission of the Foreign Office might have been due to the fact that Mallet, head of the Eastern Department who gave the permission, had not yet had much experience.

bribed, and sufficient wealth had to be displayed by the ruler to outshine not just rivals but also the British agent, who was not to appear before Kuwaitis in a more prestigious light than the Shaikh.

The diminution of the arms trade forced Mubarak to generate new income. He seems to have grown tired of continuing to draw on what he considered his private means for public business. What happened was very reminiscent of European states in the 15th–17th centuries. The ruler tries to maximize income from existing rights, and meets with opposition and opprobrium. Part of the reason for the Netherlands' emergence as an independent republic in the 16th century was the attempt by its ruler to make fiscal provisions for what we now would consider the running of a modern state. In Kuwait matters did not go as far as that. There were indeed some attempts at what we now would call enlarging the public sector beyond mere defence, administration and foreign affairs: the first initiatives in education, water transport, harbour construction, health care and suchlike were taken. These first steps were important in the development of Kuwait and did indeed give the country the lead it always held over other Gulf states, but they did not count for any significant slice of the "budget". Mubarak's attempts to generate new income were essentially an effort to safeguard the capital of a wealthy family against further bleeding by the expenses of the state machinery, itself owned by the family. This is not especially glorious, but neither was it entirely without justification.

The main cost item was desert diplomacy, backed up in some cases by military mobilization. As already argued, it may not be right to see Mubarak's desert policy as overly aggressive and uncalled-for, as some British observers and Salwa Al-Ghanim have presented it. It was rather more defensive in character, its purpose being a regional equilibrium of forces. The idea that Mubarak had ambitions to be a second Ibn Saud cannot really be substantiated. Bribes for the Turks were another cost item. This was unavoidable because Mubarak was unable to depend on the British alone. Either Kuwait would become a colony or – more probably – his rights would not receive sufficient protection because of the British habit of backing out to protect other diplomatic interests. Mubarak's chosen path was to maintain his ties with the Turks at a level which enabled him to maintain as much autonomy as possible. This he contrived to do very well. Then there were his "private" expenses. These were partly practical: a steam yacht, used for easy transit to his Basra possessions, which partly supported the Kuwait budget, or to Muhammara, which kept him abreast of affairs in the outside world. A somewhat ostentatious palace and associated paraphernalia were needed to show that Mubarak was a more puissant personage than the agent, as a visual assertion of Kuwait's independence. A single motorcar, admittedly a costly item, did not constitute an enormous expense, and made a good show.

The decline in arms trafficking lent urgency to Mubarak's search for other sources of revenue. At the same time his income from the date groves had diminished, because he had had to cede a share to his cousins. He could also argue with some justification that the difficulty and expense of collecting his income in Basra province were incurred in the service of maintaining the financial basis of Kuwait's independence. He would have had no problems with the Ottoman Government if he had formally declared himself an Ottoman subject, but that he could not do without jeopardizing the independence of Kuwait, so he was justified in feeling that his private income suffered in the interests of the state.

Revenue generation is not a recipe for a ruler's popularity. It is also very difficult in a traditional political structure. Mubarak tried various methods. The obvious way was to establish or increase taxes on trade. As a sovereign ruler he was free to do this, but there were limitations. Too much taxation might harm Kuwait's economy and make him unpopular with the merchants. The increase in taxes and customs duties at the beginning of 1907 coincides with the change in the general political situation in Arabia whereby the Saudis were becoming sufficiently powerful to constitute a threat. There was, as we have seen, Saudi pressure on Mubarak's friends in Qasim, and there were also disputes over the allegiance of nomadic tribes. Meanwhile Mubarak had overcome the Ottoman danger and could act more freely in Kuwait. At the outset of 1907 there was trouble with the 'Ajman tribe too, and Mubarak began campaign preparations against them. The merchants were required to contribute to the costs, which aroused some discontent.[145] This was no route to popularity, and it could not go unnoticed by the agent who was forever walking and talking in the bazaar.

---

[145] *Political Diaries*, Vol. 2, pp. 102 and 111–12 (March 1907). It caused the British to consider once again issuing a warning to Mubarak about interfering in desert affairs, but the war was over before the British had come to a decision: IOLR, R/15/1/479, Crow to O'Conor 17 April 1907, and Viceroy to India Office 21 June 1907.

In 1908 the merchants had a new reason for discontent when Mubarak increased the taxes on the shops in the bazaar. He now claimed 50 per cent of the annual rent instead of a fixed amount of 20 rupees. As the average rent was estimated by Knox at 50 rupees, this meant a minimum tax increase of 25 per cent.[146]

Mubarak's increase in customs duties does not seem to have been excessive, but no increase would find favour with the merchants. Given the level of duties elsewhere there was, however, no serious risk of damage to the Kuwaiti economy. The only real such harm was inflicted by the British suppression of the arms trade, because this reduced shipping movements to Kuwait.[147] Mubarak also increased taxes on newly built houses, which according to Knox caused much resentment. The total revenue raised by this measure was estimated by Knox at 16,666 pounds sterling.[148]

Mubarak no doubt regarded internal stability as being in the interest of the merchants, and that marriages between his nephews and other members of his family were conducive to it. Hence, notwithstanding their protests, he could with some justification claim large contributions from the merchants for such marriages.[149] Another important component of Mubarak's income came from pearl diving. Here too he increased taxes.[150]

Alongside these financial claims, Knox's diary also reveals Mubarak's first attempts at modernizing Kuwait. Ways and means of improving Kuwait's water supply were investigated. Mubarak imported a steam yacht for his own use, mainly for communicating with his friend and ally Khaz'al in Muhammara. He also acquired a motor car. An important initiative was his attempt to introduce social reforms into the pearling industry. The most important part of the measure was a firm regulation about the repayment of the debts of the divers to their bosses. In the past, divers had needed to obtain loans from the *nakhuda*s for their families' livelihoods, and for as long as such loans were not repaid in full the divers remained tied to that *nakhuda*. The new regulation placed a maximum limit on the loans, and stipulated that as long as the diver paid the agreed annual

---

[146] *Political Diaries*, Vol. 2, p. 214 (June–July 1907).

[147] *Political Diaries*, Vol. 2, pp. 30 (January 1907) and 184 (May 1907).

[148] *Political Diaries*, Vol. 2, p. 17 (December 1906–January 1907); pp. 29–30 (January 1907); and p. 46 (January 1907). It concerned houses up to six years old.

[149] *Political Diaries*, Vol. 3, p. 162 (April–May 1908).

[150] *Political Diaries*, Vol. 2, p. 193 (May 1907). Knox estimated that Mubarak would now receive about 10,000 pound sterling per season.

instalment he was free from that particular *nakhuda*. It is little wonder that this caused disquiet among the big entrepreneurs. Knox doubted, moreover, whether Mubarak would be able to enforce the measure.[151] The following year Mubarak tried to save both shopkeepers and pearl divers from financial ruin by regulating schedules of payment of pearl divers' debts to the shopkeepers in the bazaar.[152]

In 1908 Knox's diary also mentions that Mubarak levied a small tax on ships' carpenters, but it is not clear whether this was an innovation or the collection of an existing tax.[153] Taxation of real estate was yet another means for Mubarak to increase his income. According to Salwa Al-Ghanim, who gives no source for her assertion, Mubarak used to claim that the whole of Kuwait was his "*mulk*". The use of this term is interesting because of its specific meaning in Ottoman law. If Mubarak used this term in his discussions with the Ottoman Government it would mean that Kuwait was his property and not an administrative district in the Ottoman imperial system.[154] But Salwa Al-Ghanim gives no indication of the context in which the term was used, and in other cases it could simply mean freehold property. Whatever the case, it is clear that Mubarak, as head of the Al-Sabah family, claimed ownership of the land on which Kuwait was built. Mubarak felt that he was justified in introducing taxes on real estate because, with the growth of Kuwait's importance in this period, real estate had increased in value.

All these measures met with Knox's strong criticism. He was warning Cox in July 1908 that, low though taxes in Kuwait might still be, there was a risk of Mubarak's demands strangling the Kuwaiti economy. He feared that popular discontent in Kuwait might become directed against Britain, which in protecting Mubarak enabled him to act in a despotic fashion.[155] It is a plausible interpretation, but on the other hand Knox bore a grudge against Mubarak, nor was Mubarak so very dependent on British protection. In the same report Knox wrote: "I cannot disguise from myself

---

[151] *Political Diaries*, Vol. 2, pp. 382–3 (September–October 1907).

[152] *Political Diaries*, Vol. 3, p. 162 (April–May 1908).

[153] *Political Diaries*, Vol. 3, p. 208 (June 1908).

[154] In the world of feudal semantics, already encountered with "suzerainty", the meaning of *mulk* would approach that of "allodium": a free possession over which the suzerain had no rights.

[155] IOLR, R/15/5/18, Knox to Cox 8 July 1908; *cf.* Salwa Al-Ghanim, *Mubarak*, pp. 140–1.

the hundred little ways in which Shaikh Mubarak impresses upon me that I must play second fiddle in this town." Even Knox admits that taxes in Kuwait were still low. Moreover, the new tax revenues do not appear to have been sufficient to enable Mubarak to run Kuwait without recourse to the family income from the Basra date groves. In his annual report Knox played down his criticism. He then conceded: "Whatever may be said as to his methods, Sheikh Mubarak has the town well in hand and since the exactions recorded in connection with the shaikhly marriages, there have been no more complaints of injustice or oppression. He has been equally successful with the desert Bedouins." But in October 1908 Knox also commented, in a long letter about his difficult relations with Mubarak, that the Kuwait ruler had learnt ways of "skinning" his people from his evil friend Khaz'al.[156]

Exaggeration is to be resisted. Mubarak may have been an autocrat, but he was not out of touch with his people. Raunkiaer's description of 1912, depicting him sitting in the bazaar every afternoon, gives proof positive that Mubarak maintained a rather open system in so far as the daily running of affairs in Kuwait was concerned.[157]

While Knox's writings resound with criticisms of Mubarak, other observers heaped hyperbole upon him. The most extreme case is that of the Egyptian journalist Antaki, who visited Kuwait in January 1908 and wrote a book extolling the Kuwaiti ruler, replete with poetic panegyrics on Mubarak, his family and Khaz'al. The book contains interesting, albeit poorly reproduced, photographs, but few serious facts. It is interesting chiefly as an extreme example of the lyrical Egyptian mode of description, in stark contrast to the more matter-of-fact observations of Europeans such as Burchardt, Goguyer and Raunkiaer.[158] Antaki received a cordial welcome from Mubarak, who bestowed upon him a boat ticket for Bombay.[159]

[156] Rush, *Ruling Families*, pp. 61–9, Knox 6 October 1908 (p. 64).

[157] Raunkiaer, *Gennem Wahhabiternes Land*, pp. 40–7. The English translation by De Gaury is somewhat abridged and the town plan of Kuwait in 1912 is missing there: *Through Wahhabiland*, pp. 34–8.

[158] Abdul Masih Al-Antaki, *Al-Riyad al-muzhira bayn al-Kuwayt wa-'l-Muhammara*, Cairo 1908. Antaki had visited Muhammara when Mubarak was there and met with him and Khaz'al. Mubarak invited him to Kuwait. The book contains photographs of Mubarak, Khaz'al, a Kuwait market, a part of Mubarak's palace, and Mubarak's steamer.

[159] *Political Diaries*, Vol. 3, pp. 27 and 37 (December 1907–January 1908).

10

Mubarak and the Young Turks
1908–1912

10.1 The new Ottoman Government, 1908

For a long time now strong criticism of Abdulhamid II's regime had been voiced both internally and by exiles abroad. Discontent among the intelligentsia, independent-minded officials and army officers bred dissenting movements, the most prominent of which was the Committee of Union and Progress, an offshoot of the so-called Young Turk Movement. The opposition's goal was to create a modern, more democratic state. But the movement also contained an ethnic Turkish nationalist element that promoted the ideology of pan-Turkism, the aim of which was to turcify the multi-ethnic Ottoman empire.

But how was a democracy to be created out of the loose agglomeration of pluralisms, containing so few forces for cohesion, that was the Ottoman Empire? Sultan Abdulhamid II had understandable reasons for opposing nationalist tendencies within the Empire and had suppressed them ruthlessly, promoting Islamic institutions in their stead as the binding ingredient of the ramshackle structure. Abdulhamid and his predecessor had revived the claim of the Sultan to the status of Caliph, which had been exploited hardly at all in previous Ottoman centuries. Midhat Pasha had used this concept to breathe new life into the Ottoman claim to the Arabian Peninsula. For the Sultan to present himself as Caliph, however, could be no more than a partial solution to his problems, because a Turkish claim to the Caliphate was distasteful to many of the Empire's Arab subjects. Such a claim, furthermore, could be exposed as a double-edged

sword – as we have seen, Mubarak had deftly exploited it to acknowledge
the Sultan as his spiritual overlord and no more. The Young Turk
movement attracted adherents among those Arabs who saw democratic
reform as conferring more freedom to pursue Arab nationalist aims. The
incident with the *Khilafat* newspaper shows that Mubarak himself had
connections in these circles.

However, the currents of pan-Turkism and Arab nationalism were by
their nature incompatible, and it was inevitable that greater democracy in
the Ottoman Empire would unleash the antagonism inherent in them. The
Sultan was right to be wary of such nationalist currents in his multi-ethnic
Empire, but his oppressive methods were ultimately counterproductive. In
July 1908 he was forced to reinstate the former reformist constitution. A
liberal government was appointed that was considerably influenced in the
background by the Committee of Union and Progress. The Sultan was
forced to abdicate when, after just a few months, he attempted a coup to
evict the new government.

The Young Turks faced a dilemma. They had accused Abdulhamid of
letting the Empire fragment, but in the Arab provinces their efforts to
restructure it clashed both with existing Arab power structures and with
rising Arab nationalism. In the region adjoining Kuwait this gave rise to a
complex state of affairs. The new democratic elections in the wake of the
Young Turks' rise to power produced in Talib, the ill-famed son of the
Naqib, a dangerous member of parliament for the Basra district. The Turks
were in no position to bend the existing local powers to their will, and so
Ottoman control of the district remained as weak as it had been before.
The Young Turks inherited the situation left by Abdulhamid in Basra
province – British influence, powerful landowners, and unruly shaikhs in
the border zone – and on the whole the new administration was
ineffective in solving the region's problems.

The Young Turks drew inspiration from Midhat Pasha. They resumed
Abdulhamid's policy of asserting the former Ottoman claim to the whole
of the Arabian Peninsula. In the Gulf, new Ottoman officials were
appointed for 'Udayd (part of Abu Dhabi adjacent to Qatar) and Zubara.
The British lodged an immediate protest and the Turks retired, pretending
as usual that the appointments had been made by local officials acting
without instructions from Constantinople. The matter caused the Foreign
Office in London to consider clarifying the situation by concluding a

treaty with Qatar. The Government of India saw little point in such a blatant provocation of the Turks. It came up with another proposal, originating with Cox, that Britain should issue the new Ottoman Government with a clear statement of its claims and policy in the Gulf, so to pre-empt future misunderstandings caused by O'Conor's soft line. The India Office proposed to back up such a statement by reinforcing the British naval presence in the Gulf, enabling it to counteract any undesirable Ottoman response by occupying isolated Turkish positions in the region of Qatar and al-Hasa.[1] This was too much for the Foreign Office, which felt that such an aggressive policy could help to make war with Turkey unavoidable. Arthur Nicolson, under-secretary at the Foreign Office, was also concerned about another danger, that conflict with the Turks in the Gulf might have repercussions among the Muslims in India and Egypt. Nicolson's not unreasonable view was that, if events were to unfold in that way, there would be no chance of Britain being able to obtain absolute control over the Baghdad Railway, and that for that very reason it would be wise to strengthen its position in Kuwait.[2]

It was nevertheless rather dangerous for Mubarak's position that a hope should be born in the Foreign Office that Britain, now that there was a new government in Constantinople, might be able to reach some compromise over the old disputes with the Ottoman Empire. The Young Turks might turn out to be less anti-British than Abdulhamid II, leading to a rapprochement between Britain and Turkey. The man to investigate the possibilities of a new relationship was Lowther, who had replaced O'Conor as ambassador in Constantinople in 1908. However, it was not easy for the British to adapt to the new political set-up. They had never cultivated links with the Young Turk movement, unlike the Germans who from the start had contacts and even friends in the new regime. When Britain was finally ready to seek improved relations, two impediments blocked the way. First, the Germans had already established good relations with the Turks by seconding modern-minded army officers to them. Second was the deep irritation felt by Turkish nationalists at the British presence in Mesopotamia and the Gulf. Lowther, who had a low opinion of the Turks, did little to follow up Foreign Office ideas about mending fences with the Ottoman Empire until it was rather too late.[3]

[1] Busch, *Britain and the Persian Gulf*, p. 321.
[2] Heller, *British Policy*, p. 49.

By that time British attempts to reach a multinational solution to the railway problem had foundered. Grey's attempts to negotiate an agreement providing for British control over the final section had estranged the Russians, a state of affairs that Germany was able to exploit by negotiating a separate railway agreement with Russia.[4] French financiers also sided with the Germans, leaving the British isolated. As Grey was convinced that at some time the railway would be built, the only solution would be for Britain to negotiate a deal with the Turks.

Nor were the Turks in an enviable position. Their grip on Mesopotamia and al-Hasa was slipping, and rumours of an imminent British takeover of Basra continued to unnerve the Ottoman establishment. Basra province had entered a state of almost total anarchy. The Banu Lam had come out in revolt and had been blocking communications between Baghdad and Basra for some time.[5] There was also a plague of banditry around Basra itself, by irregulars in the service of various Arab leaders. Mubarak was alleged to be behind some of this, but the accusation appears to have been false. It was Talib Pasha and Sa'dun who were the troublemakers, and Talib was regarded by many Turks as a British agent.[6]

Indeed Mubarak chose not to interfere in Basra affairs at that time. His foremost policy concerns were twofold: how to adapt to the consequences of weakening Ottoman authority in the region, and how to maintain Kuwait's position between threats from the desert and interference by the British political agent in the running of Kuwait. The new situation in the Ottoman Empire certainly caused problems for Mubarak. He was confronted with Ottoman officials of a new kind, ideologues intent on transforming the old imperial patchwork into a modern territorial state. Former contacts such as Abu 'l-Huda had vanished from the scene. That was more a problem for the Naqib and his son Talib than for Mubarak, but Abu 'l-Huda's disappearance none the less deprived Mubarak of a discreet private line to the highest authorities in Constantinople.[7] Mubarak would

---

[3] Heller, *British Policy*, pp. 13–14.
[4] Brünner, *Bagdadspoorweg*, p. 327.
[5] Paris AE, NS Turquie 151, fos. 62–64, Rouet 5 April 1909.
[6] See also the explanation by Crow in Basra and Knox in Bushire in March–April 1909 as to why Mubarak was not really involved in this: IOLR, R/15/5/26, fos. 2–7.
[7] Paris AE, NS Mascate 14, fo. 23v, Rouet 19 August 1908: great joy over the arrest of Ebülhuda, former floor-sweeper of a mosque in Baghdad, and over Talib's problems; Paris AE, NS Turquie 151, fos. 45–46, Rouet 29 December 1908.

be in trouble if the Turks were to revive their old policy of pressure on Kuwait. In such an event he would be more dependent than ever on the British. After 1907 the entente between Russia, France and Britain meant that there was no other power available for him to exploit to manipulate the British. This was especially undesirable in the light of his poor relations with Knox, which added to his anxiety that the British might make an agreement with the Turks behind his back that threatened his autonomy. For the time being Mubarak trod warily, and took care to maintain a friendly attitude towards the Turks.

Strange rumours were doing the rounds that Mubarak and Khaz'al had sent a secret envoy to Constantinople or Western Europe. Already in June 1908, just before the revolution, the Egyptian newspaper *Liwa* reported that an envoy of Khaz'al, Mirza Hamza (administrator of Khaz'al's possessions in Basra), had been sent to London to conspire with the British.[8] Goguyer too reported on 5 December 1908 that Khaz'al had ordered Mirza Hamza to carry out a mission for his friend Mubarak in Constantinople. Mubarak, according to Goguyer, was trying to wriggle out of his too-close ties with the British. However, he scotched this rumour just a week later, reporting that he had just received reliable information that Mirza Hamza was in fact in Paris. Goguyer now wondered who was being deceived by Mirza Hamza: was it Khaz'al or Mubarak, or was it just a ploy to spread disinformation?[9]

Relations between Mubarak and the Turks had been strained once again at the start of 1908. With the permission of the Wali of Basra, Mubarak had in 1904–5 constructed an embankment to reclaim some land in Fao, close to the Ottoman fortress there.[10] The Turks claimed that this weakened their position and demolished the embankment. This insignificant fortress at Fao, which according to a newspaper report had been deserted for quite some time, had been built on land commandeered from the Al-Sabah by the Basra authorities without paying for it.[11] Mubarak let it appear at first

[8] IOLR, R/15/5/62, translation of article in *Liwa* of 25 June 1908.
[9] Nantes AD, consulat Bagdad B29, Goguyer 5 and 12 December 1908.
[10] Bidwell, *Affairs of Arabia*, 1/1, p. 134, acting consul Monahan in Basra 28 January 1905.
[11] *Political Diaries*, Vol. 3, p. 8 (31 December 1908); Rush, *Records of Kuwait*, Vol. 6, pp. 157–83; for a French translation of an article in the Egyptian newspaper *Mu'ayyad* of 31 March concerning the now deserted fortress at Fao which had been constructed in 1890, see Paris AE, NS Mascate 14, fo. 4.

that he expected the British to intervene on his behalf. Knox investigated the affair in detail and produced a complicated report. In the end the British achieved nothing for Mubarak, despite Knox's pile of paperwork. Mubarak took his own steps and settled the matter himself, probably by the payment of suitable *douceurs*, and after some months the Turks raised no objection to the rebuilding of the embankment. Knox complained bitterly how little Mubarak confided in him on this or any other matter. But why should Mubarak have placed his trust in the British?[12]

As we saw in the last chapter, relations between Mubarak and Knox had already been poor before the 1908 revolution in the Ottoman Empire. In 1907, the British vice-consul in Muhammara had warned Knox that Mubarak was casting around for a way to get rid of him.[13] In July 1908 a new flashpoint arose. Mubarak was under constant pressure from the British to apply quarantine regulations in the port of Kuwait. Enforcing such regulations would make Mubarak unpopular with the shipping and trading community in Kuwait, and so he had dragged his heels. When the British insisted, Mubarak retaliated by making trouble for the British India Steam Navigation Company agent in Kuwait, and refusing B.I.S.N.Co. ships permission to carry goods to and from the port. This caused trouble between Mubarak and Bushire. Mubarak was also participating in the founding of an Arab shipping company in Bombay which was clearly intended to compete with the B.I.S.N.Co. A compromise over quarantine was reached, but Mubarak appears to have carried on being lax in applying quarantine regulations, and the dispute flared up again the following year.[14]

[12] Busch, *Britain and the Persian Gulf*, p. 312, also quoting Knox's words of irritation about Mubarak's independent ways.

[13] IOLR, R/15/5/59, pp. 57–9, MacDouall in Muhammara to Knox 27 July 1907. MacDouall had heard that Mubarak had been discussing how to get rid of Knox with some Kuwaitis. One of the methods proposed was said to have been "to smuggle a woman into your house and then say you enticed her". It was said that Jabir opposed this plan, but not Mubarak. Knox, however, did not believe the story. MacDouall often put unverified rumours into circulation, and it may be that Khaz'al or one of his agents spread such stories on Mubarak's behalf to unsettle the British.

[14] IOLR, R/15/5/59, fos. 44–53, correspondence between Knox and Cox August 1908; Berlin AA, R 13890 A 16536 (10 October 1908), German consul Listemann in Bushire 19 September 1908; R 13890 A 17517 (23 October 1908), Listemann 29 September 1908; and R 13890 A 12824 (1 August 1909), Wassmuss, German consul in Bushire, 11 July 1909. On the Arab shipping line, see also Paris AE, NS Mascate 39, fos. 228–229 and 246, French consul in Bombay 25 April and 28 July 1911.

Knox showed his irritation most openly in May 1908 when Mubarak was trying to prevail on the British to make an agreement with Khaz'al similar to the one they had with him. If Khaz'al, with his extensive date groves on the Ottoman side too, were also to be in formal relations with the British, the strategic position of non-Ottomans in the Fao region would be considerably strengthened. Knox was furious with Mubarak for once again pursuing a foreign policy of his own and interfering in Arab affairs. He gave vent to his anger in unusually frank terms, complaining in his report of "Mubarak's usual insolence" towards him. Mubarak's attempts came to naught, just like his efforts on behalf of the Saudis some years previously.[15]

Cox seems to have devolved the irksome aspects of dealing with Mubarak to Knox. In a letter of 14 September, he told the agent that he had not kept in frequent touch with him because communications were slow. He stated that he had submitted all the issues between Mubarak and the agent to the Government of India: the position of the B.I.S.N.Co., the quarantine, the Fao embankment, and the excessive rent Mubarak claimed for Knox's house. It was up to the Government to decide them. In the meantime he assured Knox that he realized the difficulties of his position because "Mubarak is suffering from wind in the head", but that he also had the impression that Knox was "too much infected with the atmosphere of your surroundings". He agreed that "Shaikh Mubarak clearly deserves a set down", but he did not wish Knox to administer this without the explicit permission of India, because he feared that Mubarak "would not take it lying down". In short, Cox understood that Mubarak was boss in Kuwait and that the British were there on his terms unless India opted for a more forcible style of engagement. He urged Knox to try to improve his personal relations with Mubarak, because that was the way to achieve results. He told Knox about his own experiences as agent in Muscat with the Sultan of Oman, but confessed that he appreciated that Mubarak could be somewhat harder to handle, being friendly to the agent in the coffee shop, but then following his own policy in disregard of Knox's opinion.[16]

---

[15] Rush, *Records of Kuwait*, Vol. 6, pp. 647–9, Knox to Cox 17 May 1908.
[16] IOLR, R/15/5/59, fos. 53–57, Cox to Knox 14 September 1908: a long letter in which Cox tried to smooth Knox's ruffled feathers.

Knox was clearly unhappy. He applied for a long leave and continued to communicate his vexation to Cox, uttering dire warnings. In the end he concluded that Mubarak had two political priorities: friendship with the British and his own independence in Kuwait. Knox observed regretfully that if these two priorities came into conflict, Mubarak always opted for the second. He also deplored Khaz'al's bad influence on Mubarak. Khaz'al heaped fulsome praise on his ally, taught him how "to skin his people", and encouraged an extravagant lifestyle.[17]

However, the chief cause of Mubarak's woes at that time was the stricter attitude adopted by the Ottoman authorities towards his efforts to expand his land holdings in Basra province. It was understandable that he should seek new ways of investing his surplus income securely. Kuwait offered few prospects, and its running was partially dependent on income from outside. In the past there had been investment in India, but the conflict with Yusuf Al-Ibrahim had shown how unsafe that could be. The date groves produced a considerable revenue flow and were close at hand. Experience had shown that, while there might be trouble with the Ottoman authorities from time to time, such problems did not stem the flow of income generated.

So Mubarak was continuing to expand his possessions by buying from owners in the district. The Ottoman authorities always took a jaundiced view of such activity, as they watched a large part of the land in the strategic region of the Shatt al-'Arab fall into the hands of Khaz'al and Mubarak, neither of them Ottoman subjects. After a new purchase of land near the Shatt al-'Arab in 1908, they intervened. For the old lands Mubarak held old titles of possession (*hüccet*s or "notarial" deeds of the local *qadi*s) which remained valid. Ownership of the new properties, however, was to be transferred according to the new Ottoman legislation, and the local authorities refused to enter the transfer in the records unless Mubarak formally declared himself to be an Ottoman subject. Progress in this matter was slow and British endeavours to afford Mubarak their "good offices" were feeble at best. Nor did the whole business serve to improve relations between Mubarak and Knox, who was still smarting over the Shuwaikh affair. The matter was left simmering, while Mubarak

[17] IOLR, R/15/5/59, fos. 59–63, Knox to Cox, 6(?) October 1908, also published in Rush, *Ruling Families*, pp. 61–9.

himself tried to negotiate a solution with the Ottoman authorities in Basra.

One of the options considered was to have the new properties registered in the names of family members who would take Ottoman nationality. The least damaging course was for ladies of Mubarak's family, or Mubarak's blind son Nasir, to apply for Ottoman nationality. The British were hesitant about this, and Mubarak himself was clearly unhappy about it.[18] Mubarak's occasional attempts to solve the problem involved excessive friendliness to the Turks, which was bound to arouse British suspicion because it cast doubt on Mubarak's loyalty. This is demonstrated by the graphic description, by the British consul in Basra, of a party given by the attorney of the vendor of the land in question, Abdul Wahab Al-Kirtas (the real seller was Shaikh Ahmad Pasha Al-Zuhair of Zubair), at Saraji near Basra. The Wali attended on the Ottoman warship *Marmaris* and a Turkish military band enhanced the festivities. The host delivered a fulsome encomium on Mubarak, a true Ottoman in the Young Turk sense, who had lavishly contributed to the Ottoman cause despite having been oppressed by corrupt officials of Abdulhamid's regime. He continued with a paean to the Persian Shaikh Khaz'al, also a true Ottoman at heart.[19]

10.2 Capt. Shakespear as political agent in Kuwait

Knox had outlived his usefulness as agent in Kuwait, and had repeatedly asked to be replaced. In April 1909 he was succeeded by Captain Shakespear.[20] The new agent was a man of different stamp, and from Mubarak's perspective considerably more dangerous. Knox was a stiff-backed man, while Shakespear was a good deal more supple. Knox had not shirked outright confrontation with the Ruler, while Shakespear seems occasionally to have gone in for surreptitious intrigue. Shakespear also seems to have been more gullible and easier to manipulate by all parties involved.[21]

---

[18] IOLR, R/15/5/59, fo. 65(95), Lowther 28 February 1909, asserting that there was no prospect of reaching any conclusion over the registration with the new Ottoman Government. Many documents on the affair of the registration of the properties can be found in IOLR, R/15/5/5.

[19] IOLR, R/15/5/5, fos. 71(78)–74(81), Crow 9 March 1910.

[20] *Political Diaries*, Vol. 3, p. 608 (28 April 1909).

There was little change in the agency's position in Kuwait. As hitherto Mubarak pointedly excluded the agent from the running of Kuwait, and Shakespear's role was confined to acting as messenger between Mubarak and Bushire, as self-appointed informal adviser, and as information-gatherer on the informal circuit. As Mubarak had little use for the agent's advice in his private schemes, and as communications between Bushire and Kuwait were limited, Shakespear's time was chiefly occupied by information-gathering. In Knox's time this had caused the function of agent to become essentially that of a diplomatic representative, who notified Mubarak of Britain's views while being unable to interfere in internal matters. Colonial soldiers were somewhat unfitted for such a role. Shakespear was unable to expand his very limited activity, but there is some evidence that he made better use than Knox of his informal contacts, especially among the big pearl merchants who had connections in Bahrain and India, and so were close to the British. His reports certainly reflect the pearl merchants' dissatisfaction with Mubarak's style of rule, of which they had grown critical because of the harm done to their interests by his fiscal policy. Knox too could be said to have made the same points, but Shakespear went a step further in that he seems not to have been averse to a little manipulation of the opposition.

From the standpoint of modern social institutions, the pearling economy, riddled as it was with debt and exploitation, was in disarray. But the emerging political structures were not yet capable of a remedy. Attempts at reform were doomed because the administration was too weak to impose new measures; alternatively, if reforms were too rigorously applied, they might harm the economy. Mubarak, as we have seen at the end of the previous chapter, did on the one hand try to instigate some reforms, if vainly, and, on the other, try to increase taxes for his own purposes. None of this served to increase his popularity among those involved in pearling.[22]

---

[21] As we have seen Knox came into open conflict with Mubarak, for example over Mubarak's expedition against the Turuf subjects of Khaz'al. Such conflicts do not occur in Shakespear's time. We cannot share Winstone's judgement in his biography, *Captain Shakespear*, p. 68.

[22] *Political Diaries*, Vol. 3, pp. 62, 169, 281. In 1908 Mubarak tried other ways too to increase revenues, levying taxes on shops and shipbuilding and increasing some customs duties: ibid., pp. 49, 208, 214. At the same time Mubarak put his son Jabir in charge of finances: ibid., p. 190. This may have to do with complaints about Mubarak's officials: ibid., pp. 224–5.

Mubarak's intervention in the pearling economy was but one element in Kuwait's evolution after 1906. His government became more active, not only in its external efforts to preserve Kuwait's autonomy, but also in its more direct concern for the well-being of the people. This is shown by his attempt to make pearl divers less dependent on their employers, a measure regarded by Knox as too crude to succeed. The same concern is revealed by his efforts to improve Kuwait harbour, medical care and the supply of fresh water.[23] Mubarak's endeavour to improve the lot of the pearl divers does not appear to have been in isolation, in the light of a Baghdad newspaper report of a threat by the great pearl entrepreneurs on Bahrain to leave that place, on the grounds that the British political agent there wanted to protect the interests of the divers.[24] Mubarak also played a part in the funding of the first school to be opened in Kuwait.[25]

The new initiatives were observed and neutrally reported by the political agent. Occasionally he voiced a criticism, but he was not much involved in such developments, as is illustrated by events following Mubarak's growing interest in health care. In the past, doctors and dentists from Baghdad had from time to time visited Kuwait. An Indian "assistant-surgeon" was employed at the agency primarily to maintain proper quarantine regulations during these times of serious epidemics, but this official also gave some primary medical care. The assistant-surgeon was far from being a qualified doctor, his skills tracing their lineage from those of the blood-letting barbers of the 18th century. Clearly something better was needed, and this was offered by the missionary society of the Dutch

[23] *Political Diaries*, Vol. 3, p. 428, January 1909: terminal for a steamship to bring water; ibid., p. 162, April–May 1908: an attempt at a social policy regarding pearl divers; ibid., Vol. 4, p. 292, November–December 1910: sale of land for the American hospital (soon there was one doctor and a lady doctor: ibid., Vol. 4, p. 490, January 1912). In 1913 an attempt was made to organize Islamic medical care, but according to Shakespear this attempt soon ran into trouble: ibid., Vol. 5, p. 54 of March 1913 and p. 285 of October 1913.

[24] Paris AE, NS Mascate 39, fo. 220, translation of an article in the newspaper *Zohur* of 29 March 1911. On the social problems in the pearling economy, see Villiers, *Sons of Sindbad*, p. 303.

[25] *Political Diaries*, Vol. 4, pp. 457–8 (October–November 1911). Ottoman statistics of Basra province in the early 1890s, published by Cuinet, report the presence of schools in Kuwait in the 1890s, but such statistics are fanciful paper exercises of no value. See Cuinet, *Turquie*, pp. 273–6.

Reformed Church of America, which since 1892 had been sending out medically trained personnel to Arabia, more to present a positive face of Christianity than for the hopeless task of converting the population. Such missionaries had occasionally visited Kuwait and wanted to establish a small hospital there, as it was rapidly becoming one of the most important economic centres in the Gulf. The British looked with disfavour on foreigners settling in Kuwait, and Mubarak seems to have contacted the Americans without consulting the British agent about it. After that the Americans made an agreement with the British undertaking not to embroil the latter in any future disputes with the Kuwaitis.[26] At about the same time Mubarak also invited an Arab doctor to set up in Kuwait, but that gentleman performed poorly and soon disappeared again.

10.3 War with the Muntafiq, 1910–11

Relations between Sa'dun and Mubarak had been deteriorating since the aborted land sale of 1907. Early in 1910 the Muntafiq and 'Ajman had conducted raids in the territory of tribes loyal to Mubarak. The Muntafiq retired speedily and returned half of their spoils, but already by that time preparations were in hand for a general campaign by the Saudis and Mubarak against Sa'dun. Abdul Aziz Al-Saud himself had visited Kuwait in March 1910 as part of those preparations – relations seem to have recovered since the quarrel of 1908. The strong Saudi interest suggests that the expedition was at least as much a Saudi as a Kuwaiti project. Mubarak called a council of prominent Kuwaitis. The meeting decided in favour of a great expedition against Sa'dun and the levying of special taxes.[27] Initially the plan was for Mubarak himself to lead a combined Kuwaiti-Saudi force against the Muntafiq. In the end, however, the Kuwaiti force was commanded not by Mubarak, who was elderly and in poor health, but by

[26] Rush, *Records of Kuwait*, Vol. 7, pp. 702–3, Kuwait Diary, January 1910.
[27] Many British documents on this war are to be found in IOLR, R/15/5/26. See also *Political Diaries*, pp. 23, 42–3; and Berlin AA, R 13891 A 7328 (28 April 1910), a report by Hesse, German consul in Baghdad, of 6 April 1910, quoting from Baghdad newspapers that a raid by Sa'dun against a tribe subordinate to Mubarak, sparked by the capture of a falcon belonging to one of his relatives, was at the root of the conflict. See also a French report, which also gives detailed information on Sa'dun's activities at that time, in Paris AE, NS Turquie 152, fos. 25–29, Wiet 21 February 1911.

his eldest son Jabir. The timing was not especially auspicious, as the Saudis had been considerably weakened by the poor harvests of previous seasons, and when the allies encountered Sa'dun's unexpectedly large force near Zubair they suffered a crushing defeat. Shakespear observes that the Kuwaiti forces fought rather badly and that the campaign was unpopular in Kuwait.[28] In the event it seems to have been a matter of an army demoralized beforehand in the face of superior odds, and as a result losses were not too heavy.

The defeat was a setback, but not a disaster. Mubarak, probably believing Sa'dun incapable of keeping a body of men together for long, immediately began preparing an even larger force. He postponed preparations for the pearling season until half way through May, when the approaching summer could be counted on to ward off Sa'dun. During the summer months, nonetheless, Mubarak kept a considerable force in readiness while his raiding parties went marauding in the desert. In August Sa'dun was reported to have moved to the neighbourhood of Zubair, amidst rumours that he had the support of the Wali of Basra.[29]

Then, all of a sudden, Mubarak's attention was distracted by an internal crisis, as opposition to his policy flared into the open. It is difficult to assess the true character of the challenge because the only explicit documentary source on it is the writings of the British political agent. As Shakespear describes it, open dissent was fuelled by discontent over the Shaikh's financial or military demands. At times when his relations with Mubarak were bad, the agent described Mubarak as a ruler who laid heavy charges on Kuwait's population to pay for his over-ambitious military adventures against Sa'dun. Discontent there undoubtedly was, but there is no hint in Shakespear's reports or diaries of a consistent opposition movement. No alternative political programme is mentioned, and some kind of action against Sa'dun apparently found general support in Kuwait.

From such scarce and one-sided source material it is difficult to characterize the opposition to Mubarak with any precision. Thus far three

[28] IOLR, R/15/1/478, Kuwait Diary 20 March, and letter of Shakespear to the Resident 30 March 1910. The question remains whether the unpopularity was general or just prevalent among Shakespear's merchant cronies. One important Kuwaiti pearl merchant in Bombay, by contrast, was strongly supportive of Mubarak: see *Political Diaries*, 1910, p. 62.

[29] *Political Diaries*, 1910, pp. 159–60.

types of opposition had manifested themselves at different times. The first
had emanated from Mubarak's nephews, Yusuf Al-Ibrahim and their
adherents. There is no sign of this extending beyond a family dispute over
capital, and it had evaporated by 1908. Conservative Islamic elements,
which in Western sources are referred to, probably too generally, as
Wahhabi, constituted another potential type of opposition. Their
disapproval could be aroused by the presence of Westerners. Assessments of
the importance of this type of opposition are somewhat contradictory.[30]

The third and strongest opposition to Mubarak's policy came from
merchants and ship-owners who, possessing considerable amounts of ready
cash, were a logical primary target for taxation. But this business
community cannot have formed a united front against Mubarak, because
there were also aspects of his policy that were to its direct benefit.
Merchants and ship-owners were protected, for example, by his reluctance
to allow European merchants into Kuwait. His careful handling of the
Turks made it possible for Kuwaiti trade with Ottoman territory to
continue. And his turning a blind eye to the arms trade was greatly to their
advantage. Against this, prominent pearl merchants had reasons to be
unhappy with Mubarak. He had been putting them under financial
pressure, and his military expeditions against Sa'dun seriously interfered
with the pearling season in the summer of 1910, which is when the
discontent burst into the open.

The best description of the events is to be found in Rushaid's *History
of Kuwait*. While Shakespear's reports and diaries present an outsider's
view, he seems not to have been an entirely neutral observer.[31] According
to Rushaid, who mentioned that he had the story from one of Mubarak's
chief opponents, there was an outcry when Mubarak held the pearling
fleet back in Kuwait. Mubarak told the merchants that he was keeping it
back to deter Sa'dun, and he was able to reach a compromise with most
of them, who promised to pay money so that Mubarak could recruit other
troops. Three *tawwash*es, the big entrepreneurs in pearl diving, refused to
be won over even in the face of Mubarak's threats. These were Rushaid's

[30] IOLR, R/15/1/477, fo. 69, Gaskin 12 March 1904, mentioning Zwemer's
complaints about a strong anti-Western current in Kuwait; and Goguyer, quoted by
Rouet in Paris AE, NS Mascate 11, fo. 38.
[31] Rushaid, *Tarikh*, Vol. 2, pp. 104–11. The reports of Shakespear in Rush, *Records of
Kuwait*, Vol. 1, 543–561.

informant Shamlan bin Saif, Ibrahim bin Mudaf and Hilal Umtayri. These three decided to leave Kuwait, Hilal going to Bahrain and the other two to Qatar. The Shaikh of Qatar was delighted with his competitor's troubles and welcomed the wealthy merchants with open arms.

The historian Husayn Khaz'al tells a story very similar to Rushaid's. According to him, Hilal met with the British agent in Bahrain and with Shakespear, who coincidentally happened to be on a private visit to the island.[32] Khaz'al states that the British promised Hilal every assistance. Mubarak now saw that the affair was taking an ominous turn, and decided to try for a reconciliation as quickly as possible. His first emissaries were turned away by Hilal, and he then sent his son Salim. Salim managed to reconcile Ibrahim, who thereupon returned to Kuwait. Shamlan was also ready in principle to bury the hatchet, but was unwilling to abandon his ally Hilal. The latter blamed the quarrel on Mubarak's corrupt advisers.[33] This factor in the conflict has perhaps been overlooked by historians, for it points up an important and recurring element in Kuwait's evolving modernization: the difficulty of creating an honest and efficient administration under the Ruler. This was no easy problem to solve in a region where extreme corruption and inefficiency were the traditional norm among government officials, whether in the Ottoman provinces of Mesopotamia or in Persia. Both had enjoyed an extremely low reputation in this respect from the 16th century onwards.

Ibrahim's desertion broke the opposition front, but Hilal remained adamant, even, according to Shakespear, going rather too far in writing injudicious letters to Mubarak. Then Mubarak, who was always ready to swallow his pride when circumstances demanded, himself wrote to the Ruler of Bahrain and to Hilal personally in a most conciliatory tone, and this brought the affair to an end.[34]

British reports give the affair considerable prominence, but no mention of it has been found in the Ottoman archives or in the reports of other

[32] For the story of the pearl merchants, see Husayn Khaz'al, *Tarikh,* Vol. 2, pp. 280–6. *Political Diaries,* Vol. 4, p. 194, gives Shakespear's version, in which he claims that the report of his involvement had "of course" no foundation.

[33] The two advisers are identified in Shakespear's diary, *Political Diaries,* Vol. 4, p. 194 (August–September 1910): Abdallah bin Hajri and Yusuf bin Munis. This mention may be evidence that Shakespear was in Hilal's confidence.

[34] Rush, *Records of Kuwait,* Vol. 1, p. 560, Shakespear to Mackenzie 4 October 1910. The letter is published in Husayn Khaz'al, *Tarikh,* Vol. 2, p. 286.

European consuls. This is remarkable, considering that it could have afforded the Turks a good opportunity to meddle. It seems that the *tawwash*es had moved with discretion, while taking good care to keep the British agencies in Kuwait and Bahrain well-informed. It looks rather as if these gentlemen, with their strong business ties with India, were hoping for British support for their case. This was not unrealistic, as the British had no sympathy for Mubarak's Arab policies and desert adventures. One may thus legitimately ask whether the *tawwash*es' action was limited to their business interests, or whether there was a political dimension. This would not have included any sympathy for Sa'dun in Kuwait, for which there is no evidence. But it certainly did amount to a move to stop Mubarak letting his political priorities weigh too heavily on one particular sector of the Kuwaiti economy. One should bear in mind that, while during his career Sa'dun had made himself unpopular with everybody in the region, Mubarak's quarrel with him may at least partly have been also a business conflict between two wealthy landowners in Basra province, and the Kuwaitis might justifiably feel disengaged from that aspect of it.[35]

The other puzzling aspect of the *tawwash* affair is the rapid dissolution of the trio, who themselves in any case constituted a tiny minority in the larger class of *tawwash*es. Was it a case of Mubarak once again promptly and astutely bribing part of the opposition, or did they have different interests and motives from the start? Possibly Hilal had more profound reasons than

[35] The whole affair has been described in somewhat over-dramatic terms by Salwa Al-Ghanim, *Mubarak*, pp. 146–7. She regards the event as an attempt by the *tawwash*es to bring about a tribal split, a massive emigration, just as the Al-Khalifa and their adherents had done in the 18th century. She also stresses the *tawwash*es' great courage in taking this risk, because they left their families and houses at the mercy of the despotic Mubarak. This well may be true, but there is no support for it in the documentary sources. The entries in the *Kuwait Diary* and the reports of the agent show discontent with Mubarak, but the affair was conducted in a more low-key fashion than Salwa Al-Ghanim's hypothesis would demand: a quiet departure, followed almost immediately by Mubarak's effort to reach a compromise. Mubarak may have been an autocrat, but it is probable that in matters such as these his freedom of action was much more circumscribed by family members and local notables than it was in matters of international policy. That the *tawwash*es risked the safety of their families is an allegation based on a personal view of Mubarak's character, and cannot even be supported by the words of the most extreme of the trio, who feared only for his own personal safety on his return. Taking revenge on harmless family members was an Ottoman, not an Arab, habit.

the others to feel aggrieved by Mubarak and his officials. The latter may well have been the case, but even so a compromise was reached in the end.

The outcome of the dispute remains as vague as the background to it. The sources simply state that Mubarak promised to do the three no harm or dishonour when they returned. Did the three extract any substantial concessions from Mubarak? No word of this can be found in Shakespear's reports or diaries. Possibly, however, we should read these papers with an eye for what is not in them: there are no further reports of charges on the pearling economy. This is an *argumentum e silentio*, to be sure, but it is a compelling one. Interesting too is that the British, while well-informed about the crisis, were never really called in by any of the parties. During it Shakespear had two vague talks on the issue with Mubarak, who took care to appear as relaxed as possible about the whole business and not in the least vindictive. Shakespear reported that Mubarak at first suspected him of involvement because of the timing of his trip to Bahrain, but that he had been able to allay his suspicion.[36] The matter was a setback for Mubarak, but the old man was never too old to learn, and in the years that followed he pursued a less controversial policy towards the pearling economy.

Reconciliation with the *tawwash*es did not mean that the conflict with Sa'dun had blown over, and Mubarak began new preparations for war during the last months of 1910. Sa'dun had some ongoing difficulties with the Turks,[37] but these were soon resolved and he became a prime favourite with the Young Turk administration in Iraq. This made him more of a threat to Mubarak than ever. The Turks had decided that the best way to keep the troubled Basra province under control was an alliance with Sa'dun and Talib Pasha. Both could be powerful allies. Unlike Mubarak or Khaz'al they had their power base inside imperial territory and so were easier to manage than the two other big landowners, who were based outside it. Talib was the most powerful man in the town of Basra, but he was weak in the countryside around. Sa'dun was powerful in the countryside, but needed Ottoman support against his adversaries. It suited Talib to have a Wali of Basra who went along with his control of the city.[38]

Manipulation of the local balance of power in Basra province may not have been the only reason for the tripartite alliance between the Turks, Sa'dun and Talib. The Young Turk administration was less complaisant than

[36] Rush, *Records of Kuwait*, Vol. 1, p. 557, Shakespear to Mackenzie 12 September 1910.
[37] *Political Diaries*, Vol. 4, p. 291 (November–December 1910).

Abdulhamid towards Mubarak's relations with the British, who they feared might try to consolidate their interest in Lower Mesopotamia. They were strengthened in that view because their attempt to punish Khaz'al for his interference in Basra province had failed in the face of British opposition.[39]

Reports of relations between Mubarak and the Ottoman authorities in Basra at that time are contradictory. Shakespear, who was just then experiencing difficulties in Kuwait and hence may not have been well informed, reported excellent relations between Mubarak and the Wali of Basra. He even noted Kuwaiti rumours of Mubarak being ready to accept an Ottoman garrison in Kuwait as protection against Sa'dun, and of him having been appointed to the lucrative position of *mütesarrif* (governor) of the *sancak* of Najd, the official Ottoman term for al-Hasa.[40] All this seems to derive from a friendly meeting between Mubarak and the Wali. The German consul in Bushire was less impressed by the news. He reported pressure by Cox on Mubarak to be less pro-Turkish, but rather thought that "the sly old fox" was just playing the British off against the Turks to increase his importance to both parties at a time when the railway seemed to be at last in prospect.[41] In the late summer of 1910 the Porte modified

[38] Berlin AA, R 13871 A 17170 (15 October 1910), German consul in Baghdad 19 September 1910. In the autumn of 1910, Suleyman Nazif Bey, the Wali of Basra who was hostile to Talib, was recalled. This report also mentions the involvement of Talib in banditry, which is confirmed by reports of the French consul in Baghdad: Rouet Paris AE, NS Turquie 151, fos. 45–46 (28 and 29 December 1908). On fo. 46 occurs the remark: "In this town [Basra] the population speaks only with fear about the deeds of this *'condottiere'* [a term used of the notorious mercenary commanders in the bloody wars of 15th–16th-century Italy] who moves around surrounded by hired killers armed to the teeth."

[39] Berlin AA, R 13871 A 10980 (25 June 1910), Hesse in Baghdad 30 May 1910; R 13891 A 13840 (13 August 1910), Listemann in Bushire 23 July 1910.

[40] Rush, *Records of Kuwait*, Vol. 2, pp. 331–5. In May 1910, the German consul in Baghdad was already reporting that Mubarak's relations with the British were so bad that he was looking to the Ottomans to protect him against them: Berlin AA, R 13891 A 10572 (18 June 1910), Hesse 16 May 1910.

[41] Berlin AA, R 13891 A 11434 (3 July 1910), Listemann in Bushire 11 June 1910. This offers a rather interesting view in comparison with Cox's note on a meeting with Mubarak of 12 August 1910 in IOLR, R/15/5/59, fo. 67 (97)–70(100). Here Cox started a discussion with Mubarak on whether to make the relations between Mubarak and the British more public, in which Mubarak described attempts by the Wali to bring him over to the Turkish side.

its policy again. The Wali of Basra, Suleyman Nazif Pasha, was removed, apparently because of his bad relations with Talib.[42] But the Turks maintained their policy towards Mubarak, who stayed on his best behaviour. There came news, probably true this time, that the payment of a subsidy to Mubarak was to be resumed, but that he had refused it.[43]

The Turks none the less continued to regard Mubarak's properties on the Shatt al-'Arab as a danger to the strategic border province of Basra for as long as Mubarak refused to register as an Ottoman national, while Mubarak remained angry with the Turks over the land registry issue.[44] Sa'dun was easier to control and it would be good if he could be detached from his supposed allegiance to the British.[45] In the autumn of 1910, Sa'dun made an official visit to Baghdad and reached a reconciliation with its Wali, Nadhim Pasha. He was recognized as principal Shaikh of the Muntafiq and obtained the dignity of *mütesarrif* of the Muntafiq sub-province.[46] Finally Sa'dun had achieved the position among the Muntafiq he had aspired to for so many years. But Ottoman policy towards Sa'dun had its disadvantages. It represented a break with the former policy of controlling the Muntafiq through the settled portion of the tribe. Sa'dun's power base was narrow. He could levy a large army of tribesmen, but discord among the Muntafiq always loomed. Worse still, Sa'dun was a most unreliable character.

In the winter came rumours that he was preparing for war against Mubarak.[47] Now the Turks tried to intervene as mediators.[48] Mubarak was

[42] Berlin AA, R 13871 A 17170 (15 October 1910), Consul Hesse in Baghdad 19 September 1910. The Wali was in dispute with Talib over the latter's involvement in banditry.

[43] IOLR, R/15/5/5, fos. 273 (250)–274 (251), Wali of Basra to Mubarak, with reply of October 1910.

[44] Berlin AA, R 13871 A 19989 (2 December 1910), German Consul in Baghdad 6 November 1910.

[45] Talib had a quarrel with the Wali of Basra over the involvement one of Talib's men's in a robbery. The Wali threw a chair at Talib's head, and was dismissed shortly after: Berlin AA, R 13871 A 17170 (15 October 1910), Consul in Baghdad 19 September 1910.

[46] Berlin AA, R 13871 A 19989 (2 December 1910), Consul in Baghdad 6 November 1910. In the French-inspired Ottoman regional administration, a *mütesarrif* is the chief of a *sancak*, one rank above a *kaymakam*, chief of a *kaza*. See also Paris AE, NS Mascate 14, fo. 193: French ambassador in Turkey to Minister 16 November 1910.

[47] *Political Diaries*, Vol. 4, p. 324 (December 1910–January 1911).

[48] *Political Diaries*, Vol. 4, p. 337 (January–February 1911).

well-connected in Baghdad, where his agent Mansur bin Sulayman Al-Salih is mentioned as a member of the local council, and knowledge of Sa'dun's standing with the Turks may well have influenced his handling of the situation. In Baghdad it was thought that in the autumn of 1910 Mubarak had been trying to form a general coalition of Arab tribes, comprising the Saudis, Khaz'al and the Muntafiq; it was for that purpose that he had initiated peace negotiations with Sa'dun. The Turks felt this to be a threat, especially in the light of close British ties with Khaz'al, and they had been pressing Sa'dun to adopt a hostile attitude towards Mubarak.[49]

Isma'il Hakki Babanzade, a Kurdish member of parliament for Baghdad, wrote a series of articles in the newspaper *Tanin* containing dire warnings about the decline of Ottoman authority in Iraq and the danger of a British takeover. Hakki's theme was that Britain, by means of Khaz'al and Mubarak, was encircling Basra province in a ring of steel. These articles attracted much attention in Europe. Hakki shared the usual distorted Ottoman view of British aims. One article accused "the nominal *kaza*" of Kuwait of being the focal point of the British imperial plot, and his advice was that discreet efforts should be made once again to bring Kuwait under Ottoman authority.[50]

His preparations complete, Sa'dun began a new offensive against Kuwait, with the reputed intention of attacking Jahra and Kuwait City while Mubarak was assembling a new army. Mubarak claimed, to the British, that Sa'dun had Nadhim Pasha's blessing for this attack. According to him, the Turks perceived an opportunity to impose their arbitration between Kuwait and the Muntafiq should Sa'dun succeed. Shakespear for once felt that Mubarak had sound arguments for this suspicion. He judged Mubarak's behaviour to be exemplary in its lack of provocation, and was much impressed by some correspondence with the Wali of Basra that Mubarak showed him. This expressed the Turks' eagerness to mediate and so to increase their hold over Kuwait. Shakespear then wrote to Bushire that "nearly every one of Shaikh Mubarak's difficulties has its origins in

[49] On this agent, see Berlin AA, R13867 A 12894 (18 August), Richarz 25 July 1906.
[50] Vienna HHSA, PA 12 K, 1 F (5 January 1911), report of the Austrian ambassador in Constantinople, where the part of the article about Kuwait attracts special comment. See also Berlin AA, R 13871 A 45–46, reports from the German embassy in Pera (Constantinople), 29 and 30 December 1910.

Turkish intrigues".[51] The British seriously feared that Sa'dun might try to conquer Kuwait. Mubarak did not appear unduly worried about this, according to Shakespear, because he was putting on a brave face. This would have been somewhat out of character, for when Ibn Rashid and the Turks were at their most dangerous in 1901 he had successfully obtained British assistance by a great display of alarm. It may well be that the inexperienced Shakespear was exaggerating the Muntafiq peril. Sa'dun might occasionally be able to parade hordes of warriors in the field, but his power was notoriously unstable and his economic means slight.

The danger to Mubarak blew over by itself. By the beginning of 1911, the Turks were growing disenchanted with Sa'dun and were having to use military means to force the Muntafiq to pay taxes. Sa'dun moreover wanted the Wali of Baghdad to help him in his conflict with Mubarak or at least allow him to take action on his own, but Nadhim Pasha had come under pressure since Hakki's newspaper attacks in the *Tanin*, and above all wanted peace in the province. Sa'dun presented himself to the Baghdad press as a victim, through Mubarak, of British intrigues, but to little effect.[52] In January Shakespear was still much exercised by Sa'dun's movements, but his anxieties seem, as so often in this affair, to be inflated. Very soon, in February, Sa'dun concluded a peace with Mubarak, allegedly mediated by the Turks.[53]

Mubarak's relations with the Turks rapidly improved, while Sa'dun got into serious trouble, embroiling himself in a fierce tribal conflict with the Dhafir at whose hands he suffered a crushing defeat in March 1911. When he tried to resume the initiative he was attacked by more tribes, while Mubarak was said by the French consul in Baghdad to support the Dhafir. Sa'dun's enemies complained about him to the Ottoman authorities, and in July the Wali of Basra treacherously arrested him with the help of Talib.[54]

---

[51] IOLR, R/15/5/26, fos. 117–118, Shakespear 18 January 1911.

[52] Paris AE, NS Turquie 152 (Bagdad), fos. 25–29, Wiet, consul in Baghdad to minister, with translations of Baghdad newspaper articles concerning the conflict between Mubarak and Sa'dun.

[53] *Political Diaries*, Vol. 4, pp. 323–4 (December 1910–January 1911) and 337 (January–February 1911). Sa'dun already had tax problems by the end of 1910: ibid., p. 292 (November–December 1910).

[54] Berlin AA, R 13873 A 13619 (28 August 1911), German consul in Baghdad 3 August 1911; Paris AE, NS Turquie 152 (Baghdad), fos. 71–71 *bis*, 72, 79, Wiet, consul in Baghdad, to minister, 5, 17 and 28 July 1911.

He was transported to Syria and died there.[55] His son and successor 'Ajaimi was troublesome to the Turks on occasion, but never to Mubarak. Hence, early in 1911, Nadhim Pasha's policy of controlling Basra province through an alliance with the Muntafiq and Talib was abandoned.

The decline of the Muntafiq gave Mubarak a breathing space. The alliance against the Muntafiq had improved his relations with the Saudis. His policy swung away from the British towards the Turks – after all it had been the Turks and not the British who had in the end removed the Muntafiq menace. Strange rumours about Mubarak went the rounds in Baghdad. Hesse, the German consul there, reported that "this sly fox, who has always been able to exploit his double status as Ottoman subject and British protégé, is said now to be against the British and to be trying to create a general coalition of all Arab rulers in a similar position, from Oman to Najd, including Bahrain and Muhammara."[56] Once again the spectre of an Arab federation was raising its head. This was in all probability just wild speculation among the Turks in Baghdad, but it cannot be denied that Mubarak had an anti-British air about him. The German consul in Bushire reported that he had planted a large Ottoman flag in front of the customs building, had sabotaged the British quarantine regulations, was smuggling arms, and was supporting an Arab shipping line to rival the British one.[57]

10.4 Negotiations over the Railway and Kuwait's status

The frequently expressed fears of the Young Turks about British intentions in Iraq gave new impetus to the Baghdad Railway project. Communications between Constantinople and Iraq could only improve when the railway became a reality. In 1910 the project made considerable progress. The British had underestimated the Germans. German engineers had contrived to forge a railway through the Cilician Gates, those formidable passes through the Taurus mountains in Eastern Anatolia familiar to every European schoolboy classicist from his reading of Xenophon's *Anabasis*, the first ancient Greek author in the curriculum. Colossal viaducts had been constructed and the remaining route was over

---

[55] Berlin AA, R 13873 A 16028, German consul in Aleppo 28 September 1911.
[56] Berlin AA, R 13873 A 14257, Hesse in Baghdad 14 August 1911.
[57] Berlin AA, R 13873 A 15439, Consulate Bushire 4 September 1911.

comparatively easy terrain. The Germans also appeared to have devised a way to finance the railway to Baghdad.

In 1910 the Anatolian Railroad Company sent an English engineer, Money, to explore the route for the railway down to the Gulf. He came to Kuwait where he was interrogated by Shakespear.[58] Loud alarm bells rang in India. Once again the three possible locations for the terminus on the Gulf came under the spotlight. The choice was still between Basra, the Khor Abdallah at Umm Qasr, or some point on the Gulf of Kuwait. Basra was technically feasible, but strong currents and the ever-shifting bar would make it very costly to maintain a sufficiently deep shipping channel to the Gulf. For the same reason the Khor Abdallah was not as attractive as previously thought, and it would be difficult to build port facilities in such an isolated and inaccessible spot. In Kuwait the choice was between Kazima (unattractive due to lack of water), Kuwait City or Shuwaikh. Shakespear had been intrigued to note that the railway planners were not as yet aware of the potential of Shuwaikh, the best site, which was already occupied by the British – with, as we saw in Chapter 9, a neat little enclave reserved by Mubarak himself.

By the end of 1910, the British had come to the conclusion that the Baghdad Railway again demanded top priority. The preliminary agreement of 1907 between Russia and Germany took concrete shape in 1911 and eliminated Russian opposition to the railway.[59] It was obvious that the project might imperil Britain's geopolitical pre-eminence in the Indian Ocean. The Ottomans then hinted at a willingness to make concessions to the British in the matter of the control of the section to the Gulf. Babington-Smith, the man in charge of the British side of the railway negotiations, met with the Grand Vizier, Hakki Pasha, on 29 December 1910. Hakki took a vaguely conciliatory stance on the railway issue while bitterly deploring the British attitude to Turkey's claim to sovereignty over Kuwait:

> Hakki Pasha said that the question of Koweit was at the root of Turkish feeling about British action in that part of the world. On this subject he spoke quite strongly. He said that he regarded it as beyond doubt that British action in relation to Koweit had been unjust. Under British

[58] Rush, *Records of Kuwait*, pp. 442–4, Shakespear to Cox 13 April 1910.
[59] Brünner, *Bagdadspoorweg*, p. 327; Busch, *Britain and the Persian Gulf*, p. 322.

protection although there was not a protectorate in the technical sense of
the word, Kuwait was the centre of the contraband arms traffic, and a
source of continual conflict with its neighbours. So long as this
anomalous state of affairs existed it was impossible to restore peace and
order in that part of the world. Koweit was like a thorn stuck in the side
of Turkey; and it was British action there more than anywhere else that
had created suspicions of British aims in Mesopotamia.

Babington-Smith weakly parried these allegations by stating that "the
British action regarding Koweit was not directed against Turkey, but against
the possibility of Koweit falling into other hands." This was a paraphrase
of Godley's old adage that Britain did not want Kuwait, nor did she want
anyone else to have it.[60] The Grand Vizier had a ready answer: he offered
an undertaking of some kind that no power other than Britain would be
allowed to construct a naval station in Ottoman Kuwait. In his letter to the
Foreign Office, Babington-Smith argued that he did not see why the
British should not "give the Turks some satisfaction regarding Kuwait",
were Britain to receive from the Turks a binding engagement that it would
not be given to another power.[61]

Marling, who as chargé d'affaires in the winter of 1910–11 had
temporarily replaced Lowther in Constantinople, wrote a lengthy
commentary on Babington-Smith's meeting with the Grand Vizier. He
believed Hakki Pasha to have been influenced by Isma'il Hakki
Babanzade's articles in the Constantinople newspaper *Tanin*, but he could
imagine that the Turks might be contemplating serious negotiations were
there to be a linkage between the railway project and the issue of
sovereignty over Kuwait. Using somewhat different wording, Marling
sharpened Babington-Smith's suggestions, making them even more
dangerous to Kuwait:

> It is quite possible that if that question [i.e. the railway] and that of
> Koweit were treated together we should find a genuine and effective
> desire on the part of the Turks to come to an agreement. The prospect of
> gaining something at Koweit would be a powerful inducement to them
> to obtain from the Germans the latitude requisite for them to satisfy our

[60] Busch, "Britain and the Status of Kuwait", p. 196.
[61] IOLR, R/15/1/610, fos. 16–17, Babington-Smith to Arthur Nicolson 30 December 1910.

requirements in the railway question. It should be remembered that the main object in view when, eleven years ago, we entered relations with Sheikh Mubarak was to prevent the Baghdad Railway from reaching the shores of the Gulf, except under conditions consonant with our interests, and I venture to suggest that it is worth while considering whether the moment is not now approaching when we should endeavour to turn our acquired position at Koweit to account, and whether, if we do not now seize the opportunity, we may not eventually find that we have saddled ourselves with responsibilities towards the Sheikh involving us in particularly thorny questions vis-à-vis of the Turks, without having reaped commensurate advantage.

Marling would have liked to use Kuwait as a bargaining counter for concessions to the Turks, but he grasped that he did not live in an ideal world in which British diplomats could do as they liked: "We have, unfortunately, if I may say so, been led into such intimate relations with him [Mubarak] that it would be impossible for us, with the examples of Albania and Macedonia before us, to abandon him to the tender mercies of the Turks; the loss of reputation to us both in Arabia and Persia would be immense …"[62]

Foreign Secretary Grey appreciated that, were he to make too many concessions over Kuwait, he would be exposed to opposition from India that would find vocal expression in the press, just as in 1903. He may have hoped to obtain some concessions from the Turks in view of Britain's recent support for the Porte over such thorny issues as Bosnia and Bulgarian independence.[63] He made his view clear that Britain should await an Ottoman overture so as not to appear the supplicant party. A good idea of his was to introduce, as a bargaining counter in the negotiations, the matter of British permission for the raising of Ottoman customs duties.[64] This would reduce the chances of Britain finding itself forced to make unavoidable concessions over Kuwait itself. The Foreign Office then took a remarkable step. It had not yet fully penetrated the official mind that references to Ottoman sovereignty over Kuwait would be

[62] IOLR, R/15/1/610, fos. 17v–18, Marling to Grey 4 January 1911.
[63] Translation of an article in the *Ikdam* newspaper of Constantinople, enclosed with a letter of Lowther to Grey of 15 February 1911: IOLR, R/15/1/610, fo. 52(62).
[64] IOLR, R/15/1/610, fos. 18v(24v)–19(25), Mallet, head of the Eastern Department of the Foreign Office, to India Office 16 January 1911.

misconstrued. British officials might intend some kind of lofty but nebulous and purely nominal authority, but to most other people sovereignty meant "primary real authority, not to be limited unless by formal international agreements". It is no wonder that eyebrows were raised when Grey announced, to the Russian and French ambassadors, that Britain was ready to recognize Ottoman sovereignty over Kuwait, on condition that the Turks respected the status quo.[65]

Lowther meanwhile had taken over again in Constantinople. He was a realist with no high opinion of the Turks, and was politely critical of Grey's offer to recognize Ottoman "sovereignty or suzerainty" (a wise modification) provided the territorial status quo in Kuwait were respected. He argued that Kuwait's boundaries had become undefined since the days of Namiq Pasha and Midhat Pasha, because the Turks had considerably encroached on Kuwait's territory, as could be seen from the map in Palgrave's book, which shows the Fao peninsula as part of Kuwait.[66] It is interesting to see here, for the first time, a British ambassador in Constantinople showing willingness to examine the Kuwait affair in a historical perspective.

Lowther was also disturbed by a crescendo of debate in the press over the status of Kuwait. On 23 and 28 January 1911, *The Times* had presented a strong case for Britain's claims on Kuwait and the final section of the railway. The Turks tried to play down the coverage and Tawfiq Pasha, who was now Ottoman ambassador in London, advised the Porte to react cautiously. Lowther suspected that one of the notorious articles in the *Tanin* by the MP for Baghdad, Isma'il Hakki Babanzade, considering its author's virulent views, had been toned down in response to pressure from Tawfiq. This article trumpeted the old Ottoman claim to the entire Arabian Peninsula, thus putting the Kuwait issue on an almost equal footing with the Ottoman claim to the Trucial States, Bahrain and Qatar – just as in 1871 the Baghdad newspaper *Zawra* had claimed the entire Arabian coast from al-Hasa to Oman for the Sultan.

Lowther was sceptical too of the real value of a Turkish undertaking not to alienate Kuwait. He grasped the weakness of the Ottoman Government of the day, and believed the Porte unable to offer an undertaking

[65] IOLR, R/15/1/610, fo. 21, Grey to Bertie 18 January 1911.
[66] Lowther refers to W. G. Palgrave's *Narrative of a Year's Journey through Central and Eastern Arabia*, Macmillan, London, 1865.

satisfactory to the British without arousing the ire of the Committee of Union and Progress. Grey had already made it clear that such an undertaking should include the recognition of Kuwait's autonomy and the acceptance of the existing agreements between Britain and Mubarak. The Turkish government of the day would certainly be unwilling to concede so much.[67]

The following weeks saw little shift in the Ottoman stance, while the Constantinople press ran commentaries on non-existent negotiations between the British embassy and the Porte. Hakki Pasha, the Grand Vizier, told Lowther that negotiations could begin only after the German railway company had agreed to surrender its rights to the final section of the railway. Hakki at least slightly adjusted the Ottoman position by declaring that if no satisfactory deal could be reached on Kuwait, the Turks would consider making Basra the terminus. He probably wanted to jolt the British with the suggestion that Kuwait might very well lose its value in the bargaining over the railway.[68] The Turks apparently failed to appreciate how such a move might actually strengthen India's hand in the negotiations. India cared little about the railway *per se*; its concern was its impact on British dominance of the Gulf. Britain's current hold on the Gulf meant that communications between a terminus in Basra and the head of the Gulf would be subject to total British control. This would be especially the case given that Germany had never shown the slightest intention of challenging Britain's pre-eminence in the Gulf.

The *Tanin*, meanwhile, continued to run articles by Isma'il Hakki on the possibility of a Gulf understanding between Britain and Turkey. There was no real difference of opinion, he wrote, between Britain and the Ottoman Empire over the Baghdad Railway; the only substantive issue was that Kuwait should be effectively Ottoman with Ottoman police and customs. Isma'il Hakki wanted an agreement that would "put an end to the dubious position of Kuwait". He repeated the Ottoman mantra that Kuwait was a regular Ottoman administrative district because Mubarak was an Ottoman *kaymakam* and had the Ottoman title of Pasha, and so was an Ottoman subject. Lowther responded with a strong rebuttal of the old Ottoman arguments for their rights in Kuwait. Such arguments might in the past have impressed the less intelligent O'Conor, but his successor

---

[67] IOLR, R/15/1/610, fo. 52(62), Lowther 15 February 1911.
[68] IOLR, R/15/1/610, fo. 112 (125), Lowther 21 February 1911.

Lowther was better informed. Lowther quoted the examples of the German officer von der Goltz Pasha and of Prince Ferdinand of Bulgaria, who bore the nominal title of Wali of Eastern Rumelia. Eastern Rumelia was an Ottoman province in name only, to all practical purposes being part of Bulgaria. Lowther saw the Ottoman territorial claims to Kuwait as more or less equivalent to those to Qatar and Dubai. The Turks based these claims on Ottoman conquest in the 16th century or on arguments of Islamic religious hegemony. Lowther was perfectly correct in rejecting the Islamic argument, because the new Ottoman constitution defined the Ottoman Empire as a secular state, and hence the religious position of the Caliph could no longer entail any territorial rights.[69]

The Foreign Office in London went ahead with preparations of the package of proposals that Britain would submit in response to the expected Ottoman overture. A rough list of these proposals was then transmitted to India for consideration. For Kuwait, it was recommended that Britain would insist on full self-government, including customs administration, while Kuwait was to recognize Ottoman suzerainty. As token of this suzerainty the Shaikh was to pay a tribute to the Sultan, but only on condition of fair treatment in the matter of the Basra date groves. The administration of the port of Kuwait was to be shared between Britain and Mubarak. The proposals contained quite considerable concessions to the Turks.[70]

Cox was instructed to ask Mubarak for his opinion about a possible settlement with the Turks without arousing his suspicions that negotiations might be afoot. Cox had a good opportunity to do this, as he had to

[69] IOLR, R/15/1/610, fo. 112 (125), Lowther 21 February 1911. It should be remarked that the claims of past Ottoman conquest of Kuwait, Dubai and Qatar in the 16th century are very weak. Dubai was at that time mentioned only as a temporary camp of pearl divers, and there is no reference to any Ottoman activity in that region except for an Ottoman raid on Khorfakan. There is no indication of any military presence in Kuwait apart from the simple passage of Ottoman troops in 1871. In the case of Qatar there may have been an Ottoman presence in the 16th century, but by 1629 the Ottomans were not in power there because they asked the Portuguese to attack Qatar, which they duly did, plundering a few villages. For these ancient events, see Slot, *Arabs of the Gulf*, p. 133 (Qatar); and *Relation des voyages de Sidi-Aly fils d'Houssain nommé ordinairement Katibi Roumi*, translated by M. Moris (Paris 1827), p. 37 on Khorfakan.

[70] Busch, *Britain and the Persian Gulf*, pp. 322–3. The draft proposal was sent on 20 January 1911 to India, and on 27 January to Bushire for consideration.

discuss the matter of the registration of the newly acquired Basra properties with Mubarak. Mubarak seems to have adopted his usual tactic of listening to the British proposals with great sympathy and restraint, no doubt in order to lull Cox into revealing more than he intended. Mubarak was probably under no illusions. It is inconceivable that he was unaware of the reports in the Constantinople press of discussions between Britain and Turkey about the railway, if not about Kuwait too. The Shaikh politely agreed with Cox that his problems with the Turks could be solved if his independence were guaranteed by them and his sons took Ottoman nationality. The guarantee should take the shape of a firman (official document) of the Sultan, given to Mubarak and confirmed in a written promise of observance by the Sultan to the British. It appears that London's suggestion of a tribute to be paid to the Sultan was not mentioned to Mubarak. Cox warned not only that the Shaikh would deeply resent it, but also that it could adversely affect Britain's prestige among Arab shaikhs. Cox agreed broadly with the other points, such as the demand that the rail terminus should be in Kuwait. Cox also reported that Mubarak had told him of an Ottoman promise to confirm his autonomy if he applied for Ottoman nationality.[71]

India broadly concurred with Cox's opinion and the matter was sent back to London, where the India Office took some time to formulate its recommendations for submission to the Foreign Office.

On 1 March 1911, while the India Office was still preparing its formal opinion, Lowther sent the Foreign Office the formal Ottoman proposal. The Turkish proposals were that the railway might end in either Basra or Kuwait. There was a preference for Kuwait, but only if the status of Kuwait were regularized, because the terminus should be under effective Ottoman control. The railway could be an international venture with 40 per cent for the Porte and 20 per cent each for Germany, France and Britain.[72]

This was just the opening Ottoman bid in the bargaining process. Now the British could respond, but it took time for India, the India Office and the Foreign Office to agree on a compromise bid. On 3 March 1911, just two days after the Turkish proposal had been submitted, the India Office

[71] IOLR, R/15/5/65, fos. 3–5, Cox 10 February 1911.
[72] Busch, *Britain and the Persian Gulf*, pp. 324–5; Gooch and Temperley, *British Documents*, Vol. 10, Part 2, pp. 24–6, Lowther to Grey 1 March 1911, with Ottoman proposal added.

sent the Foreign Office its ideas on the offer to be made to the Turks. The India Office was broadly in accord with the recommendations of India and Cox. The railway, not Kuwait, might be the main preoccupation of Foreign Office officials, but India had little concern for that project unless it was under British control, seeing instead Kuwait's status as the top priority. In brief, the India Office proposals were that there should be a British controlling interest of the Baghdad–Kuwait section of the railway, that Kuwait should be the terminus, that Kuwait harbour should be under the joint control of the British and Mubarak, and that there should be a clear agreement between Mubarak and the Turks over the sharing of customs and transit duties. This was all to be under the following conditions: Kuwait would accept formal Ottoman suzerainty, but its full autonomy was to be confirmed by a firman of the Sultan, and the Turks were to recognize Umm Qasr, Bubiyan and Warba as part of Kuwait. The issues of the Basra province properties and the tribute were left open: Mubarak's son could become an Ottoman subject, and as long as the Turks did not demand tribute Mubarak should be amenable to the sharing of customs duties. Finally the India Office insisted that Britain could not drop Mubarak without a fatal loss of prestige. The wording of India's reaction reveals its anxiety about the Kuwaiti ruler, who had frequently demonstrated his susceptibility to a rapprochement with the Turks, on his own terms, if Britain failed to meet his expectations. India stressed that Kuwait and Muhammara were the only firm footholds Britain held in the upper Gulf, in view of which it would be highly inopportune to alienate Mubarak, who since 1910 had been making friendly overtures to the Turks.[73] This response by India was determined by two factors: fear of another European nation gaining control over the fastest route to India, and recognition that Mubarak would deeply resent the tribute proposal.

On the face of it these proposals manifest a certain resolve, but on closer inspection they embody the India Office's apparent lack of conviction that India's desires would be acceptable *in toto* to the Foreign Office. The day before sending this letter, the India Office had enquired of the Viceroy whether there might be any room for negotiation on these points.[74] India

---

[73] Rush, *Records of Kuwait*, Vol. 1, pp. 447–9, India Office to Foreign Office 3 March 1911.
[74] The question was forwarded to Cox in Bushire, see IOLR, R/15/1/610, fos. 24(31)–25(32), Foreign Department of the Government of India to Cox 20 March 1911.

had already shown a clear preference for conceding a Turco-German-controlled line to Basra if that was the price of maintaining the status quo of Kuwait. The Viceroy was adamant about this, but the India Office was reluctant to relinquish all influence over the railway, and felt that the Kuwait status quo might become untenable were the railway to Basra to be constructed without British participation. The India Office considered that the opening of such a railway would make it impossible for Britain to maintain its position in Kuwait.[75] In the light of such British vacillation between relinquishing Kuwait because it was untenable, or forcing Mubarak to become a Turkish tributary as part of a general agreement with the Turks, we can only conclude that Mubarak's oft-displayed distrust of British intentions was justified.

Meanwhile the Foreign Office maintained its view that a combined general solution of all Gulf matters, including the railway and Kuwait, was necessary. A new urgency had been injected into the affair by the Ottomans, who had made progress in reaching a compromise with the Germans to facilitate the railway negotiations with the British: the Anatolian Railroad Company had relinquished its concession for the section below Baghdad in exchange for a promise of an equal share in a new company for that section.[76]

At the end of March 1911, the India Office and Foreign Office agreed on a number of points for negotiation with the Turks. Britain would be willing to accept a temporary increase in Ottoman customs duties, in exchange for various undertakings concerning the railway, the status of Kuwait, and Ottoman territorial claims in the Gulf. On the railway issue, Britain now wanted the final section to be under a separate company that would be 50 per cent British-owned, with two British members on the board and a British chairman each alternate year, while the terminus was to be in Kuwait. The railway port in Kuwait was to be constructed by the

---

[75] The Viceroy's reaction is in a telegram of 7 March 1911, IOLR, R/15/1/610, fo. 23 (30): "Proposals of the Porte are [...] absurd, while they imply absolute surrender of our position at Koweit and our desertion of Sheikh Mobarak for the sake of participation in the Gulf section to the extent of a 20% share"; Busch, *Britain and the Persian Gulf*, p. 324.

[76] Busch, *Britain and the Persian Gulf*, p. 325; see also IOLR, R/15/1/610, fo. 134(147), Seymour at the German embassy in Berlin to Grey 10 March 1911, about the conciliatory attitude adopted by both Germany and Britain at that juncture.

British and policed by the Kuwaitis under British supervision, and its revenues were to be equally divided between the British and the Shaikh. An arrangement would be made for the levying, "in the interest of Turkey", of customs duties on merchandise transported by rail to and from the Ottoman Empire; this delicate point was very vaguely formulated. Kuwait would not be fortified and its territorial status would be guaranteed by Britain and the Ottoman Empire. Here Britain was proposing a solution very much along the lines of the international guarantee for Kuwait proposed several years previously by Goguyer – a status somewhat like that of Belgium.[77] "The administration of local affairs in Koweit shall remain as heretofore in the hands of the Sheikh and his successors. The suzerainty of the Sultan of Turkey over Koweit shall be recognised and the limits of the Sheikh's jurisdiction defined (territorially)."

While not obviously threatening to Kuwait, this was in reality a rather soft position. The proposals make no mention of the validity of existing treaties between Mubarak and the British, and thus seem to deny Mubarak any sovereignty over his external affairs. The territorial definition of Kuwait is also very vague. Another dangerous clause proposed that Kuwaiti subjects outside Kuwait should "enjoy" Turkish consular protection. This clause is understandable from the point of view of British diplomats, who sometimes found the protection of Kuwaitis tiresome, but it impugned Kuwait's international status. The compromise otherwise demanded that the Turks should accept Britain's position elsewhere in the Gulf, where the British were nervous of new Ottoman intrigues. The Turks would have to relinquish all ambitions beyond 'Uqayr, including their claims to Bahrain and Qatar.[78] In essence, the whole package represented a partial desertion of Kuwait in exchange for advantages elsewhere.

India was displeased. The Viceroy suggested a number of significant amendments and clarifications. The Ottomans should accept Kuwait's ownership of Bubiyan and Warba, more benefit to Kuwait in the matter of customs duties, and a statement to the effect that the agreement to construct the port at Shuwaikh should be legally expressed as a concession

---

[77] Goguyer had died in October 1909 in Baghdad: Paris AE, NS Mascate 48, Rouet 10 November 1909.
[78] IOLR, R/15/1/610, fo. 171, "Memorandum by Mr Parker" about the meeting of 30 March 1911.

by Mubarak to the British.[79] Ritchie of the India Office also kept up the pressure. He made it clear to the Foreign Office that the India Office regarded the British promise of "good offices" as extending to the entire territory of Kuwait as defined in Lorimer's *Gazetteer,* and that Lansdowne's restriction of these good offices to the immediate surroundings of the Gulf of Kuwait had been of only temporary application.[80] Thus Britain's position was inching in favour of Mubarak. It was also to Mubarak's benefit that Lowther in Constantinople kept up his derisive comments on Ottoman claims to sovereignty over Kuwait as promoted in the *Tanin.*[81]

From April to July 1911, the India Office, India and Grey continued to disagree about the central question in the negotiations, the British role in the railway. The India Secretary, Morley, argued that Britain should try to reach an agreement with Germany first; the Turks would then have to accept it in exchange for some formal concessions. Grey, however, wanted a deal with Turkey first on the final section of the railway, as part of an overall Gulf agreement.[82] In the end the British negotiating position crystallized: one condition of Britain agreeing to an increase in Ottoman imperial customs duties would be a 20 per cent share in an international company for the final stretch of the railway, in which France, Russia and Germany would also participate – which embodied, of course, a 60 per cent share for the Entente of Britain, France and Russia.[83]

While London and India were debating their response to the Ottoman proposal, remarkably little attention was paid to a somewhat inopportune

[79] PRO, FO 371/1233, Hardinge to Morley 6 April 1911.
[80] Lorimer, *Gazetteer,* Vol. 2, pp. 1059–61; IOLR, R/15/1/610, fos. 170 (192)–171(193).
[81] Lowther to Grey 10 April; IOLR, R/15/1/610, fos. 185(199)–186(200). The article in the *Tanin* of 10 April was written by Abdul Wahhab Al-Kirtas, the Basra landowner who mediated in the sale of property to Mubarak that all the recent trouble had been about. While the purpose of the article seems to be to prove that Mubarak was a most loyal Ottoman, Lowther discovered in it clear arguments that Mubarak was independent. The crux of the article is the description of a meeting in Al-Kirtas's house, which had previously been the cause of some concern to consul Crow in Basra: IOLR, R/15/5/5, fos. 71(78)–74(81), Crow 9 March 1910.
[82] Busch, *Britain and the Persian Gulf,* pp. 326–7, quoting Morley: "While it will no doubt be necessary to pay all outward respect to Turkish susceptibilities, they can in practice be treated as negligible."
[83] Busch, *Britain and the Persian Gulf,* pp. 327–8.

report by Rear-Admiral Slade, commander of the Indian Navy, on a recent survey of the Shatt al-'Arab. Slade came to the novel conclusion that Basra, not Kuwait, would be the best site for a rail terminus, because port installations would be much easier to construct there than at Kazima or Shuwaikh. Slade did not think it would be difficult to make the Shatt al-'Arab navigable up to Basra for large vessels. He was well aware that Britain would thereby lose control of the railway project. Slade's conclusion was that Britain should simply take firm action when Turkey became "recalcitrant" in the negotiations; Fao could be occupied while, on the other side of Arabia, Turkish communications could be cut with the remote port of Hudayda in Yemen, thus isolating the Ottoman troops in that rugged region.[84] The report was not extensively discussed, but the Government of India would certainly have brought it to the fore if negotiations with the Turks had broken down.

It would have been folly to believe Mubarak to be ignorant of these developments. Cox had consulted him about the general nature of his relationship with the Turks when preparing his advice to the Government of India about how to react to the London negotiating position of January 1911. The Shaikh always managed to be one step ahead and, just to stir things up a little, in April 1911 he went out of his way to inform Shakespear of matters that, had they been true, he should have divulged long before. He announced that some time previously he had received a French offer to construct a railway from Kazima to Kuwait, and had piously rejected it. Of course no such plan is to be found in the French archives, so this story was merely intended to keep the agent on his toes. The Shaikh furthermore revealed "that he had been intimated that the Germans wanted to lease all the ground near Kathama point". This too is uncorroborated. From Shakespear's account, Mubarak simply seems to have been dangling a carrot in front of the British to tempt them to lease the land from him! He also hinted that he did not entirely trust the English over the integrity of his territory, given past events at Umm Qasr, Safwan and Bubiyan. It was clear to Shakespear that people in Kuwait were quite well-informed about the state of negotiations over the railway. Rumours were flying about the Kuwait bazaar, and the Shaikh too was abreast of it. Of interest is Shakespear's remark that the prospect of an increased British

[84] IOLR, R/15/1/610, fos. 54(64)–63(74), Slade 23 April 1911.

presence resulting from the rail terminus inspired "merchants and townspeople with the hope that the Shaikhs absolute power will be gradually attentated [Shakespear, no intellectual, and often shaky in his spelling, presumably meant attenuated]".[85] This is typical of Shakespear, reflecting as it does his relatively limited contacts with a few individual merchants, for it is scarcely credible that the majority of Kuwaitis would welcome a strong European presence in Kuwait. On the whole it looks as if Mubarak was discreetly warning the British that he knew what was going on, and at the same time opening the door to negotiations on the lease of further sites. These he would ultimately try to manipulate to clinch new guarantees – the ploy he had used during the Shuwaikh negotiations with Knox.

Mubarak also brought the Kazima matter to Cox's attention, but in a different way. Cox warned the Government of India on 24 April of Mubarak's growing wariness. The Shaikh tried a little provocation. He wrote a reproachful letter to Cox complaining that Britain had taken no action in the past to protect his rights to Umm Qasr, Safwan and Bubiyan, and pretending to be afraid that the accelerating railway plans had now imperilled Kazima too. He asked Cox either to purchase a lease on Kazima, or to allow him to grant a leasehold to Britain against the promise of effective British protection in future. Cox hurriedly gave Mubarak the desired assurances of protection and so the danger blew over.[86] It is noteworthy how swiftly the British could act in their own interest in an emergency. In other cases they could be painfully slow, as in the case of the artillery promised after the Shuwaikh lease. These guns had arrived only after a long delay, in October 1909.[87]

In July 1911, after all the pressures from the various sides, the British at last managed to submit a formal offer of compromise to the Turks. The final product was quite differently worded from the earlier drafts, and had the merit of being clearer and simpler. Britain's claims concerning her position in the Gulf generally were less hardline, but Kuwait's status was better defined and dangerous concessions had been eliminated. There were three basic proposals: Britain was ready to recognize Ottoman suzerainty

[85] Rush, *Records of Kuwait*, Vol. 1, pp. 450–3, Shakespear 19 April 1911.
[86] IOLR, R/15/1/610, fos. 66(78)–67(79), Cox to Foreign Office 24 April; Mubarak to Cox 23 Rabi II 1329; and Cox to Mubarak 23 April 1911.
[87] *Political Diaries*, Vol. 3, p. 736.

over Kuwait and accept that Mubarak was "a Turkish *kaymakam*", provided the Turks recognized the Shaikh's total autonomy, would not interfere in Kuwait even in matters of succession on Mubarak's death, would accept that Bubiyan and Warba were part of Kuwait, and would also accept the validity of Mubarak's "treaties" with the British. Furthermore, Mubarak was to have the right to own and acquire land in Ottoman territory.[88] Comparing this with the first drafts, one can see that the dangerous concepts of tribute, Ottoman sovereignty, and Ottoman nationality had now been dropped from the formal offer. The British memorandum contained the significant statement that any British offer of a concession in the Kuwait negotiations would be "*sans préjudice*" if no agreement were ultimately reached. This statement is important for Kuwait's legal position: any British concession to the Turks would have legal consequences only in the case of a full agreement being finally ratified.[89]

In the event the British only offered the Turks concessions that were devoid of practical import. Suzerainty was an almost totally empty concept. The title of Kaymakam was futile when the Turks had no say in Kuwait or the ruler's succession. Formal Ottoman recognition of the validity of Mubarak's agreements with the British entailed that Mubarak was *ab origine* externally sovereign, and that this sovereignty was limited only by the 1899 Agreement with the British. In theory this also meant that, if the British agreed, Mubarak was free to make a pact with the French or whomsoever he pleased. One now sees the primordial importance of the clause added by Mubarak in 1899. Suzerainty might entail no more than that he would not be entirely free to make a military alliance directed against the Sultan, but even here there were enough precedents for wars by vassals against their suzerains to make this an empty clause. The question of Kuwait's boundaries had also been on the table in the internal British discussion. In the end only the northern border was explicitly mentioned in the memorandum given to the Turks. India and the India Office had thought that, in the negotiations with the Turks, the vague line of demarcation of tribal loyalties as laid down in Lorimer's

[88] IOLR, R/15/5/65, memorandum communicated to the Turkish ambassador in London, 29 July 1911.
[89] "His Majesty's Government will gladly contribute in such a resolution on the understanding that their rights and claims are not to be regarded as prejudiced by any proposals which may now be put forward, should such proposals prove abortive."

Gazetteer should be claimed, but the Foreign Office had not been entirely persuaded and was still mindful of Lansdowne's old statement about the immediate surroundings of the Gulf of Kuwait.[90]

There remained one bitter pill for the British to swallow. After more than twelve years they had to come clean about their secret agreements. Fortunately Russia and France, which in the early 1900s had protested so loudly about British infringements of Ottoman territorial integrity, were now bound to Britain in a grand alliance. It was now just Germany, Austria and Turkey who were in a position to cast aspersions. Of this illustrious trio, Austria had no leg to stand on because it had itself occupied Ottoman Bosnia out of turn, and Germany was clearly not in search of a dispute with Britain. India agreed that only the agreement of 1899, the 1900 engagement about the arms trade, and the 1904 undertaking to allow only a British post office, would be made known to the Ottomans. Mubarak opposed the revelation to the Turks of the Shuwaikh lease agreement of 1907, a stance shared by India, so this remained secret.[91] The Viceroy's letter concerning the communication of the secret agreements proposed that the Turks should also have sight of the telegrams from the India Secretary to the Government of India of 4 December 1901 and 14 October 1902, which in India's view implied an obligation on Britain's part to protect Kuwait against Ottoman attacks by land or sea. But the India Office was of the opinion that these telegrams were valid only for the particular circumstances of the time and did not constitute a general engagement to protect Kuwait against the Turks. The India Office was keen to maintain the vague notion of "good offices".[92]

Hence the British took some time to decide exactly which documents to communicate to the Turks. On 24 October, the Foreign Office at last sent the Ottoman ambassador the documents of 1899, 1900 and 1904.[93]

But just at this point new problems arose to thwart the railway once more. In September 1911 Italy, formally an ally of Austria and Germany, attacked the Ottoman Empire and occupied Tripolitania. In a paradoxical twist, the Ottomans proved powerless on the ground in North Africa, but in the Muslim world at large there was a wave of resistance to Christian

---

[90] IOLR, R/15/1/610, fo. 170 (192), Ritchie (India Office) 8 April 1911.
[91] IOLR, R/15/5/65, fos. 19–20, Viceroy to India Office 30 August 1911.
[92] IOLR, R/15/5/65, fo. 23, India Office to Foreign Office 30 October 1911.
[93] IOLR, R/15/5/65, fo. 25, Grey to Tewfiq Pasha 24 October 1911.

occupation of Muslim territory. In this parlous situation some local Ottoman authorities began to take provocative action against whatever representatives of Christian powers might be to hand. Thus hostile measures were taken in Basra against Bahraini subjects who were regarded as under British protection.

This in turn led the British seriously to contemplate, for the first time since 1895, the possibility of open hostilities with the Turks. A study was undertaken of possible options in the event of significant Turkish action against British interests. The committee, on which Cox figured, identified a key role for Kuwait as the base for operations against Basra.[94] Mubarak, meanwhile, was leaning once again towards the Turks.[95] This was to be expected. Not only did he doubtless feel sincere disquiet at the defeat of Muslims by Christians but, on a more expedient level, he would be courting vilification by the entire Muslim world were he to break Islamic ranks at such a time. So Kuwait contributed money to Ottoman coffers.

It was probably not by a mere slip of the pen that, just at that juncture in 1911, the Porte drafted a message to Mubarak addressing him not as "Kaymakam of Kuwait", as was usual, but as "Ruler of Kuwait and Chief of its Tribes", the titles Mubarak himself used to sign his documents.[96] Thus, in their dire emergency, the Turks were at last able to bring themselves to accept Mubarak's sovereign status in a bilateral contact.

10.5 Internal troubles

There is no doubt that Mubarak aroused some ongoing criticism from

[94] Busch, *Britain and the Persian Gulf*, p. 329.

[95] Berlin AA, R 13891 A 15439 (30 September 1911), Listemann in Bushire 4 September 1911. One of the signs of Mubarak's growing hostility towards Britain was his support for an Arab shipping line which was beginning to compete with the B.I.S.N.Co. steamers. See also Berlin AA, R 13891 A 19589 (28 November 1911). See cutting from the German newspaper *Frankfurter Allgemeine Zeitung* of 28 November 1911, for Mubarak's financial support of the Turkish war effort. See also French records in Paris AE, NS Mascate 39, fos. 228 and 247 (25 April and 28 July 1912).

[96] Anscombe, *Ottoman Gulf*, p. 139 and n. 131, quoting Istanbul BA, BEO 297912. This was a letter addressed directly to Mubarak (a later letter mentioned by Anscombe, *Ottoman Gulf*, n. 131, again using the word *kaymakam*, was an internal document of the Porte). It should be noted that Shakespear had already mentioned in May 1910 that the Wali of Basra had stopped addressing Mubarak as Kaymakam of Kuwait: IOLR, R/15/5/5, fo. 113, Shakespear 25 May 1910.

within. While being a highly visible personality who did not duck debate, he also kept a very tight rein, exacting funds and services as needed. There was bound to be opposition in one form or another. Mubarak's priorities were not everyone's priorities, and it can easily be imagined that leading notables would have liked more influence in the running of affairs. In January 1912, however, an incident of a different order occurred: a violent reaction by Mubarak against a supposed coup attempt.

It is difficult now to reconstruct the exact course of events from the three groups of sources extant: the reports and diaries of the British political agent; the almost contemporary early Kuwaiti historiography; and a single Ottoman document. The Ottoman document is of little information value, being a simple order from the Porte to the Wali of Basra to discover the truth behind reports of an assassination attempt on Mubarak. The British reports and diaries suffer from the agents' lack of sound information on internal matters in Kuwaiti society. Knox and Shakespear both tended sympathize with any opposition to Mubarak, as they stood to benefit from him being weakened. The Kuwaiti histories, by contrast, draw upon local tradition and opinion close to the events in question, and contain much that is absent from the British reports.

Shakespear reported the sudden arrest of several people in Kuwait.[97] He was unable to obtain any clear idea of the reasons why, and the tone of his story implies his belief that those arrested may have been more or less innocent. His account ends with the news that Saqr Al-Ghanim, the most prominent of the detainees, had been blinded with a needle.

The Kuwaiti historian Rushaid gives considerably more background. According to him, Mubarak made a sudden visit to Jahra, where he gave orders to guard the road to Zubair and arrest all passers-by. A nomad from the Zubair district was apprehended and found to be in possession of a letter. It was addressed to Saqr Al-Ghanim and referred to a plot to replace Mubarak as ruler of Kuwait. On being clapped into jail, the man revealed that the ringleader was Saqr Al-Ghanim, whose arrest Mubarak then ordered. The blinding was carried out on the advice of Shaikh Khaz'al of Muhammara. Another detail to emerge from Kuwaiti tradition is that one of the plotters had a brother who worked for Mubarak, who had alerted the Shaikh that something was up. This may explain Mubarak's sudden trip to Jahra.[98]

[97] *Political Diaries,* Vol. 4, p. 489 (14 January 1912).

The entire story as told by the Kuwaiti historians looks quite straightforward. According to one, Husayn Khalaf Al-Shaikh Khaz'al, the conspirators' aim was to kill Mubarak and his sons Jabir and Salim. The plot was apparently linked with Basra or Zubair though not with Mubarak's nephews, as Mubarak's trusted agent Abdul Aziz Salim Al-Badr took great pains to assert and Mubarak seems to have accepted. It will forever remain a mystery who was really behind the plot. Possibly Mubarak believed Saqr Al-Ghanim to be its leader, as to blind him was to render him, according to Islamic law, permanently unfit to be ruler. Shakespear's scepticism of Saqr's guilt carries little weight as he was rather poorly informed about the whole affair, and Kuwaiti tradition seems to indicate Saqr as at least a leading conspirator.[99]

The sources do not point to any Ottoman involvement in the coup, rather the contrary. The Ottomans were taken by surprise, Constantinople being informed only after the event by the Wali of Basra.[100] The incident thus seems to have been a purely local matter. Mubarak had little to fear from the Turks. He had shown solidarity with them by sending money both for the war against the Italians and for charity after the Constantinople fire of June 1911. His reward had been a very high Ottoman decoration, the Mecidiye 1st class, conveyed to Kuwait with much pomp and ceremony by a deputation from Basra, and formally presented on 3 February by the Naqib in the presence of a large crowd.

---

[98] Abdallah Khalid Al-Hatim, *Min huna bada't al-Kuwayt* (1962), pp. 356–7. According to Husayn Khaz'al, *Tarikh*, Vol. 2, pp. 280–6, the name of the man who informed Mubarak was Sa'd Al-Dukhaymi.

[99] Salwa Al-Ghanim tries to show how loyal and important a servant Saqr was, notably by citing his part in the operations against Sa'dun in 1910, but this sits a little uncomfortably with her scathing description of the same ill-fated campaign against Sa'dun: Salwa Al-Ghanim, *Mubarak*, p. 193, *cf.* p. 143. It should also be noted that she rather distorts the reference by Shakespear to Yusuf bin Salim Al-Badr's intervention (*Political Diaries*, p. 503, February 1912) – which served to deny the involvement of Mubarak's nephews, and not, as she suggests on p. 193, to deny the existence of the plot.

[100] Istanbul BA, Dahliye Siyasi, 25/19, report of the Wali of Basra, 8 Yenayir 1319 Rumi (=21 January 1912).

[101] *Political Diaries*, Vol. 4, pp. 469 and 504 (January–February 1912).

[102] Al-Qasimi, *Bayan al-Kuwayt*, p. 378, Mubarak to Hasan Ridha, Pasha of Basra, January 1912.

[103] IOLR, R/15/5/25, fo. 291, Kuwait diary of the week ending 9 February 1910.

Shakespear was not invited.[101] The British, somewhat alarmed, instituted serious measures to award Mubarak a knighthood, something mooted years before during Curzon's visit. In truth they had little reason to worry. Mubarak had written a cordial letter notifying the Wali of Basra of the arrival of the deputation in Kuwait, pointedly signed in his customary style as "*Hakim al-Kuwayt wa Ra'is al-Qaba'il*", Ruler of Kuwait and Chief of its Tribes[102] – an explicit repudiation of any ties to the Ottoman administrative structure.

Whether Mubarak's harsh suppression of the coup was entirely justified we shall never know. In the context of the rough justice of the time, a reasonable verdict would be that it was tough but to the purpose. He had eliminated his rival without executing him. If there had been an attempt to oust him, then it failed. For a while he surrounded himself with a larger than usual bodyguard, but there is no evidence of any substantial danger persisting. This implies that the plotters were a small group without broad-based support. It is also difficult to assess the gravity of the episode. Attempts to bring about change by violence were a not uncommon feature of regional politics. Just two years previously, for example, two nephews of the Saudi Amir, Abdul Aziz Al-Saud, had tried to poison him.[103]

11

Turkey and Britain Agree Kuwait's Legal Status, 1912–1913

11.1 Repercussions of Ottoman defeats

By the beginning of 1912, relations between Mubarak and Shakespear were still far from easy. The agent was critical of Mubarak's handling of the Saqr Al-Ghanim affair, and of the great public pomp attending his decoration with the order of the Mecidiye. And Mubarak continued to view the B.I.S.N.Co. with disfavour.[1] In April, the agent gave rein to his frustration in a tirade that castigated the Shaikh for undermining the old system of powerful merchant shaikhs with his "iron rule", and denounced his extravagant penchant for luxury and ostentation. While conceding that taxes were still low, Shakespear argued that they had increased sharply in recent years and ran the risk of driving important people away. He reiterated that Kuwaitis looked to the British for deliverance, and expressed fear for the consequences should they wake up to the fact that it was British support that "had enabled Mubarak's despotism to flourish".[2]

It is difficult now to assess how far the agent's report paints an objective picture of the true state of affairs. Certainly Mubarak had increased taxation, but it is an open question whether this should be judged as justifiable compensation for past disbursements from the family fortune, and perhaps current ones too, on behalf of the state. Wittingly or not,

---

[1] *Political Diaries*, Vol. 4, p. 504 (February 1912).
[2] IOLR, R/15/5/18, Shakespear 25 April 1912.

Shakespear was the mouthpiece of wealthy merchants with India connections who had good reason to object to Mubarak's exactions. It is noteworthy that complaints by British agents about Mubarak's character always coincided with business conflicts between the merchants and the Shaikh. This does not entirely invalidate Shakespear's strictures, but one should be aware that he was not impartial.

His 1912 outburst was the last utterance of this kind, however. Contacts between Shaikh and agent soon improved, and there were no more aspersions to mar Mubarak's declining years. The Ottoman award ceremony jolted the British into grasping the urgency of restoring the equilibrium. In April 1912, with almost indecent haste, they invested Mubarak with the insignia of Knight Commander of the Most Eminent Order of the Indian Empire. On Shakespear's advice this was bestowed upon him with even greater pomp and circumstance than the Mecidiye had been in February.

The British still suffered the occasional attack of anxiety lest Mubarak, out of pique at their lack of co-operation, might align himself more closely with the Turks. This was largely unjustified, as the Turks were in serious difficulties in the Basra district. Talib Pasha had quit the Union and Progress party to join the moderate Liberals – an understandable departure, given that the Committee of Union and Progress had become so focused on the Turkish aspects of its programme that it had grown inimical to Arab aspirations. Such were the problems of the Wali, Ali Ridha Pasha, with Talib that he offered his resignation. Talib entered Basra amid great pomp and was greeted by Mubarak's and Khaz'al's steamers. He appears to have enjoyed complete control of the city for some time, undisturbed by the powerless Wali. At the end of 1912, however, the Muntafiq, under 'Ajaimi, made moves to avenge Sa'dun by attacking Talib. In March 1913, the president of the municipality and 150 Basra notables sent a telegram to the Porte demanding autonomous status for Basra province, while Arab nationalist propaganda leaflets circulated in Mesopotamia demanding decentralization of the Ottoman Empire. The official Ottoman newspaper in Baghdad, *Al-Zohur*, denounced Talib and his allies Mubarak and Khaz'al for stirring up unrest in Iraq and sidelining the Basra Wali.[3] In 1913 a new Wali was appointed, while Talib persisted in

[3] Paris AE, NS Turquie 152 (Baghdad), fos. 176–178, Wiet, French consul in Baghdad, to minister 13 March 1913.

his demands for concessions by the Porte to the Arabs. After a few weeks the new Wali was assassinated. Talib was accused of being behind the murder, and riots broke out soon after.[4]

The Ottoman Empire in Europe first began to disintegrate during 1912. In May of that year the Italians occupied the Dodecanese, including the beautiful island of Rhodes, a place of luxurious exile for high Ottoman officials. October brought the outbreak of the disastrous First Balkan War, which deprived the Turks of almost all their European territory. By the end of 1912 the Turkish position in Europe was looking hopeless.

Mubarak's sympathies lay with the Turks in this conflict. The Ottoman establishment's predicament afforded him a good opportunity to improve his relations with it. To every Muslim the conquest by Christians of a large part of the Ottoman Empire was a catastrophe, and it is in this light that the remarkable interview given by Mubarak to the Baghdad newspaper *Destur* of 8 January 1913 should be seen. Wiet, the French consul in Baghdad, to whom we owe the translation of this article, regarded the publication of an interview with a Muslim leader from the region as a novel event. The article takes the form of a perhaps fictitious interview between Mubarak and the British consuls in Basra and Muhammara, on the occasion of his visit to Basra. Its gist is that the Basra consul asked Mubarak whether he had seen the conditions for peace that the Balkan powers – Greece, Bulgaria and Servia – had proposed to the Porte. Mubarak retorted that he would urge the Porte to reject them, stating:

> I am ready to help with all my forces. The Porte should fight back. I have 200,000 [!] warriors on horse and camel without counting infantry. ... They are ready to respond to the first appeal of the Commander of the Faithful. May Europe know this!

Interesting too, in the context of the Ottoman defeats in Europe, is the following interpretation allegedly placed by Mubarak on Yemen's declaration of independence from Turkey:

> The Imam and all the people of Yemen are with the Porte with their hearts and with their arms. However bad the situation may be, they do

[4] Paris AE, NS Turquie 152 (Baghdad), fos. 202–3, 207, Wiet, French consul in Baghdad, to minister and Dozon, acting consul, 1 May, 15 May, 28 June, 3 August and 9 August 1913.

not desire to secede from Turkey. They are connected to it by ties of religion and race. I am sure that they will obey the first appeal from the Sultan, so strong is their devotion to the Caliphate. I know the nobility of the Arabs and their patriotic pride.[5]

The article amounts to no more than the profession by an Arab leader of willingness to assist the Commander of the Faithful. This did not stop the French consul, Wiet, giving a rather confused interpretation of it. He was trying to find a profession of loyalty by Mubarak to the Porte, but he had to concede that this was neither implicitly nor explicitly stated. He read into the article portents of a crisis in Britain's relationship with the Arabs, following incidents between the British and the rulers of Dubai and Bahrain. One cannot deny that there existed a certain degree of irritation with the British as a consequence of the Balkan Wars and British interventions in Gulf states. The article, however, contains no declaration of subordination to the Ottoman Empire. There is merely a verbal offer of help to the Caliph as chief of all Muslims. The article's significance lies elsewhere: at this desperate juncture the Ottoman press apparently felt free to present so notoriously disobedient a person as Mubarak as offering succour to the Sultan from a position of equality.

Interestingly, the purport of this article in *Destur* exactly mirrors that of an Ottoman document dated just one day before it. This is a report by the Wali of Basra in the Istanbul archives of a visit to him by Khaz'al and Mubarak. Khaz'al presented himself as a friend, despite being a Persian subject. Mubarak declared his readiness to sacrifice himself and his fortune for the Ottoman cause, and to stand shoulder to shoulder with the Caliph. The Shaikh of Kuwait expressed his anxiety about the deleterious effects of the Balkan Wars on the Ottoman Empire, and asserted that "millions of Arabs" were waiting for the Caliph's call to arms. The Ottoman Minister of the Interior sent thanks to both Shaikhs and announced appropriate rewards to them.[6]

[5] This document is described and translated in Paris AE, NS Mascate 15, fos. 97–99 (6 January 1912).
[6] Istanbul BA, Dahliye Siyasi 25/62, coded telegram of Ali Ridha Pasha of Basra, 12 Disember 1328 Rumi (7 January 1913); ibid., 25/64, for a similar telegram with a more detailed report of 6 Safar 1331 (15 January 1913). The Minister of Interior had already sent the above-mentioned promise of rewards already on 10 January 1913 (also in 25/64).

The events in Europe not only made a deep impression in the Gulf, but also forced the Porte to adopt a more amenable attitude in its negotiations with Britain. Italy's aggression towards Turkey had at first brought negotiations to a standstill but, as tension grew during the course of 1912, the Turks returned to the negotiating table.

11.2 Anglo–Ottoman negotiations resume

Negotiations between the Ottoman Empire and Britain continued to be determined by Grey's desire to settle all disputes in the Gulf in a single package. Their problems in Europe predisposed the Turks to speed up negotiations. In the Ottoman view the main obstacle to a general agreement was Britain's demand that the Porte should accept the validity of Britain's Kuwait agreements.[7] This indeed was the crucial point from a legal perspective: if the Porte were to accept the 1899 Agreement as valid, the Turks would thereby implicitly accept that Kuwait was a sovereign state at that time. This they were not yet ready to do.

On 15 April 1912, the Ottomans finally issued a reply to the British proposals of 29 July 1911.[8] This contained virtually no concessions. The Turks maintained their claim to Qatar and pressed for joint Anglo–Ottoman maritime policing of the Gulf. They rejected outright the British view on the status of Kuwait, arguing that Britain could base its claim that Kuwait was sovereign on just two factors: on its disregard of the Ottoman protectorate of Kuwait, and on the terms of the Status Quo Understanding of autumn 1901. The Turks argued that, as the Porte was unaware of the 1899 Agreement when they concluded the Status Quo Understanding, the situation created by the 1899 Agreement could not be part of the status quo. This was rather too much of a legal nicety. The Turks were perfectly well aware that some agreement existed between Mubarak and the British, although they were ignorant of its precise contents. The Turks repeated the usual false story that the Al-Sabah had "always" been Ottoman subjects and simple *kaymakams* of Kuwait. They conveniently forgot that at that precise moment the Ottoman official yearbook still

---

[7] Berlin AA, R 13891 A 6912 (19 April 1912), internal note of the German foreign ministry regarding information received from the Ottoman embassy in London.
[8] IOLR, R/15/5/65, "Aide-mémoire communicated to the Foreign Office on April 15th 1912".

made no mention of a *kaymakam* of Kuwait, that there had never existed a regular *kaza* of Kuwait, and that so far from shaikhs of the Al-Sabah having "always" been *kaymakams*, only Mubarak and his elder brothers Abdallah and Muhammad had been granted what was in reality this purely honorific title. The Porte added the interesting, though exaggerated, assertion that Mubarak had only just recently demanded that his sons be registered as Ottoman nationals, apparently based on an inflated interpretation of the outcome of the dispute over the registration of his Basra lands.[9]

The immediate British reaction was consternation. Hirtzel, the official in charge of the matter in the India Office, even suggested (internally) chucking it onto the fire. The tension eased a little when the Ottoman negotiator, Djavid, made it clear that the reply was a bargaining bid.[10] The sticking point in the negotiations at that juncture was the Ottoman claim to Qatar. This obscure peninsula had suddenly, for no obvious reason, taken on prime strategic importance in British eyes. The Ottoman attitude to Kuwait was almost equally unacceptable to the British. The British objection was that the Turks were demanding, in exchange for a British share in the railway, the recognition of rights that the Turks did not effectively possess. The Turks had no more than a small besieged garrison at one location in Qatar, and they wielded no power whatever over Kuwait. In the matter of Kuwait the British held to their position that they were willing to accept some Ottoman authority in name only, but that in practice Kuwait's autonomy should be complete. Moreover they rejected outright the Ottoman view that Britain's position in Kuwait should be confirmed by a special convention between London and the Porte.

The validity of Britain's existing agreements with Mubarak was a legal issue of crucial importance, for Mubarak as well as for the British. Any concession on this point by Britain would be tantamount to a confession that it had been violating international law in dealing with Mubarak. By

---

[9] In reality this application for Ottoman nationality had been discussed only occasionally for Mubarak's sons, for some of his womenfolk and for his blind son Nasir, in order to obtain registration of ownership of recently purchased date groves in Basra province. The Ottomans had never accepted this overture. See IOLR, R/15/5/5, fo. 132(120), Cox 7 June 1910; ibid., fo. 143 (156), British consul in Basra to Cox 6 June 1910; and ibid., 193(127), Shakespear 19 July 1910.
[10] Busch, *Britain and the Persian Gulf*, p. 331.

the same token, a recognition of even one of these agreements by the Turks would entail their recognition that Kuwait had the right to conclude binding international agreements without reference to the Sultan, and consequently that it had been an independent state, not only internally but externally too, before allowing Britain a say in aspects of its international relations.

In the discussion between Turkey and Britain the Kuwait question boiled down to two issues: Kuwait's legal status and the extent of its territory. On both points much separated the two parties. The official proposition as presented by the British on 29 July 1911 had mentioned only the demand that the Turks should recognize Warba and Bubiyan as belonging to Kuwait, but it seems from the text of the Ottoman reply that in informal contacts the British had also claimed that Kuwait's remaining boundaries should be as defined by Lorimer in his *Gazetteer*.[11] These were based chiefly on data from Knox's expeditions in the years 1904–8 and ascribed a quite extensive territory to Kuwait.[12] This British claim was not put forward with any great conviction. In an internal British memorandum the issue was formulated as follows. Lansdowne had limited Britain's protectorate obligation to the outskirts of Kuwait town. The Foreign Office had later decided that the Kuwaiti claim on Bubiyan and Warba should be upheld, but not the claims to Umm Qasr and Musallamiya Island. The Government of India took the view that the British obligation of protection was valid for the territory as defined in Lorimer's *Gazetteer* and supported the Kuwaiti claim to Musallamiya. The India Office agreed with India, with the exception of the claim to Musallamiya.[13]

In their reply of 15 April, the Turks had refused to accept Kuwait's

---

[11] The border question was not mentioned in the British memorandum of 29 July 1911, but appears to have been discussed informally, because in the Turkish reply ("Aide-mémoire communicated to the Foreign Office on April 15th 1912") there is explicit mention of a claim by the British Government of a territory of 160 by 190 miles.

[12] Lorimer, *Gazetteer,* Vol. 2, pp. 1060–1. It is to be noted that the Danish traveller Barclay Raunkiaer, in his book published in 1913, included a map showing an excessively large Kuwait: Raunkiaer, *Gennem Wahhabiternes Land,* p. 63. This map was omitted for obvious reasons from the translation published in 1969 by the former British political agent in Kuwait, Gerald de Gaury.

[13] IOLR, R/15/5/65, fos. 60(50)– 61(52), "Précis of the negotiations".

borders as the British presented them. They accepted only a much-reduced Kuwait: west to Kazima and Jahra, north to Jabal Sanam, and just 20 miles to the south of Kuwait town. The Porte was, however, willing to settle the Kuwait matter if the British offered certain concessions. These were recognition of Ottoman rule over Bubiyan and Warba, and the replacement of the "invalid" agreements between Mubarak and the British by a convention between Britain and Turkey protecting British economic interests but respecting Ottoman sovereignty. The Turks promised to respect Mubarak's rights to his Basra properties provided they were placed under Ottoman law.[14]

This was still far from acceptable to the British. Hirtzel and Parker, the officials of the India Office and the Foreign Office in charge of formulating the British position, took little more than a week to come up with a clear analysis. The division of railway shares proposed by the Turks still entailed Turco-German control and was therefore unacceptable. There was basic concurrence that Basra should for the time being be the terminus of the railway, but for additional security Hirtzel and Parker wanted Britain to insist that the proposed general agreement should include a clause that any extension of the line to the Gulf should be to a terminus on Kuwaiti territory. The Ottoman desire to consolidate their position in Qatar should be rejected. Hirtzel and Parker now came up with a clearer solution to the Kuwait problem. Britain should propose its willingness to recognize the suzerainty of the Sultan over Kuwait

> provided that in other respects the status quo is guaranteed and the validity of certain agreements which the Shaikh has concluded with the British Government is recognized; provided the islands of Warba and Bubiyan are admitted by Turkey to be within the confines of Kuwait and Turkish military posts are withdrawn; and provided finally the Shaikh is admitted to the full and undisturbed enjoyment of any properties he may own or hereafter purchase on Turkish territory; Kuwait would thus form a sort of enclave within, and forming part of, the Ottoman Empire enjoying complete self-government under Turkish suzerainty.

Finally Hirtzel and Parker rejected the Ottoman suggestion of joint

---

[14] IOLR, R/15/5/65, fos. 27(30)–29(31), "Aide-mémoire presented on 15 April to the Foreign Office".

Anglo-Turkish policing of the Gulf, as this would be to grant the Turks a position in the Gulf that they had never previously enjoyed.[15]

Meanwhile the India Office and Foreign Office discussed a compromise solution to the frontier question. This was to be in the same vein as other parts of the treaty regarding Kuwait: a nebulous formal concession to the Turks which did not on the whole detract from the integrity of Kuwait as delineated by Lorimer. The compromise that was being formulated for proposal to the Turks was in a sense to perpetuate Lansdowne's distinction. The limited territory surrounding the Gulf of Kuwait should be as independent as possible in reality as well as formally, while the remainder should be regarded as territory over which Mubarak would continue to exercise his tax-collection rights, but which he would govern as Ottoman *kaymakam*. Neither the British who concocted this compromise, nor the Turks who later accepted it, seem to have grasped that this would mean that, in the nucleus of Kuwait, Mubarak's title of *kaymakam* would have a different and more restricted application that was in no sense practical but merely nominal.

Preparation of the British reply was clouded by a sudden squall when out of the blue India introduced an unduly onerous demand for the remainder of the agreement: at least 50 per cent of the railway (where they had earlier demanded 20 per cent like the four other Powers) and no Ottomans in Qatar. This time the Foreign Office was understandably perturbed and stated bluntly that an overall agreement was essential because the railway would enable the Turks to attack Kuwait. This overall agreement was all the more vital in view of the British withdrawal of most of their warships from the Mediterranean as a consequence of the entente with France. They had thus lost the means of exerting pressure on the Ottomans there. The Foreign Office was sensitive to the risk of pressing the Ottomans too hard, and so driving them into an alliance with Germany – a very present danger that was in any case soon to be realized on outbreak of the First World War. Moreover the Foreign Office, as of old, considered Britain's claims on Kuwait to be "very vulnerable", and proposed to offer concessions in the matter of Qatar.[16]

[15] IOLR, R/15/5/65, fos. 32(33)–35(36), joint memorandum by Hirtzel and Parker on the memorandum of the Turkish Government, 24 April 1912.
[16] Parker to Hardinge 26 May 1912, quoted in Busch, *Britain and the Persian Gulf*, pp. 333–4.

Understandable as Foreign Office irritation over India's claims might be, it does not reveal a wholly comprehensive grasp of international affairs. The Foreign Office must have been aware of the quite different thunderclouds gathering over the Ottomans. Just three days after the India view was rejected, Bulgaria and Greece concluded the alliance that was to launch an almost fatal attack on the Ottoman Empire in the Balkans, and the Turks were soon to face serious threats from elsewhere. For the time being the Ottomans posed a minimal military threat, and India was justified in regarding concessions to the Turks as premature at that stage. India defended its increased demand with the theoretically correct argument that the Turks had rejected the British offer of equal shares of 20 per cent for Turkey, Germany, Britain, France and Russia, and so the bidding was open again. India proposed a hawkish policy: Britain should demand a controlling share, or else break the status quo, declare a full protectorate over Kuwait and take complete naval control of the Gulf.

The Foreign Office held firm in rejecting the 50 per cent proposal, but India and the India Office won the day over Qatar. This was because the negotiation package had to satisfy two conflicting remits, that of the Foreign Office for the railway and that of the India Office for the Gulf. India had the last word on the Gulf and the Foreign Office on the railway. Another interdepartmental conference was held and a final compromise reached that was by no means ill-conceived. By making a sufficient number of the formal concessions the Ottomans were so much attached to it allowed them to save face, while it satisfied most of the British practical demands. The Baghdad Railway would for the time being terminate at Basra and not on the Gulf – a strategic concession to the India viewpoint. The Ottomans were to relinquish all territorial claims on Qatar and Bahrain, but could keep the small existing garrison at Bida (later Doha). As regards Kuwait, the compromise proposal of splitting the territory controlled by Mubarak into two zones was now formulated. The Gulf of Kuwait and its immediate surroundings were to be an enclave in the Ottoman Empire with a special status as a fully autonomous entity acknowledging Ottoman suzerainty, while the status quo of 1901 was to remain in force in the desert areas. The distinction between the two zones would probably have no practical meaning because the British could claim the right to intervene if the status quo (i.e. Mubarak's authority) in the outside area was violated by the Ottomans at any time. The British added a clever sweetener to make the whole more palatable to the Turks: the Sultan would be allowed a representative in Kuwait on the same footing as the one he had in Egypt.[17]

London worked up to the eleventh hour exploring further concessions that might be offered to the Turks over Kuwait. On 1 July 1912 the India Office tried to find out whether some of these would be acceptable to the Government of India. The first was a proposed return to Lansdowne's old idea that British "good offices" to Mubarak should be limited to the immediate surroundings of the Gulf of Kuwait. This would mean Britain giving up its obligations under the status quo agreement for the outer area. What would be a bitter pill for Mubarak was sweetened somewhat by the maintenance of Kuwait's claim to Warba and Bubiyan. The next concession considered by the India Office was the option of confirming the agreements between Mubarak and Britain in a special convention between Britain and Turkey. In that this would entail a recognition that such agreements required Ottoman confirmation, this would certainly be a serious climb-down.[18]

Just at this point in the negotiations, it appears that Mubarak succeeded in playing a time-honoured trick on the British. He managed yet again to kindle alarm by hinting that he might abandon the British alliance for another. Mubarak was sufficiently alert to international affairs to know that his old ploy of using the Russians would no longer work. This time he was able to exploit the growing British fear of German expansion. Mubarak spread a story that an agent of Wönckhaus, a Baghdadi Christian named Alexander Forage, had come to him; this man had suggested that, were the Shaikh to lease any part of his territory to the Baghdad Railway Company, the German Emperor would intervene with the Turks to have Safwan, Umm Qasr and Bubiyan returned to him. It is a pretty tale, but the German sources offer no evidence of such a plot. The British nevertheless fell for it. Shakespear reported it to Cox, who immediately sent a long telegram to India, which was duly forwarded to London. Such playful manipulation by Mubarak was the reason why British documents

[17] Busch, *Britain and the Persian Gulf*, pp. 333–4.
[18] IOLR, R/15/5/65, fo. 42, India Office to Viceroy 1 July 1912.
[19] IOLR, R/15/1/611, fos. 121–122, 156,177, Cox to Government of India 10 July 1912; Government of India to India Office 11 July 1912; and Shakespear to Cox 2 July 1912.

from time to time express such concern over his possible reactions to certain proposals.[19]

India could now pour cold water on the idea of extra concessions: "The necessity of carefully avoiding any concessions which Turkey may be able to transfer to Germany to our detriment or that may estrange the Shaikh and drive him into the hands of the Germans is emphasized by the news we have just received of an attempt on the part of the Germans to intrigue with Shaikh." Mubarak's little news item could not have been better timed. India saw no problem in the proposed Turkish agent in Kuwait, provided there were time to explain to the Shaikh "that the presence of an Agent is the natural result and price of autonomy and direct recognition as is illustrated by the Khedive having a Turkish Agent in Cairo". India strongly warned against any concessions that might diminish British prestige in the eyes of the Arab Shaikhs of the Gulf or show that British promises were unreliable.[20]

In the end no further concessions were offered to the Turks and all turned out well for Mubarak. On the whole the British negotiating position had now shifted. Britain was gradually surrendering influence over the railway, which was as the Turks had proposed not to be extended beyond Basra, in exchange for control of the Gulf. The British presented the Turks with a new memorandum on 18 July.[21] This was somewhat hasty, as discussions within the administration about the boundaries of Kuwait had not yet concluded. A map was nevertheless added to this memorandum showing the borderline of Kuwait according to the British view of where it ran at that moment – a rather premature step. It diverged from the modern border of Kuwait principally in extending much farther to the west and south than the present border with Saudi Arabia. The southern end of Mubarak's territory on the Gulf was determined as Jabal Manifa, at about 27° 30'. To the north-west the border ran along the Jabal Sanam range until it reached the Wadi Batin, and then along the Wadi Batin to the Hafar wells.[22] Embracing these wells as part of Mubarak's territory, the borderline then made a sharp turn to the south-east, running in a straight line to a point on the track between the Wabra wells and

---

[20] IOLR, R/15/1/611, fo. 156, telegram of Viceroy 13 July 1912.
[21] Busch, *Britain and the Persian Gulf*, p. 335. For the British proposal see IOLR, R/15/5/65, fos. 43(41)–52(46), Grey to Tewfiq Pasha, Ottoman ambassador in London, 18 July 1912.

Riyadh near the Dahna sand-hills. From there a straight line to the north-east left the Wabra wells inside Mubarak's territory, and continued up to the Na'riya hill near Wadi al-Miya. From there it ran in a straight line to the coast at Jabal Manifa.

As for the railway, the British proposed that they would be willing under certain conditions to withdraw their claim for British participation in the Baghdad–Basra section provided it terminated at Basra. The conditions were that the line could be extended farther to the Gulf only under conditions acceptable to Britain, and if two British subjects were appointed to the board. In exchange for thus yielding over the railway, Britain wanted Ottoman concessions over Kuwait and Qatar.

The question of the delimitation of Kuwait remained a thorny issue. The entire question of Kuwait's borders had always been treated by the British in a rather casual manner, and their behaviour now became distinctly odd. Some time after having issued to the Turks a map and a description of Kuwait's borders, they suddenly decided that Lorimer's findings required verification. It would, of course, have been more sensible to check the reliability of the data *before* submitting a proposal to the Turks. Shakespear was despatched once more to clarify a number of points enumerated by Cox in a letter dated 31 July.[23] He quite reasonably went to work on the basis that the areas in which the water wells belonged to tribes acknowledging Mubarak as their overlord could be regarded as Kuwaiti territory. By and large Shakespear confirmed the borders as defined in Lorimer's *Gazetteer*, but on various details reached different conclusions. He agreed with Lorimer's western border along the Wadi al-Batin down to Hafar, but proposed a different trajectory for the southern borderline. The British proposal of July 1912 had drawn three straight lines there, intruding a large wedge of Mubarak's territory between Hafar al-

[22] This is the borderline as abstracted from the map. On this point there is a probable mistake in the textual description of the border, where it mentions that it follows the Wadi Batin down to the crossing with the Wabra–Riyadh road, but no such road can be seen on the map, nor can it exist. It is probably a slip of the pen, maybe for Jahra, because a track from Jahra to Riyadh is indeed shown on the map passing that point. It is clear from the map and later documents that the borderline was to change direction near Hafar al-Batin, near King Faisal Military City, about 95 kilometres down the Wadi al-Batin from the western extremity of Kuwait today.

[23] IOLR, R/15/5/65, fos. 56(26)–58(28), Cox to Shakespear 31 July 1912. Cox took this action on receipt of instructions from India dated 26 July: ibid., fo. 59 (49).

Batin and Wabra into "Ottoman" Najd, and a smaller wedge of "Ottoman" territory north up to the Na'riya hill. Shakespear appears not to have been convinced about the extension of Mubarak's territory as such a deep wedge southwards between Lisafa and Wabra, but also observed that the Ottoman wedge up to the Na'riya hill in reality stood under the authority of Mubarak. According to Shakespear, Mubarak's authority extended southwards from Na'riya about 30 kilometres as far as the Anta'a (Nita') wells. Shakespear proposed a borderline in a wide circle to include Hafar, Lisafa, Wabra and Nita' inside Mubarak's territory. He also considered Mubarak to have a valid claim to Musallamiya Bay, which was the centre of Kuwaiti pearling activities, although the British had previously, in 1902, refused to support this claim. Finally, Shakespear was of the opinion that Mubarak's claims to Umm Qasr and Safwan were more solid than the British had earlier believed, but there was no longer anything to be done about that after O'Conor's lackadaisical handling of the affair.

It was up to Cox to present the matter to the Government of India. He considered that the coastal area claimed by Mubarak could not extend beyond the *Gazetteer* line near Jabal Manifa which had already been proposed by Grey to the Turks. The only extension originating from Shakespear's revision of Kuwait's borders which came to be accepted was the rectification of the Ottoman wedge to include Anta'a (Nita').[24] In general terms, Shakespear and Cox somewhat reduced the extent of Kuwait in the mostly empty extreme southern point of the rectangle proposed to the Turks on 18 July, but in exchange awarded Mubarak some places of more value in the area between Na'riya and Nita'.

One cannot commend the manner in which the British conducted these boundary negotiations. The verdict must be that, both by O'Conor's and Lansdowne's past negligence and by the premature presentation of borders to the Turks in July 1912, the British had done considerable damage to Mubarak's interests.

The Turks were unable to reach a quick decision on the British offer of July 1912 and the matter was stalled for several months. Then, in February 1913, more terrible Balkan disasters placed the Turks in a weaker bargaining position. They accepted the Qatar deal, but still sought more

[24] IOLR, R/15/1/65. Cox sent a preliminary account of Shakespear's findings to India on 4 August and a detailed account by Shakespear on 19 August.

concessions over Kuwait. They requested right of way for their troops through Kuwaiti territory, and possession of Warba and Bubiyan.

Meanwhile on 26 February the India Office approached the Foreign Office with a sketch of a final compromise over Kuwait's borders which had been written by Cox. The India Office urged the Foreign Office not to use it "except in case of real necessity, since the Shaikh will regard it with suspicion". Cox had expressed the fear that Mubarak would be "greatly disappointed by the loss of Umm Qasr, Safwan and Musallamiyya, to say nothing of Anta'a", and the India Secretary still urged the Foreign Office to try to claim Anta'a for Mubarak. An enclosure was appended to this India Office document with a tentative formulation of a compromise on the borders. This document was still based on the old map of 1912, but as a concession to the Turks the large territory claimed for Mubarak was now split into two: "total autonomy" was now limited to a territory circumscribed by a circle with Kuwait City at its centre, while in the remainder the status quo was to be maintained. The circled segment would run from the Khor Zubair to Qrain and outside the island of Qubar. There was immediate confusion because the India Office described this circle as having a radius of 60 miles, while in fact it was only slightly more than 60 kilometres. Nobody seems to have envisaged how this geometric circle might be applied to daily desert practice. The India Secretary saw no sense in the Turkish request for right of passage of their troops through Kuwaiti territory and requested that, if the compromise was to be used, the India Government should be given time to explain the matter to Mubarak before the news reached Kuwait through Turkish channels.[25] Cox reacted by urging that right of passage for Turkish troops within a 60-mile circle or from seaward should be refused.[26]

On 11 March, Mubarak wrote to Cox informing him that the Ottoman authorities had asked his representative in Basra for a statement on his borders. Mubarak had responded with a detailed list of his territorial claims: in the north the Khor Abdallah, Umm Qasr and Safwan; west to the Wadi al-Batin and down it to include Hafar; from there south-east to

[25] IOLR, R/15/5/65, fos. 108(94)–109(95), India Office to Foreign Office 26 February 1913. In this copy kept in the archives of the British Agency in Kuwait, the mention of 60 miles is corrected in pencil (by Shakespear?) to 42. Schofield, "Britain and Kuwait's Borders", p. 84 has, probably by mistake, 80 miles.
[26] IOLR, R/15/5/65, fo. 110(96), Cox 28 March 1913.

Haba (i.e. al-Lihaba, just south of al-Qar'a) and from there just south of eastwards to the south of Anta'a and on to the coast at Jubail. The main discrepancies between this list and the British claim are the northern border where Mubarak maintained his claim to Umm Qasr and Safwan, and the southern border where Mubarak's claim extended farther to the south, to include the wells of Haba just to the south of the British line inland, and on the coast beyond Musallamiya Island. The British were, as we have seen, persuaded that Mubarak's claim to Musallamiya was justified, but deemed it impossible to support it. The distance in a straight line between the southernmost point of Kuwait as claimed by the British (Jabal Manifa) and Musallamiya is about 50 km, from there to Jubail being a further 40 km. This means that the difference between Mubarak's claim and the British one of 1913 in the coastal zone was a stretch of some 90 km. It looks as if Mubarak had intended his piece for British consumption too, considering the clear definition of his rights to Musallamiya and the area beyond it. The British, however, saw it as no more than a useful document to demonstrate to the Turks how moderate Britain's demands were in comparison with Mubarak's.[27]

In the meantime rapid progress was being made in London. On 27 March 1913, the Foreign Office sent the India Office a draft agreement written the day before. Kuwait was to be autonomous under Ottoman suzerainty, the Shaikh was to have the formal title of Kaymakam, and an Ottoman official was to reside in Kuwait. The Turks were not to interfere in internal administration or the succession. The validity of British agreements with Mubarak was confirmed. A new map was offered displaying two arcs: a smaller one around Kuwait town (possibly intended to include Bubiyan and Warba) representing the territory of the

[27] IOLR, R/15/5/65, fos. 102(89)–106(94), Mubarak to Cox 28 Rabi I 1331, with an Arabic copy of Mubarak's statement to the Wali, and letter of Cox to Mubarak 1 April 1913. In his statement to the Wali, Mubarak states that the Subiyeh and Amayer tribes had been settled between Jubail and Musallamiya by Sabah I when this founding father of the Al-Sabah dynasty settled in Kuwait, and that these tribes had paid taxes to Kuwait ever since. Mubarak identifies the following locations as marking the southernmost part of his territory between Hafar al-Batin and the coast at Jubail: al-Safa [= al-Lisafa], al-Qar'a, al-Haba [= al-Lihaba], Iqrayat, Qaswan and Qaraya Anta'a [Nita' village]. Down to Nita this line conforms almost exactly to the British claim, differing only in including the long, narrow coastal stretch from Jabal Manifa to Jubail.

autonomous state, and a wider arc in which the Ottomans were not to make administrative changes to Mubarak's rule of the area. The status of the territory within the wider circle was defined as follows in Article 6 of the proposal:

> Great Britain and Turkey recognise as subordinate to the Sheikh of Koweit the tribes within the territory defined in article 7 of this agreement. The Sheikh shall continue to levy tithes from such tribes as at present, and shall conduct such administration as may be necessary as Turkish kaïmakam. Within the territory defined by article 7 of this agreement Turkey undertakes not to set up any administration apart from that of the Sheikh of Koweit, and not, without previous agreement with Great Britain, to station any garrisons nor take any military or other action.

This Article 6 may be justifiably regarded as a monstrosity in international law, but in practice it presented little danger. The Turks would be unable to intervene in the outer zone without previous permission from the British, and one can hardly imagine circumstances in which such permission would be granted.[28] The India Office agreed some days later with a few minor amendments.[29]

The only remaining hoop was for Mubarak to agree to this British draft before it reached the Turks. It was a compromise arrangement and there were various points to which the Shaikh would take exception, but it seems that the British very properly wanted his approval before signing the treaty. It would be Shakespear's unenviable task to explain the draft to him.

But this was not to happen because Mubarak was very ill. Instead Shakespear protested most vehemently to his superior about what in his opinion was a very poor and ignoble deal. In Shakespear's words, Mubarak "has left his case in our hands with the expectation that we will at least see his just demands satisfied; consequently we shall have to bear the odium and any resentment resulting from such disappointment". Shakespear particularly deplored the India Office proposal of the end of February to divide Mubarak's territory into two zones of different status. His fierce reaction is understandable. He was the man who would have to deal on

[28] IOLR, R/15/5/65, fo. 115(99), draft agreement dated 26 March 1913.
[29] IOLR, R/15/5/65, fo. 132(110), India Office to FO 31 March 1913.

the ground with the consequences of the India Office draughtsmen's abstract geometrical exercises. He complained that the inner circle was merely a paper arrangement with no naturally definable boundary, and he foresaw opportunities for the Turks to undermine Mubarak's authority by intriguing with Bedouin tribes.[30] Even at this late stage he proposed an extension of Kuwait's southern border, because the Haba wells belonged to Mubarak. Shakespear's defence of this sudden inclusion is remarkable: "How I came to omit the al-Haba wells from my previous report [...] dated the 12th August 1912 I cannot now understand." One cannot but wonder at the casualness if not incompetence of the British handling of the border issue. Another amendment Shakespear proposed was the upgrading of Mubarak's title from Kaymakam to Mütesarrif (governor of a *sancak* or arrondissement) instead of chief of a *kaza* or canton. Shakespear voiced strong objections to the establishment of a Turkish agent in Kuwait and urged the restriction of the right of passage of Ottoman troops, if granted at all, to a single remote track to Najd.[31]

Shakespear's objections had come at the eleventh hour. London was unwilling to forego the momentum of the negotiations and decided to carry on regardless. In truth the draft did not represent such a poor deal. Though incorporating a certain amount of face-saving for the Sultan, in essence it excluded Ottoman interference in both the administration of Kuwait and in the outer territory. It was vital that the Turks should have no say in the succession of the Shaikh, which was to remain a totally internal matter for the Kuwaitis. The old treaties with the British remained in place, implying Ottoman acceptance that the Shaikh had the authority to conclude internationally binding agreements without consulting the Sultan. Bubiyan was to be returned and Warba remained Kuwaiti territory. Furthermore the agreement entrenched the rights of the Al-Sabah to their possessions in Basra province more firmly, in that now, as they were defined by treaty, any Ottoman chicanery became subject to international scrutiny. In fact ultimately it was not so much the London officials who had unnecessarily compromised Mubarak's interests, but the Indian Government officials in the Gulf who had so deplorably handled the border issue.

[30] IOLR, R/15/5/65, fos. 122(104)–126(106), Shakespear to Cox 30 April 1913.
[31] IOLR, R/15/5/65, fos. 122(104)–126(106), Shakespear to Cox 30 April 1913.

What was truly remarkable was Shakespear's notion that Britain had made legal concessions to the Turks that would be a great blow to Mubarak. In reality the concessions were purely symbolic and Mubarak's full autonomy was confirmed. The implication of the treaty was that within the inner circle Mubarak was a sovereign ruler under purely symbolic Ottoman suzerainty, and that in the outer zone the situation was different only theoretically but not in practice. Cox watered Shakespear's proposals down slightly in a letter to the Government of India. He supported Mubarak's promotion and one border correction, to include the Haba wells. Cox also supported Shakespear's opposition to Ottoman right of passage, but had understood in the meantime that this clause had been dropped.[32]

Various amendments to the draft had already come from the India Office earlier, on 31 March. There was a clear legal mind at work in the India Office and the amendments proposed were intended to make the limitations of Ottoman authority as clear as possible. The India Office maintained that the assertion of autonomy in foreign affairs was of primary importance – an important statement because the Turks kept disputing this point. Furthermore the India Office wanted to limit the activities of the Turkish agent to the inner circle. And it once again opposed the right of passage of Ottoman troops.[33]

It is indicative of the essentially face-saving character of the Ottoman negotiating position that the final stages of the negotiations were over empty terms. The Ottomans still wanted Kuwait to be declared as being under Ottoman sovereignty, apparently unaware that the other clauses of the treaty would then empty Ottoman sovereignty of any meaningful import. The British clung to the equally meaningless feudal notion of suzerainty. In the end they wisely agreed to omit such terms and simply declare Kuwait an autonomous district (*kaza*) of the Basra province. Perhaps the British should have opposed this point but, in the light of the clear definition of Kuwait's independence both explicitly (no interference in anything) and implicitly (de facto recognition of the right to conclude international agreements), any reference to its position as part of some Ottoman district was an empty shell. This, at any rate, was the opinion of the British negotiators: Britain would accept the mere term *kaza* in

---

[32] IOLR, R/15/5/65, fos. 138(116)–139(117), Cox 11 May 1913.
[33] IOLR, R/15/5/65, fo. 132(110), India Office to Foreign Office 31 March 1913.

exchange for "satisfactory definitions in the following articles". There was also a debate about the clause that the Sultan was not to interfere in the affairs of Kuwait. Hakki Pasha wanted to this to be formulated as "not to interfere in the internal affairs of Kuwait", while the British insisted on both internal and external affairs. In the end a compromise was reached, whereby the Turks agreed to add a separate secret note to the Convention stating that both internal and external affairs were included in the term "affairs of Kuwait". Hakki wanted this note to stipulate too that the Shaikh would not have the right to conclude formal international treaties, but this was opposed by the British. Here by way of compromise it was stated that the Shaikh would not have the right to conclude treaties that contained an infraction on the Convention – which implied no practical diminution of Kuwait's existing independence.

Next Hakki Pasha "claimed to regulate the succession in the Shaikh's family". Here too the British refused to budge and Hakki accepted an innocuous formula: "The Sultan will appoint the successor of the Shaikh as Kaymakam". Designation of the successor remained a purely internal Kuwaiti affair in which the Turks had no say, and the meaning of the word *kaymakam* here is purely ceremonial. As we shall see, the subtlety of this empty British concession was entirely lost on the British representatives in the Gulf, who managed over the following months to cause Mubarak much unnecessary anxiety over this point. So the only role for the Ottomans in the succession was the Sultan's obligation to issue a new Shaikh of Kuwait with a formal document of appointment. This was to be a firman, a document issued by the Sultan himself, not by the Basra Wali. Thus in legal terms the theoretical *kaza* of Kuwait was now entirely separated from Basra province.

The British negotiators did indeed bring into play the concession previously contemplated to divide Kuwait into an inner and outer zone. In exchange they obtained a correction of the southern borderline to include Anta'a, and managed to formulate the distinction in such a way that there was "the same autonomy for the Shaikh in the larger as in the smaller area". Thus too this British concession was reduced to a mere formality. The right of passage for Ottoman troops was excluded in both parts of Kuwaiti territory.[34]

---

[34] IOLR, R/15/1/613, fos. 122–125, "Bagdad Railway and Persian Gulf, the Negotiations with Hakki Pasha", report by Mallet and Hirtzel of 3 May 1913.

Possibly the Ottomans intended to appoint a Basra province official to be their representative residing in Kuwait, but the wording of the treaty makes it all too plain that this poor man would have absolutely nothing to do, except maybe to pay formal visits to the Shaikh on festive occasions. The man's accommodation and upkeep would have to be paid from the hollow Ottoman treasury, and in view of Mubarak's methods on other occasions this might turn out to be very costly. In the circumstances of 1913, this symbolic Ottoman presence in Kuwait would in any case be of little substance, in the light of the anarchy in Basra province described in the previous section.

11.3 The Anglo-Ottoman Convention of 1913

Although at times the Foreign Office and even the India Office had been ready to surrender much of their bargaining position, in the end the deal went well for Kuwait. A balanced appraisal of the outcome, as formulated in the Convention of 1913, should conclude that Britain had relinquished a role in the Baghdad–Basra railway in the belief that a terminus at Basra conferred on Turkey no great strategic advantage in the Gulf. This was a tenable judgement given Britain's naval dominance of the Gulf, now reinforced by the treaty. To give the terminus any strategic value the Ottomans would either have to extend the line to British-controlled territory, or dredge a channel through the Shatt al-'Arab, a task which the British – probably rightly – judged the Turks incapable of carrying out. In exchange the British had gained firm control of the Gulf and a satisfactory agreement over Kuwait. To reiterate: Ottoman influence over Kuwait had been completely defined away.[35]

Article 1 of the Convention regarding Kuwait appears prima facie to represent a concession by the British of Ottoman claims: "The territory of Kuwait [...] constitutes an autonomous kaza of the Ottoman Empire."[36] The next article, however, after granting Kuwait the use of the flag proposed by Cox in 1906, makes it clear that this position as *kaza* is a mere

---

[35] For the text of the agreement with its annexes see Rush, *Records of Kuwait*, Vol. 1, pp. 408–21.

[36] The official French text of Article 1 is: "Le territoire de Koweit, tel qu'il est délimité par les articles 5 et 7 de cette convention, forme un kaza autonome de l'Empire Ottoman."

formality, because the Ottoman Government enjoys no influence whatsoever in Kuwait:

> [the Shaikh] will enjoy complete administrative autonomy [...]. The Ottoman Imperial Government will abstain from all interference in the interior affairs of Kuwait, the matter of succession included and from all administrative action as well as from any occupation or military action in the territories which are part [of Kuwait].[37]

The Ottoman Government will have the right to have a commissioner in Kuwait "to protect the interests of natives of other parts of the Ottoman Empire".[38] This formulation in effect amounts to a denial of the statement in Article 1 that Kuwait is a *kaza* of the Ottoman Empire. The commissioner is not an official in a province of the Ottoman Empire, rather his duty is defined as that of a consular representative "*auprès du cheikh*": his role is limited by the prohibition of interference in internal affairs. He may protect the interests of non-Kuwaitis, precisely the job of a diplomatic agent, but there is no mention of diplomatic privileges.

Kuwait's borders were defined in Articles 5–7 as a compromise that was not entirely according to Mubarak's theoretically justified claims, but the removal of the Ottoman garrison on Bubiyan was stipulated. The treaty was not only a broadly satisfactory solution to Kuwait's status and frontiers, but also conferred protection on Mubarak's own family fortune. The matter of the Basra province date groves was satisfactorily addressed by Article 9, which prevented the Ottomans from impeding him or his heirs in their legitimate possession. Mubarak was even entitled to acquire new ones without taking out any nationality documents.

A small remark is called for at this point on a detail of the treaty. The original French text of Article 2 is perfectly clear on the matter of the Shaikhly succession. First comes the stipulation that the Ottoman

---

[37] The official French text is: "[le cheikh] jouira d'une autonomie administrative complète [...]. Le Gouvernement Impérial Ottoman s'abstiendra de toute immixtion dans les affaires de Koweit, y compris la question de la succession, et de tout acte d'administration ainsi que de toute occupation et tout acte militaire, dans les territoires qui en font partie."

[38] The official French text is that the Ottoman Government "aura la faculté de nommer auprès du cheikh un commissaire pour protéger les intérêts et les indigènes des autres parties de l'Empire".

Government must refrain from any intervention in the affairs of Kuwait, the succession included. Next follows a clause to confirm this: "*En cas de vacance le Gouvernement Impérial nommera kaïmakan, par firman impérial, le successeur du cheikh défunt*". The meaning is: "In the event of a vacancy, the Ottoman Imperial Government will appoint as *kaymakam*, by imperial firman [diploma], the successor of the deceased Shaikh." The French text leaves absolutely no room for any interpretation other than that the Sultan *is obliged* to issue a diploma of appointment to the rank of *kaymakam* to the person who is named as successor by the internal Kuwaiti procedure. In an English translation appearing in a much-used collection of texts of Middle East treaties, a serious error appears. There the text is formulated in a much weaker and misleading way: "In the event of vacancy, the Ottoman Imperial Government will appoint by imperial ferman a kaymakam to succeed the deceased Shaikh".[39] This has in recent years caused regrettable misunderstandings. A publication of the Iraqi Foreign Ministry in 1961 gave an even more remote paraphrase: "in case there being a vacuum the Ottoman Government was to appoint by decree another Qaimmaqam to succeed the Shaikh."[40] It should be stressed that the official version is the French text: the Turks are obliged to appoint the successor as *kaymakam*. The erroneous English translation that the Turks may appoint a successor has no status at all.

The chapter on Kuwait in the Convention of 1913 ends in a rather curious manner, with a joint statement by Britain and the Ottoman Empire that the Convention may not serve as a pretext to the Ottomans to interfere in Kuwaiti affairs, nor may it serve as a pretext to the Shaikh to interfere in the affairs of adjacent Ottoman provinces. The treaty in itself is very clear in forbidding Ottoman interference in Kuwaiti affairs, but the Ottomans seem suddenly to have felt the need to protect their troubled provinces from Mubarak's long arm.

An additional clause was also added secretly recording the Ottoman Government's agreement that the phrase stipulating non-interference in

---

[39] The English translation is in Hurewitz, *Diplomacy in the Near and Middle East*, Vol. 1, p. 269. The mistranslation, which was later used as an argument by the Iraqi side to back their claim to Kuwait, had already been pointed out by Gehrke and Kuhn in *Grenze*, Vol. 2, p. 24.

[40] The Republic of Iraq, *The Truth about Kuwait* (1), Baghdad, Ministry of Foreign Affairs, July 1961, p. 11.

Kuwait's affairs covered foreign policy too (*aussi bien les affaires intérieures qu'extérieures*). The sole limitation was that the Shaikh was prevented from concluding treaties incompatible with the 1913 Convention. In practice this meant that Kuwait was free to conduct its own foreign affairs, albeit limited in certain points by the obligation to obtain the consent of Britain as stipulated in the Agreement of 1899, which was recognized as valid by the Turks in Article 3 of the 1913 Convention.

On the whole the Convention can be regarded as a victory of the India Office line over that of the Foreign Office. The prize won was not the railway of the FO officials, but control of the Gulf and Kuwait. Perhaps this shift of emphasis came about because, somewhere in the back of the British decision-makers' minds, there lurked the fear that surrendering Britain's position in Kuwait would cause not just loss of face, but would also show Britain to be an unreliable party to a contract.

On 6 May 1913, British and Ottoman representatives initialled the final agreement. Local events, however, took their own ominous course. During that very month, the Saudis expelled the Ottoman garrison from al-Hasa. This was to expose a large part of the agreement on Kuwait's borders as mere shadow play. In July the Convention was formally signed and sealed by Hakki Pasha and Foreign Secretary Grey.[41]

11.4 Mubarak's reaction to the Convention

It was late in the day, but now Mubarak, who had recovered somewhat from his illness, had to be informed of the agreement reached. Shakespear had to go to the "old gentleman", who once again showed his usual astuteness in such matters. Cox and Shakespear had apparently been afraid of a major scene of fury, recrimination and even outright rejection. Shakespear in particular adopted a tone of sympathy and compassion for the Shaikh's predicament. But Mubarak showed himself more artful. Indeed Shakespear's compassion may have been misplaced, for there is a real possibility that Mubarak in fact exploited the treaty, which after all was not unsatisfactory, to make the Indian administration feel at fault, and so put himself in a position where he could extract even more from the British.

---

[41] Istanbul BA, Muahedename 242/8, the original version signed and sealed by Grey and Hakki.

The matter had to be broached carefully, as the Shaikh was still very weak from his illness. Despite this Mubarak seems to have lost little of his acuity, because he pressed not on issues that were already irretrievable, but on those that were sensitive to the British too. Shakespear reported that at their first meeting the Shaikh was much more acquiescent than he had anticipated, finding most of the agreement acceptable as a compromise. However he kicked up a most emotional fuss about allowing an Ottoman official into Kuwait. He could do this with justification because there had been a time when Britain was sending warships to avert that very thing. The treaty as a whole rendered it a triviality, but it would have been none the less repellent to the India officials. But Mubarak's legal advisers were capable people. The very next day the Shaikh, sick old man though he was, visited Shakespear with some very sound arguments.

He did not protest about Kuwait being described as part of the Ottoman Empire, for an Empire that had to settle the status of parts of its own territory by international treaty, as was now the case with Kuwait, could hardly be considered a sovereign state in any modern sense. Previously such anomalies had heralded full separation from the Ottoman Empire, as the recent case of Bulgaria demonstrated. Instead Mubarak hammered away on the issue of the Ottoman representative in Kuwait, complaining that the British had awarded the Turks a right they had never before enjoyed. He was able to put on a convincing act of betrayed innocence, especially as Cox and Shakespear themselves felt that the diplomats had conceded too much on this point. We may suspect Mubarak of relishing such histrionics, as he was perfectly alive to the implications of what he was doing. He lamented that Britain had always wanted him to keep foreigners out of Kuwait – something desired not only by the British, but that also accorded with the Kuwaiti desire to keep out foreign competition. This in fact was the only point in his remonstration with Shakespear that hinted at a desire for a British clarification, as it was something about which he clearly needed reassurance. He enquired too about the remainder of the treaty, specifically about the Baghdad Railway. Shakespear detected a suspicion that Kuwaiti interests had been bartered for advantages elsewhere, but he was probably incorrect to do so. The railway had in fact been sacrificed by the British, and the Reuters news, of which Mubarak was also aware, gave no hint of Britain having obtained concessions on this issue.

Cox took up Mubarak's misgivings in a slightly unintelligent letter to the Government of India. He concurred with the Shaikh that the Turkish agent was a "modification of the status quo". He then came up with a remarkable, but imprudent, compromise proposal. Since Mubarak was Kaymakam he was a representative of Turkey, and Cox proposed that he might therefore charge one of his sons "with Turkish cases and interests". Cox was a military and not a legal mind, and had not discerned that the Turkish agent was described in the treaty as a simple consular representative, the implication being that he represented a foreign power, and that Mubarak would thus be much better off if Turkish cases and interests, if they really arose, were dealt with by the agent.

India was wiser and rejected Cox's proposal. There was no problem with a Turkish agent because the Shaikh's autonomy was recognized, and it could be explained to him that the presence of an agent was actually the consequence of his autonomy. India again adduced the example of the Khedive, who also allowed an Ottoman agent in Egypt.[42]

In July, when the treaty had already been initialled by both parties, Cox and Shakespear held a meeting with Mubarak in Muhammara, at which Cox gave Mubarak an Arabic translation of the text of the articles on Kuwait. This translation, which Cox had concocted with the aid of the residency interpreter, appears to have been a peculiarly inept piece of work, as we shall see below.[43] Mubarak still raised half-hearted objections about Umm Qasr and Safwan, but focused his main protests on three points: the Ottoman agent, the fact that the treaty mentioned "his successors" instead of "his sons", and the reference in Article 8 to a customs office in the event of the railway reaching Kuwait. The Turkish agent was the main stumbling block, and most of the meeting centred on that. Cox finally managed to reconcile the Shaikh by giving him in writing the purport of his instructions from India of 13 July 1912, in which the Ottoman demand for an agent was explicitly linked to the fact of Kuwait's autonomy. The other points were less contentious. As the Turks

[42] IOLR, R/15/5/65, fo. 159(138), Cox to Shakespear 27 May 1913. This contains a literal quotation of the passage in the telegram from India to Cox presenting the position of the Turkish agent as a consequence of Kuwait's autonomy.
[43] Regrettably we do not have this translation. Cox wrote that he had given the original to Mubarak and had torn up the only other copy by accident: IOLR, R/15/5/65, fo. 216(187), Cox to Shakespear 3 August 1913.

were forbidden to intervene in the succession, little hinged on the distinction between sons and successors. The customs office was a hypothetical matter: as matters stood the railway would not reach Kuwait.[44] In fact Article 8 stated merely that in the event of Britain and Turkey agreeing on an extension of the line to the autonomous territory of Kuwait, they would negotiate on all railway-related installations such as warehouses and customs offices.

At the end of the Muhammara meeting Cox felt obliged to give Mubarak a letter formally stating, on behalf of the Government of India, that Britain had conducted the negotiations over Kuwait's status on his, the Ruler of Kuwait's, behalf, and that the outcome, being the confirmation of Kuwait's independence, had been in exchange for concessions that he, Mubarak, had made. In the new situation, Britain pledged, in even stronger terms than before, to support Mubarak: "You have the formal assurance of the British Government to support you in your affairs." If the Turks had had sight of this letter they would have felt terribly deceived. They would never have entered upon negotiations if Britain had stated in advance that it was acting on behalf of Kuwait. Curiously, once again, the "old gentleman" had been sufficiently "astute" to seduce the English into going rather too far in order to please him.[45]

There can be little doubt that the treaty of 1913 was an unexpectedly good result for Kuwait – that is, the treaty as originally worded, and not as apparently translated by Cox. On his return to Kuwait, Mubarak approached Shakespear to complain about various terms used in the Arabic translation of Article 1 of the treaty given to him by Cox. Mubarak had qualms about the use of the word *infasl* for "vacancy", about *tashkhas* for the "appointment" of a successor in the event of vacancy, and about *khalaf* or "successor" used instead of "son". In combination, these three words seem to suggest that Cox had not clearly understood the French wording of the treaty. It is indeed not so easy to render in a literal translation the exact meaning of the French sentence "*en cas de vacance le Gouvernement Impérial nommera kaïmakan, par firman impérial, le successeur du cheikh défunt*". As we saw above, the English translation should be: "In case of a vacancy, the Imperial Government will appoint as *kaymakam*, by

---

[44] IOLR, R/15/5/65, fos. 188(161)–190(162), Cox 10 July 1913.
[45] IOLR, R/15/5/65, fo. 192 (163), Cox to Mubarak 6 July 1913.

imperial firman, the successor of the deceased Shaikh." What it certainly does not mean is that the Imperial Government will appoint the successor, this having been explicitly excluded in the previous sentence stating that the Ottoman Government may not interfere in the succession.

It is a reasonable deduction that Cox's translation perpetrated a serious ambiguity on this essential point. *Infasl* can be taken to mean something like "separation" or "absence" and is inappropriate in the context. *Tashkhas* however may also mean "choose" or "elect", and creates an ambiguity if the Turks were to be allowed to do those things. And then the use of *khalaf* instead of son compounded the uncertainty (the word son was explicitly used in the 1899 Agreement). The three terms together could be interpreted to mean that under certain circumstances the Turks might intervene in Kuwait to appoint a new Shaikh![46] Of course such an interpretation would only be based on the erroneous translation by Cox, a man with no very sparkling reputation in Kuwait's later history. The first two words were the most important, and it seems that Mubarak was on strong ground, for Cox seems to have fallen into exactly the same trap as Hurewitz in mistranslating the obligation of the Sultan to recognize the successor appointed by the internal procedure in Kuwait. As for the term *khalaf*, it is also clear that Mubarak was justified in opposing it in this context, as it would open the door to the Turks to manipulate factions in the ruling family, whereas, if the word "son" were used, the scope for Ottoman interference would be considerably diminished. Shakespear's defence was vague and unsatisfactory. In the discussion of *tashkhas* he told Mubarak "that he did not think that the dismissal of a reigning Shaikh was imported", when he should simply have stated that it was excluded. No wonder Mubarak remained sceptical and kept badgering him about *khalaf*.

Next day Shakespear wrote again to Cox about the offending words "with the greatest diffidence because I do not want to appear to be quibbling with the residency translation, second because I do not have the English or Arabic texts." He and his Indian clerk had themselves made an Arabic translation from the French text of the offending passage in Article 1, about which he wanted to consult Cox. Shakespear thought that this translation would satisfy the Shaikh. This version was even less helpful than Cox's opus. It runs somewhat as follows: "If he [the Shaikh] leaves his

---

[46] My thanks are due to Mr Malik Al-Wazzan, of the Kuwait Embassy in The Hague, for pointing out the serious discrepancies between the treaty and Cox's translation.

position the High State will appoint [but the word may also mean choose or elect] by a firman of the Sultan a kaymakam who will be the successor of the deceased Shaikh." In an extreme interpretation this could be taken to mean that if a Shaikh stood down he might be killed and a successor appointed by the Turks.[47]

Cox had thought of another way to satisfy Mubarak. This was just as well, because it pre-empted Shakespear's exercise in linguistics reaching the Shaikh. Cox suggested that Shakespear should try to discover, in a discreet talk with Mubarak, whether he would be interested in an official recognition by the British of his son Jabir as successor designate. In the long term this was an unsatisfactory proposal because it covered only a single succession. Worse, it looked hypocritical if, having just signed a convention excluding interference in the succession in Kuwait, the British then did just that. Shakespear now forgot about his own translation and happily obeyed Cox's orders. He told Mubarak that the English and French texts (was Shakespear really unaware that there existed no official English text?) were perfectly safe concerning interference in the succession, and that it was impossible to alter the word *khalaf/successeur* because the Convention had already been signed. The Shaikh responded that in that case he would accept the British intimation that they would support the succession of members of his own house. He then asked for an official copy or translation of Article 1. He also asked for this copy to include a reference to his objections and the statement that *khalaf* merely meant "successor". Finally Mubarak demanded "that as he was rendered anxious thereby the British Government were prepared to extend that to mean 'Mubarak and successors from his progeny', or in Arabic *Khalaf al-Shaikh min dhariati*". Shakespear thought that Mubarak's main aim in this was to exclude his brothers and their offspring from the succession.[48] This may be part of the truth, but Mubarak had a more objective reason too because the unfortunate Arabic translation did not exclude Turkish

[47] IOLR, R/15/5/65, fos. 198(168)–200(171) and 202(173)–203(174), Shakespear 21 and 22 July 1913.
[48] IOLR, R/15/5/65, fos. 204 (175) and 205(176)–206(177), Cox to Shakespear 22 July, and Shakespear to Cox 29 July 1913. See also fo. 216(187), Cox's explanation of 3 August about the Arabic translation given to Mubarak: it was not in any way authoritative and he was unable to check it, because in error he had torn up the only copy. This does not show Cox's competence as an administrator in a very flattering light.

interference in Kuwait's affairs.

India quite rightly thought little of Cox's suggestion of a succession guarantee. It is quite possible that India had wearied of the often untimely amendments put forward recently by Cox and Shakespear. The Government of India told Cox that it would be best not to approach Mubarak again on the succession question, unless the Shaikh kept harping on about it. India had consulted London about the question raised by Mubarak of the agreement opening the door to the presence of foreigners in Kuwait, and the response had been satisfactory: Cox could now tell Mubarak that he should not admit foreigners before he had consulted the British. On 26 October, Cox revisited Kuwait. Mubarak raised the succession question once more and Cox stressed that the Turks had agreed to abstain from all interference in it. Cox tried to find out what Mubarak's real motive was in placing such emphasis on this matter, and the Shaikh now declared quite openly that he feared that after his death some of his kinsmen might cause dissent and "undo his life's work in the direction of consolidation and improvement". He felt that the British had no reason to disagree with his testamentary dispositions, and expressed the hope that in the event of his sudden death they would "stand by and intervene to regulate the situation". Cox felt that Britain should "put the mind of our venerable protégé at rest" by issuing a written promise.[49] As Mubarak's health was failing, Shakespear's successor Grey urged Bushire to hurry with this document. However, the Government of India's not unreasonable response was that such a promise could only be issued once the 1913 Convention had been ratified.[50]

As we have seen, Shakespear was mistaken in supposing that Kuwait's interests had been used by Britain as bargaining counters to obtain a better negotiating position in other Gulf matters.[51] In reality Britain had sacrificed a role in the railway to keep Mubarak as independent as possible and to maintain its position in Kuwait. The irony of history is that in 1899

---

[49] IOLR, R/15/5/65, fos. 209–210 and 212–213, Government of India to Cox 30 September, and Cox to Government of India 9 November 1913. Cox sent India a proposal for a formal letter to Mubarak on 7 December: ibid., fos. 216–217.

[50] IOLR, R/15/5/59, Grey to Bushire 23 March 1914, and Government of India to Bushire 24 March 1914.

[51] Such pessimistic views of the agreement are reflected in more recent works such as Finnie, *Shifting Lines*, pp. 38–9, and Salwa Al-Ghanim, *Mubarak*, pp. 187–90.

the British acquired an influence in Kuwait in order to control the railway plans, while in 1913 they relinquished the railway in order to uphold Kuwait. The 1913 agreement was nothing less than a clear acceptance by the Turks of the British view of the Status Quo Understanding of 1901 in its widest sense. The few substantive disadvantages for Mubarak to have entered into the agreement were a consequence of Britain's past negligence – territorial erosion in the north caused by Lansdowne's and O'Conor's lack of interest – and, more recently, Shakespear's belated explorations. Cox and Shakespear caused Mubarak unnecessary anxiety by their misguided and bungled translations of Article 1.

One may cogently argue that Mubarak was the overall winner in the game. His autonomy had been defined in terms as strong and wide as possible. This independence had been formulated as much in relation to Turkey, by the total exclusion of Turkish interference, as in relation to Britain, by its formal undertaking not to establish a protectorate over Kuwait. What emerges most obviously of all is that the 1913 Convention was a much better deal for Mubarak than the original negotiating package of 1911.

11.5 Legal consequences of the Convention

A debate took place in the 1960s about whether the 1913 agreement was legally binding. The consensus of international law experts has always been that treaties become valid after ratification, but it has been suggested that this was a simple agreement not requiring ratification. The opinion of Pillai and Kumar was that it possibly did not need to be ratified. This was a mistake. Kuhn rightly pointed to the clause (Article 18) stipulating ratification within three months, and was able to show that ratification was in fact postponed several times due to matters unrelated to Kuwait, concerning remaining uncertainties over the financing of the Baghdad Railway.[52] Their error fatally weakens Pillai and Kumar's otherwise interesting speculations about the legal consequences of the treaty. But their entire description of the Convention is vitiated by their use of the erroneous English translation.[53]

---

[52] Gehrke and Kuhn, *Grenze*, p. 144.
[53] Pillai and Kumar, "Political and Legal Status", p. 118.

Kuhn's remarks about the legal implications of the treaty are more significant. He rejects Pillai and Kumar's thesis that Kuwait remained under Ottoman *sovereignty* because the word *suzerainty* was not used in the Convention. Kuhn rightly observed that the word sovereignty was also studiously avoided, and that the treaty in fact implies the classical definition of suzerainty: no Ottoman interference in anything, with the Shaikh even being able to conclude international agreements provided only that they did not run counter to the 1913 agreement. Kuhn rightly concludes that this amounts to the acceptance of an almost complete independence of Kuwait in international law.[54] An essential point here is that, as both parties had confirmed the status quo, neither Britain nor the Ottoman Empire could make any alteration to Kuwait's status as a formal vassal of the Ottoman Empire; any such change would legally require the consent of the Shaikh of Kuwait.[55]

Kuhn also demonstrates that any claim that Kuwait was a *kaza* of Basra province would be terminated by the 1913 treaty. There Kuwait is identified as a *kaza* not of Basra but of the Ottoman Empire, and Article 7 explicitly refers to a border between Kuwait and Basra province. Kuhn also points out that even in the Ottoman proposal of 1912 there is a mention of Mubarak's properties in Basra province, so implicitly confirming that Kuwait was not part of that province.[56]

Kuhn then observed that the right of the Sultan to appoint a representative or "commissioner" to Kuwait seriously undermines the statement in Article 1 that Kuwait is a *kaza* of the Ottoman Empire. If Kuwait were a regular *kaza* then the *kaymakam* would be the representative of the Sultan. If the chief of the *kaza* (i.e. Mubarak) is not the representative of the Sultan, and if the new representative of the Sultan is not allowed to interfere in the administration of the *kaza*, then the *kaza* cannot be a real *kaza*. Thus Kuhn makes more explicit the argument used by the Government of India to counter Mubarak's objection to having a Turkish representative. The acceptance by the Turks of the validity of the old agreements between Mubarak and the British entailed, according to Kuhn, the effective recognition by the Turks of Kuwait as an independent Ottoman vassal in the old style of Egypt and the like.

[54] Gehrke and Kuhn, *Grenze*, p. 148 and n. 97a.
[55] Gehrke and Kuhn, *Grenze*, p. 147.
[56] Gehrke and Kuhn, *Grenze*, p. 148.

Kuhn's final conclusion that the 1913 agreement changed nothing of substance in Kuwait's status is correct. Less convincing is his remark that Mubarak acted as if the treaty did not exist by granting Britain an oil concession on his own authority on 27 October 1913, in blatant disregard of the fact that the first term for ratification ended on 29 October. One might claim with equal justification that Mubarak was simply anticipating his rights according to the treaty.[57]

There is one further important legal aspect to the treaty. Its text concerning Kuwait was acceptable as such to the Ottomans, the delay in ratification having other causes. One might therefore reasonably conclude from this that the concept of the title of Kaymakam as a mere honorific, and thus not exclusively denoting an administrative rank, was acceptable to the Turks. The readiness of the Turks to sign the Convention also amounts to their confirmation, once again, of the existence in practice of a vassal entity enjoying almost complete sovereignty in international law, including the power to conclude treaties.

The outside world had no illusions about the contents of the treaty. Britain could expect its French and Russian allies simply to keep quiet about it. The German Government was taken aback, but not seriously. Their view was that the Turks had suffered a loss because of their bungling of the affair. The German press was another matter. Theodor Ling's fulminations in the *Reichsbote* went to the heart of the matter in more robust language than that available to diplomats:

> The Shaikh of Kuwait is the man upon whom centres the most important decisions concerning relations between Germany, England and Turkey. This man is the reason why the terminus of the Baghdad Railway has been wheedled away from the German people, why Turkey has been forced out of its Arab territories on the Persian Gulf, and why the English ring around the Gulf is now completely closed. The Shaikh of Kuwait is the cause of all this, since the Shaikh of Kuwait is – **a traitor!**[58]

At the end of August 1913, the same author penned an article in *Der Tag* extolling the advantages of the Khor Abdallah as a possible terminus

[57] Gehrke and Kuhn, *Grenze*, pp.145–7.
[58] German newspaper *Reichsbote* of 21 July 1913, in Berlin AA, R 13891 A 15584 (cutting).
[59] Berlin AA, R 13891 A 17430, German newspaper *Der Tag* of 26 August 1913.

for the railway.[59] He was aware that the definition of Kuwait's borders made this a contentious issue, but urged Turkey and Germany to press for a modification of the treaty. But this was just the empty sound and fury of the nationalist press. The matter had been settled by Britain and Turkey without German involvement, and this constituted just one more small drop in the bucket of German frustration contributing to the outbreak of the First World War.

12

Mubarak's Last Years
1913–1915

12.1 Towards the First World War

During the later months of 1913 Mubarak was chiefly absorbed by
internal affairs. A new steamer for bringing fresh water to Kuwait arrived,
and he had to reorganize Kuwait's customs service, which was still
functioning unsatisfactorily.[1] But in the course of 1913 there were
considerable developments on the international scene. More locally, Basra
province was in a state of permanent unrest, and there was also continuing
tension between the Ottoman authorities and the Muntafiq. There were
changes in the interior too, as the star of the Al-Rashid was in the
ascendant once more.[2]

The moving spirit in the Basra province troubles was Talib. At the
beginning of 1913 this unpredictable character had set himself up as leader
of an Arab popular movement. Then came further news, this time of an
impending rebellion by Talib, which was averted by the intervention of his
enemy 'Ajaimi of the Muntafiq.[3] This was accompanied by rumours of a
grand Arab alliance, to be inaugurated in a conference to be held in
Kuwait of representatives of all the Arabian Peninsula rulers.[4] In January

---

[1] *Political Diaries*, Vol. 5, p. 285 (October 1913) and p. 313 (November 1913).
[2] Berlin AA, R 13874 A 10140 (18 May 1913), Wangenheim 14 May 1913.
[3] Paris AE, NS Turquie 152 (Baghdad), fos. 207 and 215: Dozon, acting consul, 28 June
and 3 August 1913; *cf.* Berlin, AA, R 13874 A 21526 (28 October 1913), Hesse 8
October 1913. Hesse's view was that Talib posed little danger to the Turks because, as
a Sunni leader in Shiite Basra, his faction was limited to Sunni Arab officers and liberal
Turks.

1914, meetings were held in Muhammara between Talib, Khaz'al and Mubarak's son Jabir, the agenda of which is unknown but possibly concerned the Muntafiq raids that had recently resumed.[5] In February 1914, in the course of a visit to his friend Khaz'al in Muhammara, Mubarak had a final informal meeting with a Wali of Basra. The recently appointed Suleyman Shafiq Pasha, arriving from Constantinople by ship, was welcomed en route in Muhammara by an intriguing group of dignitaries: Mubarak, Talib and various Basra notables. Mubarak told the British agent in Basra that the Wali had asked anxious questions about British intentions towards Ibn Saud, and that he, Mubarak, had told the Wali that the British had no plans regarding Central Arabia.[6]

This was a decidedly economical description of the actual state of affairs. In reality the Saudi conquest of al-Hasa had confronted the British with a serious diplomatic dilemma. They could hardly maintain their old resistance to dealings with the Saudis now that the latter were their immediate neighbours in the Bahrain area. On the other hand, the grounds for that resistance had now strengthened. The British had avoided significant contacts with the Saudis in the past in order not to arouse Turkish suspicions of British intrigues, not only in Kuwait but also against Ottoman control of the coast between 'Uqayr and the border of Kuwait, which had been formally recognized as Ottoman in the Convention of 1913. A wrangle between the Government of India, which was interested in the Bahrain border zone, and the Foreign Office, which shied away from a quarrel with the Turks just when the old disputes had been resolved, was inevitable.

The Foreign Office was unable to oppose India's encouragement of informal discussions between Shakespear (who had just been replaced as political agent in Kuwait by Grey and was free for a new task), Trevor (the

---

[4] Paris AE, NS Turquie 123 (Syria 1913), fos. 142–144, Ottavi, French consul in Damascus, 21 November 1913.

[5] *Political Diaries*, Vol. 5, p. 385 (January 1914). Shortly after, however, there was a brief little quarrel between Mubarak and Khaz'al, ibid. p. 416. At the same time, though, the Naqib was visiting Kuwait.

[6] *Political Diaries*, Vol. 5, p. 434 (March 1914). There were rumours in Constantinople too at this time that Mubarak was supporting an Arab nationalist movement in Basra, but this seems improbable, and the British did not believe it: IOLR, R/15/5/26, fos. 140–141, Government of India to Bushire 20 April 1914, enclosing a report by Mallet in Constantinople of 24 February.

political agent in Bahrain), and the Saudis, and occasional meetings took place. The Saudis were seeking a deal of some kind with the British because pressure was building up against them. It seems that opposition to their domination of the Arabian tribes was intensifying. A German report that three-quarters of the tribes of Arabia were now more in sympathy with the Rashidis, testifies to the growing strength of Haïl.[7] Moreover the end of the Balkan wars had freed the Ottomans to send more troops to Iraq. Under such circumstances the Saudis had to keep open the option of a reconciliation with the Turks.

However the Saudis still preferred a deal with the British, who might help them acquire arms and ammunition to counter the Rashidi threat. Mubarak too felt more secure at the prospect of an Anglo-Saudi alliance. The Turks meanwhile were smarting over the loss of al-Hasa, and set about trying to reach an accommodation with the Saudis. The Porte still saw Mubarak as an important influence in Arabia, so an official of the Ottoman War Department visited him with a request to arrange a meeting with Ibn Saud. Mubarak informed the British agent that he had not been very co-operative, and said that a meeting between the Wali and the Saudis would be futile in view of the hostility to the Turks in Najd.[8] German reports describe the new Wali, Suleyman Shafiq, as entirely under the influence of Talib and Khaz'al, and facing growing opposition from the Muntafiq and Ibn Rashid in the background.[9] Under such circumstances the Wali would be wise to show the Porte that he could achieve results with the Saudis. Mubarak showed little interest in these proceedings, possibly because an alliance between Talib, the Turks and the Saudis could hardly redound to his advantage.

The Saudis kept the Turks waiting while they pursued an arrangement with the British. Their plan was to obtain something in the nature of Mubarak's 1899 Agreement, and they tried to oil the wheels by promising not to interfere with the Arab Shaikhs under British protection. In the end this failed because of Foreign Office reluctance to offend the Porte, especially at a time when Hakki Pasha was repeatedly urging British officials not to support the Saudis against the Turks.

---

[7] Berlin AA, R 13874 A 10140 (18 May 1913), Wangenheim in Constantinople 14 May 1913.
[8] *Political Diaries*, Vol. 5, pp. 434–5 (March 1914, sections Kuwait and Muhammara).
[9] Berlin AA, R 13891 A 8867, Baghdad 18 April 1914.

Meanwhile the Wali tried to approach Abdul Aziz Al-Saud through Talib[10] – a risky operation in view of Talib's dark reputation for intrigue.[11] At the same time the Turks tried to exert discreet pressure on the Saudis by supplying Haïl with large shipments of arms.[12] Abdul Aziz Al-Saud, having long delayed negotiating with the Turks while awaiting a British decision, yielded at last and a meeting was planned on Kuwaiti territory. The Ottoman delegation went via Kuwait to a point in the desert where the Saudi delegation was to meet them. Mubarak facilitated the journey, for which he was rewarded with a high Ottoman decoration, but did no more. The Ottoman delegates were eager for Mubarak to accompany them, to which the political agent Grey saw no problem – a remarkable response in view of persistent British objections to Mubarak's meddling in desert affairs. This time it was Mubarak who refused to involve himself in the negotiations.[13] Possibly it was no more than a matter of his failing health, but there may have been other reasons for his refusal. He may for example have had an understandable distrust of a venture in which Talib was to play a prominent part. Mubarak's equilibrium policy may also have informed his calculations: a Saudi-Ottoman agreement would create a power bloc in the region that could pose a threat to Kuwait.[14] And Mubarak traditionally preferred larger alliances of Arab leaders, whereas the Turks aimed to curb Saudi power, as demonstrated by their despatch of another large consignment of arms to Haïl immediately after reaching an agreement with the Saudis. The German consul in Baghdad considered this a wise step, arguing that the Turks had to support the Rashidis in order to avert their subjugation by the Saudis, whom he regarded as under British influence.[15]

The negotiations of May 1914 opened in the usual manner with the Turks making extreme demands: the al-Hasa fortresses were to be restored

[10] Berlin AA, R13876 A 14051, German consul Baghdad, 16 July 1914.
[11] Opinion on Talib by Shakespear in a letter to Hirtzel: IOLR, R/15/5/27.
[12] Berlin AA, R 13875, German ambassador in Constantinople 22 March 1914.
[13] *Political Diaries*, Vol. 5, pp. 434–5 (March 1914); IOLR, R/15/5/27, Grey to Bushire 29 April and 6 May 1914, with enclosed correspondence between Grey and Mubarak. See also an Arab point of view in Musil, *Northern Negd*, p. 286.
[14] Salwa Al-Ghanim, *Mubarak*, p. 195, presents a different interpretation: by refusing to participate, Mubarak lost the last opportunity to exercise influence in Central Arabia.
[15] Berlin AA, R13875 A 5891 (25 March 1914), German ambassador in Constantinople 22 March 1914.

to them and the Saudis were to have no independent foreign relations. The Saudis gave no ground over al-Hasa, counting on the British to prevent Ottoman ships transporting troops there. The land route was very arduous and dangerous and an overland march by troops was unfeasible with the approach of summer. The Ottomans urged the British to make it clear that no British help would be forthcoming, and the British Foreign Secretary co-operated by deciding to have nothing to do with the Saudis, so forcing the latter to negotiate as well as they could with the Turks.[16] The Saudis tried to reach a deal of the same kind as the Safwan agreement of 1905, allowing the Turks to instal symbolic garrisons in the al-Hasa fortresses. A formal agreement was reached on this basis and ultimately ratified by Abdul Aziz Al-Saud and Suleyman Shafiq Pasha.

It is interesting to compare this treaty with the 1913 Anglo–Ottoman Convention regarding Kuwait. The treaty gives the superficial impression that the Saudis made very heavy concessions to the Turks. One should, however, bear in mind that there was a precedent for an agreement between the Turks and Riyadh in which the Saudi concessions had proved to be meaningless. Najd was elevated from a *sancak* to a *wilaya*. Abdul Aziz Al-Saud was made Wali of Najd for life, and the dignity was to be hereditary. As many soldiers and gendarmes as the Wali might deem necessary were to be stationed in seaports such as Qatif and 'Uqayr. This is a very watered-down version of the original Ottoman right to garrison the al-Hasa fortresses. The revenues from customs, ports, post and (illusory) telegraph could be used to make good any deficit in the provincial administration, the remainder to be sent to the Porte. The Turkish flag was to be hoisted on government buildings, and Turkish postage stamps were to be used. The Wali of Najd was forbidden to engage in foreign affairs, conclude treaties or grant concessions to foreigners. The Wali was to come to the aid of the Porte with troops as occasion demanded.[17]

Though in purely legal terms these concessions made Najd into what almost amounted to a regular Ottoman province, they meant very little in practice. Najd might differ formally from a normal province only in that the office of Wali was hereditary. But nothing was said about the appointment of lower officials, and that meant that the Wali could appoint

[16] Goldberg, *Foreign Policy*, pp. 102–5.
[17] Goldberg, *Foreign Policy*, pp. 191–2, gives an English translation of the treaty as found in the Basra Turkish records.

his own men without consulting the Porte. However, a degree of Ottoman sovereignty was established by the revenue provisions. Customs dues, for example, essentially belonged to the Porte, in contrast to Kuwait where Mubarak had always levied such revenues on his own authority. Also, the Wali was precluded from making agreements with foreign powers. Hence one might follow Kuhn's line and conclude that Najd lacked external sovereignty.

In internal affairs, however, things were very different. The Wali was the sole Ottoman official, and the Porte had no influence on local administration or legislation. The original right to appoint the *qadis* in Najd arrogated by the Ottomans had not been enforced, so internally the authority of the Sultan over Najd was essentially symbolic. On the other hand it would not be legally correct to characterize the Ottoman relationship with Najd as mere suzerainty rather than sovereignty, because the revenues of Najd were still under the authority, albeit symbolic, of Constantinople. In the proper feudal context of "suzerainty", revenues normally belonged to the vassal, not to the suzerain. But such limitations to Saudi independence should not be overestimated. They had substance more in legal theory than on the ground. The Turks had no physical means of preventing the Saudis from dealing with the British if they felt like it. And in the absence of any Ottoman officials, the revenues went in practice to the Saudi treasury.

The British disapproved of the 1914 Saudi-Ottoman agreement.[18] It was of dubious value and could mean little more than a token submission by the Saudis to the Ottoman Empire. It amounted to mere face-saving by the Turks, and the Wali of Basra, Suleyman Shafiq Pasha, gained little credit for it. Soon new trouble erupted with the Muntafiq, and the Turks could find no other way to restore order than by recalling the Wali, who was over-friendly with Talib.[19]

[18] IOLR, R/15/5/25, summary of the agreement in a telegram by Cox to Foreign Department in Delhi, 28 (or 26?) January 1915. A probably fanciful news item about a completely different treaty between Ibn Saud and the British appeared in May 1914 in a Calcutta Persian-language newspaper: see Berlin AA, R 13875 A 13794, German consul in Bushire 20 June 1914. See also Musil, *Northern Negd*, p. 286, and Anscombe, *Ottoman Gulf*, pp. 164–5.

[19] Berlin AA, R 13891 A 8867 (6 May 1914), and R 13875 A 10320 (24 June 1914), Hesse in Baghdad, 18 April and 9 May 1914. The letter of 6 May 1914 is also interesting because it contains the last mention of the "Republic of Kuwait".

Mubarak had been wise not to involve himself in the negotiations. His own position was secure while the Ottoman grip on the region was slipping. In April 1914 he approached Shakespear with a remarkable request. The elderly Shaikh wanted to visit India, Cairo and London – an initiative that shows the extent to which he was still animated by his old curiosity about everything that might influence the future of Kuwait. He wanted to see the outside world for himself. It is significant too that he felt sufficiently confident to absent himself from Kuwait for such a long time. The request went through the hands of Mubarak's old sparring partner Knox, at that time acting resident in Bushire.[20] Knox was not enthusiastic. He advised the Government of India that Mubarak's "strong personality" should not leave Kuwait "for however short a period" because of the unrest in al-Hasa, by which he meant the trouble that had broken out between the Saudi-Kuwaiti alliance and the 'Ajman, and because the 1913 Convention had not yet been ratified. India informed London, with a reminder that such a visit by Mubarak had already been considered several times since 1905. The Government of India was positive about a visit to India, with the qualification that it could be considered only once the 1913 Convention had been ratified. But India was opposed to Mubarak travelling to Egypt and Britain. The reason given, which was based on protocol, looks decidedly flimsy: on such a journey an Ottoman *kaymakam* would be under an obligation to visit Constantinople. This seems a feeble argument. The normal route would be Kuwait – Bombay – Suez – Cairo – Port Said – London, and then back to the Suez Canal and through the Red Sea again. At no point does this route pass close to the Ottoman capital. A more convincing, but tacit, reason would have been that Mubarak might make undesirable Arab contacts in Cairo. Another British motive could have been an aversion, common among colonial powers, to native rulers under their protectorate visiting Europe. The 1913 Convention was never ratified, and Mubarak's travel plans were finally abandoned in September 1914, this time because of the outbreak of the World War.[21]

[20] Lorimer, author of the famous *Gazetteer of the Persian Gulf,* had succeeded Cox in 1914, but soon after his arrival in Bushire died under somewhat mysterious circumstances while cleaning his gun. Knox then became acting resident.
[21] IOLR, R/15/1/513, Knox to Foreign Department, 5 April 1914; Government of India to Secretary of State for India 28 May 1914; Foreign Department to Knox, 22 September 1914.

War had broken out in August 1914. There followed a few months during which Britain tried to persuade the Turks to remain neutral. Research carried out only quite recently has shown how hopeless these British diplomatic efforts were. Previous Foreign Office policy for settling differences with the Turks aimed at keeping them from the German embrace, and had simply failed to appreciate the power of pro-German circles in the Ottoman Empire. This pro-German influence gradually prevailed. It was the pro-German Ottoman Ministers of War and Marine who gave authority to German warships to attack Russia from Ottoman bases. This was not sanctioned by the Ottoman Cabinet, but it was an act of war. Russia's ally Britain responded with an ultimatum. The Ottoman Cabinet was slow to react, and the British declared hostilities against the Ottomans on 1 November 1914.[22]

By that time the Ottomans appear to have moved troops to Fao, and there were rumours that they wanted to occupy Kuwait and Bahrain. The British agents in these places even fled to Bushire for a short time, but they soon returned.[23] The German consul in Bushire reported rumours there that Kuwait was tense because the pro-British Mubarak's son and heir, Jabir, had come out in revolt against him, and that British troops were being sent there. This seems to have been false.[24] The region felt the impact of the war in Europe straight away. Shipping was restricted, and already by the early autumn of 1914 the prices of European goods had doubled.[25]

The Government of India had already for some time been preparing for an eventual conflict with the Turks in the Gulf, as one of the regions where the Ottoman Empire directly bordered on the British sphere of influence. India had devoted so much attention for so long to largely hypothetical means of communication with Europe via the Gulf that it is little surprise

[22] The complex course of events by which the Ottoman Empire came to war with Britain is explained by Fromkin, *A Peace to End All Peace*, pp. 58–73.

[23] Paris AE, NS Mascate 15, fos. 121v–122, French consul in Bushire 13 October 1914. The French consul spoke about "fled" to Bushire, but this was perhaps just a temporary stay to assist at the residency in the composition of Arabic correspondence, as mentioned in Schofield, *Arabian Boundaries*, Vol. 10, p. 513, Knox 14 September 1914.

[24] Berlin AA, R 13876 A 31421, Listemann in Bushire 6 October 1914, is entirely different from *Political Diaries*, Vol. 5, p. 560 (December 1914). The rumours also contrast with previous reports of Mubarak's son Jabir having the reputation of being more pro-British than his father.

[25] Paris AE, NS Mascate 15, fo. 121, French consul in Bushire 13 October 1914.

that the British attacked the Turks in Iraq almost immediately. In itself this was a reasonable strategy. The British did not yet have a firm strategic position in the Gulf and their main base at Bushire was situated in Persian territory. In the light of the Ottoman army's weakness in Iraq, British occupation of southern Iraq was a logical step to prevent the Turks from ever pursuing their tenuous claims in the Gulf. Britain's main fear in a war with the Turks was that the latter might appeal to Muslim solidarity. This was allayed somewhat by Mubarak's apparent suggestion to the British that it might be possible for him, Khaz'al and local notables, with the more remote support of Abdul Aziz Al-Saud, to neutralize Basra or allow the British peaceful occupation of that place. To this end it was considered expedient to make various promises to Mubarak, Khaz'al and Abdul Aziz Al-Saud.[26] This development seems to have been inspired in part by talks between Mubarak and Cox after the outbreak of war in Europe in the late summer of 1914, before the Ottoman Empire had effectively entered the war. From the start Mubarak tried to bring over the Saudis to the side of the Entente against the Ottoman Empire, although he was rather slower in committing himself publicly. Meanwhile the Saudis were in a somewhat difficult position because Saud bin Subhan, the Rashidi regent of Haïl, had declared holy war on the Saudis as traitors to the Ottoman Empire, and was some way to restoring Rashidi power.[27]

On 6 November, British troops landed at Fao. At the beginning of that month, Cox in Bushire was aiming to press Mubarak into making a clearer pro-British commitment. Mubarak received a request to attack Umm Qasr, Safwan and Bubiyan, and to try to expel the Turks from Basra with the help of the Saudis and Khaz'al, while the British attacked Basra with warships. In exchange, Cox promised Mubarak that the British, having conquered Basra, would keep the place, that they would protect Mubarak from the consequences of attacking Bubiyan, Umm Qasr and Safwan, and that the British Government would recognize Kuwait as "an independent Government under British Protection". Mubarak's possession of the date groves in Basra province would be guaranteed for him and his heirs, and would be immune from taxation. Mubarak hardly had time to go into action for, on 20 November, Basra was occupied by the British.

[26] Correspondence, partly through Mubarak as intermediary, with Ibn Saud, in IOLR, R/15/5/25, from 5 October 1914, fos. 176–94.
[27] Musil, *Northern Negd*, p. 249.

What happened next is less clear. No mention is to be found of attacks by Mubarak's troops on the Turks, although a few weeks later it was reported that the Ottoman troops had retired from Umm Qasr. This made an Ottoman presence on Bubiyan untenable, while Safwan too had probably been evacuated.[28] The British were relieved to hear that the populace of Kuwait evinced no audible pro-Ottoman sympathies. Mubarak then clearly demonstrated his intentions for all the world to see by replacing the Ottoman flag with a special Kuwaiti one lacking the Ottoman emblem. The final form of this flag – a red one with the word "Kuwait" in Arabic characters – had been determined in consultation with Bushire.[29]

The British agent in Kuwait, Grey, was very explicit in his praise for Mubarak, who was active in dissuading other Arab Shaikhs from joining the Sultan. The *Times of India* published a letter from a certain Mr Chandarvarkar from Malabar, who wrote: "Arab merchants, followers of the Shaikh of Kuwait on the Arabian coast who come here for the purpose of trade, are becoming helpful in enlightening the Mahomedans on the correct situation about the war and the folly of Turkey in allowing herself to be made a catspaw of German ambition." It remains highly questionable whether the Ottoman Sultan's attempt to combat Britain by declaring a *jihad* ever had a realistic chance of success, but the British were none the less fearful of the religious zeal the Sultan might unleash, and were seemingly happy for Mubarak to help neutralize that Ottoman weapon.[30]

Minimal though his war effort on Britain's behalf might have been, Mubarak seems to have reaped the full benefit of it. The British considered themselves fully bound by their promises of 13 November, as can be seen from a later list of British obligations in the Gulf.[31] Mubarak could feel considerable satisfaction. He was now rid of all ties with the Ottoman Empire, and Kuwait had been clearly confirmed as an independent government – the later list of British obligations even uses the word

[28] *Political Diaries*, Vol. 5, p. 560 (December 1914).
[29] Rush, *Records of Kuwait*, Vol. 1, pp. 537–9.
[30] IOLR, R/15/1/504, fos. 86–88 (90–92), Grey to Bushire 9 June 1915.
[31] IOLR, R/15/1/513, Knox to Government of India 5 April 1914; Government of India to India Office 28 May 1914; and Government of India to Knox 22 September 1914.

"principality". The British had now recognized Kuwait's sovereignty as being entirely separate from the Ottoman Empire. Now, at last, all the carefully contrived devices of previous years for saving Ottoman face could be dropped. A British post office was finally opened in Kuwait.

The legitimacy of this belated British recognition of Kuwait's independence was questioned in 1962 by Pillai and Kumar. Their thesis is that the 1914 promise was invalid since it constituted a breach of the 1913 Convention, because vassals are not allowed to make war on their suzerains.[32] This opinion was strongly opposed by Kuhn, who argued that it is difficult to apply the tools of international law to this situation because the concept of suzerainty is so vague. Kuhn observes that the obsolete term suzerainty, which belongs to medieval feudal law, can be defined in two ways. First, it can be seen as a kind of authority of one element over another within a single state; Kuwait's secession would then be not a matter of international law, but simply of the fragmentation of a state and therefore an internal matter. The Turks would be entitled to punish Mubarak and reverse the situation should they be able to do so, but otherwise the secession would become an established fact. The second option is to consider suzerainty as the unifying bond amongst a number of separate territorial entities. In that case, suzerainty would indeed be a matter of international law, but then Kuwait's action would amount to a simple revocation of an agreement. Once again, if the other party is unable to reverse it, the revocation becomes a fact. Finally, Kuhn rejects Pillai and Kumar's thesis that a vassal may not make war on his suzerain. Kuwait's behaviour is no different from other rebellions which international law "has been forced to countenance" by recognizing the legitimacy of the secession.

Comparison between Pillai and Kumar's position on the one hand and Kuhn's on the other shows that, for Kuhn, the essential event is not the recognition by the British, but the act of secession by Mubarak. Secession from the Ottoman state is simply a de facto issue: the question is simply whether the secession has become effective, as was the case with Mubarak. If it was a revocation of an agreement, then the question is whether the revocation was accepted or was legitimate. Kuhn puts forward the option that a revocation may become effectively lawful when the other party (the

[32] Pillai and Kumar, "Political and Legal Status", pp. 122–5.

suzerain) becomes unable to defend his claims. Kuhn states that in any case the secession of Kuwait was later implicitly accepted by the Ottoman Empire or its legal successor the Turkish Republic by the peace treaties of Sèvres and Lausanne. Another important legal factor was the recognition by the Turkish Republic of the right of self-determination of territories with an Arab majority.[33]

Joining the British in 1914 was Mubarak's final gamble. It accorded with his previous inclinations, and in any case was forced upon him: with British naval power in the offing he could hardly afford to declare himself a supporter of the Sultan. It was none the less a gamble, because in the years that followed it sometimes looked as if the Germans might win the war. The German-trained Ottoman army proved to be an unexpectedly capable force. This would be demonstrated not only at Gallipoli, but also in Iraq where the Ottoman forces, commanded by the German von der Goltz Pasha, painfully exposed the inadequacies of the British Indian forces.[34] It took the British more than three years to reach Baghdad, but Basra remained firmly in their hands throughout and there was no real danger for Kuwait.

The British had good reasons to be grateful to Mubarak in the First World War. Had it not been for his antics in previous years delaying the construction of the final section of the Baghdad Railway, the weak British Indian Expeditionary Force would have been faced with a much stronger enemy in Iraq. And given the extent to which the Germans showed themselves capable of fomenting trouble in Iran and even Afghanistan, British domination of the Gulf could have been under threat. Old Col. Meade, in retirement in Britain, would have been entitled to feel greatly satisfied by his work in 1899.

Not that Kuwait participated in the war in any active manner. The only clear instance of Kuwaiti military participation is Mubarak's despatch of a considerable military force of 1500 men to help his friend Khaz'al protect his oilfields from attack by pro-German Persian leaders. This provoked

[33] Gehrke and Kuhn, *Grenze*, pp. 149–51. On pp. 152–7, Kuhn concludes that in any case all this clearly demonstrates that the issue of Kuwait's statehood is entirely distinct from the yet-to-emerge issue of Iraqi statehood.

[34] Already in 1910 the British had observed that German training had improved the quality of Ottoman troops in Baghdad: IOLR, R/15/5/5, fo. 221 (200), confidential information forwarded by Lorimer, consul in Baghdad, 18 August 1910.

discontent among Kuwaitis. A deputation followed Mubarak to Muhammara and obtained the return of 1200 men to Kuwait. Mubarak was unhappy about this and manifested his deep displeasure before a meeting of notables. At the same time there were reports in Basra about agitation against the pro-British Shaikh in Kuwait. They originated from the Basra police commissioner, and seem to have been exaggerated. According to Grey, most Kuwaitis were anti-Turkish and pro-British, and would remain so even if France, Britain or even Russia were to occupy Constantinople. The Basra police produced the names of three opponents of Mubarak. Grey was not impressed. One of the trio was unknown in Kuwait, and the other two did not look especially sinister. The first, a certain "Sheikh Muhammad Shangaiti" had lived in Jahra for two years and had made it clear that he was pro-Turkish. Grey had intended to speak to Mubarak about him. The other was a schoolmaster, Hafiz Wahabi, who had married in Kuwait about seven months earlier. Grey had been warned by the Government of India against somebody by that name, but had no complaints about him and was not even certain that it was the same person.[35]

All doubts about possible fifth columnists in Kuwait were resolved quite simply. Mubarak summoned the two men and told Muhammad that he would be executed immediately were he to indulge in "any further attempt to seduce my people". Both gentlemen professed their innocence and were dismissed after a discussion about *jihad*. Grey thought that it would be wise to keep an eye on Muhammad, but that Hafiz was harmless.[36]

12.2 The final two years

Mubarak's importance to the British did not fade away and, at the end of January 1915, the Viceroy Lord Hardinge came on a visit to Kuwait. On

---

[35] Very probably Hafiz Wahba is referred to. An educated Egyptian, Wahba worked in Kuwait as a schoolmaster. In open opposition to the British, he had to leave Kuwait soon after the outbreak of the First World War. He went first to Dawra and then Bahrain, whence he was deported to India by the British. He later entered the service of Ibn Saud, and was appointed first Saudi Arabian Minister to London, later becoming a highly respected ambassador to the Court of St James's. Rush, *Al-Sabah*, p. 105 n. 12.

[36] New Delhi NAI, Foreign and Political, 1915 Secret War, August, 15–19.

his arrival, Mubarak's son Jabir, accompanied by Cox, came on board to welcome the Viceroy on the Shaikh's behalf. Mubarak himself came on board later to be decorated with the ribbon of Knight Commander of the Most Exalted Order of the Star of India. Naturally he needed some such new honour, now that he was no longer able to sport his three Ottoman decorations. He was now firmly in the British camp.[37]

As the campaign in Mesopotamia ground on, another almost forgotten front in the war was opened: the confrontation between Saudi and Rashidi forces in Central Arabia. No clear result emerged either from this confrontation as a whole, or from the complicated battle at the wells of Jarrab in February 1915 where Captain Shakespear, formerly political agent in Kuwait, met his end.[38] The Germans thought the Rashidis to be intent on letting this war drag on for as long as possible, as that would immunize them from Ottoman requests for help against the British on the Mesopotamian front.[39] The hostilities meant that Mubarak had to take extra care to keep his desert front in good order, and thus to maintain good relations with the Saudis, the idea being to present a solid front to the Ottomans and their Rashidi allies.

In the framework of this alliance, Mubarak helped the Saudis in their conflict with the 'Ajman tribe between Kuwait and al-Hasa.[40] Mubarak's sympathy with the Saudis had its limits. The conflict is said to have had its

[37] Paris AE, NS Mascate 15, fos. 149–150, French consul Dejean in Calcutta, with cutting from *Times of India* containing a report on the Viceroy's visit to Kuwait on 31 January 1915.

[38] Reports of how Shakespear came to his end were somewhat contradictory. The French consul in Bushire agrees with this version, stating that Shakespear had been killed while photographing the battle (NS Mascate 15, fo. 160, French consul Bushire 27 February 1915), and moreover that this was a great loss to the British because Shakespear was one of the few British officials to have mastered the Arabic language. Such praise is exaggerated: the confusion over the translation of the 1913 Convention gives an inkling of the standard of Shakespear's Arabic. Musil's history of the Rashidis, however, states that Shakespear was killed while standing next to a piece of artillery during the battle while the Saudi warriors were fleeing: Musil, *Northern Negd*, p. 248; and Musil, *Zur Zeitgeschichte von Arabien*, p. 20.

[39] Berlin AA, R 13876 A 16092 (15 May 1915), copy of a letter of the Austrian consul in Damascus, 10 April 1915.

[40] New Delhi NAI, Foreign, Secret War, September 1917, fos. 408–434, *Précis regarding the relations of the British Government with Bin Saud*, by the Iraq Section of the Arab Bureau in Basra, p. 6 (12 January 1917) gives a good summary of the events.

roots in discontent over the tough regime the Saudis had imposed on Al-Hasa, and it was exacerbated by the presence of dissident members of the Al-Saud family with the 'Ajman. The Saudis also claimed that Ottoman agents had fanned this unrest, but Mubarak did not believe this. Abdul Aziz Al-Saud's first attempt to quash the rebellion ended in a disastrous battle at Kinzan near al-Hofuf, where he was wounded and his brother Sa'd killed. Kuwaiti help was needed, and Mubarak's son Salim marched south with a Kuwaiti force.[41] Mubarak's support, however, was not unconditional. He had discussed a plan with Grey, the British political agent in Kuwait, who had entirely concurred with it. Salim was to go into action only if the Saudis accepted this plan: evacuation of al-Hofuf by the majority of Saudi forces, protection of the date gardens instead, and later an attack on the 'Ajman from three sides simultaneously. The 'Ajman were defeated in a battle in which Salim played a prominent part, his horse being shot from under him.[42] They had to leave their country, and Mubarak allowed them to settle in Kuwaiti territory. This was strongly resented by the Saudis, and it was even claimed that Mubarak had played a double game from the start of the campaign. This would not have been inconsistent with Mubarak's policy. The stock explanation for it, that Mubarak was merely jealous of the Saudi leader, is too simplistic: it was clearly not in his interest to have the Saudis to both west and south, and the 'Ajman could form a good buffer. Also, in the course of time Mubarak's feelings about Ibn Saud had cooled somewhat. The American missionary Mylrea quoted him as saying of the latter: "He has no 'siasi' [diplomatic sense], no courage, nothing."[43]

These interpretations may, however, be too deep. One of the few really contemporary sources comes up with a quite innocent explanation. Grey describes how the 'Ajman shaikhs, while retiring from battle, entreated Salim for peace. Salim replied that it was not up to him, and that they should apply either to Ibn Saud or to Mubarak. According to Grey, it was logical for the 'Ajman to apply to Mubarak, as Ibn Saud's sentiments against them were "ferocious in the extreme" and they could expect "a

---

[41] *Political Diaries*, Vol. 6, p. 87 (July–August 1915) and p. 119 (September–October 1915).
[42] IOLR, R/15/5/25, fos. 282–283, Grey to Bushire 23 July 1915.
[43] IOLR, R/15/2/32, fo. 261 (278), Keyes, Political Agent in Bahrain, to Resident, 2 March 1918.

general massacre". They came into Kuwait on 20 November 1915, and Mubarak accepted their plea. Two days later a Saudi messenger arrived requesting Mubarak not to deal with the 'Ajman, but by then Mubarak could not renege on his promises even had he wished to, which is improbable. Grey thought that Ibn Saud had reason to be unhappy about this, but not excessively so because without Kuwaiti help he would not have been able to keep up the fight against the 'Ajman. Grey himself was not unhappy with the final outcome.[44] During the conflict between the Saudis and Salim in 1918–21, Salim's attitude in the 'Ajman crisis was seen by various observers as the reason for Ibn Saud's animosity towards him.[45] This looks tenuous in the light of the above, as it is clear from Grey's reports that the whole incident was much more Mubarak's doing than Salim's.

Kuwait's economy, like that of the entire Gulf, suffered badly from the war. Trade fell to a minimal level and the prospects for the pearling industry, with the slump in wartime sales, were bleak. Mubarak seems to have responded to hard times by actively trying to reduce the debt burden on the impoverished population of pearl divers, and to streamline the collection of revenues. The collection of customs duties had always been a problem, because Kuwait lacked a well-established and reliable bureaucracy, and over the years several serious problems had arisen over it. After an initial approach to the political agent, Grey, in July 1915, in September Mubarak proposed to Cox that the British should take over the financial administration, simply paying him the revenue after deduction of expenses. In the light of the British administration of customs in Bahrain and Muscat, which had gone quite smoothly and to the satisfaction of the

[44] IOLR, R/15/5/25, fos. 305–307, Grey to Bushire 25 November 1915.
[45] It is even stated by some authors that the Saudi furore was partly caused by a correspondence between Salim and Mubarak which had come into the hands of the Saudis, see for instance Dr Abdallah Al-Salih Al-Uthaymin, *Tarikh al-Mamlaka al-Saʿudiyya*, Vol. 2 (1422/2001 edition), p. 153; and Husayn Al-Shaikh Khazʿal, *Tarikh al-Kuwayt*, Vol. 2 (1962 edition) p. 218. A rather strange version of the anti-Salim version is given by Alois Musil, *Northern Negd*, pp. 287–8. Musil mentions that, during the last months of Mubarak's life, a dispute flared up between his sons Jabir and Salim; Salim was anti-Saudi and was behind the operations of the 'Ajman against the Saudis. This is at complete variance with the fact that Salim commanded the Kuwaiti forces assisting the Saudis! Anyhow, Musil's *Zeitgeschichte*, p. 77, gives a totally different story from the one in *Northern Negd*.

Rulers there, this initiative of Mubarak's is not so extraordinary, especially at a time when the disappearance of other European shipping from the Gulf meant that what remained was under British control. Mubarak, now an old and very sick man, went even further in proposing to Cox that the British Government should be appointed as a kind of neutral executor for the financial arrangements with his heirs after his death. Cox supported Mubarak's proposals in a letter of 14 September 1915 to the Government of India.

This episode would be of minor importance, were it not for Salwa Al-Ghanim devoting a quite astonishing piece to it in her book.[46] She describes it as follows: "His proposal was one of the oddest ever made to a British official in all the centuries of British involvement in the Gulf: *in effect Mubarak proposed to give Kuwait to Britain.*" She follows this up with a mix of quotations and interpretations purporting to show that Mubarak had in effect offered the British effective control of Kuwait, and that the Government of India was shocked by this offer. This account is a blatant misrepresentation. Cox's letter is clearly limited to this point: "He [Mubarak] wanted the Government of India to *farm* from him or *manage* for him, now and in future, all sources of revenue and simply pay him the income. He can then in his Will leave his various beneficiaries their inheritance in the form of specific sums ..." The reason given for this by Mubarak was his fear that after his death his heirs would enfeeble Kuwait by squabbling.[47] In no sense can this affair carry the interpretation that Mubarak's first biographer places upon it. She seems to assume that a senile Mubarak had taken leave of his senses, and that the Government of India was "horrified" by the proposal, but this opinion was certainly not shared by Cox. He describes it as "an ingenious scheme, worthy of his fine old character and I very much hope that [...] the Government of India will vouchsafe a response which will not disappoint him". In short, it was nothing very exceptional, and there is no evidence that the Government of India was horrified.

As usual it took some time for a reply to come, and when it did it was simple: if the political agent was to undertake such a task, his staff would

[46] Salwa Al-Ghanim, *Mubarak*, p. 197.
[47] IOLR, R/15/5/59, Cox to Government of India 15 September 1915; also in IOLR, LPS /11/72, file 618/14.
[48] IOLR, R/15/5/59, Foreign Department to Cox 18 November 1915.
[49] *Political Diaries*, Vol. 6, pp. 146 and 158.

have to be multiplied, and the costs of this might be considered excessive by the Shaikh; furthermore, Mubarak's successor might oppose the scheme, and so it might cause conflict between him and the British.[48]

Mubarak died on 28 November 1915, a few days after the good news of victory over the 'Ajman had reached Kuwait. The cause of death was an attack of malaria aggravated by his bad heart. The succession was rapidly and smoothly arranged without British intervention, and to everybody's satisfaction. Mubarak's eldest son Jabir succeeded, and was able easily to gain general approval by repealing one of his father's most unpopular financial measures – the old man had left financial elbow-room for that.[49] Kuwait's security was assured. There may have been a little trepidation in 1916 when British Indian forces were driven back in Iraq for a while, but Ottoman forces were never again to approach Kuwaiti territory.

Conclusion

MUBARAK AL-SABAH was an imposing and likeable personality. Even opponents like Knox could sometimes be won over by his charm. His influence on Kuwait's emergence as a sovereign state was crucial, although it has not always been correctly understood. His policy was a far more subtle one than simply to inveigle Britain into commitments to protect him from the Turks. In reality it aimed at preserving his independence by means of a complex balancing act between the two great regional powers. Thus he was trusted as pro-Ottoman in parts of the Ottoman system, while the British never really doubted his fundamental loyalty to them.

Despite the quantity of contemporary written sources on Mubarak's life, many of them are contradictory, and it remains impossible to establish his real feelings and ideas with any degree of certainty. The historian may describe events, and the biographer may describe his subject's actions, but Mubarak's true personality remains elusive. One senses that he approached his problems with a certain sense of humour and an appreciation of the incongruous, but also with a detached appraisal of possible risks. He was a consummate actor who could conceal his cool calculations behind a deceptive façade. If he acted dumb, angry or afraid it was usually to manipulate a situation, and most often had the intended effect. He was a man who enjoyed life, who dressed well and who was open to innovations: he had a steamboat and a motor car, his palace was illuminated by electricity, and he was probably the most photographed Gulf personality of his time.

Contradictions in the sources preclude a conclusive version of how

Mubarak's rule began. Nor is much known with any certainty about the rule of his predecessor Muhammad. Lurid tales abound, both contemporary and later, of Mubaraks's role as mastermind of the bloody events of May 1896, but his denial, and the telegrams sent to the Ottoman authorities in 1896 by Kuwaitis in support of him, cannot be dismissed out of hand as irrelevant. Contradictory reports of Yusuf Al-Ibrahim's part in the whole affair also muddy the waters.

A dominant principle of Mubarak's policy was never to take a step without having covered his back somehow. Thus when things went wrong he usually had a safe fall-back position. Another vital characteristic was his prodigious bargaining ability. He was able to exploit the – often imaginary – activities of other powers, notably Germany, Russia and Turkey, to railroad the nervous Government of India, and sometimes even the Foreign Office in London, into actions they would not have contemplated had they kept a cool head. He seems to have had an uncanny instinct for the hidden fears and wishes of those he negotiated with. This is especially clear in his dealings with Meade in 1899, when he managed to get the second clause into the agreement, containing a concession that could be granted only by a sovereign ruler. A no less significant example of this ability was his manipulation of Knox and Cox into the Shuwaikh deal, by which he obtained a repeated British promise of protection against the Ottomans, while at the same time safeguarding Kuwait's autonomy against possible British infractions too. Obtaining Cox's letter of 1913 "on behalf of the British Government" further strengthened his position. Impeccable too was his tactic of keeping the agents in Kuwait at a distance while being most friendly to the resident Cox in Bushire.

Mubarak acted as a sovereign ruler, never countenancing any interference by the Ottomans or the British in the affairs of Kuwait. He rightly felt that the Ottoman Empire was not a state in the Western sense with clearly defined borders. In Arabia the Ottoman Empire tried to impose its sovereign rights over something that amounted to little more than a self-proclaimed sphere of influence. It was thwarted in this by internal disputes and incompetence, and by Mubarak's ability to bring external pressures to bear. By accepting without qualification the British 1899 Agreement with Kuwait, which implied Mubarak's full power to sign away elements of his internal and external sovereign rights, the Ottoman Empire in 1913 implicitly conceded that Mubarak in 1899 had possessed the right to make internationally binding agreements.

Mubarak's intention in his relationship with Britain was simple and straightforward: to maintain the Agreement without being restricted too tightly in his actions. The British, however, made a very complicated meal of their relationship with Kuwait. As an expanding empire, Britain subscribed to the imperial belief that it had the right to bring under its control those entities on the margins of their territories that enjoyed no clear sovereign status according to Western standards. Britain understood and accepted the expansionist policies of other empires, provided they did not conflict with British claims. The Ottomans had put forward a claim to Kuwait that was no more than verbal. It can hardly be taken seriously in terms of the modern concept of self-determination, but in the context of 1899–1913 the British were not ready openly to contest it. British reluctance to contest the legitimacy of the Ottoman claim is understandable. But it ran very deep, as is highlighted by the British unwillingness to adopt a firm position on territorial disputes on Kuwait's margins. Mubarak had arguments in support of his rights that may have been somewhat vague, but the British took seriously Ottoman claims that had no valid argument at all to support them.

The British seem to have felt vulnerable to the charge of having breached international agreements over the territorial integrity of the Ottoman Empire, perhaps not in actual fact given the weakness of Ottoman claims, but at least in theory. This view of Ottoman legitimacy was shared both by those British politicians and officials who were willing to go furthest in the Kuwait affair, and by the most hesitant, the former's motive being "Let's grab and who cares what the world thinks". Under Salisbury the latter attitude was prevalent, but Lansdowne as Foreign Secretary was more sensitive to world opinion, and at one point was afraid of war with Germany. British diplomats, who never had a proper understanding of the true character of the Ottoman state, never really believed in the ultimate legitimacy of the British stand on Kuwait and never tried to find serious arguments for it.

Much of the diplomatic trouble the British had to endure over Kuwait stemmed from their inability to implement a clear policy. A radical declaration at an early stage of a protectorate over Kuwait was felt to carry too high a risk of a diplomatic furore in Europe. As a result, the British were to suffer the full consequences of half measures, as Mubarak grasped the opportunity to have the best of both worlds. The Turks would not be allowed by the British to attack him, but the British could not allow themselves to be seen to be in control of Kuwait. Mubarak was thus free to do as he pleased. The Turks did not dare confront the British openly and resorted to underhand interference. In theory this could have worked, but they estranged their potential European allies by their mistimed hesitancy and inopportune aggression. On the whole, however, it is clear from the German archives that Germany was unwilling to extend more than verbal support to the Ottomans against the British. Britain, for its part, feared German intentions more than was necessary. Germany was ready to exploit the Kuwait affair to cause embarrassment to the British, but nothing more, while London was at one point fearful of war with Germany. The Germans had already concluded at a very early stage that the Turks were too unreliable to merit substantive support.

A conspicuous cause of inconsistency in British policy was the disparate positions adopted by the Foreign Office on the one hand and, on the other, the Government of India and its local representatives in the Gulf. The Foreign Office was above all concerned to pursue correct diplomacy and to balance Gulf affairs with global requirements, but the Government of India had a more limited purview: to maintain its prominence in the Indian Ocean and to prevent other powers acquiring a foothold in the Gulf. International attention had been drawn to the strategic position of Kuwait, and the Government of India wanted at least to be able to take control of it should international developments force its hand. This caused considerable friction between the Government of India and the Foreign Office. The India Office, the official intermediary between India and the British Government, showed little political consistency in its efforts to smooth the differences.

The relationship between Mubarak and the British acquired a new dimension once a British political agency was established in Kuwait. The proximity of British officials inspired Mubarak to assert his independence more forcefully. The agents Knox and Shakespear had reason to feel vexed, both by Mubarak's disparagement of them and because their best contacts in Kuwait were elements of the population with material reasons to resent Mubarak's policy. The agents obtained their information from those in Kuwait they could most easily talk with: pearl merchants with Bombay contacts and shopkeepers.

Mubarak's first biographer, Salwa Al-Ghanim, characterizes the complaints of these groups simply as discontent over the funding of his grandiose schemes by over-taxing the populace. This is too extreme a view. Mubarak's ambition was more focused and political, his real aim being to prevent his neighbours from growing too mighty to be managed. His strategy was to create a balance of power between them. It was a costly policy, and he had been dipping into his private income to run Kuwait for years when, in 1908, he at last felt sufficiently strong to increase taxes. The most positive view of this would present Mubarak – not without evidence – as trying from then on to finance Kuwait and his "representation expenses" out of taxes, instead of out of the Al-Sabah private fortune. The sources are clear that the Al-Sabah fortune was essential to the funding of Mubarak's policies. Hence, if one accepts that his policy was in general sound, he was justified in claiming some compensation for monies spent. One might counter this by arguing that, in that case, Mubarak should have kept clear accounts distinguishing between disbursements from his private fortune and the state treasury. If he had indeed done so, he would have added yet another exceptional honour to his record, for no Gulf ruler of that era, or even of later times, would ever have entertained such distinctions. In this Mubarak remained a man of his time. A historian cannot really reach an unequivocal verdict. A new analysis might question whether Mubarak's private disbursements were really on the scale that was sometimes claimed, and criticize him for his sometimes unfriendly methods of raising revenue. In his favour, the latter were extenuated by Kuwait's primitive administrative structure, which made generating income no easy matter. And it is reasonable to argue that he was quite right to try to generate public revenues in an emerging state. In his public finances he might not always have been Mubarak the Great, but nor was he Mubarak the Terrible.

Mubarak showed his finest qualities in his dextrous manipulation of Kuwait's international position, with which this work has been primarily concerned. He would have been unable to demonstrate such skills had he not been well-informed about world affairs, and all kinds of European sources confirm that he was so. Interestingly, this view of him emerges particularly sharply from the accounts of intellectuals with whom he was less inhibited about speaking plainly, such as Burchardt or Goguyer.[1]

---

[1] It should be noted that Mubarak's father Sabah was also described as well-informed about international affairs: Pelly, "Remarks on the Tribes", p. 76.

Mubarak might have had a quaint way of expressing himself in speech and writing, but this was in part the traditional style to be expected of a prominent Shaikh, and in part a façade to deceive his interlocutors. Behind the screen of oriental verbosity can be discerned a keen instinct for the extent to which European or Ottoman policy-makers might be manipulated to do his bidding.

One report by a British political agent describes Mubarak as running Kuwait through his slaves, even his close family being kept out of government affairs. This statement is contradicted by other sources which, for instance, show his son Jabir being placed in charge of finances.[2] Jabir also handled delicate international business during Mubarak's not infrequent absences. Mubarak's son Salim was responsible for desert affairs and carried out a delicate mission to the *tawash*es in Bahrain. And every afternoon Mubarak held open court in his office in the market. Far from being a remote autocrat, he cannot have been as out of touch as various remarks by political agents make him out to be. Shakespear's outburst, that the great merchant shaikhs were no longer able to provide a counterweight to Mubarak, is a case in point, locating and emphasizing the discontent precisely within the group with which Shakespear was intimate. It was Shakespear who was perhaps out of touch with Kuwaiti society at large. If Mubarak was a despot, at least two aspects of his behaviour were most untypical of real tyrants. The first was that he presented himself in public every day. The other was that he absented himself from Kuwait frequently and without hesitation, and in 1913 even planned an extended trip abroad. The conclusion must be that, while some aspects of his rule might have provoked opposition in some quarters, he was still universally regarded as the best choice as ruler.

It is possible that Mubarak's need to manoeuvre with extreme prudence in external affairs made him internally more autocratic. Kuwait's public order and cleanliness, visible symptoms of strict rule, were usually noted with approval by visitors. Mubarak seems to have regarded cleanliness as a virtue, as testified by Burchardt's remark on the nice towels and fine soap in the palace. Kuwait's cleanliness, however, was not exclusively to Mubarak's credit, for it was noted as early as 1863.[3] More significant was the matter of public order. Kuwait really was a haven of security in a very

---

[2] *Political Diaries*, Vol. 3, p. 190 (1908).
[3] Pelly, "Remarks on the Tribes", p. 73.

troubled region. Such recommendations can even be found in sources hostile to Mubarak, but there they are often accompanied by negative comments on his very autocratic governance.

Positive views of Mubarak are commonly to be found in the accounts of Europeans who had dealings with him. Such observers were not usually representative of European diplomatic interests, and found Mubarak's methods of manipulating the great powers amusing. Other Europeans were not so complimentary, especially those connected with the British Foreign Office who had no direct dealings with him, but whose lives were complicated by his astute power play. One just has to recall Lord Lansdowne's angry comment about Mubarak as a "savage".

Mubarak's image in Kuwaiti tradition is also double-sided. Appreciation of his preservation of Kuwait's identity under difficult circumstances is coupled with criticism. His subjects were on the receiving end of his autocratic style of government and nobody likes tax increases, so discontent on this score is to be expected.

The contemporary Arab press occasionally described him in hostile terms. This view was a consequence of the confusion created by Sultan Abdulhamid's "pan-Islamist" policies. When opposing Ottoman expansion with British support, Mubarak was sometimes seen as breaching Islamic solidarity. Some criticism also emanated from adherents of enemies such as Abdul Aziz Al-Rashid of Haïl. Nor was Mubarak insensitive to the power of the printed word. He received journalists and was the first Gulf ruler to have a kind of interview published in a newspaper.

One can speculate as to the nature of Mubarak's actual thoughts. They were probably more complex than his allies and enemies suspected. He almost certainly shared the general Arab dislike of Turkish domination of much of the Islamic world, but he seems to have accepted the Ottoman Empire as an Islamic "superstate" as long as it remained a very loose structure. This brought him into collision with the ambition of Midhat Pasha, Sultan Abdulhamid II and the Young Turks to refashion the ramshackle old structure of the Ottoman Empire into a territorial state in the Western sense. Mubarak was not unwilling to recognize the Ottoman Caliphate – even Abdul Aziz Al-Saud was willing to do this under certain circumstances – but only if it carried a no more than symbolic meaning. Occasionally it seems that his political ideal was a kind of Arab federation as the dominant element in the region, which was to be a sovereign entity in some vague relation with the Ottoman Empire. During the reign of Abdulhamid, some Arabs may have hoped that such ideals might find sympathy with the Young Turks. A sign of this is Mubarak's connection with the *Khilafat* newspaper, which later printed an article penned by Goguyer promoting this early Arab nationalist tendency.[4]

It would be fanciful to believe Mubarak's "friendship" with Britain to be anything other than opportunistic and expedient. His attitude to the British was often mistrustful, while non-British outsiders could find him very friendly. In 1905 Mubarak figured as one of just two Gulf subscribers to an anti-British Arab publication.[5] Sometimes the British attributed Mubarak's unfriendliness to his belief that they had not kept their promises to him. It could be that he had other reasons too to keep the British at arm's length – in order to preserve his own freedom of action, and to spare the anti-British feelings of at least part of the Arab population.

It is only results that create the unfolding tapestry of the past. In writing about them, is a historian obliged to make moral judgements about the personalities who are the agents and victims of events? This is a rash undertaking unless one is describing a life either of unblemished saintliness or of undiluted evil. Normal human beings are a mixture of good and bad, and solid judgements can be reached only if well-balanced testimonials by close associates are available, together with personal documents by the subject himself. In the absence of such materials, it is difficult to pass judgement on Mubarak. The real person remains hidden behind the many masks he assumed to suit varying circumstances. He was undoubtedly an autocrat, but one who could be extremely open and charming. He could, as required, appear very intelligent and widely informed on international affairs, or dumb or uncommunicative, as when he painted himself as just a nomad sitting on the edge of the desert. He wanted himself and Kuwait – to his way of thinking hardly distinguishable from one another – to be prosperous and independent. Even if its pursuit took him down complex and devious byways, he worked tirelessly for that ultimate goal. For him the end to a large extent justified the means. This may not be the way of saintliness, but saints make very bad rulers, especially in troubled times. It

[4] Paris AE, NS Mascate 48, copy of Goguyer's article in the *Khilafat* annexed to a letter of the French consul in Muscat of 8 February 1906.

[5] According to IOLR, R/15/5/62, the only subscribers to the anti-British *Fatih al-Hassayer* in the Gulf area were Mubarak and Abdul Rahman Al-Saud.

would be equally wrong to see him as a sour tyrant. Mubarak enjoyed life, and particularly good company. He was loyal to his friends, as can be seen from his unceasing efforts to get his Basra agent released. An interesting insight into his private personality is also afforded by a collection of private letters by him to a Kuwaiti family that he counted among his friends: in his close personal circle he appears as a warm and caring character.[6]

Mubarak's friendship with Shaikh Khaz'al of Muhammara has generated much discussion. Some have seen Khaz'al as Mubarak's evil genius. Mubarak's frequent visits to Khaz'al and his lands in Fao served to refresh his knowledge of current affairs in the region. Muhammara was blessed with a discreet telegraph office, and was also an excellent neutral venue for meetings with Ottoman officials. Khaz'al seemed for long the richer and the more powerful of the pair, but in the end it was Mubarak who managed to bind the British with undertakings that conferred on Kuwait an exceptional degree of autonomy for a Gulf state. Khaz'al, by contrast, lost his position and ended up in house arrest in Teheran.

A somewhat despotic ruler who ruled with an iron hand is perhaps not cut out to appeal to people at the beginning of the 21st century, but standards were different in the Gulf region during Mubarak's lifetime. Bloody palace revolutions and family power struggles were typical of the Arabian politics of his day. In comparison with his contemporaries, Mubarak appears a good deal less terrible than he does in comparison with modern democratic presidents and prime ministers.

Are Kuwaitis justified in referring to him as Mubarak the Great? It is a grandiloquent title that makes inevitable a comparison with other rulers in world history also known as "the Great". Of the various rulers who are so named, some conquered very short-lived empires (e.g. Alexander), while others gave shape to a state (e.g. Peter) or led it through difficult changes (e.g. Frederick). In comparison to such titans, Mubarak worked on a very small canvas, but that aside he achieved very tangible and remarkable results under extremely difficult circumstances. It is difficult now to imagine how Kuwait could have maintained its independence under any other ruler. Mubarak's biographer, Salwa Al-Ghanim, seems to deplore what she sees as a lack of bedouin nobility in him, but it was only by the sometimes devious means he employed that a small city state under

---

[6] A collection of original letters, condolences and wishes to members of the Al-Khalid family, now in the possession of the Centre for Research and Studies on Kuwait.

threat from a much stronger neighbour was able not only to preserve its independence but also to achieve statehood.[7] Mubarak can now be seen to have shown consummate skill in exploiting the greed and fears of great empires to accomplish his objective. He did so with supreme perspicacity and imagination, that cannot but claim the admiration of posterity. In some other aspects of his rule he was not innovative, or perhaps even not very capable. The same can be said of all other rulers dubbed "the Great".

Mubarak's crowning achievement was Kuwait's firm status under international law. This was no easy matter for a non-European. The Ottoman state had achieved international recognition as a great "empire" in the European sense and was regarded as possessing the right to imperial expansion. Kuwait, however, did not originate as an Ottoman administrative district and had an equal right to oppose this expansion. As part of Ottoman attempts to expand its authority in the Arabian Peninsula, a little blackmail had forced Kuwait to recognize a vague overlordship of the Sultan, but not one that led to any exercise of sovereign rights by the Ottomans. For twenty-five years there had been no serious attempt from the Ottoman side to strengthen the ties. When the Ottomans eventually set about trying to convert the situation into the substance of real sovereignty, Mubarak could justifiably oppose the Sultan. The Ottoman imperial ideology appears to have regarded the Sultan as having sovereign rights over the entire Arabian Peninsula that might for a period lie dormant, but were capable of being legitimately revived at any time. This meant that Kuwait stood forever in peril of the Turks exercising their so-called rights. The only permanent solution for Kuwait would be its recognition, by the two powers directly involved, as a legitimate independent state with clear borders. The detailed story of how Mubarak accomplished this has been the subject of this work.

To conclude, Mubarak was a prodigiously gifted player on the regional political stage. The sporting analogies used by outsiders to describe his methods have perhaps led to them being seen in too amusing a light, but closer analysis shows them to be of considerably greater weight, interest

---

[7] Salwa Al-Ghanim, *Mubarak*, especially pp. 202–5. One cannot take too seriously the simplistic ethnographic-moralistic contrast Salwa Al-Ghanim makes between the noble son of the desert, Abdul Aziz Al-Saud, and Mubarak, the hard-headed representative of the merchant nation of Kuwait, especially where it is based on the over-selective use of sources.

and significance. Internal affairs may reveal Mubarak's career and personality from a less attractive angle, but even here much can be explained in more sympathetic terms than is sometimes done. As far as Kuwait is concerned, only a negotiator of Mubarak's rare ability could have preserved its independence by largely peaceful means – for Kuwait had no substantial military muscle – and won international recognition as a sovereign state.

Sources

MUBARAK AL-SABAH'S activities were of interest to many countries. The most voluminous material on him is to be found in the British archives. The structure and character of British archival sources has been summarily described in many publications on the history of the region. For the period of Mubarak's life and times, the principal British sources are the British diplomatic records kept as Foreign Office records in the National Archives (formerly the Public Record Office) at Kew in west London, and the records of the India Office and of the British residency and agencies in the Gulf which are kept in the British Library, London.

Foreign Office records include the records of British embassies and consulates. The most important of these are the records of the British embassy in Constantinople. There are some important exceptions to this rule because of the ambiguous position of the consuls-general in Bushire and Baghdad who, as political agents in the Gulf and in Turkish Arabia were also subordinate to the Government of India. The records of the Baghdad residency were transferred to India and are now kept in the National Archives of India, while the Bushire residency records constitute the series R/15/1 of the India Office Records in the British Library in London.

The most important Foreign Office documents for Mubarak's time are to be found in three series: the general correspondence of the Foreign Office (FO 79), the correspondence of the embassy in Constantinople (FO 195), and the correspondence of the Basra consulate (FO 602). This should be understood as follows. FO 79 forms part of the records of the

Foreign Office itself, while FO 195 contains the correspondence as it was kept in the embassy records, and FO 602 contains the correspondence as it was kept in the Basra consulate records.

Much of the diplomatic correspondence was printed for circulation among the departments involved. These files of "confidential print" also contained, in the case of Kuwait, correspondence of the Government of India and of officials in the Gulf that had been forwarded to the Foreign Office. Part of this confidential print has been published.[1]

The India Office Records in the British Library contain the archives of the British institutions most closely connected with Kuwait. From top to bottom these were: the India Office in London, with the reports from the Government of India (LPS), and copies of the reports of the Bushire residents to India; the Bushire residency (R/15/1); and, from 1904, the Kuwait political agency (R/15/5). The two latter groups of records are rather incomplete, but nonetheless comprise the most important groups of records concerning Kuwait. The India Office Records are also complemented by various private collections of papers from high officials, those of Curzon and Pelly being the most important for Kuwait.

A large but far from complete collection of British documents of varied origin, but chiefly from the India Office collections, has been published by Archive Editions. These usually consist of selections of records from different groups. Problems with these are that the selection criteria are not always clear or logical, and that the documents have in some cases been ordered in a rather arbitrary way. This is the reason why most documents cited in the present work have been referred to exclusively by their original archive notation. However, the series published by Archive Editions, *Political Diaries of the Persian Gulf*, 1904–1958, is especially useful. This series presents no problem of selection criteria and has been used extensively in this work. The series of Arabic documents from the archives of the Kuwait agency also has the merit of a clear method of selection and is ordered in an objective way, just as they are in the original files. Regrettably, many of the most interesting Arabic documents regarding Kuwait are not in the agency archives (R/15/5), but in the Bushire residency archives (R/15/1), and so fall outside the scope of this Archive Editions publication.

---

[1] See Bibliography under Bidwell.

The records of the Government of India are kept in the National Archives of India in New Delhi. The central series for Gulf affairs in the National Archives is the set of Foreign Proceedings, which can be accessed by huge printed annual indexes. Files relevant to Kuwaiti history can be found via the keywords *Persian Gulf* and *Kuwait*. It looks as if most of the items relevant to Kuwait, however, can just as well be consulted in the India Office Records in London. Of most relevance to Kuwaiti history is the existence in the National Archives of India of rather incomplete, but quite voluminous, archives of the British residency (or consulate-general) in Baghdad, including Basra diaries for part of Mubarak's lifetime. Abstracts of these diaries exist in the records of the British embassy in Constantinople in the London Foreign Office records, but these are less complete.

Extensive records on the Gulf are held in French archives. Of most importance are the files of political correspondence on Muscat and the Persian Gulf, which also include reports from Baghdad and newspaper cuttings from India, and the files of diplomatic correspondence on Baghdad, all kept in the Paris Foreign Ministry Archives. As the French were interested in international public opinion on "the Kuwait affair", many newspaper cuttings or translations (British, Indian, German, Russian, Ottoman and Egyptian) are included in the correspondence. Of considerable importance too are the archives of the consulate in Baghdad containing the copies of letters and telegrams sent by the consuls, and a file in the archives of the French embassy in Constantinople concerning Kuwait. The archives of French embassies and consulates are held in the Diplomatic Archives in Nantes. Here the archives of the embassy in Constantinople and of the consulate in Baghdad contain especially good material on Kuwait. Some reports of French naval expeditions have also been found in the archives of the French navy in the Château de Vincennes, series B4.

The sources at the German Foreign Ministry are structured in a relatively simple way. There is a series Türkei 165 Arabien (modern numbers R 13840–13882), which contains correspondence and reports concerning the Arabian Peninsula, as well as correspondence with local German representatives and correspondence with diplomats and experts elsewhere on Arabia. In 1900 a sub-series containing papers on Kuwait was separated off from this main series (Türkei 165 Arabien adh. 1 Kuweit, modern numbers R 13883–13891). It should, however, be noted that there continues to be material of interest for Kuwait in the main series too after 1900.

There are two other series that should be mentioned. One is a series of reports by the German consul in Baghdad (Türkei 134 Bagdad, modern number R 13203–13209). Those specifically relating to Kuwait can also be found in Türkei 165 Arabien, but the general file is interesting for wider information about German-Ottoman relations in Iraq. Secondly, there exists an extensive series of reports by the German representative in Egypt, Max von Oppenheim (R 14554–14566). Oppenheim was the leading European expert of his time on the Arabian Peninsula, and his information is of great value. Duplicates of most of Oppenheim's reports can be found in the Türkei 165 Arabien series, but not all of them, so this series too remains important.

Inside the bound volumes of the series Türkei 165 Arabien and Türkei 165 Arabien adh. 1 Kuwait, the documents are ordered, as is usual in continental European archives, according to the sequence in which they were dealt with at the Berlin Ministry, not according to the dates of the documents themselves. For purposes of easy retrieval by other historians, documents are cited in the footnotes to this work not only by their dates, but also by the sequence number (preceded by "A"), with the date on which they were dealt with given between parentheses.

No parts of the archives of German diplomatic missions in the Ottoman Empire that might relate to our subject appear to have survived. The German navy never visited Kuwait, so neither are naval records relevant.

Austria was never directly involved in Gulf affairs, but diplomatic relations with the Ottoman Empire had been an important factor in Austrian policy ever since the 16th century, and it is clear that Austrian diplomats were well-informed on the affairs of Kuwait. In the present work a few selected reports by the Austrian ambassador in Constantinople and the consul in Baghdad have been used, from the Vienna State Archives.

The Netherlands had been active in the Gulf region since the 17th century, and some of the earliest documents on Kuwait are of Dutch origin. In the present work some use has been made of reports of 1902 by the Dutch Legation in Constantinople, and of papers concerning the visit of a Dutch warship to Kuwait in 1870.

Russian documents were used extensively by Bondarevksy in his book on Kuwait, and some Russian documents have also been published by Rezvan (see Bibliography). In a few instances the author of the present work was also able to consult some copies of Russian documents available at the Centre for Research and Studies on Kuwait.

It is thanks to Anscombe that Ottoman documents have been now introduced into the study of the history of Kuwait. In a number of instances the author of the present work has been able to add to Anscombe's data from the large collection of copies of documents in the Bashbakanlik archives in Istanbul.

Contemporary newspapers are a source that should not be neglected for the history of the Mubarak era. It is not so much that they impart information of any value on events, for their articles on the Gulf were usually much-delayed and based on second-hand and often distorted data. They are important because, during the course of the 19th century, the press grew to have an influence on the politics of most powers, even of the Ottoman Empire. The press influenced public opinion, and was exploited by different groups in order to do so. In Britain, political interests relating to India used the press to promote their views. The German attitude in the Kuwait affair was strongly influenced by the press, as to a lesser extent was the French and Russian attitude. Even Mubarak himself used the press at certain times, through intermediaries, to bring pressure to bear. It is thus important to take into account the interaction between the press and policy-makers. French and German diplomatic correspondence in particular is larded with cuttings from newspapers – not only their own, but also from British, Indian, Ottoman, Egyptian, Russian and Austrian ones.

For all their interest, press reports can be even more contradictory than the official documents. The latter frequently conflict with each other, not only because they reflect different national viewpoints, but also because discrepant views competed with each other within national institutions. It is often difficult to extract the germ of truth from conflicting data.

It is of vital importance never to lose sight of the fact that reports tend to be written from the perspective of the interest group to which the authors belong, and may even reflect the authors' personal views. Reports can also be influenced by the nature of the informants used. Conspicuous examples of this are the reports of the French consul in Baghdad, who obtained much of his information either from Ottoman military contacts or from the French arms merchant Goguyer, who had stayed in Mubarak's palace for some time and hated the English. Such factors need to be recognized, and reports judiciously weighed and decoded accordingly. The lack of direct, reliable information from contemporary Kuwaiti sources means that one is often reliant upon biased information from outsiders with conflicting interests. It is sometimes necessary to study the texts as if they were medieval documents in order correctly to evaluate the information they give.

Bias in the sources used in this work comes in two forms, voluntary and involuntary. Involuntary bias stems from the writer's unconscious assumptions determined by his social and political background. Thus it is little wonder that a middle-class French republican with egalitarian views should give a different version of events from a member of the British upper classes. In German officialdom it was not so much class-consciousness as dry, solid erudition that earned advancement, and so German reports contain much information of a scholarly nature. A certain general bias is also created by the social assumptions of an era in which rather static and entrenched attitudes prevailed in favour of monarchy, firmly established territorial borders, and rules of conduct laid down at the Vienna Congress of 1814–16.

Voluntary bias is less common. For an official to deliberately communicate false information, or more commonly information that is blatantly incomplete, is highly undesirable behaviour. It tends only to occur in systems in which different branches of the bureaucracy are in conflict. This was clearly the case in the Ottoman system, though one is also justified in suspecting that British officials on the spot were not always above such methods of deception. German representatives in the region too passed on to their superiors a fair amount of incorrect intelligence fed to them by Ottoman officials.

A more insidious form of voluntary bias can be a product of bureaucratic "tribalism". This is best illustrated by the conflicting viewpoints prevalent in different parts of the British system. The main institutions responsible for the affairs of Kuwait were: the Government of India and its representatives in the Gulf, in particular the Bushire political residency and the Kuwait political agency; the India Office in London; and the Foreign Office in London with its regional representatives (the embassy in Constantinople, the consulate in Baghdad and the vice-consulate in Basra). The Baghdad consul, at the same time as being political resident for Turkish Arabia subordinate to the Government of India, was also, as consul, subordinate to the Constantinople embassy.[2] Although everybody was regarded as working in the British national interest, there were strong differences of opinion and position.

The Government of India, like all European colonial establishments, was of a somewhat nervous disposition where its security was concerned. It had only limited military means at its disposal to maintain order over a vast territory, and was deeply sensitive to the possibility of foreign powers gaining easy access to the region – especially the Gulf, where direct contacts with the Mediterranean or Russia (through Persia where Russia held a dominant position) were a distinct possibility. Because of this the Indian Government was predisposed to a somewhat expansionist policy in the Gulf, in order to counteract any possible adventures by other powers. The Foreign Office, on the other hand, had a tendency to oppose any forward policy involving real or imaginary Ottoman territory, because of the diplomatic trouble this would cause in Europe, where the powers had agreed not to violate Ottoman territorial integrity. And it was also reluctant to cause the Ottomans any offence that would make the life of the British ambassador in Constantinople more difficult. The India Office tended to adopt an intermediate position, that was sometimes also tinged by a certain apprehension, common to all the European powers, about the possible impact, on colonies with Islamic populations, of any conflict with the Ottoman Sultan as Caliph.[3] These disparate standpoints engendered divergent opinions and policies. Closest to Kuwait, the Bushire residency tended to be the most aggressive in promoting British engagement, while the embassy in Constantinople just wanted to avoid complications. The consul in Basra too was inclined to avoid problems with the Basra government, but could occasionally, because of increasing contacts between the British representatives in Basra and Bushire, consider the attitude of his superior the ambassador to be over-cautious.

Naturally such differences provoked squabbles, but one must be careful not to exaggerate. There is little justification for describing, as Dr Al-

---

[2] Such a dual role was played by the Bushire resident too: as consul for the Persian ports he was also subordinate to the British diplomatic representative in Teheran.
[3] Though this issue generated files that were sometimes thick, it was of much less practical consequence, and the fears decreased as Ottoman power waned.

Ghanim often does, a certain official as "shocked" or suchlike by the forward actions of another. They may have been irritated or intent on opposing another's actions, but this was done in a polite manner – these were gentlemen of similar background and they were not at daggers drawn. However, the press campaigns fuelled by elements in the Indian Government to further their aims were less polite. The Indian newspapers vigorously promoted a forward policy and such propaganda was often reflected in the British press too.

Another feature of the age that is important to an understanding of the sources is the time factor. Communication was painfully slow before the mass introduction of voice telephone and fax. In 1900 the situation was not quite as bad as in the 16th-century empire of Philip II as described by Braudel, but the transport of letters could still take many weeks.[4] Anscombe depicts Sultan Abdulhamid sitting in Yildiz much alarmed by a short telegram, and then having to wait a month for a detailed report to reach him from distant Baghdad, much like Philip II awaiting news in the Escurial. The Gulf had been connected to the outside world by telegraph since the 1870s, but the capacity of one set of copper wires was sufficient only for short messages, and not for a two-way debate about the best course of action. Consequently most decisions were prepared by exchange of correspondence. That might take months, as the people involved in deliberations might be scattered between Bushire, Constantinople, London and Calcutta. A proper appreciation of this time factor is essential to a correct interpretation of events.

Finally, bureaucratic language is another factor to take into account. Western European observers tend to couch their accounts in a cool, detached style, while Ottoman officials are prone to exaggeration, which helps to explain the Porte's hesitant reaction to their reports of events. Hyperbole mars the reporting of some Russian representatives too, as it does Russian and Ottoman press reports. Wild allegations do occasionally appear in the Western European press, but the Russian and Ottoman newspapers in general contain more exaggeration and less solid fact.

[4] Braudel, *La Méditerranée*, pp. 320–5.

Bibliography

Abu Hakima, Ahmad Mustafa, *The Modern History of Kuwait*, London, 1983.

Abu Manneh, B., "Sultan Abdulhamid II and Shaikh Abulhuda al-Sayyadi", *Middle Eastern Studies* 15, no. 2 (May 1970), pp. 131–53.

Ahmad, Feroz, *The Young Turks: The Committee of Union and Progress in Turkish politics, 1908–1914*, Oxford, 1969.

Akarli, Engin Deniz, "The Problems of External Pressures, Power Struggles and Budgetary Deficits in Ottoman Politics under Abdulhamid II (1876–1909)", unpublished thesis, Princeton, 1976.

Alawi, Hassan, *Aswar al-tin 'uqdat al-Kuwayt wa aydiulujiya al-dhama*, Beirut, 1995.

Anscombe, Frederick F., *The Ottoman Gulf: the creation of Kuwait, Saudi Arabia and Qatar*, New York, 1997.

Antaki, Abdul Masih, *Al-Riyad al-muzhira bayn al-Kuwayt wa-'l-Muhammara*, Cairo, 1908.

B., F. L., "Voyage du Catinat dans le Golfe Persique", *Le Monde Illustré*, 1902, p. 202.

Bagdadbahnprojekt, Bericht der von der Anatolischen Eisenbahngesellschaft in September 1899 ausgesandten Studienexpedition, Berlin, 1900.

Banse, Ewald, *Auf den Spuren der Bagdadbahn*, Weimar, 1913.

Banse, Ewald, *Die Türkei: eine moderne Geographie*, Berlin, 1916.

Barth, Jacques. "La contrebande des armes dans le Golfe persique et la question de Mascate", *Asie Française* 11 (December 1911), pp. 548–56.

Bidwell, Robin, *The Affairs of Kuwait, 1896–1905*, 2 vols., London, 1971.

Bidwell, Robin, *The Affairs of Arabia, 1905–1906*, 2 vols., London, 1971.

Bode, F. H., *Der Kampf um die Bagdadbahn 1903/14*, Breslau, 1941.

Bondarevsky, Grigori, *Al-Kuwayt wa 'alaqatuha al-duwaliyya khilal al-qarn al-tasi' 'ashr wa awa'il al-qarn al-'ashrin*, Centre for Research and Studies on Kuwait, Kuwait, 1994.

Bondarevsky, Grigori, "Mubarak's Kuwait in Russian and German Policy", in Ben J. Slot (ed.), *Kuwait, the Growth of a Historic Identity*, London, 2003, pp. 49–57.

[Bowier, M.W.], "Zending van Z. M. Schroefstoomschip *Curaçao* naar de Persische Golf", *Mededelingen betreffende het Zeewezen 1870–2*, pp. 1–99 and separate map.

Braudel, Fernand, *La Méditerranée et le monde méditerranéen à l'époque de Philippe II*, Paris, 1949.

Brünner, E. R. J., *De Bagdadspoorweg: Bijdrage tot de kennis omtrent het optreden der mogendheden in Turkije 1888–1908*, Groningen/Djakarta, 1956.

Burchardt, Hermann, "Ost-Arabien von Basra bis Maskat auf Grund eigener Reisen", *Zeitschrift der Gesellschaft für Erdkunde zu Berlin* (1906), pp. 305–22.

Busch, Briton C., "Britain and the Status of Kuwait, 1896–1899", *Middle East Journal* (Spring 1967), pp. 187–98.

Busch, Briton C., *Britain and the Persian Gulf*, Berkeley, 1967.

Busch, Briton C., *Britain, India and the Arabs, 1914–1921*, Berkeley, 1971.

Butterfield, Paul R., *The Diplomacy of the Bagdad Railway*, (Inaugural Dissertation), Göttingen 1932.

Cambon, Paul, *Ambassadeur de France, 1843–1924*, Paris, 1937.

Chapman, Maybelle Kennedy, *Great Britain and the Baghdad Railway*, Massachusetts, 1948.

Chiha, Habib K., *La province de Bagdad, son passé, son avenir*, Cairo, 1908.

Chirol, Valentine, *The Middle Eastern Question or Some Political Problems of Indian Defence*, London, 1903.

Cuinet, Vital, *La Turquie d'Asie: Géographie administrative*, 4 vols., Paris, 1894.

Curzon, G. N., *Persia and the Persian Question*, 2 vols., London, 1902.

Curzon, G. N., *Tales of Travel*, London, 1923.

A. E. Deniz, "The Problem of External Pressures, Power Struggles and Budgetary Deficits in Ottoman Politics under Abdulhamid II", unpublished thesis, Princeton, 1976.

Dickson, Harold R. P., *The Arab of the Desert,* London, 1949.

Dickson, Harold R. P., *Kuwait and her Neighbours,* London, 1956.

Dieulafoy, Jane, *La Perse, la Chaldée et la Susiane: relation de voyage,* Paris, 1887.

Dieulafoy, Jane, *À Suse: journal des fouilles 1884–1886,* Paris, 1888.

Encyclopaedia of Islam, 2nd edition, 11 vols., Leiden, 1980–2003.

Esmaïli, Malek, *Le Golfe Persique et les Isles de Bahrein,* Paris, 1936.

Facey, William, and Grant, Gillian, *Kuwait by the First Photographers,* London, 1998.

Finnie, David, *Shifting Lines in the Sand: Kuwait's elusive frontier with Iraq,* Cambridge, Mass., 1992.

Floor, Willem, "Le Karūn et l'irrigation de la plaine d'Ahwaz", *Studia Iranica* 28/1, pp. 95–122.

Fontanier, V., *Voyage dans l'Inde et dans le Golfe Persique par l'Égypte et la Mer Rouge,* 3 vols., Paris, 1844–6.

Fromkin, David, *A Peace to End All Peace: The fall of the Ottoman Empire and the creation of the modern Middle East,* London, 2000.

Geary, Grattan, *Through Asiatic Turkey,* 2 vols., London, 1878.

Gehrke, Ulrich, "Historische Aspekte des irakischen Anspruchs auf Kuwait", *Orient* (Hamburg) 2, (1961 heft 4), pp. 160–8.

Gehrke, Ulrich, and Kuhn, Gustav, *Die Grenze des Irak: Historische und rechtliche Aspekte des irakischen Anspruchs auf Kuwait und des irakisch-persischen Streites um den Schatt al-Arab.* Stuttgart, 1963.

Genthe, S., *Der Persische Meerbusen, Geschichte und Morphologie,* Marburg, 1896.

Al-Ghanim, Salwa, *The Reign of Mubarak Al-Sabah, Shaikh of Kuwait 1896–1915,* London, 1998.

Gillard, D. (ed.), *British Documents on Foreign Affairs,* Part 1, Series B, Vols. 16–17: *The Ottoman Empire, Arabia and the Gulf,* London, 1985.

Gillard, D. (ed.), *British Documents on Foreign Affairs,* Part 1, Series B, Vol. 18: *Arabia, the Gulf and the Baghdad Railway,* London 1985.

Goguyer, Antonin (aka Antoine), *Choix splendide de préceptes cueillis dans la loi [par Ahmad ibn al Khoga]: petit manuel de droit immobilier suivant les deux rites musulmans orthodoxes de la régence de Tunis,* traduit sur la première éd. du texte arabe et annoté par A. Goguyer, Paris, 1885

Goguyer, Antonin (aka Antoine), *La pluie de rosée: étanchement de la soif* = *Qatr al-nada wa-bal al-sada,* Leiden, 1887. [A translation of Ibn Hijam.]

Goldberg, Jacob, *The Foreign Policy of Saudi Arabia: The formative years, 1902–1918,* Cambridge, Mass., 1986.

Gooch, G. P., and Temperley, H., *British Documents on the Origins of the War, 1898–1914,* 11 vols., reprint, New York, 1967.

Gothaischer Hofkalender 171, (1934).

Graves, Philip, *The Life of Sir Percy Cox,* London, 1941.

Griessbauer, L., *Die internationalen Verkehrs- und Machtsfragen an den Küsten Arabiens,* Berlijn, 1907.

Grohmann, Adolf, "Kuwait", *Encyclopaedia of Islam* (1), Vol. 2, pp. 1259–62.

Hansard's Parliamentary Debates, 3rd Series, London, 1892–1908.

Harrison, Paul W., *The Arab at Home,* New York, 1923.

Al-Hatim, Abdallah Khalid, *Min huna bada't al-Kuwayt,* Kuwait, 1962.

Heller, Joseph, *British Policy towards the Ottoman Empire, 1908–1914,* London, 1983.

Helfferich, Karl, *Georg von Siemens, ein Lebensbild aus Deutschlands grosser Zeit,* Berlin, 1923.

Hewins, Ralph, *A Golden Dream: The Miracle of Kuwait,* London, 1963.

Hughes Thomas, R. (ed.), *Selections from the Records of the Bombay Government,* New Series no. XXIV, Bombay, 1856.

Hurewitz, Jacob Coleman, *Diplomacy in the Near and Middle East, 1535–1914,* Princeton, 1956.

Hüsni, Hüseyin, *Necd kitasin'in Ahval-i Umumiyesi,* Istanbul 1328/1910.

Iraq, Republic of, *The Truth about Kuwait* (1), Ministry of Foreign Affairs, Baghdad, July 1961. [Leiden University Library 8264 F 29]

Jedina, Leopold von, *An Asiens Küsten und Fürstenhöfen,* Wien and Olmütz, 1891.

Jouannin, André, "Les influences étrangères dans le Golfe persique", *Asie Française* 3, (January 1904), pp. 23–7.

Jouannin, André, "Sur les rives de la Golfe persique: notes de voyage (1903)", *Bulletin de la Société de Géographie Commerciale de Paris*, 26 (1904), pp. 62–73.

Jwaideh, Albertine, "Midhat Pasha and the Land System of Lower Iraq", in: Albert Hourani, ed., *St Antony's Papers* 16, *Middle Eastern Affairs* 3, Carbondale, 1963.

Kelly, J. B., *Britain and the Persian Gulf, 1795–1880*, Oxford, 1991.

Keun de Hoogerwoerd, R., C., "Die Häfen und Handelsverhältnisse des Persischen Golfs und des Golfs von Oman", *Annalen der Hydrographie und maritimen Meteorologie* 17 (1899), pp. 189–207.

Khaz'al, Husayn Khalaf Al-Shaikh, *Tarikh al-Kuwayt al-siyasi*, 5 vols., Beirut, 1962.

King, Peter, (ed.), *Travels with a Superior Person, by the Marquess Curzon of Kedleston*, London, 1985.

Kochwasser, Friedrich H., *Kuwait: Geschichte, Wesen und Funktion eines modernen Asiatischen Staates*, Tübingen, 1975.

Kumar, Ravindar, *India and the Persian Gulf Region, 1858–1907*, London, 1965.

Lepsius, Johannes, Mendelsohn-Bartholdy, Albrecht, and Thimme, Friedrich, *Die Grosse Politik der Europaischen Kabinette, 1871–1914*, 40 vols., Berlin, 1927.

Lienhardt, Peter, "The Authority of Shaikhs in the Gulf: An Essay in Nineteenth Century History", R. B. Sergeant and R. L. Bidwell eds., *Arabian Studies*, Vol. II, London, 1975, pp. 61–75.

Lindow, Erich, *Freiherr Marschall von Bieberstein als Botschafter in Konstantinopel, 1897–1912*, Danzig, 1934.

Locher, A., *With Star and Crescent: A full and authentic account of a recent journey with a caravan from Bombay to Constantinople*, Philadelphia, 1890. [This journey took place in 1866.]

Longrigg, Stephen H., *Four Centuries of Modern Iraq*, Oxford, 1925.

Longrigg, Stephen H., *Iraq 1900–1950: A Political, Social and Economic History*, London, 1958.

Lorimer, J. G., *Gazetteer of the Persian Gulf, 'Oman and Central Arabia*, 2 vols., Calcutta, 1909–15.

Mahan, A. T., "The Persian Gulf and International Relations", *National Review* 40 (September 1902), pp. 27–45.

Marsigli, Luigi Ferdinando, *Stato Militare dell' Imperio Ottomanno/ L'état militaire de l'empire Ottoman, son progrès et sa décadence*, La Haye, 1732.

Midhat, Ali Haydar, *The Life of Midhat Pasha: a record of his services, political reforms, banishment and judicial murder*, London, 1903.

Midhat, Ali Haydar, *Midhat Pasha Hayat-i syasiyesi*, Istanbul, 1325/1907.

Moris, M., *Relation des voyages de Sidi-Aly fils d'Houssain nommé ordinairement Khatibi Roumi*, Paris, 1827.

Morley, G., *Recollections*, London, 1917.

Musil, Alois, *Zur Zeitgeschichte von Arabien*, Leipzig/Wien, 1918.

Musil, Alois, *Northern Negd: A topographical itinerary*, New York, 1928.

Mylrea, S. G., "Kuwait, Arabia", *Muslim World* 7, no. 2 (April 1917), pp. 118–26.

Niebuhr, Carsten, *Beschreibung von Arabien*, Copenhagen, 1772.

von Nolde, Eduard, *Reise nach Inner Arabien, Kurdistan und Armenien 1892*, Braunschweig, 1895.

Oestrup, J., *Arabien's Historie*, Koebenhavn, 1933.

von Oppenheim, Max, *Vom Mittelmeer zum Persischen Golf*, Berlin, 1900.

Palgrave, William Gifford, *Narrative of a Year's Journey through Central and Eastern Arabia (1862–3)*, 2 vols., London, 1865.

Parfit, J. T., *Marvellous Mesopotamia, the World's Wonderland*, London n.d. [1924?].

Pelly, Lewis, "Remarks on the Tribes, Trade and Resources around the Shore Line of the Persian Gulf", *Transactions of the Bombay Geographical Society* 17 (1865), pp. 32–112.

Pelly, Lewis, "Account of a Recent Tour around the Northern Provinces of the Persian Gulf", *Transactions of the Bombay Geographic Society* 17 (1865), pp. 113–40.

Philby, H. St J. B., *Arabia*, New York, 1930.

Philby, H. St J. B., *Sa'udi Arabia*, London, 1955.

Pillai, R., and Kumar, M., "The Political and Legal Status of Kuwait", *The International and Comparative Law Quarterly*, 1962, pp. 108–130.

Plass, Jens Barthold, *England zwischen Russland und Deutschland: Der Persische Golf in der Britischen Vorkriegspolitik, 1899–1907*, Hamburg, 1969.

Political Diaries of the Persian Gulf, 1904–1958, 20 vols., Slough, 1990.

Preller, Hugo, *Salisbury und die Türkische Frage im Jahre 1895*, Stuttgart, 1930.

Al-Qasimi, Sultan bin Muhammad, *Bayan al-Kuwayt*, Sharjah, 2004.

Al-Qina'i, Yusuf bin 'Isa, *Safhat min tarikh al-Kuwayt*, 5th edition, Kuwait, 1988.

Raunkiaer, Barclay, *Gennem Wahhabiternes Land paa Kamelryg*, Kjobenhavn, 1913.

[See also the abridged English translation by Gerald de Gaury, below.]

Raunkiaer, Barclay, *Through Wahhabiland on Camelback, 1912*, introduced, translated and abridged by Gerald de Gaury, London, 1969.

Reclus, E., *Nouvelle géographie universelle*, Vol. 9, Paris, 1884.

Rezvan, Efim, *Russian Ships in the Gulf, 1899–1903*, Reading, 1993.

Rihani, Amin, *Ibn Sa'oud of Arabia: His people and his land*, London, 1928.

Rihani, Amin, *Around the Coasts of Arabia*, London, 1930.

Rittter, Carl, *Die Erdkunde Asiens* 2, Vols. 12–13, Berlin 1846–7.

Rosen, Friedrich, *Oriental Memoirs of a German Diplomatist*, London, 1930.

Rush, Alan de Lacy, *Al-Sabah: History and genealogy of Kuwait's ruling family*, London, 1987.

Rush, Alan de Lacy, *Records of Kuwait, 1899–1961*, Slough, 1987.

Rush, Alan de Lacy, *Ruling Families of Arabia: Kuwait: the ruling family of Al-Sabah*, Slough, 1991

Al-Rushaid, Abdul Aziz, *Tarikh al-Kuwayt*, Baghdad, 1926.

Saldanha, J. A., *The Persian Gulf Précis*. Vol. 4: "Précis of Bahrein Affairs, 1854–1904", and Vol. 5: "Précis of Kuwait Affairs" and "Précis of Nejd Affairs". Reprint, Slough, 1986.

Salnama-i devlet-i aliye Osmaniye, 19 vols., Istanbul, 1895–1913.

Schläfli, A., "Skizze der politisch-territorialen Verhältnisse der Gestädeländer des Persischen Golfes", *Mitteilungen aus Justus Perthes' Geographischer Anstalt*. Gotha, 1863, pp. 210–12.

Schmidt, W., *Der Kampf um Arabien zwischen der Türkei und England*, Hamburg, 1918.

Schofield, Richard, *Arabian Boundaries, Primary Documents*. Vols. 7–8: *Kuwait–Iraq*, and Vol. 9: *Saudi Arabia–Kuwait, Saudi Arabia–Iraq*. Farnham Common, 1988.

Schofield, Richard, *Kuwait and Iraq: Historical Claims and Territorial Disputes.* London, 1994.

Schofield, Richard, *The Iraq-Kuwait Dispute.* Vol. 1: *Evolution of the Iraq-Kuwait International Boundary on Land and Sea.* Farnham Common, 1994.

Schofield, Richard, "Britain and Kuwait's borders, 1902–1923", Ben J. Slot (ed.), *Kuwait, the Growth of a Historic Identity*, London, 2003, pp. 58–94.

Schott, Gerhard, "Geographie des Persischen Golfes und seiner Randgebiete", *Mitteilungen der Geographischen Gesellschaft in Hamburg* 31 (1918), pp. 1–110.

Sitki, Bekir, *Das Bagdadbahnproblem, 1890–1903*, Freiburg, 1935.

Slot, B. J., *The Arabs of the Gulf*, Leidschendam, 1998.

Slot, B. J., *The Origins of Kuwait*, 2nd edition, Kuwait, 1998.

Stocqueler, J. H., *Fifteen Months' Pilgrimage through Untrodden Tracts of Khuzistan and Persia*, London, 1832.

Stuhlmann, Franz, *Der Kampf um Arabien zwischen der Türkei und England*, Hamburg/Braunschweig/Berlin, 1916.

Stürken, Alfred, "Reisebriefe aus dem Persischen Golf und Persien", *Mitteilungen der Geographischen Gesellschaft in Hamburg*, 22 (1907), pp. 71–124.

Tauber, Ebenezer, "Sayyid Talib and the Young Turks in Basra", *Middle Eastern Studies* 25 (1989), pp. 3–22.

Tschirner, Hans-Erich, *Streifzüge um den Persischen Golf*, Berlin, 1917.

Tuson, Penelope, *A Brief Guide to Sources for Middle East Studies in the India Office Records*, London 1982.

Al-Uthaymin, Abdallah Al-Salih, *Tarikh al-Mamlaka al-Sa'udiyya*, Riyadh, 1422 AH/AD 2001.

Villiers, Alan, *Sons of Sindbad*, London, 1940.

Vivien de Saint-Martin, Louis, *Nouveau dictionnaire de géographie universelle*, Paris, 1897–1900.

Whigham, Henry J., *The Persian Problem: An examination of the rival positions of Russia and Great Britain in Persia, with some account of the Persian Gulf and the Bagdad Railway*, London, 1903.

Winstone, H. V. F., *Captain Shakespear: A portrait*, London, 1978.

Wratislaw, A. C., *A Consul in the East*, Edinburgh and London, 1924.

Index

Arab names are, with a few exceptions, given in full without inversion. In alphabetizing al-, Al-, bin and Ibn are ignored.

Some significant place names in or near Kuwait's desert borderlands are accompanied by a fully transliterated version, shown in brackets. These spellings are gleaned from S. G. Knox's investigations in the field, carried out while he was political agent in Kuwait and recorded in Arabic script; from Shaikh Mubarak's own description of his southern border, in IOLR, R/15/5/65; and from the most reliable maps.